THE CAMBRIDGE
ANCIENT HISTORY

THE
CAMBRIDGE
ANCIENT HISTORY

EDITED BY

J. B. BURY, M.A., F.B.A.
S. A. COOK, Litt.D.
F. E. ADCOCK, M.A.

VOLUME IV

THE PERSIAN EMPIRE
AND THE WEST

CAMBRIDGE UNIVERSITY PRESS

Published by the Syndics of the Cambridge University Press
Bentley House, 200 Euston Road, London NW1 2DB
American Branch: 32 East 57th Street, New York, N.Y.10022

ISBN: 0 521 04486 3

First published 1926
Reprinted, with slight corrections 1930 1939
1953 1960 1964 1969
Reprinted 1974

Printed in Great Britain
at the University Printing House, Cambridge
(Brooke Crutchley, University Printer)

PREFACE

THIS volume takes us into the very middle of the current of Greek history as its limits were generally conceived fifty or sixty years ago. From the beginning of the sixth century B.C. onwards we have a more or less continuous story of the principal states in Greece, and a more or less accurate knowledge of the maritime conditions and political relations which existed both in the eastern and in the western portions of the Mediterranean world, when the hour came for the supreme struggle between the Persian Empire and the West, the main theme of the present volume. How the Greek world had come to be what it was when this struggle began has already been partly shown in the previous volume, in the preface to which it was explained that volumes III and IV were projected and written simultaneously.

We have then, first, formally to introduce the Persian Empire, explaining its origin and character. The chapters (I and VII, sections I–VI) on this theme were entrusted to the late Dr G. Buchanan Gray of Mansfield College, Oxford, and were almost finished, but in manuscript and unrevised, at the time of his death. In chapter VII Dr Gray has given a description of the organization of the Empire under Darius and of Persian culture and religion. The account of the Scythian Expedition and of the Ionian Revolt, with which the chapter closes, is from the pen of Dr M. Cary, who shows how the attention of the Great King was, perforce, turned to the West.

Now that the history of the Greek States has become more continuous and comparatively fuller, we can see much more precisely than hitherto the political talent of the Greeks at work in the city-states. This is especially true of Athens, the growth of whose Constitution can be followed from the beginning of the sixth century, that is, from the time of Solon, onwards. The early structure of the Attic State was described in volume III (ch. XXIII), and in this volume Professor Adcock traces Athenian history from the second half of the seventh century down to the fall of the Peisistratid Tyranny. In chapter II he shows the nature and the significance of the economic and political reforms of Solon, and in chapter III he follows the fortunes of the city under Peisistratus and his sons. The further development of the Athenian Constitution is taken up by Mr E. M. Walker in chapter VI, who examines the reform of Cleisthenes, so that in chapters II

and vi we have a history of the first steps in the development of
the Athenian Republic towards the democracy of the fifth century,
a development of which the instructiveness and interest have
always been recognized, exhibiting as they do the exceptional
political gifts of the Greeks.

A survey of the leading cities of Hellas, east, south, north and
west, excepting those of Greece Proper and of Sicily, which are
treated later, will show us how the stage was set for the imminent
struggle, and contribute to the picture of what Greece meant at
this time. This survey has been entrusted to Professor Ure who,
in chapter IV, guides us to all parts of what we call the 'outer
Greek world.' In the seventh and sixth centuries the use of
coined money became common to all Greek States, and an account
of the origin and spread of coinage up to the beginning of the
fifth century follows from the pen of Dr G. F. Hill, the Keeper of
Coins and Medals in the British Museum.

At this stage of politics and culture the Greeks came into
conflict with the Persian Empire. In chapters VIII, IX and X,
Mr J. A. R. Munro recounts the campaign of Marathon and the
repulse of the Generals of Darius, with its sequel in the struggle
against the forces of Xerxes. No wars in history have provoked
more debate among scholars, and this fact, together with the
importance of the issue for the future of European civilization,
justifies the fullness of Mr Munro's criticism and re-interpretation of the ancient evidence. In chapter VIII he advances strong
reasons for adopting the view that, contrary to the received
opinion, which has always assigned the Battle of Marathon to the
year 490 B.C., it was really fought a year earlier, in 491 B.C. In
sections VI–X of chapter VIII, Mr E. M. Walker[1] describes the
unsuccessful expedition of Miltiades to Paros and the important
events of Athenian political life and Greek inter-state relations
which were happening between Marathon and the Great Persian
Invasion, especially the outbreak of war between Athens and
Aegina.

We then pass to the parallel struggle which was being carried
on in Sicily, and was decided at much the same time, between the
Greeks and Carthaginians. In chapter XI Mr Hackforth describes
the rise of Carthage in competition with the Hellenic settlers in

---

[1] Mr Walker adheres to the accepted view that Marathon was fought
in 490 B.C., and adopts the corresponding dates for the events of the years
which immediately precede and follow it. Cross-references and footnotes
in the chapters and the chronological table at the end of the volume make
clear the implications of this difference of view.

the West, which culminated in the deliverance of the island from the Carthaginian menace at the Battle of Himera.

From Sicily we turn to Italy. Professor Conway explains and discusses our knowledge of the people who lived there during the period after the Bronze Age, the centuries in which the Etruscans were the most influential and powerful folk in the peninsula. Chapter xii is devoted to the character and culture of the Etruscans themselves, and to the question of their origin and the notorious enigma of their language. In chapter xiii Professor Conway goes on to survey the different Indo-European communities which inhabited Italy at or before the beginning of recorded history. Any conclusions suggested at present in this field must mainly depend upon the linguistic materials, and the exposition is, of necessity, very largely concerned with the evidence of language. Readers who are not deterred by the formidable appearance of some of this evidence will find in it, on the one hand, the means of at least estimating our knowledge of the Etruscans and, on the other hand, of distinguishing the different degrees of kinship which linked together the other Italic peoples, so far as such links can be measured by language. The final section of chapter xii, that on Etruscan art, is from the pen of Mr S. Casson, who describes the extant remains of that art with its ill-paid debt to the inspiration of Greek artistic ideas.

Rome is not included in this survey of early Italy. The origin of the city and the traditions of early Roman History are postponed to a later volume, where they will be treated in more immediate connection with the period when Rome is making her entry upon the stage of the world's history.

Greeks and Greek States have been leading actors in the events recorded in the present volume, and Greece will be the main subject in volume v. It is therefore opportune to review what they had achieved in thought and in artistic creation by the beginning of the fifth century B.C., when they were about to enter on their most brilliant age. Accordingly, in chapter xiv, Professor Bury gives a survey of their Literature from the period immediately succeeding Homer down to the end of the Persian Wars. The early development of Attic Drama, which it is more convenient to consider in immediate connection with the account of the maturity of Athenian Tragedy and Comedy, is reserved for treatment in the next volume. What the Greeks did for religious speculation, especially in the Eleusinian and Orphic mysteries, is explained in chapter xv by Mr F. M. Cornford, who also passes under review the early philosophical systems of the sixth and fifth centuries. In chapter xvi the history of Greek art of the Geometric and Archaic periods is traced by Professor Beazley from the beginning of the first millennium B.C. down to the year 520 B.C., the end of the period of black-figured Attic pottery. The rise and principal monuments of early Greek architecture have been treated of by Mr D. S. Robertson, who carries his account down to the Persian Wars.

In the spelling of Greek names the practice adopted by the *Journal of Hellenic Studies* has in general been followed, but here and there consistency has been yet further abandoned in order to present to the reader familiar names in their familiar forms. On occasion convenience has been the guide. For example, what seems to have been the earlier and more correct Greek form Artaphrenes is used for the brother of Darius, while the later, more familiar, Artaphernes is retained for his son, the defeated Commander at Marathon.

Throughout the volume asterisks have been employed to indicate objects which are to be illustrated in the Volume of Plates to volumes i–iv which Mr Seltman is preparing for publication in the autumn.

Mr Munro wishes to thank Mr Jerome Farrell of Jesus College, Cambridge, for the information acknowledged in the note to p. 295; and Messrs N. Whatley, Headmaster of Clifton College, and B. Ashmole, Director of the British School at Rome, both of Hertford College, Oxford, for the use of photographs and explanations of the neighbourhood of Eleutherochori. Mr Robertson desires to express his indebtedness to Mr A. S. F. Gow for criticisms and suggestions. Professor Conway wishes to acknowledge the valuable assistance which he has received from Professor J. Whatmough on all that concerns the dialects of the early peoples of north-west Italy (Ligures, Lepontii and Raeti) and the antiquities and place-names of the Sicels. Professor Whatmough's direct contributions he has indicated by the initials J. Wh. in footnotes. He also wishes to thank Professor G. E. K. Braunholtz for help in the section on the Gauls and Mrs Elizabeth Johnson (*née* Jackson) for placing at his disposal the manuscript of her part of 'The Prae-Italic Dialects.' Mr Casson would acknowledge the assistance of Dr G. Schnyder of Utrecht University; Professor Adcock has to thank Mr A. B. Cook and Mr D. S. Robertson for criticism and help in matters archaeological.

The editors would express their thanks to the contributors for their cordial and ready co-operation and to them and to other scholars for their courteous help and advice. They are under particular obligations to Mr H. M. Last of St John's College, Oxford, Mr Sidney Smith of the British Museum and Mr C. T. Seltman. Acknowledgments are due for Map 1 to the Austrian Kartographisches Institut, for Map 3 to the Delegates of the Oxford University Press, for Map 5 to Messrs Philip and Son, for Maps 6, 7, and 9 to Messrs Macmillan and Mr Munro, for Map 8, which is based on Karte 5 in J. Kromayer's *Antike Schlachtfelder*, vol. II, to the publishers, Messrs Weidmann, for Map 10 to Messrs Leroux, to the Royal Geographical Society and for both 8 and 10 to Mr Munro. The editors are indebted to Professor Conway for Map 11 and for the Table of Alphabets facing p. 402. The table facing p. 470 is derived from that published in volume III facing p. 432 and the editors would repeat their thanks to Mr S. G. Campbell. The sheet containing plans of temples at the end of chapter XVI has been arranged by Mr D. S. Robertson and acknowledgments are due to Messrs Macmillan for Nos. 1 and 2, to Messrs J. B. Gebhardt for No. 3, to the Greek Government for No. 4, to the authorities of the British Museum for No. 5, and for No. 6 to the Archäologisches Institut des Deutschen Reiches. The general index and index of passages have been made by Mr W. E. C. Browne, M.A., formerly scholar of Emmanuel College. Finally due acknowledgment must be made of the skill and care of the staff of the University Press, for which the editors have every reason to be grateful.

The design on the cover is the figure of Darius from the Darius Vase, now at Naples.

J. B. B.
S. A. C.
F. E. A.

February 1926

TABLE OF CONTENTS

CHAPTER I

THE FOUNDATION AND EXTENSION OF THE PERSIAN EMPIRE

By the late G. Buchanan Gray, D.Litt., D.D.
Of Mansfield College, Oxford

CHAPTER II

THE REFORM OF THE ATHENIAN STATE

By F. E. Adcock, M.A.
Professor of Ancient History in the University of Cambridge

CONTENTS

CHAPTER III

ATHENS UNDER THE TYRANTS

By F. E. ADCOCK

CHAPTER IV

THE OUTER GREEK WORLD IN THE SIXTH CENTURY

By P. N. URE, M.A.

Professor of Classics, University College, Reading

CHAPTER V

COINAGE FROM ITS ORIGIN TO THE PERSIAN WARS

By G. F. HILL, M.A., D.LITT., LL.D., F.B.A.

Keeper of Coins and Medals, British Museum

CONTENTS

CHAPTER VI

ATHENS: THE REFORM OF CLEISTHENES

By E. M. WALKER, M.A.

Pro-Provost of Queen's College, Oxford

CHAPTER VII

THE REIGN OF DARIUS

By G. B. GRAY and M. CARY, D.LITT., Reader in Ancient History
in the University of London[1]

[1] Sections I–VI are by Dr Gray, Sections VII and VIII by Dr Cary.

CHAPTER VIII

MARATHON

By J. A. R. MUNRO, M.A., Rector of Lincoln College, Oxford, and E. M. WALKER[1]

[1] Sections I–V are by Mr Munro, Sections VI–X by Mr Walker

CHAPTER IX

XERXES' INVASION OF GREECE

By J. A. R. Munro

CHAPTER X

THE DELIVERANCE OF GREECE

By J. A. R. MUNRO

CHAPTER XI

CARTHAGE AND SICILY

By R. HACKFORTH, M.A.

Fellow and Lecturer, Sidney Sussex College, Cambridge

CHAPTER XII

ITALY IN THE ETRUSCAN AGE

A. THE ETRUSCANS

By R. S. CONWAY, LITT.D., D.LITT., F.B.A., Hon. Fellow of Gonville and Caius College, Cambridge, Hulme Professor of Latin in the Victoria University of Manchester, and S. CASSON, M.A., Fellow of New College, Oxford, and University Lecturer in Classical Archaeology[1]

[1] Sections I–VII are by Professor Conway, Section VIII (Etruscan Art) by Mr Casson.

CHAPTER XIII

ITALY IN THE ETRUSCAN AGE

B. THE INDO-EUROPEAN COMMUNITIES

By R. S. CONWAY

CHAPTER XIV

GREEK LITERATURE FROM THE EIGHTH CENTURY TO THE PERSIAN WARS

By J. B. Bury, M.A., F.B.A.
Regius Professor of Modern History in the University of Cambridge

CHAPTER XV

MYSTERY RELIGIONS AND PRE-SOCRATIC PHILOSOPHY

By F. M. Cornford, M.A.

Fellow and Lecturer, Trinity College, Cambridge

CHAPTER XVI

EARLY GREEK ART

By J. D. BEAZLEY, M.A., Lincoln and Merton Professor of Classical Archaeology and Art in the University of Oxford, and D. S. ROBERTSON, M.A., Fellow and Lecturer, Trinity College, Cambridge[1]

[1] Sections I–IV are by Professor Beazley, Section V (Architecture) by Mr Robertson.

CONTENTS

CHAPTER I

THE FOUNDATION AND EXTENSION
OF THE PERSIAN EMPIRE

AFTER the fall of the Assyrian empire, related in the last
volume, the next most momentous event in the chronicle
of ancient history is the rise of Persia, which succeeded Assyria
as the great power of western Asia, and during the period covered
in this volume the might of the Persian state is the central fact.
In this chapter its origins will be discussed, and it will be shown
how the foundations of its empire were laid by the conquests of
Cyrus and how it was expanded by Cambyses. These conquests
meant the disappearance, sooner or later, of four great states—
of the two, Media and Babylonia, which had joined forces to
pull down Assyria, and of Egypt and Lydia, which had counted
for much in the Assyrian period. After these rapid initial successes, which in the lifetime of a generation established her
dominion to the shores of the Mediterranean and brought under
her yoke the Asiatic Greeks and the Phoenicians, the further expansion of Persia westward was arrested by the Greeks of the
motherland. Having turned back to follow the political and commercial development of the Greek states throughout the sixth
century, we shall resume the thread of Persian history in the reign
of Darius and see how the clash came between this immense
monarchy, so much larger in extent than any of its predecessors,
and the cities of free Greece. In the perennial debate between
East and West this clash is the first of which the story is known
in detail, and perhaps it is the most dramatic; it is certainly one
of the most important, for it frustrated the probable prospect of
Persia controlling the Aegean and becoming the sovran power in
south-eastern Europe.

While Persia is casting her shadow over the lands and waters
of the eastern Mediterranean, the western Mediterranean is beginning to come within the radius of 'recorded history,' and we
can discern the rivalries of the three powers which are striving for
supremacy in the western seas, the Etruscan, the Carthaginian,
and the Greek. The foundations of the Greek cities in Sicily and
Italy have already been described, but we shall have to go back to
examine the rise of Carthage and the origins and growth of the
Etruscan state which in this period reaches the summit of its power.

The Persian wars define an epoch in the history of Greece. After her victory in this conflict she will enter on her great age, the age in which the achievements of her sons as thinkers and artists are the facts that matter most in the history of the world. This volume will close with a review of what her genius had already accomplished in literature, philosophy and art.

I. THE RISE OF CYRUS: PERSIA

The Persian is vastly more than a mere successor to the Median empire: with the Medes the Aryans first took a conspicuous place in world-history; but it is their kinsmen the Persians who first became a world-power[1]. The Persian empire was created within the space of a single generation by a series of conquests that followed one another with a rapidity scarcely equalled except by Alexander, and by the Arabs in the first generation after the death of Mohammed. The defeat of Astyages the Mede in 549 B.C. and of Croesus the Lydian in 546, the capture of Babylon in 538 and the conquest of Egypt in 525, gave to the Persian empire within thirty years an extent exceeding that ever obtained by the greatest of the monarchs of Mesopotamia or the Nile valley, and consequently greater than that of any earlier empire west of China. Confirmed and rounded off by Darius, this empire was maintained by the same family that created it, for two centuries undivided and unbroken, whereas Alexander's dominions were separated from his family and divided immediately after his death, and within the first century and a half of Islam great dynastic changes occurred and the unity of Arabian rule was broken. It was the house of Achaemenes, which down to 549 B.C. had enjoyed the simple style and exercised the restricted dominion of kings of Anshan, that created and maintained the empire; it was the people from whom they sprang, the Persians, who were their mainstay, first in conquest and, subsequently, in peaceful administration.

The Persians are all but unknown till with Cyrus, Cambyses and Darius they suddenly became the centre of world-history. If, and this is none too certain, the Persians are twice alluded to by Ezekiel

---

[1] Whatever the origin of the Medes (cf. vol. II, pp. 13, 15), they appear among the enemies of Shalmaneser III and his successors (vol. III, pp. 26, 34, 51). Their later history (which is only slightly known), in particular, the rise of Phraortes and Cyaxares, has been noticed in connection with the history of Urarṭu, etc. (see vol. III, pp. 127 *sqq.*, 188 *sq.*, 220). For the late notions of a Median empire in Babylon and a Median Darius prior to Cyrus, see the commentaries on the Book of Daniel.

(xxvii, 10, xxxviii, 5), they contributed soldiers to Tyre at the beginning of the sixth century, and were expected by the prophet to form part of the army of Gog. If, and this again is doubtful, they gave their name to a region known as Parsua by the Assyrians in the ninth century, who mention its inhabitants along with the Madai (Medes), they moved, within a century or so before Cyrus, south from some region south-west of the Caspian to the country to which they permanently gave their name, and whence the family of Achaemenes sprang. Into these or other earlier wanderings of the Persians in particular it is unnecessary to enter further here, but the country named after them may be briefly described[1].

In modern western usage the term Persia is applied to the whole Iranian plateau stretching from the Caspian in the west to the Hindu Kush in the east, and from the Persian Gulf in the south to the steppes of Turkestan, the region of the Oxus and the Yaxartes in the north. But the name for this vaster district is in modern Persian usage Iran or Eran, while Fars, perpetuating the ancient name Persia, is the name of the south-western corner only. Persia, according to the older usage of the term, or Fars, consists of a long and little-broken coastline with a narrow belt of flat country generally some 15 to 30 miles in width, from the landward edge of which mountains rise abruptly to some 6000 feet, and then an extensive high plateau cut in places by valleys or interrupted by mountain ranges. The coast of Fars, the ancient Persia, is the western end of that long coastline which stretches some 1200 miles from just south-east of the mouth of the Shatt el-Arab (Tigris-Euphrates) to the mouths of the Indus. This entire coast is poor in harbours, and approach is also rendered difficult by shallows and rocks. The maritime plain, moreover, with its stifling heat and soil unfertilised by the mountain torrents, too full and turbulent in the rainy season and then for a longer part of the year dry, was always, as it still is, ill-suited to maintain any strong or considerable population. For these reasons their coastline never induced the Persians to become a sea-faring people, nor rendered their country easily accessible on this side to others. And as the sea cut them off on the south-west, so did the great deserts of Gedrosia, Carmania and the Sagartii, broken only by infrequent and inconsiderable oases, on the north and east.

In contrast with these inhospitable surroundings, the mountainous interior of Persia, though naturally not thickly populated, was able, in virtue of its many fertile valleys and high plains

[1] On the movements of the Aryans, see vol. II, ch. I, and the *Camb. Hist. of India*, vol. I, chap. III.

between the mountain ranges, to sustain a vigorous and healthy race. It was yet in the words of Darius 'beautiful, possessing good horses, possessing good men.' It is part of that vast mountain mass that stretches south-westwards from Armenia to India; and the main communications of Persia, hindered by the sea on the south and the deserts in the east and north, were north-westwards by mountain roads, of which the chief led to Susa and Babylon along the westerly, and to Ecbatana along the easterly chains[1]. With these none too easy lines of communication even north-westwards, Persia was necessarily retired and relatively inaccessible, capable of producing a race equal to great conquests, but, like Arabia later, unequal to offering a suitable administrative centre for the empire their conquests won. On the other hand, in this high country, and on the bank of a river, the modern Pulwar, the Persian monarchs were well content to build their greatest buildings, though neither 'Persepolis' nor Pasargadae as cities ever rivalled the capitals of earlier empires like Babylon and Nineveh.

So little does the ancient land of Persia offer a site for the capital of a great empire, that, before the conquests of Cyrus began, the centre even of the small kingdom which he had received from his ancestors seems to have lain outside Persia. Cyrus was the fourth at least of his family to enjoy the title of king of Anshan; none of them so far as we know was called king of Persia, and Cyrus only received this style after his career of conquest began, and because, as may be surmised, he was the first to bring all the Persian tribes under a single sceptre. If Anshan lay outside Persia, it would be possible to explain these facts by the supposition that Cyrus and his ancestors who were kings of Anshan before him, were not Persians, Cyrus first becoming king of Persia, as later of Babylon, by conquest. But this simple supposition requires a complete disregard of other evidence: not only to the Greeks, but to Darius, Cyrus was Persian; for Darius, who lays great stress on his own Persian origin, claims 'Cambyses, the son of Cyrus' as 'of our family.'

For the history of the Persians and the Persian royal house before the time of Cyrus, the monumental evidence has substituted a few certain facts for the vague legends of the Greek writers. But the new evidence raises fresh questions, and leaves various details in uncertainty. We know the names of the Achaemenids in two lines of descent for several generations: we know the title enjoyed by one of these lines, though the significance of

[1] The very difficult roads over the south Iranian mountains from Bunder-Abbas or Bushire to Shiraz and thence to Isfahan and Teheran are the chief line of communication of the empire from south to north.

it has been much disputed; but we are ignorant of the title, if any, borne by members of the other line before Darius. The facts, monumentally attested, may be conveniently presented in a genealogical table in which everything—the names, the titles and the filiations—is directly attested by the monuments, except the identity of Teispes the ancestor of Cyrus and Teispes the ancestor of Darius: this identity, which, though not unchallenged, is generally admitted, is established if some old Persian inscriptions at Pasargadae (Mashad-i-Murghab, *c.* 30 miles north-east of Persepolis): 'I (am) Cyrus the king, the Achaemenian' are records of a Cyrus that was king, and not, as an alternative theory proposes, of Cyrus the younger, a descendant of Darius I, and son of Darius II, who never was king.

	Achaemenes
	|
Teispes, the Great King, King of Anshan (=)	Teispes
|	|
Cyrus, the Great King, King of Anshan	
|	|
Cambyses, the Great King, King of Anshan	Ariaramnes
|	|
Cyrus, 1. the Great King, King of Anshan	Arsames
2. King of Persia (*c.* 550 B.C.)	|
3. King of the All, King of Babylon	
| &c. (539 B.C.)	Hystaspes
Cambyses, King of Babylon, King of the Lands	|
	Darius, K. in Persia,
	K. of the Lands,
	K. of Babylon

Whether or not the ancestors of Cyrus, without using the title, were in fact kings of Persia, they were kings of Anshan, the title being both used by Cyrus of himself and his ancestors, and applied to Cyrus by his contemporary Nabonidus, the last native king of Babylon. Anshan (or Anzan), which appears both as the name of a city and as that of a country or district, is an ancient term which may in the course of centuries have undergone some modification in its exact application. At all periods, however, in which it can be traced Anshan is closely associated with (though at times clearly distinguished from) Elam, and at times it is more particularly connected with Susa. Gudea in the third millennium refers to 'the city of Anshan in (or of) Nimki,' *i.e.* Elam; the native rulers of Elam towards the end of the twelfth century style themselves king of Susian Anzan (or of Anzan and Susa); and Sennacherib a little more than a century before Cyrus mentions Anzan as one of the lands summoned by the Elamite king to oppose him. To these particulars, which leave in some uncertainty the exact limits of the Anshan which gave to Cyrus his earliest title, the monuments of his own age add nothing. We may dismiss the theory which would identify the Anshan of Cyrus with Media; to identify it with a *part* of Persia would no doubt offer an easy explanation of the order in which the three different titles used by or of Cyrus— king of Anshan, king of Persia, king of Babylon—appear; but this seems to depart too widely from the other known usages of the term. It remains, therefore, to identify Anshan with southern Elam and especially perhaps the district around and including Susa.

Cyrus was already king of Anshan in the sixth, if not in the third, year of Nabonidus king of Babylon, *i.e.* in 550 or 553 B.C. His reign began as early as 558 B.C. if we may accept, on the authority of Herodotus (1, 214), twenty-nine years as the total length of his kingship. His great-grandfather, Teispes, is the first of his family known to have been, and probably the first who actually was, king of Anshan. Of the date or manner of the capture of Anshan from the Elamites there is no direct record; but it is possible that the Israelite prophetical writings contain in- direct evidence of it: in 588 Ezekiel (xxxii, 24 *sq.*) looks back on a destruction of Elam which was perhaps still anticipated by Jeremiah (xlix, 34 *sqq.*) in 597.

Whether before this Teispes had been king of Persia, or rather of that small part of it that belonged to the Pasargadae, 'the most noble tribe of the Persians' (Hdt. 1, 125), and lay in the valley of the Medus (modern Pulwar) in the western part of Persia ad- jacent to Elam, and if so, whether at his death, while bequeathing the new kingdom which, from its ancient capital of Susa, was in direct connection with the great cities of the ancient world to his eldest son Cyrus, he left the older, smaller and remoter kingdom to his younger son Ariaramnes, is uncertain; though considera- tions already referred to make some such arrangement not im- probable. No advance in dominion is marked by the reigns of the son and grandson of Teispes; on the other hand it is to be inferred that, while they certainly kept the style and title of king of Anshan, they did so as vassals of Cyaxares and Astyages, the rulers of the Median empire; and to this vassalage, as well as to the kingly title of his father Cambyses, Cyrus succeeded; and indeed, according to one interpretation of an ambiguous pronoun, Nabonidus, in his earliest reference to Cyrus, describes him both as king of Anshan and 'petty vassal' of the *Umman-manda*, the people from whom Astyages took the title king of the *Umman- manda* under which he appears in the inscriptions of Nabonidus.

II. CONQUEST OF MEDIA AND LYDIA

Born heir to the small kingdom of Anshan, Cyrus was destined for far greater things: as he himself, after his main achievements had been accomplished, states the case, Marduk, god of Babylon, looking about for a righteous prince found such an one in the king of Anshan, whom he accordingly called to lordship over the entire world. His first step in the fulfilment of his destiny was to unite under his sway the Iranian peoples, from Persia in the south to Media in the north, with all others whom the kings of Media or the *Umman-manda,* and principally Cyaxares and Astyages, had already subjected to themselves. Whether or not there is any substance in the stories perpetuated by Greek writers of the close connection by marriage between Cyrus and Astyages—according to one he was son of Mandane, the daughter of Astyages, according to another he married (though only after the defeat of Astyages) Amytis, the daughter of Astyages—neither family-ties nor his position as vassal hindered Cyrus from overthrowing Astyages.

In this first step he was assisted, while his own troops were relatively few, by dissatisfaction among the subjects and treachery in the army of Astyages, facts which underlie the elaborate legends in Herodotus, and are briefly recorded in the contemporary Babylonian Chronicle. Astyages, who appears to have been attacked by Cyrus as much as three years previously, now anticipated Cyrus' designs, and took the initiative in the final campaign (550–49 B.C.) which ended so disastrously for him: 'he assembled his troops,' as the mutilated text of the Chronicle appears to say, 'and marched against Cyrus, king of Anshan, to conquer him; and Astyages' troops mutinied, and he was captured, and they gave him over to Cyrus.' Cyrus brought him a prisoner to his country (Anshan), but spared his life, as Herodotus directly asserts, and as the silence of the Babylonian Chronicle allows us to believe. Where the battles, if any, were fought is not stated in these sources; a picturesque legend preserved by Ctesias asserts that the last conflict took place at Pasargadae.

Having captured Astyages, Cyrus proceeded to the Median capital Ecbatana, entered it apparently without serious opposition, and transferred its treasures to Anshan; otherwise Ecbatana does not appear to have suffered, except indirectly from the fact that Susa, which had been the capital of the kings of Anshan from Teispes to Cyrus, continued to be the capital of the rulers of the Persian empire, who however maintained Ecbatana as a summer residence.

A change in the centre of government, a change in the ruling house, a certain increase in the number of southern Iranian officers, but not to the exclusion of the Medes, in the army and the state—these are the principal changes, so far as the Iranian peoples were concerned, occasioned by the fall of Astyages. For the house of Astyages was substituted the house of Cyrus, but the Medes became thereby a conquered people scarcely more than the English, when the house of Orange was substituted for the house of Stuart. The new state, the nucleus of the greater empire which Cyrus was yet to create and Darius to solidify, consisted of the Medes and Persians; the greater empire itself, in the words of Darius, of 'Persia and Media and the other lands.' Whether under Cyrus the Persians obtained even so much ascendancy as later under Darius is not clear, and is scarcely to be inferred from the fact that, soon after his overthrow of Astyages, Cyrus appears in the Babylonian Chronicle no longer as king of Anshan but in a single passage as 'King of Persia' (548 B.C.), a title which he was soon to exchange for others of greater antiquity and wider significance.

In what precise circumstances and for what precise reasons Cyrus assumed—if, from the fact that it is once used of him, we may infer that he did—the title King of Persia, and whether he ever also—as Xerxes for a few years did later—employed the style King of Persia and Media, and whether his assumption of the title meant depriving of it, or of some other less wide royal title, the younger branch of the family of Teispes, are unknown or matters of uncertain speculation. Herodotus (I, 125) seems to say that Cyrus at the time of his conflict with Astyages could influence only three of the many Persian tribes—the Maraphians and the Maspians in addition to his own tribe of the Pasargadae. The extension of his influence and the establishment of his dominion over the remaining Persian tribes, agricultural and nomadic, may in this case have formed part of his task in establishing and enlarging the position which the defeat of Astyages had won for him.

Between his conquest of Media and his attack on Lydia two years later (547 B.C.) the movements and activities of Cyrus cannot be followed in any detail. In spite of the assistance he had received from some of the Medes and part of the Median army, many districts which had been subject to Astyages may have refused allegiance to the new ruler and required military operations on his part. In 547 according to the Babylonian Chronicle he was engaged in northern Mesopotamia: 'in Nisan (April) Cyrus, King

of Persia, levied his troops and crossed (?) the Tigris below
Arbela.' In the following month he opened hostilities against a
country whose name is mutilated on the cylinder, and whose king
he finally captured and put to death. Though complete certainty
cannot be attained, there is very strong probability that the country
concerned was Lydia and that Croesus was the unhappy king.

The peril to themselves involved in the rise of Cyrus had
already been perceived in the neighbouring states, particularly by
Croesus. He had no confidence that Cyrus would respect the
boundary of the Halys which, since 585, had divided Asia Minor
among the Lydians to the west of it and the Medes to the east
of it, or that the peaceful relations which had been cemented by
marriage between the royal houses of the Lydians and the Medes
could be maintained with the new ruler. Accordingly, in the year
547 he secured alliances with Egypt, Babylonia and the Spartans.
In the spring of the next year, persuaded by the ambiguous replies
of the oracles that he would be victorious, he crossed the Halys
into Cappadocia, and besieged and captured Pteria(vol. iii, p. 523).
Cyrus, according to Herodotus, first attempted to parry this invasion of his territory by soliciting the Ionians to revolt from
Lydia. Failing in this, he himself began the campaign to which
the Babylonian Chronicle refers, and fought a severe but inde-
cisive action near Pteria. Cyrus showed no sign of immediately
renewing the attack, and, as it was late in the year, Croesus, expecting to be left alone till the spring, retired to Sardes and dis-
banded his mercenaries; but immediately despatched envoys to
his allies, bidding them prepare for united action in the spring.
Cyrus, however, instead of waiting for the spring, quickly advanced to Sardes; and in the plain outside the city defeated
Croesus, who opposed him stubbornly with his Lydian cavalry.
After a short siege he succeeded in capturing the city, before the
Egyptians and Babylonians, to whom Croesus renewed his
appeals and this time for immediate assistance, had had time to
respond, or the Spartans, to whom he also sent, had despatched
their ships. Thus the kingdom of Lydia passed out of history and,
if we may believe the contemporary Babylonian evidence against
the tales later current among the Greeks, with it went Croesus
its king (see vol. iii, p. 524).

With the overthrow of the kingdom of Lydia (546 b.c.) the
dominion of Cyrus was extended over nearly the whole of the
interior of Asia Minor. Within the next year or two the hold on
what Croesus had directly ruled or influenced was strengthened,
and the remainder—i.e. principally the coasts—of Asia Minor

actually incorporated in the Persian empire or, as in the case of
Miletus, which had agreed with Cyrus that the same relations
as had existed between Miletus and the Lydians should be
maintained between Miletus and Cyrus, brought within the sphere
of its commanding influence. Cyrus left this work of completion
in Asia Minor to his representatives and generals. The city of
Sardes he left at first in the hands of Tabalus a Persian and
Pactyas a Lydian—giving to the latter, according to Herodotus,
charge of the finances. Pactyas used his position to lead a revolt
of the Lydians: this was put down by a Median general, Mazares,
and the population was entirely disarmed. Mazares also com-
menced the subjection of the Ionian cities; and after his death
Harpagus, formerly the leader of the revolting Medes who helped
Cyrus to secure his victory over Astyages, completed the subjection of the Ionian cities of the mainland and received the
submission of the Ionian islands. He then turned to the subjection of the southern coast of Asia Minor, actually raising for this
purpose troops from among the Ionians.

Whereas Cyrus, in obtaining the empire of the Medes, had
extended his dominion over a state of which the nucleus consisted
of peoples kindred to his own, of similar customs, culture and
religion, his conquest of Lydia, which had become intimately
connected with Greece, and deeply affected by Greek ideas and
culture, and of the Greek cities of Asia Minor, brought him into
relation with a totally different civilization and religion, and with
other conceptions of life and government. Some aspects of the
action and reaction of Persia on Greece and Greece on Persia
may be left to be referred to in the sequel; but among the points
on which Herodotus touches in narrating the conquest of Lydia
and Ionia are the contempt of Cyrus for the commercial habits
of the Greeks, and his rejection of the proposal of the Spartans
when, unwilling to give more material help for the Ionian cities,
they put forward a kind of Monroe doctrine in behalf of Greek
city life. His accommodation to Greek religious institutions—
anticipating his policy in Babylon—can be seen in the use made
by him of the Greek oracles, as may be inferred from the way in
which, after Cyrus had so remarkably revealed his power by the
defeat of Croesus, the oracular replies were in favour of Persia.

III. CONQUEST OF BABYLON

Though neither Babylon nor Egypt actually assisted Croesus
in his distress, the alliance between the three must have been well
known; and this must have sharpened the intention of Cyrus to

deal with the remaining members of it. The expectation of an
Iranian attack on Babylon, probably before Cyrus defeated
Astyages, can be traced in the poem of a Jewish exile in Babylon,
who anticipates the complete destruction of the city by the Medes
(Is. xiii, 17 *sq*.). Certainly, at any time after 546 Babylon had
good cause for anxiety in the Perso-Median empire under its
new and successful ruler. Egypt, till Babylon had fallen, or Cyrus
could threaten the command of the Mediterranean, may have felt
more secure.

Yet the attack on Babylon was not made for a few years after
the fall of Lydia. Of the reasons for this delay, and of Cyrus'
activities during the interval, we are ignorant; he may have had
to direct his energies to the far east: Herodotus speaks of the
Bactrians and Sacae in addition to Babylon and Egypt dividing
his attention. But when he acted he acted decisively, and the
conquest of Babylon, begun only in 540, was completed by the
late summer of 539. The army he now led was large; and, as
formerly in Media, so now in Babylon, Cyrus was assisted by
divisions within the empire he was attacking. Nabonidus, the
last king of Babylon, himself, unlike the kings of the Chaldean
house of Nebuchadrezzar, a native of Babylonia, had been raised
to the throne as the result of a conspiracy, and, in contrast to the
short reigns—three in six years—of Nebuchadrezzar's immediate
successors, maintained it for 18 years. But he failed to maintain
internal union and content; possibly by his personal indifference to
national security—for a good part of his reign military affairs seem
to have been handed over to his son Belshazzar—and clearly to
some extent by his religious policy as well, he provoked much
discontent, of which Cyrus availed himself in his rapid conquest
and occupation of the country (see p. 13 n.). The course of this
conquest can be traced in considerable detail. It was probably in
the year 540 B.C. that Cyrus opened his Babylonian campaign.
Whether he approached from the east, descending through the
Zagros gates, or (as seems more probable in view of the presence
of the governor of Gutium) from the north, which also had long
been his, along the Tigris, is not stated, but the first notable
success to which the operations led was the capture, after hard
fighting, of Opis, which lay on the Tigris to the north of Babylon.
This secured northern Babylonia for Cyrus, who seems now to
have divided his forces. He himself at the head of one army
within a fortnight captured Sippar, near the Euphrates and 50
miles nearer the capital, without having to strike a blow. Two days
later the second army, under Ugbaru (Gobryas) the governor of

Gutium, marched unresisted into Babylon, and took Nabonidus prisoner before he had time to escape. Gutium was a district north of Opis, enclosed between the Tigris, the Diyala, the lower Zab and the mountains to the east; but about Gobryas, its governor, there is some doubt. Though it is clear that he is not the same as the conspirator of that name who helped Darius seventeen years later to overthrow the Magian pretender, complete certainty cannot be claimed for the attractive conjecture which would identify him with an important officer of the Babylonian army who held high positions even before the death of Nebuchadrezzar[1].

If the two are identical, we must conclude that Cyrus had secured the allegiance of Ugbaru before moving south, and that the rapidity of his conquest was greatly accelerated by the amount of sympathy which the revolting Babylonian general commanded within the Babylonian empire. Ugbaru forced his way into Babylon on the 16th day of the month Tishri (October); on the third of the following month, Markheshwān, Cyrus himself entered the city; and eight days later (if a somewhat mutilated passage is so to be understood), Ugbaru overcame the last remnant of opposition by killing the king's son. The month Markheshwān marks the transition in Babylon from the reign of Nabonidus to that of Cyrus[2].

Making all allowance for the natural bias in Cyrus's own inscriptions, and for the Nabonidus-Cyrus Chronicle written and completed after his success was achieved and he had become king of Babylon, it is clear that Cyrus obtained the throne and empire of Babylon with the acquiescence, not to say on the invitation, of a large part of the population. He came to free them from a ruler who had forfeited their adhesion: he accepted the throne as the gift of their own god Marduk: 'Nabonidus, the king who did not fear him (Marduk), he delivered into his (Cyrus') hand. All the people of Babylon, Sumer and Akkad, princes and governors, fell down before him and kissed his feet. They rejoiced in his sovereignty, their faces shone.' Bel and Nebo loved the rule, rejoiced in the sovereignty of Cyrus. He was the founder of a new

---

[1] In a letter (*Revue d'Assyr.* 1914, pp. 165 *sqq.*) written late in the reign of Nebuchadrezzar a man named Gubaru holds office in southern Babylonia.

[2] Among the numerous dated business documents of the time one is dated the 24th of Markheshwān in the beginning of the reign of Cyrus: whether down to the 10th of this month Nabonidus was still held to be king, as has sometimes been inferred from another of these documents, is doubtful, and the last certain date in the documents of Nabonidus' 17th year is the 28th of Elul, the month next but one before to Markheshwān.

dynasty over a willing people, not a foreign conqueror indifferent to them and their interests. Such at least was the light in which Cyrus put himself forward, and he made it his first concern to secure peace and freedom from hostile attack, and to care for the needs of 'Babylon and all its cities.'

Cyrus immediately reversed the religious policy of Nabonidus, which had provoked great resentment, and in other respects in his attitude to the Babylonian gods he put himself right with the people. Whereas Nabonidus, especially apparently under threat of invasion, had gathered into the capital the images of the gods from various outlying temples—with the exception of Borsippa, Cuthah and Sippar—to the annoyance not only of the gods thus removed, but of Marduk also whose city they overcrowded, Cyrus sent back the gods and human beings, also, who had been exiled, to their own cities and re-established them there[1]. Among the districts to which he sent back the gods was western Elam from which they could hardly have been removed by Nabonidus, but by some predecessor of his[2]. He does not mention any cities or districts of the west which Nebuchadrezzar had incorporated in the Babylonian empire, but the Jewish tradition, that Cyrus fulfilled the expectations of the prophet of the Exile (Is. xl *sqq.*) that he would rebuild the cities of Judah and re-erect the Temple of Yahweh at Jerusalem, only ascribes to him what his general policy might well have led him to do. This restoration of the gods was begun in the month (Kislēw) after Cyrus entered Babylon, and continued till the month of Adar (March) following. The care now shown by Cyrus for the national religion had already been anticipated by Ugbaru, while Cyrus tarried at Sippar; the Chronicle relates that 'to the end of the month (viz. in which Ugbaru entered Babylon) the shield-bearers of the country of Gutium guarded the gates of E-sagil (*i.e.* the temple of Marduk at Babylon): no one's spear approached E-sagil or came within the sanctuaries, nor was any due rite transgressed.' In another inscription Cyrus describes

[1] It would appear from a recently-published verse account of Nabonidus, evidently emanating from a Persian source hostile to the Babylonian king, that he had been an energetic worshipper of the moon-god Sin of Harran, and had made a number of changes at the various cult-centres which, though claimed by him (and perhaps rightly) to be a restoration of ancient rites, were detested by the priests, or certain of them, 'who willingly lent themselves to the vilification of his memory in accordance with the political aims of Cyrus, and represented him as a kind of heretic, which he certainly was not' (Sidney Smith, *Bab. Hist. Texts*, pp. 62 *sqq.*).

[2] See the translation of the Cylinder Inscription (*E.Bi.* col. 982; Whitehouse, *Isaiah*, II, 343).

himself, presumably in reference to some work of reparation or extension such as Nabonidus had carried on freely in other cities near Babylon, as 'builder of E-sagil and E-zida' (the temple of Nebo in Borsippa).

Cyrus adopted the palace of the Babylonian kings as his own, and Babylon became one of the capitals of his now vast empire. Certainly he did not degrade Susa, nor abandon Ecbatana: but in Babylon, whose dominion since the time of Nebuchadrezzar had extended westward to the Mediterranean, he received the tribute and the homage of 'all the kings dwelling in palaces of all the quarters of the earth, from the Upper to the Lower Sea—all the kings of the West-land dwelling in tents.' Yet he appointed Ugbaru governor of Babylon, and Ugbaru appointed sub-governors under himself. And further, perhaps in view of the necessity for his own absence from Babylon, after the first few months, in the first month of the first full year of his reign, he for a time made his son Cambyses king of Babylon, keeping for himself the more comprehensive title of King of the Lands; but before the close of his first year he had, for reasons unknown, resumed for himself the double title 'King of Babylon, King of the Lands,' which is henceforward attested for every year down to the ninth and last, though occasionally during this period one or other of the two titles is used alone.

The capture of Babylon gave Cyrus a claim to the countries of the west—to Phoenicia and Syria down to the borders of Egypt. As his first conquest of Media threatened Babylon, so his last threatened Egypt; but as the threat hung for ten years and more in suspense over Babylon, so now Egypt, though exposed to attack and the object of military preparations entrusted by Cyrus to Cambyses, remained untouched by Cyrus during the last ten years of his life; and the last great conquest of the Persians was left for his son Cambyses. Even so, Cyrus, by uniting under his single sway what had been the dominions of the Medes, the Lydians, and the Babylonians, became master of the whole of western Asia, sovereign in Asia Minor which none of the greatest conquerors of Assyria or Babylon had brought under their sway, and at the same time sovereign in the east far beyond the farthest limits to which these conquerors had penetrated.

Between the years of active conquest and between 538 and his death in 529, Cyrus must have had enough and more than enough to occupy his attention in organizing and securing his rapidly increasing empire. In this, as in the actual acquisition of it, he must have been assisted by the readiness of large parts of the populations to receive him, and, also, by his tolerance. Even if religion was one of the vital factors in the rapid rise of Persia, Cyrus, unlike Mohammed and his successors, made no attempt to impose his own religion on his new subjects; on the other hand in his newly-won countries, at least in Babylon, he publicly appears as the devotee and servant of the religion of the country. He made no attempt to continue the Assyrian and Babylonian methods of transporting conquered populations to distant parts of his empire, largely perhaps because the earlier Assyrian and Babylonian treatment had broken the national spirit of the peoples of whom he had become the ruler, and because, in any case, in these countries the resistance offered was less general and less obstinate than that offered to the earlier conquerors: on the other hand he in certain cases at least reversed that policy and restored exiles to their countries. The administration of the empire through satraps, and much more belonging to the form or spirit of the government, was the work of Cyrus, but it will be more convenient to describe this policy later.

In spite of the extent of conquest already achieved by Cyrus ten years before his death, and the thoroughness with which he had established his authority in great kingdoms or empires which he had overcome, Cyrus died fighting. In details and even in naming the people with whom he was fighting the various stories, of which that given by Herodotus was but one of several known to him, differ widely; but that the last war of Cyrus was on the far eastern confines of his empire they are agreed. His opponents were the Massagetae, a savage race who occupied the great plain to the east of the Caspian, according to Herodotus; the Derbices assisted by the Indians, according to Ctesias; and the Dahae, a term meaning 'robbers' applied by the Persians to the wild desert tribes, according to Berosus. It is significant of the importance attached to securing the eastern frontier and subduing the wild peoples about it that Cyrus undertook this campaign himself, leaving Cambyses to carry forward the preparations for the attack on Egypt.

IV. THE CONQUEST OF EGYPT BY CAMBYSES

The opening years (529–526 B.C.) of the reign of Cambyses, like the closing years of Cyrus, are involved in considerable obscurity; the one conspicuous achievement of his reign is the conquest of Egypt (525). Of this Cambyses himself left no record that has yet been discovered, and, apart from an inscription, written in the reign of Darius, of an Egyptian, Uzahor-resenet, who received

Cambyses on his visit to Saïs, the history of this king and of his conquest of Egypt in particular must be constructed almost entirely from Greek sources, especially Herodotus, who drew mainly on a Persian and an Egyptian source, both alike hostile to the king.

Merely as successors to the Assyrian and Babylonian empires, the Persians, apart from any special provocation, would probably have sought to add Egypt to their empire; and certainly, as a matter of fact, in establishing their authority in that country for over a century (with one or two brief interruptions) they far surpassed the achievements of the Assyrians who, under Esarhaddon and Ashurbanipal, conquered and for a few years held it, and even more that of Nebuchadrezzar who, barely forty years before the accession of Cambyses, attacked Egypt, but proceeded to no permanent occupation of it.

Egypt had, immediately before the Persian conquest, passed through a period of considerable activity and prosperity, which concealed, however, the seeds of its decay. This was during the long reign of Amasis, to which native records and Herodotus agree in assigning a length of 44 years. Since Amasis died just before the Persian invasion, his accession, which he owed to a revolt of the native Egyptian troops against Apries, is to be placed in 569–8 B.C. Amasis, who was not of low birth (Hdt. II, 172), but born of parents highly placed at the court of Apries (Breasted, IV, 1000), found himself obliged, in the opening years of his reign, to secure the country from the mercenaries who had supported Apries, and also to withstand the Babylonian attack. This, as a contemporary Babylonian inscription records, took place in the thirty-seventh year of Nebuchadrezzar (c. 568–7 B.C.). Whether Nebuchadrezzar's attack was merely a revenge for the help which Egypt had given in the past to the tottering Assyrian empire against its Babylonian enemies, or whether, coinciding with the recent change of dynasty in Egypt, it was intended to utilize the distractions and weakness of the country to establish a permanent occupation such as the Assyrians had attempted in the previous century, it proved as a matter of fact but a passing menace, and for the remainder of the reign of Amasis Egypt remained, on the one hand, free from attack and even, till the menace of Persia became obvious, from fear of attack, and, on the other, abstained from any attempt at annexation, except in the case of Cyprus which was conquered and made tributary. (On the history viewed from the Egyptian side, see vol. III, pp. 305 *sqq.*)

From the circumstances, already referred to and related in detail elsewhere (see vol. III, p. 302 *sq.*), in which Amasis became

king, it might have been anticipated that his policy would have
led him to react against the reliance of recent kings on foreign
and particularly Greek mercenaries, and to rely more upon the
native troops. But whether because Amasis perceived the inade-
quacy of the latter, or for other reasons, his reign is marked by
no such reaction, but rather by more intimate relations with the
Greeks. He was pre-eminently Philhellene: in addition to connecting himself with the dynasty he had overthrown by marrying
the daughter of Psammetichus II, he married also Ladice, a
Greek lady of Cyrene. He made rich presents to various Greek
shrines: after the destruction of the temple at Delphi (548 b.c.)
he contributed a thousand talents weight of alum for its rebuilding; he presented a gold-covered image of Athene to Cyrene,
and made gifts also to the temples at Lindus and Samos. With
Polycrates of Samos in particular he established close and friendly
relations.

In one respect, indeed, Amasis may have given satisfaction to
Egyptian anti-foreign feeling by appearing to restrict the freedom
of Greek merchants, and actually limiting the points of contact
between Greeks and Egyptians: he made Naucratis the sole Greek
emporium in the Delta, even compelling cargoes driven by
weather to any other point on the coast to be transported thither.
But the restriction proved no serious hindrance to Greek trade,
and the new city, situated on the Canopic arm of the Nile and not
very far from Amasis' capital, Saïs, continued to flourish as an
almost exclusively Greek city, in close touch with and engaging
the interest of the whole Greek world, which contributed to the
building of its Greek temples.

But while the prosperity of this important Greek city on
Egyptian soil is one of the distinctive features of the reign of
Amasis, the king may have appealed to Egyptian feelings by his
numerous activities in the building or restoration of Egyptian
temples, notably at Saïs and Memphis; and the Serapeum stele
states that he buried the Apis which was born in the fifth and
died in the twenty-third year of his reign with pomp unsurpassed
before[1]. By nature, if he may be judged by the impressions received by Herodotus from the stories current in the next century,
he would have done all that was possible to secure the attachment
both of the native and the foreign elements in his country; for in
these stories he appears as a man of resource and versatility and
industry, as one who had largely broken away from the court
conventions that had greatly restricted the Egyptian kings, and

[1] See Breasted, *Ancient Records*, iv, p. 513 *sq.*

who yet had the wit and good humour to turn aside as far as possible the offence which his liberalism tended to occasion.

But in the course of his reign, and as we may believe under the pressure of events in the east, Amasis was compelled to lean heavily on his mercenaries: Herodotus significantly records that he removed the Ionians and the Carians whom Psammetichus had settled in encampments below Bubastis and 'established them at Memphis, making them into a guard for himself against the Egyptians.' In spite of the prosperity of the country the cost of these mercenaries proved burdensome, and Amasis appears to have drawn for their support on the revenues of the temples. Thus when from about 550 B.C. onward the danger lurking in the rising power of Persia became clear, and to meet it Amasis was seeking or acquiescing in alliances with Croesus of Lydia, Polycrates of Samos, and Nabonidus of Babylon, he had two causes of weakness or insecurity at home: (a) there was always the possibility that the mercenaries, bound to him by no patriotic ties but on whom he relied for the effectiveness of his army and his fleet, would fail him at the crucial moment, and (b) the discontent among the Egyptians occasioned by his reliance on these foreigners and the means he was compelled to use in order to support them.

Though the rapidity of Cyrus's movements in 546 prevented Amasis from actually supporting his ally Croesus, his opposition to Persia, as implied by the alliance, would be sufficient occasion for Persia to mark down Egypt for conquest in due time. Babylon, however, naturally came first, and Babylon was not occupied by the Persians till 539; and with the inclusion of this ancient empire in his already vast domains and with warfare on the troublesome far eastern frontier the last ten years of Cyrus were sufficiently engaged. With Babylon, the Babylonian provinces in Syria, which however had not remained entirely quiescent under Nabonidus (vol. III, p. 218 *sq.*), fell to Persia. In this way the Phoenicians would come under Persian control—according to Herodotus, 'the Phoenicians had delivered themselves over to the Persians of their own accord'—and Persia gained possession of an important means to the subjugation of Egypt—the Phoenician fleet. The value of this can be easily guessed from the fact that Cambyses was tempting the Cyprians to throw off the yoke of Egypt and constitute a contingent in his forces, and was persuading Polycrates of Samos to abandon his understanding with Egypt and to place his fleet at the disposal of the Persian king. (See vol. III, p. 305 *sq.*)

It was not till four years after his accession that Cambyses found himself ready to attack Egypt. His first task must have been, if not to pursue the offensive in prosecuting which Cyrus had died, at least to make secure the conquests of Cyrus in Asia. He may also have been called upon to defend the sovereignty over the dominions which passed from Cyrus to himself. Cyrus, indeed, had indicated Cambyses, his eldest son by Cassandane[1], the daughter of Pharnaspis, an Achaemenid, as his successor; and had thus so far as possible freed the empire from the dangers of a disputed succession. But there are some uncertain indications of conflicts within the realm, and even of the connection of these with dissension between Cambyses and his brother Smerdis (Bardiya). Herodotus speaks incidentally of Cyrus, and again afterwards of Cambyses, 'having subdued' Asia; and, in spite of its romantic character, the *Cyropaedeia* of Xenophon may preserve a good historical tradition when its author says that after the death of Cyrus 'immediately his sons quarrelled and immediately cities and nations revolted, and everything took a turn for the worse.' Darius in the Behistun Inscription directly asserts that before proceeding to Egypt Cambyses had his brother murdered, keeping the death concealed from the people. It is reasonable to find a cause for the murder, not in the fable of Herodotus which assumes that Smerdis had accompanied Cambyses to Egypt, but in suspicions of Cambyses of the loyalty of his brother and a desire to have him out of the way before undertaking the conquest of Egypt.

As Cyrus in his conquest first of Media and then of Babylon, so Cambyses in his conquest of Egypt found his task lightened by treachery within the country he was attacking. How far this may have been the result of definite overtures on his part cannot be said; but Polycrates at the crucial moment transferred his support from Egypt to Persia, and Phanes who had held an important position among the mercenaries of Amasis on the eve of war fled from Egypt and placed his skill and knowledge of Egyptian conditions at the service of Cambyses. Of treachery on the part of the priests there is no direct record, but the inscription of Uzahor-resenet gives some ground for suspicion of disaffection, and has even given rise to the suspicion that he had used his position as Admiral to keep the Egyptian fleet out of action. Amasis died before the Persian attack developed, and his son Psamatik or Psammetichus III, a man at that time in middle life, succeeded him.

One important detail in the preparations for the invasion of Egypt was, according to the picturesque narrative of Herodotus,

---

[1] And not by Nitetis the daughter of Apries (Hdt. iii, 2, 3,) nor by Amytis the daughter of Astyages (Ctesias, 29). See Xenophon, *Cyr.* viii, 8, 2.

worked out on the suggestion of Phanes. Whether on this point Cambyses actually needed the advice of the Greek renegade from Egypt, or was otherwise acquainted, as Esarhaddon and Ashur-banipal before him had been, with the essentials to a successful passage of the desert lying between Palestine and Egypt, he secured the water-supply for his army by establishing good rela-tions with the Arabs. Of the action of the fleet, which supported the land army, no details are known; its base was at Acre[1].

Cambyses led his army by the coast road from Gaza to the confines of Egypt where, at the city of Pelusium, he found the Egyptian army, including the Ionian and Carian mercenaries, awaiting him. Here he decisively defeated them, the garrison in Pelusium itself for some time offered a stubborn resistance before capitulating; but the defeated troops retired in disorder to Memphis, and there endured a siege of some duration. With the capture of that city and, together with it, of the Egyptian king Psammetichus III, who had reigned but six months, Cambyses found Egyptian resistance at an end, Heliopolis alone of the other cities offering any opposition[2]. By the end of May 525 B.C. he was recognized as king of Egypt. Cf. vol. III, p. 310.

V THE WORK OF CAMBYSES AND DARIUS IN EGYPT

But the plans of Cambyses had not been limited to the conquest of Egypt alone: he aimed at an African empire as extensive as his Asian dominion. Libya and Cyrene avoided attack by making their submission. In three directions he planned to extend his conquest so as to bring within his empire Carthage, Ethiopia and the oasis of Ammon. But for the conquest of Carthage a fleet was required, and the Phoenicians who formed the main naval strength of Cambyses proved so reluctant to operate against their kinsmen that this plan had to be abandoned. Cambyses undertook the conduct of the Ethiopian campaign himself, detaching at Thebes a force of 50,000 men (according to Herodotus) for the expedition to the west. These troops reached the seven-days' distant city of Oasis (el-Khargah), which, perhaps as the result of the initial success of this expedition, was tributary to Cambyses' successor Darius, but in their further march west towards the oasis of Jupiter Ammon they were overtaken by disaster, being, according to the story, buried under a sand-storm (Hdt. III, 26).

[1] As a passing reference in Strabo XVI, p. 758 implies.
[2] Iamblichus, *Vita Pyth.* 4.

The Ethiopian campaign undertaken to the south from Thebes, probably closely following the Nile, also failed to achieve all that was intended. But it is probable that it was far from being the complete failure that Herodotus represents it to have been, nor was the measure of ill-success that attended it due to the fact that the capacity for organization displayed by Cambyses in the invasion of Egypt itself had given place to the folly of a madman allowing his troops to undertake the difficult marches through the southern deserts unprovided with supplies. On the other hand, unless the name of a place near the third cataract recorded by Strabo and others is merely due to Greek confusion with some similarly sounding Egyptian name, the storehouse of Cambyses (Καμβύσου ταμιεῖον) is evidence of the Persian king's commissariat department at four-fifths of the distance from Thebes to Napata, the sacred city of the Ethiopians which had served as their capital, and two-thirds of the distance to distant Meroe to which the capital had been transferred[1].

Complete subjugation of Ethiopia would have involved the capture of Meroe, and this Cambyses failed to achieve, in spite of statements of some late Greek writers which might seem to imply that he did. Circumstances still unknown to us compelled Cambyses to retire, his troops now suffering from lack of supplies, though scarcely to the extent implied in the highly coloured Egyptian story preserved by Herodotus. The measure of success achieved by Cambyses south of Thebes, whence this campaign was undertaken, is to be seen in the securing of the southern boundary of Egypt—Elephantine continued for more than a century to be held by a strong Persian garrison—and the establishing of some degree of Persian authority extending from Elephantine over northern Ethiopia, *i.e.* the country immediately to the south of Elephantine, the southern gate of Egypt. It is significant that Herodotus, while in his narrative of the Ethiopian campaign he speaks of unqualified failure, elsewhere not only mentions Ethiopians as the subjects of Persia in the time of

---

[1] In an inscription, the Ethiopian king Nastesenen speaks of defeating, at some place north of Meroe, K-m-b-s-u-d-n, who had led against him a well-planned expedition by land and water. The attempt to identify this K-m-b-s-u-d-n with Cambyses (B. Schäfer, Lehmann-Haupt in *P.W.*) has been strongly criticized by Reisner who on the basis of his discoveries in Nubia constructs a sequence of Ethiopian kings in which Nastesenen is 21st from Taharḳa (+ 663). His earliest possible date would therefore be *c.* 482–472, and his more probable date *c.* 307–287 B.C. (*Harvard African Studies*, vol. II). See, on the other hand, the view of Hall, vol. III, p. 312.

Darius (VII, 9), but actually refers to 'the Ethiopians who border upon Egypt whom Cambyses subdued as he marched against the long-lived Ethiopians,' and who, he further asserts, were still tributary to Persia under Darius: he also speaks of 'Ethiopians who dwell above Egypt' forming a part of Xerxes' army against Greece under Arsames the son of Darius. The result of Cambyses' campaign, then, was that, though it failed to reach Meroe and to enable the Persian king to overthrow the Ethiopian as he had overthrown the Egyptian monarchy, it carried the Persian arms and finally established Persian authority much farther south than any previous Asiatic conqueror had come: the success of Cambyses far exceeded in this direction that of the Assyrians in the previous century.

In another important respect Egyptian contemporary sources have corrected the one-sided Egyptian stories concerning the activity of Cambyses current a century later and preserved by Herodotus. According to these he from the first outraged Egyptian sensibilities by desecration and sacrilege: immediately after the fall of Memphis he proceeded to Saïs, and there violated the corpse of Amasis; after his return to Memphis from Ethiopia he slew Apis the sacred calf and openly mocked at the religious customs of Egypt, treated the priests with violence and contumely, desecrated temples, destroyed images and freely interfered with the observance of religious festivals. This policy or conduct, contrasting so strikingly with that of Cyrus towards the Babylonian gods and religious customs, cannot be altogether the invention of a conquered people: the destruction of Egyptian temples, for example, is not only attributed to Cambyses in hostile Egyptian tradition, but is neutrally attested by the tradition current a century later among the Jews of Elephantine, according to which 'when Cambyses came into Egypt...the temples of the gods of the Egyptians were all of them overthrown,' while the Jewish temple at Elephantine was left unharmed[1].

The violation of the corpse of Amasis may be doubted, and, in any case, Cambyses at first adopted a very different policy towards the Egyptian religion, and indeed a policy precisely similar to that of Cyrus in Babylon. Immediately after he had obtained effective possession of the country he came to Saïs, the seat of the dynasty which he had just overthrown, and there, according to the statement of Uzahor, who received him in the temple of Neith, he sought by acquiescence in Egyptian religious custom and rites to give to the crown he had won by conquest the sanction of the

---

[1] Cowley, *Aramaic Papyri*, 30, l. 13 *sq.*

native religion. As king of Egypt he received the name Re-mesuti,
born of Re; he worshipped and made offering to Neith and all
the great gods in Saïs, as all good Egyptian kings had done before
him. In particular he granted to Uzahor authority to eject the
foreigners, presumably foreign mercenaries, from the precincts of
the temple, and to restore the temple revenues.

Later in the inscription—it was not written till the reign of
Darius—Uzahor refers to 'the heavy misfortune which had be-
fallen the whole land, such as this country had never experienced
before,' in which he is perhaps alluding with a discreet vagueness
to a change of policy on the part of Cambyses, of which a severe
treatment of the priesthood and a less tolerant attitude to the
Egyptian religion were characteristic. Apart from the violation of
the corpse of Amasis, even in Herodotus the charges of sacrilege
all relate to what was done by Cambyses after his return from
Ethiopia. Herodotus attributes this later conduct to a mental break-
down of Cambyses, and some, accepting this, have traced the
madness to the hardships and ill-success of the Ethiopian campaign. Possibly it was due to political plots in which priests
and officials of the temples were conspicuously involved.

Be this as it may, before he died—by his own hand, on his way
to Persia, whither he was recalled, in the spring of 522—Cambyses appears to have been able to establish Persian rule in
Egypt with the same thoroughness with which he had achieved
the initial conquest of the country. The Egyptians took no part
in the revolts against the Achaemenidae which broke out at the
end of his reign and took Darius many months to quell (see on
these, pp. 173 *sqq.*). Babylon at this time produced more than one
brief occupant of the throne of Babylon, but no Egyptian disputed with Cambyses or—till the very end of his reign—with
Darius the throne of Egypt. The Persian Aryandes, whom
Cambyses had appointed governor of Egypt unchallenged by
the native population, maintained his position till Darius himself
deprived him of his office and life on the ground or suspicion of
arrogating to himself royal prerogatives. It was not till 485 B.C.,
more than thirty years after the death of Cambyses, that an
Egyptian revolt led to the enthronement of a native chief, a
break, brief even then, in the rule of Persian monarchs of Egypt.
Thus for a generation the Persian dominion over Egypt established by Cambyses remained unchallenged.

So far, then, as Egypt was concerned the main task of Darius
was to maintain what Cambyses had won. In one direction,
indeed, viz. westwards, the African dominions of Persia were

enlarged under Darius, while they suffered contraction in none. Aryandes the governor of Egypt utilized dissensions in Cyrene and Barca to extend Persian control as far west as Euhesperides, west of Barca. Pheretime of Cyrene having appealed to Aryandes against Barca, Aryandes despatched the Persian army under Amasis (or Arsames) the Maraphian, and the Persian fleet under Badres the Pasargadan to attack Barca. The expedition was completely successful and a large part of the population was deported to the other end of the Persian empire, to Bactria. It is possible that the independence of Aryandes' action in this matter may have been one of the counts against him with Darius—another was that he had struck a peculiarly pure silver coinage; but in any case the ultimate result was an enlargement of Darius' dominions: included in the satrapy of Egypt were 'the Libyans bordering on Egypt' and Cyrene and Barca.

The country won by conquest had to be maintained by force, though Darius tempered the force it was necessary to employ by resuming and perhaps enlarging the conciliatory policy of Cambyses' early months in Egypt. The army commanded by a Persian general and the fleet commanded by a Persian admiral at the disposal of the government in Egypt have just been mentioned. Strong garrisons were established in the central city of Memphis, at Daphnae at the eastern extremity and (in all probability) Marea at the western extremity of the Delta, and at Elephantine the frontier town between Egypt and Ethiopia. The support of the troops was maintained by contributions in kind from the Egyptians. The troops largely consisted of Persians, but far from exclusively: Herodotus speaks also of others ($\epsilon\pi\iota\kappa\text{o}\upsilon\rho\text{o}\iota$) at Memphis; and at Elephantine Jews and other Semites formed part of the garrison, and indeed (at least in 411 B.C.) Egyptians[1]. Egyptians also served in Xerxes' fleet against Greece. Nor were the officers entirely drawn from the Persians, though it is noticeable that, at any rate somewhat later than the reign of Darius, native Egyptians occupy no offices in the Persian army in Egypt. Military considerations, the need for facilitating at all times the movements to and fro of Persian troops, may have had much to do with the systematic provisioning with water of the desert road from Palestine to Egypt: this was secured by a service organized at Memphis.

Darius was not concerned to conceal the fact that he held Egypt as a conquered country: in an inscription erected by the side of the canal which he re-opened he describes himself as Persian and relates that 'from Persia I seized Egypt.' Yet by his attitude

[1] Cowley, *Aramaic Papyri*, 30, l. 8.

towards the Egyptian religion and by his care for the economic prosperity of the country, he must have done much to soften the hardness of alien rule and to correct the ill-feeling engendered by the later policy of Cambyses. Like Cambyses, Darius adopted as king of Egypt a name, Stitu-Re, that proclaimed his devotion to the god Re. He repaired the temple of Ptah at Memphis, and built the great temple in the oasis of Khargah. He made offerings to the god and gifts to the priests. Uzahor in his inscription at Saïs describes how Darius commanded him to re-establish the Temple-school there, and concludes eulogistically 'all this the king did because he knew that such was the best means of awakening to new life all that was falling into ruin, in order to uphold the name of all the gods, their temples, their revenues, and the ordinances of their feasts forever.' Later in his reign, in the thirtieth year, the architect Khnum-ab-Re who carried out much work for Darius speaks of him as 'the friend of all the gods.'

Among the measures known to have been taken by Darius for the economic welfare of the country the chief was the completion of the canal connecting the Nile (a little above Bubastis) with the Red Sea (near Suez) which Necho nearly a century before had attempted and abandoned. The careful measures for keeping in repair the great dam at Memphis, attested by Herodotus for his own days as one of the activities of the Persian government, may also go back to the time of Darius.

The tribute exacted from the entire satrapy of Egypt was 700 talents (rather under a quarter of a million sterling) and the yield of the fish taken from Lake Moeris, which was estimated at a talent a day for six months in the year and 20 minae for the other six months. The country had also to supply corn for the troops. Next to Babylon with Assyria, which paid 1000 talents yearly, Egypt yielded the largest tribute of the Persian satrapies, but in proportion to the population and prosperity of the country it can scarcely have weighed very heavily on the taxpayers, even though the large priestly element was exempt from payment.

CHAPTER II

THE REFORM OF THE ATHENIAN STATE

I. CYLON

DURING the first half of the seventh century B.C. Attica was an obscure corner of Greece. It had achieved one thing—unity; the farmer of Eleusis, Marathon or Sunium felt himself an Athenian. There was one central government and when its word went out to levy men for war or cattle for sacrifice, it was obeyed. This government was aristocratic and the Attic peasant left high affairs of state to his betters, while he busied himself in farming or learning to plant olives. As yet there was little overseas trade. Athenians went down to the sea in ships, for the paths of the sea are easier than the roads of Greece, and many scholars see in the naucraries evidence for a navy on a small scale, while Attic vases of the Dipylon style often display what may be Athenian galleys guarding against pirates (vol. III, pp. 595, 596.) Athens herself belonged to the Amphictyony of Calauria, a religious league of the cities which lay around the Saronic gulf, but across her way farther afield lay Aegina the jealous island of merchants, while nearer home, within sight of the city, was Salamis, now in the hands of the Megarians, who had their neighbourly feuds with the city of Pallas. As yet, indeed, there was little enough to export and little power to win markets. Other states had made the venture of colonization and they had their reward. The one Attic industry of note was pottery but the day of its dominance was yet to come and Corinthian, Sicyonian and Chalcidian ware held the field as pottery *de luxe*. The greater part of Attica was poor land from which the peasantry could hardly earn a living. The good land lay chiefly in the plain behind the city and most of this belonged to nobles, whose clans gave their names to many places in this area. Enriched by this fertile land the nobles were learning to live in some kind of splendour which may still be seen depicted on Attic vases of the time. They spent their substance like gentlemen in competing at the athletic festivals of Greece and so the name of Athens was sometimes heard at Olympia. In neighbouring states, Corinth, Megara and Sicyon, there were brilliant tyrannies, and the Athenian gentry learned at these courts ambitions and desires alien to the home-keeping peasantry of Attica.

MAP I

ATTICA

C. 600 B.C.

Scales

0   5   10   15   20
English Miles.

0   5   10   15   20   25
Kilometres

To face p. 27

It is thus not surprising that the first event we know of in the political history of united Attica is the attempt of a noble to copy his friends abroad and set up a tyranny. A young aristocrat Cylon had brought glory to Athens and himself by winning a victory in the footrace at Olympia (640 B.C.[1]) and had added to his athletic distinction the social triumph of marriage with the daughter of Theagenes the tyrant of Megara. The marriage implies that there was peace between Athens and Megara at the time, but the relations of the two states were not friendly and Theagenes himself might well feel more secure if Athens was ruled by a tyrant and a kinsman. Sure of Megarian support, Cylon found nobles of his own age ready to help in the overthrow of the governing aristocracy. The attempt was made in the year of an Olympian festival when Cylon's chief claim to distinction might be remembered. It is likely that his marriage and his *coup d'état* were not very long removed in time from his victory in the footrace, and that the conspiracy was a young man's adventure. The plot was at first successful and Cylon and his friends helped by Theagenes' hoplites seized the Acropolis. But the archon of that year was Megacles the Alcmaeonid, the first of a long line of determined, tenacious aristocrats. He sent out word through the naucraries—the local districts of Attica—and the levies poured into the city under their headmen, the prytaneis. Tyranny found its best soil in commercialized states, and the Athenian peasantry and farmers were still loyal to their aristocracy. The Acropolis was blockaded and its defenders were starved into surrender, though Cylon himself and some of his followers escaped into exile. The remainder trusted for their lives to the terms of the surrender and the protection of the gods. But Megacles and his followers, possibly already at feud with the nobles who followed Cylon, massacred their opponents, some even, it was said, at the altar of the Eumenides near the Areopagus.

The state was saved, but this massacre stirred the conscience of the Athenian peasantry which had more superstition or a deeper moral sense of guilt than the more sophisticated aristocrats. Possibly, too, other nobles resented the high-handed action of Megacles. The result was dissension in Attica aggravated by the feeling that the land was polluted by this bloodshedding. An inevitable consequence of Theagenes' support of Cylon was that Megara and Athens came to open war in which the Megarians held at least their own. The Alcmaeonidae, though the taint of bloodguiltiness clung to them, maintained themselves for a time

[1] For the date of Cylon see Chronological Note 1.

but were at last forced to submit to judgment. They were tried before a court of nobles, the living were banished, the bones of the dead cast outside the Attic border. Their accuser was Myron of Phlya; the fact that his name is preserved suggests that he was a man of note, perhaps the head of a rival noble house. There was a tradition that Epimenides, a Cretan seer, was brought in to conduct the formal purification of the city. Later writers however give contradictory accounts of the date of Epimenides and it is likely enough that he really lived a century later. But a formal purification must have taken place. There is another tradition that it was Solon who persuaded the Alcmaeonidae to submit to trial. But it is not likely that the trial was so long after the massacre that Solon would have become eminent enough to intervene. Nor is there anything in the history of the Alcmaeonid family to suggest that they would yield to the moral suasion of any statesman however respected. By the banishment of the guilty the land had peace but the moral ascendancy of the nobles was shaken.

II. DRACO

In consequence of all this the Athenians realized the need for a lawgiver to put an end to this lawlessness and fix and make accessible in a code the practice of the judges, the Thesmothetae (see vol. III, p. 593). The nobles were to be bound by their best judgments. Accordingly in the closing decades of the seventh century—the traditional date is 621 B.C.—Draco was given powers to make a code of laws[1]. There was a belief that the penalties in his code were unduly harsh according to the notions of later times, so that 'Draconian' became a synonym for 'severe.' Otherwise hardly a trace remains of most of Draco's work. For his laws were superseded by the code of Solon and we have no means of disengaging from Solon's laws any part which he may have inherited from his predecessor. There is one exception. Draco's lawgiving about homicide was important and permanent. The troubles of the state had been largely caused by blood feuds and the new code sought to set definite bounds to this evil. The conscience of the Athenians had been roused by their domestic troubles and no less by their growing enlightenment, and Draco's laws about homicide are significant of the moral atmosphere of his day.

[1] If the intervention of Solon is not historical the banishment of those responsible for the Cylonian massacre may be set before the legislation of Draco as above, but the evidence does not admit of certainty.

The blood feud was deeply rooted in Attic sentiment. It arose from the belief that the spirit of a man killed cries to his kin for vengeance and cannot be appeased until blood has had blood. If the injured spirit is not thus set at rest, it remains hostile and has for its allies the powers of the earth, which refuse fertility to a land tainted with guilt. The son inherits the feud as he inherits his father's goods and has no choice but to seek revenge. This was the belief which clung to the soil of Greece proper, where the close bond of the family was strongest. In the society of the Homeric poems, a society uprooted from its mother country, these ideas appear shadowy. There killing is an injury which gives the kin of the deceased the right to vengeance or to compensation. Killing is hardly murder; the dead man is little more than a chattel with a sentimental value; it is not discreditable to take goods in place of the son lost by murder. The state has no direct interest in the matter which is a diplomatic incident between families.

But in Greece proper the old belief continued and was strengthened by the teaching of the Delphian Shrine, which, probably from the eighth century onwards, had declared that killing involved the defilement of the killer and of his city until vengeance had been taken and rites of purification performed. The moral quality of the act did not at first challenge inquiry. The spirit of a man killed by accident was no less angry, his kin no less injured than if the killing was wanton and deliberate. The duty of vengeance, the pollution of the act was just as great. Where the killer was unknown so that the next of kin could not pursue the feud, the state was obliged to step in. Thus at Athens the Basileus and the four Tribal Kings, the representatives of the state in its earliest form, meet outside the Prytaneum and solemnly pronounce their ban on the unknown homicide and thus the land is cleared of guilt. So in the *Oedipus Tyrannus* of Sophocles, the King standing at the doors of his palace in Thebes bans the unknown slayer of Laius:

> That man, whoe'er he be, from all the land
> Whose government and sway is mine, I make
> An outlaw. None shall speak to him, no roof
> Shall shelter. In your sacrifice and prayer
> Give him no place, nor in drink-offerings,
> But drive him out of doors...for it is he
> Pollutes us, as the oracle Pythian
> Of Phoebus hath to-day revealed to me[1].

[1] ll. 236–243, trans. J. T. Sheppard.

But the state must do more. If the family vengeance falls on the innocent and the guilty goes free, the dead man is still hostile, the land is still cursed. And so the Areopagus was made a sanctuary whither a man might flee before the feud and declare his innocence of the act. Standing at the rock of Offence facing the pursuer of blood on the stone of Implacability he swears to his innocence and the Council of the State judges if his plea is true, and if it acquits, the avenger of blood must turn elsewhere. The homicide may, if he will, abandon his plea and, if he can, escape into exile. The state protects itself and also the next of kin, who must run down the actual killer and no one else. But presently reason began to struggle against the doctrine that the moral quality of the action was indifferent. It was realized that when a man wantonly attacks another's life or goods or honour and in doing so meets his death, he is himself the true cause of his killing and his spirit has no claim to be avenged. In the old Greek formula 'his death is without blood-price.' From the idea that the guilt of the killed implies the innocence of the killer may have arisen the conception of justifiable homicide, and this conception, no doubt already put into practice, was made law by Draco. It is laid down that where a man has killed in defence of himself, his goods, or his honour, he may flee to the sanctuary of Apollo Delphinios and there a court of Ephetae decides if his story is true and, if it is judged to be so, he is admitted to purification and protected[1].

A further advance was made by the setting up of a legal distinction between premeditated and unintended homicide. This is a greater break with the old ideas and, as Draco expressly makes it retrospective, it may not have been the regular practice until his code was published. Where a homicide could plead that he had not intended to kill his neighbour, he might take refuge at the sanctuary of Pallas outside the city. There the court of Ephetae judged his story and, if they judged it true, the kinsmen of the dead man must allow him to go into exile to remain there until the kinsmen, or, failing them, representatives of the dead man's phratry granted him pardon ($a\check{\iota}\delta\epsilon\sigma\iota\varsigma$). This is a compromise between the anger of the dead man, the guilt of blood and the moral ideas of a more enlightened time. Further, so as to restrict the area of the vendetta, Draco gave the protection of the law to the homicide in exile so long as he avoided the frontier markets of Attica and the general meeting-places of the Greeks. If the exiled homicide returns to Attica still unpardoned he may be

---

[1] Accidental killing at the games or in battle was apparently viewed as a variant of justifiable homicide and tried at the same sanctuary.

killed or haled to judgment, but not mutilated or held to ransom. Thus private vengeance is restricted to the duties of religion, and neither is cruelty allowed on the one hand nor cynical blackmail on the other.

The exclusive right of the family to prosecute for murder is expressly stated and, in the absence of relatives, the right falls to the phratry of the dead man. In the fragmentary inscription which contains a part of the law of Draco about homicide the Ephetae are found elaborately described as 'the Fifty-one, the Ephetae,' which suggests that a regular court of Fifty-one members had been instituted by Draco to supersede other bodies which bore the same name. The word probably meant those who 'admitted' to trial or to purification and the earliest Ephetae may have been priests at the several sanctuaries, for whom the Athenians, ever jealous of priestly authority, now substituted civil officials, who went in circuit to these *asyla* to judge the cause of suppliants. The Ephetae were presided over by the Basileus, the old tribal kings probably sitting as assessors with him. There was yet another court, at Phreattys near the harbour of Zea, where men in exile for unpremeditated homicide might defend themselves against a subsequent charge of deliberate murder. They pleaded their cause from a boat so as not to forfeit the protection of the law by setting foot on Attic soil. But as this court seems to imply some experience of the operation of Draco's other laws, it may have been set up later, possibly by Solon.

These laws of Draco are a skilful compromise between the claims of the family and of older religious ideas on the one hand and a more enlightened morality and more active intervention by the state on the other. They became a permanent part of Athenian jurisprudence and when Plato wrote his Laws he accepted for his model state the statutes which Draco had laid down for Athens[1].

III. FROM DRACO TO SOLON

Towards the end of the century Athens appears to have pursued a vigorous foreign policy. Her nearest enemy was Megara, and the possession of Salamis by the Megarians was a constant menace to Athens and a check on Attic sea-going trade. Unfortunately the ancient traditions about the wars over Salamis are vitiated by the absence of any clear chronology and by the disturbing

[1] The constitutional order ascribed to Draco in Aristotle's *Constitution of Athens*, c. IV, is almost universally regarded as unhistorical, and throughout this chapter it is not used as evidence.

attraction of the personality of Solon. For in periods without fixed chronology events gravitate towards the leading personality of the time. It may be taken as likely, though no more, that not long before the year 600 B.C. the Athenians had gained possession of Salamis and so made more possible a certain naval activity. This activity was directed towards the mouth of the Dardanelles, to wrest from the people of Lesbos the town of Sigeum in the Troad. Tradition records the name of the Athenian commander, one Phrynon, who had won a victory at Olympia in 636 B.C. The war may be set in the last decade of the seventh century. After a prolonged struggle which speaks well for the tenacity of the Athenians, the war ended in the arbitration of the Corinthian tyrant Periander about the year 600 B.C. In accordance with his award the Athenians remained in possession of Sigeum but the Lesbians took advantage of Athenian weakness later to retake the city (see vol. III, p. 516 and below, p. 69). The motive of this Sigeum adventure can hardly have been to secure a market for export trade. At least there is no evidence that Athenian products found a sale in these regions at this time. It had been suggested with some probability that Athens had already begun to import Black Sea corn to supplement her own scanty crops and that this war was an attempt to secure the free and unchallenged passage of these supplies. Whatever the motive, the city could hardly have committed herself to so distant and arduous an enterprise unless her own borders were secure, so we may suppose that she had successfully asserted herself against Megara, where the tyranny of Theagenes had collapsed. Thus at the beginning of the sixth century Athens was beginning to make herself felt in Greek affairs and was pursuing a spirited foreign policy. Athenian merchants were learning to engage in overseas trade and to travel abroad even as far as Cyprus and Egypt.

But at this very time the internal condition of Athens had become steadily worse and there was impending an economic crisis which the strain of these enterprises helped to hasten. The Athenian small farmers, though ready to fight their neighbours in times of need, may have resented being taken from their farms to distant wars—especially if these only resulted in easier importation of foreign and competing corn.

In the days of Hesiod in Boeotia the small peasant led a hard and anxious life, but on his own plot of land, excluded from political power, but his own master (see below, p. 478). Between the days of Hesiod and the days of Solon lies a great change due to the invention and spread of coined money. The old days of

barter were now coming to an end and the peasant must more
and more exchange his produce for coin, while the prices are fixed
by powers beyond his understanding and control. If he lacks the
new medium of exchange he must buy it or borrow it. The great
noble and the merchant who buys his way into the nobility has
at his command the luxuries of the world, fine cups and vases
from Corinth, handsome cloaks from Miletus, purple from
Laconia, metalwork from Chalcis the city of bronze. But the
peasant discovers new needs without the means of satisfying
them, and upon him falls the chief stress of the new epoch. In
any case Attica was bound to find the strain greater than most
Greek states, for the balance of trade was against her. The country
had not yet reached its full production of oil, wine or pottery;
it grew no more corn than was needed at home; the silver mines
of Laurium were as yet hardly touched. The needs of Attica grew
with a growing population in a country where the good land was
limited. Had all the Athenians been content to remain primitive
and simple, it might have been a second Arcadia, happy and un-
distinguished. But the nobles were not content. Wealth seemed
so worth while at any cost. This is the significance of the thought
that recurs in poems of the seventh and sixth centuries B.C., that
'money makes the man,' that if a man attains wealth he attains
everything, that men will do anything, even go far out to sea, to
win wealth and avoid poverty.

If the Athenian nobles were to keep abreast of their neighbours,
they must put away the idea of modest contentment, forget the
Delphic lesson of moderation and wring out of Attica the last
drops of wealth. They must find ever more things to sell abroad
for money, even the corn the Athenians needed to eat, even, if
need be, Athenians themselves. Draco's code had stereotyped
harsh laws protecting property and had failed to meet a grievance
still not clearly formulated. While it marked an advance in restricting the blood feud, in other ways the codification of law had
stood in the way of progress. The nobles were the judges and
without wrenching the law they might make it their tool.

The law of debt, above all, framed to protect the creditor in a
less advanced society, was turned into a great instrument of oppression. In ancient societies where the rich were rather hoarders
than capitalists men must be given the maximum of security
before they were willing to lend. The state, controlled by the rich,
used such power as it had to support the extreme rights of the
creditor against the debtor. On the other hand, especially in rather
primitive agricultural countries such as was Attica in the last half

of the seventh century, the peasant who was forced to borrow, first cattle or seed-corn and later money, had little security to offer except himself, his family and his land. A friend might stand surety, but the bitter experience of the Greeks was distilled in the sage maxim 'Be surety and destruction is near.' There may have been a time when even the peasant's land was not his to pledge, as it was really the common property of his clan. This stage had passed in Attica; private property had taken its place and now the peasant's land might be surety for him.

Land thus pledged was marked by boundary pillars (ὅροι), and Solon speaks of their removal as the freeing of the land in a passage which deals with the relief of debtors. These boundary pillars are commonly called 'mortgage stones' and such have been found in Attica, but none earlier than the fourth century. This last fact has aroused doubt whether Solon's 'boundary pillars' really recorded mortgages in his day, but there is no reason to assume that the pillars were of stone indelibly inscribed, or that, once private property in land was established, anything would prevent a peasant, under stress, from pledging his farm before he pledged himself. That the rich had accumulated much land before Solon is certain. It is hard to evade the conclusion that the poor had lost some. Sentiment may have been strong, but the stress of need is stronger and law was on the side of the rich who wished to add field to field. The word 'mortgage' may be in-exact[1]. The form of pledge is more likely to have been something more familiar to the needy which the Greeks called πρᾶσις ἐπὶ λύσει 'sale with a provision for redemption.' The land passed into the legal possession of the creditor at once, subject to the debtor's right to redeem it by the repayment of the loan, so the boundary pillars marked an effective, though possibly temporary, extension of the creditor's estate. How long the right of re-demption was to last would be a matter for bargaining. But the same stress which drove a peasant to borrow might prevent him from repaying, and thus by the sixth century there was a steady expropriation of the poor, and these boundary pillars were the silent witnesses to many hard bargains.

[1] See Lipsius, *Att. Recht*, p. 692 *sq*. For the arguments in favour of mortgage (ὑποθήκη) see Sir P. Vinogradoff, *The Outlines of Historical Juris-prudence*, vol. II, pp. 252–4. The view that until Solon the land of Attica was distributed in inalienable family holdings appears to the present writer hard to reconcile with the historical evidence. No deduction either way can fairly be drawn from Aristotle, *Politics*, II, 7. 1266 b 16. See on this passage Glotz, *La Solidarité de la famille etc...*, p. 329 *sq*.

A second form of security was for the peasant to pledge his labour or the produce of his labour. From being a peasant proprietor working for himself he might become a serf working for his creditor. Such a condition is reflected in the name *Hektemoroi* which came down in Attic tradition from the times of Solon. The word means 'Sixth-parters' and was explained in the fourth century as meaning those who worked on other men's land, paying to the owner one-sixth of the produce and keeping the remainder for their own use. Such a condition and its origin may be well illustrated from the Book of Genesis. 'Then Joseph said unto the people, Behold, I have bought you this day and your land for Pharaoh: lo, here is seed for you, and ye shall sow the land. And it shall come to pass at the ingatherings, that ye shall give a fifth unto Pharaoh, and four parts shall be your own, for seed of the field, and for your food, and for them of your households, and for food for your little ones. And they said, Thou hast saved our lives' (xlvii, 2 3 *sqq.*). The condition of the *Hektemoroi* was, however, something more grievous than that of *métayers* or of tenants paying a bearable rent. The name suggests some kind of state-recognized institution in that the quota was not subject to the processes of bargaining or to variation in different parts of Attica. It may be, then, that in these *Hektemoroi* is to be seen an incipient serfdom like that of the Helots in Lacedaemon or the Penestae in Thessaly, except that in Attica there was no difference of race or right of conquest to plead in its favour. That such a serfdom might arise from debt may be seen from the Laws of Gortyn where there are found debt-serfs who are in a position between complete freedom and absolute slavery, and are distinguished from those who have been adjudged the slaves of their creditors.

In Crete the rights of the former were defined by the law, and when the debt was paid off they resumed the full rights of citizens. It is possible that the institution began in that way in Athens but was unfairly exploited by the rich who may have usurped rights to labour which hindered repayment, and may have then gone further and seized the *Hektemoroi* as slaves if ever they failed to pay their quota at the right time. For besides this institution of the *Hektemoroi* there was a yet more drastic weapon in the hands of the creditor. He might impose the condition that if a debt was not repaid, the debtor with wife and children became his slaves. The poor peasant might be forced to accept such a bond if his land was already pledged, and such an arrangement suited better nobles hastening to be rich. Thus Athenians were not only losing their land and becoming bound to make over part of the produce of their labour but were being made slaves and even sold abroad, 'some unjustly' says Solon, as though the noble judges did not enquire too closely into the claims of the rich and the rights of the poor.

So harsh a law harshly administered in times of economic stress is in itself enough to explain the discontent of the mass of the Athenians who had suffered or feared to suffer from it. The loss of land, the loss of independence, the loss of freedom, in an age in which the divine right of the nobles was challenged and money seemed at once the root of evil and the root of power, set abroad ideas of revolution.

For there was no easy road to redress. The constitution gave no power to the poor and very little to the lower middle class. In the words of Aristotle 'The cruellest and bitterest grievance of the many against the existing order was their slavery. But they were, too, discontented with all else. For at this time they had a share in almost nothing.' The aristocracy, by absorbing those who had succeeded in the race for wealth, was becoming more and more aloof from the mass of the people. A generation before, the peasantry had flocked into Athens to defend the existing order against Cylon; now it seemed as if a revolution or a tyrant would be the result, if not the remedy, of the economic ills which were so keenly felt. What the moment demanded was one who would face boldly the problem of debt, make just and fair laws for all, and discover means of relieving Attica of the economic inferiority which was the deep-seated cause of the social crisis. Fortunately for Athens and for the generations who have gained by the greatness of Athens, such a man was found in Solon the son of Execestides.

IV. SOLON AS ECONOMIC REFORMER

Solon is the first Athenian whose personality we can grasp. The evidence for his character lies in his poems, of which rather less than 300 lines have come down to us. He was not an inspired poet, he was a statesman with a philosophy of life who wrote in verse because as yet one did not write in prose. A travelled man of some wealth and position, he possessed, together with a genuine sympathy for the oppressed, a cool detachment from the partizanships of Attic politics; he was lacking in personal ambition though not unconscious of his own deserts as a statesman and reformer. The motive of his policy was a strong ethical desire to see fair dealing between the strong and the weak. To achieve this end

he was bold and resolute, otherwise he was no idealist and not
at all a doctrinaire. He was as bold in resisting the undue claims
of the poor as in assailing the injustice of the rich. In politics he
did not aim at democracy but at making a contented people and
a stable government.

To secure this was needed a radical reform of the law of debt
and a drastic handling of the grievances to which the old law had
given rise. Accordingly Solon, appointed Archon and 'reconciler'
in 594 B.C.[1], made these his first task. It was the practice for the
Archon on entering office to declare that he would maintain
existing rights of property during his rule. Instead of that, Solon
made a new proclamation, his programme for healing the evils
of the state. First he declared void existing pledges in land. In
his own words

> Best witness with me at the bar of Time
> Were the great mother of the Olympian gods
> Black Earth herself: for I pluck'd up the host
> Of boundary marks that pierced her everywhere.
> After long years of bondage, she is free.
>
> (fr. 24. Diehl, ll. 3–7.)

Further, he granted freedom to all men enslaved for debt and,
it is reasonable to assume, cancelled all debts which involved any
form of personal servitude. For the future he declared it illegal
to accept the person of a debtor as security for a loan. Thus all
debt slaves or debt serfs within Attica gained complete freedom.
It is no wonder that these measures were called the *Seisachtheia*,
the 'Shaking off of burdens.' For the new order meant freedom,
and to many, what the Greeks prized almost as much as freedom,
return to their country:

> Many I brought back to their fatherland
> To god-built Athens, who unlawfully
> Or by strict right were sold, or under stress
> Of debt had fled the land and wandering far
> Had unlearnt Attic speech: while others here
> Suffered a slave's despite and cower'd beneath
> Their masters' humours—these I have set free.
>
> (*ibid.* ll. 8–15.)

For those who had fled or were still in Attica the proclamation
of freedom was enough. There remained the Athenians who had
been sold abroad as slaves. These could not be liberated by the

---

[1] On the date, see the discussion in De Sanctis, *Atthis*[2], pp. 203–4. A
possible alternative is 591 B.C

bare *fiat* of the Athenian state. We may assume that they were ransomed by the Athenian treasury, by private benevolence, or by compulsion applied to the creditors who had sold them.

The grievances which Solon had to meet were agrarian or due to personal bondage for debt. That he went beyond the grievance and cancelled also commercial debts and contracts in which personal servitude was not involved is most unlikely. Solon was himself too well versed in the ways of trade to destroy such rudimentary credit as there was, from a desire for formal consistency. The action he did take was in itself bold and drastic enough but plainly necessary, as is shown by the fact that it was carried through without recourse to violence and without entirely destroying the power of the creditor aristocracy.

Many of the rich nobles must have lost much land which they had counted theirs, for such land as was recorded as gained by pledge was freed and restored to its former possessors. But the great estates with long-established titles were beyond the scope of Solon's enactment and the old Athenian aristocracy remained great landowners. This fact gave rise later to scandalous reports that Solon had deliberately played into the hands of his friends among the nobles. The land taken from the rich could not be enough to re-establish as independent farmers all those who had been set free. There accordingly arose a cry for a 'redistribution of land.' The Greeks readily invented for themselves an ideal past in which every citizen had an equal share in the land of his city state. But Solon would yield neither to the ideal past nor to the over-exigent present. Neither to win favour nor power was he willing 'to give to base and noble alike an equal share in the rich soil of their fatherland.' And his resolution prevailed. The result was that there remained in Attica many landless men who must gain a livelihood by handicrafts or by working as labourers on the land in place of the debt slaves or serfs who had tilled the estates of the rich. Among those who had gained freedom but not economic independence a leader who made great promises might easily find a following. And there were nobles, too, who had suffered most severely from the incidence of Solon's measures and were ready for any desperate venture to repair their fortunes. Thus the economic reform of Solon, great and permanent as were the benefits it brought to Attica, did not produce at once a millennium of contentment, but left behind the raw material of future discontents. It was reserved for the next generation to complete the creation of the small peasantry which made the agrarian prosperity of Attica.

Solon had achieved his first and immediate purpose but much remained to be done. The economic inferiority of Attica must be removed. To this end he sought to facilitate the growth of Athenian trade both westwards and eastwards. The carrying trade to the west was mainly in the hands of Corinth, to the east it was divided between Euboea and Aegina. Before Solon's time Athens had moved in the orbit of Aeginetan trade, no doubt with growing reluctance. Her commercial dependence on Aegina was manifested and in part maintained by the fact that such currency as circulated in Attica was on the Aeginetan monetary standard. What Athens needed was a coinage of her own struck on whatever standard was most convenient for the development of her overseas trade (see below, p. 129). This standard was that used by Corinth and later by Euboea when the cities of that island struck coins for their own use. It was believed in the fourth century that it was Solon who changed the standard of currency at Athens from the Aeginetan standard to what was called the Euboic. The effect of this would be to substitute a lighter for a heavier standard, as the Euboic didrachms contained little more than two-thirds as much silver as the Aeginetan. The democratic politician and antiquary Androtion was naïve enough to suppose that Solon's object was to enable the debtor who had borrowed the heavier silver drachmae to clear himself by paying an equal number of the new lighter drachmae, as if a man borrowed ten half-crowns and paid back ten florins. This theory was hardly advanced when it was refuted by Aristotle who pointed out that the Seisachtheia with its cancelling of debts preceded the reform of the currency. And indeed the financial juggle assumed by Androtion did not meet the grievance of the moment. The main grievance was that Athenians had been enslaved, and a slave could no more procure light drachmae than heavy ones, and Androtion's scheme of repayment without tears would only mock him.

It is not necessary here to discuss the discrepancy between the details of Solon's monetary reform as given by the two ancient accounts which we possess, the one in Aristotle, the other derived from Androtion (see below, p. 134). For, as regards the main fact, we may appeal to the numismatic evidence. It is most likely that one or both of the two ancient authorities reached their statistics by comparing Aeginetan coins with the Athenian coins bearing the owl and the head of Athena which were current in their own day. But numismatists are generally agreed that Athenian coins of this type were not struck as early as the archonship of Solon but first in the times of Peisistratus. On the other hand there remains the ancient tradition that Solon was concerned with a new currency standard, and laws which certainly seem Solonian imply the existence of one fixed standard of coinage recognized if not issued by the state. We must therefore assume as probable an Attic currency set up not later than the times of Solon. Such a currency is to be found in the so-called 'heraldic' coins, most of which have been attributed, for no very good reason, to Euboea. The coins form a continuous series: at least the combined evidence of punch-marks and of types implies that they were issued by the same mint[1].

These coins, which bear no letters, are stamped with heraldic badges, some of which, such as the owl and the amphora, may well be town-badges of Athens; others may be the badges of noble families[2]. They are silver didrachms of what is called Euboic weight (approximately 8·4 gms.). There is also a small series of didrachms of Aeginetan weight (approximately 12·3 gms.) which also bear an amphora, and these are in all probability a short-lived pre-Solonian coinage which was superseded by the lighter amphora coins when Solon made a change from the heavier to the lighter standard. As there is no tradition that coins of Aeginetan weight were ever struck in Euboea, we may suppose that both series of amphora coins were minted in Attica and, if so, the whole continuous series of heraldic coins. See further, pp. 134, 63 sq.

The Athenians had already begun to work the silver mines at Laurium in the south of Attica though it was not till the end of the century that the rich vein at Maroneia yielded its treasures, for it has been shown that that vein would not be reached until after a good deal of mining had taken place. It is at least possible that at this time the cities of Euboea availed themselves of this series of coins produced by the Athenian mint. Perhaps of more importance was the fact that the Corinthian stater was on the same standard as these heraldic coins. It is interesting to observe that the Corinthian stater was divided into three drachmae each equivalent to a quarter of the Aeginetan stater. This looks like an ingenious device to make the best of both worlds, and in that case the Athenian break with the Aeginetan standard is more marked, in as much as Athens did not adopt this compromise but divided the stater into two drachmae. The practical result was to make easier Athenian trade both with Corinth and with Euboea and with the outer world with which those states traded both as producers and middlemen. The days of Attic mercantile subordination to Aegina were over.

[1] C. T. Seltman, *Athens, its history and coinage*, p. xviii, and below, p. 129.
[2] See Volume of Plates i, 304.

Solon was also regarded as the founder of the Attic system of weights and measures. There is a fifth-century decree 'to use the laws and weights and measures of Solon.' The commercial weights introduced by Solon were the coin weights with the addition of one-twentieth[1], that is a mina of produce weighed rather more than a mina of coins. There are very few extant Attic weights which can be assigned to the sixth century. As far as they go, they bear out this statement, but it is certain that Athens also used other weights including some of the Aeginetan standard. It has been suggested[2] that the overweight given to the commercial mina as against the coins was borrowed, with a difference, from the overweight which kings and temples claimed in western Asia Minor and Babylon. The difference was that while in Asia the poor must give the overweight, in Attica when the peasant buys his salt or figs it is he who gets the extra fraction, thanks to the good Solon.

Of greater importance in a country which mainly produced corn, oil and wine were the measures of capacity. It was believed in the fourth century and it is probable enough, that Attica had hitherto used the 'Pheidonian' measures which obtained in the Peloponnese. Solon now set up measures which were larger than the Pheidonian. Here our knowledge ends, for it is not possible to establish beyond doubt the size of the Pheidonian measures. But at all events another step was taken away from the Peloponnesian system of trade. The increase in the measures, besides its superficial suggestion of Jack Cade's promise that 'the three-hooped pot shall have ten hoops,' had a political effect. For it was in these measures that the limits of the Athenian property classes were to be reckoned (see below, p. 47).

V. THE SOLONIAN CODE

Like Tyrtaeus Solon had sung the praises of Eunomia, the Reign of Law. On good laws faithfully observed rested the happiness of states and people. So to make good laws was the duty of one who would serve his city, as respect for law was the higher loyalty of the city state. But besides this impulse, Solon recognized the need to modernize the Athenian laws.

He, even more than Draco, belongs to the class of lawgivers who definitely made an advance in Greek ideas of right. Such lawgivers had arisen in the vigorous and progressive colonies of

---

[1] Aristotle, *Const. of Athens*, x, 2. See G. F. Hill cited in Sandys (2nd edit.) *ad loc.*　　[2] Lehmann-Haupt, *Solon of Athens*, pp. 28 *sqq.* and n. 34.

the west, at Locri in Italy and at Catana (see pp. 116, 355 *sq.*). The lawgiving of Solon is a symptom that Athens was rousing herself to become a modern state. For so far as we can judge of his laws they were instinct with a sense of the future. And, just as Solon had sought to reconcile rich and poor with his economic reforms, so it was his pride to set up laws before which rich and poor should stand equal. The Athenian code, for which he did more than any other man, was destined to become as widely current as the Athenian drachma. The completeness, simplicity and flexibility which it attained were to make it the model for the codes of Alexander's successors[1] and a rival of Roman Law under the Roman Empire. It bore, in fact, the imprint of the Greek mind just as Roman Law embodied the spirit of Rome.

It is not possible to say exactly how far Attic Law as we know it in the fourth century B.C. is the work of Solon and how far that of the generations which followed him. Attic pleaders did not hesitate to attribute to him any law which suited their case, and later writers had no criterion by which to distinguish earlier from later laws. Nor can any complete and authentic collection of his statutes have survived for ancient scholars to consult. But the evidence of such laws alone as are undoubtedly old is enough to establish Solon's claim to be by far the greatest Athenian legislator.

The law of Draco concerning homicide was taken over by the new lawgiver without alteration except that, possibly, he set up the court and jurisdiction at Phreattys (see p. 31). The rights of the family and the ideas of the past had been reconciled sufficiently with the claims of the state and the needs of the present. But the law of Solon governing bequest marked an advance. The Greeks had long outlived the stage, if it ever existed, when property was held in common by the clan and private ownership was unknown. But down to the seventh century property, especially in land, was generally considered as belonging to a family in the narrower sense rather than to an individual. The possessor at any time might be said to have a life interest in it. Then came inevitable modifications of this idea. There was no privilege of primogeniture to surround the heir with impoverished younger brothers. Without violating the idea that the family estate must stay in the family a man might divide his possessions among his sons. But the dowering of a daughter meant the alienation of property to another family, so that early lawgivers were inclined to limit the amount of a dowry. Besides, when a man died leaving

[1] A law of Solon's was borrowed verbatim by the municipality of Alexandria; of. the third-century Papyrus published in *Dikaiomata*, pp. 64 *sqq.*

no sons but a daughter, if the daughter inherited the estate, it might presently pass into another family, for a daughter is a potential alien. Hence came the rule which obtained at Athens that a daughter left heiress must marry within her own family, and thus keep the property together. A further problem would arise where a man had no children at all. In the earliest times his blood-relatives[1] or, failing them, his phratry would then become entitled to his property. But as the differentiation of property advanced, it seemed unreasonable that the phratry should thus be the heir of the individual member. During the seventh century there grew up the practice of adoption, which was a compromise between the possessor's right of disposal and the idea that property must remain in the family. By the adoption of a son the continuity of possession in the family was maintained. This had become the practice at Athens in the time before Solon.

Solon's laws first laid down that where there were legitimate sons they had an indefeasible right to their father's property, together with the obligation to provide a dowry if they had a sister. If there were no legitimate sons a man had the right to bequeath his property to whomsoever he would. Very often this took the form of adoption by testament, and, where property was left undivided, a will may be regarded as a form of posthumous adoption. That adoption was still viewed as a form of keeping property within the family may be seen from the fact that Solon excluded from the right of free bequest those who had been adopted before his archonship. For those persons were adopted in order to keep property in a particular family and so might be regarded as having only a life interest in it. At Thebes the legislator Philolaus seems to have made adoption compulsory where there were no legitimate sons. In Crete the laws of Gortyn as codified in the fifth century allowed adoption *inter vivos* even where there are legitimate sons[2], but recognized no adoption as a form of bequest.

Solon's law is a compromise. While it is more conservative than the law of Gortyn in maintaining the rights of sons, it is bolder in allowing the free disposal of property in the absence of sons. Thus the law of inheritance was laid down once and for all in a clear and reasonable form taking account both of the claims of the family and the rights of the individual.

---

[1] See Swoboda, *Beiträge zur griechischen Rechtsgeschichte*, Zeitschrift der Savigny-Stiftung, Bd. xxvi (Roman. Abt.), p. 244.

[2] x, 34 ff. In such cases the adopted son receives a daughter's share, see Kohler and Ziebarth, *Das Stadtrecht von Gortyn*, p. 71 *sq.* The form of the fifth-century codification implies that some form of adoption had existed before.

There is also attributed to Solon a group of laws regulating agriculture and pasturage such as might well be enacted at a time of agrarian changes. The small farmer was protected from encroachments on his boundaries or his water supply, this last so precious to the Attic peasant. According to Demetrius of Phalerum, a careful student of Attic law, Solon bound the state to pay a reward of five drachmae for the killing of a full-grown wolf, one drachma for a wolf-cub, that is, the value of an ox or the value of a sheep. More doubtful is the statement that a reward of 100 drachmae was appointed for a victor at the Isthmian games, of 500 for a victor at Olympia, and proportionate sums for victories at other festivals[1]. The precedence first of Olympia and then of the Isthmian games may suggest that this law is early; but on the other hand, for an age when a drachma might buy a sheep, the rewards seem unreasonably high, especially in Greek states which were lavish in compliments and frugal in gifts.

That such matters should be thus regulated in a code of laws is not in itself surprising, for the Greeks believed that a lawgiver might care even *de minimis*. But it is hard for the historian to tell where the lawgiver has obeyed this theory and where the theory has excited the imagination of later writers. And when a lawgiver was also a sage, if he uttered a maxim, the maxim presently reappears as a legal enactment. Thus Solon is said to have made one law forbidding evil speaking against the dead, and another against personal abuse in temples, public buildings, courts of law or at festivals. The former may represent the maxim *de mortuis*, the latter was to the Athenians a counsel of perfection. The legend is very likely based on some wise moral saw. So too, it was widely believed in antiquity that Solon made a law punishing those who, in time of civil strife, failed to take up arms on one side or the other. Such a law could hardly be enforced or would only be an instrument of injustice in the hands of victorious partizans. More probable, because more demanded by the crisis of the time, was an elaborate regulation of expense and display at funerals. Extravagant spending had helped to cause the discontents which Solon had faced, and it is certainly true that the funerals depicted on the Attic white *lecythi* after Solon are far simpler than the lavish pomps of the earlier Dipylon vases. According to Plutarch, Solon also laid down laws strictly regulating the behaviour of women on the rare occasions when they appeared in public[2].

[1] Plutarch, *Solon*, 23; Diogenes Laertius, I, 55.
[2] See Cicero, *de legibus*, II, §§ 59–66, and compare the laws of Ceos (*Inscriptions juridiques grecques*, I, p. 10) and of Delphi (Michel, *Recueil*, 995).

Of even more importance was a law granting citizenship to aliens on condition that they settled permanently in Attica to pursue some skilled craft (see p. 145). This law, to Greek notions so liberal, was to prove of great value to the industrial development of Attica[1]. For instance, master-potters from Corinth presently transferred their skill to help the artistic advance of Athenian pottery. Consistent with this is the alleged enactment that a parent who failed to teach his son a handicraft had no claim to support in his old age. But Greek sentiment both about handicrafts and the claim of old age makes highly unlikely a law so sweeping.

A more probable tradition ascribed to Solon penalties against those who followed no trade or occupation, though both Draco and Peisistratus are credited with a similar enactment. If the law was made, and made by Solon, his motive may have been not so much the moral reprobation of sloth as a desire to limit the idle and dangerous retainers of the nobles. Solon realized that the chief danger to the constitution lay in the feuds and ambitions of the Athenian aristocracy, and he made any attempt to set up a tyranny involve the outlawry of the author, and excluded from a general amnesty those who had been condemned for attempted tyranny or for massacre ($\sigma\phi\alpha\gamma\alpha\acute{\iota}$). The first exception was presumably aimed at the followers of Cylon and their descendants, the second at the house of Alcmaeon and its followers who had slaughtered the main body of Cylon's adherents. But this last exception failed of its object, for a member of that family is found in office at Athens soon after Solon's archonship (see below, p. 59).

Fragments of laws and phrases preserved by the caprice of orators or grammarians show that Solon laid down penalties for crimes of passion and of violence and protected even slaves from the wantonness of their masters. Daylight theft, so easy in Greek villages where the men go out into the fields all day, was visited with fines and in some cases with imprisonment in the stocks. The right to search the house of a suspect for stolen goods was legally established as it was in early Rome, and the householder was held guiltless if he killed a nocturnal housebreaker. And while it is not possible to determine with certainty those parts of fourth-century criminal law which are Solonian in origin, it may fairly be assumed that his code was at least the foundation on which succeeding generations built. What is characteristic of this as of

[1] A like liberality is evinced in a law quoted as Solonian by Gaius (*Dig.* XLVII, 22–4) which accepts the validity of rules laid down by associations whether social or mercantile so far as they do not conflict with the laws of the city.

other codes of the time is that fixed penalties or penalties assessed according to the loss or hurt inflicted are prescribed by the laws. Thus the power of judges and juries is limited by the considered moral values of the lawgiver. The laws of a Greek city were its great possession and not lightly abandoned, and even when time brought inevitable changes these were made with all solemn deliberation and formality. The laws were not to be the *arcanum* of a favoured class but the common familiar heritage of all Athenians. For this good reason Solon not only inscribed his code on the famous *axones* which were preserved in the Prytaneum, the official centre of the state, but had copies made on pillars called *kyrbeis* which were placed where all citizens could see and study them.

VI. THE CONSTITUTION. THE CLASSES

Solon was above all an economic and legal reformer. He swept away the main abuse of the past and equipped Athens for the commercial and social progress of the future. Besides this, he made constitutional changes which were to prove more significant than he can well have expected or intended. Many Athenians of the fourth century saw in him the authentic founder of the democracy under which they lived, while others attributed to him 'the democracy of their fathers,' that is, the democracy less what appeared to be manifest evils due to empire and demagogues. A third opinion was that Solon aimed rather at the stability of a contented state than at making the commons supreme. A variant of this is the view that his work consisted in the adroit tempering together of aristocratic, oligarchic, and democratic institutions. These discordant judgments betray the fact that the ancients had no means of determining with decisive certainty the exact character of Solon's constitutional achievement. Modern scholars, in turn, are and must remain at variance, as they have not only to deal with conflicting statements but are often reduced to conjecture as to the evidence, if any, on which these statements rest. Fortunately fragments of Solon's poems, which reveal his intentions, here and there afford a criterion of the ancient evidence. And it is to be remembered that Attica was not so cut off from the rest of Greece as to remain unaffected by the constitutional ideas which were abroad at the time. Solon himself was a travelled man who may well have seen the new democracy at Chios and the timocracies in Colophon and Aeolian Cyme or, nearer home, in Chalcis and Eretria. And a third criterion is the fact that he must have been most influenced by the crisis which he was chosen to face, the reconciliation of a people, in Aristotle's phrase 'enslaved and hostile,' with an aristocracy prepared to abandon a dangerous exercise of oppressive power. But, even after the ancient evidence has been sifted with every care, any account of Solon's constitutional reforms must contain judgments which are subjective and deductions which are hazardous, and no synthesis can claim with confidence to be true in every part.

The new economic order demanded a partial restatement of social distinctions. Before Solon's time the Athenians had been roughly divided into classes. Of these the highest as in other Greek states were the *Hippēs* (Knights) who could afford to keep horses and serve as cavalry or mounted infantry, the second were the *Zeugitai*, that is, according to the most probable explanation, those who could equip themselves to fight in the ranks of the hoplite phalanx. After these came the *Thētes*, the labourers. This old division was rather military and social (see above, vol. III, p. 594) than based on any exact census. Solon took these classes and fixed definitely the property qualification of each. It is significant that he takes into account only property in land. Land is measured by its annual production in units which may be either a *medimnus* (about $1\frac{1}{2}$ bushels) of grain or a *metrētes* (slightly over $8\frac{1}{2}$ gallons) of wine or oil. Land producing 200 units qualifies the owner as a Zeugite, 300 as a Knight. Those whose land produces less than 200 units are classed as Thetes.

We may further attribute to Solon the introduction of a division of the first class of Knights. He separated off those whose land produced 500 units or over and made of them the class called *pentacosiomedimni*, 'the five hundred bushel men.' The word has the air of a popular name like 'millionaire' and may have been current before Solon made it a legal definition of status. The name too suggests that the chief product of Attica was still grain, which was measured by the *medimnus*. No doubt economic progress had begun to increase the number of those who counted as Knights and it would suit Solon's idea of fair dealing to separate off the richest of these for the heaviest burdens of the state. For we may assume that some at least of the liturgies or public services performed by the richest men are as old as Solon and that the limit of the census classes would be used to make a rough grading of any taxes levied on the community. From such taxes as from military services as hoplites, the lowest class, the Thetes, would be exempt. There is however no evidence or probability to support the view that Solon went further and introduced a method of taxing according to a sliding scale. If the exact fixing of the limits was the work of Solon and not of his predecessors, it could be made after taking into account the increase of the measures which Solon had carried through. Otherwise we must suppose either that Solon rectified the existing limits and of this there is no hint in the tradition, or that, if existing limits were maintained, the increase of the measures had the effect of raising the standard of the property-classes. Such a result would be regarded as a grievance and certainly seems reactionary and out of harmony with the general tenor of Solonian legislation. This consideration, taken for what it is worth, supports the tradition followed above that Solon was responsible for the limits of these property-classes.

At a later time the qualification in produce was changed into a qualification in terms of money and as the value of money fell no man even moderately well to do remained in the lowest class. In Solon's day, however, the social prestige of land still stood high, and the effect of his economic legislation would be to throw on to the market a good deal of land which though freed from obligations due to debt could not be farmed for lack of capital to provide the equipment which in the fifth century made the Athenian farms the best appointed in Greece. Thus the rich merchant might easily achieve his ambition to become a landowner. The equation of the *medimnus* of grain with the *metrētes* of oil or wine is significant. In the fifth and fourth centuries a *metrētes* of olive oil was worth up to four times as much as a *medimnus* of barley, the grain most grown in Attica. Solon's equation suggests that grain was comparatively scarce and oil comparatively plentiful in Attic markets. The growth of import trade in grain and of export trade in oil accounts largely for the later change in value. Thus Solon's law prohibiting the export of natural commodities except oil resulted in the destruction of his parity.

This definition of the property-classes was followed by important political consequences. The first of these affected the high offices of state. Before Solon's archonship the Athenian magistrates had been appointed from those distinguished by good birth as well as wealth—and it may be assumed that office had been monopolized by the old aristocracy. Now the qualification to hold office was fixed in terms of the property-classes in which the only definition was in terms of landed wealth. Athens thus ceased to be in form an aristocracy and became a timocracy, a change which, in itself, had little practical importance at the moment but was destined to lead to the most far-reaching consequences in the future (see below, p. 57).

Of far greater immediate importance was the political enfranchisement of the Thetes, who received the right to vote in the

Assembly of the Athenian people. This Assembly, which came to be called the Ecclesia, was no new invention of Solon. Such a body, the gathering of freemen, was an integral part of the oldest Greek institutions. But in what may be called the aristocratic period popular Assemblies had in many cities ceased to be popular and those outside a privileged class had lost all voice in affairs of state (see vol. iii, p. 700). So at Athens aristocratic government and the economic depression of the poor had combined to exclude the mass of Athenians from such political powers as the Assembly might claim, until, in the words of Aristotle, they 'had no share in anything.' This grievance had been keenly felt and as 'reconciler' Solon met it by this measure of enfranchisement. To many such a course must have appeared revolutionary, and Solon defends himself against that reproach in verses of which fragments have survived. 'I have given to the people just so much privilege as is enough for them, neither diminishing their rights nor seeking to extend them.' 'The commons will follow their rulers best if they are neither left too free nor are too much crushed.' These are not the words of a statesman who aimed at making the commons supreme or at laying the foundations of a democracy. And having made the concession which the crisis demanded he set himself to devise safeguards to protect the stable order which was what he prized.

As members of the Assembly the Thetes might help to elect magistrates and might vote on measures proposed to them. But under Solon's constitution their choice was limited by the property qualification for office and no measures were voted upon until they had first been considered by a body specially appointed for that purpose (see below, pp. 53 *sqq.*). Thus, in normal times, the gain of the Thetes was rather in self-respect than in active political power, but their admission to these rights removed the sense of grievance which had helped to produce the danger of a revolution.

VII. THE CONSTITUTION. THE MAGISTRATES

It is now necessary to consider in detail the magistrates whom the Assembly might elect. The duties of the archons and lesser officials were left unchanged. The chief archon continued to be the leading executive officer in the state, the Basileus or King performed the few civil and sacred functions which were all that time and change had left him, and the Polemarch led the Athenian army in war. The other officials whom Aristotle mentions as existing at this time are the Stewards or Treasurers of the Goddess, the Pōlētae, the Eleven and the Colacretae. The Stewards, whose existence is attested by an inscription which may well belong to the first half of the sixth century, were officials of dignity rather than of importance. The treasures of Athena included the reserves of the state, as well as the offerings of the devout, but at this time these reserves cannot have been great. The ordinary revenues and expenditure were left in the hands of the Colacretae, who, with the local Naucrari, administered the taxes levied from the forty-eight naucraries of Attica, which like the four Ionic tribes remained unchanged (see vol. III, pp. 583, 595). Associated with these officials were the Poletae, the 'sellers,' whose primary duties would be to turn into money confiscated goods and let out contracts such as for the exploitation of the silver mines at Laurium which were already being worked. The Eleven, the keepers of the public prison, who became also a rudimentary police and a court of summary jurisdiction, may be as old as Solon though we cannot say with confidence how far their powers extended in his day. How these lesser magistrates were chosen we are not told, except that Aristotle quotes a law of Solon prescribing that the Stewards should be chosen by lot from the Pentacosiomedimni. There is no reason to doubt this statement, as the office was, in a way, sacred, did not demand any special qualifications, and was not a very proper object of competition. The other minor magistrates were presumably chosen by direct election.

It is almost certain that direct election was employed also in the choice of the nine archons, though here the ancient evidence is conflicting. Before Solon the archons were either elected by the Assembly, that is by those who were then full citizens, or were appointed by the Council of the Areopagus. That the former method was employed was the orthodox Attic tradition which Aristotle seems to have followed except in one passage. In the *Constitution of Athens* (VIII, 2) he says that in ancient times, that is, before Solon, the Areopagus after summoning and choosing (or judging) them according to its discretion appointed suitable persons for the year to the several offices. In its context this passage seems to describe the whole process of election, and Aristotle may be here correcting a tradition which elsewhere he accepts. But the words may mean no more than that the Areopagus tested the qualifications of candidates whom the Assembly had elected, and assigned to each that one of the archonships or other offices for which he was suited. What evidence Aristotle possessed except a firm belief that the Areopagus had been dominant in the state we cannot say. Solon's own appointment as 'reconciler and archon' is described as an election made jointly by the nobles and the commons, but the phrasing may be inexact or based on no clear evidence.

Whatever was the procedure before Solon, the accepted view of the Athenian antiquarians and of Aristotle himself in the *Politics* and in some passages of the *Constitution of Athens* was that after Solon the people chose the archons by direct election. In one passage however (*Constitution of Athens*, viii, 1) Aristotle states definitely that Solon introduced a method of election by lot from previously selected candidates (κλήρωσις ἐκ προκρίτων). This may be no more than a deduction from the law about the Stewards of the Goddess mentioned above which Aristotle quotes in this connection. If so, the deduction is hardly worthy of its author, and it is most unlikely that the Athenians allowed the lot to decide who should lead them in war or superintend the administration at home. And the history of the following decades is unintelligible unless the chief archonship was to be gained by influence and not by the caprice of chance even operating among a limited number of candidates. It seems then necessary to believe that until 487 B.C., when the archonship lost its practical importance (see below, p. 156), appointment to this office was by direct election.

As has been said the qualification to be a candidate for this and the lesser offices of state was defined in terms of the property-classes. The Stewards of the Goddess might only be taken from the highest class and the same may possibly be true of the archons[1]. We have no means of discovering what was the qualification needed for the other magistrates, but it is certain that Thetes were excluded from all offices.

VIII. THE CONSTITUTION. THE AREOPAGUS AND THE FOUR HUNDRED

The power of the executive had been limited by the authority, if not the direct control, of the Council of the Areopagus which had been perhaps the most effective organ of government in pre-Solonian Athens (see vol. III, pp. 587 *sqq.*). It is true that in the time of Aristotle it was widely believed that this Council was

[1] This would follow from a strict interpretation of Aristotle, *Const. of Athens*, vii, 3, in which the archons are mentioned before the Stewards of the Goddess in what appears to be a descending order of dignity. But if Knights were eligible before Solon (p. 47) it may be that they remained eligible after him. And it is doubtful if the Pentacosiomedimni were so numerous as to supply enough archons in view of the fact that there was not the practice of re-election to these offices, which were annual.

created by Solon. The powers of the Areopagus had been the subject of acute political controversy in the fifth century, and it is easy to see how those who wished to challenge its title to political power would be tempted to maintain that while Athena may have made it a court, it was only Solon who made it a Council. And a like conclusion would be reached by antiquarians who wished to attribute to Solon as lawgiver *par excellence* as many institutions as possible. But the evidence for this tradition was not as strong as the will to believe it. Aristotle, whose study of Greek constitutions had led him to expect an aristocratic council in an aristocratic state, declared the Council of the Areopagus to be pre-Solonian, and the evidence of Solon's amnesty law is decisive in his favour (see vol. iii, p. 589).

After Solon, as before, the Areopagus was recruited from those Athenians who had held the high offices of state, the archonships. Thus, like the Roman Senate, it embodied the administrative experience of its time and, as membership was for life, it might pursue a continuous policy. Now that the archons were elected by the free choice of all the Athenians, the Areopagus might claim to represent the will of the people, once removed. But it need not be supposed that it would leap to interpret the people's will. Its effect in the state would be rather conservative and oligarchical, as befitted the social position of its members, and it would look back and not forward. Its influence must have been great in a community possessed of little political education. To this body, permanent in personnel and paramount in influence, Solon gave the high duty of guarding his laws and assigned to it independent rights to ensure their application.

For more than a century after Solon the Areopagus was the public prosecutor and might step in when the machinery of the public courts was not set in motion by a private citizen. Such a power of selective intervention in the name of justice might well become an abuse, and, with a state police which did not exist to detect but only to execute criminals, might often be ineffective. Yet when these powers of the Areopagus were swept away by Ephialtes, the democratic alternatives of the Cleisthenean Council and professional accuser were hardly an improvement. If it would, the Areopagus might defend the freedom of Athens by impeaching a would-be tyrant when no private citizen dared to assume the dangerous duty. To secure the permanent validity and even-handed application of his code was to Solon all-important, and he therefore devoted to this purpose the most august and eminent body in the state. And to this end it must, like himself.

stand above the partizanships and political emotions of the day. It was withdrawn therefore from its old position as the real centre of administration, the source of political power, and in guarding the laws ceased to maintain the stability of the constitution and to direct the policy of the state.

With the Areopagus thus removed from an active share in current politics there was need of a body to control the deliberations of the enlarged Assembly. Such a body is to be found in the Council of the Four Hundred, an institution which Athenian tradition attributed to Solon, regarding it as the predecessor of the Five Hundred established by Cleisthenes to prepare business for the Assembly. This tradition was most likely accepted as early as the fifth century, for in the Oligarchical Revolution of 411 B.C. a Council of Four Hundred was set up as a return to ancestral practice. Herodotus, too, in his account of the events of the year 508 B.C., speaks of a Council which cannot in fact have been either the Cleisthenean Council or the Areopagus, but his evidence is weakened by the suspicion that he wrongly assumed the Cleisthenean constitution to be in existence at that time, and so misconceived the Constitutional position (see p. 140). The last decipherable letter of the famous Attic decree about Salamis is most likely the first letter of *Boule*, but the inscription itself (I.G.[2] 1, 1). need not be earlier than the Cleisthenean democracy.

There is no mention of this Council in our very scanty records of the political struggles in the period between Solon's archonship and the tyranny of Peisistratus. All that is recorded of the method of its appointment is, first, that a hundred councillors were drawn from each of the four tribes, and second, that when Solon instituted it, he selected its members. This second statement appears only in Plutarch's *Life of Solon* (19) and the phrasing may be inexact, though at this point in the biography Plutarch's ultimate source was the accepted fourth-century tradition. Scholars generally assume that the whole Council changed every year like the holders of the executive offices, but this deduction is insecure because it is not rare to find in Greek states an annual executive and a permanent deliberative Council. And a primitive state could not easily contrive or practise the repeated election or sortition of so many as a hundred members from each tribe. Cleisthenes overcame these difficulties by a species of devolution which was his invention, and so could make his Council annual, partly in order to educate the Athenians in government, partly to prevent it from being a clog on the immediate will of the people (see pp. 149 *sqq.*). It therefore seems safest to follow the tradition in

Plutarch that Solon chose its members in the first instance and to assume that only vacancies which occurred by the death of members were filled by election from time to time. Election would be a more likely method of choice than sortition, as being more consistent with the method of the Council's first appointment. It may fairly be assumed that membership was not open to the Thetes who are definitely said to have received no rights except to belong to the Assembly and sit as judges in the Heliaea (see below).

Solon's purpose in constituting this Council is described by Plutarch as to set a check on the unruly motions of the popular Assembly, emboldened as it was by the remission of debts. The Council was to deliberate before the Assembly and allow no measure to reach that body before the Council had discussed it. To the Areopagus Solon had given general oversight and the protection of the laws, and these two Councils were to be like two anchors holding the city and keeping the commons from becoming restless. It has been well suggested that the vivid pro-verbial phrase of the two anchors may reflect Solon's expressed intention. In that case his intention was rather constitutional stability than progress, and this agrees with the attitude of mind reflected in his poems.

Scholars have urged with force that the business of the Assembly cannot have been so great that Solon need have instituted a special Council to prepare it. This objection, which incidentally assumes the elaborate machinery of an annual election, is weakened if the view is taken that some such body was needed to prevent hasty decisions in times of excitement. We need not attribute to Solon, what no ancient writer attributes to him, the establishment of the Four Hundred as a stepping stone to democracy, and scholars who rightly refuse to believe that Solon created a democracy need not therefore deny the existence of this Council[1].

[1] Other and further duties have been attributed to this Council. A new 'council of the commons' at Chios, a small body of fifty members, included among its duties the hearing of appeals from magistrates' decisions at law. But there is no evidence that the Four Hundred possessed such powers, which were among those of the Heliaea (see p. 56), and, had the Four Hundred possessed them, we should expect to hear of their disappearance when the Cleisthenic Council was set up. An undivided Council of Four Hundred seems too large to be designed for administration. Some scholars have seen in it the survival of an older Council of the Four Tribes, but of that there is no trace unless it is assumed to be the organ of the forty-eight naucraries or local districts. Even so the distribution of 400 seats over 48 naucraries presents arithmetical difficulties.

As the safeguard of the property qualification for office proved vain when nobles turned demagogues, a phenomenon not rare in Greek states at this time, so this safeguard of the second Council, perhaps from lack of established prestige and inherited wisdom, is shown by the subsequent history of Attica to have been ineffective. The Areopagus maintained the prestige of the Solonian code, but the second anchor was not firm enough to hold. But Solon may well be forgiven the belief that he had given stability to the state. The effect of his limitations on the Assembly was to keep administration and the initiative in policy in the hands of the well-to-do or middle classes. It was true that years of aristocratic government had left the commons politically uneducated, the easy dupes of ambitious leaders, and Solon's poems show him well aware of the dangers of their uninstructed hopes. But the alternative, to deny to the commons all political power, was a greater evil and a greater danger, and Solon might hope that the new economic order would keep the poorer Athenians too busy or too contented to lend themselves to faction. Given that little power which was enough, the people might not be misled into grasping at more. And both policy and justice demanded that if they did not really govern they should be protected from misgovernment and injustice. The code of Draco had been an instrument of injustice in the hands of noble judges: the new code was to be administered before the eyes and with the assent of all Athenian freemen.

IX. THE HELIAEA

With this end in view Solon established the right of the people to sit in judgment. There is no good reason to attribute to him any anticipation of the elaborately organised democratic courts of the fifth and fourth centuries. The Athenian population was still too much occupied on its farms to devote much of its time to deciding legal cases. The Thesmothetae continued to judge between citizens and administered the new laws under the supervision of the Areopagus. But Solon gave the right to every citizen to claim justice for himself or others and the right to be judged by a meeting of the citizens. This meeting of the citizens was called the Heliaea. The word means 'Gathering' and elsewhere, as in Argos and Epidamnus, is the name of a political assembly. It is at least likely that it is the old name for the political Assembly of the Athenian people who now became judges as well as voters, and the phrase 'the Heliaea of the Thesmothetae' may reflect the function of the Assembly as a Court.

Aristotle says that Solon established the right of appeal to the Heliaea, and it is tempting to compare this with the Roman *ius provocationis* or the Macedonian right of appeal to the army. On either analogy this right of appeal would be rarely exercised and only in serious cases. But there exists a fragment of a law clearly old in form and attributed to Solon which prescribes that in cases of theft the offender may be sentenced not only to restitution and a fine of double the value of the theft, but also to a season in the stocks 'if the Heliaea add that penalty.' This implies that the Heliaea might be concerned with a trial of so unimportant a character which was rather civil than criminal in form. We may then suppose that the magistrates judged cases regularly with the help of a meeting of citizens. Possibly the judges sat on market days and their courts were attended by such citizens as had the leisure. Thus the administration of justice was popular and the sense of grievance aroused by the absolute judgment of the nobles was removed. The gradual organisation of the floating body of jurymen into panels would be a natural development. Solon's aim was not so much the triumph of democracy as of Dike, Justice: his ideal was fair dealing. He would have men equal before the goddess of Justice though not in the counsels of the state.

By a kind of extension of this right the commons gained a retrospective control over their magistrates. It was the regular practice in Greek states for magistrates on retiring from a term of office to submit to judgment on their actions. Such a judgment (εὔθυναι) was in some states conducted by special commissions or by a permanent Council. At Athens before Solon we may assume that it was conducted by the Areopagus, in the case of the archons as a preliminary to entering the dignified security of that body. This regular judgment was now transferred to the Heliaea, though the elaborate machinery found in fourth-century Athens was still far in the future. But the prospect of facing a popular court in which any aggrieved Athenian might be a prosecutor was enough to deter magistrates from flagrant oppression or misuse of power.

The verdict on the new order which Aristotle repeats is significant for his day. 'There are three points in Solon's constitution which appear to be its most democratic features; first and most important, the prohibition of loans on the security of the debtor's body; second the right of any person who wishes to claim redress on behalf of those who are wronged; third, and this, they say, has most given power to the masses, the appeal to the jury court, for when the commons is master of the juryman's ballot, it is

master of the state' (*Constitution of Athens*, ix, i). Those words
were written after generations of political trials before jealous
democratic juries, and the last phrase represents the ultimate
effect rather than the intention of Solon's constitution.

Solon would have disclaimed the praises which democrats
heaped on him in later times. To those who declared that he
purposely made his laws obscure to ensure constant reference to
the popular courts, he would have found a vigorous answer. The
executive stayed in the hands of the landed rich, and the commons
were rather protected from misgovernment than allowed to govern.
But the timocracy which he set up, with the limits and rights of
the property-classes clearly defined, was at the mercy of economic
forces. As long as the census remained in terms of natural
produce from land, it tended to maintain the interests of the well-
to-do farmers. But as Athenian industry and trade increased,
these values were presently translated into terms of money. This,
together with a fall in the value of the drachma, had the result that
the lower limits of the classes became so low that they were no
bar to democracy, and a hundred years after Solon there were
comparatively few Athenians legally excluded from any office by
poverty. Thus, for reasons which Solon can hardly have foreseen,
his ordering of the state, which for the time had an oligarchical air,
proved in fact a stage on the road to democracy.

When all is said the greatest positive immediate achievements
of Solon were a solution of the economic problem of Attica in
his day, the equipment of Athens for commercial progress, and
the establishment of an up-to-date and even-handed justice. These
notable results were attained without violence and were permanent
and of growing value. But there was a danger to Athenian peace
and prosperity against which Solon made no sufficient defence,
and that was the ambition of the Athenian nobles. One remedy,
which lay near to hand, was for the lawgiver to set himself over
nobles and commons alike as tyrant.

Solon had held for a time the most absolute control of the state.
His position may best be compared with that which Pittacus held
about the same time at Mitylene (p. 98). Pittacus was Aesymnetes, an extraordinary magistrate with power to order the affairs
of the state, such a position as Sulla held as Dictator at Rome.
Alcaeus the political opponent of Pittacus declared that in setting
him up the Mityleneans were choosing themselves a tyrant, and
a Greek popular song spoke of Pittacus as king in great Mitylene.
The possession of such power was to the Greek of the time the
supreme temptation, and as at Mitylene so at Athens many men

thought that Solon's character would not stand the strain. A popular programme would have made him tyrant though very likely not for long. Solon himself speaks the language of his tempters who declared him witless and timid because he would not take the prize which the gods had placed in his reach. 'The fish was in the net, he let it escape.' But the moderation of character which had won him power was proof against the temptation to retain it. Assailed by the hopes and the reproaches, the grievances and ingratitudes, of his friends and enemies, he stood at bay 'like a wolf surrounded by a pack of hounds.' At last with a final gesture of renunciation he bound the Athenians by an oath to maintain his laws and left Athens to go into a voluntary exile for ten years.

This, almost the greatest sacrifice a Greek could make, crowns the moral dignity of his career. But it may well be doubted if it was not really the 'great refusal,' an act which did not serve the best interests of Athens. In his own words Solon had stretched his stout shield over both parties in the state; now the arm which held the shield was withdrawn. His economic and legal reforms persisted by their inherent merit: his constitutional work was too tentative to do more than make men able to be contented, if they were willing. Neither the executive nor the popular voice had power enough to defend the constitution against a resolute ambition. It was Athens' fate to try both means: to see a tyrant make a strong executive, and a democrat, if a newly converted one, make Athens in practice a democracy. It was to take two generations and Peisistratus and Cleisthenes to complete Solon's political work, and in those two generations there was much loss as well as much gain. That the gain outweighed the loss was due to the personality of Peisistratus. Athens was fortunate: it may have lain in Solon's power to make her need no such good fortune. But Solon's great services are certain, his failure hypothetical. His claim to fame rests on his bold economic settlement and his code which gave the Athenians that respect for law which steadied them even in the days of their extreme democracy. Athens' neighbour, Megara, faced by such an economic crisis, failed to find a Solon, and the result was first a red terror and then a generation of civil strife. If anyone would criticize Solon, let him read Theognis on Megara.

CHAPTER III

ATHENS UNDER THE TYRANTS

I. FROM SOLON TO PEISISTRATUS

SOLON left the Athenian state for the moment vigorous and united, able to resume the spirited foreign policy of the last decade, and an opportunity of playing a part in Greek affairs soon offered itself. Shortly before 590 B.C. Thessaly, then at the height of its military power, intervened in Central Greece (vol. III, p. 604). At Anthela near Thermopylae was the meeting-place of the Amphictyony or Sacred League of Northern and Central Greece. This body, which was overshadowed and controlled by the power of Thessaly, now sought to gain influence farther south. The people of Delphi, the servants of the oracle of Apollo, appealed to be freed from the power of Crisa the leading town of Phocis which shut them off from the sea. It was alleged that the Crisaeans exacted tolls from the pilgrims who came to enquire of the god, and this violated the common rights of Greeks of which the Amphictyony was champion. Accordingly a sacred war was declared against Crisa[1] and an army led by the Thessalian Eurylochus besieged the city. The Amphictyones found a powerful ally in Cleisthenes the tyrant of Sicyon who sought to gain a sanction for his rule and possibly to crush a commercial rival. The Athenians, too, took the opportunity of flying to the help of the strong cause and sent a contingent under Alcmaeon the son of Megacles who had effected his return to Athens (p. 45). It is possible that Athenian policy was influenced by the Sicyonian tyrant who may have afforded shelter to the exiled Alcmaeonidae. At least Alcmaeon's son Megacles was destined to marry Agariste the tyrant's daughter, winning her from suitors who came from all over Greece. Crisa was presently forced to surrender and the city was destroyed; its territory was dedicated to the Delphian god, and Delphi became the second seat of the Sacred League. Athens was rewarded for her help by gaining the monopoly of one of the two votes assigned to the Ionians in the congresses of

---

[1] Aeschines, III, 108 and Aristotle, quoted in Plutarch, *Solon*, 11, attribute to Solon's influence the Amphictyonic decree against Crisa. See however De Sanctis, *Atthis*[2], pp. 261–3. The date of the fall of Crisa is probably 591/0 B.C. See F. Jacoby, *Marmor Parium*, p. 165 *sq*.

the Amphictyony. Thus the Athenians won recognition and influence in Central Greece and among their own kin (see vol. III, p. 605).

But this energy was short-lived, for the internal peace of Athens was soon broken. In the lists of Athenian Archons twice—against the years 590/89 and 585/4 B.C.—stood the significant word 'anarchia.' This must mean that in those years there was no generally recognised head of the state. The rivalries of the nobles and the divergence of interests in Athens were too strong for the constitution or the peace which Solon had hoped to establish. The natural result of such strife was the rise of a tyrant. In 582/1 B.C. Damasias, a nobleman of old family, was made Archon and stayed in office for two years and two months. It became clear that he was aiming at tyranny and at the end of that time he was overthrown.

On his fall the government of Athens was entrusted to ten archons, five from the Eupatridae or nobles; three from the *agroikoi* or small farmers and two from the *demiourgoi* or craftsmen. The most natural assumption is that these ten archons were chosen to govern in turn during the ten months which remained of Damasias' last year of office. The fact that they were drawn from different grades of society points to a coalition of all classes to overthrow the would-be tyrant. It must be assumed that, under stress, the Solonian property qualification for the archonship was set aside. At least it is hard to imagine that either 'agroikoi' or 'demiourgoi' can have normally been eligible for high office at this time. This constitutional experiment of the counter-revolution was short-lived and temporary union was succeeded by lasting division.

Ancient tradition speaks of three factions in Athenian politics in the period between Solon's archonship and the tyranny of Peisistratus, those of the Plain (*pediakoi*), of the Coast (*paralioi*), and of the Hill-country (*diakrioi*). But the last of these three is credibly associated with the personality of Peisistratus who can hardly have formed his party as early as the time of Damasias, so for the next decade we may assume the active existence of only the first two of these factions.

The men of the Plain were the nobles and well-to-do farmers who held the best land in Attica and looked back with regret to the days when the power of birth and land was still unimpaired by reform. This was no doubt the party which had made a temporary concession to the small farmers and craftsmen in order to overthrow Damasias. Their leader was Lycurgus the son of Aristolaïdes, possibly a member of the ancient noble house of the Eteobutadae. Opposed to this party were the men of the Coast, the fishermen and sailors and craftsmen of the city. Their interest lay in the commercial development of Attica, in the recognition of other wealth than land. They were led by Megacles the son of Alcmaeon. The Alcmaeonidae were aristocrats as proud as any, but their ambition made them ill-content to take an equal place with other nobles and the taint of blood-guiltiness still rested on them. Their return to Athens and the recovery of their estates can have been no easy matter, and it is possible that they owed it to the support of men of the coast and had so adopted a policy of championing the more modern elements in the Solonian settlements. In this century as in the next the ambition of their house was to be the handmaid of Athenian democracy. These were the two parties which strove for mastery and their strife weakened the state, so that when Solon returned to Athens about 580 B.C. it was to find Athens far other than he had hoped.

A result and a sign of Athenian weakness was that the Megarians had regained their hold on Salamis. Solon who knew what the island meant to Attica came forward and poured scorn on the inertia of the Athenians in indignant verses, calling on his countrymen 'to go out and fight for the lovely island and be clear of the cruel shame.' These lines which are full of youthful fire voiced the patriotism of the younger Athenians who found a general in Peisistratus, a nobleman from Brauron in the south of the Hill-country. Megara itself was by now torn by the dissensions between nobles and commons which find an echo in the poems of Theognis, and Athens seized her opportunity. The traditional details of the war can hardly be trusted. The one fact that seems fairly certain is that Peisistratus succeeded in taking Nisaea the port of Megara. With this pledge in their hands the Athenians admitted the arbitration of the Spartans who assigned Salamis to Athens while Megara regained Nisaea. According to an ancient tradition the Athenians supported their claim to the island by quoting as Homeric a line (*Iliad*, II, 558) in which Ajax the Hero of Salamis is posted with the Athenians, and the credit for this diplomatic master-stroke was given to the wise Solon or the wily Peisistratus. This time the annexation was permanent and in the course of the century the island was occupied by settlers from Attica.

II. THE RISE AND EXILES OF PEISISTRATUS

The winning of Salamis may be set shortly before the year 570 B.C., and the next decade saw the rise of Peisistratus to a dominant position in the state. There had been, as has been said, two factions, the Plain and the Coast; there remained a part of

Attica which waited for a leader. The Hill-country (the Diacria) could share neither in the agricultural prosperity of the Plain nor in the commercial progress of the Coast. Here, in a tangle of glens, lived shepherds and herdsmen and crofters, many, no doubt, men to whom Solon had given freedom but not land. In Peisistratus they found a leader who would urge their claims and could win their affection so that they stood firmly by him even in failure and exile. And Peisistratus, though he made the men of the Hills the instruments of his personal ambition, was to prove able and willing to fulfil the promises by which he had won their support. With this backing and with the prestige gained by his exploits in war he now took his place among the party leaders of Attica.

He might have been well content, like Megacles and Lycurgus, with a share of power, for an adroit politician might hold the balance between the other two parties. But personal ambition and the claims of his followers forbade such a course; to satisfy the men of the Diacria he must control the state. Accordingly he prepared quietly to make himself tyrant. The Athenians did not go unwarned. Solon's shrewdness was not deceived, but his wisdom went unheeded. There are lines of Solon's which may be referred to this time and contain more than half the truth about the Athenian people[1]:

> With fox-like gait each several one of you
> Walks slily, but, collected, all your cunning
> Turns folly: while you watch the subtle play
> Of a man's speech, you fail to see the deed
> That is afoot the while.   (fr. 8. Diehl, ll. 5–8.)

The Assembly granted to Peisistratus on the proposal of Aristion, one of his followers, a bodyguard of men armed with staves. There is a fine funeral stele set up not long after this time which bears the name Aristion[2]. This stele was found north of Brauron and it is very possible that Aristion was a neighbour who was used by Peisistratus. The bodyguard with their staves seemed harmless compared with the mercenary spearmen who were to the Greeks the outward sign of tyranny[3].

But there must have been some excuse for such a guard and Herodotus describes how Peisistratus drove into the market-place

---

[1] It is of course also possible that these lines refer to Damasias and belong to the years immediately following Solon's return to Athens if that is placed just before 580 B.C.   [2] See Volume of Plates i, 284.

[3] Possibly, however, 'stavebearers' is an old nickname, here as elsewhere, for rustics (see *P.W.* s.v. κορυνηφόροι) and really meant a troop of Peisistratus' Hill-men.

with wounds on himself and his mules and told how his enemies had sought to kill him by the way. There is no reason to doubt the story, for, if it was a comedy, Peisistratus was quite clever enough to have staged it. The number of the guard might be quickly increased and in the archonship of Comeas (561/0 B.C.) there was a *coup d'état*, the Acropolis was seized and Peisistratus was master of Athens. Solon's warning had come true, and Solon lived just long enough to see a tyrant at Athens.

But this new Damasias was soon faced by a coalition. Before his tyranny had taken root, the leaders of the Plain and Coast composed their differences and joined to drive the tyrant from the city. Whether he was forced to leave Attica or merely retired to the Hill-country is not certain. At least he clearly remained near at hand and with a following worth the consideration of his rivals: the coalition soon broke down and Megacles intrigued with Peisistratus and secured his return to Athens (560/59 B.C.)[1].

Herodotus tells a charming story how Megacles brought back the tyrant in peace by dressing up as Athena a fine upstanding lady who rode to Athens in a chariot with Peisistratus at her side while the story was spread through the villages that the goddess was bringing him home. Heralds went before to the city saying 'Men of Athens, welcome Peisistratus whom Athena herself, honouring above all men, brings back to her own Acropolis.' And those in the city believed the lady to be the goddess herself and worshipped the mortal woman and received Peisistratus. This incident Herodotus finds 'by far the most naïve of devices,' but he does not disbelieve it. The story may only reflect the fact that Peisistratus believed himself to enjoy the especial patronage of the goddess. It was he who set the head of Athena on the currency of the city together with the owl, the city badge. Before this the coins of Athens, the so-called 'heraldic' coins, which were didrachms, had borne either badges of the city as the owl or the amphora or of noble houses as the trisceles or the galloping horse which was perhaps the badge of Peisistratus' own family. Now the tyrant, tyrant by grace of the goddess, set on the new tetradrachms of the city the head of his patroness[2].

The political alliance between the parties of the Coast and the Hills was confirmed by the marriage of Peisistratus and the daughter of Megacles. But the ambitions of the two leaders soon made shipwreck of both political and matrimonial alliance.

---

[1] The view taken here of the dates and historicity of both exiles is defended in *C.Q.* xviii, 174 *sqq.* For variant views see the Bibliography.

[2] See above, p. 39, Vol. of Plates i, 304 and Seltman, *Athens*, pp. 19–38.

Megacles had perhaps hoped that the successor of Peisistratus would be a son by this new marriage, but the tyrant had no such intentions. He had already sons of his own and had no desire to sacrifice their claims to a grandson of Megacles. Nor was the new dynasty to be tainted with the guilt which rested on the Alcmaeonidae. So it presently became clear that there would be no children by this marriage of policy. In anger at this Megacles turned once more to the party of the Plain, and Peisistratus with his family was driven from Attica (*c.* 556 B.C.).

On the northern coasts of the Aegean there was still room for a determined adventurer, and Peisistratus settled at Rhaecelus in the north-west of the Chalcidic peninsula. There he united the people of the countryside into a city and won the friendship of the king of Macedon, so that when his dynasty was finally overthrown the shelter of Macedon was offered to his son Hippias. From Rhaecelus he presently established his power in the region of Mount Pangaeus near the mouth of the Strymon. Here there were rich mines, and gradually he gathered a store of money and raised a small mercenary army. He was equally diligent in making friends among the enemies of Athens and the Athenian government and intriguing with the Thebans and with the Argives, who no doubt were hostile to Megacles the son-in-law of their old enemy Cleisthenes tyrant of Sicyon. And it may be that Peisistratus was helped at Argos by his marriage with an Argive lady, Timonassa. These states supplied him with the sinews of war, and he was further strengthened by the assistance of Lygdamis a rich adventurer like himself, who aimed at becoming tyrant of Naxos.

Meanwhile his victorious enemies at Athens had returned to their old ways and heraldic badges appear once more on the Athenian coins[1]. All the written record of their doings which the irony of time has left us is to be found in two broken inscriptions, one for a victory which Alcmaeonides won in the *pentathlon*[2], the other the dedication of a statue of Apollo in which the same Alcmaeonides son of Alcmaeon commemorates his swift steeds and the skill of his Boeotian jockey 'when Pallas' high festival gathered at Athens[3].' As the statue was dedicated at the Ptoion in Boeotia, it would seem that Alcmaeonides won his victory during Peisistratus' exile, only to celebrate it during his own.

[1] Seltman, *op. cit.* pp. 47 *sqq.*
[2] See Hiller v. Gärtringen, *Hermes*, LVII, 478 *sqq.*
[3] See Bizard, *B.C.H.* 1920 and the further restorations by Wilamowitz, *Pindaros*, p. 155.

At the end of ten years Peisistratus felt strong enough to attempt the recovery of his power at Athens. A base near Attica was needed and this he found in the city of Eretria where, for whatever reason, the oligarchic government favoured his enterprise. Here he gathered his forces, including a thousand men from Argos, and opened up communications with the Hill-country of Attica where his old followers were still looking for their leader's return. At last about 546 B.C. the time was ripe and he landed near Marathon. The government of Athens, which had underrated their enemy, were only just in time to occupy with their levies the gap between Pentelicus and Hymettus, and the two armies faced each other near the temple of Athena at Pallene. The citizen levies were careless and very likely half-hearted, and they were soon surprised and scattered to their homes where they were very ready to remain. The way to Athens was clear, and Peisistratus' enemies fled into exile. The sons of those whom Peisistratus did no more than suspect were taken as hostages and interned in the island of Naxos where Peisistratus helped his friend Lygdamis to become tyrant.

III. THE FINAL TYRANNY OF PEISISTRATUS

Peisistratus was now lord of Athens by right of conquest. His power was maintained by troops of mercenaries, not only Greek but barbarian; and Scythian archers, who were the police of the tyrant, make their first appearance on Attic vases[1]. His possessions on the Strymon afforded him revenues besides those which he was able to draw from Attica. By shrewd diplomacy he maintained good relations with his neighbours, and he knew how to attach to himself the goodwill of a great part of the Athenian people. His rule was mild and he avoided the proverbial faults of a tyrant, so that for the rest of his lifetime no one was found able and willing to essay the dangerous adventure of attacking his power.

The domestic policy of Peisistratus, though possibly its chief motive was to secure support for his power, was of great benefit to Attica. What was needed to complete the work of Solon was to provide with farms those to whom Solon had given freedom but nothing more. After Solon the great bulk of the best land in Attica had remained in the hands of the wealthiest nobles, while many Athenians were forced to work as labourers or make a poor living on the bad land of Attica. These it was who had been the followers of Peisistratus, and now the tyrant was able to fulfil the promises of his early days and settle a great number of Athenians on small farms. For the rich nobles who held the great part of

---

[1] See Volume of Plates i, 282.

the land were his defeated enemies; many of them were dead or in exile and Peisistratus could reward his friends by dividing the estates of his enemies. He imposed on the land of Attica a tax of one-tenth or one-twentieth of the produce, a tax which brought in a steady revenue and can have seemed no great burden at least to those who before had been landless. He used his wealth to advance money to the new smallholders, and their intensive culti-vation did much for Attic agriculture. Judges were appointed to go round Attica and judge suits in the villages to meet the con-venience of the local peasantry. The security of a settled govern-ment no doubt went far to reconcile to the tyranny those who gained nothing else from the tyrant's return. A sign and a result of this security was the spread of olive growing. For an olive plantation, so slowly grown and so speedily destroyed, was the product of peaceful times, and now at last Attica had peace at home and abroad.

A secondary though most important result of this was the in-creased production of pottery for the growing export of oil and wine. During the reigns of the tyrant and his sons, the Attic black-figure style reached its climax and was succeeded by a new style full of life—that of the red-figured vases. Before the fall of the dynasty the pottery of Corinth had forfeited its predominance to the new Attic ware and the workshops of Boeotia and Eretria had become no more than provincial offshoots of Attic decorative art. Nor was this the only sphere in which the Athenians showed a newer, more modern spirit. Attic sculpture began to have a life of its own and to free itself from the stiff almost grotesque manner of the early sixth century. The new era of peace at home and enterprise abroad, the increasing intercourse with other Greek states especially those of Ionia, and the patronage of the tyrant dynasty which attracted artists from abroad, all combined to quicken the artistic life of Athens.

New buildings arose which attested the greatness and helped to ensure the popularity of the new régime. The fountain of the Nine streams, the *Enneakrounos*, showed the care of the tyrant for his people. And the care of Athena for her favourite did not go unrewarded. Besides the precincts of Pandrosos and probably of Erechtheus and Athena Polias, there stood on the Acropolis a temple of the goddess[1]. This the tyrant or his sons glorified by surrounding it with a colonnade and adorning it with marble sculptures. As if in reply, the democracy, when the dynasty

[1] See L. B. Holland, *Erechtheum Papers*, I–IV. *A.J.A.* XXVIII (1924), esp. pp. 402 *sqq.*

fell, planned to build a temple to the same goddess where the Parthenon now stands, and its marble columns were rising when the great Persian invasion broke upon Athens[1]. The ascent to the Acropolis was adorned, as well as fortified, with a columned gateway, the predecessor of the splendid Propylaea of Pericles. Apollo did not go short of honour, for Peisistratus laid out a precinct of the Pythian god, in which his grandson and namesake built an altar to commemorate the year of his archonship. Finally the new dynasty began a vast temple of Olympian Zeus, though it was reserved for two aliens, Antiochus Epiphanes and the Emperor Hadrian, to continue and to complete the work.

Even more significant was the establishment at Athens of a state cult of Dionysus, a god not so much of the old aristocracy as of the common folk who had worshipped him with rude rejoicings in their villages. Now the cult which had belonged to Eleutherae was transferred to Athens and the tyrant set up the great city Dionysia, the festival which made the city the patron of dramatic art. At this festival in 534 B.C. Thespis the reputed founder of Greek Tragedy was victor in the first of the long line of Athenian dramatic contests. The new state worship of Dionysus was no doubt a solvent of family and tribal cults and so, here as elsewhere, politically convenient to a tyrant. But Peisistratus was not merely a shrewd politician; he was 'a lover of the city' and believed that the greatness of his house was reflected in the dignity of Athens. He may have instituted, and certainly he raised to splendour, the Great Panathenaic Festival which was held every four years. The original motive of the festival in its simpler form was to celebrate the union of Attica; it now showed to the Greek world the greatness of the city and of the ruler whom Athena guarded. It was the climax of civic life, the moment caught and made immortal by the frieze of the Parthenon. At this festival rhapsodes from all over Greece recited the poems of Homer, the common heritage of the Greeks, and Peisistratus laid down rules for these recitations. That he did more or that there was more to do for Homer at this time cannot or should not be stated with assurance[2]. The multitudes which flocked to Athens for the great Festival saw a city growing in prosperity and claiming to stand with Delphi and Olympia as a centre of Greek national life (see vol. II, pp. 640 sq.).

The new coinage of Athens bearing the head of Athena and the owl, the city badge, steadily won the affectionate respect of

[1] See B. H. Hill, *A.J.A.* (N.S.), XVI, pp. 535–556.
[2] See T. W. Allen, *Homer, The Origins and Transmission*, pp. 225 sqq.

Greek traders. During his exile Peisistratus had controlled the silver mines at Mount Pangaeus and had continued there to strike his coins, though the workmanship shows a touch of barbarism. Now on his return he could add to the silver of Thrace the silver of Laurium, and his Attic currency and again that of his son Hippias[1] shows a tendency towards a regular fullness or increase of weight which helped the commercial prestige of Athens and soon forced the Corinthians to raise slightly the standard of their coins. The tetradrachms of Athens, which no political change affected for long, were the most lasting and the most manifest memorial of Peisistratus and his house. More than a century later, when the enemies of Athens hired rowers to man their fleets against her, they reckoned their pay in good Attic currency.

The foreign policy of Peisistratus was an adroit mixture of imperialism at a distance and peaceableness near home. His own experience had shown how dangerous it was to a government to have unfriendly neighbours. His recent return had been made possible because Eretria had allowed him to use that city as his base against Attica and because the Thebans and Argives had lent him help in men or money. Triumphant and powerful as he was, his exiled enemies were not to be despised. Megacles and his son Cleisthenes had all the tenacity and resolution of their house and ceaselessly intrigued to secure their return. Thus one chief preoccupation of Peisistratus was to prevent these exiles from finding support and a refuge near Attica. This was only possible if Athens could maintain and extend the friendships which he had formed in exile, so that Attica should be surrounded by a protective circle of goodwill. It was no easy task. The rivalries of the Greek states made it hard for Athens to be the friend of all the world, but for nearly a generation Peisistratus and his sons were successful. With Thessaly, still the most famous military state in Greece, Peisistratus maintained a close friendship; a hint of this is the fact that one of his sons bore the name Thessalus. He avoided arousing the jealousy of the Euboean cities, maintained peace with Aegina and Corinth and the states which bordered on Attica. With Sparta his house had old ties of friendship. It is true that it was impossible for Athens the friend of Argos to be for ever not the enemy of Sparta, and it was hard to avoid friction with the growing and grasping power of Thebes. But the statecraft of Peisistratus was equal to the task.

[1] Some scholars attribute to Hippias a doubling of the nominal value of the Attic coins so that what had been called a didrachm was now called a tetradrachm, see below, p. 134.

Thus he secured for Attica peace and for himself security. Farther afield his policy was more ambitious. The enterprises in the northern Aegean which had occupied his long exile were not allowed to drop, for here in case of need was a second home and a second source of power. Accordingly he recaptured Sigeum, which the Athenians had lost to the Mityleneans, and settled there as governor his illegitimate son Hegesistratus. This was to prove in the end the last refuge of his house. The holding of Sigeum meant no doubt acknowledging the suzerainty of the Persians who were now overlords of the coast of Asia Minor. But that as yet could arouse no scruple in a Greek tyrant. Besides this dynastic consideration Peisistratus realized how vital it was to Athenian interests to control the trade route to the Pontus. The population of Attica was increasing and its production of corn very possibly declining as olive-growing proved itself more profitable. Thus the harvests of the Pontus were becoming more and more necessary to Athens. Sigeum guarded the southern side of the passage through the Dardanelles; on the north lay the Thracian Chersonese.

This was already in Athenian hands. Miltiades, son of Cypselus of the Philaid house, had made himself lord of the Chersonese during the early days of Peisistratus' tyranny. The story how he embarked on this adventure was no doubt preserved in the traditions of his family and is related by Herodotus. The Thracian Dolonci lived in the Chersonese and were harassed by their neighbours the Apsinthii. They hoped to find protection in the settlement of a Greek colony, and so an embassy of Thracians set out to Delphi to enquire of the god. The god bade them ask the first man who invited them into his house to lead a colony of Greeks to the Chersonese. They accordingly retraced their steps along the Sacred Way and neither in Phocis nor in Boeotia did anyone invite them in. They pursued their journey into Attica and passed by the house of Miltiades son of Cypselus, and he, seeing their strange garb and spears, asked them to be his guests, whereupon they invited him to obey the god and lead a colony to the Chersonese. And he, finding the rule of Peisistratus irksome and wishing to leave Attica, did as they requested. He led a body of Athenians to the Chersonese and the Dolonci made him tyrant. That there was collusion between the Dolonci, Apollo and Miltiades is more than likely. Peisistratus, too, may have been willing enough to see the departure of a possible rival and the extension of Athenian influence in the north-east Aegean. Miltiades protected the peninsula by building a wall across the

isthmus which joins it to the mainland. This Athenian intervention brought on a war with Lampsacus, probably during the
long exile of Peisistratus when he could not help Miltiades.
Miltiades was taken prisoner but released on the intervention of Croesus the king of Lydia. After this he maintained
himself against his Greek and barbarian neighbours until the death
of Peisistratus (see below, p. 76 *sq.*).

In the central Aegean the tyrant extended the influence if not
the dominion of Athens. He had rewarded Lygdamis for his
support by setting him up by force of arms as tyrant in Naxos.
Lygdamis in turn helped the notorious Polycrates (pp. 75, 90 *sqq.*)
to make himself tyrant of Samos, no doubt with the countenance
of Peisistratus. There was an old religious bond between Attica,
especially Marathon and Oenoe in the Hill-country, and the
Ionian sanctuary at Delos. This was now strengthened and
Peisistratus carried out a purification of Delos to win the favour
of Apollo. The Athenians became more ready to assert their
kinship with the Ionians. A hint of this may be seen in the fact
that the figure of Theseus, the symbol of Athenian race-con-
sciousness, appears more and more often on Attic vases. Thus
was laid the foundation of sentiment on which in the next century
the Confederacy of Delos was to be built.

At Athens itself the tyrant found that the Solonian constitution
could be made a good servant. Archons were elected as before,
except that they happened always to be those whom the tyrant
could trust. The Council of the Areopagus still met; indeed it
became more and more a convenient instrument. For it had been
purged of Peisistratus' chief opponents and it was recruited from
those trusty men who had held the archonship, and so, as time
went on, was bound to become pro-Peisistratean. The tyrant himself even appeared before it to answer a charge of murder, an act
which enabled the tyrant to show his respect for the law and
might have enabled the Areopagus to show its respect for the
tyrant had not the accuser failed to appear. The code of Solon
remained in force—not even the law against tyranny was repealed—and justice was made more accessible by the creation
of the local judges for the country districts, though their
appointment may have been inconsistent with the idea of the
Solonian popular courts. The remaining organs of the Solonian
government continued to exist and to be active so far as they
did not inconvenience the tyrant. Peisistratus was no constitutional reformer; he was content to be the first man in an obedient
state.

MAP 2

THE PELOPONNESUS

c. 550 B.C.

Scales.

0   10   20   30   40

English Miles.

0 10 20   40   60

Kilometres.

Some scholars, it is true, have attributed to him the institution of the ten tribes with their subdivisions which Herodotus and Aristotle, following the Athenian tradition, describe as the work of Cleisthenes (see below, pp. 142 *sqq.*). It is possible to interpret the grouping of the tribal divisions as they appeared in the fifth century as a kind of 'electoral geometry'[1] which was to increase the importance of the Hill-country from which Peisistratus had drawn his supporters. But there are two things which we do not know for certain: the exact boundaries of the Hill-country and whether that area remained the home of a political faction during the established rule of the tyrant. What is more certain is that, when the tyranny fell, its victorious opponents would not have allowed to survive any arrangement of Athenian tribes which might give a political advantage to the tyrant's followers. And, as is shown in a later chapter, the organization of the tribes and their subdivisions can be convincingly explained by the conditions with which Cleisthenes had to deal (see below, pp. 146 *sqq.*).

At last, in the year 527 B.C., after a long period of peace to which the Athenians looked back as a golden age, Peisistratus died in his bed and his power passed without challenge to his sons. It is hard to gather from the scanty records of the time what manner of man he was. The lines of Solon already quoted (p. 62) suggest that he had the eloquence which an Athenian politician needed. His career shows him tenacious and supple, no doubt a patient enemy and a faithful friend. Under his easy and enlightened despotism Attica recruited the strength which made possible the brilliant career of the democracy which succeeded his dynasty.

IV. THE PELOPONNESIAN LEAGUE

The reign of Peisistratus witnessed the appearance of the most permanent organization in Greek politics, what is called the Peloponnesian League. Before this time Greek states had joined in Amphictyonies with their centre at a temple, held together by a bond like that which bound together members of a clan, or they had made short-lived alliances for definite purposes[2]. Now,

---

[1] Beloch, *Griech. Gesch.* I², 2 § 124. The same scholar, *ibid.* § 123, attributes to Peisistratus the organization of the naucraries as the foundation of an Athenian navy, a view which is shared by De Sanctis, *Atthis²*, pp. 305 *sqq.* Their view implies a later date for the conspiracy of Cylon (see p. 27) than that which is here adopted (see Chronological Note 1).

[2] Boeotia and Thessaly, where is found a kind of league, may be regarded as racial units. See above, vol. III, pp. 608 *sqq.*, 601 *sqq.*

by a striking innovation, there arose a lasting combination of
separate states which rested on the political power of a single
state. As a league it was secular, as an alliance it was permanent.
The term 'league' is strictly a misnomer, for the members were
not bound to each other but only each to Sparta. Subject to the
claims of this alliance with Sparta the several states were left
entirely free to manage each its own foreign policy; they might
even make war on each other. The official title of the league was
'The Lacedaemonians and their allies[1].'

The underlying assumptions of the league, as can be reconstructed from its later history, were two—the military hegemony
of Sparta and the autonomy and territorial integrity of the several
members of the confederation. Until the middle of the sixth
century Sparta had constantly sought to acquire territory at the
expense of her neighbours. She was now satisfied, or at least her
need for new land was no longer commensurate with the sacrifices
required to obtain it. That had been made clear by her struggle
with Tegea (see vol. III, pp. 565 sqq.). Sparta now offered security
to her neighbours in return for security for herself. There were
two quarters from which danger might come: from Argos and
from the helots who were becoming over-numerous compared
with their masters and cherished the unfading memory of their
old freedom. The power of Argos was declining; the offensive
had passed to Sparta and after a crushing victory in 546 B.C.
Sparta had little to fear from her enemy if her enemy was isolated.
But a century before Argos had been the head of a group of
states and might be so again. The alliances which bound her
neighbours to Sparta were a means to forestall such a combination.
The treaty, for instance, with Sicyon or Corinth was for ever, and
it precluded any other engagement which might conflict with it,
and bring these states into the field as allies of Argos against
Sparta. Equally, a rising of the helots lost half its terrors if the
helots were shut in by states which were pledged to help Sparta
to defend herself and were pledged to help no one to attack
Sparta[2]. By limiting herself strictly to these principles and being
careful to avoid any infringement of the domestic rights of her
allies, Spartan policy, ever guided rather by fear than hope,
achieved a solid if not brilliant success. She succeeded in capital-

---

[1] See Kahrstedt, *Griechisches Staatsrecht*, I Sparta und seine Symmachie, especially pp. 81–118, and 286–294.

[2] It is possible that these treaties, like that of Sparta with Athens in
421 B.C. (Thucydides, V, 23), expressly pledged her allies to help Sparta
in case of a helot-rising.

izing her military prestige. The policy was the reflection of a
wider movement, for in social life Sparta had deliberately cut
herself off from progress: she shut her frontiers to art and to
the new phase of commerce, and so avoided the crisis which
through strife and suffering issued in the larger life of Athens.
While the Athenian state was growing up from youth to manhood, the Spartans set before themselves the ideal of a well-pre-
served middle age.

The growth of the confederacy is not easy to trace, but it was
sufficiently rapid to show that most of the Peloponnesian states
welcomed the security which the new system seemed to offer.
The states which lay under the shadow of Argos had not forgotten
the days when that city had been dominant and were well content
to lean on Sparta. Corinth, far enough removed to have no immediate fear of Spartan arms, might derive moral and, if need be,
material support for the sober aristocratic government which had,
a generation before, replaced the brilliant and ambitious tyranny
of the house of Cypselus. The Arcadians followed the example
of Tegea which made a treaty with Sparta (see vol. iii, pp. 565 sqq.).
Elis, the second largest state in the Peloponnese, was an old ally.
At some time in the closing decades of the century Megara, after
establishing an oligarchy, became a member of the Spartan league
and so opened the road which led to central Greece. It is significant that Sparta did not secure the adhesion of Achaea, that
happy land without a history. The reason may be that Achaea,
hemmed in by allies of Sparta, could neither help Argos nor the
helots and so might be left to herself. It was not until Athens
became active in the Gulf of Corinth during the next century
that it became necessary to bring Achaea into the league. By the
end of the sixth century the league included the whole of the
Peloponnese except Argos and Achaea, also the island of Aegina
which was Dorian, oligarchic, and connected with the Peloponnese
by the strongest ties of commercial interest. In the main the
league was a Dorian league, but there is no sign that Lacedaemonian policy was narrowly racial. The removal of the bones of
Orestes to Sparta was a claim to an ancient primacy which preceded and transcended the limits of what was Dorian (see vol. iii,
p. 566). This claim pressed by an ambitious king like Cleomenes
(see p. 137 sq.) might and sometimes did break through the
tradition of defensive caution which was inherited from ephorate
to ephorate. But in the main, even when fear of Argos was faint,
the ever-present danger of a helot-rising armed with an invincible
argument the party which opposed a policy of aggression. And,

besides, the ephors who were in general the prophets of traditional policy were able to rely on the eternal rivalry of the two
Laconian royal houses.

There is an apparent exception to the general defensive attitude
of Sparta. At the very earliest stage of the league she was credited
with carrying out a mission to put down tyrants. According to
a papyrus fragment, 'Chilon the Lacedaemonian, having become
ephor and general, and Anaxandridas put down the tyrannies
among the Greeks[1].'

They are said to have driven the Cypselids from Corinth and
Ambracia, Lygdamis from Naxos, the sons of Peisistratus from
Athens, Aeschines from Sicyon, Symmachus from Thasos, Aules
from Phocis and Aristogenes from Miletus. The list is impressive
but it does not mean that in every case Sparta herself intervened
in arms. Nor is it probable that when the Spartans saw a tyrant
their native egotistical caution was lost in righteous indignation.
We may suppose that they waited as in the case of Athens until
a tyranny had outlived its welcome and then gave or inspired the
final blow to secure the good will of the government which succeeded it. To the several states concerned such intervention did
not seem an infringement of their autonomy if autonomy meant the
enjoyment of rights which the tyranny had set in abeyance. Spartan
policy which aimed at a permanent distribution of power, no
doubt, preferred to deal with a more settled government than a
tyranny. As the Spartans desired to be surrounded by powers
with which they could make firm and lasting arrangements, they
viewed tyrants with the same uncomfortable dislike with which
the Holy Alliance after Waterloo would view a usurper or a
republic. Besides, some tyrants had liberated serfs (vol. iii, p. 554).

In the settlements which followed the age of the tyrants in
Greece proper the influence of Sparta was on the side of oligarchy
or aristocracy, which seemed to her not without reason most
permanent and most orderly. Here may be found the chief bond
between Lacedaemon and the governments of Megara and Aegina
which had to fear a democratic opposition.

When the allies of Sparta or a majority of them agreed that a
casus foederis had arisen, Sparta could place herself at the head
of a very formidable league army comprising two-thirds of the
active fighting strength of her allies, and had no rival in Greece
except Thessaly. Thucydides puts into the mouth of Pericles an

[1] Rylands Papyri 18, and, for lists of the tyrants overthrown by Sparta,
Plutarch, de malignitate Herodoti, 21, and Schol. ad Aeschinem, ii, 77.
The traditional date of Chilon's ephorate is 556 B.C. See vol. iii, p. 568, n. 1.

unflattering comparison of the Peloponnesian League with the centralized energetic empire of Athens. But the league had the qualities of its defects and, despite a clumsy and often disloyal leadership, it showed great vitality even after the Peace of Nicias.

Lacedaemonian prestige, already recognized as far afield as Lydia and Egypt (vol. III, pp. 304 *sq.*, *565*), grew with the growth of the league and soon the Spartans found themselves involved in the affairs of the Aegean seafaring states. Polycrates tyrant of Samos, a buccaneer with a taste for art and letters, had made himself intolerable[1]. He had been the ally of Egypt but had evaded the hostility of Cambyses the Great King by an adroit *volte-face* at the right moment. Samians had plotted against him in vain and exiles from Samos now appealed to Sparta. Their appeal was strongly supported by the Corinthians who had plenty of grievances old and new against the island, and a Lacedaemonian force was sent to join an expedition to suppress the tyrant (*c.* 524 B.C.). After forty days the siege of Samos was abandoned and the Spartans returned. Herodotus relates a story, which he does not believe, that the Lacedaemonians were bribed by Polycrates. Where Herodotus is sceptical, we need not be credulous. The failure of the expedition was not of very great moment, for soon after Polycrates fell a victim to the treacherous cunning of the Persian satrap at Sardes and 'was miserably put to death in a manner unworthy both of himself and of his high ambitions.' It is, however, likely enough that the incident strengthened the Spartan dislike for adventures overseas.

V. THE SONS OF PEISISTRATUS

On the death of Peisistratus his power passed to his sons. As in mediaeval Italy, so in Greece it was not rare for a tyrant to leave his rule to be held jointly by his sons though in practice the eldest or ablest would take the lead. The eldest son of Peisistratus was Hippias, who appears to have inherited much of his father's ability and all his father's tenacity of purpose. The ancient authorities are not in agreement as to the other sons of Peisistratus. Aristotle says his legitimate sons were Hippias and Hipparchus and that there were two others by his Argive wife Timonassa, who in Attic law did not count as legitimate, namely Iophon and Hegesistratus who was also called Thessalus. Iophon is not known otherwise and may have died young. At least he does not come

[1] For a slightly more sympathetic account of Polycrates see below, pp. 90 *sqq.*

into the history of the period. Hegesistratus according to Herodotus was ruler at Sigeum and presumably took no part in
Athenian affairs. It is doubtful if he should be identified with
Thessalus, as Thucydides[1] appears to count Thessalus among
Peisistratus' legitimate sons and the traditions about him imply
that he lived at Athens during the rule of Hippias. Plutarch[2],
it is true, mentions Thessalus as a son of Timonassa as does
Aristotle, but he is probably using the same source and so his
testimony has no independent value.

The two sons who play a part in history after the death of
Peisistratus are Hippias and Hipparchus, and it must be regarded
as certain that of these two Hippias was the effective head of the
government. He had in later times the reputation of being a
prudent and competent ruler, and for more than ten years he
maintained his power unassailed. His brother Hipparchus, who
lacked his solid and respectable character, was a patron of arts
and letters. He delighted to gather round him poets like Anacreon
and Simonides of Ceos (see pp. 500, 505 *sq.*). Anacreon, who was
born to live in tyrants' palaces, had for some years adorned the
court of Polycrates, and, now that fate had overtaken that tyrant,
he accepted the honorific invitation of Hipparchus to remove to
Athens. Simonides, a greater poet, was younger and it may have
been Hipparchus who first recognized his talents which were at
the disposal of tyranny and liberty alike. Lasus of Hermione, an
innovator in music, who founded the Athenian school of Dithyr-
ambic poets, was as welcome as Pratinas of Phlius the champion
of the older tradition, who did much to advance the dramatic
performances which were to be the pride of Athens. And among
these poets and musicians appeared the strange personality of
Onomacritus who was learned in the lore of the Orphics[3] and
dealt largely in oracles (p. 532). He was doubly welcome, for
while Hipparchus loved a mystic, Hippias was a great connoisseur
of oracles, 'having the most accurate knowledge' of them. Indeed
the Peisistratidae had collected on the Acropolis a great store of
such which were later seized by the Spartan king Cleomenes,
possibly to the satisfaction of the priests at Delphi. Onomacritus
sought to increase the collection by adding sundry forgeries but
was discovered in the act by Lasus and dismissed by his indignant
patron.

Meanwhile in the Chersonese, that outpost of Athenian influence, the first Miltiades had died and left his realm to Stesa-

---

[1] I, 20. 2; VI, 55. I.   [2] *Cato Major*, 24.
[3] Orphism and its influence at this time are described below in chapter xv.

goras the son of his half-brother Cimon (p. 70). Stesagoras fell
in the intermittent wars with the neighbouring city of Lampsacus
and there must have been a moment when the Athenian hold on
the Chersonese was in danger. The government at Athens could
not remain indifferent, and had to find someone to take over the
power with all its dangers. Cimon himself, the father of Stesagoras,
had been driven from Athens by Peisistratus but had returned
trusting to a reconciliation with the tyrant, only to be assassinated
by the agents of the tyrant's sons as soon as he showed signs of
asserting himself. There remained his son Miltiades, who was at
Athens, and the Peisistratidae were glad enough to send out to
the Chersonese an able young man who might, if he stayed at
home, prove a formidable enemy. The young Miltiades, by
treachery, mercenaries and a marriage of policy, established
himself and presently conquered the island of Lemnos which was
gradually settled by emigrants from Athens.

In Greece proper Hippias for a time pursued the peaceful
policy of his father, with its careful neutrality, but such a policy
was increasingly difficult to maintain. The relations of the Peisistratid house with Thessaly were of the closest, and this friendship
Hippias continued to enjoy. But the power of Thessaly was declining. It had reached its zenith early in the century, after the
Sacred War, when the Thessalians had invaded central Greece
and were for a moment overlords of Phocis. They even marched
through Boeotia as far as the territory of Thespiae but were there
defeated near the stronghold of Ceressus. After this defeat, which
may be set before 570 B.C., their influence in central Greece waned
before the rising power of Thebes. The Thebans had helped
Peisistratus to regain his power but that may have been as much
from enmity to Athens as from friendship to the tyrant, and as
Athens grew in prosperity and power they became more and more
jealous and hostile. A strong Athens was bound to exercise an
attraction on the southern Boeotian states, which could thus hope
to find support against the increasing claims of Thebes to dominate
the whole of Boeotia. And the Peisistratidae had to reckon with
the patient and skilful intrigues of the Alcmaeonidae who never
abandoned hope of return. Argos, the remaining support of Peisistratus and his house, had been isolated in the Peloponnese by the
arms and diplomacy of Sparta, and its friendship had become a
liability rather than an asset.

The growth of the Peloponnesian League had not only brought
Sparta into contact with Boeotia and Attica but had allied her
with two mercantile states, Corinth and Aegina, which looked

askance at a tyranny that did so much to encourage the growth of Athenian commerce. Megara, a new ally of Sparta, had defeats to remember and to avenge. Against the influence of these states the Peisistratidae could only set their old personal friendships at Sparta which were outweighed by their connections with Argos the enemy of Sparta, and Thessaly her possible rival in the politics of central Greece.

Thus Sparta gradually became hostile but was, as ever, slow to move. In 519 B.C.[1] arose a dangerous crisis. Plataea, the city which lay at the Boeotian side of the western passes from Attica to Boeotia, was hard pressed by the Thebans who claimed the hegemony of Boeotia, and the Plataeans appealed to king Cleomenes and the Lacedaemonians for protection. The Spartans acted with their usual caution and even more than their usual cunning. The opportunity of spreading Spartan power north of the Isthmus was tempting and they had an army near the Isthmus. But, we may assume, the able young king Cleomenes realised that to help Plataea might drive Thebes to seek an alliance with Thessaly and Athens. For the Thebans would make any sacrifice to further their ambition to dominate Boeotia. A triple alliance of Thessaly, Athens and Thebes would be an effective answer to the Peloponnesian League. So Sparta chose a more excellent way and urged the Plataeans to seek help from Athens their neighbour. The Plataeans did so and Hippias accepted them as allies with the result that the Thebans marched against Plataea while the Athenian army advanced to meet them. The Corinthians offered their mediation which was for the moment accepted. Their ruling that the Thebans should not coerce states which did not wish to join the Boeotian League was naturally unacceptable to Thebes. The Boeotian army attacked but was defeated and the Athenians, pressing their advantage, annexed the northern slopes of Mt Cithaeron. Thus for the moment Athens had won a brilliant success. The annexation no doubt gratified old ambitions and the alliance with Plataea strengthened the western defences of Attica against Boeotia. But the price was the lasting hostility of the Thebans on which the enemies of Athens could always count. The immediate result was that Boeotia though forced to make peace allowed the Alcmaeonidae to use its territory as a base against Attica. The protective circle of friendly states was broken, while Spartan ill-will to Athens was not lessened by the momentary success which they had placed in the tyrant's way.

---

[1] See Wells, *Studies in Herodotus*, pp. 81 *sqq.*

About the same time as this the influence of the Peisistratidae in the Aegean was shaken by the overthrow of Lygdamis the tyrant of Naxos, an event which removed a good friend and meant the release of the hostages whom the tyrant was guarding. It was said that Sparta had a hand in his downfall, and this alone was sufficiently ominous. The power of Persia became more of a reality in the regions of the Hellespont and the campaigns which followed the Scythian expedition ended any Athenian ambitions in that quarter (p. 214). Possibly with a shrewd foreboding Hippias sought Persian friendship; at least he chose out Aeantides, son of the tyrant of Lampsacus who stood high in favour with the Great King, as husband for his daughter Archedice. The lady thus became the daughter, wife, sister and mother of tyrants and yet, if we may trust her epitaph, 'was not uplifted to presumptuousness.' But not all the Peisistratid family were so virtuous, and a lapse into the faults of a tyrant weakened the dynasty at Athens itself.

In 514 B.C. arose a conspiracy aimed at Hippias and his brother Hipparchus. Its leaders were Harmodius and Aristogeiton, two members of the Gephyrean clan which had migrated to Athens from Tanagra. The ancient tradition agrees that the conspiracy was not inspired by political principle but due entirely to a private wrong inflicted by Hipparchus or, as some said, his younger brother Thessalus. About the whole story the democratic tradition was active; the truest account is probably that of Thucydides[1]. According to him few shared in the plot, which was directed primarily against Hipparchus but also against Hippias, as their private revenge could only be securely gained if the tyranny was overthrown. The chosen time was the Great Panathenaic Festival when the Athenians gathered in arms for the procession up to the Acropolis. Only on such an occasion could the conspirators hope for immediate support against the mercenaries of the tyrant. When the day came they armed themselves with daggers and first turned their attention to Hippias who with his guards was in the outer Ceramicus. But, as they saw one of their number talking with him, they believed that the plot was being betrayed and rushed off to the Leocoreum, where Hipparchus was ordering the procession. They struck him down, but there their success ended. Hippias acted with resolution—the conspirators were killed or taken, the Athenians did not rise in revolt, and suffered themselves to be tricked into surrendering their arms. Harmodius was killed on the spot, Aristogeiton taken soon afterwards and put to death.

[1] I, 20; VI, 54–60.

The democracy glorified them as martyrs of liberty, and they were celebrated by a statue and by the singing of their praises in a famous song. There was an epigram attributed to Simonides which told how liberty dawned at Athens when Aristogeiton and Harmodius struck down Hipparchus. The same false perspective which caused these two to be seen as heroes and martyrs of freedom caused Hipparchus to be viewed as the tyrant. Popular tradition made him the tyrant in order to turn murder into tyrannicide. Thucydides is severe in correcting this popular misconception, though indeed while Hipparchus was not the head of the government he was just as much a tyrant as his elder brother Hippias.

The one result of the murder which really undermined tyranny at Athens was its effect on the character of Hippias. He became embittered and suspicious. By disarming the Athenians he deprived himself of his chief security against a foreign intervention and was reduced to rely on his mercenaries and on his Thessalian allies. His enemies the exiled Alcmaeonidae, now led by Cleisthenes the son of Megacles, saw their opportunity. They raised a force and invaded Attica, apparently from Boeotia. As Plataea blocked the western passes, they took the longer route by Mount Parnes. But little support came from Athens and the enterprise ended in the occupation of Leipsydrium which overlooks Paeonidae. After fighting which served to show that the *émigrés* were worthy of their fathers, the raid ended in utter failure.

It was now clear that only foreign intervention could restore the Alcmaeonidae and overthrow the tyrant, and to secure that intervention they turned to Sparta. They had on their side the powerful influence of Delphi. In 548 B.C. the temple of Apollo at Delphi was burnt down. The Amphictyons decided to rebuild it with magnificence worthy of the god, and collected funds amounting to 300 talents throughout Greece and even from Lydia and Egypt. The Alcmaeonidae had received the contract for the rebuilding. According to Herodotus, who no doubt follows the tradition of that family, they carried out the work with yet greater splendour than the contract required, using Parian marble instead of tufa for the front of the temple. Their munificence was rewarded by the goodwill of the god and of his servants[1].

Aristotle follows a malignant and cynical tradition, which found acceptance at Athens in the fourth century, that the Alcmaeonidae, receiving the money to rebuild the temple, used part of it to bribe

[1] See Volume of Plates i, 288.

the Pythian priestess, and made their restoration at Athens a first charge on the remainder. The magnificence of the temple marked their gratitude for the success of their speculation with Apollo's funds. Neither version is dictated by a pure love of truth: the second is slightly more probable, as the Alcmaeonidae must have needed money for their earlier enterprise[1]. And it is hard to see from what other source they could get sufficient funds.

It is however doubtful if it was so necessary to bribe the Pythian priestess. Her message to all Spartans whenever they consulted the oracle was 'first free Athens.' But the influence of Sparta was powerful at Delphi and the oracle pointed her along the path she was inclined to go. Hippias was the old friend of Argos and the new friend of Persia, and that was enough. Besides, an Athenian government which owed its establishment to the help of Sparta might be a useful instrument of her policy, and her policy was for the moment dominated by the able and restless king Cleomenes. The exiles would be ready enough to make any promises. The Spartans accordingly prepared to put down tyranny at Athens as they had done in other Greek states. Possibly deceived as to the resistance they would meet, they first sent by sea a small force under Anchimolius which landed in the Bay of Phalerum (511 B.C.). The expedition was no doubt convoyed by the fleets of Aegina or Corinth so that the small naval force of Athens could make no opposition. But Hippias was not taken unawares. Besides his mercenaries he had the help of 1000 Thessalian horse and in the country between Phalerum and Athens, which had been cleared so as to suit cavalry, this force defeated the Lacedaemonians and killed their commander.

But Hippias was not deceived by his success, and busied himself fortifying the hill of Munychia at the Piraeus as a last refuge on Attic soil. For Spartan prestige was now deeply engaged, and this reverse only made it more necessary to vindicate the valour of Spartan hoplites as against Thessalian cavalry. So in the next year (510 B.C.) Cleomenes himself took the field at the head of a large army which marched through the Megarian passes and thence on Athens. Hippias advanced to meet it, but the Thessalian horsemen proved ineffective and rode home after a skirmish—a poor display which was to be followed a few years later by a disastrous attempt to invade Phocis. The military prestige of Thessaly was finally eclipsed by that of Sparta, and Hippias, thus deserted, was driven into Athens and besieged on the Acropolis where the old

[1] This may explain an issue of heraldic silver and electrum coins at Delphi and in Phocis; see Seltman, *op. cit.* pp. 80–84. See Vol. of Plates i, 304, *n, o, p.*

fortifications had been strengthened and a good store of provisions
had been collected. Herodotus says that the Spartans had no mind
to maintain a longdrawn siege and would soon have retired but for
a fortunate accident. The tyrant's children fell into their hands
as they were being smuggled out of the country, and to save them
he agreed to capitulate and leave Attica within five days. So
Hippias and his kinsmen retired to Sigeum and the rule of the
house of Peisistratus was ended.

CHAPTER IV

THE OUTER GREEK WORLD IN THE SIXTH CENTURY

I. INTRODUCTION. SOURCES

AT the beginning of the sixth century B.C. the period of colonial expansion was practically at an end. From then onward till the time of Alexander the Great the limits of the Greek world remained practically unchanged. Where changes occurred they were mainly adverse to the Greeks. Massilia was founded by the Phocaeans about 600 B.C., Miletus was captured by the Persians in 494, and these two events may be taken as typical. Both in the far east and the far west the Greek city states flourished during the sixth century in a way that they never did in any succeeding age.

The early history of the Greek cities of the far west, in Italy, Gaul and Spain, has an importance that has not always been fully recognized. It is only from recent researches and discoveries that historians have learned how very much of a half truth is the statement of Horace that captive Greece took captive her wild conquerors. Italy was first taken captive by Greek culture when the Greeks in Italy were still their own masters and the Roman power was still in its infancy. This fact is vital for a proper understanding of ancient Rome as well as of ancient Greece, and it will be developed and documented later in this chapter. But before dealing with the youthful west it will be well to consider the eastern Greek world, the region where in the sixth century B.C. life was probably fuller and civilization more developed than even in Greece proper.

Here in the east the centre of interest is different, and needs a word of explanation. The source of all Greek achievement is generally admitted to have been the city-state (see above, vol. III, p. 687). The ideal of all the best and most typical Greek thinkers was a Greece consisting of as many such states as possible, none of them overgrown, each of them independent, and all of them co-operating harmoniously. The practice was of course different. From the early part of the fifth century onwards the Greek cities were invariably under the hegemony of some centralizing power.

But in the sixth century the Asiatic Greeks were under no such central authority. What they suffered as a result is notorious. Their lack of cohesion led to enslavement by the great power farther east. But their intellectual activity and independence of thought were extraordinary. It is true that they eventually sacrificed first political and then (as a result) intellectual freedom to this perhaps impossible ideal of absolute autonomy. But the fact that their losses came after their gains does not prove that they outweighed them. The balancing of the account can only be accomplished by examining in detail the history of the period.

Unfortunately the sixth century comes before, though only just before, the fully documented epoch of Greek history. Hence it becomes doubly necessary to review briefly the sources on which our knowledge of it is based.

The principal source of our information is the history of Herodotus, written in the third quarter of the century succeeding. Of the nine Books into which his work is divided the first five are devoted to the earlier history of the conflict between East and West, and deal in special detail with the exploits of Croesus of Lydia, Cyrus, Cambyses, and Darius. These five prefatory Books, leading up to the invasions of Greece by Darius and Xerxes which are narrated in the last four, contain many minor digressions into the history of Greece itself during the sixth century. A writer so invariably entertaining is plainly not exhaustive in his treatment of any subject. His accuracy too may be a matter of opinion. But recent research tends to show that his statements are not untrustworthy where he was in a position to ascertain the facts, and this he unquestionably was in the case of many of his statements about sixth-century events. For those with which this chapter is concerned his testimony is especially valuable. He was a native of south-west Asia Minor, spent some time as a refugee in Samos, and finally settled in south Italy when the Athenians re-colonized the site of Sybaris.

Still more valuable where available are the writings of sixth-century poets and philosophers, the more so since the philosophers tended to be also statesmen and the poets were apt to write about their own immediate surroundings. Unfortunately these writers are preserved only in scanty fragments, known partly from papyri, partly from the accident of their being quoted by learned writers of later ages. Where they are quotations the context in which they are quoted often becomes a valuable commentary.

There are of course also numerous incidental references to this period in many later writers both Greek and Latin, such as

Aristotle, Plutarch, Livy. The value of these later sources varies very greatly, but it should not be forgotten that not only these ancient writers but also their earliest readers had access to a large literature that has since perished.

Finally an important mass of material is supplied by archaeology. Remains of the architecture and sculpture of the period exist in some numbers, coins and inscriptions are fairly abundant, while vases, many of them elaborately painted, have been unearthed in thousands. An ever-increasing number of these finds come from sites that have been excavated under more or less expert control. There are already many known types of statues, coins, and vases that can be assigned with some certainty not merely to sixth-century Greece, but to a closely defined period within the century and to some precise locality. Finds like these are of particular value for a period such as the sixth century B.C., where the literary evidence is sufficiently abundant to add immensely to their significance, but at the same time so incomplete that archaeology serves not merely to illustrate the written documents but also to fill gaps in our knowledge.

II. THE EASTERN POWERS

We may now turn to the first and main division of this chapter, that namely which deals with the history of the eastern Greeks. For the reasons already given the basis of study must be the individual city-state. But before dealing with these separate units a word must first be said about the great eastern powers that so decisively influenced the course of events in western Asia Minor throughout this period. See chaps. I and VII, and vol. III, chaps. XIV, XXI.

During the first great phase of Ionian civilization, which coincides roughly with the seventh century B.C., the Asiatic Greeks had had as their immediate neighbour to the east the newly consolidated kingdom of Lydia, which had become the foremost power in Anatolia at just about the time when civilization began to make rapid strides in Ionia and Aeolis. The seventh-century kings of Lydia were not always on the best of terms with their Greek neighbours, but the Greek question seems not to have been that with which their foreign policy was most concerned. To the east they had the great power of Assyria, and within their own borders they had the Cimmerian invaders. The main object of their foreign policy had been to drive out the Cimmerians without becoming permanent vassals of the Assyrians. But at the end of the seventh century the situation changed. The Cimmerian peril passed away; Assyria was overthrown by the united efforts of the Babylonians and the Medes, and the Assyrian empire divided between the two conquerors (vol. III, pp. 126 *sqq.*). Lydia's new neighbours, the Medes, held only about half the dominions of the Assyrian empire, and king Alyattes tried long and hard to extend his power eastwards at the Medes' expense. It was not till more than twenty-five years after the fall of Nineveh that the two parties gave up the struggle by mutual agreement and sealed the peace by a marriage between the king of Lydia's daughter and the heir to the throne of the Medes (see above, vol. III, p. 512 *sq.*). This peace with the Medes (585 B.C.) allowed Alyattes to turn his attention to the west. Previous kings of Lydia had made occasional wars against individual Greek cities, but Alyattes seems to have initiated a policy of periodic invasions. His chief success was the capture and destruction of Smyrna, that most suffering of Greek cities. His campaigns against Miletus were less successful and ended in a negotiated peace (vol. III, p. 513). Alyattes was succeeded about 560 B.C. by Croesus, who completed the subjugation of the Greek cities of the western coast, conquering and annexing not only the Aeolic cities of the north and the Ionians of the centre, but also the Dorians of the south. When about 546 B.C. Croesus was overthrown by Cyrus and Lydia became a Persian satrapy, the Greeks of the coast were also incorporated in the Persian empire. The Persians do not appear to have been particularly cruel conquerors. The various cities continued to be treated as separate political units. But the government in each city was put into the hands of a tyrant, a pro-Persian Greek who depended for his position on Persian support, and even the able administration of Darius, who employed Greeks in positions of high responsibility, failed to reconcile the Greek cities to the rule of the Great King. Hence perhaps arose the Persian policy of favouring Phoenician shipping as against Ionian, which may in turn explain why the opening of the fifth century witnessed the great Ionian revolt. The rebels, aided by the Athenians, who had themselves so recently expelled their tyrants and established a democracy, set up democracies in their various cities, proclaimed their independence of Persia, and actually succeeded in burning Sardes. The revolt was soon crushed, but it proved to be only the prelude to the great Persian wars. Its effects therefore go beyond the limits of the present chapter (see below, pp. 214 *sqq.*).

One other great foreign power exercised such an influence on sixth-century Ionia that a brief notice of it is here necessary. Egypt had witnessed a revival of its ancient civilization just at the time when the Ionian and Aeolic renaissance was in its first great phase. This Egyptian revival was the work of the Saïte dynasty, of which the real founder, Psammetichus I, had made himself pharaoh about the year 663 B.C. (vol. III, pp. 286 *sqq.*, 299 *sqq*). His ascendancy over the numerous petty chiefs who had previously divided up the country was established by the aid of Ionian and Carian mercenaries, and for the next century and a half Ionian mercenaries continued to be the basis of the pharaohs' power. When Necho, the successor of Psammetichus, had defeated at Megiddo Josiah the pro-Babylonian king of Judah, he sent a thank-offering to the temple of Apollo at Miletus. When Psammetichus II sent an expedition against the Ethiopians, Greek troops took part in the advance to the far south. Some of these Greek soldiers scratched their names on an ancient monument at Abu-Simbel, and a kind chance has preserved these vandalisms for incorporation in modern handbooks of Greek epigraphy. Apries (the Biblical Hophra), who reigned from 588 to 566 B.C., rested his power on 30,000 of these mercenaries, and though their unpopularity with the Egyptians brought about his downfall, his successor was soon forced to adopt the policy which he had been put on the throne to abolish. Some forty years later, just after his death, the Greek mercenaries are still found playing a prominent part in the struggle between Psammetichus III and Cambyses of Persia. Cambyses however proved the victor. Egypt became, like Lydia, a Persian province, and the event was disastrous not only to the Greek military establishment in the country, but also to the prosperous trading settlement of Naucratis (see p. 218).

III. MILETUS, SAMOS AND EPHESUS

This eastern background must be constantly before the eye when we turn, as we may now do, to the individual histories of the various Greek cities.

Of these the most important was Miletus, which is described by Herodotus as having been at this time the pride of Ionia. He tells us that during a period which must coincide roughly with the sixth century B.C. Miletus enjoyed two phases of great prosperity separated by two generations of disastrous civil strife. There can be little doubt that these phases of prosperity and eclipse are to be correlated with the changes just recorded in the policy of Lydia and Persia. The earlier period of prosperity must coincide with the tyranny of Thrasybulus, a ruler who is dated by his dealings with the Corinthian tyrant Periander (see above, vol. III, p. 553).

Of the subsequent period of dissension practically nothing is known. Its origin is perhaps to be sought in the tyrant's persecution of the aristocracy, which he sought to teach his friend Periander to imitate by the acted parable of the cutting off of all the tallest ears of corn. The decline of the city must have been hastened by the wars it had to wage against Croesus and Cyrus. The second period of prosperity embraced the reign of a new tyrant, Histiaeus, who was a personal friend of the Persian king Darius. He had won the favour of Darius by help rendered during the Persian campaigns in Scythia and Thrace (p. 213). He ultimately fell because he had sought to extend his own personal power in that same direction. After the Persian annexations in Thrace he begged Darius to make him a present of Myrcinus, a site on the Strymon rich both in timber and mines, and with a population, both native and settlers, ready to be employed in exploiting these riches. The request brought upon him the suspicions of the Great King, who sent for him and kept him in Persia in a sort of honourable confinement. Ultimately he is found again in Ionia involved in the great revolt that broke out there in 499 B.C. The part assigned to him by Herodotus is picturesque but incomprehensible (see below, p. 217); but at this stage in his career the personal adventures of the tyrant cease to have much historical significance. The great and tragic fact was that the Greek cities of the west coast of Asia Minor had revolted and been crushed. The capture of Miletus in 494 B.C. ends its history as a free city-state (p. 227).

It is interesting to notice how little these political occurrences appear to have reacted on the great movement in philosophy and natural science that was the chief glory of sixth-century Miletus. Thales may have begun his work during the first period of prosperity and Anaximenes have finished his after the opening of the second, but much of their scientific activity and most of that of Anaximander must have fallen within the two generations of civil strife (see below, pp. 539 sqq.).

The material prosperity of Miletus was due in the first place to her shipping, which also can have suffered only relatively from her internal dissensions. Except perhaps during the brief period of the Samian thalassocracy (see below, p. 91), Milesian merchantmen and the trades and industries that supplied both ships and cargoes must have been ceaselessly active. The colonization of the Black Sea coasts went on far into the century, and the

Black Sea trade presumably right till the end. At Naucratis, the Greek emporium in Egypt, the Milesians held a position apart and presumably one of privilege, down to the Persian conquest of Egypt in 525 B.C. The trade with Sybaris, the greatest and richest Greek city in south Italy, flourished till the Sybarites were overthrown in 510 B.C. by their neighbours and rivals the Crotonians. When Sybaris fell the Milesians were the chief mourners, 'for these two cities more than any others that we know of had been closely united from of old.' The bond was a commercial one. The Sybarites were the middlemen of the trade between Miletus and the Etruscans, and further supplied Miletus with raw wool from which she manufactured her famous textiles.

Another industry of the seventh and earlier part of the sixth century that probably had its centre in Miletus is known from the numerous specimens to be found in modern museums. This is the pottery characteristic of sites (so far excavated) that fell at this time within the Milesian sphere of influence. It is a white-ground ware decorated with friezes of animals whose heads are drawn in outline but the bodies in silhouette. The best and most numerous examples of this pottery come from Rhodes[1], but that may be because Rhodes has been more fully excavated than most Anatolian sites. It is the characteristic pottery of Miletus itself so far as the site has been explored, and it is equally characteristic of the Milesian colonies. Milesian sculpture of the sixth century is best known from the series of draped seated figures that once adorned the approaches to the temple of Branchidae but are now for the most part housed in the British Museum. One of them bears an inscription which declares that it represents Chares of Teichiussa. These statues are easily distinguished from contemporary products of Greece proper by a certain massiveness and fleshiness that is a common feature in sixth-century Ionic art. It will be found reappearing in works found at Ephesus and Samos and in the Parian colony of Thasos.

Next to Miletus in importance, and even before it during the period of Milesian civil strife, was the island state of Samos. Till well into the sixth century it appears indeed to have been largely in the power of a landed class called *geomoroi*, but side by side with these landowners there was a strong and enterprising mercantile community. Well before the end of the seventh century a Samian named Colaeus made a voyage to Tartessus and became famous from the cargo that he brought back from the region of the Spanish mines. About 600 B.C. the city founded the colony of Perinthus on the north coast of the sea of Marmora. Some-

---

[1] See Volume of Plates i, 348, *b, c.*

where towards the middle of the sixth century a certain Aeaces[1] had a statue erected in his honour. The statue with its inscription was unearthed in 1906. The meaning of the inscription is uncertain, but a very plausible interpretation regards Aeaces as a priestly official engaged in collecting tithes for the state temple from the merchant-adventurers of the city. However that may have been, it is probable that this Aeaces is to be identified with Aeaces the father of Polycrates, the most outstanding figure in Samian political history.

Something like a biography may be constructed for Polycrates, though at the best it is a meagre one and some of the incidents are only weakly documented. If the father had a statue erected to him the son must have moved early in prominent circles. Hence it is not surprising that mention is made of his doings before he became the chief man in his state. The story, which is unfortunately not from the best extant authority, tells how in those early days of his career he used to lend out coverlets and drinking vessels to people who were holding great receptions or celebrating weddings. His next step was to make himself tyrant, at first in conjunction with two of his brothers, but subsequently as sole ruler. Herodotus mentions the bowmen who formed his bodyguard. These bowmen were needed, for the tyrant had disaffected subjects. On one occasion he tried to get rid of them *en masse* by sending them to help in the Persian invasion of Egypt. The plan failed. The disaffected contingent came back regardless of instructions and turned their arms against the tyrant, being helped in this undertaking by a force from Sparta. Polycrates however overcame the rebels, and the Spartans returned ingloriously home (see p. 75). The report of this incident in Herodotus was derived by him from the grandson of one of the Spartans who took part in it.

Polycrates acquired his power just about the time when Miletus submitted to the Persians. The coincidence was no accident. Samos and Miletus had been rivals from the days of the Lelantine war[2] (see vol. III, p. 622).

When Miletus became subject to a foreign conqueror the Samians saw their opportunity. They took the place of Miletus not only as the chief trading port in the east Aegean but also as the chief opponents of expansion any farther westward on the

---

[1] See Volume of Plates, I, 368, *b*.

[2] Their alliance against Priene in the days of Bias is probably to be dated about the time of Cyrus' conquests and to be explained as an attempt to make common cause against the Persian invader when Priene was already in Persian hands, see Wilamowitz, *Berl. S B* 1906, p. 44.

part of the great eastern power. There is mention in late writers
of a war waged by Polycrates against Cyrus himself. The account
is obscure but not in its main outline improbable. The chief object
of Polycrates' foreign policy was to keep Samos independent of
Persia. The chief means to this end were a strong navy and
alliances with actual or potential enemies of the Persians, notably
with Amasis the Egyptian pharaoh. The tyrant established something of a thalassocracy in the Aegean, where numerous islands
were brought under his sway. One of them was Rheneia, the
larger neighbour of Delos. As he dedicated this island to Apollo
and celebrated the Delian games, there can be little doubt that he
aimed at being recognized as having some sort of suzerainty over
the whole archipelago. With a considerable naval power he maintained what was practically a blockade of Persia, during which
neutral and even friendly ships were systematically searched. The
blockade was of course described as piracy by those whom it in-
convenienced. Polycrates himself justified it by declaring that
friends whose ships he captured and released were more grateful
to him than they would have been if he had never interfered with
them. The success however of this struggle with Persia depended
on the Great King being much pre-occupied in the east. When
Cambyses began to concentrate his policy on the conquest of
Egypt and the raising of a powerful fleet in his western dominions,
Polycrates abandoned the struggle, broke off his alliance with
Egypt, and sent a force to take part in the Persian invasion
(525 B.C.). The picturesque narrative in Herodotus casts only the
thinnest of disguises over these hard and disagreeable facts. But
it shows also how reluctantly the Samian tyrant bowed to circumstances. The force he sent to help Cambyses consisted of the
disaffected contingent whose subsequent proceedings have been
already described, and he himself took the first possible opportunity to turn again against the Persian king. He was led to believe that the Persian satrap at Sardes had quarrelled with his royal
master and needed Samian help. The treacherous satrap promised
him that if he gave it he should receive such sums of money as
would make him rich enough to become tyrant of all Greece.
Polycrates was induced to cross to the mainland for an interview,
and was there taken prisoner and put to death with barbarous
cruelty.

When Polycrates set out on his disastrous visit to the mainland
he left in charge of the island a Samian of low birth named
Maeandrius, who had a sad experience. 'He sought,' so Herodotus
tells us, 'to show himself the justest of men, but found it im-

R.-2

possible.' What he proposed was to hand over all the tyrant's power and wealth (except a priesthood of Zeus the Liberator and a sum of six talents) and establish freedom and equality in the island. But he quickly discovered that the proposal was too dangerous for himself personally to be carried into execution, so he changed his mind and established himself in Polycrates' place. The murdered tyrant however had left surviving one of the two brothers who had originally shared his tyranny. This brother, Syloson by name, had some years before become a personal friend of the Persian prince Darius. Syloson now persuaded Darius to restore him to his native island. Maeandrius fled to Sparta where he sought in vain to purchase the support of king Cleomenes with the Samian drinking vessels that he had brought with him, and Syloson was left tyrant of Samos but only after it had become almost depopulated by massacres and reprisals. The saying 'thanks to Syloson there's lots of room' was long remembered in Samos, and though the citizen roll was to some extent made good by the admission to it of manumitted slaves, the island ceased altogether to be what it had been under Polycrates, 'foremost among all cities, Greek and barbarian.'

Herodotus dilates the more over Samos because, as he explains,

they have executed three works that are among the greatest in all Greece. The first is a tunnel through a mountain one hundred and fifty fathoms in height, that starts from below and runs right through. The length of the tunnel is seven stades, the height and breadth eight feet each. The whole length of this is traversed by another channel twenty cubits deep and three feet broad, through which the water conveyed in pipes reaches the city from a great spring. The architect of this tunnel was Eupalinus son of Naustrophus, a Megarian. This is one of the three works. The second is a mole round the harbour, twenty fathoms deep and more than two stades long. Their third work is a temple, the greatest of all temples that I know. Its first architect was Rhoecus son of Philes, a native of the island. This is why I have dilated the more over the Samians (III, 60).

So writes Herodotus with the superficial irrelevance and inconsequence that help to make him so attractive. There is little doubt that these three works were all begun or completed during the reign of Polycrates. Rhoecus is associated with Theodorus who is known to have worked for the tyrant. The mole is naturally connected with the thalassocracy. All three, and especially the waterworks, are typical of the tyrannies of this period. The temple, mole and tunnel at Samos may therefore be identified fairly safely with the 'public works of Polycrates,' which Aristotle says that that tyrant executed to ensure that his subjects were kept fully employed and inadequately paid.

All three works are still partially extant. Of the temple there remains one headless column and of the foundations enough to confirm Herodotus' dimensions. The line of the mole may still be traced in the waters of the harbour. The tunnel, rediscovered forty years ago, shows that the engineers had sufficient skill and confidence to begin simultaneously at both ends. When the two gangs met, the errors to be rectified amounted to under six yards in direction and about half that amount in height.

One other work that was erected in Samos at this time is definitely ascribed to Polycrates himself. It was called a *laura* and is said to have been put up as a rival to the 'Sweet Corner' at Sardes. Whether this laura was a bazaar or something less reputable is doubtful, but austerity was certainly not the predominant feature of life under Polycrates. Poets of love and wine such as Ibycus and Anacreon found a congenial home at his court. Pythagoras the philosopher migrated to south Italy.

Sculpture and the minor arts flourished in the island throughout the century. The artists Rhoecus and Theodorus are said to have invented the casting of statues in bronze, and though such legends generally sacrifice accuracy for simplicity and use the word 'invented' in a very loose way, they still bear witness to the fame of the artists they refer to and indicate the character of their achievements. Various works by both these artists are mentioned by ancient writers—more particularly the ring that Theodorus made for Polycrates which the tyrant cast into the sea when he was advised by his friend Amasis to try and avoid the consequences of his excessive prosperity by casting away his most precious possession. Another famous Samian gem-cutter of this period was Mnesarchus the father of the philosopher Pythagoras.

The extant material for forming an idea of the works of these artists is meagre. The statue of Aeaces has marked affinities with the Milesian figures from Branchidae. A draped standing male figure similar in style to the Aeaces statue has features that recall a figure carved in relief on one of the sculptured columns from the temple of Artemis at Ephesus which were dedicated by king Croesus.

On the Ionian mainland the one city that rivalled Miletus in importance was Ephesus. About 600 B.C. the aristocratic government of the Basilidae was overthrown by a certain Pythagoras who established himself as tyrant. This ruler is said by a plainly unfriendly authority, a certain Baton of Sinope who wrote a history of the tyrants of Ephesus, to have been cruel and avaricious and to have confiscated the property of those who enjoyed reputation or power, 'But with the people and the multitude he both was and appeared to be well liked, sometimes making them hopeful by his promises, sometimes secretly distributing small gratuities.' At the command of the Pythian oracle he built a temple, possibly the first great temple of Artemis[1]. Four other tyrants are found ruling Ephesus in the course of the sixth century. Of these the earliest was probably Melas who became son-in-law of the Lydian king Alyattes. Melas was succeeded by his son Pindarus, who however failed to maintain his father's good relations with Lydia, where Croesus had now succeeded to the throne. But even the story of this failure suggests the great wealth and importance of Ephesus at this time, when Miletus was no longer under Thrasybulus and Samos not yet under Polycrates. When Alyattes died there was a struggle for the Lydian throne between Croesus and his half-Greek half-brother Pantaleon. Croesus secured financial support from Ephesus, but it came from Pamphaes the son of Theocharides, not from any member of the house of Melas which may plausibly be supposed to have been backing the half-Greek candidate. The result of this mistake was that Croesus, when established on the throne, marched against Ephesus. Pindarus realized that the attack was directed more against him than against his city, advised the Ephesians to put themselves under the protection of Artemis, which they did by tying the city with a rope to the temple of the goddess, and himself retired to the Peloponnese. Ephesus must have become in fact if not in name a Lydian protectorate, but continued to enjoy internal freedom. The Ephesians were able to invite from Athens a certain Aristarchus who, under the title of Aesymnetes, held for five years a position not unlike that held in Athens by Solon (p. 57), and established in Ephesus a limited democracy.

Under this new régime the city recovered the friendship of Lydia. Croesus was one of the chief contributors to the rebuilding of the Artemisium, and the Ephesians refused to side against him when attacked by Cyrus of Persia. To the time just after the Persian conquest should probably be assigned the rule of the obscure tyrants Comas and Athenagoras, of whom little is known except that they expelled from the city the somewhat provocative satiric poet Hipponax. The banishment of Hipponax must be roughly contemporary with the birth of the philosopher Heracleitus, whose whole life was spent in his native city (pp. 486 *sq*., 553).

The material remains of sixth-century Ephesus are limited to the finds made in excavating the great temple of Artemis. From

[1] See Volume of Plates i, 388, *b.*

these it appears that the earliest temple of any size dates from about the beginning of the sixth century. The enormous temple that made the city famous was in course of construction in the time of Croesus, though it appears to have been completed and dedicated more than a century later. The building was about 360 ft. long by some 180 ft. broad, with a double row of columns running all the way round. The lower parts of these columns were sculptured in relief with human figures of which one or two are preserved fairly complete. The work is of the highest excellence. One of the columns as restored in the British Museum (from fragments that may have not all belonged originally to the same column) has a mutilated inscription that can however be interpreted with certainty as saying that it was dedicated by king Croesus. The epigraphical evidence thus bears out the statement of Herodotus about the contributions made by Croesus to the temple. Theodorus of Samos, who is credited also with other work for Croesus, is said to have had a share in the building (p. 607).

IV. THE NORTHERN IONIAN CITIES

Chios, the more northerly of the two great Ionian islands, never played a leading part in the sixth century. About 600 b.c. the government was some sort of democracy with a demarch who seems to take precedence of the king and a public council containing 50 members from each tribe (*phyle*) and meeting at least once a month to transact general public business and to act as a law court with the right of revising judgments and inflicting penalties. Unfortunately this early Chian constitution, which shows affinities with that of Solon, is known only from a single mutilated inscription and a possible reference in the *Politics* of Aristotle. The island became early a slave-owning state, and the land was largely given over to the cultivation of the vine. The wine-jar and vine-branch that appear on early coins of Chios[1] suggest that by the second half of the sixth century wine making was one of the great industries of the island. The slaves and vineyards may account for the fact that the island seems to have been in constant need of food-supplying lands on the mainland opposite. Hence perhaps the constancy with which the same types are repeated on the Chian coins, the object of which may have been to preserve the credit of the Chian currency outside the island. Hence too perhaps the war with Erythrae of about 600 b.c. (in which the Chians were supported by Miletus) and the sacrilegious surrender to Cyrus of the Lydian refugee

[1] See Volume of Plates i, 302, *i*.

Pactyas in return for which the islanders received the rich corn-lands of Atarneus on the mainland. Under the Persians the island prospered. It had not been too well treated by the Lydians and may at first have welcomed the new masters of Ionia. A tyrant named Strattis is found attending Darius on his campaign of 516 B.C.; but in the Ionian revolt it came out strongly on the Greek side. At the battle of Lade in 494 B.C. it supplied 100 ships as against the 80 of Miletus, 70 of Lesbos and 60 of Samos, numbers which show how prosperous the island had been growing during the period of Persian suzerainty.

The elegant refinement of Chian civilization in the latter part of the sixth century is reflected in Chian art. A famous family of sculptors worked in the island, notably Archermus, who was reputed to have 'invented' the winged type of victory, and his sons Bupalus and Athenis who excelled in the rendering of draped female figures. The signature of Archermus has been found both at Delos and at Athens, and with the help of epigraphy and literary tradition one group of the great find of archaic female statues from the Athenian acropolis has been recognized as Chian[1]. Clothes, coiffure, and facial expression are all elaborately delicate and graceful, while in technique these statues are beyond dispute superior to contemporary Attic work. Chian influence appears to have ceased with the fall of the Athenian tyranny in 510 B.C. The Chian statues were of Parian marble and probably imported into Athens ready made. The favourite pottery was the delicate fabric known generally as Naucratite (p. 586).

On the mainland Ionia extended northward to a point about level with the northern extremity of Chios and included the hammer-headed peninsula that faces the island. In this region the chief cities were Colophon, Teos, Clazomenae, Smyrna, and Phocaea. Three of the five soon fell on evil days. Smyrna, where at the opening of the sixth century Mimnermus may have been still composing his despondent elegies (p. 487), was destroyed by Alyattes, and centuries elapsed before it was restored. Teos had been proposed by Thales as a federal capital of Ionia when he was trying to unite the Ionians in a federation to resist the Persians; but the scheme failed, Cyrus reached the Aegean, and the Teians, rather than submit to him, sailed away and founded Abdera on the Thracian coast. Phocaea at the same time lost a great part of its population. Its earlier importance is shown by the tradition of a Phocaean thalassocracy and by archaic electrum coins[2] with the *type parlant* of a seal (*phoca*) and struck on a standard that became widely known as the Phocaic. About 600 B.C. it

---

[1] See Volume of Plates ii, 18, *b*.   [2] *Ib.* 302, *b*.

founded Massilia (Marseilles) and a generation later Alalia in Corsica. When the army of Cyrus threatened the city a large contingent of the Phocaeans fled to their Corsican colony.

Colophon had in the seventh century become the mother-city of Smyrna and reached an importance which was lost only temporarily, if at all, when for a while it fell into the hands of the Lydian Gyges. In the first part of the sixth century it waged with Alyattes a war in which the cavalry was prominent (vol. III, p. 514). But its chief claim to fame is that it produced the philosopher Xenophanes. The works however of that remarkable critic of received opinions belong to the period after he had been driven from his native city (about 530 B.C.) and begun his long wanderings in south Italy (see p. 559). More may be known about the city if ever circumstances allow the archaeologists of the American school at Athens to resume the excavations that they began while the Greeks were administering western Asia Minor in the spring of 1922.

Of Clazomenae ancient historians have still less to say; but this lack of literary evidence is to some extent made good by archaeology. The city is now best known for its seventh- and sixth-century sarcophagi of painted terracotta. Some seventy of these were known to the French archaeologists who studied them in 1913. Systematic excavations were begun there by the Greek archaeologist Oikonomos in 1921 and were being successfully prosecuted in 1922 when the city once more passed out of Greek hands and the work and most of the finds had to be abandoned. The subjects depicted include scenes of war (Greeks fighting Cimmerians), of legend (the *Doloneia*), games (chariot races with Ionic pillars for turning-posts), and hunting. The style is distinctive but has a close kinship with that of the vases usually ascribed to Miletus. There is the same use of a combination of outline and silhouette, and the ornamental motives are also very similar. Vases decorated in the same style as these coffins have been found in Ionia, Aeolis, Rhodes, Athens, Egypt, the Black Sea, and Italy. The human figures on this pottery show a distinctive type of face that is presumably Ionic. The women with their receding foreheads, almond-shaped eyes, tiny mouths, and ears ornamented with pendant earrings are attractive in a naïvely sophisticated way. A few of the sarcophagi are decorated partly in the technique just described, partly in what is practically the red-figure style[1] that was used from about 530 B.C. onwards by the great vase painters who worked in Athens. It may have been refugees from Ionia, perhaps from Clazomenae itself, who introduced the new style into Attica (see further below, p. 599 *sq.*).

[1] See Volume of Plates i, 292, *c*.

V. AEOLIANS, DORIANS AND THE CYCLADES

North of Ionia the land was occupied by another branch of the Greek race, the Aeolian, whose greatest achievements belong to an earlier epoch. These mainland Aeolian cities never became great naval powers. The best known of them is Cyme, the near neighbour of Phocaea. The attitude of the people of Cyme towards their harbour (Strabo XIII, p. 622) is enough to show that it long remained a dominantly agricultural state.

On the other hand, the great city of Mitylene on the island of Lesbos was in the year 600 B.C. in some ways the most advanced community in the whole Greek world. Sappho, Alcaeus and Pittacus were all Mityleneans, and all three were very probably flourishing at that date. In the preceding period the hereditary aristocracy had been displaced by a series of tyrants, the last of whom had been overthrown by a movement in which Pittacus and Alcaeus were leaders. The two however soon quarrelled. The poet Alcaeus, himself an aristocrat, wished for a return to the old régime, while Pittacus aimed at a moderate democracy. The party of Pittacus triumphed: he was given a position much like that of Solon at Athens, and he used it with similar good sense and moderation. Like Solon he revised the laws of his city. One of his statutes imposed a specially severe penalty on any offence if committed under the influence of drink, another put a limit to the expenditure on funeral ceremonials. This position of constitutional dictator or Aesymnetes was held by Pittacus for ten years during which Alcaeus and perhaps Sappho were exiled from Mitylene. A brother of Alcaeus who was also banished took service as a soldier under the king of Babylon. At the end of the ten years Pittacus gave up his position voluntarily and Alcaeus returned from exile (see vol. III, p. 516).

The time of these internal struggles in Mitylene was seized by Miletus to strengthen her control over the Hellespont, which was constantly threatened by a powerful and unfriendly Lesbos. It may have been with Milesian help that during the time of the Mitylenean tyranny Athens, the mother-city of Miletus, seized Sigeum in the Troad, just outside the entrance into the straits. Pittacus renewed the struggle and himself killed in single combat the Athenian commander. In the negotiations which ended the war Periander the tyrant of Corinth acted as arbitrator. Sigeum reverted to Mitylene, but only for a while. It was again seized for Athens by the tyrant Peisistratus who appointed one of his own sons to be ruler of the city.

The moderation and practical wisdom of Pittacus won him a place among the seven sages of archaic Greece, but in fame and importance he is easily eclipsed by the two great Lesbian poets, Alcaeus and Sappho (pp. 494 *sqq.*). In one respect Sappho gives Mitylene a unique position. Not only her own achievements in poetry but also her band of women disciples show that in the Mitylene of her day women, at least of the most prosperous class, enjoyed a freedom found elsewhere only in Sparta and an opportunity for self-development without parallel in Greek history.

Of specifically Aeolic works of art very little is certainly known. There is a rare and curious form of the volute capital which is found among the temple remains at Mitylene and a few mainland Aeolic sites[1]. The style of these capitals recalls Egypt, and they have often been regarded as belonging to the type from which was developed the mature Ionic. A connection between Mitylene and Egypt is attested at least from the time of Sappho, whose brother exported Greek wine to Naucratis.

A third group of Greek settlements, Dorian by race, lay to the south of Ionia in the south-west corner of Asia Minor. Of the six chief cities of this group two, Cnidus and Halicarnassus, were on the mainland; three, Ialysus, Camirus, and Lindus, on the large island of Rhodes; the sixth being Cos, the second largest island of the Dodecanese. These six cities held periodically a common festival from which however Halicarnassus was early expelled, perhaps as not being of pure Doric stock (see however Herodotus I, 144). Within this group the three Rhodian cities showed a remarkable tendency to act as a unity. Rhodes for instance, not any particular Rhodian city, is mentioned by Herodotus as one of the four Dorian cities that had part in the Naucratite Hellenium. (The other three were Halicarnassus, Cnidus, and Phaselis.) In 580 B.C. Rhodians, presumably from the whole island, combined with the Cnidians in an expedition which first attempted to seize Lilybaeum in west Sicily and ultimately founded a Greek state in the Lipari islands (see below, p. 354). This Lilybaeum expedition formed part of a wider colonial scheme, which, if successful, would have excluded the Phoenicians from Sicily and profoundly affected the history of the middle Mediterranean. About the same time Gela in south-east Sicily, itself a Rhodian foundation of about a century earlier, was establishing the great city of Acragas (Girgenti) about half-way along the south coast of the island. The two enterprises cannot have been quite independent of one another. It looks as though the Dorian hexapolis was aiming at the subjugation of the whole of

[1] See Volume of Plates i, 390, *b.*

west Sicily, perhaps in conjunction with the Dorian Selinus, the
most westerly of Greek cities in Sicily. Any such projects were
however dealt a fatal blow by the advance of Cyrus to the Aegean.
The Dorians seem to have offered the Persians singularly little
resistance. The only effort was made by the Cnidians and even
that did not get as far as fighting. The Cnidians consulted the
Delphic oracle on an engineering project for digging a canal to
turn into an island the long peninsula on which their city was
built, but the oracle discouraged them and they took its advice.
Some of them may have migrated and taken service under Amasis
of Egypt. At the battle of Pelusium in 525 B.C., where the
Egyptians were defeated and their country left at the mercy of the
Persians, the Caro-Greek contingent which fought on the Egyptian
side distinguished itself by the treachery of its Dorian commander, by the way it began the battle by sacrificing the deserter's
children and drinking their blood mingled with wine, and by the
heroism with which it then proceeded to fight against the Persians.
Cnidus was sufficiently important about the middle of the sixth
century to erect a treasury of its own at Delphi, but the remains
are too scanty to give any idea of Cnidian art at the time.

The archaic pottery of Greek Asia Minor is best known from
finds made in Rhodes[1], notably by Biliotti, the British consul on
the island some seventy years ago, and more recently from the
carefully conducted and admirably published excavations at
Vroulia of the Danish scholar Kinch. Whether the typical pottery
of the seventh and sixth centuries that has been found in such
abundance on the island is a local fabric, as Kinch held, or
Milesian, as is held by many archaeologists, it bears witness to
the commercial importance of Rhodes at this period.

The Cyclades, in spite of their central situation, never held a
dominant political position in Greece. No single island was big
enough to play for long the leading part, and as a group they
were too much separated by the sea for any effective synoecismus
or federation. The largest and most important was Naxos. Its
early prosperity and the main source of its riches are alike indicated by the coins[2] which it began to strike about 600 B.C. with
a large wine cup (*cantharus*) as type. About the same time or only
a little later the Naxians began to quarry their beautiful coarse-
grained marble and to develop a school of sculpture of which
remains attested by inscriptions are to be seen at Delos and at
Delphi[3], while on Naxos itself there are several statues that from
their unfinished condition as well as from their material are plainly
local products. Some too of the earliest archaic statues found on

---

[1] See Volume of Plates i, 348, *b, c*.   [2] *Ib.* 302, *j*.   [3] *Ib.* 294, *a*.

the Athenian Acropolis are of Naxian marble and are held on high authority to be of Naxian workmanship[1]. About the middle of the sixth century the island fell under a tyrant named Lygdamis, who had led a popular movement against the governing aristocracy. This Lygdamis was a close ally of the Athenian tyrant Peisistratus. Each helped the other with men or money to secure the tyranny of his native city. Polycrates too is said to have received support from Lygdamis when he seized the tyranny at Samos. The Naxian tyranny, which was overthrown by the Spartans, perhaps in connection with their expedition to Samos, was followed by a reversion to an oligarchy which in its turn was overthrown and replaced by a democratic government that was still in power in 500 B.C. when the Persians were persuaded to make an expedition against the island with the alleged intention of restoring the exiled aristocrats (see p. 216). This expedition and the success of the Naxians in repelling it, show how prosperous and powerful the island must have been at the time. It appears for a while even to have succeeded Samos as the chief independent Greek naval power in the Aegean.

The people of Paros supplied the arbitrators who ended the period of discord at Miletus by giving the government to those of the citizens whose lands they found best cultivated. This decision in favour of the landed class may mean that the landed interest was dominant in Paros itself, a state of things which would explain why so little is heard at this time about this prosperous island, the second largest of the Cyclades.

The little island of Siphnos owed its importance to the gold and silver mines which were already yielding richly by about the middle of the sixth century. The islanders distributed the output periodically among themselves. When the Samian exiles and their Spartan supporters had failed in their attack on Polycrates and Samos, the Samian exiles descended on Siphnos and extracted from the Siphnians the large sum of a hundred talents. Before this incident the Siphnians had already decorated their market place and town hall with Parian marble. Some idea of their prosperity at this period may still be gleaned from the remains of the treasury which they built at Delphi with the tithe of their income from the mines. It is of marble and decorated with finely carved reliefs[2] and sculptured female figures in place of columns. The work is Ionic but is generally held not to be by Siphnian artists.

Delos itself during the sixth century played an important but

[1] Guy Dickins, *Catalogue of the Acropolis Museum*, vol. i, p. 151.
[2] See Volume of Plates i, 292, *a*, *b*.

somewhat passive part. The Athenian tyrant Peisistratus established a sort of protectorate over the island and purified it by
removing all the graves within sight of the sacred precinct. We
saw how Polycrates of Samos celebrated Delian games and presented Delos with the larger neighbouring island of Rheneia,
which he joined to it by a chain stretched across the narrow
intervening strait. By these particular attentions to the religious
capital of the Aegean the tyrants of Athens and Samos sought
successively to gain some sort of presidency among the island
cities such as republican Athens secured in the succeeding century
as president of the Delian confederacy (see p. 70). Actual remains of this period are comparatively scanty on the island, but
the series of sixth-century female figures from the temple of
Artemis excavated by the French in the seventies of the last
century was the most striking of its kind known till the Athenian
Acropolis revealed its treasures. They have been attributed to the
younger school of Chian sculptors.

One other island of the Aegean that claims a brief notice is
Thasos, close to the coast of west Thrace. Though so far from the
Cyclades it had a close connection with them, having been
colonized from Paros early in the seventh century. Like Siphnos
the island became wealthy and important from its mines. About
550 B.C. it began issuing a coinage[1] the type of which, a satyr
carrying off a maenad, is executed in the full and fleshy style that
is typical of Ionic workmanship. The same style is seen in sculptures of the period found on the island, as for example a relief
representing a kneeling Heracles now in the museum of Constantinople. These coins and sculptures are enough to show that
the importance of Thasos began some time before the Persian
wars when, in recorded history, it first appears as a wealthy city[2].

VI. THE BLACK SEA AND ITS APPROACHES

This concludes the survey of the chief Greek cities on the
islands and the east coast of the Aegean. It remains to consider
the principal outlets which the Greeks, starting from this centre,
had found for themselves in the eighth and seventh centuries and
continued to develop during the sixth.

Of these the most important, at least for the eastern Greeks,
was probably the Black Sea and its approaches. By the year
600 B.C. both sides of the Hellespont were fringed with Greek
cities. On the European side in the Thracian Chersonese (Peninsula of Gallipoli) Lesbos had founded Madytus, Alopeconesos

[1] See Volume of Plates i, 308, *h.*
[2] For Crete see above, vol. iii, p. 563 *sq.*; for Cyprus, *ibid.* pp. 643 *sqq.*

and Sestos, the Milesians and Clazomenians had planted Limnae and Cardia, the Teians Elaeūs. These cities must at first have been much in the nature of factories, since the native Dolonci still occupied the peninsula. Hence perhaps the fact that in the cemetery of Elaeūs, revealed by Turkish shells in 1915 and excavated by French troops during the campaign and in 1921–2, the finds appear to date only from towards the end of the sixth century. On the Asiatic side the two chief cities were the Milesian Abydos, near the modern Chanak, and the Phocaean Lampsacus nearer the Marmora end of the straits. The rivalries that must have inspired these various settlements during the days of Pittacus and Thrasybulus have left no record; but for the period from 560 b.c. onward we have a consecutive narrative in Herodotus (vi, 34 *sq*). The Chersonese was being threatened by barbarian neighbours and the Dolonci sought help at Athens, where Peisistratus had recently established himself as tyrant. With the consent of Peisistratus a rival of his named Miltiades, a rich man who kept a chariot and four and had won a victory at the Olympian games, accompanied the Dolonci home, built a wall across the neck of the isthmus, and made himself tyrant of the whole Chersonese (see above, p. 69). He became a friend of the Lydian king Croesus, and when, in an attempt to secure a footing on the Asiatic side of the strait, he was captured by the Lampsacenes, Croesus forced them to release him. This Miltiades was succeeded by Stesagoras, the son of his half-brother, and he again by his brother, a second Miltiades. This latter was sent to succeed Stesagoras from Athens by Hippias, the son and successor of Peisistratus, who later in his reign married his own daughter Archedice to Aeantides the son of Hippoclus, the ruling tyrant of Lampsacus, at that time high in favour at the Persian court. This wedding of policy may have secured for Athens, at least for a time, what wars had failed to achieve, the control of both sides of the Dardanelles (see above, p. 32 and p. 79). Within the Chersonese Miltiades followed his patron's policy and strengthened his position with his Thracian neighbours by himself marrying the daughter of their king Olorus. When Darius made his expedition to the Danube *c*. 516 b.c. Miltiades accompanied him (see below, pp. 212 *sqq*.). In later times, after the Ionic revolt, when he had fled to Athens, he claimed to have conspired against Darius during this early campaign. The statement is beyond proof or refutation, but the whole history of the Miltiades family and the Chersonese is of unique interest both for the facts and the suggestions that it offers as to the interplay in these outlying

Greek regions of the somewhat miscellaneous Greek settlements with one another, the surrounding natives, and the great powers of the period, both barbarian and Greek.

In the Sea of Marmora the foremost Greek city was Cyzicus, a Milesian foundation on the lofty peninsula that runs out from the south coast. Its early importance is shown by its coins[1], heavy electrum pieces which soon circulated all over Greece. Their type, a tunny fish, probably indicates the early source of Cyzicene prosperity. The city began early to erect imposing public buildings, as is shown from fragments of archaic sculptured reliefs and Ionic capitals now preserved in the Constantinople Museum. Its fame among the uncivilized tribes who dwelt beyond the Marmora and the Black Sea is perhaps reflected in the story of the Scythian Anacharsis and his visit to the city, from which he is said to have introduced the worship of the great mother-goddess into his native country. After the Persian conquest a Cyzicene named Pytharchus tried to make himself tyrant of his native city. He had previously been presented by Cyrus with seven obscure towns and advanced on Cyzicus with an army, but was beaten back by the Cyzicenes. The incident illustrates the considerable amount of freedom enjoyed by the city-states within the Persian dominion. In 516 however Cyzicus was under a tyrant Aristagoras who accompanied Darius on his expedition to Scythia.

A Black Sea trade such as existed from at least 600 B.C. presupposes an important station on the Bosphorus, and Byzantium, founded by Megara about 660 B.C., must soon have attained to this position. Megara was consistently friendly with Miletus and so too presumably was its daughter-city. Hence perhaps the fact that so little is heard about it till the time when Darius crossed the Bosporus and Ariston, tyrant of the city, is found along with Aristagoras of Cyzicus and other Greek tyrants of the Marmora and Hellespont districts, attending Darius on his expedition to the Danube. Byzantium appears not to have been enthusiastic in the Persian cause, for it passed under a Persian governor, Megabazus. It is to him Herodotus attributes the saying that Chalcedon, the earlier settlement just opposite Byzantium on the Asiatic coast, must have been founded by men who were blind. Two monuments of the Persian passage of the Bosphorus survived at least till the time of Herodotus, one, a pair of pillars inscribed respectively in Greek and 'Assyrian' (i.e. Persian cuneiform, see p. 201) set up by Darius, the other, a set of paintings of the crossing that had been executed for the Samian Mandrocles, builder of the bridge.

[1] See Volume of Plates i, 302, c, d.

In the Black Sea itself the opening of the sixth century probably saw the coasts already fringed with Greek settlements, mostly Milesian, along the west and north to beyond the Crimea, and along the south and east as far as the Caucasus. Sinope facing the Crimea, Trapezus (Trebizond) nearly 300 miles farther along the southern coast, and Phasis and Dioscorias on the eastern coast in the land of Colchis, supplied Miletus with raw materials such as flax, timber, and iron, and could maintain Greek trade with the far east behind the back of an unfriendly power in western Asia Minor. Our knowledge however of the Black Sea cities during the archaic period is derived mainly from excavations and is limited mainly to the Russian sites which alone have been systematically explored. At Panticapaeum (Kertch), Theodosia, and other Crimean sites, Attic vases of the latter part of the sixth century have been found in some numbers. At Taman on the Asiatic side of the Cimmerian Bosporus (the strait that connects the Sea of Azov with the Black Sea), similar Attic pottery has been found and also various Ionic fabrics of the same period. These finds establish a latest possible date at which the settlements grew to importance. It may be that the Greeks feeling their way gradually forward past Apollonia (Burghas), Odessus (Varna), Callatis, Tomi, Istrus (Costanza) and the mouths of the Danube and Dniester did not firmly establish themselves so far away till about this period, but they had reached the north-west corner of the Black Sea considerably earlier. Olbia in a sheltered position on the estuary of the Hypanis (Bug) and facing that river's junction with the Borysthenes (Dnieper) was already a flourishing Greek city before 600 b.c. Here and at the neighbouring site of Berezan (Borysthenes?) careful excavations have produced, besides some fine examples of early Ionian jewellery and other archaic objects, many examples of all the best known Greek potteries of the archaic period: Corinthian, Sicyonian (?), the Ionic fabrics provisionally assigned to Miletus, Samos, and Clazomenae, and specimens of the Greek ware of Naucratis in Egypt. About the middle of the sixth century these wares began to give way to the black-figure pottery of Athens, which again is succeeded by the red-figure pottery which Athens began putting on the market about 530 b.c. Trade connections were various as well as extensive. One fact brought out by the Olbia excavations is particularly significant. Of the graves those of the sixth century are the farthest from the city; later ages buried nearer in. This can only mean that the city was shrinking and that the sixth century was its period of greatest prosperity. Before the end of

9

the century and probably some time before it the people of Olbia
were issuing coins. They are of two kinds, the one being large
round copper pieces, the other curious pieces cast in the shape of
fish, particularly dolphins. Some of these fish coins have been
found in the hands of the dead where they are taken to represent,
like the diobol that the Athenians put into the mouth of the
departed, the passage-money for the journey to the other world.
The numerous *graffiti* on the potsherds show that writing was a
common accomplishment and that the dialect spoken till near the
end of the sixth century was pure Ionic. Ionic influence was replaced by Attic, but in some ways these remote Greek cities must
from the first have been curiously conservative. At Panticapaeum
fifth- and fourth-century graves have been held to show Mycenaean
features both in construction and furniture. Centuries later the
Olbiopolitans still regarded Homer as the last word in literature.
Early Greek products penetrated far inland. Archaic Ionian vases
have been found in the middle Dnieper district and in Podolia
near Nemirov on the upper Bug. In exchange for these articles
the Greeks must have received the raw products that they are
known in later ages to have exported to the mother-country,
namely slaves, cattle, honey, wax, dried and pickled fish, hides,
salt, timber, amber, drugs. Most important of all, perhaps even
from this early period, was the trade in corn. The corn of the
'Agricultural Scythians,' who according to Herodotus grew corn
'not for consumption but for sale,' may explain why Thrasybulus
of Miletus was able so successfully to withstand the invasion of
his territories by the Lydians in spite of their systematic destruction of the Milesian crops.

Detailed facts about these Pontic cities are wanting. The
settlers must have been men who had found life hard or un-
congenial in their old homes, or in some cases refugees from
foreign invasion like the founders of Phanagoria on the Asiatic
side of the Cimmerian Bosporus, who are said to have been men of
Teos fleeing from the violence of the Persians. The sites of their
settlements they seem generally to have rented from the previous
occupants. Certainly the natives cannot have been very unfriendly,
otherwise the colonies, depending as they did on their inland trade,
could hardly have survived. The story told in Herodotus of the
fifth-century Scythian chief who made periodic and prolonged visits
to Olbia and aped Greek dress and manners is probably typical of
the state of things from the time of the first settlers onwards. The
chiefs derived both profit and pleasure from the neighbourhood of
a superior civilization. The lower classes were less appreciative.

VII. THE GREEKS IN EGYPT AND CYRENE

In Egypt when the founder of the Saite dynasty died (609 B.C.) there were two main Greek settlements—'The Camps' at Daphnae on the east side of the Delta and Naucratis on one of its western arms. Both had grown out of the Milesians' Fort, the original head-quarters of both the Greek mercenaries and the Greek merchants within the pharaoh's dominions. Both continued to flourish till the anti-Greek outbreak that put Amasis on the throne (566 B.C.) and led to the concentration of all the Greeks in Naucratis. The Daphnae Camps were two in number; one was occupied by Carian mercenaries the other by Ionians, and the Nile flowed between them. It was from this camp that the Greeks marched out under Necho on the expedition which overthrew Josiah (cf. Jeremiah ii, 16), and it was here that Jeremiah and many of his fellow-countrymen sought refuge from Nebuchadrezzar (Jeremiah xliii, 5 *sqq.*) and found it till that monarch fell upon Egypt and led them away captive to Babylon. Daphnae was thus the scene of the first intercourse in Egypt between the Jews and the Greeks, an intercourse that was to have such notable developments four centuries later at Alexandria. The sojourn of distinguished Jewish refugees at Daphnae appears to have left its mark on the place to this day. The camp buildings, of which remains still exist, are known as Ḳaṣr Bint el-Yehudi, 'the castle of the Jew's daughter.'

A generation later the Greeks were forced to leave the site. The troops were transferred to Memphis, ostensibly to be more under the pharaoh's eye but soon to be his trusted body-guard. The merchants were removed to Naucratis. In the days of Herodotus their old homes at Daphnae and the slips for their ships there were already in ruins. The site has been excavated and the remains of Greek pottery confirm the tradition of the abandonment about 560 B.C. (see vol. III, pp. 291 *sq.*, 303).

Amasis began his reign by prohibiting Greek traders from carrying on business anywhere in Egypt but at Naucratis.

And for those Greeks who did not wish to reside but merely made voyages there he gave sites to set up altars and precincts to the gods: the greatest of these and the most famous and the most used is called the Hellenium; these are the cities which united to establish it: of the Ionians Chios, Teos, Phocaea, Clazomenae, of the Dorians Rhodes, Cnidus, Halicarnassus and Phaselis, of the Aeolians only Mitylene:...and these are the cities which supply superintendents of the mart....Apart from these the Aeginetans established on their own a precinct of Zeus, the Samians another of Hera, and the Milesians one of Apollo. (Herodotus II, 178.)

Amasis was thus in a sense a founder of Naucratis, but he was only a second founder. Excavations have shown that the city flourished from about the middle of the seventh century. The unmistakable pottery of Greek Naucratis found its way to Aegina well before the reign of Amasis. Naucratis itself was being flooded with Greek pottery of several distinctive styles, mostly of uncertain East-Greek origin, but including some Corinthian. Charaxus, brother of Sappho, was bringing Lesbian wine to the city and falling victim there to the charms of a Greek hetaera. The various precincts contained temples of the protecting deity. Column fragments of an Apollo temple have been preserved which must belong to a building erected about the middle of the sixth century B.C. in a variety of the Ionian style details of which find parallels at Samos and in south Italian Locri. The ruins of the Apollo precinct measure 80 m. by 43 m.; those of Hera are considerably larger, those of the Hellenium larger still with traces of numerous internal buildings. South of the precinct lay the quarter of the Greek residents, a labyrinth of winding streets, and south again of that, a native quarter. The area excavated measured 800 m. by 400 m.; the total area occupied must have been larger still.

From the point of view of Greek history Naucratis and Daphnae are mainly interesting as the centres from which Egyptian influence reached Greece. Their existence meant that Egypt was known at first hand not merely to occasional enterprising travellers but to a large body of Greeks from a variety of cities; at all events during the long reign of Amasis many of these Greeks were constantly passing to and fro between Naucratis and their native cities. The effect of this intercourse must have been considerable. It may be illustrated from the figures of two scribes dressed in what is obviously a Greek imitation of Egyptian garb found among the pre-Persian remains on the Athenian Acropolis[1]. Cases like this of direct Egyptian influence are few, perhaps surprisingly so; but it would be rash on that account to put a low estimate on the debt of Greece at this time to Egypt. The wise men of Greece like Pythagoras and Solon visited the land and tradition connected these visits with their search for wisdom. One service Egypt certainly rendered to Greek science. The pages of Herodotus and the fragments of his predecessor Hecataeus (born at Miletus *c.* 550 B.C.) show how much the Greeks were impressed when they discovered the extreme antiquity of Egyptian

[1] Guy Dickins, *Catalogue of the Acropolis Museum*, vol. i, p. 167 on Nos. 144, 146; cf. also No. 629. See Volume of Plates i, 296, *b*.

civilization. It seems indeed to have first inspired them with a real spirit for historical research. A particularly precious gift that the Greeks received from Egypt probably by way of Naucratis was the papyrus, the plant which provided them with a light and comparatively cheap material for book making.

The high plateau west of Lower Egypt that looks north across the sea to Greece received its first Greek settlers a little later than Egypt. About 630 b.c. Greeks from Thera and Crete established themselves on the island of Platea (Bomba) whence they moved a few years later to Cyrene on the mainland some 15 miles farther west. They brought no women with them and married Libyan wives. Some 50 years later the Cyrenaeans invited the Greeks at large to come and share in a distribution of land. The invitation was backed by Delphi and resulted in a large influx from the Peloponnese, Crete and other islands (570 b.c.). The new-comers were naturally unpopular with the natives whom they dispossessed, but the estrangement was temporary and partial. Quarrels among the Greeks themselves soon led to the foundation of Barca, which in turn became the mother of Euhesperides (Benghazi) and Taucheira (Tokrah) still farther west near the mouth of the gulf of Sydra (Syrtis Major). The natives sided with Barca, and the Libyan strain was soon stronger there than in Cyrene itself. At Cyrene the women would eat no cow's flesh. At Barca they abstained from pork as well. Libyan names occur in both cities in the most exalted families (Battus, Alazir).

The leader of the original expedition became king of Cyrene, assuming the name of Battus, a Libyan word for king which became a personal name in the family. Battus founded a dynasty that was still ruling in the days of Pindar; the kings bore alternately the names of Battus and Arcesilas. The great immigration took place under Battus II (the Prosperous). The movement that led to the foundation of Barca began with a quarrel between Arcesilas II (the Cruel) and his brothers. When shortly afterwards Arcesilas II was murdered the throne would have passed to a usurper but for the vigorous action of his widow Eryxo, who secured the succession for her son Battus III (the Lame), under whom the Cyrenaeans enjoyed the blessings of a very limited monarchy: instructed by the Delphic oracle they called in as 'reformer' Demonax of Mantinea, who left Battus a titular kingship but organized the city on democratic lines. We have few details as to his reforms, but the fact that he created or recognized three 'tribes,' the original citizens from Thera and the *perioikoi*,

the Peloponnesians and Cretans, and the islanders, shows that
the problem was largely racial. Arcesilas III set about overthrowing this constitution, and though at first driven into exile
he ultimately with the help of Polycrates of Samos established
himself as despot. The two cities, so Herodotus tells us, had been
close friends from the days of the settlement on Platea. Arcesilas
was on good terms with his cousin Alazir (Aladdeir), king of
Barca, whose daughter he married and with whom he was staying
for fear of his own subjects when both he and Alazir were murdered (about 510 B.C.). Cyrene meanwhile had been governed by
his mother Pheretime. It is noteworthy how active a part in
Cyrenaic politics was played by the women of the royal house.
Battus IV owed his throne to Pheretime and the army she
secured from the Persian satrap of Egypt. Barca was reduced,
the leading men and women mutilated and murdered by the
queen-mother, the remnant transplanted to Bactria by the Great
King and Battus became the vassal ruler of the whole Cyrenaic
pentapolis.

The prosperity of Cyrene was due to its sheep (much advertised by the Delphic oracle) and still more to its crops. The soil
is rich, and rain so abundant that the natives called it the place
where there is a hole in the sky. The great plateau rises from the
sea to a height of 2000 ft. in terraces which allowed of three
successive harvests at four-month intervals. Its most valuable
product was silphium, a medicinal plant which grew only in
Cyrenaica. When some Libyans wished to make a dedication at
Delphi they set up a column that represented a highly conventionalized silphium plant. Silphium appeared regularly on the
coins of Cyrene[1] from about 600 B.C. and also on those of Barca.
It was a royal monopoly, and a vase that may well be of local
make depicts Arcesilas, probably the second of the name, superintending the weighing of packets of the precious plant on a
ship's deck while other consignments, already weighed and ready
for export, are being placed in the hold[2]. We are told by Ephorus
that Battus I was a good ruler 'but his successors governed more
and more tyrannically, appropriating the public revenues and
neglecting the observances of religion.' This change may
perhaps be equated with the institution of the royal monopoly in
silphium (see vol. III, p. 666 sq.).

In spite of the distances that separated Cyrene and her daughter-
cities from their civilized neighbours, they maintained relations
with them that illustrate the unity of Mediterranean civilization
at this period. The earliest settlements do not indeed seem to

---

[1] See Volume of Plates i, 306, a, b.   [2] Ib. 378, b.

have attracted much notice either in Saïs or in Carthage, but the
influx of 570 B.C. had immediate repercussions. The tribes of the
interior appealed to the pharaoh Apries who sent to their help a
large expedition the failure of which directly contributed to his
overthrow by Amasis, who made friends with the Cyrenaeans,
sent them a portrait of himself and a statue of Athena (Neith)
and is even said to have taken a Cyrenaean wife. When Arcesilas II
was murdered, Battus III went in person to Egypt with his mother
and grandmother to secure recognition from Amasis. The conquest of Egypt by Cambyses led both Cyrene and Barca to
acknowledge his supremacy and send gifts. Darius incorporated
Cyrenaica in the nome of Egypt and it was as his vassal that
Pheretime made her appeal for Persian help. This constant intercourse with Egypt explains the worship of Amon at Cyrene, derived probably from the famous oasis, and that of Isis by the
Cyrenaean women. The magnificent rock tombs of Cyrene[1] recall
Egyptian tombs and imply Egyptian models. The *Telegonia* of
Eugammon, who wrote at Cyrene (see vol. ii, p. 501), introduced
an episode which may have been influenced and possibly inspired
by the Egyptian story of Rhampsinitus.

With Greece Cyrene maintained constant communication. Two
archaic female statues recently found in the city at once recall
the finds made in Delos and on the Athenian Acropolis. A Lindian
temple chronicle bears witness to early intercourse with Rhodes.
The city had a treasury at Olympia. It is probable that as early
as the sixth century Cyrenaic horses were often seen at the
Olympian games[2]. Of close ties with Sparta the most interesting
evidence is furnished by recent finds of pottery: the Arcesilas
vase described above belongs to a very distinctive fabric that was
formerly regarded as exclusively Cyrenaic. Recently, however, the
British excavations at Sparta have shown that this was the normal
kind of decorated pottery used in sixth-century Sparta[3], and the
fabric shows a continuous development there from times before
Cyrene was founded. Still more recently some fine specimens
have been found in the Spartan colony of Tarentum. There is
thus a strong probability that the pottery of this kind found at
Sparta is a local product. But for the later phases at all events there
is no need to assume that Sparta was the only seat of the industry.
Besides the Arcesilas vase there are others painted with subjects
that have been plausibly associated with Cyrene. When American

---

[1] E. A. Smith and R. M. Porcher, *Discoveries at Cyrene*, Pll. 13–27.
See Volume of Plates i, 290.

[2] According to Herodotus (iv, 189) the Libyans taught the Greeks the
use of four-horse chariots.   [3] See Volume of Plates i, 378, *a*.

archaeologists began digging at Cyrene in 1910 their rather meagre pottery finds included 'one or two fragments that showed the characteristics of the so-called Cyrenaic ware.' Whatever the place or places of origin of this pottery, its distribution is significant. It is not an all-pervading fabric like Corinthian and Attic. The places where it is best attested are Sparta, Tarentum and Cyrene. Examples have also been found at Phigalea in Arcadia, at Naucratis, Samos, Sardes and Massilia. The finds thus illustrate the written records which bring sixth-century Cyrene into special connection with Egypt, Samos and the Peloponnese (see above vol. III, pp. 304, 668). The Egyptian Amon was worshipped in Samos and Sparta as well as in Cyrene; Sparta and Egypt as well as Cyrene figure prominently in the history of Polycrates. The Spartan expedition to Samos was directed against the tyrant, but it dates from the time when he was deserting his Greek and Egyptian friends and going over to the Persians and Phoenicians. The Dorian thrust into Cyrenaica had barred the passage from Phoenicia to Carthage, and the Cyrenaeans and their friends must have been in constant fear of a combination between their Phoenician rivals to east and west. Samos, Egypt and Cyrene fell before Persia, and it was probably as a result of this that about 513 B.C. Dorieus of Sparta, half-brother of king Cleomenes, sailed to Libya and tried to settle Cinyps, the most fertile region in north Africa, roughly midway between Cyrene and Carthage. After two years he was driven out by the Carthaginians and Libyans, returned to Sparta, and set out on a still more unsuccessful expedition to wrest territory from the Punic settlers in west Sicily (see p. 359). His career suggests that the Peloponnesians were trying to prevent the Carthaginians from turning east and joining hands with the eastern Phoenicians. A Spartan Cinyps would have secured this object and held out the hope of liberating Cyrene from its Greek tyrants and Persian overlord[1]. Persia and Carthage recognized the danger, and sought to prevent a repetition of the attempt by claiming between them all the intervening coast of Libya and fixing a common frontier.

---

[1] It is not impossible that the Spartan designs on Carthage and Libya were even more aggressive: cf. the oracles (Hdt. IV, 179) that a descendant of an Argonaut should found 100 cities round lake Tritonis and that the Spartans should colonize the island of Phla in the lake (*ibid.* 178). It is worthy of note that these oracles are not attributed to Delphi and that Delphi did not encourage Dorieus. It was already medizing.

VIII. MAGNA GRAECIA AND THE WESTERN
MEDITERRANEAN[1]

In south Italy for the greater part of the sixth century the most
prominent Greek cities were Croton and Sybaris. Sybaris is said
to have had a circuit of over eight miles and a population that is
variously given as 100,000 (Scymnus) and even 300,000 (Diodorus XII, 9. 2), estimates which are sufficiently impressive even
allowing for exaggeration and the possible inclusion of de-
pendents living in the country round. Croton was much the same
size. In situation the northern city had two great advantages.
Ships from the east at this period always crossed from Greece to
Italy where the sea is narrowest and then coasted down, so that
Sybaris was the nearer city, and, secondly, the land-passage across
to the western sea is shorter and brought the trader out nearer
to the markets of central and northern Italy. The result was that
in the sixth century B.C. Sybaris became one of the greatest commercial cities in the Greek world. It had specially close connections with both Miletus and Etruria, which means that it was
the chief centre from which Ionian products found their way over
Italy. There is reason to believe that it had a practical monopoly
of the Etruscan trade, the extent of which is attested by the
abundant finds of Greek pottery. 'The Sybarites wore cloaks
made of Milesian wool, and this was the origin of their friendship,
as Timaeus states. For of the peoples of Italy they most loved the
Etruscans, of those outside Italy, the Ionians.'[2] The territory
controlled by the city was considerable. It reached at least to Siris
which lay half-way to Tarentum, while along the west coast it
extended from Laus to Paestum. The close connection between
the two coasts is illustrated by the coins of Siris, which have the
Sybarite type of the bull[3] and are inscribed on the one side with
the name of Siris and on the other with that of Pyxus (Buxentum)
on the west coast. The wealth and luxury of the Sybarites became
proverbial all over the Greek world. It is said that cooks were
encouraged to invent new dishes by the grant of a sort of patent
on their inventions, and that producers, importers, and purveyors
of certain luxuries such as eels and purple dye were exempted
from taxation. These stories plainly have their origin in satire,
but they may none the less throw light both on staple industries
and the fiscal policy of the people satirized. Something has been

[1] For the history of the Greek cities in Sicily see below, chap. XI.
[2] Athenaeus XII, p. 519 B. See How and Wells, *Commentary on Herodotus*,
vol. II, p. 71 *sq.*   [3] See Volume of Plates i, 306, *e, f.*

said already on the commercial aspects of the great Greek games. Those of Sybaris were on the same lines as those of Olympia and were deliberately held at the same time[1].

Croton, in a bracing situation[2], had a more distinguished history. Medicine and physical culture were both carried to a high pitch in the city. A Crotonian named Democedes, son of a priest of Aesculapius who had migrated there from Cnidus, attained such fame as a physician that he was employed as a public practitioner at Aegina and Athens, then as court physician first to Polycrates of Samos and later to Darius of Persia. The city was famous for its athletes: on one occasion at the Olympic games the first seven places in the foot-race all fell to competitors from Croton; Milo, the Crotonian statesman and soldier of the latter part of the sixth century, was one of the most famous of ancient athletes. But Croton's chief claim to a prominent place in history comes from its connection with Pythagoras. His doctrines are dealt with in another chapter (see pp. 544 *sqq.*), but his personal career and the way of life that he introduced first into Croton and then into other cities of south Italy is one of the outstanding facts in the history of Greater Greece. After migrating from Samos in the days of Polycrates he settled in Croton and gathered bands of devoted disciples, taught them his way of life with its doctrine of purification and inward harmony, and organized them in a sort of religious brotherhood. His appeal found in Croton a special response. Milo became one of his disciples.

The Italian Greek communities were even more quarrelsome than their parent cities. About 530 B.C. Croton, Sybaris and Metapontum combined to suppress the flourishing city of Siris (a Colophonian foundation), and in spite of assistance sent from Locri the city was annihilated. We hear of a plague that resulted from this campaign. When this had spent itself the Crotonians turned against Locri, but though the aggressor's forces are said to have been immensely superior in numbers the Locrians won the day. It was after this chastening experience that Pythagoras is said to have come to Croton. In the next war the opponents are Sybaris and Croton. The *casus belli* as given in the tradition was that Croton on the advice of Pythagoras received some refugees who had been expelled from Sybaris by the tyrant Telys, but we may suspect that Croton, checked in her attempt to expand southward, had claimed some compensation in the Sybaris direc-

---

[1] Another version attributed the great Italian games to Croton. Their significance is the same in either case.

[2] Cf. the proverb 'healthier than Croton,' Strabo VI, p. 262.

tion. In the fighting the Sybarites were completely defeated and their city utterly destroyed (510 B.C.). Herodotus gives a lively description of the dismay of the Milesians: 'they all from youth upward shaved their heads and put on great mourning' when they heard the news. This destructive rivalry is enough in itself to explain why these great cities did not make themselves more felt in later Italian history.

Tarentum stands apart as the one great Dorian foundation in Magna Graecia, a fact illustrated by the finds of pottery that have been made in the city (see above, p. 111). Its splendid harbour, now one of the chief bases of the Italian navy, and its position as the first important Greek city to be reached after crossing from Greece made it unique. When the isthmus route from Brindisi to Tarentum first came into use is uncertain, but tradition says that the founder of Tarentum died at Brindisi. The considerable collection of Greek pottery in Brindisi museum said to come from local finds dates from about 500 B.C. A still shorter passage across the Adriatic may have been secured by crossing to Hydrus (Hydruntum, Otranto) and then proceeding by land to Callipolis on the east coast of the Tarentine bay, a settlement that is known to have been a naval station of the Tarentines (Dionysius of Halicarnassus XIX, 3). The wealth of Tarentum was derived partly from agriculture and fishing, partly from industries, notably the making of fabrics and dies. To the purple dye works are due the ancient heaps of mussel shells still to be seen both at Callipolis and at Tarentum itself.

The other cities of the east coast are of less importance. Metapontum lay too far from the western sea to offer a convenient isthmus route. Its wealth depended on its agriculture, whence both the ear of corn that from about 550 B.C. appears on its coins[1] and the golden corn ear that the city offered to Delphi[2]. Caulonia seems to have followed obediently the policy of its mother-city. The chief evidence for its importance in the sixth century is its coinage[3]. Locri had outposts on the western sea which show that it must have taken advantage of its situation, which offered the nearest alternative route to the sea passage through the straits of Messina; but its early activities have left little record, the most notable remains being a fine series of terracotta reliefs that begin at the end of the sixth century. No early coins of the city are known, and the fact has been associated with the fame of its ancient lawgiver Zaleucus, who, like the Spartan Lycurgus, imposed laws that remained in force till a late period and may similarly have forbidden the use of coined money.

---

[1] See Volume of Plates i, 306, *h*.   [2] Strabo VI, p. 264.
[3] See Volume of Plates i, 306, *g*.

The Locrian lawgiver is a figure about whom we would gladly have fuller and more trustworthy information. He is represented variously as contemporary with the semi-mythical Lycurgus, as living early in the seventh century, and as a pupil of Pythagoras, while Timaeus maintains that he never lived at all. Timaeus is hardly to be taken seriously as against Plato and Aristotle, and an early date is rendered probable by the tradition that the laws of Zaleucus were the first Greek laws to be committed to writing, as also by the curious statement that they were put to music, and by the character of the laws themselves, which became pro- verbial for their severity. As with other early codes the main point gained was the simple fact of their being written, which meant that justice was administered in accordance with a fixed public code instead of the arbitrary discretion of the judge. For the first time the citizen knew definitely what the law regarded as a crime. Zaleucus is represented by Aristotle as a slave, by Diodorus as a nobleman. Both versions may have an element of truth. The lawgiver acted as a mediator between the privileged and unprivileged classes. If he did not, like Solon, belong to the middle class, he probably had connections with both extremes. Zaleucus is always associated with Charondas who a little later drew up for Catana a code which was adopted also at Rhegium. In the comparatively new communities of Magna Graecia and Sicily established usage was doubtless less sacrosanct than in the motherland, a fact that would explain the prominence that these regions play in the epoch-making change involved in the publi- cation of a written code.

On the west coast the most southerly city, Rhegium, has its history closely bound up with that of Messana on the Sicilian side of the strait. North of the straits there lay a series of cities that acted as western ports for the cities of the east coast and were important for the part they played in forwarding Greek goods to central Italy and Etruria. Medma and Hipponium performed this service for Locri, Temesa and Terina for Croton, Laus and Scidrus for Sybaris. About 600 B.C. the Sybarites had planted still farther north the colony of Posidonia (Paestum), whose walls and temples are now the chief material witness to the ancient greatness of greater Greece. The walls are three miles in circum- ference. Of the temples the oldest (the so-called basilica) is dated by some modern writers a little before 550 B.C.: it is an unusual building some 178 by 80 ft. with nine columns at either end, 18 along either side, and a third row dividing the building longi- tudinally into two equal halves; a second and smaller building[1],

---

[1] See Volume of Plates i, 384, *b.*

108 by 47 ft., known as the temple of Demeter, is dated by the same authorities only a decade or two later. The coinage[1] begins about 550 B.C. with curious pieces that show the same type (Poseidon with trident) on both sides, in relief on the one, *repoussé* on the other. This peculiar technique is used also for the contemporary coins of other south Italian Greek cities, namely Laus, Caulonia, Croton, Sybaris, Metapontum and Tarentum[2] (but not Cumae).

Paestum represents the utmost limit of this group, which embraced neither Cumae to the north of it nor Velia (Elea) to the south. Elea was founded about 535 B.C. by Phocaeans who had been ousted from Corsica by the Carthaginians and Etruscans (p. 358). It owes its fame to Xenophanes and the other philosophers who lived there and came to be known as the Eleatic school (see below, pp. 559 *sqq.*).

Cumae, the home of the sibyl who taught the central Italians the art of letters, was the most ancient Greek settlement in Italy, but still in full vigour throughout the sixth century. About 600 B.C. she founded on the magnificent bay a little farther south a settlement that was called the New City (Nea Polis), and which now, with twenty-seven centuries of history and over half a million inhabitants, still bears the same name. Detailed history begins at Cumae some seventy or eighty years later, when Etruscans and other barbarian inhabitants of Campania, attracted by the city's great wealth, made a united attack upon it. The Cumaeans successfully repelled the invaders, thanks especially to the exploits of a certain Aristodemus, who subsequently established himself as tyrant (vol. III, p. 671). He is said to have owed his tyranny to a popularity which he had acquired partly by his military prowess, partly by his eloquence, and partly by the distributions of money that he made to the poor. As tyrant he is accused of having forced the citizens to engage in manual work and wearied them with toils and labours. When the Tarquins were banished from Rome they sought refuge at his court.

In the far west Massilia (Marseilles) had been founded probably a little before 600 B.C. Greek pottery of various kinds dating from the seventh century has been found in the city. Its position was strengthened when, some forty years later, a fresh army of Phocaean emigrants founded Alalia and again when the Corsican settlement was reinforced by the refugees who left Phocaea to avoid the Persian domination. Ideas of settlement in these regions were much in the air. Bias, the 'wise man' of Priene, proposed that the Greeks should abandon Ionia to the Persians and found a new home in Sardinia. Meanwhile traders and probably settlers

---

[1] See Volume of Plates i, 306, *i.*   [2] *Ib.* 306, *g, d, f, h, c.*

were extending Phocaean influence to the west side of the gulf of Lyons and down the coast of Spain. Agathe (Agde) between Massilia and the Pyrenees and Rhode and Emporiae (Rosas, Ampurias) on the Catalonian coast just south of the Pyrenees were founded by Massilia probably about the middle of the sixth century: at Emporiae excavation has revealed a considerable amount of sixth-century Greek pottery, some as early as 550 B.C., and including a fair proportion of vases from the Greek east. Both here and at Massilia Attic pottery begins to prevail in the second half of the century. The Phocaean foundations of Hemeroscopium (Cape Nao) and Maenaca (east of Malaga) were probably due directly to the trade with Tartessus (Tarshish) at the mouth of the Baetis (Guadalquivir), an ancient town with something of a native civilization which from the seventh century was exploited by the Phocaeans for its silver. It seemed for a while as if the Phocaeans were destined to control the whole of this part of the Mediterranean; but Etruscans and Carthaginians combined against them and inflicted on them a great defeat about 535 B.C. Alalia was lost and with it all prospects of Greek political domination in the far western sea (see below, p. 358). But despite this loss of power the Phocaeans long continued to diffuse a certain amount of Greek culture, or at least its products, among the inhabitants of south Gaul and east Spain. In the latter country the natives had welcomed the arrival of the Greeks and the consequent competition between them and the Phoenicians who had been earlier in the field. At Massilia too the Greeks appear to have been on good terms with the natives, and continued so without losing anything of their own hellenism. The city maintained relations with the mother-country and had a treasury[1] at Delphi founded in 535 B.C.

IX. CONCLUSION

It remains to attempt a brief general survey of the achievements of the Greek world outside the Balkan peninsula during the sixth century, and of the conditions to which they may be attributed.

In every quarter there was a remarkable outburst of creative activity alike in architecture, sculpture and the minor arts and crafts, in poetry and thought, and in the sphere of social and political experiment.

In architecture Paestum is exceptional only in the state of preservation of its great buildings. Those of cities like Samos and Ephesus are shown both by ancient records and existing remains to have been both larger and more magnificent.

[1] See Volume of Plates i, 390, *a*.

Hand in hand with architecture went sculpture. The schools of Chios and Samos are known from literary records as well as from actual remains, while the finds made at sites such as Miletus, Ephesus, Naxos, Paros, Thasos and Delos are enough to show that sculptors were busily employed throughout Ionia and the Aegean. If similar finds have been less frequent in south Italy it is probably the result of chance. A fine but isolated example is the seated goddess[1] said to come from Locri, acquired in 1914 by the Museum of Berlin.

The best known art however in this as in all periods of Greek history is that of the potter and vase-painter. Here again sixth-century work is distinguished by the number and variety of the local schools into which it can be divided. The Ionians in particular were producing large quantities of several distinct fabrics. One of them (Phineus vase style) must be attributed to one of the islands, though it is uncertain at present to which; another (Caeretan)[2] shows African affinities, another is probably Clazomenian. All these fabrics have in common the free use of the human figure in descriptive scenes as the main motive of the painting, as contrasted with the fabrics of the seventh century, which are mainly decorated with ornamental designs of animals and flowers. It is in great part to these humble vase-painters that we owe our ideas of the progress achieved during this period by the more ambitious artists who painted frescoes on the walls of public buildings. Neither painters nor sculptors had acquired complete technical mastery of their art, even at the end of the century; but both had reached the ripe archaic stage which, in ancient as in mediaeval art, is for many people more attractive than subsequent periods of complete mastery. See further, chap. xvi.

To complete the picture of the arts and crafts it is necessary to imagine in each city whole bands of craftsmen applying the new skill and inspiration to all manner of industries, both useful and ornamental, involving all manner of materials. A glance at the illustrations of any properly published excavation of an archaic Greek site is enough to show how varied these activities were and to suggest also how large are the gaps in our knowledge.

At the opening of the sixth century the invention of coinage was only about a century old (see below, p. 126). Ionia here had led the way for Greece. It is interesting to note that throughout this century of rapid artistic development the Ionians went on striking coins of the most primitive sort. Their conservatism shows how quickly the various types won recognition, and how unwilling the various mints were to unsettle their customers by any innovation.

[1] See Volume of Plates i, 296, *a*.   [2] *Ib.* 382.

Trade both by land and still more by sea flourished exceedingly. Any city of any importance had special connections over a great part of the Mediterranean. Milesian vessels were constantly visiting Olbia in south Russia, Naucratis in Egypt, Athens and Sybaris. Phocaea was in constant communication with Massilia and Tartessus, and secured from a native Spanish prince the means of improving its fortifications. The Samian seamen were familiar with the straits of Gibraltar, the Cyrenaica, the Dardanelles.

Of the cargoes that they carried we know little in detail but can form a fairly good general idea. Samos was famous for its metal work and woollen goods, and it must have been these and the like that she bartered at Tartessus for the raw metal of the Spanish mines: the Samian wool industry was doubtless interested in the Samian connection with Cyrene and sheep-bearing Libya.

The pursuit of these mercantile adventures was intensely stimulating. The spirit of adventure permeated thought and literature; familiarity with the cities and minds of many men produced a versatility of outlook and a freedom from provincialism that has seldom been paralleled.

The poetry and the science of the period could have flourished as they did only in societies where intellectual interests were particularly acute and fairly widely disseminated. Careers such as those of Alcaeus and Sappho (pp. 494 *sqq.*) and their seventh-century predecessor Archilochus (p. 483) imply an aristocratic society where thought was singularly free and direct and the passion for self-expression almost unprecedented. But by the beginning of the sixth century aristocracy had in many cities had its day. The typical government was the tyranny. The tyrant became the centre of all the main activities of his city. Polycrates with his court poets Anacreon (p. 499 *sq.*) and Ibycus (p. 504 *sq.*), his skilled artists and physicians such as Theodorus and Democedes, his army of engineers and craftsmen erecting harbours and waterworks and temples, and his navy of warships and merchantmen scouring the Mediterranean sea, is only the latest of a whole series of similar rulers. Their government was anti-aristocratic, and the status of the middle classes was probably far higher than it had been before. Socially as well as politically the tyranny marked a transition stage between aristocracy and democracy. In the aristocratic period culture as well as power was the exclusive possession of a small class. The people consisted mainly of farmers and farm labourers whose condition in the Greek world at large was probably as pitiable as it is known to have been in Attica and Boeotia. The great development of trade and industry in the seventh century meant a sudden demand for a large new supply of skilled labour of many diverse kinds—ship-builders, sailors, miners, metal workers, masons, sculptors, and the like. In the fifth century and afterwards this demand was met by developing the slave-trade. It was the plentiful supply of slave labour that allowed the citizens of Periclean Athens to become a community of politicians and critics of art, the drama, and philosophy. But in the sixth century the citizens themselves still met the new demand. The new outlet for free labour worked in two directions. It weakened the hold of the landed classes over the landless, and it created a new class of citizen which must obviously have contained some of the most discontented and some of the most enterprising elements in the free population. This new urban industrial class was the basis of the power of the tyrants. The great constructive works that distinguished the period—the aqueducts, harbour works, temples, and other public buildings—were executed by free workers in the employment of the tyrants. When tyranny was overthrown from within, one contributory cause may have been the failure to maintain the army of employees that these undertakings involved. A considerable amount of evidence has been adduced to show that tyrants not infrequently rose to power by securing some sort of economic control over this same element of the population[1].

The features just outlined seem to have been common to all the regions where Greek communities most flourished. But there were local variations. Ionian civilization in particular had a character determined by its constant contact with the great powers of Asia and Egypt. These powers were unquestionably civilized. The nearest of them was overwhelmingly superior from the military point of view. The result of this contact was a comparative freedom from the narrow provincialism of the European Greeks, a freedom which explains alike the failure of the Asiatic Greeks to maintain their own independence and their success in planting colonies. It explains likewise their literature and science. Athenian literature centres round the city-state. The Ionian was generally concerned either with the whole universe or with his own individual soul.

In south Italy the intellectual movement took yet other forms which are best represented by the philosophers Pythagoras and Xenophanes. The fact that these remarkable men both came from Ionia shows that the movements which they set on foot

---

[1] On the tyrants in the Outer Greek World, see further, P. N. Ure, *The Origin of Tyranny*, chs. iii–v, ix; on tyranny in Lydia, vol. iii, pp. 514 *sqq.*; in Greece Proper, *ibid.* ch. xxii; in Sicily, below, pp. 355 *sqq.*

must have been largely conditioned by their new environments. But the Greeks of the far west did not merely react to their environment. They affected it widely. Greek art and artists, Greek wares and Greek traders permeated the whole Italian peninsula. Greek terracotta revetments[1] of a highly ornate character were used to adorn and protect the temples of the native gods in many 'barbarian' cities of Campania, Latium, Etruria, and still farther north. The finds show that the same mould was sometimes used in all three provinces, and make it probable that Greek artists who had worked in such cities as Caulonia, Locri, Paestum and Cumae established themselves at Veii and other places in Etruria and there founded prosperous schools[2]. Greek pottery of this period has been found in large quantities in non-Greek cities all over the peninsula, even as far north as Bologna, a fact which hardly surprises us when we remember that Spina near the mouth of the Po had a treasury at Delphi. The ancient accounts which tell how Demaratus the Corinthian fled from the tyranny of Cypselus and established himself with a band of Greek workmen at Tarquinii (Corneto) in Etruria conform entirely with all the archaeological evidence. Caere (Agylla) possessed a treasury at Delphi and consulted the Delphic oracle as early as 540 B.C. Its Greek character is borne out by the abundant finds of Greek vases and architectural terracottas made on the site. One particularly distinctive type of sixth-century Ionian vase with African affinities has been named Caeretan[3] and is known only from a fine series of specimens found at Caere. Archaic Greek finds from north Italy are not exclusively of pottery Perugia for instance has yielded some fine archaic bronzes. A fairly representative series of Greek vases[4] and architectural terracottas and other objects of the sixth century has been found in Rome itself. Most important of all, the art of writing made its way from Magna Graecia over a great part of Italy: the lettering of the earliest inscriptions in Latin and Etruscan shows that this happened in the sixth century, and points to the two languages having learned their letters independently direct from the Greeks[5]. Modern discoveries have in fact revolutionized our attitude towards the statements of ancient writers about early relations between Rome and the Greek world. The evidence shows that there is a historical basis for the stories of Rome being visited by Phocaeans and of intercourse between Rome and Ephesus in the time of Servius Tullius, as also for the obviously Greek traits in the history of the Tarquins as recorded

---

[1] See Volume of Plates i, 332, *b*.

[2] Douglas Van Buren, *Terra Cotta Revetments in Latium and Etruria*, pp. 3, 34.   [3] See Volume of Plates i, 382.

[4] *Ib.* 298, *b*.   [5] See chap. XII, pp. 395 *sqq*.

in our earliest extant authorities. Not only was Rome moulded by Greek influences from its earliest days, but so too were the states that were its earliest neighbours and first conquests. Witness the terracotta statues, Ionian in style, of about the end of the sixth century, recently found at Veii[1] and now in the Villa Giulia Museum at Rome (*J.H.S.* xli, pp. 213–215, figs. 6, 7 and Pl. IX). These splendid figures at once recall Plutarch's description of a terracotta group at Rome which he says was made by Veientine workmen for the Tarquins.

Nor did even west and north Italy mark the limit of Greek influence at this momentous and most plastic period. Finds like those from Elche[2] in Spain make it probable that in the Iberian peninsula also the influence of Greece spread well beyond the pale of the Greek settlements. Marseilles had a considerable effect upon southern Gaul. The Rhone, Saône, and Loire may already have formed a route from the Phocaean city to the outer Ocean, where a succession of coasting ships may have linked up Tartessus with the British Isles.

[1] See Volume of Plates i, 334, *a, b.*   [2] *Ib.* 294, *b.*

CHAPTER V

COINAGE FROM ITS ORIGIN TO THE PERSIAN WARS

I. ANTICIPATIONS OF COINAGE

METALLIC coinage—consisting of pieces of precious metal, refined, shaped and stamped with some mark of authority guaranteeing quality and weight—is preceded in the development of commerce, logically if not always chronologically, by three stages. The first is that of simple barter, when any commodity is exchanged against any other; the second that of trade with a recognized medium, such as stock-fish or oxen or utensils; the third that in which use is made of metallic ingots of various weights, stamped with a mark guaranteeing quality, but not divided according to a standard. The fully developed coin differs from the last only in being of standard weight, so that, by those who accept the authority issuing it, no use of scales is required. But slight as the advance on the preceding stage may seem to be, it is no less momentous in its own sphere than, in another, was the advance made by the printing-press on manuscript.

All these stages are represented in the ancient world. It is unnecessary here to dwell on the earliest stage, or on the use of amorphous pieces of metal, more or less broken up for convenience of division by the scales into quantities required at any time. Hoards of such broken metal, merely amorphous, or cast in the form of bricks, bars, plates and the like, are forthcoming from all kinds of places, from Assyria to Ireland, and at all periods from the ninth century before to the fifth century after Christ. In central Italy such rude metal (*aes rude*) was in use from about 1000 B.C. to the third century B.C. A later development is shown when the metal is cast in the form of more or less regular ingots or bars, sometimes ornamented. Such bar-money, which could be broken into smaller pieces and weighed, is found at all periods down to the Middle Ages; it was the most convenient method of keeping bullion, whether intended for conversion into coin or not.

Our literary records show that many utensils were used in the ancient Mediterranean world as units of value. With the exception of the roasting-spit, however, it cannot be said that any

specimens of them have survived in circumstances which show
that they were used as money in the Mediterranean world. The
so-called bronze axes from Sardinia, Cyprus, Crete, Euboea,
Mycenae[1] are merely ingots with incurving sides convenient for
lashing (whereas the edge of an axe must curve outwards), and
cannot be identified with the Homeric 'axes' and 'half-axes.' If
they were modelled on anything, it was ox-hides. (They doubtless
served as currency, though whether they were the equivalent of
gold talents or not, has not yet been definitely made out.) Prehistoric sites in central Europe, on the other hand, have furnished
actual bronze double-axes, pierced with holes too small for a
practicable handle, but intended for stringing them together; and
from Gaul come hoards of small bronze celts which seem also to
have been used for currency. In Crete, as late as the sixth century
B.C., fines were reckoned in tripods and cauldrons. There is as
yet no evidence of finds of such objects conforming to a weight-
standard, in the way in which the early British and Indian 'water-
clocks' conform.

The use of iron and bronze spits (*obeliskoi*) as money—whence
the names obol for a small coin, and drachm for a 'handful' of
six pieces—is thoroughly well attested. Spits of which six went
to a handful must have been quite serviceable for cooking, unless,
as one author states, they were deliberately blunted. Pheidon's
dedication of *obeliskoi* in the Heraeum at Argos[2] and the offering
by the courtesan Rhodopis at Delphi are definite examples of
such spit-money. The latter evidently consisted of current pieces.
As to Pheidon's dedication, it is in dispute whether it represented currency which had been demonetised, in consequence of
his reforms; or standards of currency which he was inaugurating
or regularising, deposited for reference; or merely specimens
dedicated without any such reference; the last view seems the
most plausible. The well-known bundle of spits actually found in
the Heraeum is reasonably to be identified as the dedication
attributed by tradition to Pheidon, whether he made it or not
(see vol. III, p. 542). Striking parallels to the Greek use of spits
come from Etruria, where from the eighth to the sixth centuries
B.C. first bronze and, later, iron spits were hung together on
ornamental handles in sets of six.

Another form in which metal was employed for currency was
the ring[3]. This was especially frequent in Egypt, and there are
many examples of what may be ring-money forthcoming from
prehistoric sites in Central Europe. For its use in the prehistoric
Aegean and allied civilizations the hoards of rings from Troy,

[1] See Volume of Plates i, 300, *a*.   [2] *Ib.* 302, *a*.   [3] *Ib.* 300, *b*.

Mycenae, Aegina and Cyprus are evidence; but the attempt to base metrological systems on the weights of the actual rings is a failure. The later wheel-money of the Gauls is probably analogous to the ring-money.

Apart from such objects bearing no formal relation to the developed coin, there are a few of coin-like form, of very early date. Such are the gold dumps[1] (hardly later than the ninth century) from Mycenaean Salamis in Cyprus, and a silver piece of similar form found in a late Minoan deposit at Cnossus; these seem to be on standards which were in use in the early Aegean. They are cast, not struck, but otherwise very like the earliest coins.

II. THE EARLIEST COINS

Such anticipations of metallic coinage are however isolated in the period of transition between the Aegean and the Ionian cultures. As early as the seventh century, perhaps earlier, the inhabitants of Lydia and the Ionian coast-towns which were in touch with that kingdom began to use the stamped electrum pieces[2] which are the earliest examples in the western world of a true metallic coinage. The metal which was used was the native 'white gold,' a mixture of gold and silver in varying quantities, which was found in the sands of the river Pactolus and elsewhere. When the foundations of the earliest basis in the temple of Artemis at Ephesus were laid, this electrum coinage was already well developed, with various types, such as the lion[3], the gryphon's head, the seal. If the date of the basis is rightly placed shortly before 700 B.C., the introduction of such currency, specimens of which were buried beneath it, is thrown back well into the eighth century. And since (whether this early coinage was issued by civic authorities or by private persons) such a type as the seal can hardly have originated far from the sea, it seems to follow that not merely Lydia, but the Ionian coast-towns also, knew the use of coins at this early date. Of our literary authorities, Xenophanes, in the sixth century, ascribed the origin of coinage to the Lydians. Herodotus, in the fifth, says that the Lydians were the first men to strike and use coins of gold and silver, by which he must mean what he says: coins of gold and coins of silver, not coins of electrum, which is a mixture of the two metals. He was doubtless thinking of the later coins attributed to Croesus which are the earliest coins of pure gold and pure silver[4]; his statement is so far specifically accurate, and is quite consistent with his other remark about the Lydians, that they were the first small dealers—for such

---

[1] *Ib.* 300, *c.*   [2] *Ib.* 300, *e, f, g.*   [3] *Ib.* 300, *d.*   [4] *Ib.* 302, *f, g.*

people need coins more than the great merchants (vol. III, p. 519 *sq.*). The solution of the Iono-Lydian controversy may be that the coast-towns must have been full of Lydian shop-keepers who may have privately inaugurated a coinage for their own purposes; or the Lydian kings may themselves have caused such coins to be struck in the towns under their influence. The extraordinarily irregular and unsystematic character of the earliest electrum coinage lends some colour to the theory that it was originated rather by private persons—such as bankers—for their own convenience than by state-authorities. The types which were impressed on them were, in any case, the signets of the private persons or public authorities who issued them, tokens, as Aristotle says, that they contained the full quantity of metal, guaranteed by the issuer. Whatever the character of a coin-type may be, religious or commercial or other, the reason for its appearance on the coin is that it is the sign by which the guarantor may be recognized. There are exceptions, but only apparent: thus at Cyzicus [1], which issued vast numbers of electrum staters, the main type varies according to the issue; but the city badge (the tunny-fish) is never absent, though placed in a subordinate position. The importance given to the main type was intended to make the coinage attractive, and win it acceptance as an international medium—an intention which was most successfully fulfilled.

The early electrum coins of Asia Minor and certain others, which there is good reason to suppose were produced in the neighbourhood of Mt Pangaeus [2] (although most of the gold of that district was exported before being turned into coin), are undoubtedly the most primitive in make that have come down to us. On the west of the Aegean, south of Macedon, there is an entire absence of that irregularity in fabric, style and quality of metal, which is characteristic of the districts we have been discussing. The metal is uniformly silver, not electrum or gold. For the most part, all the early coins can be attributed to definite places. Of these coinages of old Greece, that of Aegina is the most primitive in appearance; and this fact has been connected with various statements to the effect that coinage was invented by Pheidon, king of Argos (see vol. III, pp. 540, 542 *sq.*). Although Herodotus says that Pheidon gave Peloponnesus a system of measures, and although his famous *obeliskoi* represent a currency of iron spits, there is no evidence earlier than Ephorus, in the fourth century, connecting him with a developed metallic coinage like the silver 'tortoises' of Aegina [3]. There appears to be no other witness to Pheidon having ruled over that island. The tradition

[1] *Ib.* 302, *c, d.*   [2] *Ib.* 302, *e.*   [3] *Ib.* 302, *k, l, m.*

is however favoured by the facts that the Aeginetan coins conform
to what was known as the Pheidonian standard, and that the most
primitive of them may reasonably be assigned to the first half of
the seventh century. On the other hand the former fact, coupled
with the primitive appearance of the coins, would have sufficed
to suggest to the Greeks the connection with Pheidon which
Ephorus has preserved. The tradition must be admitted as reasonable, but insusceptible of proof. See vol. III, p. 540.

III. THE SPREAD OF COINAGE

The spread of the invention down to the time of the Persian
Wars may best be followed by taking our stand at successive fixed
periods. Whatever the date at which coinage was invented, by
the middle of the sixth century it was firmly established in widely
spread areas. In Asia Minor, not only in Lydia, but in the great
trading cities of the coast from Cyzicus in the north down to
Cnidus in the south, there circulated a large variety of coins,
mainly of electrum, but also occasionally of silver. Towards the
middle of the century a Lydian ruler, probably Croesus[1], inaugurated, as we have seen, a coinage of pure gold and of pure silver:
a great advance beyond the haphazard electrum currency, which
was thereby largely superseded. The islands near the coast, such
as Samos[2] and Cos, followed close on the heels of the mainland
cities; and there was evidently a considerable coinage among the
other islands which formed the bridge to Greece. As we move farther
from Asia Minor electrum becomes rarer; indeed (although some
small pieces have been plausibly attributed to the Alcmaeonidae
in Delphi[3], p. 81 n.) there is very little satisfactory evidence of
the use of electrum coins in Greece itself south of Macedon. There
silver is the standard metal when true coinage is introduced, and
the primitive bronze or iron ingots, spit-money and other early
forms superseded. Of the earliest currencies in silver, the first
pegasi of Corinth[4] seem to be not much less primitive than the
first Aeginetan 'tortoises.' The view that their introduction may
have been due to Periander is attractive and reasonable, in so far
as the Corinthian tyrant must have felt it necessary to support
his power by an active commercial policy. The money of Corcyra[5]
probably dates from the era of its independence, about 585 B.C.
The coinage of certain members of the Boeotian League, such as
Thebes[6] and Tanagra, began before the middle of the century.
When Athens began to issue coins is uncertain; her well-known
'owls' are reasonably assigned to the time of Peisistratus[7], and

[1] *Ib.* 302, *f, g.*   [2] *Ib.* 302, *h.*   [3] *Ib.* 304, *n, o, p.*   [4] *Ib.* 304, *a* to *d.*
[5] *Ib.* 304, *e.*   [6] *Ib.* 304, *f.*   [7] *Ib.* 304, *k, l.*

there is little doubt that before his time the Athenians issued the rare two-drachm pieces[1] with 'heraldic' types which are found especially in Attica, Euboea and Boeotia (see above, p. 40). The term heraldic is a misnomer, since all early coin-types are equally heraldic in origin, but no better name has been suggested. These, in spite of their varying types, are so uniform in fabric that they must be the product of a single mint; and the presumption is that they represent the Solonian system. Before Solon's time the Attic currency was on the Pheidonian standard, and may have consisted of the amphora coins[2] of which the attribution has so long been matter of conjecture. The middle of the sixth century saw a great expansion in Attic trade, well illustrated by the way in which Attic pottery began to dominate the market, and not unconnected with the rivalry between Athens and Aegina. One of the most effective means of capturing the Aeginetan trade must have been the introduction of an attractive coinage (p. 39 *sq*.).

It is surprising that the great trading cities of Euboea, notably Chalcis and Eretria, should be so meagrely represented in the field of early coinage. Even if the 'heraldic' pieces just mentioned were taken from Athens and assigned to Euboea, the amount of coinage would far from correspond to the commercial importance of the cities. Apart from such issues, there remain only certain small electrum coins, of which the attribution is extremely doubtful, and a few early silver coins bearing chariot and horseman types which used to be generally given to Olynthus in Macedon. It is possible that the Euboeans were content, until late in the sixth century, when the first coins certainly attributable to Chalcis and Eretria were struck, to use the coinage of Corinth, with which they were in such close relations.

Outside the districts mentioned and Sicily (of which later), the only place employing coinage before the middle of the sixth century was the important colony of Cyrene[3]. It is curious that Crete and Cyprus remained outside the movement. As to Persia, it is not certain that, on the fall of the Lydian empire, the Great King immediately inaugurated a Persian coinage on the lines of the Croesean. Persia had managed without a coinage so long that we need not be surprised that another generation should elapse before Darius, son of Hystaspes, struck the first darics and *sigloi*[4]. On the other hand, there is much to be said for the suggestion that the light gold staters of 'Croesean' types as distinguished from the heavier gold staters of 'Babylonian' weight, may have been issued for circulation in Asia Minor not by Croesus himself, but by the Persian governors who followed him at Sardes.

[1] *Ib.* 304, *h, i, j*.   [2] *Ib.* 304, *g*.   [3] *Ib.* 306, *a, b*.   [4] *Ib.* 304, *s, t*.

Phoenicia, Egypt and Mesopotamia, in spite of their vast commercial activities, never had a coinage until they were penetrated by Greek influence—possibly out of mere conservatism, aided by the fact that, where commerce is carried on mainly by great river or sea-routes, and bulky objects for barter can be transported by water with greater ease than by land, the necessity of coinage may not be so keenly felt.

By the time of the Persian Wars most of the important places in the Greek world were accustomed to a coinage of their own. Corinthian and Corcyraean trade carried the invention to southern Italy; to Sicily it came, shortly before the middle of the sixth century, probably from the mother-cities in Peloponnesus and the Aegean, although, as soon as Athenian exports and coinage began to play a large part in commerce—as they did about the middle of the century—the Athenian 'owls' began to circulate in the island in competition with foreign rivals. In Asia Minor coinage continued to spread round the coast of the peninsula, especially in the south, including in its influence the great city of Salamis in Cyprus[1].

About the middle of the sixth century the Cyzicene electrum coinage began to develop as a kind of international trade-currency on a great scale. Crete still remains little affected, although some of its cities may have been using coins[2] as early as 500 B.C. North of the Aegean there are, at the end of our period, plentiful issues in the rich metalliferous districts of Thrace and Macedon, both among the barbarous tribes—who nevertheless inscribed their coins in Greek and must have used Greek workmen—and in Greek towns. The activity of these mints may have been stimulated by the Persian invasion; except in Thasos[3] there is very little coinage in these parts earlier than 500 B.C. Most remarkable is the alleged appearance in south Russia, at Olbia[4], of a coinage of large cast bronze coins towards the end of the sixth, or early in the fifth, century.

The end of our period saw the appearance of the first coins to partake, so far as we know, of the character of medals. The Demareteia[5] of Syracuse undoubtedly, whatever be the exact facts concerning their origin, commemorate the victory of Himera. The Athenians celebrated Marathon by placing olive-leaves on the helmet of Athena[6].

IV. COIN STANDARDS

If there is much that is vague and uncertain in the account that has been given above of the origin and spread of coinage, it is clearness itself compared with any possible description of the

[1] Ib. 308, j.   [2] Ib. 308, i.   [3] Ib. 308, h.   [4] Ib. 310, a.
[5] Ib. 308, g.   [6] Ib. 304, q, r.

metrological problems with which the historian of the period is confronted. While one school seeks to establish connection between the various standards in use, and to assume that they were originated on mathematical principles, involving minutely accurate calculations, another, diametrically opposed, maintains that political jealousy caused each state to keep to its own old weight-system, which had only local currency; that the standards of antiquity did not spread from Babylonia and Egypt 'like the cholera or the Black Death'; and that each of these early local weight-systems must be investigated by itself. In attempting to steer a middle course between these extremes we are still confronted by the difficulty of ascertaining the normal weights. Usually our only evidence is provided by the coins themselves, which may be unequal in preservation and in alloy, so that nothing but an approximation to the normal can be reached. It cannot be too strongly insisted, therefore, that the figures used in the following description are merely adopted for working purposes as the best obtainable by modern methods.

It should be premised that in weighing the precious metals the scales used were a mixture of the sexagesimal and the decimal systems. The talent was divided into 60 minae, but the mina into 100 drachms. This curious combination was borrowed, like many of the Greek weight-systems themselves, from Babylonia. The word *statēr* was used by the Greeks, as was shekel by the Orientals, for the standard or unit-coin in any system; circumstances must decide what number of drachms—varying from 4 to 2—it contained. For the sake of simplicity we shall ignore the small denominations.

The subject of trade-weights, as distinct from coin-standards, is too obscure to be considered in this place. And the whole violently controversial question of the relation of Greek weights to those of Mesopotamia and of the prehistoric Aegean must also be touched upon but lightly.

The early electrum coins of western Asia Minor provide us with staters of five kinds. They are the so-called Phoenician, Graeco-Asiatic or Milesian group, with staters of about 14·10 gms. (with a maximum of 14·23 gms.); a very small group known as the Phocaic, of 16·58 to 16·22 gms.; a very large group, consisting almost entirely of Cyzicene staters, of rather more than 16·00 gms., and distinct from, though sometimes confused with, the Phocaic group; the Lampsacene group of about 15·25 gms.; and a group, chiefly connected with Samos, of staters from 17·43 to 17·32 gms. The standards used for pure gold coins in early times in Asia Minor were three: that of the heavy 'Croesus'

staters, of which but twelve are known, weighing from 10·76 to
10·64 gms. with an average of 10·71 gms.; that of the light
'Croesus' staters, weighing from 8·10 to 7·97 gms.; and the
Persian daric standard, estimated at from 8·4 to 8·34 gms.

Of these, the daric standard appears to coincide with the shekel
of the Babylonian Royal gold standard, theoretically estimated
at 8·4 gms.

The early silver of the Ionian cities was much less important
than the electrum of the same period. The silver coins before the
fifth century were for the most part small denominations, not
higher than a drachm; but there are a few early staters which
approximate to what is known as the Aeginetic standard. The
attributions of these pieces are in the highest degree uncertain;
they have been assigned to Chios, Teos, Phocaea, Cyme in Aeolis,
Cnidus, Cos and Camirus. So far as these coins are really Asiatic,
they must be regarded as outliers of the great Aeginetic system
which dominated the Aegean basin. The theories invented to
account for the origin of the various electrum and gold standards
of Asia Minor and to explain their relation to silver have always
ignored these Asiatic coins of Aeginetic weight, and considered
only other silver standards which were hardly if at all in use for
coinage at the period concerned: a fact which throws grave doubt
on the value of such speculations. Whatever may be true of Asia
Minor, however, we have in the coins of Aegina itself a vast mass
of currency of which the stater-standard is probably, judging from
recent investigations, about 12·3 gms. There is no good ground
for supposing that the earliest coins of Aegina, before about
550 B.C., are on a lighter standard than their successors. The
origin of this weight has been much discussed without any result;
but its identification with the Pheidonian standard—whether
Pheidon invented that, or merely stabilized an older standard—
appears to be reasonable. After the earliest period of the coinage,
that is the beginning of the seventh century, the standard spread
slowly to widely separated districts of the Mediterranean world.
From the west coast of Asia Minor it went eastwards as far as
Cilicia, where coins on this standard were issued, perhaps by
Aphrodisias on the peninsula of Zephyrium, for about a century
from the last quarter of the sixth century. But these coins stand
alone in this part of the world, for the supposed 'reduced
Aeginetic' coins of Cyprus were on a local standard intended not
to compete with those of normal Aeginetic weight, but to outweigh coins of the Persian standard. The same is true of the
early coins of Sinope in the north.

It is on the mainland of Greece proper that we find the empire of the Aeginetic standard most old-established and enduring. Aegina, indeed, is in this respect no island; and Crete is, in the same respect, as in so many others, but a process of Peloponnese. We know from Aristotle that Pheidonian measures were in use in Attica itself down to the time of Solon; and we know that the 'emporic mina,' as late as the end of the second century B.C., was on the old Aeginetic standard. The whole of the mainland from Thessaly southwards would have used the Aeginetic standard for centuries from the earliest days of coinage, had it not been for the influence of the trade-route from east to west across the Isthmus of Corinth, which is responsible for the fact that Athens and Corinth fell out of line, and divided the Aeginetic domain into a northern and a southern portion. At one or two points, as in Corcyra, it is possible that Corinthian influence caused a slight modification of the Aeginetic standard. The Corcyraean stater, too light to be regarded as purely Aeginetic (for its maximum is 11·64 gms.), seems to be the equivalent of four Corinthian drachms or eight Euboic obols. Cephallenia and Zacynthus were similarly affected, reducing the Aeginetic norm to suit their Adriatic trade. The supposed early Aeginetic coins of the Chalcidian colonies of Zancle, Naxos, Himera[1] and Rhegium are probably of the Corcyraean standard.

The early Corinthian, Attic and Euboic standards may be considered as one group, forming the great rival of the Aeginetic. Within this group, however, we distinguish a lighter standard, with a drachm of about 4·2 gms. and a heavier one with a drachm of about 4·3 gms. The lighter standard is that of the so-called heraldic coins; of the earliest Corinthian coins, before the introduction of the armed goddess on the reverse; of certain early coins of which the attribution as between Chalcis and Olynthus is disputed, and of some others of which the Macedonian origin is assured. The heavier standard is represented by the coins of Cyrene, the earliest of which, with incuse reverses, date from not later than the middle of the sixth century; by the earliest Athenian coins with the head of Athena and the owl; by the Corinthian double-type coins; by the early issues of certain Euboean origin; by many coinages of Macedon, and so on: in fact it is what is generally known as the Euboic-Attic standard. The standard adopted by the majority of the colonies in south Italy seems to have been derived from Corinth before the raising of the standard. The introduction of the higher weight in Greece itself was probably the work of Peisistratus (p. 68). It has been suggested

[1] See Volume of Plates i, 308, *c, b.*

that he was inspired by the example of Cyrene. But it is not certain that the earliest Cyrenaic coins precede in date the earliest Attic 'owls.' There is also no evidence for connecting the weight in question with that of the Samian electrum, which is definitely higher, or with the weight of the Egyptian *ket*.

If the heavier Attic standard dates from the first tyranny of Peisistratus, what, we may ask, is the application of Androtion's and Aristotle's accounts of the Solonian reform to the pre-Peisistratean coinage of Athens[1]? It seems clear that any such coinage must have been on the lighter standard: drachm of 4·2 gms. and mina of 420 gms. This cannot by any decent manipulation of text or figures be brought into harmony with Aristotle's story. He implies that there was a general increase of the weights all round; that a new mina was made of which the drachm (or $\frac{1}{100}$ part) was equivalent to $\frac{1}{70}$ of the Pheidonian mina previously in use. Now the old mina of 100 Pheidonian drachms (or 50 Aeginetic staters of 12·3 gms.) weighed about 615 gms.; and $\frac{1}{70}$ of this is 8·8 gms. So that the new Solonian 'drachm' was of the weight of what we should regard as a rather heavy didrachm of the later Attic weight. Aristotle himself remarks that 'the stamped coin in old times was called a didrachm,' instead of a tetradrachm; and the use of the term drachm for what later was called a didrachm is confirmed by extant archaic weights. It has been suggested that the doubling of the nominal value of the coins took place in the time of Hippias; a memory of some trick of his is preserved in Pseudo-Aristotle (*Oecon.* II, 4). Aristotle appears to know nothing of the lighter standard, the existence of which has been proved by recent research. He seems to have assumed that the weight introduced by Solon was the same as that familiar to him from the 'owls.' It is an assumption which has also been made by all numismatists down to the last few years. Androtion, however, whose work was used by Aristotle, understood that Solon made the mina which had previously contained 73 drachms consist of 100, so that the weight of the drachm was reduced, and creditors who were paid old debts in the new coinage lost heavily (see above, p. 39). We may dismiss the implication that a pre-existing mina divisible into 73 Aeginetic drachms was newly divided up into 100 reduced drachms, and what follows from it. But his figure 73 looks exact, and if we use it as we used Aristotle's 70, we find that the Solonian 'drachm' weighed not 8·8 gms. but 8·4 gms. This is much nearer to the evidence provided by the metrologists on the

[1] See Aristotle, *Const. of Athens*, x; Plutarch, *Solon*, 15.

basis of the Corinthian and Euboic or Attic coinage of pre-Solonian days.

Of the other silver standards with which we meet in the early days of Greek coinage, the three which are sufficiently important to be mentioned here are chiefly represented by Asiatic issues. The so-called Phoenician, Graeco-Asiatic or Milesian standard of about 14·10 gms. was, as we have seen, used in quite early days for electrum. The denominations of early silver on this standard in Asia Minor are usually drachms or smaller. The so-called Babylonic standard, already mentioned in connection with the heavier gold issues of Croesus, also determined his silver coins (staters of about 10·7 gms., with their halves) and those of a number of mints on the coasts of Asia Minor. Both the standards mentioned are found also in the extremely important currency of the mining districts of Macedon in the second half of the sixth century. When the Persian imperial coinage was inaugurated the silver was issued on a standard slightly higher than that of Croesus. The weight of the Persian silver *siglos* is normally 5·6 gms. This weight (so far as we can ascertain the normals) stands to the weight of the Persian gold daric in nearly the same proportion as the weight of the Croesean silver stater to the Croesean light gold stater. That is to say, when the Persians raised the weight of the standard gold coin they raised that of the silver in proportion. We know that the daric was tariffed at 20 sigloi; similarly the Croesean light gold stater must have been equivalent to 20 Croesean silver drachms, or ten of his staters. This decimal relation was curiously combined, as elsewhere, with a duodecimal division of the denominations.

The relation in value between gold and silver revealed by the weights of the Persian coins is $13\frac{1}{3}$: 1, which is not far from the figure, given by Herodotus, of 13 : 1. That figure has been corrected accordingly by nearly all recent writers on metrology. It is not possible to discuss here how far this relation is correct for earlier periods, and how far, combined with a conventional relation of gold to electrum as 4 : 3, it explains the origin of the various standards. But it provides a good working hypothesis of the origin of the 'Babylonic' standard. Thus, at the rate of $13\frac{1}{3}$: 1, one gold shekel of 8·4 gms. would be worth 111·72 gms. of silver, which could be divided up into ten pieces of 11·17 gms. or 20 of 5·6 gms.—which is the so-called 'Babylonian' standard for silver. Similarly a double-shekel of gold would be worth fifteen pieces of 14·89 gms. This has been supposed to be the origin of the 'Phoenician' standard; but the actual weights of extant coins are far too low to support any such theory, even if it be modified by taking the Croesean gold standard as the base. That there were constant attempts to attain a recognized system of interchangeable values in the different metals, and that 'a Babylonian gold unit is the root-norm which, at the ratio of $13\frac{1}{3}$: 1, accounts for some of them,' is as much as can be admitted. The scales doubtless continued even in historic times to play a much greater part in financial transactions than is generally supposed.

CHAPTER VI

ATHENS: THE REFORM OF CLEISTHENES

I. CLEOMENES AND ATHENS

DURING the twenty years that followed the expulsion of the tyrants from Athens there is no one who plays a more important part on the stage of Greek history than Cleomenes, king of Sparta. In Herodotus, who is our main authority for the career of Cleomenes, the Spartan king appears in a most unfavourable light. He succeeded to the throne by the mere accident of birth, for had the succession been determined by merit rather than by birth, his half-brother Dorieus would have been king; he was half crazy from the first, and he degenerated into a drunkard; his reign was brief, and he died by his own hands—such is the view of Herodotus. Yet most modern historians are agreed that Cleomenes was both a statesman and a general of exceptional merit, and that, directly and indirectly, he did much to determine the issue of the Persian wars. It must be remembered that Herodotus' account of him is derived from various sources, and that almost all of them are tainted. Athenian tradition, the source that flows most freely, could hardly fail to see in him the would-be destroyer of the liberties of Athens. The other sources from which it may be presumed that Herodotus derived his information were the Spartan ephors, the descendants of the first wife of King Anaxandridas, the sons or grandsons of the exiled Demaratus, and Argive and Aeginetan tradition. Were authorities such as these likely to do justice to the memory of the Spartan king? If the alliance between Plataea and Athens is correctly dated to 519 B.C. (see p. 78), the reign of Cleomenes must have begun not later than 520 B.C., and it lasted at least until 489 B.C. Thus a reign which Herodotus describes as brief extended over more than thirty years. His career was as important in the internal history of Sparta itself, as in the relations of that state to the rest of the Greek world. It is clear that he was the last Spartan king who governed as well as reigned, if we may venture to borrow from Talleyrand's definition of a constitutional monarch; but it is not so clear whether his reign was a period of reaction, or merely of arrested development. If we are to accept as satisfactory evidence the statements to be found in Herodotus as to the powers exercised by the ephors in the reigns of his predecessors, we cannot but see in his reign a period of reaction. He must have succeeded, in familiar phrase, in putting back the hands of the clock. On the other hand, it is possible that some of the details in Herodotus' narrative of earlier Spartan history are anachronisms such as are not uncommon in popular tradition. However this may be, the mere fact that the history of Sparta during this momentous period is for the most part narrated in connection with the name of Cleomenes himself indicates sufficiently that Spartan policy was both determined and carried out by the king, rather than by the ephors. Indeed, from the verdict of Herodotus we may appeal with confidence to the verdict of the king's own contemporaries. To what other Spartan king do we find such a series of appeals addressed as those recorded by Herodotus himself—the Plataeans, Maeandrius, Isagoras, Aristagoras, and, the most significant of all, the Scythians[1]?

Three parties may be distinguished in the political life of Athens after the expulsion of Hippias. In the first place, there were the adherents of the exiled tyrant. An impartial survey of the evidence renders the inference inevitable that down to the battle of Marathon the Peisistratid faction could still count on a large body of supporters in the Assembly. If we would understand Athenian history down to Marathon, we must allow for the influence of this party throughout the period. Although the Greek tyrant, unlike the English monarch of the seventeenth century, was surrounded by no halo of legitimacy, and although his claims were not buttressed up by any theory of Divine Right, yet the existence of a party whose object was the restoration of Hippias as tyrant is a factor in the political history of Athens from the fall of the tyranny to the Battle of Marathon which can as little be disregarded as the influence of the Jacobites in the politics of our country during the half century that followed the flight of James II. The second party was the old aristocratic faction, which included the great bulk of the *genē* or clans. The leader of this party was Isagoras. Lastly there were the Alcmaeonidae, probably the most important of all the clans. To the old influence of this clan was now added the popularity resulting from the part which

[1] Although Herodotus does not connect the appeal of the Athenians in 491, in regard to the medism of Aegina, with the name of Cleomenes, it is evident from the subsequent course of events that it must have been to him, rather than to the ephors, that the Athenian envoys addressed themselves (see below, p. 259).

it had played in the overthrow of the tyranny. Its leader was
Cleisthenes, whose mother was Agariste, the daughter of the
famous tyrant of Sicyon (see vol. III, pp. 554 *sqq.*).

It was natural that King Cleomenes should anticipate that what
had happened in other states in which Sparta had helped to overthrow a tyranny would happen also at Athens. In the Peloponnesian states generally, the fall of a tyranny had been followed by
the establishment in power of an oligarchy subservient to Spartan
interests, and amenable to Spartan influence. Doubtless, Cleomenes imagined that the fall of Hippias would be followed at
Athens by the ascendancy of the aristocratic party led by Isagoras.
For the moment the serious danger to the ascendancy of Isagoras
lay in the popularity of the Alcmaeonidae and their leader Cleisthenes. For more than three years, however, after the expulsion
of Hippias, the anticipations of Cleomenes were fulfilled. In the
party struggle between Isagoras and Cleisthenes the latter was
worsted, and in the spring of 508 B.C. Isagoras was elected to the
archonship, which was still the supreme executive office in the
Athenian political system. It was then that the unexpected happened. On the fall of the tyrants a revision of the lists of the
citizens had been demanded, with the result that a large number
of those who owed their position in the citizen body to the
patronage of Peisistratus and Hippias were deprived of their
rights. It is difficult to determine whether Cleisthenes was a
supporter of this measure of disfranchisement; the result,
however, of such a measure can only have been favourable
to the party of his rival Isagoras. It is not surprising, therefore, that Cleisthenes, when worsted in the struggle, should
have made a direct bid for the support of those so recently
disfranchised.

At this point it becomes a matter of some difficulty to determine
the precise order of events. If we are to follow the narrative of
Herodotus (v, 66, 69–70), we must put Cleisthenes' reform of
the constitution before Isagoras' appeal to Cleomenes. On the
other hand, the account in Aristotle's *Constitution of Athens* (xx *sq.*)
distinguishes between Cleisthenes' bid for popular support and
the enactment of his reforms, and suggests that it was the mere
bid for popular support that prompted Isagoras' appeal to Sparta,
but that the actual enactment of the reforms was subsequent to
the failure of Cleomenes' intervention. In view of the precise
chronology of Aristotle's version, in contrast to the vague indications afforded by Herodotus, it is difficult not to prefer Aristotle's
order of events. If this view is correct, it would follow that Isagoras,

in order to defeat the schemes of Cleisthenes, resolved on an appeal to Cleomenes. He suggested to the Spartan king that he should demand from the Athenian people the expulsion of the Alcmaeonidae, on the ground of the curse (ἄγος) which the clan had incurred at the time of the suppression of the conspiracy of Cylon (see above, p. 27). Cleomenes fell in with this suggestion, and demanded the expulsion of the 'Accursed.' Cleisthenes did not venture to resist, and withdrew from Athens. The first success had been scored by Isagoras. Thereupon Cleomenes appeared in person, and proceeded to exile from Athens no less than 700 families who formed the chief support of Cleisthenes and his cause. Cleomenes, whose watchword seems to have been the same as Strafford's, did not stop here. If Cleisthenes intended to convert the constitution into a full blown democracy, Sparta must secure its control of Athens by converting the constitution into a narrow oligarchy. In place of the existing Council a new council, consisting of the adherents of Isagoras, must be established. The attempt to dissolve the Council was frustrated by the courageous resistance of that body, whereupon Cleomenes and Isagoras took possession of the Acropolis. Here they were besieged by the Athenians, and as the military force which Cleomenes had brought from Sparta was small, capitulation was inevitable. After a siege of only two days Cleomenes consented to withdraw, on condition of a safe conduct for himself and his Spartan force. The supporters of Isagoras who had taken part in the seizure of the Acropolis put to death by the Athenians, although it would appear that Isagoras himself effected his escape with Cleomenes.

We are here confronted with a serious problem. What council was it that Cleomenes attempted to dissolve? If Herodotus' order of events is correct, it is clearly the new Council of Five Hundred, which owed its existence to the reforms of Cleisthenes. If, however, Aristotle's order is correct, it can only be the old Council of Four Hundred, the institution of which was ascribed by Athenian tradition to Solon[1].

The withdrawal of Cleomenes from Athens was followed by the immediate recall of Cleisthenes and the exiles, and Cleisthenes lost no time in securing the enactment of his comprehensive measures of reform.

---

[1] Unless we fall back on the hypothesis that the council in question was none other than the Areopagus.

II. THE CONSTITUTIONAL REFORM
OF CLEISTHENES

Nowhere is our debt to Aristotle more apparent than in the discussion of the measures of constitutional reform which are to be attributed to Cleisthenes. It would be too much to say that our present knowledge of these reforms as compared with what was surmised on the subject before the recovery of Aristotle's *Constitution of Athens* in 1891 is as light to darkness[1], but it is no exaggeration to say that it is as noon-day compared with twilight. Hitherto our main authority had been Herodotus, and Herodotus in his account (v, 66, 69) of the Reform of Cleisthenes is not seen at his best. Here, as in his other references to Athenian constitutional history, he is superficial and inaccurate. The change in the tribal system is to him chiefly a question of the number of the tribes, and the motive ascribed for the change is puerile. All that he has to say is that Cleisthenes altered the number of the tribes from four to ten, and that he also altered their names. Instead of their being called after the four sons of Ion, they were henceforth called after ten heroes, all of whom, with one exception, were native to the soil of Attica. In thus changing the names of the tribes, he was but imitating the action of his maternal grandfather, Cleisthenes, tyrant of Sicyon (see vol. III, p. 555). The latter, in order to show his contempt for the Dorian race, altered the names of the Dorian tribes at Sicyon to names derived from some of the less honourable of the domestic animals; his grandson, in order to show his contempt for the Ionian race, invented new tribes, and new names for them, in order that the Athenians might no longer have the same tribes as the Ionians. No one who reads this passage can fail to see that, whatever merits Herodotus may have had as an historian, an insight into things constitutional was not among them. There were in addition a couple of references to Cleisthenes in the *Politics*[2] of Aristotle, one of them extremely obscure in its terminology, and that was almost all that we had to go upon. That Grote should have come so near to the truth in what is most essential in the legislation is a singular proof of his genius as a constitutional historian.

Not the least part of our debt to the *Constitution of Athens* is that it enables us to rule out much that had been attributed to the Athenian reformer by one writer or another. Cleisthenes did not institute the popular courts of law; the Heliaea was the

---

[1] See Aristotle, *Const. of Athens*, xxi *sq.*
[2] Aristotle, *Pol.* III, ii, 3 (1275 *b ad fin.*); vii, iv, 18 (1319 *b* 20).

creation of Solon. Nor did Cleisthenes substitute sortition for election in the appointment of the archons; the change came more than twenty years later. He did not even reorganize the army on the basis of his new tribes, nor did he institute the Strategia, although both these reforms may fairly be called consequential on the change in the tribal system. The only reforms that we have any warrant for attributing to him are (1) the institution of ten tribes, based on the deme as their unit, in place of the old four Ionic tribes, whose unit was the clan (γένος), and the substitution of the deme for the naucrary as the unit of local administration; (2) the reconstitution of the council on the basis of the new tribes; and (3) the invention of the curious constitutional device known as Ostracism. Of these three changes the one that was at once the most fundamental in its character and the most far-reaching in its consequences was the change in the tribal system.

1. THE TRIBES AND DEMES

There was much in the structure of the Athenian state that Solon left as he found it. While he altered the qualification for office, he left the qualification for citizenship unchanged. Down to the time of Cleisthenes membership in the citizen body involved membership in the phratries and clans. Cleisthenes did not indeed abolish the phratries and clans when he abolished the four Ionic tribes. He allowed them to continue as religious and social institutions; what he did was to dissociate them entirely from the political system. The unit of the new tribes was to be the deme, and not the clan.

All our evidence goes to prove that the Demes were ancient divisions of Attica. They may be compared to the English parish, if it is remembered that the comparison with the parish is merely by way of illustration, and that it is not an analogy that can be pressed. Herodotus himself assumes the existence of the demes in the age of Peisistratus, and Plato in that of the Peisistratidae. From one passage in Herodotus (ix, 73) it is clear that Athenian tradition carried them back to the Heroic Age. But while there is no good ground for crediting Cleisthenes with the invention of the deme, there is some reason for supposing that the demes in the city of Athens itself were created by him for the purposes of his system. The evidence for this view is to be found in a passage in Herodotus (i, 62) relating to the return of Peisistratus from exile, in which the inhabitants of the demes are contrasted with those of the city. If the city demes were artificial in origin, they would be analogous to the artificial boroughs, such as Marylebone,

Finsbury, or the Tower Hamlets, which were the creation of the
First Reform Bill of 1832. What then was the relation of the
new tribes to the demes? It is, unfortunately, not quite certain
what was the view of Herodotus. The reading of the MSS makes
him say that Cleisthenes assigned 10 demes to each tribe, which
would imply that there were 100 demes in all the tribes. An
emendation of the text which has won wide acceptance makes
him say, however, that the demes were arranged 'in ten groups'
instead of 'in groups of ten,' which is the reading of the MSS[1].
At all events, his silence suggests that between the tribes and the
demes there was no connecting link. The evidence at our command—evidence which is partly derived from the *Constitution of
Athens*, and was partly known before its recovery—proves conclusively that Herodotus is in error. The number of demes in the
third century B.C. was 174[2], and there is no sufficient reason for
supposing that it was ever materially less; the number of demes
in each tribe was not uniform, and between the tribe and the deme
there was an intermediate link, the Trittys. Each tribe consisted
of three trittyes, but the trittys might consist of a single deme,
or it might include several. Nor were the demes in a trittys, if
more than one was included, necessarily contiguous.

A system more artificial than the tribes and trittyes of
Cleisthenes it might well pass the wit of man to devise. In the new
tribal system the demes were arranged in three groups corresponding to their geographical position. The first group consisted
of the demes in Athens itself and its suburbs; the second, of the
demes on the coast of Attica; and the third, of those in the interior
of the country. Each tribe included one or more demes in each
of the three groups. The deme or demes from each group in each
tribe made up a trittys, so that in all there were thirty trittyes,
ten in the city and its suburbs, ten in the Paralia, or coast district,
and ten in the interior or midland region. The trittys was thus
purely artificial in character, a fact which helps to explain how
it came about that down to the recovery of the *Constitution of
Athens* hardly a single reference to it was to be found in Greek
literature. Had the trittys always been a single deme, or had it
always consisted of contiguous demes, it would have been different.
As it was, it served no further purpose than that of constituting
a mere link between the tribe and the deme. Unlike the latter,
it had no separate functions of its own to discharge. While the

---

[1] Lolling's conjecture of δέκαχα for δέκα is supported by Hicks and
Hill, *Gr. Hist. Inscr.* 81, l. 35.
[2] Polemo quoted by Strabo, ix, p. 396.

tribe and the deme were corporations with officers, assemblies and property of their own, the trittys had no corporate existence.

When we come to ask the question, what was the object of Cleisthenes in this reform of the tribal system? it is clear that two questions, rather than one, are involved. The first, and much the more important, question is, what was the object of Cleisthenes in substituting the deme for the clan as the basis of the organization of the citizen body? The second, and less important, question is, what was his motive in introducing the highly artificial system of trittyes? It is unfortunate that these two entirely different questions have been too often confused.

The substitution of the deme for the clan meant in effect the transition from the principle of kinship to that of locality, or residence. The clan was based on kinship, actual or supposed; the deme was a local division of Attica. A similar transition from the one principle to the other is to be traced in Roman History also. There was a time when at Rome the legislative body was the Comitia Curiata; *i.e.* a time when the citizen body was organized on the basis of the *gens*, a unit which implied real or presumed kinship. In the historical period the Comitia Tributa has taken the place of the Comitia Curiata; *i.e.* the citizen body is organized on the basis of the tribe, a unit which was originally local in character. It is significant of the difference between the history of Greece and that of Rome—between the genius of the Greeks and that of the Romans—that a change which at Rome was effected in the course of generations by a process of slow development was effected at Athens in a moment, in the twinkling of an eye; we can put our finger on the moment and the man. To those who are familiar with the history of our own country no principle can appear more obvious than that of locality. To the Greek mind it was otherwise. Not only had Solon left the principle of kinship untouched, but even Cleisthenes, when he substituted the deme for the clan, applied the principle of locality in a modified or restricted form. Membership in a deme in the time of Cleisthenes depended on residence within its borders, and so far the deme was purely local in character. But strange as it must seem to the modern mind, the privilege of membership in any given deme was made hereditary, so that in any subsequent generation an Athenian was a *dēmotes* of a given deme, not because he was resident in it, but because his ancestor had been resident in it at the time of the Reform of Cleisthenes. Even the cleruch in a distant colony retained his membership in his deme. Thus in all the demes of Attica there were two classes of residents in the deme; the *dēmotai*, who were both members of the deme and resident within it, and the *enkektēmenoi*, who although resident in the deme were members of some other deme.

Grote, with much less evidence before him than is now available, had divined the motive of Cleisthenes in substituting locality for kinship as the principle of the organization of the citizen body. It was, as Grote puts it, in order to secure the admission to citizenship of a body of free residents in Attica who were not of pure Athenian descent, and who consequently could not be admitted to citizenship without a shock to the religious sentiment of the Athenians, so long as citizenship involved membership in the clan, which was an association largely religious in character. In the words of a modern jurist[1]: 'The Greek City State was not conceived as an aggregate of individuals, but consisted of clusters of kinsmen, strongly bound together by common interests and common religion. The earlier ages may be characterized as epochs of federation—the federation of kindreds (γένη).' Athens after the Reform of Cleisthenes was no longer to be a federation of kindreds.

The new evidence afforded by Aristotle enables us to trace the history, and estimate the importance, of this class of free residents in Attica of impure Athenian descent, whose existence was postulated by Grote. To understand the origin of this class we must go back to Solon. Plutarch, in the *Life of Solon* (24), tells us that Solon, in order to stimulate the industrial development of Athens, granted the privilege of citizenship to those resident aliens (μέτοικοι) who satisfied two conditions; they must be skilled workmen, who came to Athens for the practice of their art or craft, and they must bring wife and children with them. It is generally agreed that there are traces in Athenian art of the sixth century B.C., especially in vase painting, of the growth of Ionic and other foreign influences (see pp. 66, 595).

It is probable that under Peisistratus and his sons the class of resident aliens had increased rapidly in numbers. The growing importance of this class would explain the statement of Aristotle, in the *Constitution of Athens* (XIII, 5), that this class, those who were 'not of pure descent,' formed one of the chief supports of the tyranny. But the position of this class in the citizen body must have remained precarious, so long as citizenship was connected with the clan and the phratry, admission to either of which was so jealously safeguarded. Their motive in supporting the tyrants was clearly, as indeed Aristotle asserts, the fear of losing their privileges if

[1] Sir P. Vinogradoff, *Outlines of Historical Jurisprudence*, vol. II, p. 85.

the protection of the tyrants were withdrawn. Their fears proved
only too well founded, for (as has been described above) on the
expulsion of Hippias the register of citizens was revised, and a
large number of those citizens who could not prove pure Athenian
descent were struck off the list. What happened at Athens on
the fall of the Peisistratid dynasty was to be repeated in a similar
form a generation later on the fall of the tyranny at Syracuse.
There too those who owed their place in the citizen body to the
tyrants were deprived of their rights by the restored democracy.
The object, then, of Cleisthenes in dissociating citizenship from
the clan, and connecting it with the deme, was to facilitate the
admission to citizenship of those who could not prove pure
Athenian descent, and to render their position unassailable for
the future. There were no associations of kinship with the deme,
and there were no religious sentiments to be shocked by the
admission to the ranks of the demotae of those whose origin was
wholly or partially foreign. In order to secure still further the
position of this class of citizens, it was enacted that henceforward
the official designation of a citizen should be by his deme, and
not, as hitherto, by his patronymic. The patronymic might reveal
the secret of a foreign origin; the name of the deme could convey
no such information. For half a century or more Athens remained
faithful to the liberal policy of her great reformer, and her
citizenship was open to those who had no claim to pure Athenian
blood. It was left to the most famous democratic statesman of
the ancient world—Pericles himself—to reverse the enlightened
policy of his predecessor, and once more to impose the test of
pure Athenian descent on both sides.

To the second question, What was the object of Cleisthenes in
constituting the new tribes in so artificial a manner? the answer
commonly given is that this artificial constitution of the tribes
was directed against the danger of a recrudescence of the old
feuds between the parties of the Plain, the Coast, and the Hill-
country—the Pedion, the Paralia, and the Diacria (pp. 60 *sqq.*). As
each tribe consisted of three trittyes, each from a different region
of Attica, it was clearly impossible, so it is argued, for any one
of these factions to exercise a dominating influence in any one of
the tribes. This explanation of the motive of Cleisthenes is clearly
based on two assumptions, for neither of which there is adequate
evidence. It assumes in the first place that the rivalry of the three
factions still persisted as late as the time of Cleisthenes, and it
also assumes that the three regions of the Cleisthenean system
correspond to the threefold division of Attica into the Pedion,

the Paralia, and the Diacria, of the period which preceded the tyranny of Peisistratus. That the feuds which prevailed during the generation which separated the legislation of Solon from the first tyranny of Peisistratus, and were largely accountable for the success of the tyrant, were local in character, does not admit of doubt. What may well be doubted—what certainly cannot be proved—is that the three parties with which we have to deal at the time of the Reform of Cleisthenes—the party of Cleisthenes himself, that of Isagoras, and that of the Peisistratidae—are identical with the old local factions. It may fairly be argued that it was the firm rule of Peisistratus and his sons that had effaced the local lines of cleavage, and given to the whole country a sense of unity that it had not possessed half a century earlier. Since the middle of the sixth century new questions had come to the front, and political parties were now grouped according to new principles.

Still less ground is there for the assumption that the three regions of the Cleisthenean system are identical with the Pedion, the Paralia, and the Diacria. The town area, the city and its suburbs, could have formed but a small part of the Pedion, most of which would fall within the μεσόγειος, or 'midland,' region. It is usually supposed that the demes in the neighbourhood of Marathon were included in the Diacria; but in the Cleisthenean system these were divided between the midland and the coast districts. Finally, if the old view[1] is correct, that the Paralia in the popular sense meant the southern part of Attica, the triangle which is bounded on two sides by the sea, and the apex of which is Sunium, then there is little correspondence between the Paralia of Cleisthenes—the demes situated on the coast—and the Paralia in the popular sense.

But if this explanation of the object of Cleisthenes in constituting the tribes on the basis of the trittys is to be ruled out, what motive can be suggested for a scheme so peculiar? Much the most probable motive is the desire to weaken the influence of the old Eupatrid families, an influence which was mainly local, and found its centre in the clan. In the new tribe, composed of three trittyes taken from three different regions of Attica, no family, however great its local influence might be, could hope to control more than a third of the voters in any one tribe. There was, however, a further result of the system of trittyes which was to prove of such importance in the development of the Athenian democracy that we are compelled to surmise that it must have

---

[1] Cf. Thucydides ii, 55.

been one of his principal objects in his reform of the tribes. One trittys in each tribe consisted of a single deme situate either in the city of Athens or in its suburbs. It was in the city and its immediate neighbourhood that the new citizens, 'those not of pure descent,' were congregated. Some of this class were doubtless resident in the Paralian demes, but none can have been found in rural Attica. Cleisthenes thus secured that in each of the ten tribes there should be a compact body of voters who were his own special adherents, and who owed their position in the body politic to his reforms. The influence of this class would be out of all proportion to their numbers, for the simple reason that, being on the spot, they would be in a position to exercise their right of voting far more frequently than those members of the tribes whose homes were in the more distant parts of Attica, whether in the coast or the midland region.

It has often been pointed out that one consequence of the new tribal system was that there could be no further danger of any conscious opposition of the interests of Athens to those of Attica, since there were no tribes that were purely Athenian in this narrow sense, and none that were purely Attican. So far the working of the system was beneficial to the interests of the state as a whole. But there was another consequence, to which attention is not so commonly called, which was far from beneficial. It was inevitable that, when the interests of rural Attica conflicted with those of the city, the interests of the former should be sacrificed to those of the latter.

Down to the Reform of Cleisthenes the unit of local administration was the naucrary. The precise nature both of the naucrary itself and of its functions is obscure, but we can gather that it was a subdivision, local in character, of the old Ionic tribes, that it was presided over by a president called *naucraros* (p. 50), and that it raised and administered funds. For the naucraria Cleisthenes substituted the deme, a subdivision of his new tribes, and, as has been explained above, also local in character. Its president was the Demarch, and the deme, like the naucrary, had funds to administer. The deme varied almost as much in size as the English parish. There must have been not a few demes with less than 100 demotae, while the largest demes must have counted some thousands of members. Thucydides[1] speaks of the deme of Acharnae as furnishing 3000 hoplites to the army, a statement which would imply 4000 demotae at the least.

[1] II, 20.

2. THE REFORM OF THE COUNCIL

Our authorities, Aristotle as well as Plutarch, agree in attributing the institution of a Council, side by side with the primitive Council of the Areopagus, to Solon. Aristotle has nothing to tell us as to the prerogatives and duties of this Solonian Council, although Plutarch attributes to Solon the provision that no measure could be brought before the Assembly except in the form of a *probouleuma*, or proposal of the Council[1]. However that may be, the ancient writers are unanimous in representing it as composed of 400 members, 100 from each of the four Ionic tribes. Cleisthenes based the organization of his reformed Council on the tribe, in its new form, and the deme. The new Council consisted of 500 members, 50 from each of the ten tribes. The 50 members of each tribe were apportioned to the demes included in that tribe roughly according to the size of the several demes, and the method of selection was by drawing lots. No citizen could hold office as a member of the Council more than twice in a lifetime. One of the most peculiar features in the new Council was the system of *Prytaneis*. The year was divided into ten periods of 35 or 36 days each called by the name *Prytany*, and the 50 Councillors of each tribe held office, under the title of *Prytaneis*, or Presidents, for one of these periods. During their term of office they acted as a committee of the Council. Nowhere else in the Athenian constitution do we see the democratic principle applied with such rigorous logic as in the Cleisthenean Council. It was of the very essence of the system that the conception of special fitness or capacity was entirely set aside. Anybody who had the ambition had his chance of entering the Council, and, even if the number of citizens is computed at more than the thirty thousand suggested by a passage in Herodotus[2], something like a third of them must have served on the Council at some period of their lives. Yet the duties which the Councillors had to discharge were as multifarious as could well be imagined, and if most of them were of a routine nature, some were at once important and difficult.

A detailed account of the functions of the Council must be reserved for the chapters which treat of the Periclean age, nor is it easy to determine which of the duties that it performed in the fully developed democracy had been assigned to it by Cleisthenes. It is clear, however, that from the start it must have been the mainspring of the machinery of government. An assembly which any citizen was entitled to attend, which was convened only

<hr/>

[1] Plutarch, *Life of Solon*, 19; see above, p. 54.   [2] v, 97.

once in ten days, and might be attended by many or by few, was eminently unfitted for the business of administration. For that a much smaller and more permanent body was required, and such a body was found in the Council. It is unfortunate that Grote should have lent the great authority of his name to the employment of the word *Senate* as the equivalent for *Boulē*, the Greek name for the Council. Unless we are to misconceive completely the nature of the Athenian Council, we must get rid of all our associations with the Roman Senate, the Senate of the United States of America, or the Second Chamber of other modern states. The Athenian Council was in no sense of the term a Second Chamber. It was simply a committee of the Assembly, but it was a committee for all purposes, and its work was in the main administrative in character. It was a probouleutic body, to use the technical Greek term; that is to say, its principal task was to prepare the business for the meetings of the Assembly. Hence, as has been explained above, no measure could be brought before the Assembly except in the form of a *probouleuma*, or proposal submitted by the Council. Such a proposal when ratified by the Assembly was styled a *psephisma*. The probouleuma may be compared to the report of a Standing Committee of one of our Town or County Councils, which is presented to the Council for its approval; only it must be remembered that at Athens there was but one standing committee, the Council itself. These *probouleumata* were chiefly concerned with the work of administration, and many of them were what Austin calls 'occasional' or 'particular commands,' *e.g.* a direction to certain officials to pay certain sums to certain individuals. It is true that all legislative proposals must originate with the Council, but it is not less true that the normal duty of the Assembly, and therefore of its committee, the Council, was to carry on the business of the state, rather than to make laws. As it was the task of the Council to prepare business for the consideration of the Assembly, it fell to the Council to draw up the *Programma*, or agenda, for each meeting of the Assembly. But in addition to its probouleutic duties, the Council was charged with the transaction of any business of state that might turn up and that could not wait, and, either solely, or jointly with the various boards of magistrates, it had the superintendence of the different departments of state.

It would be difficult to exaggerate the importance of the part played by the Council in the political education of the Athenian citizen. If it is asked, How could the affairs of a great empire be conducted with success by an Assembly of the whole citizen body? the answer is that it was in his year of office in the Council that the citizen received his training for politics. It is probable that a large proportion of those who attended the meetings of the Assembly with any degree of regularity had been at some time or other members of the Council. During their term of office they had been brought into touch with every department of state, and with every branch of business. It is hardly necessary to point out that the political experience thus gained must have been of peculiar value to the inhabitants of the more remote demes.

3. OSTRACISM

By far the most peculiar of the measures of constitutional reform which are to be ascribed to Cleisthenes is the institution known as Ostracism. It is found later elsewhere in the Greek world, at Syracuse, Argos, Megara, and Miletus; but of these four states, the two last had been part of the Athenian empire, while Argos was more than once an ally of Athens, and there are other traces of the influence of Athens on the development of its democracy. At Syracuse, where it was called Petalism, we are definitely told by Diodorus (xi, 87) that it was introduced in imitation of Athens, and what we are told of Syracuse almost certainly holds good of the other states in which ostracism is found. Hence the full merit of its invention may be claimed for Cleisthenes. In the Greek world, especially in the sphere of constitutional reform, conscious imitation played a large part.

There is certainly no device of ancient statesmanship that will strike the modern reader as more curious than that of ostracism. Once a year, if the Assembly had so decided, but only once, an Ostracophoria was held, but unless at least six thousand citizens took part in the voting the proceedings were null and void. At the ostracophoria the voter might write on a piece of broken pottery the name of any citizen whom he wished to be exiled. The words ostracophoria and ostracism are derived from *ostraka*, the Greek name for these potsherds, which formed the wastepaper of the ancient world, just as the Syracusan term petalism is derived from the Greek word for leaf, the names at Syracuse being inscribed on olive leaves, instead of potsherds. The citizen against whom most votes were cast was exiled for a period of ten years, at the end of which he returned to full possession of all his rights. His exile did not carry with it the confiscation of his property.

There can be no doubt that the object of Cleisthenes in devising this strange constitutional contrivance was to provide a safeguard for the infant democracy against the risk of a restoration of the tyranny just overthrown. As we have seen, the adherents of the exiled Hippias still formed a large and well-organized body of voters in the Assembly; a struggle between the rival factions in the state might easily afford an opportunity for the restoration of the tyrant. Ostracism would furnish the means of getting rid of any prominent supporter of the tyrant's cause before his influence had become too great and before his plans were matured. And it might well appear to Cleisthenes that, even if the Peisistratid cause were discredited for good and all, the ambition of individual statesmen might constitute a standing danger to the democracy.

Aristotle, in the *Constitution of Athens* (xxii, 4), asserts not only that the object of the institution was to avert the danger of a restoration of tyranny, but that the immediate motive of Cleisthenes was the desire to get rid of the leader of the Peisistratid party, Hipparchus, the son of Charmus, a cousin of Hippias. This latter statement involves a serious difficulty, inasmuch as we learn from the *Constitution* itself that Hipparchus was not ostracized until the year 487, some twenty years after the date of the legislation of Cleisthenes. In the passage in the *Constitution* in which the date of the ostracism of Hipparchus is given he is stated to have been the first person who was ostracized under the provisions of the new law, and his name appears at the head of a list of those who were sent into exile between the First and the Second Persian Invasions. It may be suggested as a solution of the problem that the list given was derived from the *psephisma*, or decree, which provided for the recall of those who were in exile at the time of the Invasion of Xerxes. As the period of exile was limited to ten years, the name of no one who had been ostracized before the Battle of Marathon (490 B.C.) could occur in the list. As no record had been preserved of any earlier ostracism, it might have been inferred from the *psephisma* that Hipparchus was, not only the first who was ostracized after Marathon, but the first who was ostracized under the new law. It does not, however, follow that the law may not have been brought into operation at an earlier date, or that it may not have been directed against some other leader of the exiled tyrant's party.

But while there is little reason to doubt that ostracism was introduced as a safeguard against the *tyrannis*, it is evident that it soon ceased to be employed with this object in view. After Marathon the cause of the tyrants was discredited for ever, and their adherents must have formed a weak and timid faction. At any rate, after Salamis and Plataea the danger of the restoration

of any member of the Peisistratid house had passed away. The last
to be ostracized on suspicion of being an adherent of the tyrant's
cause was Megacles, the head of the great Alcmaeonid house,
and the date of his ostracism was the year 486 B.C. From this
time onwards ostracism came to be recognized as a regular
weapon of party warfare, to be used by a popular leader against
a dangerous rival. In the interval between the two Persian invasions Xanthippus, the father of Pericles, who had married
Agariste, the daughter of Cleisthenes himself, was ostracized in
484, and two years later Aristides followed him into exile. In
the period after the Second Persian Invasion Themistocles, Cimon,
and Thucydides, son of Melesias, the rival of Pericles, were all
in turn ostracized. It was the long ascendancy of Pericles himself
that led to the disuse of the institution. When it was revived in
417 B.C. to decide between the claims of Nicias and Alcibiades
it was felt that this involved a return to an obsolete stage of
political development. The weapon was never again employed,
although the law appears to have remained unrepealed down to
the time of Aristotle[1].

Critics of the democratic principle have not failed to adduce
ostracism as a proof of the inherent injustice of popular government, and one of the most memorable passages in Grote's *History
of Greece* (vol. III, pp. 368 *sqq.*) is that in which he attempts the
defence of the institution. Grote argues that, in the first place,
under the conditions of Athenian political life in the age of
Cleisthenes, some such safeguard was indispensable; that secondly,
precautions were provided against its abuse; and that thirdly, it
did not involve the confiscation of property or the loss of civic
rights. Such considerations could at best constitute a defence of
the institution at a time when the restoration of the tyranny was
a question of practical politics. They can constitute no sort of a
defence of the institution as it was worked after 486 B.C. It was, in
fact, as injurious to the interests of the state as it was unjust to the
individual. To the individual it meant the loss of all that was
best worth having during the best years of his life; to the state
it meant a fatal impediment to the proper working of the party
system. A party unfairly deprived of its leader at some great
crisis—and in the Greek democracies the leader counted for much
more than he does in our modern popular governments—is not
unlikely to have recourse to unconstitutional methods. The answer
to the ostracism of Cimon in 461 B.C. was the assassination of
Ephialtes.

[1] *Const. of Athens*, XLIII, 4.

III. CONSTITUTIONAL CHANGES BETWEEN CLEISTHENES AND THE INVASION OF XERXES

It will be convenient to describe two further changes which, although they form no part of the Reform of Cleisthenes, may fairly be regarded as consequential on them. These changes are, firstly, the reorganization of the army on the basis of the ten new tribes, which in its turn involved the institution of the ten Generals (*stratēgoi*); secondly, the substitution of sortition for election in the appointment of the archons. The first of these measures belongs to the year 501 B.C. and the second to 487 B.C., but it will be seen that the two are closely connected together.

It is probable that the Greek mind would have regarded it as almost inevitable that a change in the political system should involve a corresponding change in the military organization. In Boeotia, for example, the same unit served to determine the political representation and the military quota of each member of the League. We are almost completely in the dark as to the military organization of the Athenian state in the sixth century B.C. We know that the levies were raised by the naucraries, and we also know that the Polemarch, one of the nine archons, was commander-in-chief of the army. But this is about all that we do know. It would appear from Aristotle's *Constitution of Athens* XXII, 2 (though the passage is somewhat obscurely worded), that it was in the year 501–500 B.C. that the re-organization of the army on the basis of the ten tribes was effected. Corresponding to each tribe there was to be a *taxis*, or regiment, of hoplites, and a squadron of cavalry. The taxis was thus the tribe in its military aspect. It was commanded by a *stratēgos*, or general, who was elected by the corresponding tribe. The institution of the office of strategos was to prove one of the most important changes that were ever effected in the Athenian constitution. From the first the strategi were General Officers, as well as commanders of the regiments, though the supreme command was still exercised by the Polemarch. But three changes in their duties and position were to follow before long. New officers called taxiarchs were appointed, to whom were transferred their duties as commanders of the regiments; the Polemarch was deprived of all his military functions, which were transferred to the board of strategi; and finally a *strategos autocrator*, or commander-in-chief, was instituted.

Although it is impossible to assign a date to each of these changes, it may be regarded as certain that all three were effected in the course of the twenty years that followed the re-organization of the army. As late as the Battle of Marathon the Polemarch is still titular commander-in-chief, and he still presides at the council of war (see below, p. 240). If Plutarch[1] can be trusted, the strategi are at this date (490 B.C.) still commanders of their regiments. But the introduction of the lot in the appointment of the archons in 487 B.C. indicates that the Polemarch was at that date deprived of his military duties, and it may be surmised that the institution of the taxiarchs belongs to the same period. Finally, it is clear that the office of *strategos autocrator* was instituted at least as early as 480 B.C., since Themistocles was elected to that office in that year.

It was the formation of the Delian League, the assumption by Athens of the direction of the operations against Persia, and the gradual transformation of the League, that led to the development of the powers of the strategi. In the Periclean age the strategi acquire prerogatives other than purely military ones, and they are prerogatives of great importance. It is the *stratēgia* that gives to the Athenian democracy in the latter half of the fifth century B.C. its peculiar character. The institution of the strategia is sometimes regarded as marking a stage in the development of the democracy. If by this it is meant that it marks a stage in the development of the democratic principle in the constitution, nothing could be further from the truth. The strategia was the non-democratic element in the constitution, and it was the substitution of the strategia for the archonship as the chief executive office that strengthened the aristocratic and conservative influences in the state. It meant the substitution of an office that was military in character for one that was civil, and from this two consequences followed. Firstly, an office that is military cannot be filled by sortition, but only by election, and according to Greek ideas sortition is a democratic device, while election is aristocratic in its working. Secondly, while a civil office could be held only once in a lifetime, the holder of an office that is military must be capable of re-election. The institution of the strategia and the growth of its powers gave to the old families a fresh lease of influence, since the strategi were almost invariably chosen from their ranks. What is of still more moment is that it was the strategia that gave the opportunity for one-man power in the democratic constitution. Had the chief executive office still been at once civil in character and annual in tenure, and had there been no such office as that of *strategos autocrator*, Thucydides could not have described the constitution in the days of Pericles as still in name a democracy, although in fact it was government

[1] *Aristides*, 5.

by her greatest citizen. It is hardly too much to say that, if Athens created, organized, and held, a great empire, it was in virtue of the undemocratic principle contained in the democratic constitution. If we would trace the results of undiluted democracy, we must turn to the Athens of the fourth century—to the age of Demosthenes, not to the age of Pericles.

The last constitutional change that is to be ascribed to this period is the application of the lot to the appointment of the archons in the year 487 B.C. in place of election. It is probable that sortition had been employed from the first in the selection of the members of the new Council of Five Hundred, and it was not long before the principle of sortition was applied to all civil offices without exception. Its application to that which had hitherto been the chief office in the state marks a very definite stage in the growth of the democracy. All our ancient authorities are agreed in regarding sortition as a democratic device for equalizing the chances of rich and poor. Before the true date of the employment of sortition in the appointment of the archons was known, it had sometimes been maintained that the real object of the reform was not to equalize chances, but to avoid faction. In view of the new evidence afforded by Aristotle's *Constitution of Athens*, it may be regarded as certain that the ancient view is correct. The full effects of the change were not felt until the further step was taken of introducing payment for office. The application of the lot to the archonship in 487 B.C. affords conclusive evidence that by that time the office had lost its importance. As Grote long ago argued, the Athenians would never have entrusted to the hazard of the lot any but purely routine duties; least of all would they have entrusted to it the command of the army. Hence the Polemarch must have been stripped of the last remnants of his military prerogatives at the time the change from election to sortition was made.

The lot is another of the features in the Athenian system that critics of democracy, ancient and modern, have selected for attack. In fairness to democracy, and to Athens, it should be borne in mind that the duties of the offices to which sortition was applied were for the most part such as any person of ordinary intelligence and probity could discharge. It should also be pointed out that it was safeguarded in its operation by a process of preliminary selection, known as *procrisis*. In the appointment for the archonship, for instance, no less than 500 names were selected by the demes and it was out of these 500 candidates that the nine archons were chosen by drawing lots.

IV ATHENS UNDER CLEISTHENES

Cleisthenes was for the moment supreme at Athens. With the aid of his newly enfranchised citizens he could command a decisive majority in the Assembly. He had, however, still to reckon with Cleomenes. It was one thing to have compelled a Spartan king, in command of a small body of troops, to capitulate; it was another and a very different one to offer resistance to the whole military resources of the Peloponnesian League. Only three or four years before, Hippias had little difficulty in defeating the small force under the command of Anchimolius, but when Cleomenes had appeared in person at the head of a more considerable army, Hippias had been compelled to go into exile (p. 81 *sq*.). If anything was certain, it was that Cleomenes would not tamely submit to his discomfiture. Cleisthenes had every reason to anticipate a Peloponnesian invasion of Attica in the immediate future. It would appear that, in presence of this threatened danger, he resolved to appeal to Persia. The passage in Herodotus is so remarkable that it must be transcribed in full.

The Athenians directly afterwards recalled Cleisthenes, and the seven hundred families which Cleomenes had driven out; and, further, they sent envoys to Sardes, to make an alliance with the Persians, for they knew that war would follow with Cleomenes and the Lacedaemonians. When the ambassadors reached Sardes and delivered their message, Artaphrenes, son of Hystaspes, who was at that time governor of the place, inquired of them who they were, and in what part of the world they dwelt, that they wanted to become allies of the Persians. The messengers told them; upon which he answered them shortly that if the Athenians chose to give earth and water to King Darius, he would conclude an alliance with them; but if not, they might go home again. The envoys, 'on their own responsibility' (ἐπὶ σφέων αὐτῶν βαλόμενοι), anxious to form the alliance, accepted the terms; but on their return to Athens, they fell into deep disgrace (αἰτίας μεγάλας εἶχον) on account of their compliance. (v, 73.)

It has been generally recognized that this is one of those passages in which the influence of Alcmaeonid tradition can be detected. It is an obvious inference from the phrasing that the embassy was sent soon after the recall of Cleisthenes; that is, it was sent at a moment when his influence was at its height; at a moment when his position in the state may be compared to that of Miltiades on the morrow of Marathon. It follows that the policy of sending the embassy to Sardes must have been the policy of Cleisthenes himself. That Cleisthenes, whose family had had intimate relations with Sardes in the days of the Lydian kings[1] and who was

[1] Herodotus VI, 125.

possibly better acquainted with the circumstances of the Persian empire than most people at Athens, should have imagined that Persian aid could be obtained on any other condition than that of giving earth and water, the symbols of homage to the Great King, is incredible. He must have known that the only relation which could subsist between an empire like the Persian and a petty Greek state like Athens was that of suzerain to vassal. It is not less incredible that he should have sent the envoys without instructions on the question of earth and water. What is most incredible of all is that the envoys should have ventured to give earth and water without these instructions.

It is difficult not to find in the narrative of Herodotus a deliberate attempt to shift the responsibility for the act of homage from Cleisthenes to the envoys. Indeed it is more than probable that the attempt may have been made by Cleisthenes himself. The subsequent history of Athens affords not a few examples of the agent being made to suffer in place of the principal. No doubt Cleisthenes was careful not to explain to the Assembly the conditions on which the alliance of Persia was to be obtained. It is one of the chief dangers to which popular government is exposed that, when an end is eminently desirable, awkward questions as to the means by which that end is to be obtained are not allowed to be asked. The relations of Athens to Macedon in the age of the orator Demosthenes suggest some parallels[1]. It may be surmised that Cleisthenes calculated that when the Assembly, on the return of the envoys from Sardes, was called upon to choose between homage to Persia and capitulation to Cleomenes, it would prefer to secure the cause of democracy even at the price of submission to Persia. The first chapter of the long and squalid history of medism had been written. In after times, when the glories of Marathon and Salamis had obscured so much of the earlier history, it was easy for Athenian orators and historians to charge Aegina or Thebes with having set the example of seeking support from the Persian king. For all that, the fact remains, and it is a fact that should never be forgotten, that the first Greek statesman to invoke the intervention of Persia in the politics of Greece itself was none other than the founder of the Athenian democracy.

Cleisthenes had calculated that, when the envoys returned from their mission with the good news that the support of Persia had been secured, a Peloponnesian army under Cleomenes would be on the frontiers of Attica. As it proved, however, the danger had

[1] *E.g.* the negotiations preceding the Peace of Philocrates.

passed away when the envoys returned, and it was easy to de-
nounce their act of betrayal, when the force which had advanced
under the two Spartan kings, Cleomenes and Demaratus, as far
as Eleusis had retired into the Peloponnese without striking a
blow. But if the expedition had failed, it was not the fault of the
military dispositions of Cleomenes. His strategy was masterly.
Attica was to be invaded from three sides: from the Peloponnese,
from Boeotia, and from Euboea. While the Peloponnesian army
advanced from the Isthmus, the Boeotians were to invade Attica
from the north, and the Chalcidians were to cross the Euripus
and deliver their attack from that direction. For the hostility of
Chalcis an explanation may perhaps be found in the perennial
rivalry of that state with its neighbour Eretria, the ancient ally
of Athens. The hostility of Boeotia is easier to account for. Something like a dozen years earlier, in 519 B.C., the town of Plataea,
which stood on a spur of Cithaeron not far from the Athenian
border, had seceded from the Boeotian League, and had sought
an alliance with Sparta.The Spartans advised the Plataeans to
place themselves under the protection of Athens rather than that
of Sparta, with the result that Athens incurred the lasting enmity
of Thebes (p. 78).

In the presence of an invasion from three sides at once, the
Athenians could not hesitate as to the front on which the defence
must be made first. Herodotus' statement (v, 74) that they advanced against the Peloponnesian force which had already reached
Eleusis may reasonably be interpreted as meaning that the
Athenian army took up a defensive position on the ridge of
Mt Aegaleos, which separated the Pedion or Plain of Athens
from the Thriasian Plain in which Eleusis lay. Meanwhile dissensions had broken out in the Peloponnesian army, and Cleomenes found that he had a two-fold opposition to deal with, that
of the Corinthians, who refused to take any further part in the
invasion of Attica and drew off with their whole force, and that
of his colleague Demaratus, who supported the action of the
Corinthians. The rest of the Peloponnesian army, encouraged by
the quarrel of the two Spartan kings, were not slow in following
the example of the Corinthians. The invasion ended in a fiasco.

What was the motive of the Corinthians? The answer that is
commonly given is based on the support given by Corinth to
Athens in the Aeginetan War[1]. It is assumed that the motive
of Corinth was purely commercial, and it is argued that, as Aegina
was at the time a more serious rival to Corinthian trade than

[1] Herodotus vi, 89.

Athens, Corinth was unwilling to see the power of Athens weakened. It may well be doubted whether this reasoning is sound. The policy of Corinth was not always determined by commercial motives, and it is hazardous to conclude that either Corinth was hostile to Aegina, or Aegina hostile to Athens, in 507 B.C., because something like twenty years later (the true date of the Aeginetan War), Aegina was the rival of Corinth and the enemy of Athens. Still more hazardous is it to argue that the decision of the Corinthians in favour of Plataea in 519 B.C.[1] must have been prompted by the same desire to strengthen Athens against Aegina. A passage in Xenophon[2], which refers to the action of the Corinthians in refusing to support Lysander in his attempt to restore the oligarchy at Athens in 403 B.C., suggests a different explanation. Corinth was ready to support Sparta, so long as Spartan hegemony was confined to the Peloponnese, but Corinth had no wish to see Sparta supreme on both sides of the Isthmus. The mere geographical position of Corinth might seem to have marked her out as the exponent of the doctrine of a Balance of Power.

There still remained the Boeotian and Chalcidian armies to be dealt with. The former had occupied Hysiae, which although it lay outside Attica proper, was in the territory of Plataea and therefore in alliance with Athens, and had advanced as far as Oenoe, an important position well to the south of Mt Cithaeron. The Athenians, instead of attacking the Boeotian force, which was the nearer of the two, marched against the Chalcidians, in the direction of the Euripus. The movement had the result that was doubtless intended; it compelled the Boeotians to evacuate Attica and hasten with all speed to the support of the Chalcidians. No sooner did the Athenians get news of the retirement of the Boeotians than they turned and attacked them on their line of march, before they had effected a junction with their allies on the Euripus. It is probable that the Boeotians were taken by surprise; at any rate the victory of the Athenians was decisive, and no less than 700 prisoners were taken. The action must have been fought not far from the Euripus, for on the same day the Athenians crossed into Euboea, and there won a second and even more

---

[1] Herodotus VI, 108; see above, p. 78.

[2] *Hell.* II, iv, 30 (ἔπραττον δὲ ταῦτα, ὅτι ἐγίγνωσκον Λακεδαιμονίους βουλομένους τὴν τῶν Ἀθηναίων χώραν οἰκείαν καὶ πιστὴν ποιήσασθαι). 'They acted thus because they were convinced that it was the intention of the Spartans to reduce Attica to the position of a dependency on whose support they could rely.'

decisive victory, over the Chalcidians. That two such victories should have been won on the same day argues a commander of some military skill on the Athenian side; yet Herodotus cannot tell us his name. He must have held the office of Polemarch, but that his name should be unknown is a signal example of the fragmentary character of our knowledge, even of Athenian history at this period. It is clear from the narrative that the number of Chalcidian prisoners taken in the engagement was considerable, and they as well as those captured from the Boeotians were kept in prison at Athens until they were ransomed. The chains in which the prisoners had been fettered were preserved on the Acropolis, where they were seen by Herodotus, and from a tithe of the ransom the Athenians dedicated to the goddess Athena a bronze chariot. The victory was commemorated in an inscription which speaks of the gloomy iron chains in which the Athenians quenched the insolence of their foes, and of the bitter bondage in which they were kept fettered[1].

As we are told that their captivity lasted a long while, peace cannot have been concluded either with Chalcis or Thebes immediately after the double victory. It is probable that Chalcis was the first to make peace with Athens. The terms dictated to her were sufficiently harsh, as she had to cede to Athens the most fertile part of her territory, hitherto occupied by the Hippo- botae, the aristocracy of Chalcis. On this territory what was probably[2] the first cleruchy in Athenian history was planted; if Herodotus is to be believed, the cleruchs numbered four thousand. More will be said in a later volume to point out that the cleruchy was a colony of a peculiar kind, resembling the Roman *colonia* rather than the ordinary Greek *apoikia*; that the colonists, or cleruchs as they were called, retained their Athenian citizenship, and even their membership of tribe and deme; and that the cleruchy served a double purpose—the economic purpose of providing land for the poorer citizens, and the military purpose of establishing a garrison in a position of strategic importance. The cleruchy at Chalcis was to be the first of a long series of such settlements.

It would be difficult to over-estimate the consequences of these successes of the Athenians against so formidable a combination. The policy of Cleomenes had suffered shipwreck, and Athenian

---

[1] A fragment of this inscription was discovered on the Acropolis more than 30 years ago. Hicks and Hill, *op. cit.* 12.

[2] It is doubtful whether the early inscription relating to Salamis (Hicks and Hill, *op. cit.* 4) is really concerned with an Athenian cleruchy on the island, although this view has been widely held.

troops had proved their superiority in the field over two neighbouring states, Boeotia and Chalcis. It was these successes that
inspired the new-born democracy with self-confidence, and it was
their glamour which, as much as any other one factor, helps to
explain the century of democratic government which Athens was
to enjoy[1]. It must be admitted that the defeat of the Boeotians
is not easy to explain. The history of the next two centuries was
to prove the quality of the Boeotian infantry. We can only suppose
that at this epoch Thebes received half-hearted support from the
other towns of Boeotia. Boeotia was not so ready as Chalcis to
make peace with Athens, and Thebes was naturally anxious to
avenge her defeat. As no further help could be expected from
Sparta, it was to Aegina, at that time the first naval power in
Greece, that Thebes turned for help. An invasion from the north
combined with an attack by sea from Aegina on the south might
prove fatal to the new government at Athens. The means adopted
by Thebes to secure this end were characteristic of the age. An
oracle, couched in terms of appropriate obscurity, was obtained
from Delphi. The Thebans were told 'to seek the aid of those
nearest them[2].' It needed little ingenuity to interpret 'those
nearest them' in the light of the legend which made the nymphs
Thebe and Aegina sisters, and to base the appeal of Aegina on
the mythological kinship of the two states. The answer of Aegina
to this appeal is not less characteristic. Aegina had reasons of her
own for not wishing to precipitate a conflict with Athens. Her
answer to the appeal of Thebes was to send them the Aeacidae,
or sons of Aeacus, that is, the images of the tutelary deities of
the island. That this meant a refusal of the alliance can scarcely
be doubted. The diplomatic fictions of the modern world are
borrowed from Law; those of the sixth century B.C. were borrowed
from Religion. The grounds of the appeal were mythological;
the assistance sent belonged to the same order of ideas. It need
not surprise us that the Thebans sent back the Aeacidae with
the explanation that what they had asked was aid of a more
material nature[3]. A formal peace must have been concluded
between Athens and Boeotia not long after this, although it is
impossible to assign the precise date. It has been suggested that
the district of Oropus, which is subsequently found in the pos-

---

[1] The effects of the military successes of the French Revolutionary armies
afford an obvious parallel.

[2] Herodotus v, 79.

[3] Herodotus v, 80, 81. For a fuller discussion of the Aeginetan War
see below, chap. VIII.

session of Athens, although it never formed a part of Attica proper[1], may have been acquired by the terms of this peace.

A year or two later[2], Cleomenes made one more attempt to crush the Athenian democracy and to undo the work of Cleisthenes. This time he summoned a congress of the Peloponnesian League at Sparta, and laid before it the proposal to restore Hippias as tyrant of Athens. This meeting of the congress at Sparta was regarded by Grote as marking an epoch in the history of the Peloponnesian League. It is undoubtedly the first recorded meeting of the League, but we have no warrant for the assumption that it was the first meeting to be held. The action of Cleomenes implied a complete reversal of his previous policy in regard to Athens. It was Cleomenes who had expelled Hippias and who had lent his whole support to Isagoras, the leader of the aristocratic party. It is true that Herodotus attributes to Cleomenes on the occasion of his last invasion of Attica the design of setting up Isagoras as tyrant, but the word 'tyrant' need not be pressed; it may perhaps be used in a loose and rhetorical sense. Hippias, however, was to be restored as 'tyrant' in the strict and proper sense of the term, and no change of policy could well be more startling. The ultimate object of the proposed restoration of Hippias was, of course, identical with the ultimate object of the attempt to restore Isagoras. It was the aim of Cleomenes on the one occasion and on the other to establish at Athens a government subservient to Sparta. Once more the opposition was led by Corinth, and once more it was successful. Herodotus' statement that it was Sosicles (or Socles) who was the Corinthian spokesman may be accepted as true, but the long speech which he puts into his mouth is clearly the outcome of the historian's imagination. The proposal was rejected. In any case, it could have found little favour with the representatives of the philo-Laconian oligarchies which were in power in the great majority of the states included in the League. It looked as if the failure of Cleomenes' policy was now irretrievable. The Athenian democracy could at length breathe freely.

V. THE ARGIVE WAR

Cleomenes laid the lesson of his failure to heart. It was idle for him to attempt to extend the hegemony of Sparta to Greece north of the Isthmus so long as Sparta was not mistress in her

---

[1] Oropus was not one of the Athenian demes, nor included in any deme.

[2] Probably about 504 B.C.; but a precise chronology of the period between the Reform of Cleisthenes and the Ionic Revolt cannot be attempted.

own house; so long, that is, as there was a rival claimant for the hegemony of the Peloponnese itself. Sparta had wrested from Argos the border district of Cynuria half a century before this (vol. III, p. 569), but Argos still cherished the memory of her ancient supremacy, and she was still a possible head of an anti-Laconian confederacy. In view of the open threat of Corinthian secession to Argos at the Congress of 432 B.C. on the eve of the Peloponnesian War, and of the intrigues of Corinth to form an anti-Laconian alliance after the Peace of Nicias, it is tempting to explain the success of her opposition to the policy of Cleomenes, in the field at Eleusis as well as in the Council Chamber at Sparta, by the presence in the Peloponnese of a rival claimant to the hegemony. To Cleomenes it was evident that the destruction of the power of Argos was the indispensable condition of the recognition of Spartan supremacy in Greece as a whole. But it was not enough that Argos should be crushed; she must be crushed by a purely Spartan army. Sparta must prove to her Peloponnesian allies that she could achieve her object without their aid.

It is here assumed that the date of Cleomenes' invasion of Argos is *c.* 494 B.C. As happens so frequently in the history of Greece, and that not merely in centuries earlier than the fifth, our whole view of the meaning of an event turns on the determination of its date. Two dates have been suggested for the Argive War— *c.* 520 and *c.* 494 B.C.[1], but fortunately there can be little doubt as to which is to be preferred[2]. The only argument for the earlier date that carries any weight is the statement of Pausanias that Cleomenes' invasion of Argos was at the beginning of his reign[3]. Against this statement of Pausanias are to be set two arguments, each in its way conclusive. The first of these is based on Herodotus' statement (VI, 19, 77) that the oracle given from Delphi to the Argives when the war with Sparta was impending was given at the same time and on the same occasion as an oracle to Miletus which, on grounds of internal evidence, can only be

[1] To Grote belongs the credit of establishing the true date of the Argive War.

[2] Our two principal authorities for the Argive War are Herodotus VI, 76–82 and Pausanias II, xx, 8–10 and III, iv, 1. The arguments for either date are summarized in How and Wells, *Commentary on Herodotus*, App. XVII, 3. In questions of this nature, however, the arguments should be weighed rather than counted.

[3] His statement, however, would have more authority had it occurred in the passage in Book II (the *Corinthiaca*) which is mainly derived from an Argive source. The passage in Book III in which it is found is a mere précis of Herodotus' narrative.

dated to the interval between the Battle of Lade and the Fall of Miletus (c. 494 B.C.). Herodotus' statement has been called in question, but an oracle given on the same occasion to different states (ἐπίκοινον χρηστήριον) is unique in the records of the Delphic Oracle, and inventors are prone to invent not the unique but the commonplace. The second argument is derived from the excuse pleaded by the Argives for their neutrality at the time of the invasion of Xerxes, that their defeat by Cleomenes had been recent[1]. While 494 B.C. may fairly be called recent from the point of view of 481 B.C., it is incredible that the Argives could have alleged as an excuse the loss of life incurred in a defeat which had occurred forty years before.

It was evident that the whole effort of Sparta must be concentrated on the conflict with Argos, which was to determine the position of Sparta in the Greek world. Hence the appeal (498 B.C.) of Aristagoras met with no response. In view of the previous assertion of Spartan claims in Ionia, it might have been expected that Sparta would have given some support to the cause of the Eastern Greeks; but to have sent Spartan troops across the seas when the issue at home was so soon to be decided would have been little short of suicidal. See p. 219 sq.

Almost all would admit that Herodotus is not seen at his best as a military historian. Of the art of war and of the principles of strategy he has little understanding. Nowhere is this seen more clearly than in his account of Cleomenes' invasion of the Argive territory and of the victory of Sepeia. Yet the data recorded by Herodotus enable us to arrive at some tolerably certain conclusions. The army which Cleomenes commanded was a purely Lacedaemonian force; it is clear that no contingents from the other Peloponnesian states were engaged[2]. The direct route to Argos ran up the valley of the Oenus to Sellasia; from this point it led across the mountainous district of Cynuria, and reached the sea at Thyrea, whence it followed the coast of the Argolic Gulf to Argos itself. It was by this route that Cleomenes advanced as far as the river Erasinus, about three miles from the city of Argos. On the pretext that the omens were unfavourable for the passage of the stream, he led his troops back again to Thyrea, whence he shipped them across the Gulf to Nauplia. Having landed them here, he advanced on Argos as far as Tiryns, about four or five miles from Argos. The fact that he had collected a fleet composed of

---

[1] Herodotus VII, 148, νεωστί.

[2] Herodotus VI, 76, ad init. (Σπαρτιήτας ἄγων) compared with VI, 81, ad init. (τὴν μὲν πλέω στρατιὴν ἀπῆκε ἀπιέναι ἐς Σπάρτην).

Aeginetan and Sicyonian vessels which lay in readiness at Thyrea for the transport of his troops across the Gulf to Nauplia[1] proves conclusively that we are dealing with a carefully thought out plan of campaign, and that the advance to the Erasinus was a mere feint, designed to mislead the Argives as to the direction from which his real attack would be delivered.

The battle between the two armies was fought at a place called Sepeia in the neighbourhood of Tiryns. The victory won by Cleomenes was one of the most decisive recorded in the history of Greece, and one of the most momentous in its consequences. The total loss of the Argives is put by Herodotus (VII, 148) at 6000; an extraordinarily high number according to Greek standards. Argos itself escaped capture, and Cleomenes on his return home was brought to trial by the ephors for his failure to take the city. It may be that he distrusted the skill of the Spartans in siege operations; it is more probable that it was part of his policy to spare the city. It may be conjectured that his policy differed from that of the ephors. Their policy was inspired by blind insensate hate; it aimed at the destruction of the city and the incorporation of its territory in that of Sparta. Cleomenes realised that Sparta stood to gain more by having as its neighbour an enfeebled Argos, governed by a philo-Laconian oligarchy, than by the capture and destruction of the city[2]. It is certain that the destruction of Argos would have been fatal to the moral ascendancy of Sparta in the Greek world[3]. Sepeia is in one respect unique in Greek warfare down to the Persian Wars. We have been taught in the modern world to regard victory in the field as a means to an end, that end being the destruction of the enemy's force. To the Greeks a battle was in the nature of a duel; it was an *agōn*, in which honour was satisfied, and the pursuit ceased, when the enemy acknowledged defeat by asking for a truce for the burial of his dead. At Sepeia the Argive army was annihilated, and Argos, as a military power, put out of action for a generation. Upon the position of Sparta, both in the Peloponnese and in the rest of Greece, the effects of the victory were immediate. All opposition to Sparta within the Peloponnesian League died down, and three or four years later Athens in her appeal against Aegina virtually conceded to Sparta a supremacy in the Greek political system as great as any that Sparta had ever claimed

[1] Herodotus VI, 92.

[2] Cf. the parallel case of Agis in 418 B.C.

[3] The destruction of Thebes was the greatest political blunder of which Alexander was guilty.

for herself (p. 259). The acquittal of Cleomenes when brought to trial by the ephors proved that his policy had commended itself to the public opinion of Sparta. It was Cleomenes—not the ephors—who governed now.

VI. POLITICAL PARTIES AT ATHENS FROM THE REFORM OF CLEISTHENES TO THE YEAR 491 B.C.

To write a history of political parties at Athens, and of the relations of the party leaders to one another, is a task of some difficulty. Our available data are scanty, and Herodotus, our primary authority for these years, shows little insight into the political situation of each successive phase, and it may be surmised that the traditions which he follows were far from impartial. In any attempt to solve the problems which are presented to us, there are certain considerations which must be kept in view. In the first place we must be on our guard against anachronisms. On the one hand, we have no right to assume that the local factions of the Coast, the Plain, and the Hill-country, which were the determining factor in Athenian politics in the middle of the sixth century B.C. had the same importance at the beginning of the next century; on the other, it must be remembered that the rivalry of the Clans (γένη) is a factor of far more importance than was the case fifty years later. Secondly, it is impossible to understand the internal politics of Athens apart from the foreign relations of the state. Throughout this period we must keep our eyes fixed on the far side of the Aegean. When the vital question of the hour is a question of foreign policy, when the very existence of a nation is at stake, political combinations may be effected which would be inconceivable at other times and in other circumstances.

It has been argued above that Cleisthenes must bear the full responsibility for the embassy to Sardes, and for the instructions given to the envoys (see above, p. 157). The version of the story which we have in Herodotus lays stress on the disgrace of the envoys. His language is vague. We should like to know what lies behind the phrase 'They fell into deep disgrace.' Were they fined, or exiled, or put to death? Still more should we like to know what were the consequences for Cleisthenes himself. He is said to have been the first victim of his law of ostracism[1], but the authority

---

[1] Aelian, *Var. Hist.* XIII, 24.

for this is late and poor; yet the passage in Herodotus looks like a deliberate attempt to conceal the disgrace of the leader of the Alcmaeonid party, and few things in Athenian history are more inexplicable than the sudden disappearance of Cleisthenes from the scene. Two or three years later a second embassy was sent to Sardes[1], after the failure of Cleomenes to induce the Congress of the Peloponnesian League to restore the tyranny at Athens. Hippias had retired to Sigeum, on the Asiatic side of the entrance to the Hellespont, and was sparing no effort to secure the support of Artaphrenes, the satrap at Sardes. The menace to Athens was grave, and the answer that the envoys received was in the form of an ultimatum; Hippias must be restored. The story as told by Herodotus presents great difficulties. A couple of years before, the Athenian Assembly had repudiated the action of the envoys in giving earth and water to Darius. It is hard to conceive of a more deliberate affront to the majesty of the Great King. How could the Athenian people imagine that, under these circumstances, its efforts to detach Persia from the cause of Hippias would be successful? Or how could the envoys have obtained an audience of the satrap, unless they were empowered to offer earth and water? The return of the embassy with the Persian ultimatum marks a stage in the history of political parties at Athens. Up to this point, the Alcmaeonidae might be called the medizing party, in the sense that they were prepared to accept the intervention of Persia, if the democracy could thereby be secured. Henceforward there could be but one party at Athens which in the strict and proper sense of the term deserved to be called 'the Medizers'—the party of Hippias. For the Alcmaeonidae to have accepted Persian intervention on Persian terms would have been to commit political suicide, for the Persian terms now meant the restoration of the tyranny. The curtain falls, and for the next half dozen years we are not vouchsafed so much as a glimpse of the internal history of Athens.

It is not until the embassy of Aristagoras in 498 B.C. that the curtain is once more raised (p. 220). There are three facts to be taken into account in this connection. A fleet is sent to the aid of the Ionians; it consists of only 20 vessels; and it is recalled on the first reverse to the cause of the insurgents. Evidently, parties in the Assembly are so nicely balanced that while the one side has a majority for sending help, the other side succeeds in cutting down the number of vessels, while the retreat from Sardes and the defeat at Ephesus are sufficient to secure the triumph of

[1] Herodotus v, 96.

the anti-Ionian party. The *fundamentum divisionis* is the Ionian
question; the two alternatives presented to the Assembly were the
sending, or refusing, aid to Aristagoras. But which of the parties
that have been distinguished above voted for this alternative or
that? There can be no question as to the attitude of the Peisistratid
faction; it must have voted against, and not for the sending of
help to the Ionians. But yet it cannot have constituted so large a
proportion of the citizen body that, without the aid of any other
party, it could procure both the reduction in the number of the
vessels and the recall of the fleet. Clearly there was a coalition,
and the only party with whom common action on this question
of foreign policy can be assumed is that of the Alcmaeonidae.
Nothing is more probable than that the party which had originally
invited the intervention of Persia, and which was in such close
touch with Sardes, should deprecate action which could only tend
to exasperate the Persian Court. On the other side must have been
found the party once led by Isagoras, the party of the aristocrats—
the old allies of Sparta and the bitter enemies alike of the Peisistratidae and the Alcmaeonidae.

Two years later, in the spring of 496 B.C., the anti-Ionian party
is strong enough to carry its candidate, Hipparchus the son of
Charmus, a cousin of Hippias, in the election to the archonship,
which is still the chief executive office in the state. The evidence
of a coalition is here irresistible. Can it seriously be maintained
that the supporters of the exiled tyrant, fourteen years after the
fall of the dynasty, could have carried their candidate by the mere
votes of their own party? Once more the Alcmaeonidae must
have felt themselves constrained to fall into line with their old
rivals. But the coalition in itself hardly explains a success so surprising. In order to understand it, the fortunes of the Ionic Revolt
must be taken into account. By the beginning of 496 B.C. the
insurrection in Cyprus had been crushed; Persian columns were
advancing down the river valleys to the shores of the Propontis
and Aegean; the Hellespontine region was being reduced, and
two of the cities on the western coast, Cyme and Clazomenae, had
been recovered. Aristagoras had fallen in Thrace, and the ultimate
issue of the revolt was no longer doubtful (p. 223 *sq.*). To many
at Athens who were attached neither to the Peisistratid nor to the
Alcmaeonid faction it may well have seemed that the sending of
the twenty ships to the aid of the Ionians had been a gigantic
blunder, and that the only course open to Athens was to make
the best terms that she could with Persia. Within the next two
years two events had happened, the defeat of the Ionian fleet at

Lade and the reduction of Miletus, the last stronghold of the insurgents, which combined to produce a profound revulsion of feeling at Athens, and a complete change of policy. Grote has aptly compared the sentiment excited throughout the Greek world by the fate of Miletus to the thrill of horror which ran through Protestant Europe on the news of the Sack of Magdeburg by Tilly in the Thirty Years' War. Nowhere can this sentiment have been more intense than at Athens.

At this crisis a new party emerges into view in Athenian politics, and a new party leader is introduced to us. It is the first appearance on the scene of Themistocles, one of the two most famous statesmen in Athenian history. Themistocles was a *novus homo*; it was even said that he was of foreign origin on his mother's side. The interests for which he worked were those of the town rather than of the country—of the trading and industrial classes, of those above all who 'occupied their business in great waters.' The future of Athens to which he looked was its future as a commercial and maritime power. The party which he had gathered round him must have been largely drawn from the very class to which Cleisthenes appealed. Themistocles must have succeeded in detaching from the party of the Alcmaeonidae a large section of the newly enfranchised citizens by the aid of whose votes Cleisthenes had carried his reforms. It may well have been the medizing policy of Cleisthenes that cost his party the support of this interest. If the party was in existence at the time of the embassy of Aristagoras, it cannot be doubted that Themistocles would have been one of the strongest supporters of the Ionian cause. In the year 493 B.C. he was elected archon[1], and during his term of office, from midsummer 493 B.C. to midsummer 492 B.C., he planned, and partly carried out, the creation of a new naval harbour at the Piraeus, which was to take the place of the open roadstead at Phalerum, which had hitherto sufficed for the needs of the Athenian fleet.

To the same year 493 B.C. are almost certainly to be assigned two other events of first-rate importance in their bearing on the party politics of Athens at this period—the first trial of Miltiades

---

[1] That there were two archons of this name, an unknown Themistocles in 493 B.C. and the famous one in 482 B.C., and that the little Themistocles should have held the office when it was all-important and the great Themistocles when it was unimportant, is a hypothesis for which there is little to be said. What is now certain is that the addition of the 200 (or 100) vessels to the Athenian navy belongs, not to the archonship of Themistocles, but to that of Nicomedes (Arist. *Const. of Athens*, XXII, 7).

and the prosecution of the poet Phrynichus for the production of his tragedy, the *Sack of Miletus*. It was apparently in this year that Miltiades arrived in Athens on his flight from the Thracian Chersonese, and immediately on his return he was brought to trial 'by his enemies' before a Heliastic Court, on the charge of having been a tyrant in the Chersonese. It may be presumed that 'his enemies' were identical with his prosecutors in his second trial after the Parian expedition; that is, that they were the Alcmaeonidae, the great rivals of the Clan of the Philaidae of which Miltiades was the head. During his absence in the Chersonese the Philaidae must have counted for little at Athens. But their influence was likely to revive with the return of their leader, and the Alcmaeonidae were resolved to achieve his political ruin before he became dangerous. The charge on which he was brought to trial implies that there was an Athenian colony and Athenian citizens somewhere in the Chersonese, presumably at Sestos. It cannot have been an offence known to the Athenian law for an individual Athenian to exercise despotic authority over barbarians; there must have been Athenian citizens in the Chersonese whose rights had been impaired by the rule of Miltiades.

The charge was almost certainly well-founded, for the narrative in Herodotus[1], while it insists on the enmity between the house of Miltiades and that of Peisistratus, discloses the fact that Miltiades himself was sent out to the Chersonese by the Peisistratidae in a vessel of war. He must, therefore, in the first instance, have ruled there as the deputy of the tyrants. He was now a fugitive from the power of Persia, and his impeachment must have been supported by the partisans of Hippias, by whom he would be viewed as a renegade. Yet he was acquitted, and acquitted at the very moment when the influence of Themistocles was at its height. Can it be doubted that, if Themistocles had used his influence against Miltiades, the latter would have been condemned? Is it not then a certain inference that in the presence of the Persian menace Themistocles, although the leader of the popular party, made common cause with Miltiades, the leader of the aristocratic party[2], in much the same way as in the presence of the Irish menace, Mr Chamberlain, the author of the 'unauthorized programme,' made common cause with Lord Salisbury, the Tory chief, or as in the presence of the German menace in 1914, the leader of the Belgian Socialists made common cause with the leader of the Catholics? Themistocles can hardly have

---

[1] vi, 35, 36, 39, 103, 104; vi, 39 is the important passage.
[2] Cf. Aristotle, *Const. of Athens*, xxviii, 2.

failed to see in Miltiades a heaven-sent general against the Persians[1].

It is almost certain, too, that in the production of Phrynichus' drama we may trace the hand of Themistocles. Who so likely as he, 'who was of all men the best able to extemporize the right thing to be done[2],' to hit upon the idea of employing the tragic stage for the purposes of political propaganda? The object of the play can only have been to bring home to an Athenian audience the guilt of those who were responsible for the withdrawal of the Athenian ships and the abandonment of the Ionian cause. The fact recorded by Plutarch (*Themistocles*, 5) that Themistocles in the year 476–5 B.C. dedicated a tablet to commemorate his having acted as Chorēgus to Phrynichus, when the latter was awarded the prize in the tragic contest, affords more than a presumption of some connection between the statesman and the dramatist. The prosecution must have proceeded from the leaders of the anti-Ionian parties. Possibly the charge was one of impiety, on the ground that a contemporary event had been chosen as the subject of the play in place of one taken from myth or legend, as was prescribed by immemorial usage. If this conjecture is correct, we have in the prosecution of Phrynichus an anticipation of the attacks upon Pheidias and Anaxagoras which were designed to undermine the ascendancy of Pericles. The prosecution was so far successful that Phrynichus was fined 1000 drachmae, and the representation of the play upon the stage was forbidden for the future; it failed, however, to affect the popularity of Themistocles. That he should have carried his proposal for the new naval base at the Piraeus, and that he should have been able to make some progress with the scheme, prove that his influence remained undiminished until he laid down office in the middle of the year 492 B.C.

[1] For a different interpretation of these proceedings see below p. 231 *sq.*
[2] Thucydides I, 138.

CHAPTER VII

THE REIGN OF DARIUS

I. THE MAGIAN PRETENDER

WE have now to go back and follow the steps by which Darius had made himself king (p. 23 *sq.*). Cambyses had left Egypt three years after he entered it, not having returned to Persia in the interval. In his long absence disaffection developed and gathered around the name of the very brother whom he had had slain secretly before leaving home. A Magian, Gaumata by name, personating Bardes (Bardiya, Smerdis), the king's brother, became king within the life-time of Cambyses. Darius on the Behistun inscription merely records the main facts:

When Cambyses slew Bardiya it was not known to the people that Bardiya was slain: afterwards Cambyses went to Egypt: when Cambyses had departed into Egypt the people became hostile...afterwards there was a certain man, a Magian, Gaumata by name...he lied to the people (saying) 'I am Bardiya the son of Cyrus, brother of Cambyses': afterwards all the peoples rose in revolt, and from Cambyses they went over to him, both Persia and Media, and the other provinces: he seized on the kingdom... afterwards Cambyses died. (See Chronological Note 2.)

Where Cambyses died Darius does not record, nor precisely when, but only that the revolt broke out while Cambyses was in Egypt, and that Bardiya became king before Cambyses' death. According to Herodotus, Cambyses died at Ecbatana in Syria some weeks after the heralds of Bardiya, on their way to Egypt to demand of the army its allegiance to Bardiya, had met him there, returning with his army. Other Greek accounts agree that Cambyses died on his way back from Egypt to Persia, but differ as to the place, one naming Babylon, another Damascus. Nor is it clear how much, if anything, Cambyses knew of the development of disaffection at home before he left Egypt, nor certain that, on learning how far the revolt had gone, he committed suicide: the phrase used by Darius permits but scarcely requires this interpretation, and the story of Herodotus ascribes his death to accident.

Cambyses died early in the eighth year of his reign, *i.e.* in the spring of 522 B.C., seven years and five months (according to Herodotus) after his accession in the autumn of 529 B.C. It is

probable that the latest tablet of Cambyses' reign is that dated
the 23rd day of the first month (March-April) of his eighth year,
and therefore that he died, or at least ceased to be regarded in
Babylon as king, in the spring of that year.

Darius names as the place where the pretender raised the revolt
Paishiyāuvādā, which cannot with any certainty be identified.
Whether or not it lay in the very country from which the Achaemenidae sprang—it has even been identified by some with Pasargadae—it is certain that Persia no less than Media and the other
provinces fell away from Cambyses; but in doing so the Persians
did not intend to withdraw their support from the house of Cyrus.
In accepting the claims of Bardiya they believed that they were
transferring their allegiance from Cambyses, who had forfeited
his claim to the affection with which they had regarded his father
by his despotic government, to another son of Cyrus. And their
belief has been shared by some modern scholars who have argued
that the story of the murder of Bardiya by Cambyses rests only
on the word of Darius, who is himself rather to be regarded as
a pretender, and who to make good his claim constructed for
himself a fictitious genealogy, tracing back his descent to Teispes,
an ancestor of Cyrus as well as supposititiously of himself (cf.
p. 5 above). Yet it is hardly probable that, if this was really the
case, no suggestion of the truth should have maintained itself
in circulation long enough to have found a place in the Greek
stories about Darius; and it may be inferred that the Persians
themselves gave up the belief that the man whom Darius calls
Gaumata was the son of Cyrus, for not long after his death their
credulity fastened on another person, and they accepted a Persian
of the name of Vahyazdāta as Bardiya, the son of Cyrus.

But while the Persians accepted this first pretender as a Persian,
it does not follow that he actually was so; indeed Darius and the
stories told by the Greek writers agree that he was a Magian,
and therefore a Mede. Since he can scarcely have given himself
out in Persia as a Persian, and in Media as a Mede, his claim
to the throne cannot have been supported, as it would otherwise
have been natural to suspect, by any wide Median national
reaction against a Persian ruling family. At the same time, it is
probable enough that Gaumata relied on a certain number of
Median nobles, or perhaps rather of Median priests and Magi,
who were privy to his secret, and sought by his means to recover
the former supremacy of their nation or caste. Yet, at all events,
within the space of his brief reign, Gaumata was probably unable
to carry through any great substitution of Median for Persian

holders of high office: it is known at least that, for example,
Hystaspes, the kinsman of Cyrus and father of Darius, remained
under him satrap of Parthia and Hyrcania.

Two measures of Gaumata, one recorded by Herodotus, the
other by Darius on the Behistun inscription, indicate a wider and
not merely a sectional policy. According to Herodotus (III, 67),
he signalized his accession to the throne by proclaiming to all
peoples within his realm freedom for three years from military
service and from tribute. The intention of this is sufficiently
obvious: the pretender seeks to secure support by easing the
burdens which the policy of conquest pursued by Cambyses had
imposed. More difficult to elucidate fully is the religious policy
of Gaumata. Darius asserts that Gaumata destroyed the sanctuaries or temples (āyadanā, Bab. bitāti sha ilāni, houses of the
gods), and that Darius restored them. The one thing that is clear
is that Gaumata and Darius pursued two contrary religious
policies: what precisely the temples destroyed by the one and
restored by the other were is uncertain, and consequently whether
Gaumata or Darius was the greater innovator. Gaumata is so far
an innovator that he destroys existing temples, but if these were
the temples of a new faith, or the temples of peoples subject to
the Persian empire restored by Darius out of regard to a new
principle of toleration not native to the Persian mind, the destroyer rather than the restorer may have appealed more directly
to deep-lying conservative feeling[1].

Gaumata deceived the Persians no less than other peoples of
the empire; and he obtained from them the recognition of his
right to rule, making in return certain concessions to Persian
feeling. Yet, if a statement of Herodotus is to be accepted, 'when
he died' (in Sikayauvatish, in the Median province of Nisāya, as
Darius records), for the great benefits which he had done to all
his subjects, 'he was lamented by all in Asia except the Persians
themselves.' Moreover, Darius himself acknowledges the extent
of Gaumata's hold on the people, though he ascribes it naturally
to other reasons: 'there was no man, Persian, or Median, or one
of our family, who could deprive Gaumata of the kingdom: the
people feared him for his tyranny...no one dared to say anything
against Gaumata until I came.' Certain it is that it was on the
Persians, especially the Persian nobility, that Darius had to rely
in making good his claim to the throne to which Cambyses, dying
childless, had left no direct heir. Persians one and all, as Darius
expressly states in each case, were the six men who were with

[1] For the part played in this by a religious movement, see below, p. 210.

him when he slew Gaumata; and the same six—Intaphrenes, Otanes, Gobryas, Hydarnes, Megabyxos, Ardumanish—assisted him in the struggles that followed; and for this their families are commended by Darius to the favour of his successors.

With the death of Gaumata in the autumn of 522, Darius acceded to the throne of Cyrus and Cambyses. Darius himself with all clearness admits that Gaumata had actually though illegitimately been king, and that his own accession took place only after Gaumata's death: 'I with few men slew Gaumata the Magian, and what foremost men were his allies...in Media...I smote him; I took his kingdom from him; by the grace of Ahura-Mazda I am king; Ahura-Mazda gave me the kingdom; the kingdom which had been taken away from our family, this I put in its place.' Why Ahura-Mazda promoted the son rather than his father Hystaspes, whose connection with Cyrus was the nearer, Darius does not say; but it is easy to see that the greater skill and readier initiative of Darius gave him the crown: his father continued under him a loyal satrap of Parthia.

But Darius, even after overcoming and slaying Gaumata, obtained a kingdom which at once threatened to fall asunder. No successor to Gaumata ever claimed, as he had done, the whole empire; but simultaneously or in rapid succession men arose, some of them claiming to be members of former ruling families, and endeavoured to establish an independent sovereignty each in his own part of the empire. During the first year or two of his reign Darius was fully engaged in suppressing these sectional but formidable revolts, and so preventing his empire from falling to pieces. In his great inscription at Behistun he describes the several campaigns in which he, personally, or his generals were engaged. He accurately dates the main events by the day of the month, but in no case names a year; but it can be concluded that all the events fall in the five months of his accession year and the first year of his reign. (See Chronological Note 3.)

Darius was first of all, and, as he states, at the time when he slew Gaumata, faced by two revolts—one in Susiana, the seat of the earliest kingdom of Cyrus, and one in Babylon. In Susiana, Ashina (the Persian form is Atrina), the son of Upadaranma claimed, though on what grounds is not stated, to be king of the province, and was recognised as such by the Susians. But his reign was quite brief: Darius sent an army which suppressed the revolt and brought Ashina bound to Darius who slew him. Much more serious was the Babylonian revolt, and with this Darius dealt in person. The Babylonians had acknowledged the claims

of the would-be Persian Gaumata, but on his death they made
an effort to recover their independence, and accepted as king a
Babylonian of the name of Nidintu-Bel, who reigned under the
name of Nebuchadrezzar the son of Nabonidus, the last king of
Babylon before Cyrus.

Whether Nidintu-Bel actually deceived the Babylonians as
Darius asserts, or whether one of themselves, chosen by the
Babylonians, assumed as his kingly name the name of the last
famous and successful king of Babylon, and by a legal fiction
reigned as the son of Nabonidus, and therefore legitimate heir to
the Babylonian throne, must be left undetermined: in either case
he secured the allegiance of the entire Babylonian people. Some
half-dozen tablets survive dated from the 17th day of the seventh
month to the 21st day of the ninth month (*i.e.* Oct.-Dec. 522)
of the year of his accession. In the latter month Darius set out
with his army from Media, where he had tarried for some two
months after slaying Gaumata, for Babylon. Nidintu-Bel proceeded from Babylon to the Tigris and attempted to dispute the
passage of the river with Darius. But in vain: on the 26th day of
the ninth month (Nov.-Dec.) Darius defeated Nidintu-Bel at the
Tigris, and four days later at the Euphrates. Nidintu-Bel escaped
with his cavalry to Babylon. The city made some resistance,
though, in spite of Herodotus who speaks of a siege lasting nearly
two years, it was probably not a long one; with the city Nidintu-
Bel was captured and then slain and, as early as the eleventh
month of his accession year (Jan.-Feb. 521), as Babylonian tablets
testify, Darius was recognized in the city as king.

II. THE WINNING OF THE EMPIRE

For a few months Darius remained at Babylon, and during this
period further widespread revolts occurred. Darius mentions first,
though it is not clear that it actually broke out first, a second and
apparently also brief revolt of Susiana. The rebel king on this
occasion was Martiya, a resident in the Persian town of Kuganakā,
who as king in Susiana assumed the name of Imanish. Darius set
out for Susiana, but before he arrived the Susians themselves slew
Martiya.

News of the far more serious revolt of Media must have reached
Darius almost as soon as he reached Babylon, for the first battle
against the rebels was fought within a month of Darius's defeat
of Nidintu-Bel at the Euphrates; and consequently the revolt
itself must have broken out as soon as Darius, after slaying Gau-

mata, left Media for Babylon. The leader of this revolt, who for some time reigned as king in Media, was Fravartish (?Phraortes). He assumed the name of Khshathrita, and claimed to be of the family of Cyaxares, that is, of the old Median royal family that had been displaced by Cyrus. Thus, unlike Gaumata, he was able to appeal to all the Medes as a Mede himself and a lawful and rightful ruler against the attempt of Persia to continue, under a new dynasty, its dominion over Media. And even beyond the bounds of Media Fravartish obtained recognition. Darius states that 'Parthia and Hyrcania...declared allegiance to Fravartish.' Possibly also Armenia did the same: Darius interweaves his account of the campaign in Armenia with that of his operations against Media, and gives no indication of any native or independent Armenian claimant to the throne. Alternatively it may be conjectured that in Armenia as in Media the revolt was entirely national in character, and that the two movements, though they synchronized, were not directed towards the same end. But this view is difficult to maintain unless the entire period of the revolts extended over more than seventeen months and ran on into at least the third year of Darius.

Of these operations against Media and Armenia, if rightly regarded as nearly synchronous, those against Armenia began first. After the defeat of Nidintu-Bel at the Euphrates, but before the capture of Babylon, Darius despatched an army under the Persian Vaumisa to Armenia. The rebels advanced south to meet the Persian army, and an engagement took place at Izzila in Assyria (January, 521). The Armenians were defeated and retreated to their own country; and four and a half months later (May, 521) they were again defeated by the same general at Autiyāra in Armenia. But the Armenian resistance had been severe, and was not quashed by Vaumisa unaided. Some time, perhaps as much as two or three months after Vaumisa had set out, Darius despatched another army to Armenia under Dādarshi, an Armenian faithful to Darius; and in rapid succession this army fought three engagements in Armenia, at Zuzza, Tigra and Uyamā respectively. Both generals then awaited in Armenia Darius's arrival in Media. The operations thus extended over five months, if Vaumisa's departure is correctly fixed before, though it is related after, that of Dadarshi. This however is not quite certain. It is possible that Vaumisa set out *after* Dadarshi, and in that case the resistance of the Armenians took more than twelve months to quell—from the beginning of the month of Thuravahara (May) in one year (521), at the earliest, to the end of the same month in the next year.

Within a few days of entering Babylon, and within a week or two of the departure of the first army to Armenia, Darius received news of the revolt in Media: the Persian and Median army still left with him was, as Darius expressly states, but small; yet from this he detached a force which he sent under the command of the Persian Hydarnes to Media. Hydarnes fought with the Medes at Marush, in, but not far within, Media in January, 521. The Persians claimed a victory, but it was apparently ineffective. Hydarnes was unable to push on to Ecbatana the capital, but awaited Darius's arrival in the region of Kampada, well to the west.

At some time between May and September in the same year (521) Darius himself left Babylon for Media. Fravartish advanced to meet Darius, offered battle at Kundur, and was defeated. Fravartish with a few of his horsemen fled to Ragā (Ragae) in eastern Media, pursued by Darius's army. Darius himself appears to have captured Ecbatana and to have remained there till the pursuers captured Fravartish. The captive pretender was brought to Darius at Ecbatana, mutilated and slain.

With the fall and death of Fravartish the Median resistance was broken. Hyrcania and Parthia still called for settlement. Darius indeed claims that his father Hystaspes obtained a decisive victory over the rebels, shortly after they had declared for Fravartish, at Vishpauzātish in Parthia on the 22nd of Viyakhna (i.e. in March, 521). Hystaspes, it is true, appears to have maintained his position in Parthia, yet only with difficulty, and the revolt was not really brought under till Darius months later was able to send him reinforcements. After Darius had secured the whole of Media up to Ragae in the extreme east, from that town he despatched an army to assist Hystaspes. Thus reinforced, Hystaspes decisively defeated the rebels at Patigrabana in Parthia (probably in April, 520).

Farther east in the Bactrian province of Margush (Margiana), an independent rebellion led by one Frāda, a Margian, was suppressed by the Persian satrap of Bactria, Dadarshi, the decisive battle being fought in December, 521. No date is mentioned in connection with the revolt in Sagartia, where the Sagartian Citrantakhma claimed the throne of Sagartia as a member of the family of Cyaxares. He was captured, mutilated and at Arbela in Assyria put to death.

After the outbreak of Media, but before Darius himself left Babylon to deal with it in person, Persia, or perhaps in particular the nomadic tribes of Persia, renounced allegiance to him and accepted as king Vahyazdāta of Tārava in the Persian province of

Yautiyā (Οὔτιοι), who, like Gaumata before him, claimed to be Bardiya son of Cyrus. Vahyazdāta maintained his position in Persia for some months and attempted to establish his power also in the far eastern province of Arachosia on the borders of India. Dividing his forces so as to take part with him to Media, Darius despatched the rest under a Persian general, Artavardiya, to Persia. Here (in May, 521) he defeated the rebels at Rakhā. Vahyazdāta retreated to Paishiyāuvādā, where Gaumata had formerly raised the standard of revolt; and it was probably as late as in April, 520, that he was defeated again, captured and slain. In the interval the army sent by Vahyazdāta into Arachosia was defeated by Vivāna, the Persian satrap of the province in December, 521, and seven weeks later it was again defeated, its leaders being put to death.

After Darius had left Babylon in the summer of 521, and while he was still engaged both with the Median and the Persian revolts, the Babylonians made a second attempt to regain their independence of Persia, though curiously enough on this occasion the king who reigned for a month or two was an Armenian. Like Nidintu-Bel before him, this Armenian, Arakha by name, took the style of Nebuchadrezzar son of Nabonidus, and indeed his reign was perhaps accounted a continuation of Nidintu-Bel's: tablets apparently dated from his reign exist for the sixth and seventh months of his first year, but none for this accession year. Darius detached a force under a Persian general Intaphrenes, who captured Arakha (probably in November) and put him to death.

Media, Armenia, Persia—these with Babylon were the countries that offered to Darius the most obstinate resistance: Persian disputed with Persian the succession to Cyrus and Cambyses; the Medes attempted to recover from their fellow-Iranians the supremacy of which Cyrus had deprived them; the more distantly related Armenians sided with the Medes or attempted independence on their own account. Babylon alone of the three non-Iranian empires which together with Media had been conquered and united with the Persian empire showed active opposition to Persia and efforts to re-establish a native dynasty. Lydia and Egypt showed no opposition to the Persian satraps that governed them; Phoenicia and Syria remained quiet (cf. p. 23, and vol. III, p. 411). It was the eastern half of the empire that revolted, and for the suppression of the revolt Darius had to depend almost entirely on the Persian and Median army which he speaks of, in his inscription, as small. The necessity for dividing this small force to meet several simultaneous revolts was more than offset by the fact that the revolts though simultaneous were not co-ordinated. But it says much for the skill and energy of Darius that he was able in spite of this far-spread opposition to obtain recognition of his right by descent to rule, and to secure peace and quiet throughout his dominions within a year or two of Cambyses' death.

At the end of the second year of Darius[1], in December, 520, the still recent political convulsions in the empire led the prophet Haggai (ii, 22) in Jerusalem to anticipate that 'the throne of kingdoms' would be overthrown, although his fellow-prophet Zechariah (i, 11) two months later recognizes that there is no indication of further disturbance within the empire: 'the earth sitteth still, and is at rest.' (Cf. vol. III, p. 409 sq.)

Yet something remained for Darius to do before he could rest satisfied that his empire was secured both within and without. Further conquests such as Cyrus left to Cambyses in Egypt he scarcely set before himself; and such extensions as the empire received under Darius are rather to be looked on as rectifications and a strengthening of its frontiers.

Within the empire Darius had to assert his authority in two important satrapies where, not the native population, but the Persian satraps appointed by Cyrus and Cambyses respectively, had shown signs of independence. Among the provinces which Darius names in the Susian version of the Behistun inscription— the corresponding places of the Persian and Babylonian texts are mutilated—as rebelling from him while he was in Babylon, is Egypt; but the inscription contains no account of the suppression of any Egyptian revolt, and it is probable[2] that what is referred to is the failure of Aryandes the satrap of Egypt to lend Darius any active support. In any case, Darius had reasons for suspecting Aryandes, and as already related, when he came to Egypt, probably in 517 B.C., relieved him of his office, and put him to death (cf. p. 24). The satrap of Sardes, Oroites, laid himself under similar suspicions and suffered, perhaps rather earlier, a similar fate. In the story told by Herodotus Oroites is charged with having done the Persians no service at the time of the Median revolt, with having slain Mitrobates, satrap of the neighbouring province, and his son Cranaspes, and with having disregarded

---

[1] Or, his first year, according to Meyer (*Entstehung d. Judentums*, p. 2), on the ground that the Jews ante-date, the Persians post-date.

[2] Unless, indeed, 'Egypt' is an error in the Susian translation (Meyer, *ibid.* p. 82, n. 3).

Darius's instructions, and even putting to death a messenger that carried them. Since this happened while Darius was still occupied with the revolts and had no army to send against him, he secured the death of Oroites by treachery, a sufficient measure since it was the satrap personally and not the province that was inclined to become independent of Darius. One of the achievements of Oroites had been to entrap and then put to death Polycrates of Samos (see above, p. 91). After Oroites's death Darius despatched Otanes to take possession of the island and to leave Syloson, Polycrates's brother, to govern it as a Persian vassal. Herodotus counts Samos as the earliest of Darius's conquests. It was the prelude to the extension of his dominions westwards and northwards, into Thrace and Macedonia, and to his attempt to bring all Greece into his power.

A last attempt at revolt was made by Susiana: this is recorded by Darius in the fifth and later inscribed column of the Behistun inscription. The year in this instance was given, but the monument is mutilated and cannot be deciphered with certainty; possibly the statement at the beginning of the column read: 'This is what I did in the fourth and fifth years after I became king,' *i.e.* in 518–16 B.C.[1] In this case the Susian revolt may be placed in the former year; the Scythian expedition, of which a brief account follows, in the latter. The unfavourable incidents in this expedition are naturally enough passed over. Darius claims that the province became his, and that he deposed the rebel chief, putting another in his place. The latter statement need not be questioned; the former is vague, though it suggests an over-favourable interpretation of what Darius actually achieved on his northern frontiers against the Scythians. The details of this expedition are related below (see pp. 212 *sqq.*), and all that need be noted here is that it may be regarded as part of the policy for securing his northern frontiers against the inroads of the nomads. Herodotus half perceived this when he asserts that 'Darius formed the desire to take vengeance on the Scythians, because they had first invaded the Median land'; but Darius's action was not determined merely by a Scythian peril that had been realized a century before, but was for the purpose of putting an end to a peril that had since continually threatened and was still threatening; it was directed by a right perception of the connection among these northern peoples, though its success was seriously qualified by insufficient knowledge of the vast extent and the difficult character of the steppe country over which they

[1] *Z.D.M.G.* LXII, 641; cf. L W. King, *History of Babylon*, p. 286

roamed. Cyrus had died fighting against one section of these northern nomads; and there is evidence suggesting—what might independently have been surmised—that the Sacae or Scythians had attacked the frontiers of Darius[1].

To the extreme east Darius made an extensive and what must in many respects be regarded as an important enlargement of his dominions. Among the countries enumerated by Darius on the Behistun inscription as having come to him with the crown are Gandāra and Sattagydia, from which it may be inferred that Cyrus had already pushed the Persian conquests to the north-western frontier of India and even to the southern slopes of the Hindu-kush. In the later inscriptions of Persepolis and Naksh-i-Rustum, Darius includes among the provinces brought into his possession by his Persian army and tributary to him, along with Gandara and Sattagydia, India. Herodotus refers allusively to Darius as having subdued the Indians; but neither the Persian nor the Greek sources define either the date of the conquest or, at least with any precision, its extent. The Persian province of India scarcely extended east of the Indus; but it paid in tribute far more than any of the other provinces, and is likely therefore to have included a very considerable tract of country between the mountains that separate Afghanistan from India. The conquest is to be placed relatively early in the reign of Darius, but it was not necessarily due to the activities of Darius's satrap in Arachosia immediately after the suppression of the revolt in that country in 521.

Thus, within a few years Darius had secured his position as ruler of the wide empire that Cyrus and Cambyses had created, and in certain directions had even added to it. But his more peculiar task was not to be the fresh conquest of ancient empires. He did not and perhaps did not need to possess the military genius of Cyrus, though he showed discernment in the choice of generals when he was not taking the field in person, and a power of rapid and successful action when he commanded himself. He exhibited great skill, moreover, in the distribution of his relatively small forces over the various areas of conflict; and against his failure in Scythia may be set the circumstances in which Cyrus died. The widespread revolts that followed the death of Cambyses showed only too plainly how easily the empire might fall to pieces; and the peculiar genius of Darius is to be seen in the completion of the organization of the empire which his predecessors had created. Much of the organization must indeed go back to

[1] See Polyaenus, VII, 11, 6, and VII, 12.

beginnings under Cyrus, but, on the whole, it is the stamp of Darius that is set on the forms of life and state which were maintained under his successors, and in some important respects long outlasted the overthrow of his house, and with it of the Persian dominion, by Alexander. It is at this point, therefore, that it is most convenient to take a survey of the constitution and institutions of the Persian state so far as they can be discovered.

III. THE ORGANIZATION OF THE PERSIAN EMPIRE

Not only in extent did the Persian empire far surpass any that had gone before, but in the organization to which it was subjected; it may indeed be regarded as the first attempt to bring a large number of different races and nationalities under a single government which assured to the whole the rights and privileges as well as the burdens and responsibilities of members of the state.

At the head of the state was the king, and the Persian monarchy was hereditary. As the ancestors of Cyrus had been for generations kings of the small kingdom of Anshan and the succession had regularly passed from father to son, so the empire which Cyrus created passed to his son Cambyses. The pretender, too, who later challenged the rule of Cambyses, appealed to the hereditary principle by claiming to be son of Cyrus; and the people in accepting his claims held fast by the principle that the house of Achaemenes had the right to rule. Darius recovered for the family 'whose possession,' as he expresses it, 'it had been from long ago' the kingdom of which Gaumata had wrongfully and by deception for a few months deprived it. From Darius it passed to his son Xerxes by Atossa the daughter of Cyrus, and to later descendants successively down to the time of Alexander.

The discussion as to the respective merits of democracy, oligarchy and monarchy attributed by Herodotus to Darius and his six companions after the death of Gaumata, interesting as it may be as an illustration of Greek political philosophy, is valueless for the Persian theory or practice of government. The kingdom of Cyrus did not fall to Darius, as in the story of Herodotus, accidentally as the result of a clever trick, nor merely by force, but in virtue of his being a member of the oldest surviving line of the hereditary royal family. A strict law of primogeniture, indeed, did not hold with the Persians, or his father Hystaspes and not Darius himself should have succeeded; and Darius in turn was succeeded not by his eldest son, but by Xerxes, his eldest son by Atossa the daughter of Cyrus, the son first born to him after he had succeeded to the throne. Thus, the reigning king had apparently the right of choosing his successor among his sons, and this right, according to Herodotus, he was expected, in accordance with Persian custom, to exercise before making a foreign expedition.

The hereditary principle enjoyed a religious sanction: 'By the grace of Ahura-Mazda I am king; Ahura-Mazda gave me the kingdom,' are the words of Darius in the Behistun inscription[1]; and Xerxes and Artaxerxes in their inscriptions speak of Ahura-Mazda 'who made Xerxes (Artaxerxes) king.' As the empire grew and incorporated ancient empires of other faiths, the Persian kings sought and obtained the sanction of the religion of these countries for their sovereignty: Cyrus was called to the throne of Babylon by Marduk, and Cambyses and Darius in Egypt took names claiming relationship with the Egyptian god Re. The great variety of the nations subject to him, the universality of his dominion which united them, the unshared and undisputed supremacy exercised by him, are the claims which Darius, and after him Xerxes and Artaxerxes, make for themselves in their inscriptions: Darius is 'one king of many, one lord of many; the great king, king of kings, king of the countries possessing all kinds of peoples, king of this great earth far and wide.' The unity of rule was never weakened by any of these kings dividing the empire among two or more sons. In his lifetime Cyrus made Cambyses king of Babylon, but strictly in subordination to himself as 'king of the lands,' and even this experiment was not perpetuated. Cyrus throughout most of his reign used 'king of Babylon' as part of his own style, as did Cambyses, Darius, and at first Xerxes. Nominally, the kingdom of Babylon for a time continued, but the occupant of the Babylonian throne was the king of Persia. So in Egypt the native monarchy nominally continued, but with the Persian king himself as monarch. Certain smaller countries and city-states which had submitted voluntarily to the Persians retained their monarchies in vassalage to Persia. The satraps of Cilicia drawn from the native royal house are termed 'kings' (βασιλεῖς) by Greek writers; and in Phoenician inscriptions of Byblus, of Sidon, and of Citium (in Cyprus), belonging to the Persian period, the native rulers term themselves kings. Yet the title 'king of kings,' which, so far as is known, was first used as a standing title by the supreme monarchs of the Persian empire, expresses less the relation of the Great King to these petty vassal monarchs than the uniqueness of his kingship: to the Greeks he was *Basileus*, the one and only real king in the world.

[1] See Volume of Plates i, 311, *a*.

The monarchy was an absolute monarchy: the king's will expressed in word was law. What that word was, however, was generally determined in consultation with the Persian nobles and officials (which custom required of the king), and by regard for the usages of the country concerned.

The 'royal judges' as Herodotus calls them, or 'law-bearers' as they were probably called in Persian (*dātabara*), advised the king what was law or custom: in such cases, for example, as whether it was lawful for a man to marry his sister, how many Egyptian nobles should die in retaliation for each Mitylenean slain at Memphis, what ought to be done to Queen Vashti 'according to law' (*dāt*) for refusing to come to the king at his bidding: these three instances, though not all of them historically real, may serve to illustrate how, though 'the king of the Persians might do whatsoever he desired,' yet, in practice, he generally had regard to law and custom. In certain respects, also, he was practically limited by the privileges enjoyed by the Persian nobles, and among these pre-eminently, though not exclusively, the families of the six men who were associated with Darius in the overthrow of Gaumata. Only from these families might the king take his wives, and they enjoyed the right of unannounced access to him. They were endowed with great territories, and within them enjoyed princely positions. Of the house of Otanes, one of the six, Herodotus relates that 'at the present time this house alone remains free...and submits to rule only so far as it wills to do so itself, not transgressing the laws of the Persians,' thus making Otanes practically as absolute—within his own dominions —as the king himself. On the other hand, the power of the king over even the six is illustrated by the fate of Intaphrenes, who was put to death by Darius, though not, as Herodotus states, immediately after the suppression of Gaumata, for he appears with the others whose families are commended to the favour of future kings by Darius in the Behistun inscription.

In administration the king acted in consultation with his ministers, the heads of great departments of state, which must have existed in the capital, though of them little is directly known. Ezra, in the letter given to him by Artaxerxes, is described as sent to Judaea by 'the king and his seven counsellors,' and the seven counsellors are associated with the king in the gift to the Temple at Jerusalem (Ezra vii, 14).

Certain lines of policy characteristic of the Persian government seem clear. While supreme authority resided in the king, great regard was paid, so far as the supremacy of the central authority allowed, to the traditional life and custom of the many diverse allowed, to the traditional life and custom of the many diverse peoples gathered into the vast empire. The Persian was a tolerant government. The supreme and absolute character of the king required the suppression of the existing dynasties in the greater states that had been conquered, and even the avoidance of creating in these countries native vassal kings. But the Persian kings were ready to continue the forms and the religious associations of these monarchies. In Babylon Cyrus, Cambyses, Darius and—at first—Xerxes, all reigned as king of Babylon, and Cyrus proclaimed himself king as the chosen of Marduk. And similarly in Egypt: the earlier Persian kings ruled as successors of the pharaohs and adopted Egyptian names. Nothing similar is known in relation to the Median monarchy; that, however, was but a recent institution, and the religions of the Medes and Persians were closely akin.

As the sentiments of the people were considered in this continuation of the ancient forms, so at times were the persons of the conquered and deposed monarchs: not only was the life of Astyages spared by Cyrus, but he was treated with consideration; and Cambyses apparently treated or was prepared to treat Psammetichus similarly; and it was only, if we accept the story of Herodotus, after a breach of parole that Psammetichus was put to death, although, according to Ctesias, he was kept alive at Susa. Certainly Darius's treatment of the kings who gained a brief recognition in various countries during the revolts was marked by the greatest severity and even barbarity: they were not merely put to death, but previously mutilated. But their case was different: they were, as pretenders claiming to be what they were not, servants of 'the Lie,' abhorrent to Darius's own object of worship, Ahura-Mazda the True; they were not as still independent sovereigns but as subjects of the Persians disputing the supremacy of the Persian king, and that was not to be tolerated. So, too, as, towards the end of the reign of Darius and in the reign of Xerxes, repeated efforts at a renewed national independence were made in Babylon and Egypt, the Persian kings ceased to use the style King of Babylon—in form as well as in reality the kingdom of Babylon came to an end—and Artaxerxes no longer takes as king of Egypt an Egyptian name of religious significance, as Cambyses and Darius had done.

Not only were the Persians prepared to be tolerant to the various religions within their empire; they went further and actively supported the temple-worship of the gods of their subjects, or contributed to the building of their temples, and conferred on priesthoods and religious institutions special privileges.

Cyrus in his cylinder-inscription records 'I gave daily care to his (Marduk's) worship'; and Cyrus and Darius not merely permitted the rebuilding of the Jewish temple at Jerusalem, but laid the cost of it on the royal treasury; that is to say, they decreed that the cost should be defrayed from the taxes levied in the province by the king's government. Darius and Artaxerxes also provided the cost of the sacrifices offered in the Jewish temple for the life of the king and his sons (Ezra vi, 4, 8, 10). Darius's general Datis not only assured the fugitive Delians that he was bound by the king's command to respect the sanctity of the island where Artemis and Apollo had been born, but also offered on the altar of the Greek gods three hundred talents weight of frankincense. Cambyses, at the request of the Egyptian priest Uzahor, had the temple of Neith at Saïs freed from the foreigners who had taken up their quarters in it (p. 22 *sq.*). Not only this, he 'restored the temple of Neith in person. He testified in every good way his reverence for the great, exalted, holy goddess Neith the great mother, and for all the great gods in Saïs as all the pious kings had done...the king bestowed all that was good on the temple of Neith. He caused the libations to be offered to the Everlasting One in the house of Neith as all the kings of former times had done.' Darius charged Uzahor to restore the number of the temple-scribes and 'ordered that all favour should be shewn to them...the king did all this...in order to uphold the names of all the gods, their temples, their revenues and the ordinances of their feasts for ever.' Darius also undertook the repair or building of temples to Egyptian gods, especially the building of the temple of Amon in the Great Oasis (el-Khargah). Definite instances of the exemption of priests or sacred classes from taxation are the decree of Artaxerxes forbidding tribute, impost or toll to be levied on the priests and on the temple personnel at Jerusalem (Ezra vii, 24), and the requisition by Darius I that his officer Gadatas should cease exacting tribute from the gardeners of Apollo at a place which is probably Magnesia on the Maeander in Asia Minor. In the latter case Darius distinctly stated that the action of Gadatas had violated the intention of his predecessors with regard to the service of the Greek god.

As the king, sprung from the noble Persian house of Achaemenes, was the head of the state, so the Persians were the ruling race within it and next to them the Medes. While the rest of the empire, including even Media, was, from the time of Darius onwards, subject to regular taxation for its support, Persia proper was not. For geographical reasons the real administrative centre of the empire was indeed Susa outside the ancestral home and country of the ruling family; but it was in Persia that the kings erected or carved in the rock their tombs and built their most magnificent palaces. At Mashad-i-Murghab on the Pulwar within the region inhabited by the Pasargadae, the clan from which the Achaemenidae sprang, still stands the marble-like limestone structure which, in spite of contending theories, is rightly regarded as the tomb of Cyrus[1]; the ruins around it represent the city built by Cyrus and called Pasargadae after the name of his clan; on an artificial terrace in the neighbourhood of the tomb stand the scanty remains of a palace, amongst them door-posts and a pillar with a winged figure carved in relief which has often, but mistakenly, been regarded as a portrait of Cyrus. These bear the legend written in Persian, Susian, and Babylonian: 'I [am] Cyrus the king, the Achaemenid.' The attempt to refer these inscriptions, the only surviving Persian inscriptions of Cyrus, to Cyrus the younger, who was never king, must be dismissed as unsuccessful[2], and they may be accepted as proof in support of the statements of Greek writers that Cyrus, like his successor, built on, and was buried in, Persian soil.

Of Cambyses' buildings in Persia nothing certain is known; but in the neighbourhood of the modern Istakr, 30 miles to the south-west of Pasargadae (Murghab), inscriptions sufficiently and clearly attest the devotion of Darius and his successors to their home country. Here they built the city known to the Greeks as Persepolis, here on a great artificial platform they erected magnificent pillared palaces and sculptured staircases[3], which inscriptions directly attribute to Darius, Xerxes and his son Artaxerxes. Here, too, they were buried. Carved in the rock immediately behind the platform at Persepolis, and there and in the rock at the neighbouring Naksh-i-Rustum, are four tombs, one of which bears an inscription of Darius. Pasargadae was moreover the Rheims or Westminster of the Achaemenidae[4]; here they were externally invested with the kingship, putting on the robe of Cyrus and partaking of the simple meal consecrated by custom. In another way, too, the bond between Pasargadae and the Persian royal family is shown by the practice of the kings to present the women of Pasargadae with a gold piece whenever they visited the city. The very fact that the kings continued to lavish expense on their Persian city, in spite of the fact that reasons of state made their visits to it relatively rare and—in comparison with their periods of residence in Susa, Ecbatana and Babylon—brief, is

---

[1] See Volume of Plates i, 312, *b*.   [2] Herzfeld, *Pasargadae* (1908).
[3] See Vol. of Plates i, 314, *b*; 316, *a, c*; 318, *b*.   [4] Cp. Plut. *Artax.* 3.

proof of the continued hold of Persia on the monarchs of a now far vaster empire. Darius's praise of Persia has already been referred to and in part cited; in another inscription he regards the welfare of his own house as bound up with that of Persia: 'If thus thou shalt think, "May I not fear an enemy," protect this Persian people: if the Persian people shall be protected, welfare for a long time and undisturbed will thro' Ahura descend upon this house.'

The army, which was organized in divisions of 10,000 divided into ten battalions of a thousand each, and then again into hundreds and tens, each with their respective officers, was drawn in time of war from all the nations composing the empire, but the flower of it then, and the standing army in peace, consisted of Persians and Medes. It was with the Persian and Median army that Darius overcame Gaumata and suppressed the subsequent revolts; the soldiers before the throne of Darius sculptured on the staircases at Persepolis are alternately Persians and Medes. At the head of the list, in Herodotus, of national contingents to the army of Xerxes stand the Persians and Medes; the kernel of the army was the Persian foot—the ten thousand 'immortals'— and the Persian cavalry. The command of the army was predominantly though not exclusively in the hands of Iranians, and especially of Persians. Thus, of eight generals mentioned by Darius in the Behistun inscription, six are called Persians, one a Mede, and one an Armenian; the non-Iranian as well as the Iranian elements in Xerxes' army were commanded by Iranian leaders—e.g. the Assyrians by Otaspes the son of Artachaeës, the Indians by Pharnazathres the son of Artabates, the Arabians and Ethiopians by Arsames the son of Darius.

The garrisons in various cities and at strategic points throughout the empire consisted mainly of Persian soldiers, and were commanded by Persian officers: Oroites at Sardes had a bodyguard of 1000 Persian spearmen; the Persian garrison at Memphis, to judge from the amount of corn supplied to it, was much larger, though associated with the Persians were some foreign mercenaries. The garrison at Syene consisted in part of Jews, in part of Egyptians; but it was commanded towards the close of the fifth century by Persians, first by Waidrang, and then by his son Naphayan[1]. The names of the officers after whom the various 'companies' of the military colony at Elephantine-Syene were called are chiefly Persian—Warizath, Haumadāta, Artabanus, Artaphernes; but some are Babylonian—Iddin-Nabu and Nabukudurri.

[1] Cowley, *Aramaic Papyri*, 6, 3; 7, 3; 9, 2; 20, 2; 28, 2.

Important alike for appointments to the army, to court offices, and to administrative posts in the provinces, was the existence of something like cadet schools. At the court of the king himself, or at the minor courts of the satraps, 'all the boys of the foremost Persians,' as Xenophon phrases it, were educated[1]. The stress laid on old Persian habits of life and accomplishments—riding, shooting with the bow, plainness of diet, the chase—formed a counteractive to the luxury which tended to increase with the increase and increasing wealth of the empire; though Xenophon already complains of decadence and perversion: where virtue once, now vice too often is learnt. Instruction in history and religion, attendance at judicial proceedings, familiarity with the king's methods of awarding or withholding favours, are other elements in this education on which the Greek writers who describe it lay stress.

Thus, as the mass of the Persian population formed the nucleus of the army, the chief Persian families supplied, not indeed exclusively, but very largely, the generals and officers of the army, the ministers of the central administration, and the satraps and governors of provinces and districts throughout the empire. So far afield had conquest and expansion dispersed the Persians from their home; though the story with which Herodotus closes his history may reflect an actual opposition of the government to any unnecessary permanent settlement of Persians away from Persia. The importance of maintaining a sufficient nucleus of hardy mountain peasants for the army, and of retaining in the education of the ruling classes a place for the virtues which had contributed to the original conquering vigour of the race, may have been consciously realized and come to form a principle of state action. In the conquest of the empire 'the spear of the Persian had gone forth afar,' and 'the Persian had fought his foe far from Persia,' in the words of Darius's eulogy: in the maintenance of it, as often as was needed this must happen again, but it could only happen with effect if Persia resisted the temptation to migrate to richer lands opened to it by conquest, and retained a sufficient reserve of man-power in its rugged home.

Though Cyrus built and adorned Pasargadae, and Darius and his successors Persepolis, they could scarcely, even had they tried, have created in the valley of the Pulvar or elsewhere in Persia a suitable administrative centre of the empire. The very features that made that country a cradle of a hardy race of soldiers left it lacking a site for the centre of a far-extended empire; and what-

[1] Xenophon, *Anab.* I. 9, 3; *Cyr.* VIII, 1, 6.

ever their desire to limit the emigration of their people, the Persian kings themselves found it necessary for the most part to reside beyond the borders of Persia, returning thither indeed to be buried, but in their lifetime only on brief infrequent visits. Susa, the ancient capital of Elam, perhaps even the capital of the kingdom of Anshan over which the ancestors of Cyrus had ruled, was from the time of Darius, if not of Cyrus, to the last Achaemenid king the capital of the empire: 'the city where,' as Herodotus phrases it, 'the Great King has his residence' and where 'the money is laid up in treasuries.' In the height of summer the king transferred his residence to the more northerly, high-lying and cooler Ecbatana, formerly the capital of the Median empire, and, at first at least, in the winter to Babylon—though Xenophon's statement that Cyrus resided regularly for more than half the year in Babylon is very doubtful.

Susa, some 200 miles south of Ecbatana, 225 east of Babylon, and nearly 300 north-west of Persepolis, situated midway between the distant eastern and western extremities of the empire, less centrally in reference to the much less widely separated southern and northern borders, had the advantage of being so much the closer to Persia, the cradle of the royal house, and the great reservoir of its man-power. Whether it was the ancestral city of Cyrus as king of Anshan, as early Greek writers (Aeschylus and Herodotus) imply, or was first made the capital by Darius (as others have surmised), it certainly owed much to Darius. The building inscriptions of Susa record the activity of Darius and Artaxerxes II, the fame of Darius's buildings at Susa lives in the classical writers, and modern excavation has revealed the chief features of these. The city, situated in a fertile plain at the foot of the Zagros mountains between two rivers, the Karun, at a few miles distance to the east, and the Kercha (Choaspes) to the west, occupied for a distance of several miles the area between the eastern banks of the latter river and the western banks of a third (the Shapur, Ulai) which separated it from the citadel and palace which was the work of Darius. Artaxerxes II, in the inscription recovered by excavation, says of the *apadāna* or throne-room: 'this *apadāna* Darius (I) my ancestor made: later under Artaxerxes (I) my grandfather it was burnt: by the grace of Ahura-Mazda, Anahita and Mithra I built this *apadāna*.' This great hall, some 250 feet square, had roof-beams of cedar supported on 36 pillars of fluted limestone, and topped with elaborately carved capitals[1], in front were colonnades with friezes of enamelled bricks depicting processions of lions and of royal life-guards[2]. It was the audience-

[1] See Volume of Plates i, 320.   [2] *Ib.* 322.

chamber of the empire whither, along the roads that con-
verged upon Susa, came from all parts those who sought
the king, and whence, along the same roads, went the administrators or messengers who carried letters containing the word
of the king which was law, and the troops who enforced it,
and inspectors who reported to the king how his will was
carried out (see below, p. 197 *sq.*).

The development of older lines of communication into the
Persian road-system, which in some degree achieved the completeness and excellence of the communications of the later empire
of Rome, may have been initiated by Cyrus, and owed much to
Darius: Herodotus speaks of it as something long and well-
established. In detail he describes only one of the roads, viz. that
which connected Ephesus and Sardes with Susa at 90 days'
distance[1]; Ctesias in the lost close of his Persian history gave
similar details for the road to Bactria and India, and incidental
information is found in other writers. These roads were accurately
measured by parasangs (= $3\frac{2}{5}$ miles); at intervals of, on an average,
about four parasangs there were posting-stations and inns, which
Herodotus describes as excellent; and at certain strategical points
there were garrisons: of these Herodotus mentions four between
Sardes and Susa—one at the Halys, two on the borders of Cilicia,
and one in Armenia. The larger rivers which were not bridged
were crossed by ferries. At posting-stations along the routes
messengers mounted on swift horses stood always in readiness
to carry forward the king's letters and despatches, so that these
passed as fast as a horse could travel without delay by night or
day from Susa to the farthest limits of the roads; and whereas
travellers normally took nearly three months from Sardes to Susa,
the king's correspondence may have passed over the same road in
less than a week. These roads of course served not only for the
royal despatches and the movement of the royal troops, but also
for trade, which would naturally be stimulated by the great improvement in transport and communication, and for the private
movements of the king's subjects. At the same time, the administration of the roads served to keep the government informed
about their subjects: private correspondence passing along the
roads was carefully examined by the king's officers, and private
persons could only hope to escape the vigilance of these and
maintain the privacy of their communications with one another
by resorting to ruses such as that described by Herodotus (v, 35).

---

[1] On the course of this road see W. M. Calder, in *C.R.* 1925, pp. 7 *sqq.*

IV. THE SATRAPIES

Under Darius, after his conquest of India but probably from an early period of his reign, the empire was divided into twenty satrapies, or provinces, under satraps or governors appointed by the king; and within these large provinces there were again smaller districts under subordinate governors to whom however, at least often, the same term satrap was applied. The appointment of satraps and the organization of provinces goes back to Cyrus and Cambyses, not to speak of similar organizations in the Assyrian, Median and Babylonian empires that preceded the Persian; what Darius did was to complete the organization: to modify the limits of some of the satrapies and the functions of the satraps.

The Persian term satrap, meaning protector of the realm, is applied to two Persian officials in the Behistun inscription, Dadarshi, who is described as 'satrap in Bactria,' and Vivāna, 'satrap in Arachosia' in the early months of the reign of Darius when the revolts broke out. There is no suggestion that these appointments had been made by Darius himself: they dated rather from one of the previous reigns. The same is true of Darius's father Hystaspes, who is represented in the same inscription as occupying a corresponding function in Parthia and Hyrcania, though the title of satrap does not happen to be applied to him in the inscription. In a passage of Xenophon (*Cyrop.* VIII, 6, 7–8), which may rest on good information, Cyrus is said to have appointed satraps over (1) Arabia, (2) Cappadocia, (3) Great Phrygia, (4) Lydia and Ionia, (5) Caria, (6) Hellespontine Phrygia and Aeolis; but to have appointed no Persian satraps over Cilicia, Cyprus or Paphlagonia. Herodotus attributes to Cyrus the appointment of Oroites to be satrap of Sardes, *i.e.* of Lydia, implying that he filled the office continuously into the reign of Darius, and to Cambyses the appointment of Aryandes to be satrap (ὕπαρχος or ἄρχων) of Egypt. He also mentions Mitrobates as satrap of Dascylium before the time of Darius. As the empire was extended by Cyrus and Cambyses, other provinces were no doubt set up and placed under similar government, though no sufficient data exist for determining the limits of several of these provinces before the reign of Darius. Two things, however, are clear in regard to this earlier as also to the later periods: (1) the satraps were appointed for indefinite terms, often retaining their position over a long period of years and through more than one reign, and (2) from the first the Persian provinces were large in comparison with those of earlier empires. Indeed, it is probable

MAP 4

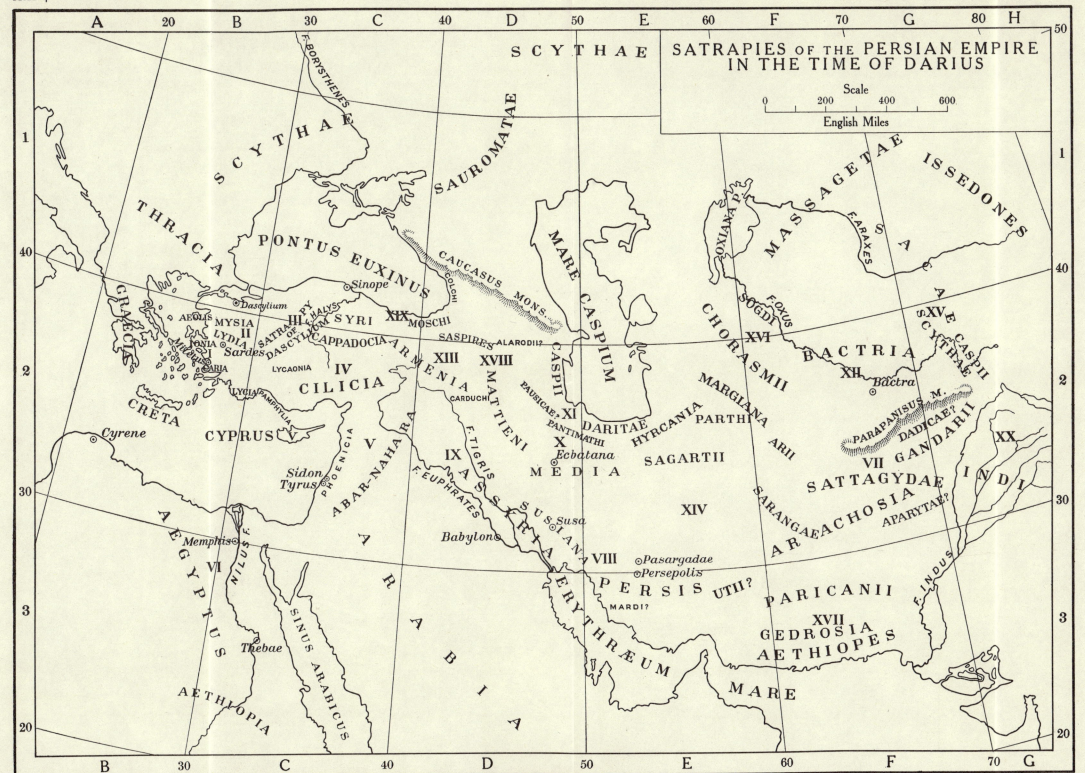

SATRAPIES OF THE PERSIAN EMPIRE IN THE TIME OF DARIUS

Scale

0   200   400   600

English Miles

Abar-Nahara, C 2
Aegyptus, BC 2, 3
Aeolis, B 2
Aethiopes, EF 3
Aethiopia, BC 3
Alarodii?, D 1, 2
Aparytae?, F 2
Arabia, CD 2, 3
Arachosia, F 2
Araxes, F., FG 1
Aria, B 2
Arii, F 2
Armenia, CD 2
Assyria, D 2

Babylon, D 2
Bactra, F 2
Bactria, F 2
Borysthenes, F., C 1

Cappadocia, C 2
Carduchi, D 2
Caspii, D 2
Caspii, G 2
Caspium, Mare, DE 1, 2
Caucasus M., D 1
Chorasmii, EF 1, 2
Cilicia, C 2
Colchi, D 1
Creta, B 2
Cyprus, C 2
Cyrene, B 2

Dadicae?, FG 2
Daritae, E 2
Dascylium, B 1
Dascylium, Satrapy of, C 2

Ecbatana, D 2
Erythraeum Mare, D–F 3
Euphrates, F., D 2

Gandarii, FG 2
Gedrosia, F 3
Graecia, B 2

Halys, F., C 1, 2
Hyrcania, E 2

Indi, G 2
Indus, F., FG 2, 3
Ionia, B 2
Issedones, G 1

Lycaonia, C 2
Lycia, BC 2
Lydia, B 2

Mardi?, E 3
Margiana, EF 2
Massagetae, FG 1
Mattieni, D 2
Media, DE 2
Memphis, C 2, 3
Miletus, B 2
Moschi, CD 1
Mysia, B 2

Nilus, F., C 2, 3

Oxiana P., EF 1
Oxus, F., E–G 1, 2

Pamphylia, C 2
Pantimathi, DE 2
Parapanisus M., FG 2
Paricanii, F 3
Parthi, E 2
Pasargadae, E 2
Pausicae?, D 2
Persepolis, E 2, 3
Persis, E 3
Phoenicia, C 2
Pontus Euxinus, B–D

Sacae, FG 1, 2
Sagartii, E 2
Sarangae, F 2
Sardes, B 2
Saspires, D 1, 2
Sattagydae, FG 2
Sauromatae, D 1
Scythae, B–E 1
Scythae, G 2
Sidon, C 2
Sinope, C 1
Sinus Arabicus, C 3
Sogdi, F 1
Susa, D 2
Susiana, D 2
Syri, C 1

Thebae, C 3
Thracia, B 1
Tigris, F., D 2
Tyrus, C 2

Utii?, E 3

that the satrapy of Egypt, in comprising the whole of a conquered empire, was an exception, and that the empires of Babylon and Media were from the first, as they were under Darius, divided into more than one satrapy; yet, even so, the satrapies were extensive and in many cases included several different nations or peoples, and in some several formerly sovereign states.

Of the twenty satrapies into which the empire of Darius was divided, Asia Minor contained the first four in the list of Herodotus: (i) the first, including the Ionians, Aeolians, Carians, Pamphylians and others, and (ii) the second, including the Lydians and others, covered the west; (iii) known as the province of Dascylium, was in area much the largest and included the centre stretching from the northern to the southern coast; and (iv) consisting of Cilicia on the south-east. The fifth satrapy (v) known as Abar-Nahara, *i.e.* Beyond-the-River, consisted of Syria, Phoenicia, Palestine and Cyprus; (vi) Egypt together with Libya and Cyrenaica. The seventh satrapy in the list lies to the far east, between India the twentieth and Bactria the twelfth, and included (vii) the Sattagydae, the Gandarii, Dadicae, and Aparytae. Then follow (viii) Susiana, (ix) Assyria, which included Babylonia; (x) Media and (xi) the district north of Media and west of the Caspian Sea inhabited by the Caspians, Pausicians, Pantimathi and Dareitae; (xii) Bactria, (xiii) Armenia; (xiv) the vast district east of Persia inhabited by the Sagartians, Sarangians, Utians and others; (xv) the district to the north-east inhabited by the Sacae (Scyths); (xvi) the area westwards from Bactria to the south-east corner of the Caspian through the country of the Areians, Sogdians and Parthians, including the outlying oasis inhabited by the Chorasmians just south of the Aral Sea; (xvii) covered much of the area of the modern Baluchistan, and was inhabited by the Paricanians and 'Ethiopians.' The eighteenth satrapy (xviii) was the country of the Matieni, Saspeires and Alarodians, with the Urmia Lake more or less in its centre; the next (xix) lay along and behind the south-eastern shores of the Black Sea, having amongst its inhabitants the Moschi and Tibareni, and the twentieth (xx) consisted of the latest won territory—India, *i.e.* the Indus water-basin west of the Indus.

A comparison of the satrapies under Cyrus as given by Xenophon and under Darius reveals a number of differences: Arabia under Darius no longer forms either the whole or part of a satrapy; if Cyrus actually appointed a satrap of Arabia, his successors found it expedient to withdraw him; they were content with maintaining a good understanding with the Arabs, which was essential for the safety of their communications with Egypt, without persisting in the attempt to subject them to more direct Persian government. There are in both cases four satrapies in Asia Minor, but differently constituted: for example, Lydia and Ionia are combined in one case, and in the other belong to different satrapies; Caria, which under Darius is merely part of the first satrapy, appears in Xenophon's *Cyropaedeia* as an independent satrapy under Cyrus; this it certainly became, whether for the first time or not, from 404 B.C. onwards. Modifications in the satrapies subsequent to Darius may be illustrated not only by the case of Caria just mentioned, but also by the division of the ninth satrapy of Darius: Assyria, perhaps about or soon after 478 B.C., was detached from Babylonia (which henceforward was a separate satrapy) and was attached to the fifth satrapy of Darius. In Xenophon's list of provincial rulers Belesus is ruler of Syria and Assyria, Roparas of Babylonia. Again, Areia, part of the sixteenth satrapy, is, under Darius III, a separate satrapy. At times the same governor was placed in charge of two or more complete satrapies: for example, Ushtanni, as a Babylonian contract-tablet attests, was in the third year of Darius *pakhatu* (the Babylonian translation of 'satrap') of Beyond-the-River and Babylon, *i.e.* of the satrapies v and ix, and under Darius III, Mazaeus (Mazdai) governed Beyond-the-River and Cilicia, as the legends on his coins attest.

The satraps were men of high birth, such as Hystaspes, Artaphrenes, Cyrus the younger, in some cases members of the royal family by birth or marriage, appointed for indefinite periods and actually remaining in office for many years if not for life, administering provinces great in area and frequently including several nations, and extending the policy recommended, according to Xenophon, by Cyrus to the satraps 'to imitate him' to the pomp of their courts. They enjoyed a state that, in the history of the western Asiatic empires, was apparently something new. In some provinces, too, at some periods the office became in practice hereditary, though in theory terminable at the will of the king. Cilicia is the one instance in which, thanks to the timely recognition by its native ruler of the expediency of being on the side of the Persians, a previously existing kingdom became a satrapy with the native ruling house still providing the satrap from generation to generation. This lasted throughout the fifth century: in the next, probably as a result of unsuccessful accommodation of the Cilician ruler to the conflict between Artaxerxes II and Cyrus the younger, the satraps are no longer Cilicians but

Persians. In the neighbouring satrapy of Dascylium, the office continued to be filled by members of the house of the Persian noble Artabazus who was appointed satrap of this province by Xerxes in 476 B.C. Caria in the fourth century became a satrapy under successive members of the house of Hecatomnus.

The functions and powers of the satrap were of the widest in civil administration, and were wide also in military matters. It was his duty to maintain security of communication within his province not only for the king's interests, but also for those of all well-disposed subjects. He was the highest judicial authority within the province, which in Aramaic was termed *mĕdīnah*, judicial district. He received envoys from neighbouring states, and determined action with regard to them, though larger matters of policy were normally referred to Susa, as for example by Artaphrenes, when he referred the question of an expedition against Naxos for the approval of Darius before undertaking it. He had to maintain good relations within his own province, and here again questions often arose which required reference to the king, such as was made by Tattenai (? Ushtanni), the satrap of Beyond-the-River, in the matter of the rebuilding of the Jewish Temple which had been associated with disputes between the Jews and Samaritans. Within certain satrapies, older or local forms of government were in a measure and with modifications perpetuated, such as the Phoenician city-kingdoms, and the Jews under high-priestly government and the law-book of Ezra (to which was given the force of state-law for the Jews by Artaxerxes, in the satrapy of Beyond-the-River) and many of the Greek cities in the satrapies of Asia Minor, though even so their representatives were subject to the satraps.

These powerful administrators, as early as the reign of Darius, showed a tendency to independence, and later the satrapic system facilitated the break-up of the empire. The experience of Darius with Oroites in Lydia and Aryandes in Egypt may have drawn his attention to these dangers, and to him may be attributed the creation or perfecting of measures for a due control of the satraps. Important was rapidity of communication, for this at all events diminished the need for the satrap to undertake independent action without prior reference to Susa. Along the greatly improved roads and by means of the rapid government post, communications passed in great numbers and with frequency to and from the satraps, to each of whom a royal secretary was attached who attended to the receipt and despatch of the correspondence between the king and the satrap. Periodical inspections of the

satrapies and of the way in which the governors discharged their
duties were made by a person specially appointed by the king—
his brother, for instance, or his son, or that high official who
bore the significant title 'the King's Eye'—who travelled accompanied by a military force supplied from the king's Persian army.

A further check on the satrap could be exercised by the commander of the Persian troops in the garrisons within his province.
The satrap, indeed, was himself the military as well as the civil
head of his province: he secured the requisite levy for the army
from the Persians resident in his province and the native inhabitants: the subordinate officers of these troops were natives,
but the satrap himself in war took the general command of them,
or, in cases where the troops of a province fell under more than
one command, of the principal part of them. Thus in the Behistun
inscription Vivāna and Hystaspes clearly appear as commanding
the troops of the provinces which they governed; and the naval
force furnished by Egypt for Xerxes' expedition against Greece
was commanded by Achaemenes, his brother, the satrap of Egypt,
similarly the Cilician fleet by the *Syennesis* of Cilicia. So, at the
end of the Achaemenid period under Darius III, the Bactrians,
for example, were under the command of the satrap of Bactria,
the Areians of the satrap of Areia, the Arachosians of the satrap
of Arachosia. The garrisons of citadels like those of Sardes,
Celaenae, Ecbatana, Memphis, and of the fortified places along
the royal roads were provided from the Persian army under the
direct central authority of the king: the commanders of them,
also directly appointed by the king, were independent of the
satrap, and satrap and garrison-commanders exercised a mutual
control over one another.

An important function of the satrap, and one which, in association with his administrative and military supremacy, contributed greatly to his power and facilitated later the tendency on
the part of satraps to independence, was the control of finance.
As there were satraps and satrapies before Darius, so also the
conquered countries must have contributed tribute or taxes to
the state, and indeed Gaumata had sought popularity by promising
to remit the charges for some years. But the regular and equitable
distribution of taxation based on an exact measurement of the
empire for the purpose and with reference to the varying fertility of different lands was one of the principal achievements of
Darius, and he placed on the satraps the duty of raising the
specified amount from their respective provinces. According to
the list given by Herodotus, the total amount raised annually

from the twenty provinces (including the Indian contribution paid in gold-dust) by this regular taxation was 14,560 Euboic talents, or in round numbers about three and a half million pounds sterling. The heaviest contribution was the gold-dust of India valued at 4680 talents; after this the largest contribution was made by the province of Assyria and Babylon (1000 talents); the next largest by Egypt and the other African dominions (700 talents); the four satrapies of Asia Minor together paid 1760 talents; the fifth satrapy (Phoenicia, Syria, Cyprus) 350 talents; Bactria 360, Susiana 300. Some of the larger but much less thickly populated provinces paid considerably less than these sums: the seventh satrapy with its contribution of 170 talents paying the least. The proceeds of this taxation were forwarded annually by the satraps to Susa, where the surplus that remained, after defraying the annual outgoings, accumulated in the king's treasury as a reserve fund. After this fund had been largely drawn upon by Darius III for the war with Alexander the Great, and after he had carried off with him 8000 talents in his flight, there remained a rich spoil for Alexander: he is said to have obtained from Susa, Persepolis and Pasargadae metal coined and uncoined to the value of 180,000 talents, of which far the greater amount was in uncoined metal: of this from Susa he obtained 40,000 silver talents, as against darics to the value of 9000 silver talents only.

The income of the government from the provinces was not limited to this fixed taxation in money. Much was paid in kind; and there may have been other occasional payments such as tolls. Passages in Ezra (iv, 13, 20; vii, 24) distinguish three kinds of charges, one of which must have been the fixed annual land-tax (cp. Neh. v, 4), another may cover contributions in kind, and the third, on one view of the etymology of the term, may refer to *way*-tolls. Of the contributions in kind there is more information: they were made especially for the support of the army and of the households of the king, the satraps and even sub-satraps. The Great King and his army for four months in the year, according to Herodotus, 'had their support from Babylon, and for the remaining eight months from the whole of the rest of Asia': here as in the matter of the money tax Babylon is most heavily charged. On the march in warfare the army was maintained by the country through which it was marching or quartered for the time being. The household of each satrap was provided for by his own province, and that of each sub-satrap by the district under his charge: the governor even of a small district like the Persian sub-satrapy of Judah dined at his table 150 officers daily and, at all events in the poorer communities, the cost of such entertainment was felt to be burdensome (Neh. v, 14 *sqq.*). Other contributions in kind were 1500 horses, 50,000 sheep, 2000 mules exacted yearly from Cappadocia, and nearly double this number from Media, also 360 white horses from Cilicia; 1000 talents of incense from Arabia, ebony and ivory from Ethiopia. The sculptures of Xerxes and Artaxerxes at Persepolis depict various types of tribute brought to the king, including camels and zebras.

The extent and value of these contributions in kind and other charges cannot be accurately estimated: they may possibly have amounted to two or three times as much as the fixed money tax. Still less is it possible to compare at all precisely the burdens imposed on their subjects by the Persian and earlier empires, or the value received in return for them in the form of peace, security, good administration and public works, though in general it is sufficiently clear that the subjects of Persia were far more favourably placed than those of Assyria, and it is possible to specify some of the public utilities of the Persian government. After the period of conquest was over, *i.e.* from the early years of Darius onwards, in spite of certain border warfare and with the exception of the struggle with Greece, the Persian proved a peaceful government. The great road-system, though constructed primarily for military and government purposes, must have served also the interests of trade and commerce; and the same may be said of another of the great works of Darius—the completion of the canal connecting the Nile with the Red Sea (see above, p. 25): 'I commanded,' he says in an inscription, 'to dig this canal from the Nile...to the sea which goes from Persia; afterwards this canal [was dug] thus as I commanded, and [ships] passed from Egypt by this canal to Persia as was my [will].' The interests of commerce were also served, and may have been directly considered by Darius, in sending out the expedition of Scylax: this Carian traveller sailed down the Indus, and then, after exploring the Indian Ocean, seems to have found his way into the Red Sea and finally to have arrived in the neighbourhood of Suez; thereafter water-communication between India and Persia, as well as between Egypt—and by means of the Nile canal, the Mediterranean—and Persia, was for a time maintained. A later expedition under Sataspes, commanded by Xerxes to circumnavigate Africa, by sailing down the west coast, after proceeding not very far beyond the Pillars of Hercules (Gibraltar) gave up its task and returned by the same way that it had set out. Under the later kings, when Egypt in the fourth century had regained its independence, the use of the canal by the Persian empire was lost, and the canal itself allowed by the Egyptians to fall into disuse and decay; and in other respects the commercial results of the organization and policy of Darius may have gradually diminished under the later Achaemenid rulers.

V. THE ARTS

Two sides of Persian life and achievement remain to be considered—art and religion. Persia proper, before the rapid rise of the Persian empire, was the home of a simple hardy race which had found no opportunity for the development of great art; the extension of dominion beyond Persia proper under the ancestors of Cyrus had already brought the Persians closer to Babylon, one of the centres of ancient art, and, if this extension included Susa, had put them in possession of a city which must have contained great artistic monuments. The conquests of Cyrus, besides making Persia heir to all that Media had already developed through its contact with the civilizations of the Tigris-Euphrates valley and of Asia Minor, gave the Persians possession of Babylon and other Asiatic centres, and brought them into close contact with Greece. The conquests of Cambyses added the other great home of ancient art—Egypt. In general, Persia did not owe its art to a native development, but borrowed and skilfully adapted to its own particular purposes the arts of other peoples. Having no deep native roots, and serving essentially imperial ends, it passed, as it arose, with the empire.

The art of writing was borrowed from Babylon. Cuneiform signs were used for expressing the Persian language on monuments, but the innumerable variations employed by the Babylonians and Assyrians were reduced to forty-three, and these with fixed and substantially alphabetic values. That this method of writing was the invention of Darius, as some have inferred from an obscure passage in the Behistun inscription, is improbable in view of the brief inscription of Cyrus—who cannot well be Cyrus the younger—at Murghab (Pasargadae); it must rather go back to Cyrus, unless, of which indeed there is no proof, it should be traced to his ancestors in Anshan or to the Medes. No instance of the use of Persian cuneiform later than the fall of the Achaemenid empire is known. Utilized by Darius in the greatest of rock-inscriptions at Behistun, by him and his successors on their buildings and tombs, it died with the overthrow of his empire

and house, and exercised no abiding influence on future developments of writing. Of greater moment for the future was the
adoption by the Persian kings of the Aramaic language and the
Aramaic alphabet for communications with their subjects in the
west. Though this language and alphabet were already used
alongside of cuneiform in Babylonia and Assyria before the rise
of Persia, the Persian empire promoted the extension of its use.
Whether or not the Achaemenidae and their subjects employed
the Aramaic alphabet for writing Persian otherwise than monumentally there is at present no evidence to determine; but subsequently the Aramaic alphabet was so used, and from it the Pehlevi
alphabet is derived. Under the Persian empire Aramaic was used
in India: a recent discovery at Taxila of an inscription in the
Aramaic alphabet and language proves what had formerly been
surmised; and as it became in Persia the source of the Pehlevi,
so did it in India of the Kharoshthi alphabet[1].

The greatest examples of Achaemenian art are architectural
and sculptural. In these, too, the influence of Babylon is obvious;
and at the same time we see that power of adaptation, as distinct
from mere servile borrowing, that gives to the great buildings
and sculpture of the Persian kings a character of their own. In
them ancient western Asiatic art culminates and also expires;
even the Arsacids and Sassanids drew their inspiration for their
works of art from elsewhere, and not from the earlier Persian
monuments.

Borrowed from Babylon is obviously the plan followed alike at
Pasargadae, Susa and Persepolis, of erecting the royal buildings
on large artificial terraces or platforms. In these platforms, however, as well as in the buildings, the Persians, instead of using
bricks, as the Babylonians (and largely the Assyrians also) had
been forced to do by the nature of their country, took advantage,
especially at Pasargadae and Persepolis, of the excellent marble-
like limestone which was to be found close at hand merely waiting
to be quarried.

The buildings themselves differ strikingly from the royal
buildings of Babylon and Assyria: whereas these had consisted
of many chambers opening on to an interior court and presenting
an uninteresting and forbidding exterior, the most characteristic
Persian buildings are the single-chambered audience halls whose
columnar construction lent beauty and dignity to interior and
exterior alike. Particularly in its use of the column did Persian
architecture differ from that of the Tigris-Euphrates valleys,

[1] See *The Cambridge History of India*, I, p. 62.

where it had been most sparingly employed. Whether, as some have suggested, the Persian architectural column should be traced back to timber-columns similar to those of modern village houses in the province of Mazandaran on the southern shores of the Caspian, or to those of Median palaces—Polybius (x, 27, 10) refers to columns supporting porticoes in the palaces at Ecbatana —or whether it derives rather from Egypt, and whatever may have been the influence of Greece on some of its features, it underwent developments in its structure and use that account for much of the distinctive character of Persian architecture.

The Persian columns are more slender than the Egyptian and placed at greater intervals from one another: the ratio of the height to the diameter, which in Egypt rarely exceeds 6 : 1, is in the hall of Xerxes[1] at Persepolis 12 : 1, a ratio which is not quite reached by the slenderest of the Athenian columns. The intervals between the columns, which in Egypt is one or two diameters, and in Greece varies from rather over one to something under three, ranges in the different Persian buildings between three and a half and six or even seven diameters. Distinctive of the Persian columns are also the fluting, and both the bases and the capital. The fluted is in Persian more frequent than the unfluted column, which appears only at Pasargadae and in the rock-tombs; the flutings are much more numerous than in Egypt where they are mainly confined to the earlier buildings, and about twice as numerous as those which are found in the Greek orders. The bases—though at Pasargadae a plain round disc appears—have more frequently a very characteristic bell-shape with rich drooping leaf-ornament[2], and as a whole they present an effect not to be traced previously elsewhere. In the elaborate and equally distinctive capitals[3] the use of the two fore-quarters of two beasts (generally horse or bull), with knees and heads forming a strongly marked projection and directly supporting the architrave, is perhaps the most striking but not the only peculiar element.

In sculpture which is used so profusely at Persepolis, and in the enamelled bricks which were used for the friezes at Susa, as they had previously been used with great effect in Babylon, the influence of Babylon or Assyria is obvious enough in the choice and treatment of subjects. The colossal winged-bulls[4] with human faces which adorn the Persian entrances unmistakably recall, in spite of certain refinements, the similar colossi of Nineveh; and the depiction of the king in conflict with monsters has a similar origin, as also has the treatment of the king enthroned and of the processional subjects. Further, the one religious symbol that

---

[1] See Vol. of Plates i, 318.   [2] *Ib.* 320, *b*.   [3] *Ib.* 320, *a*.   [4] *Ib.* 318, *a*.

appears in these Persian sculptures—Ahura-Mazda in a winged disc—closely resembles the Nineveh representation of the god Ashur, which again, in virtue of the use of the winged disc, appears to betray Egyptian influence; and alike at Nineveh and Persepolis the divine symbol is depicted above the head of the king[1]. In the greater refinement of the sculptures—for example, in the draperies of the human figure and in the human figure itself—may perhaps be detected the influence of Greece: Greek craftsmen and artists in some way and for one reason or another found their way to the Persian court, and it is likely enough that specimens of Greek art from rifled temples, and elsewhere, were by no means unknown in Persia. To what extent the work was actually carried out by foreign or by native workmen cannot be determined; in either case the workmen were maintained by the court and for court purposes and, as already remarked, on the fall of the empire they and with them the art they had practised ceased to be employed.

In addition to their palaces and state buildings, the Persian kings constructed massive architectural tombs. In these, if the buildings at Pasargadae and Naksh-i-Rustum—which have by some been judged to be fire-temples—are actually tombs, two influences exercised at different periods are to be discerned: the square detached buildings of Pasargadae, Naksh-i-Rustum and Naubandajan, a few miles south-east of Faza, recall the Lycian tombs, and the 'tomb of Cyrus' at Murghab presents features in which Ionian treatment has been suspected. These, if they are tombs, are remains of the earliest reigns—of Cyrus and Cambyses. With Darius a new influence comes in: the effect of closer acquaintance with Egypt after the conquest by Cambyses is telling; and Darius, as the inscription above his tomb makes clear, and his successors cut their tombs in the sides of the rock and provided them with an architectural façade and a sculptured frieze.

Ancient Persia has left nothing corresponding to the temples of Egypt, Babylon, Greece; and, in general, Persian art found little in religion to serve or to represent. The representation of Ahura-Mazda has been already mentioned; apart from that, sculpture is entirely secular in subject. The Persian religion afforded no scope for great religious buildings. Fire-altars[2] were required and were constructed, but hardly fire-temples, though, as we have seen, some would regard as temples the buildings at Naksh-i-Rustum and elsewhere. The character of the houses of the gods, possibly not intended for Persian worship, which Gaumata destroyed and Darius restored, remains uncertain.

[1] See Volume of Plates i, 312, *a*.   [2] *Ib.* 314, *a*.

VI. RELIGION

If the art of the Persian empire was neither deeply rooted in the earlier Persian life, nor destined to outlast it or exercise any marked influence on the future, the same cannot be said of Persian religion. It is true that neither the greatest figure nor the most notable development in the religion commonly designated as Persian was Persian in the stricter sense of being connected with the particular district whence the Achaemenidae sprang; but Iranian they were, and if not the origin, yet important stages in the history of the religion fall within the period of the Persian empire, and are intimately connected with it. The religion itself survived the empire and exercised a larger and wider influence after it had fallen than while it stood. The origins and history and character of this religion present many still keenly-disputed problems—which cannot be fully discussed, and indeed can be little more than mentioned, if even that, in the brief sketch which alone is possible here—of the Persian religion in relation to the history and abiding influence of the first Persian empire.

Herodotus has recorded his information or impressions as to the Persian religion in the latter half of the fifth century B.C. They count it unlawful, he relates, to set up images and shrines and altars, 'but their custom is to ascend the highest peaks of the mountains, and offer sacrifices to Zeus, calling the whole vault of sky Zeus, and they sacrifice also to Sun, Moon, Earth, Fire, Water, and Winds. To these alone they have sacrificed from the beginning; but they have learned from the Assyrians and Arabians to sacrifice also to Urania. . . .The Persians call Aphrodite Mitra.' Herodotus goes on to describe the manner of sacrifice, the spreading out of the flesh on a carpet of herbage, while a Magian, without whom it is not lawful to sacrifice, 'stands by and chants a theogony. . . .Other things are talked of as secrets and not openly, with regard to the dead—how the corpse of a Persian is not buried before it has been torn by bird or dog. Now I know the Magi do this, for they do it without concealment; but the Persians cover the corpse with wax and bury it in the earth.' The Magi, Herodotus concludes, differ from Egyptian priests in 'slaying with their own hands all animals except a dog and a man, and they make this an object of rivalry, slaying alike ants and snakes and other reptiles and birds.'

These statements are remarkable alike for what they contain and for what they do not contain. Judged by its objects of worship —great natural phenomena—the Persian religion in the time of

Herodotus retained much of the character of the earliest Aryan religion; but it had already had a history; it had introduced from without the worship of Urania; it had also developed, out of or alongside of the natural phenomena, a personal deity, Mithra—a name which Herodotus mistakenly attributes to a female deity. The priestly caste of the Magi are prominent, and are distinguished from the Persians by their greater or exclusive devotion to certain practices, viz. the exposure of the corpse prior to, if not instead of, burial, and the slaying of certain animals, which in later stages of the religion become obligatory on all its adherents.

But while Herodotus is aware that the religion has had a history, he has nothing to say of Zoroaster. Obviously Zoroaster occupied no such position in the Persian world of his day as Mohammed occupied in the Arabian empire from the time of the earliest caliphs onwards; not only does the Greek traveller not mention the name of the Iranian prophet, but he describes as Persian a religion that differs markedly from that of the earliest Zoroastrian literature—the Gathas. Is this due to the fact that an earlier prevalence of the purer Zoroastrian faith, having contributed more or less powerfully to the establishment of the Achaemenian empire under Cyrus or its recreation by Darius, had been affected by a reaction which had reintroduced much that was pre-Zoroastrian, or by other influences that had brought about beliefs or customs alien to Zoroaster's teaching? or had that teaching never yet, at least widely, affected the Persian world? In either case, was it mainly the teaching of Zoroaster himself, or was it other religious beliefs and customs, that affected the political development of the empire, or through that empire gained wider influence?

The answers to these questions are affected by many uncertainties: the age in which Zoroaster lived, the region where he lived and taught, the religious significance of the inscriptions of the Persian kings, and the criticism and interpretation of the various sacred writings of the Persians. The attempt to treat Zoroaster as a purely mythological figure having no place in actual history may be said to have failed, yet though his age and country remain disputed, one thing seems certain: he neither was born nor worked in Persia proper, the home of the Achaemenidae—in a word, the greatest figure in Persian religion and the family of the Persian monarchs did not spring from the same country.

The highest antiquity claimed for Zoroaster is that assigned

by certain Greek writers of the fourth century B.C., and Xanthus
the Lydian of the fifth century, also by Diogenes Laertius
(flourished *c.* 300 A.D.). According to them, he lived 5000 or
6000 years before their time. Their curious statements can be
explained as due to misunderstanding; but the misunderstanding
could scarcely have arisen in regard to a prophet whose lifetime
was actually quite recent. Persian tradition as given in the
Bundahish which, whatever its exact date, is not earlier than
the seventh century A.D., assigns to him a date some 300 years
before Alexander, and, more precisely, according to one interpretation, indicates 660–583 B.C. as his lifetime. Various considerations would point to an earlier date rather than a later such
as would be suggested, if not demanded, were the identification
of Hystaspes the father of Darius with Hystaspes (Vishtaspa), the
royal patron of Zoroaster, accepted; but in spite of the coincidence
of names, so late a date for Zoroaster, though defended by many
scholars, seems to the present writer to involve grave difficulties
and he would prefer to place the prophet about 1000 B.C.[1]

The scene of Zoroaster's activity was not Persia proper: it
was Media, according to one theory, Bactria according to another;
or it may have included both regions.

In the Persian scriptures, the Avesta, the only parts that have
gained any general recognition as the work of Zoroaster himself
or his age are the Gathas—metrical hymns in a distinct dialect.
The Yashts, other metrical parts of the Avesta, are later, but
may fall within the Achaemenian period; they show a greater
affinity with the religion of the Persians as described by Herodotus than do the Gathas. Later still as literature is the prose
Vendidad, a ritual work dealing with defilement from the dead
and the correct treatment of corpses, though much of the
custom is, or is intimately connected with, practices of great
antiquity.

Zoroaster is best regarded as a reformer who, over against
such a nature-worship as Herodotus describes, recognized no
independent objects of worship in Sun, Moon, Stars and so forth,
but rather, in a series of questions, implied that Ahura-Mazda
(*i.e.* the Wise Lord, often in the Gathas in the reverse order
Mazda Ahura, or simply Ahura, or Mazda) determined the path
of the stars, upheld the earth and the firmament, caused the moon
to wax and wane, yoked swiftness to winds and clouds, created
light and darkness, sleep and waking, morning, noon, and night.
No other deity is by name or implication associated in the Gathas

[1] For further reference to the various views proposed, see the Bibliography.

with Ahura-Mazda; his companions are certain qualities or attributes of his nature—Good Thought, Right, Dominion, Piety,
Welfare, Immortality, as the terms may be more or less adequately
rendered. So far there is nothing that precludes the application
of the term monotheistic to the religion of Zoroaster in the
Gathas. But from the beginning, and so far as the present world
and age are concerned, Ahura-Mazda is in conflict with an evil
spirit. There is nothing in common between him and the enemy
—*angro*, the first element in the later Angromainya, Ahriman
(which does not itself occur in the Gathas), as the evil spirit is
once described. 'Neither thought nor teachings nor wills nor
beliefs nor words nor deeds nor selves nor souls of us twain agree.'
The 'two primal spirits' are 'the Better and the Bad in thought
and word and action.'

The demons—the *daēvas*—the (nature) gods of the older
religion, which Zoroaster set out to reform, attached themselves
to the evil spirit and 'infected the world of men.' In the conflict
in the spiritual world mankind is involved: men are free to choose,
but choose they must, whether they will be followers of the Right
(or Ahura-Mazda), or of the Lie (or the evil spirit). The issue of
the conflict is not uncertain: victory will rest with Ahura-Mazda:
the Lie is ultimately to be vanquished, to be delivered into the
hands of Right. Then, too, the human adherents of Ahura-Mazda
and the Lie will receive their respective requitals—cruel torment
for the liar, blessing, delight for the righteous: 'in immortality
shall the soul of the righteous be joyful, in perpetuity shall be the
torment of the liars.' Thus, sharp as is the conflict, absolute as is
the antithesis between the two spirits, in view of the ultimate
victory of the Good Spirit, the monotheistic may be said to prevail
over the dualistic element in Zoroaster's conception of God.
The strongly ethical character of the religion is obvious; and its
activism stands in sharp contrast to the passivism of Aryan religion
as it developed in the great religions of India.

How widely or how thoroughly this teaching of Zoroaster
made way is difficult to determine: the prophet's aim was, by
presenting the two destinies, 'to convert all living men.' His outlook was wide: to the one Good Spirit all men irrespective of
nationality might, if they would, adhere, and in him find salvation.
But of the actual extent of Zoroaster's converts the Gathas tell
little: among them the king, or as the Gathas call him, *kavi*,
Vishtaspa; but unless this Vishtaspa be identical with the father
of Darius, which is improbable, his age and region are uncertain
like those of Zoroaster himself.

Later ages numbered Zoroaster among the Magi, who were already in the time of Herodotus the indispensable priests of the religion. But the Gathas fail to confirm this; and it may be that the later religion is due to a fusion of two originally distinct streams—the Zoroastrian, and the Magian with its insistence on the exposure of corpses, on next-of-kin marriage, on ritual, and, generally, with its intimate and more detailed application to life of a dualistic principle. Be this as it may, the various elements —old Aryan nature-worship, Gathic religion, and Magianism— fused in various ways or confused, maintained various degrees of vitality through the Achaemenid period: Herodotus vouches for the prevalence of the first and the power of the third, the mere fact of the survival of the Gathas for the second.

Which of these three elements of the religion affected the development of the empire and in what way? What religious forces were liberated during the period, to affect the future? It has been suggested, on the one hand, that the rise of Zoroaster within the Median empire had the result that it was so weakened by religious divisions as to fall a ready prey to the energy and vigour of Cyrus and the Persians; and, on the other, that it was the acceptance of the religion of Zoroaster by the Achaemenidae that supplied to them much of the power that made their conquests possible. These and other speculations must remain unsubstantiated till the time and place of origin and the progress of Zoroaster's teaching can be more closely and certainly determined. The records of the Achaemenid kings themselves in reference to their religion are in many respects incomplete and ambiguous. One point is clear: the tombs of the kings show that Cyrus and his successors did not conform to the Magian practice of exposing the dead; but that for this reason they also acted contrary to the teaching of Zoroaster cannot be proved: the Gathas nowhere require this treatment of the dead, and possibly in a single passage imply without disapprobation burial as the existing custom.

In another respect the kings fall short of what the Gathas allow us to attribute to Zoroaster—a belief in Ahura-Mazda unqualified by the recognition of other gods: the difference, so far as the recognition by the kings in their dealings with other nations of Egyptian, Babylonian and other gods is concerned, might indeed be attributed to policy. But Darius even in his own home in Persepolis speaks of Ahura-Mazda as 'the greatest of the gods'—a phrase which may indeed occur as a survival of polytheism in a monotheistic faith—and prays that Ahura-Mazda may bear him aid 'with the royal,' or 'the clan,' or 'all the gods' as the phrase is variously rendered, and at Behistun records that 'Ahura-Mazda and the other gods which are bore me aid.' Yet in spite of these qualifications Ahura-Mazda dominates the inscriptions of Darius scarcely less than the Gathas: no god is *named* beside him, nor referred to except in the phrase just mentioned. To Darius—and Xerxes and Artaxerxes later repeat the faith—Ahura-Mazda is he 'who created this earth, who created yonder heaven, who created man, who created welfare for man,' who gave the kingdom to his house and defends his empire from evil.

Over against Ahura-Mazda stands, not indeed, in the actual terminology of the inscriptions, a primal spirit of evil, but, as often in the Gathas, the Lie: the Lie made the provinces rebel against Darius whom Ahura-Mazda had made king and assisted, because he was not an enemy nor a liar nor a deceiver nor a wrong-doer. With certain differences which have been indicated, there appears to be too considerable agreement between the religion of the prophet as revealed in the Gathas and that of the statesman in the inscriptions for the latter to be independent of the former. At a distance in time and place, not at present to be exactly determined, and by ways which cannot be closely traced, Zoroaster had powerfully affected Darius and perhaps with him in particular the Persian nobles as distinct from the people in general, who were more closely held by the kind of worship indicated in Herodotus. Whether Darius is the first of the Achaemenidae to have come under the influence of Zoroaster's teaching cannot be either asserted or denied with certainty: of the predecessors of Darius no inscription exists in Persian, except the five words of Cyrus at Pasargadae; and there is consequently no means of judging what expression of religious belief they would have made in their own country. On the other hand, the evidence, from inscriptions and other sources, that Cyrus and Cambyses recognized in countries not their own the gods of those countries, is in itself no proof that they were less affected by Zoroaster than Darius; for Darius made the same recognition.

In the successors of Darius it is possible to observe an important change which would appear to indicate that they were led further away from the religion of Zoroaster, partly by the pressure of the still-surviving pre-Zoroastrian religion, partly by the influence of the religions of peoples incorporated into the Persian empire. Whereas Darius, as we have seen, invokes no god but Ahura-Mazda by name, Artaxerxes II prays 'may Ahura-Mazda,

Anahita and Mithra protect me,' the same king, according to Berosus, 'first taught the Persians the worship of the gods in human form, and set up the image of Aphrodite-Anaitis at Babylon, Susa, Ecbatana, Damascus and Sardes.' Mithra, a divine figure of the Aryan past, regarded perhaps by Zoroaster as a *daēva* or demon, had maintained his position even under the earlier Achaemenidae, as proper-names compounded with Mithra attest; the worship of Anahita, the goddess of fertility, is to be traced mainly to Semitic (Babylonian) influence. The direct influence of these cults was for long wider and deeper than the teaching of Zoroaster.

Thus, (1) the belief in a conflict between two opposite and opposed spiritual principles—a good spirit, with whom at last will lie the victory, and an evil spirit—in the division of mankind into adherents by free choice of one or other of these spiritual powers, and the different destiny that awaited them at the End, (2) the worship of Mithra the unconquerable Sun and maintainer of compacts, or (3) of Anahita the mother-goddess, are some of the religious factors that entered into the life of the Persian empire, and gained the power which enabled its religion to spread beyond it and survive it.

But it lies beyond the scope of the present chapter to trace in detail the working of these ideas and the modification of the Persian or Zoroastrian religion in the obscure Arsacid period, and during the striking revival with its keen propaganda that marked the rule of the Sassanids; or to examine the extent to which indirectly the Persians affected the religion of Islam forced upon them by their Mohammedan conquerors; or to compare with the ancient religion that of the still surviving followers of Zoroaster—some 10,000 in Persia, some 90,000 in India (Parsis). Nor is this the place to trace the march and growth of Mithraism through the late pre-Christian and early post-Christian centuries, or to determine precisely how far the religion of Persia actually introduced fresh ideas into, or forced the growth of ideas latent but previously undeveloped in, Judaism, and so affected the conditions under which the Christian religion came to birth; or again what heretical ideas that gained currency in the earlier centuries of the Christian Church proceeded from Persia. Merely to refer to these movements must suffice to indicate the general fact that the influence of Persian religion which in various ways affected and was affected by the empire of the Achaemenidae extended far, lasted long, and is not really exhausted even to-day.

VII. THE SCYTHIAN EXPEDITION[1]

Shortly after his re-organization of the Persian empire, in or about 516 B.C., Darius delivered the first historic attack of Asia upon Europe. Like the Ottoman Sultans of the fourteenth century, he did not in the first instance direct his march upon Greece but upon the Balkan hinterland.

This 'Scythian expedition' of Darius, as it is commonly called, can only be described in skeleton outline, for Herodotus, who is practically our sole informant on it, has drawn most of his detail from the realm of fable.

Since Darius took command of the expedition in person, the forces engaged in it must have been considerable. But the traditional estimate of 600 ships and 700,000–800,000 men is a gross exaggeration. The fleet, being drawn exclusively from Darius' Greek subjects, cannot have numbered more than 200–300 sail; from the nature of the work in hand we may conclude that the army did not exceed one-tenth of the traditional total. Darius crossed over to Europe by a bridge with which a Greek engineer, Mandrocles of Samos, had spanned the Bosphorus. Proceeding in a northward direction he traversed Thrace to the Danube, and effected the speedy submission of the natives, most of whom were overawed into an unwontedly tame surrender. But instead of pausing on the Danube to consolidate his gains he pushed on at once into Scythia.

The purpose of Darius' plunge into the trans-Danubian wilderness is not at all clear. Was he reconnoitring for a suitable frontier, or in quest of new sources of wealth, or bent upon adventure? Perhaps he aimed vaguely at all these objects. In that case his Scythian foray may be compared with Caesar's excursions into Germany and Britain.

The Persian force effected the passage of the Danube by means of a bridge of boats which his fleet had built for him at a distance of two days' sail from the river mouth, near Galatz or Braila. Its subsequent line of advance cannot be traced with any certainty. According to Herodotus, it followed the easterly bend of the Black Sea towards the Don steppes and eventually reached a river Oarus, presumably the Volga, on whose banks eight ruined 'forts of Darius' were exhibited in later times. But these 'forts' were probably ordinary Scythian *kurgans* or burial mounds: they can no more be used to define Darius' route than can the 'Caesar's camps' in Britain to trace Caesar's line of march. Had Darius'

[1] For an account of Scythia at this time see vol. III, chap. IX.

objective really been the east Russian steppe, assuredly he would not have approached it by a toilsome overland march across the Dniester, Bug, and Dnieper, but by the commodious water-way up the Azov Sea and the Don. Moreover Herodotus tacitly corrects himself in mentioning that the tribes attacked by Darius retreated upon the land of the Agathyrsi, *i.e.* towards the Carpathians. From this we may infer that Darius marched north or north-west through the Moldavian plain.

But whatever the direction of his march, Darius now found himself in a steppe land similar to the Bactrian prairie which had baffled Cyrus, in his last campaign, and he encountered like difficulties (p. 15). The Scythians, not daring to face him in battle, drove off their herds and left their primitive timber shacks to be fired by the invader, and by this elusive strategy they won the campaign. After a protracted but ineffectual pursuit Darius was forced to turn back by the failure of his supplies; and as the Scythians doubled back upon him he had to race for the Danube, abandoning his transport and sick.

Meanwhile the Greeks whom Darius had left in sole charge of the Danube passage were being incited by Miltiades, tyrant of the Thracian Chersonese, to unmoor their ships and sail home. But a fellow-tyrant, Histiaeus of Miletus, pointed out that a Persian catastrophe in Scythia would be followed by domestic revolutions in the Greek cities, in which the rule of the despots would be swept away. This warning, which subsequent events proved true, was not lost upon the Greek commanders, for most of them were tyrants. Consequently the bridge was preserved until Darius had recrossed it, and a Persian disaster was averted. But while the Greeks in the field safeguarded the Persian line of communications at its most vital point, their compatriots at the base, misled perhaps by exaggerated reports of Darius' misadventure, rose in revolt and broke down the Bosphorus bridge. Thus Darius was compelled to prolong his retreat through Thrace and to seek a new return road to Asia. Having found a crossing-point at Sestos he retired to Sardes and took no further personal part in European warfare.

The king's '1812 campaign' ended far differently from Napoleon's, and the retreat across the Danube was attended with no such disaster as the passage of the Beresina. Yet his failure sufficed to deter him from further adventures in the interior of Europe. After Darius' departure operations in Thrace were resumed under his lieutenant Megabazus. This officer reduced the coastland from the sea of Marmora to the Strymon. In order to secure the passage of this river he deported to Asia some of the native tribes which bordered upon it, and he induced Darius to revoke a gift of land under Mt Pangaeus which had been bestowed upon Histiaeus in recompense for his loyalty. In asking for this territory Histiaeus probably had no other object than to develop the adjacent mining fields. But the Persian was less impressed by its wealth than by its strategic position on the narrow strip between Lake Prasias and the sea. We may also count among Megabazus' victims Histiaeus' former antagonist Miltiades. According to Herodotus, Miltiades was expelled from his dominions by the Scythians (see p. 232, n. 1). But even if they did ever make a raid to the Dardanelles, Miltiades could safely have defied them behind his fortifications on the Bulair isthmus, so in all probability it was Megabazus who expelled him. On the other hand, Megabazus failed to reduce Macedonia. The envoys whom he sent to demand its submission were murdered by the Crown Prince Alexander, and this affront remained unpunished.

Megabazus was eventually relieved by an officer named Otanes, who recaptured Byzantium and Chalcedon, and with a Greek flotilla subdued Lemnos and Imbros. With these operations, which secured the whole border strip between the two continents and brought Persia's frontiers within easy distance of the Greek homeland, Darius' European campaigns ended for the time being.

VIII. THE IONIAN REVOLT

With the fifth century, however, began a conflict of nations which probably went further than any other ancient war to determine the world's history.

Of the two antagonists in this struggle, the Greeks were ill-organized and unready, whereas the Persians possessed the most formidable war machine which the world had yet seen. This machine, moreover, was seldom allowed to rest. The king of Persia, as Herodotus truly fabled, was driven on by a 'daimon.' Though he might doubt the wisdom of war piled on war, the traditions of the Persian people and its powerful nobility and the need of distracting the realm from the internal dissensions which had shaken it closed every career to him save that of conquest. The direction in which his next blow would fall was plainly indicated. On its northern, eastern and southern sides the Persian empire had reached the limits of profitable advance; but the Greek lands on its western frontier, though deficient in material wealth, lay within easy reach of a Persian attack, and their inhabitants were known to the Persian king as the most restless of neighbours and the most useful of subjects. Besides, though so energetic a king required no prompting, Darius was spurred on by numerous Greek renegades who aspired to re-enter their country in the baggage-train of a Persian army. That the alleged grievances of these refugees might become a pretext for aggression against Greece had been shown in the case of the ex-tyrant Hippias, whose suit was taken up by Darius' brother Artaphrenes as a means of opening a quarrel with Athens (p. 168). But, as Herodotus has aptly pointed out, the chief danger to Greece lay in the impression of divided strength which these *émigrés* produced. Like the Macedonian, the Roman and the Turkish conquerors of later times, the Persian invaders were solicited by the Greeks themselves and could reckon on internal feuds within the Greek nation.

About 500 B.C., therefore, a Persian attack upon Greece appeared imminent. In point of fact, Persians and Greeks came to blows at this very time. But in this round the Greeks were the aggressors, and for the first time in their history made an Anabasis into Asia.

The Ionian Revolt, as this passage of arms is called, is the first war in Greek history of which we have a detailed account. The *Persika* of Charon and of Dionysius, who lived at the time of the Revolt or soon after, and included the history of it in their works, have not come down to us. But we still possess the account of Herodotus, and the Ionian Revolt marks the very point at which he begins to attempt a continuous narrative. Unfortunately this chapter of his story reveals Herodotus almost at his worst. It forms a string of more or less incoherent episodes, of which the sequence and causal connection are often hard to establish. As there are no means of supplementing Herodotus' account from other sources, the task of reconstructing the story of the Revolt is like the re-assembling of a mosaic whose pattern is lost. Herodotus' story also suffers from a strong bias against his own countrymen. Nowhere else is the 'malignity' for which Plutarch rated him more manifest. The reason of Herodotus' prejudice may partly be sought in the antipathy of a Dorian from Halicarnassus against the Ionian cities which took the leading part in the Revolt. But where Herodotus judges unfairly, the cause usually resides less in him than in his informants. These were principally drawn from the island of Samos, which played a most equivocal part in the Revolt. By way of apologizing for the uncertain support which the Samians gave to this movement,

Herodotus' authorities were set on depreciating the rebellion as a headstrong piece of mischief-making, of which men of sense could but seek to wash their hands. By faithfully mirroring a distorted presentation of events, Herodotus reduced his picture to a caricature. Thus not only the proper grouping of events but also the discovery of their true causes offers great difficulties to the modern historian of the struggle.

In seeking the causes of the Revolt, we have to remember that when the Greeks were first conquered by the Persians they surrendered their independence without any serious struggle, and that they had since borne the Persian yoke with apparent resignation. A few years before the Revolt, the Greek contingents which accompanied Darius on the Scythian Expedition had deliberately thrown away a good chance of marooning the Persian army in the wilderness and thus regaining their freedom at one blow. The uprising of the Greeks against the Persians at first sight appears like an attack upon a wolf by a sheep.

In Herodotus' eyes the Ionian Revolt was indeed a mere impulsive fling, and its cause lay no deeper than the sudden inspiration of two Greek adventurers bent on fishing in troubled waters. Aristagoras, tyrant of Miletus, so his story runs, was solicited by political refugees from Naxos to reinstate them in that island. With the ulterior purpose of winning Naxos for himself, he pressed their claim before Artaphrenes, the governor of Lydia, on the ground that the conquest of the Cyclades would provide Persia with a row of convenient stepping-stones for an ultimate invasion of Greece itself. Artaphrenes was so impressed with this argument that he invoked his brother Darius' consent to an expedition and proceeded to raise from the seaboard of his province a fleet of 200 sail, double the size suggested by Aristagoras. In 499 B.C. the expedition set out under a cousin of Darius named Megabates, with Aristagoras second in command. To such an armament Naxos should have fallen an easy prey. But on the journey a quarrel broke out between the two leaders over a question of discipline, and Megabates, having got the worse of it, took his revenge by giving the Naxians notice of the coming attack. Thus forewarned, the islanders prepared for a siege and held out successfully. At the end of four months Aristagoras raised the blockade for lack of funds and sailed home. Having thus damaged Persian prestige and squandered Persian money, Aristagoras became apprehensive of punishment at Darius' hands, and his thoughts turned to rebellion as the only means of saving his face.

At this juncture the Milesian tyrant received a message from his father-in-law Histiaeus, who was chafing in honourable detention at Darius' court and had set his hopes on an Ionian insurrection as the readiest means of procuring his return to Ionia. To evade detection, the message was tattooed on the skull of a slave who presented himself to Aristagoras with the bald request, 'please to shave my head.' Aristagoras, having removed the covering of new-grown hair, read a summons to rebellion. He was now emboldened to sound his political confidants. The most distinguished of these, the geographer Hecataeus (p. 518 *sq.*), could speak from his own experience of the vastness of Persia's resources and so discountenanced all rebellion as hopeless. But his voice was lost in a general chorus of approval. Thereupon Aristagoras played his master-stroke. First setting a good example by restoring a free constitution in Miletus and exchanging his tyranny for an elective office, he conducted a campaign against the despots of the other Greek cities. This campaign was facilitated by the arrest of those tyrants who had served in the Naxian expedition and had not yet been demobilized. A general *dégringolade* of despots was the result. But this series of revolutions was also a series of declarations of war against Darius, for the tyrants were his agents and enjoyed his support. The whole of Ionia and the island of Lesbos were thus involved in rebellion.

In analyzing this story we may begin by pruning away some improbable and unessential details. Aristagoras' failure to surprise Naxos should rather be ascribed to the bad discipline which he abetted against Megabates than to treason on the latter's part. That a keen and competent commander, and a Persian nobleman, should have turned traitor out of pure spite is incredible. Again, however much we may cherish the anecdote of Histiaeus' cryptogram as a classical example of evading the censor, we must admit that it is *ben trovato* and nothing more. The exile of Susa could not possibly foresee that his message would find Aristagoras already half inclined to revolt, and without such foreknowledge the sending of the message ceases to be plausible, for Histiaeus could not have been so naïve as to imagine that Aristagoras and all Ionia to boot would mobilize at a mere gesture of impatience on his part.

When these excrescences have been trimmed away, Herodotus' tale may be accepted as substantially true. An expedition to the Cyclades was obviously in Persia's interest, and it promised to be even more profitable to its originator, for Aristagoras could reasonably hope to be rewarded with the lordship of the isles.

His failure to reduce Naxos is no more surprising than Miltiades' similar failure at Paros ten years later. But Herodotus recounts only the immediate antecedents of the Revolt without indicating its ulterior causes. Though he explains satisfactorily why Aristagoras in person was driven to rebellion, he fails to solve the key problem in his own story, why the Ionian cities followed suit.

Two reasons for this apparent mystery may be suggested. The system of government by tyrants, which the Persians maintained in the Greek cities as they had found it at the time of the conquest, had outlived its usefulness and had come to be resented as a burden and a humiliation. At the time of the Scythian Expedition Histiaeus had predicted that the removal of Persia's protecting hand would be followed by a general revolution in Asiatic Greece. In 499 B.C. Aristagoras proved by his own abdication that he considered the revolution to be imminent in Miletus; and the success of his campaign against tyranny in the other Greek cities shows that the feeling against tyrants had become general.

Secondly, at the end of the sixth century the Asiatic Greeks were going through an economic crisis which was bound to react on their politics. Though many of the minor cities of Asiatic Greece were self-contained agricultural states, the leading communities such as Miletus, Samos and Chios were largely dependent on an industry and commerce which in the sixth century showed signs of decline. At the great Egyptian mart of Naucratis Ionian pottery was being displaced by the superior products of Corinth, and in the Black Sea it was losing ground to the still better black-figure ware of Athens. Worse still, some of Ionia's best markets had eventually been lost outright in consequence of various political catastrophes. The conquest of Egypt by Cambyses had ruined the prosperity of Naucratis and indirectly dealt a blow to the Asiatic Greek cities which had the principal share in Naucratic trade. In 510 B.C. the destruction of the Italian city of Sybaris threw Miletus into mourning, and not without reason, for the commercial connection between the two cities had been close. The opening of the western Mediterranean by the Phocaeans had been checked by the combined opposition of Carthage and Etruria (see below, p. 351), and Histiaeus' attempt to exploit the Eldorado of Myrcinus in Thrace had been frustrated on political and military grounds by King Darius (see above, p. 214). It is only fair to add that these reverses, as we have already seen, were due to different causes; and there is little evidence that the Persian kings ever injured Greek trade of set purpose, or gave preferential treatment to the rival commerce of Phoenicia. Yet part at least of Ionia's losses was plainly the result of Persian interference, and when the Greeks felt the shoe pinching it was but natural that they should throw the entire blame on Persia as being the most obvious cause of the pressure. But whatever the precise causes of the Revolt may have been they were certainly more deep-seated than Herodotus suggests; only a widespread sense of grievance could have created an insurrection on such a scale.

In the winter of 499–498 B.C. the rebels were left unmolested by the Persians, who had evidently been taken by surprise. During this respite they set to work, though without any great success, to organize their existing forces and to recruit fresh ones. The κοινὸν τῶν Ἰώνων or confederacy of Ionian cities, which had played a vigorous part in the politics of the seventh century but had since relapsed into inactivity, was now resuscitated as a war parliament. It was probably at this time too that the rebel states entered on a monetary convention which bound them to issue a uniform coinage according to a common weight-standard derived from Miletus. The extant specimens of this mintage prove definitely that Chios, Samos, Clazomenae, Cyme, Priene, and eventually also Lampsacus, Abydos and Dardanus joined the convention, and it is not unlikely that other insurgents took part in it. By this arrangement the various communities not only facilitated commercial intercourse but provided a suitable money for paying the federal forces. But apparently no steps were taken to establish unity of command in the field, and each contingent served under its own general.

The task of extending the area of revolt does not seem to have been pursued at first with much energy, for nothing is heard at this stage of missionary propaganda among the neighbours of the Ionians. But in the winter of 499–498 B.C. Aristagoras in person undertook a tour in the Greek homeland with a view to obtaining support for the movement. Had this support been granted in any generous measure, the combined Greek forces should have had a good chance of fighting the Persians to a standstill, and the European Greeks need not have had to repel a Persian invasion of their own soil.

Aristagoras first had recourse to Sparta. If we are to believe a Spartan tradition reproduced by Herodotus, he brought with him a map of the world (based, no doubt, on a treatise of Hecataeus, the so-called Γῆς περίοδος or 'Tour round the World'), and with the help of this pictorial argument explained to King Cleomenes how easy and lucrative a Greek Anabasis into the heart of Asia would be. This tradition further declares that Aristagoras reinforced his arguments with bribes and had raised his own bid to the colossal sum of fifty talents, when Cleomenes' little daughter Gorgo, who had overheard these proceedings, broke in with wisdom from a babe's mouth and bade her father break off the interview. In this story the parts assigned to Aristagoras and Cleomenes are not merely knavish but downright silly, and no words need be wasted in refuting it. Aristagoras could readily have offered some cogent reasons in favour of Spartan intervention, such as the nearness of Persian peril to Sparta itself, and we need not doubt that he used some such plea. But whatever his arguments were, his suit was rejected. Although Cleomenes was subsequently to show that he appreciated the danger from Persia more fully than most of his countrymen, for the time being the memory of Sparta's past failures in overseas ventures, and the prospect of imminent conflicts in Peloponnesus itself, committed him to a policy of inactivity (p. 165).

There is no record of Aristagoras having visited any other Peloponnesian city. A famous Delphic oracle which was delivered about this time to the Argives and prophesied the destruction of Miletus for its ill deeds, suggests that Aristagoras made an appeal for help to Argos, for unless the Argive consultants had sounded Apollo on the subject of their relations to Miletus his allusion to the fate of that city would appear quite gratuitous. But whether the Argives were approached by Aristagoras or not, they kept their head within their shell, as in every pan-Hellenic crisis.

Of the two old-standing allies of Miletus in the Greek homeland, Aegina and Eretria, Aristagoras appears to have visited the latter only. In this city he obtained promises of support, and he achieved a similar success in Athens. The participation of Athens in the Ionian Revolt was hardly due to commercial considerations, for she was a competitor rather than a trade ally of the Ionians, and the claim which these could make upon her as their reputed mother-city had no binding force. But, as we have seen, the Athenians had a grievance against Artaphrenes for befriending their ex-tyrant Hippias and had reason to believe that the Persians intended to pick a quarrel with them. Therefore it does not require Herodotus' caustic comment, 'that it is easier to fool thirty thousand men than one,' to explain why the Athenian Ecclesia rushed in where Cleomenes feared to tread (see above, p. 168 *sq.*).

The isolated and delusive successes of Aristagoras at Athens and Eretria did not, however, suffice to redeem his mission from failure. To all intents and purposes the Asiatic Greeks were left to fight out their quarrel with Persia unaided. In spite of these disappointments the rebels opened the campaign of 498 B.C. with a daring offensive stroke. With the temporary assistance of twenty ships from Athens and five from Eretria, they advanced upon Artaphrenes' headquarters at Sardes, captured most of the town and penned up the Persian commander in the citadel. The boldness of this onset and its complete initial success raise two questions: with what object did the Greeks attack Sardes, and why were the Persians caught defenceless?

In considering these problems we must remember that the Greeks had apparently no reason for engaging in operations by land, and every reason for putting their trust in their fleet. For a people whose communications were mainly maritime a powerful navy was the surest shield against attack. And it was also their strongest offensive weapon, for their best hopes of propagating the revolt lay among the remaining Greek towns of the Asiatic seaboard. Moreover, in case these plain truths should have escaped the insurgent leaders, Hecataeus had warned them at the outset that they must obtain command of the seas at all costs, and, if necessary, must impound the treasure in the temple at Branchidae for the upkeep of the fleet. By all the tokens therefore the Greeks were committed to a Periclean strategy of making the seas safe and eschewing adventure by land. Again, it cannot be supposed that in 498 B.C. Artaphrenes' province was entirely denuded of troops. Though the reinforcements despatched from up-country had not yet reached him, the Persian commander certainly was no worse off for men than in 499 B.C., and in that year he had been able to draft a considerable force of land troops for service on the Naxian Expedition. In the ensuing year Artaphrenes must have had sufficient troops under his command to contest the Greek advance.

A satisfactory answer to both problems has been furnished by an otherwise unknown Greek author, Lysanias of Mallus, whom Plutarch fortunately quoted on this particular point (*de malign. Herodoti*, 24). According to Lysanias, the march upon Sardes was the Greek reply to a Persian attack upon Miletus. This explanation fits all the known facts of the case excellently. From the Persian point of view, a swift blow against the rebel headquarters was clearly indicated as the best means of paralyzing the movement of revolt, and Artaphrenes lacked neither the men nor the energy to carry out such a stroke. Conversely, though Miletus was probably not in serious danger at this stage, the insurgents were bound to do all that they could to protect their capital, and an active defence promised not only to be as effective as a passive one, but also to have a good influence on Greek morale. In view of these facts, we need not be deterred by the obscurity of Lysanias and the silence of Herodotus from accepting the former's account. The Greeks, we conclude, were first put into check by the Persians, but they relieved the pressure by offering check to the Persians in turn, and as Artaphrenes had thrown his pieces too far forward they caught him at a disadvantage.

Viewed in this light, the Greek offensive fully accomplished its main purpose, for the pressure upon Miletus was completely relieved; and the eventual consequences, as we shall shortly see, were considerable. Not that the Greeks could hope to hold Sardes permanently. Persian reinforcements from all western Asia Minor were closing in and the Lydians were converted from onlookers into enemies by an accidental conflagration which wrought much havoc in the town and destroyed the national sanctuary of Cybebe. Indeed the invaders retired none too soon, for on their retreat they were roughly handled. And this misfortune gave rise to another, for the Athenian forces, and no doubt also the Eretrian contingent, which had lost its leader, now returned home, and in spite of fresh appeals for help no further assistance was sent to the Ionians from the Greek homeland (p. 168 *sq.*). But these losses were more than counterbalanced by the rapid spread of the revolt among the Asiatic Greeks which followed upon the capture of Sardes. Towards the end of 498 B.C. a federal fleet which was sent to cruise along the Asiatic seaboard as far as the Bosporus roused to revolt all the Greek cities on its passage, and doubling back to the south it won over not only the maritime communities of Caria, which had been associated with the Greeks in the Naxian Expedition, but a large portion of the Carian hinterland. Among the adjacent Dorian cities the insurgents do not appear to have made any recruits, except perhaps at Lindus on the island of Rhodes, which subsequently figured on the Greek side. But the insurgents were presented with an important success by the spontaneous accession of the Greek communities of Cyprus at the instigation of Onesilus, the ruler of Salamis. At the end of 498 B.C. the rebellion had become general among the Asiatic Greeks, and its high-water mark was now attained.

It was probably at this stage that Darius accepted an offer by Histiaeus to pacify the Ionians. Though Herodotus represents Histiaeus as boastfully undertaking to deliver Aristagoras to Darius and to make Sardinia, 'the biggest of all islands,' tributary

to Persia, in all likelihood Histiaeus merely promised a diplomatic mediation, which indeed was all that he could hope to
accomplish. The acceptance of this offer shows that Darius saw
no present prospect of crushing the rebellion. But before Histiaeus
could accomplish anything the tide of war had turned against
the Greeks. In 497 B.C., a new Persian force which had assembled
in Cilicia was sent to recapture Cyprus. On this island Onesilus
had invested the Phoenician town of Amathus which had remained loyal to Persia, but as his fleet was unequal to the Phoenician squadron which escorted the Persian reinforcements he was
unable to oppose their landing. The Cypriote Greeks were now
thrown on the defensive and had to appeal to the Ionians for help.
The rebel war council lost no time in sending out a strong fleet.
In the first set battle between the two chief seafaring people of
the Levant the Greeks gained the upper hand, and as nothing
further is heard of the Phoenician fleet for three years, its defeat
was probably complete enough to cripple it. But the Persian land
force, which had now no base except the Phoenician towns of
Amathus and Citium on Cyprus itself, retrieved its own fortunes
and decided the fate of the whole island in a no less decisive land
battle. In this action, which was fought on the plains of the
Cyprian Salamis with a medley of foot, horse and chariots, the
Greeks were their own worst enemies, for during the engagement
the contingent of Curium went over to the Persians, and the
chariot corps of Salamis followed suit. In the ensuing rout
Onesilus, who had fought gallantly, was killed, and as the Ionian
fleet now sailed home from an apparently hopeless venture the
insurgents were left without a leader. The example of Salamis,
which capitulated promptly, was not followed by the other Greek
cities; but none of these, except Soli, which held out for five
months, was able to stand a prolonged siege. Towards the end
of 497 B.C. all Cyprus had fallen back into Persian hands.

On the mainland the Persian re-conquest proceeded at a less
even rate. In the spring of 497 B.C. Artaphrenes attacked the
Greeks at three different points. One Persian force began a
lightning campaign on the Hellespont, where it carried five towns,
including the key positions of Abydos and Lampsacus, in as
many days. This army was eventually told off for a more arduous
service in Caria, and its place was taken by a force which had
previously operated with indifferent success on the Propontis and
now proceeded to recapture the numerous little agrarian settlements in the Troad. The third Persian army, which had been
directed against the western seaboard, recovered Clazomenae and

Cyme, but failed to take any of the larger cities. Thus the campaign of 497 B.C. on the mainland brought the Persians many minor successes; but all the principal towns, such as Miletus, Ephesus, Cyzicus and Byzantium, and all the islands, still held out. Moreover the Persian victories against the Greeks were balanced by a disaster in Caria which brought the Persian offensive to a standstill along the whole line.

The revolt of Caria, which had deprived the Persians of their communications along the Maeander valley and of access by land to Miletus, was a more serious blow to them than the poverty and the remoteness of the country would indicate. Therefore as soon as Artaphrenes could spare his first army from the Hellespont he despatched it to the Maeander front. The Carian levies allowed the Persians to cross the Maeander at a point near its confluence with the Marsyas, with a view to driving the invaders into the river; but their force was inadequate even for purposes of defence, and the Persians pushed the Carians back upon Mt Latmus. The defeated army, which had begun to talk of surrender, was here rallied by a Milesian force; but in a second battle it was dislodged from the heights and driven down into the plain of Mylasa. The road to Miletus now lay open to the Persians, but their commander, hoping to keep the Carians on the run, pursued them towards Pedasa. The capture of this stronghold would probably have ended the Carian revolt; but at the eleventh hour the Carians turned the tables on their pursuers by means of a night surprise in which the whole Persian force, generals and all, was destroyed. The Carian campaign, which probably did not extend over more than a few weeks, paralyzed the Persian offensive for several years.

In 496 and 495 B.C. the Greeks enjoyed a respite by land and sea, but lack of leadership prevented them from putting their leisure to any good use. At the time of the Persian advance into Caria the Milesian leaders lost their nerve and contemplated the evacuation of their city. Hecataeus proposed a temporary retreat to the adjacent islet of Leros, and Aristagoras actually led an exodus of faint hearts to Myrcinus. It is idle to speculate whether he could have secured himself here against a Persian pursuit; before the year 497 B.C. was out he and all his company had been massacred by the Thracians.

A double opportunity was also lost to the Greeks through Histiaeus' successive failures as a mediator and as a general. The journey of Histiaeus to Sardes appears to have occupied him until 496 B.C. On his arrival there he made an attempt to win

over some of Artaphrenes' staff to a policy of conciliation. But
the satrap himself, who could not but resent Histiaeus' officious
interference, took good care that his diplomatic mission should
miscarry. Roundly accusing Histiaeus of 'having stitched the
shoe which Aristagoras put on,' he frightened his rival away from
Sardes. Having stolen across the Persian lines to the coast,
Histiaeus made his way to Chios. From this refuge he made a
futile attempt to resume negotiations with his accomplices at
Sardes; but at the same time he trained himself to play up to the
part which Artaphrenes had imputed to him by giving himself
out as the real author of the revolt, and he eventually persuaded
the Chians to escort him to the insurgent headquarters at Miletus.
It would have been fortunate for the Greek cause if Histiaeus
had been received back by the Milesians, for here was a leader
who knew the enemy's position from the inside and could be
trusted to fight with the desperate determination of a renegade.
But the Milesians would have none of him, and the Chians, who
had distrusted his intentions from the first, refused to give him
any support. Unable to escape from the false position into which
his adventures had thrust him, Histiaeus now took to privateering.
With a small squadron which the Lesbians had entrusted to him
he took up his station at Byzantium and detained the Greek
merchantmen from the Black Sea. Though the other Greeks did
not think it worth while to send a fleet against him, the effect of
this blockade upon them must have been considerable, for the
larger Ionian towns at all times drew much of their raw materials
from the Black Sea, and it is probable that during the revolt
they looked to that quarter for a great part of their food supply.
Thus Histiaeus, instead of rescuing the Greeks, became a thorn in
their side.

The history of the campaigns of 496 and 495 B.C. is almost a
blank. The defeat of their fleet at Cyprus and of their army in
Caria compelled the Persians to mark time; the disunion of the
Greeks prevented these from making a counter-attack. By 494 B.C.
however, the Persians had prepared for a new offensive. A new
Phoenician fleet, reinforced by contingents from Egypt and
Cilicia, and even from Cyprus, set out in that year for Greek
waters. At the entrance of the Aegean Sea this armada was
checked by the resistance of Lindus, and the timely intervention
of a fleet from Ionia might have brought the Persian advance to
a definite standstill. But the Greeks were unprepared to seize this
chance and left Lindus to arrange a favourable capitulation with
the Persian admiral. Having thus secured an entry into Ionian

waters, the Persian fleet made its way to Miletus. Simultaneously
Artaphrenes, who had won a passage through Caria by promising
part of the Milesian territory to the neighbouring community of
Pedasus, sent a force to invest Miletus by land. At this critical
moment the Greeks were again caught unprepared, and only
eight of the Ionian states (Miletus, Priene, Myus, Samos, Teos,
Erythrae, Chios and Phocaea), together with the cities of Lesbos,
took any common measures of defence. But this small group by
an eleventh-hour effort raised a fleet such as had never yet
met in Greek waters. The lesser mainland states, handicapped by
the abstention of Ephesus, only contributed forty-three ships; but
Chios equipped 100 galleys, Lesbos 70, and Samos 60, and
Miletus spared from the defence of its own walls a force sufficient
to man 80 vessels. The standard ships of this fleet were probably
not triremes but some lighter type of vessel. But ship for ship,
the Greeks were a match for their antagonists, and although
Herodotus relates that the Persian fleet was 600 strong, the
subsequent course of events indicates that in reality it was barely
superior to the Greek navy. Instead of proceeding at once to
battle, the Persians first endeavoured to break the Greek front
by underhand negotiations with the several communities.

These intrigues had their effect before long; but at first the
insurgents, as Herodotus says ungenerously, 'refused to see
reason.' Nay more, by an unwonted effort of self-denial they consented to confer the unified command of their whole force upon
their ablest captain, Dionysius of Phocaea, and to exercise their
fleet in united action. But these good resolves only lasted some
seven days. The story of Herodotus, that the Ionians refused any
longer to expose their delicate complexions to the sun, reads like
a gratuitous libel on an active and seamanlike people; but there
is no denying the jealousy of city against city which prompted the
Samians to parley with their former tyrant in the Persian camp,
and the whole fleet to disobey their generalissimo.

The Persians now waited no longer, but forced an action off
Miletus, hard by the islet of Lade. This battle showed that the
Greeks could have repeated their victory off the Cypriote coast,
if they had but held together. The Chians in particular fought
superbly, and though Herodotus is probably wrong in saying
that they rowed clean through the enemy's lines—for this purpose
their vessels probably lacked sufficient oarage and carried too
many marines—they more than held their own. But the decisive
part in the engagement fell to the Samians and Lesbians. The
former by a deliberate act of treason hoisted their sails and bolted

out of the fighting-line; the latter, on finding their flank exposed by this desertion, fled in similar fashion. Thus Greek disunion and disloyalty presented the Persians with a crushing victory. A hundred years later, at the battle of Cnidus, the same causes gave the Persians their only other great triumph over a Greek fleet.

The rest of the story is soon told. Dionysius escaped from Aegean waters and turned buccaneer in the western Mediterranean. Miletus was hemmed in by land and sea and was shortly after carried by storm; and in the same year the rebellion was ended in Caria. In 494 and 493 B.C., the Phoenician fleet received the surrender of the remaining Greek insurgents in the Aegean and Propontis. Miltiades the Athenian, who had been governor of the Thracian Chersonese under Hippias but, unlike that ex-tyrant, had risen against the Persians, raced back to his native town and so saved himself for another trial of strength with the Persians. Histiaeus returned to Aegean waters after the battle of Lade and for a brief hour became the champion of a forlorn hope. With his Lesbian squadron he carried the island of Chios and made it a rallying-point of the leaderless Greek rout. But the campaign which he waged against his Phoenician pursuers was nothing more than the distracted dodging and doubling of the quarry before the hounds. He was finally run down on a foraging expedition in Aeolis and delivered to Artaphrenes. The Persian satrap, fearing no doubt that if his captive could gain the ear of Darius he might excuse his treason by throwing the blame for it upon Artaphrenes himself, put Histiaeus to death at once.

In the first flush of victory the Persians committed some unwonted acts of frightfulness. The population of Miletus was partly transplanted to farthest Mesopotamia; the seaboard quarter of the town was razed so effectively that the later Milesians never rebuilt it, and the temple of Branchidae was burnt down. A similar treatment was meted out to the other cities, and though Samos received immunity from reprisals as a reward for its treason, the victors undertook a systematic man-hunt in the other islands. But the reign of terror did not last long. King Darius, as usual, was more bent on reconstruction than revenge and imposed a saner policy upon his subordinates. In the Lydian satrapy Artaphrenes not only maintained in general the old moderate rates of tribute, but he secured a better distribution of the burden by means of a new land-measurement and assessment. In addition, he compelled the Greek towns under his charge to set up courts for

the settlement of claims between their citizens and interdicted
forcible reprisals. In 492 B.C. Mardonius, a son-in-law of Darius,
was sent on a special commission to the Ionian and Hellespontine
towns and astonished these by ridding them of their returned
tyrants and setting up democracies in every community except
Chios and Lampsacus. The wounds caused by the six years' war
were thus healed up, and in 481 B.C. King Xerxes was not afraid
to levy contingents from the Asiatic Greeks for service against
their European compatriots.

But although Asiatic Greece was pacified, it failed to recover
its ancient prosperity. The economic decline which had preceded
and partly caused the revolt was merely hastened by the strain
of an unsuccessful war; and it was henceforth accompanied by a
decline in general culture. Ionia, which in the seventh and sixth
centuries had led Greece in commerce and industry, in literature,
art and science, fell into the background for two centuries, and
not until the new Anabasis of Alexander did Asiatic Greece regain its pre-eminence.

Such was the tragic ending of a war which the Ionians entered
on, not light-heartedly, but with a genuine sense of grievance,
and waged without proper cohesion, yet not without dash and
courage. But if the Ionians sacrificed themselves in the revolt,
they helped to save the Greeks of the homeland. Far from
hastening on the invasion of European Greece, the Ionian Revolt
tended to delay it. The respite thus gained, and the lessons which
the revolt conveyed, were precious. They enabled the European
Greeks to realize and secure the two conditions of success, control
of the seas and unity of command. In liberating the Asiatic Greeks
after the Great Persian Wars the Athenians but made amends for
their previous desertion of them, and repaid service rendered by
them to the Greek homeland.

CHAPTER VIII

MARATHON

I. THE RECONQUEST OF PERSIAN EUROPE

AFTER the battle of Lade and the fall of Miletus, which shattered the Ionian revolt (p. 227), the navy of King Darius wintered near Miletus, and in the following spring, 493 B.C., sailed northwards to continue the work of re-establishing Persian rule. Having captured Chios, Lesbos and Tenedos, and the Ionian cities on the mainland, the fleet, or at least the Phoenician fleet, entered the Hellespont and took all the towns on the European side as far as Byzantium. The Byzantines and the Chalcedonians fled into the Euxine and left their homes to be burnt. The Phoenicians turned back, and finished the subjugation of the Asiatic side by giving the island cities, Proconnesus and Artace, to the flames. Cyzicus had already made terms with the satrap of Dascylium.

So far Herodotus is lucid, although he has not made it clear whether the Phoenicians are the whole or a part of the Persian fleet. Now he surprises us with the information that the Thracian Chersonese had not been completely conquered. The Phoenicians return to it and subdue the cities which they had not ravaged before. Again the conquest is incomplete. They did not take Cardia on the north coast.

It was from Cardia that Miltiades son of Cimon, the Athenian prince of the Chersonese, fled with five triremes on the news that the Phoenicians were at Tenedos. He encountered them at the western extremity of the peninsula, and narrowly escaped to Imbros, losing one ship captured with his son Metiochus. The Phoenicians were obviously neither advancing up the Hellespont nor returning to the south, but making for the outer shores of the Chersonese. Why then had they put back to Tenedos? and why was Cardia omitted? Is not the explanation this—that Herodotus has combined into one year operations which belong to two? The Phoenicians did not take Cardia on their first campaign because it was defended by Miltiades, who was fighting for his neck and held out to the last. They retired southwards from the Hellespont to winter quarters, but returned the next spring (492 B.C.) to finish the job in preparation for the advance of Mardonius.

The recovery of the Hellespont had cleared the way for the reconquest of the Thracian and Macedonian province. Darius committed this task to Mardonius son of Gobryas, who had perhaps distinguished himself in the war at the siege of Lindus and had now been married to one of his daughters. He put him in supreme command not only of the forces already at the front, but also of fresh levies naval and military. From Cilicia Mardonius sailed in the spring of 492 B.C. to Ionia, where he occupied himself in disarming disaffection by setting up democracies instead of tyrants in the cities, while his troops journeyed by land to the Hellespont. When all were assembled, he put his army across the straits in his ships, and marched (past Cardia) through Thrace into Macedonia. Nowhere did he encounter any serious resistance. The Thasians surrendered to the fleet without a blow, the Macedonians tamely submitted. Two misadventures, however, marred the triumphal progress. A storm caught the fleet doubling the promontory of Mount Athos, and wrecked part of it. The Thracian Brygi (Phrygians) attacked the camp under cover of night, and succeeded in inflicting some loss and wounding Mardonius himself. But these incidents are evidently much exaggerated. The Greeks afterwards imputed to Mardonius the intention of reaching Athens and Eretria, or even wider designs. Xerxes a dozen years later followed the same route and his march suggested the same objective. But it is clear that Mardonius aimed at no more than he achieved, the reconquest of Thrace and Macedonia. Having first enlarged his scope, and probably his forces, the Greek version reproduced by Herodotus had then to magnify his disasters. He had crossed the Hellespont too late in the year for an invasion of Greece, for which there is no hint of any preparation. He had made the most of his time. It was the attainment of his goal at the close of the campaign, not defeat or failure, that turned him back to Asia. Herodotus elsewhere represents him as thoroughly complacent with his performance, and acknowledges his success.

Meanwhile Miltiades came to Athens, a fugitive from his Thracian principality before the king's fleet; he cannot have awaited in Imbros the advance of Mardonius from the Hellespont. His arrival at Athens precipitated a political crisis.

A declared and inveterate enemy to Darius, twice hunted from his dominion in the Chersonese, the conqueror of Lemnos, a patrician of the highest lineage, and kinsman (one may infer) to

Isagoras the rival of Cleisthenes, he was just the man whom the Opposition wanted. His rank, connections, and traditions approved him to the nobility. To the merchants and artisans, in close touch with the cities of Ionia (whence some perhaps were immigrants) and deeply interested in Athenian trade and enterprise in the Aegean, his imperial record was a strong recommendation. He was acclaimed the champion of the malcontents against the government and came forward as a candidate for the office of General. It was a test election to decide momentous issues. Was Athens to beg peace and pardon from the king and receive back Hippias, or was she to confront his anger with what forces she could muster? The question was complicated by considerations of domestic policy. A war against Persia would be madness without Spartan assistance. But the Alcmaeonidae had good reason to apprehend what might be the price eventually to be paid for an alliance with Sparta—their own expulsion and the repeal of their new Constitution. Better come to terms with Hippias, restore the monarchy, and by sacrifice of the form preserve the substance of the democracy. The Agrarians, the old followers of Peisistratus, who had gained most by the constitutional developments of the past century and were little concerned for trade or expansion abroad, were probably solid in support of the government. On the other side, the Eupatrids or Patricians would welcome the Spartan alliance as a check to the progress of the Demos or an instrument of reaction. The Parali, the commercial and industrial class, held the balance. Their normal temper was no doubt democratic, but they were now incensed at the betrayal of the Ionians and in revolt against their Alcmaeonid leaders. Miltiades carried his election in his own tribe, the Oeneis, and presumably secured a majority on the board of generals.

But the Alcmaeonid faction had one more card to play. 'His enemies,' Herodotus tells, 'brought Miltiades before a court of law and prosecuted him for his Tyranny in the Chersonese.' It is difficult to see how despotism in the Chersonese over the Thracian Dolonci could have been a criminal offence in Attic law. It was surely a compliment to Athens that a barbarous people should have accepted one of her citizens for its prince. Miltiades' antagonism to Hippias refutes the suggestion that his reign could have been represented as a survival of the Peisistratid Tyranny. The elder Miltiades, it is true, had taken with him to the Chersonese Athenians who volunteered to accompany him. But it is incredible that their settlement in his dominion under his patronage and protection could have furnished a capital charge against his nephew half a century later. The proceedings will become intelligible if we may suppose that Herodotus has misunderstood the case, and, betrayed by his memory and by a literary temptation (the double escape), has imported the death penalty from the second trial of Miltiades. On this first occasion his enemies did not prosecute Miltiades, but essayed to disqualify him for office at his examination before admission and annul his election. Tyranny in the Chersonese would be a perfectly relevant objection. Miltiades (like Theramenes later, Lysias XIII, 10), was a danger to the constitution. He had been a tyrant abroad, and would presumably become a tyrant at home[1]. This interpretation of the proceedings is confirmed by the close connection implied by Herodotus between the acquittal and the appointment of Miltiades[2]. At all events Miltiades won both his election and his case. The votes had decided on war with Persia, alliance with Sparta, and Miltiades as protagonist of Athens.

Herodotus (VI, 103–4) implies that the election and acquittal of Miltiades came almost immediately after his arrival at Athens, and that the battle of Marathon followed during the year of office for which he was then elected. The implication is incompatible with his formal chronology. The advance of Mardonius from the Hellespont marks the latest date possible on any theory for the flight of Miltiades from Imbros, and Herodotus interposes a complete year between the year of Mardonius' campaign and the year of the invasion of Attica. But as a general rule the historical contents of his narratives are a more trustworthy guide than the chronological scheme into which he tries to adjust them, and in particular this intrusive year is altogether suspect. He assigns to it three transactions—a 'second' surrender of Thasos to the Persians; a mission of heralds from Darius to Greece to demand earth and water; and a charge of 'Medism' brought against the Aeginetans, which had far-reaching consequences for Sparta and Athens (pp. 259 sqq.). The attribution of each one of these items to that year excites the gravest doubts. Moreover Herodotus himself entirely obliterates that year in a later passage where he refers Mardonius' expedition to the year before the invasion of Attica. The best argument for retaining the year, that it is required in order to build a new fleet after the wreck at Mount Athos, is

---

[1] One can reconstruct the argument on both sides from Herodotus IV, 137 and VI, 39–41 (where Σκύθας ἐκφεύγει is of course the hardy, but easy and plausible, perversion of the accusers, instead of Σκύθας φεύγοντα βασιλέα Δαρεῖον ἐκφεύγει). Cp. Corn. Nep. Milt. 8.

[2] For a different interpretation of these proceedings see above, pp. 170 sqq.

heavily discounted by the admitted exaggeration of the disaster in Herodotus' story, and the probably limited scale and comparatively late start of the next year's expedition. The 'curiously explicit chronology' which has been noted[1] in 'the Annals of the Triennium' (493–2–1 B.C.) seems to betray an uneasy conscience in the annalist, and suggests that Herodotus, finding himself approaching the battle of Marathon with his narrative a year in arrear of his schematic chronology, and thinking that he has a year too many in hand, is driven to mete out his historical material to cover the gap. If Miltiades fled to Athens on the advance of Mardonius, and Mardonius reconquered Thrace in the year before the invasion of Attica, then Herodotus is entirely accurate in placing the election of Miltiades. But if the year between the two expeditions drops out, is the campaign of Mardonius to come down a year, or the campaign of Marathon to go up? The usually accepted date of the battle of Marathon is 490 B.C. But Herodotus, Thucydides, and the Aristotelian *Constitution of Athens*[2], simply and naturally interpreted, all indicate a date one year earlier, and their consensus is the more cogent because they reach it by different methods. In the account of the Marathon campaign which follows, the battle is put in the year 491 B.C.[3]

II. THE ADVANCE ACROSS THE AEGEAN

Mardonius had recovered the Persian province in Thrace and Macedonia. It remained to complete the suppression of the revolt by the punishment of the Athenians and the Eretrians for their aid to the Ionians. Athens was indeed herself a rebel; and Darius, with Hippias to importune him, needed no attendant to remind him of the Athenians. Naxos too, where the trouble had begun, was still to be subjugated; and, if peace was to be secured in Ionia, the Cyclades must be taught to recognize the Persian supremacy. Neither the authorities, nor the force employed, nor the plan pursued in the campaign now undertaken warrant us in supposing that the king had any aims beyond these or as yet contemplated a conquest of Greece. The route chosen was by sea across the Aegean. The troops required were not too many to be carried on ships, and the fleet could put them straight on to their objectives. No hostile or neutral territory had to be traversed, no unnecessary fighting incurred. Darius dominated the sea.

[1] Macan, *Herodotus*, IV–VI, vol. II, p. 77.

[2] Herodotus VII, 1, 4, 7, 20; Thucydides VI, 59 (cp. VIII, 68), I, 18, 118; Aristotle, *Const. of Athens*, XXII.

[3] See also below, p. 245, note, and p. 253, n. 1.

The winter and spring (492–1 B.C.) after Mardonius' return were spent in preparations. The new fleet, or at all events transports, ordered for the expedition picked up the troops mustered in Cilicia, and conveyed them along the coast to Samos. The subsequent operations are so brief, and finish so late in the season, that we may infer that either the start was delayed until towards midsummer, or there was a long stay at Samos, where some of the contingents and most of the naval forces may well have assembled. Mardonius, perhaps disabled by his wound rather than discredited by his campaign, was not appointed general. The king entrusted the command to his nephew Artaphernes, son of the satrap of Sardes, and Datis, a Mede, who was no doubt an experienced officer, possibly his admiral at Lade. On the numbers of the forces there is scarcely any trustworthy evidence. Herodotus puts the fleet at 600 triremes (warships), and twice notices the horse-transports, and implies them in a third passage. The 600 are a stock figure, given too for Lade and the Scythian expedition. In view of the slight resistance to be expected, this figure is highly improbable. The Platonic *Menexenus* gives 300, a more modest computation, but of dubious authority, and still too large to be acceptable. The transports, horse or other, are not enumerated. The interest which Herodotus shows in the horse-transports seems to indicate that it was a novelty to ship cavalry overseas. For the army he records no number. Later writers assign various figures, from 200,000 infantry and 10,000 cavalry (Nepos) to 600,000 men (Justin), all absurd. Perhaps we may estimate the infantry at 25,000, half a Persian Army Corps, which would well fit the history of the campaign. The proper quota of cavalry would be 5000, but so large a number is barely credible. Let us say 1000, and surmise that they really embarked in Ionia. There presumably Hippias also joined, although Thucydides vouches that he had been to the king, and Herodotus is aware of Peisistratidae at Susa. Hippias was himself a powerful reinforcement, not only by his political influence and his intimate knowledge of Attica and Eretria, but also by his skill and experience, bred up (as his name and his brother's suggest) in the saddle, and familiar (as his story proclaims) with cavalry tactics. Was it he who first proposed to ship the horsemen across the Aegean?

Herodotus does not give any details as to the composition of the forces. His mention of Persians and Sacae at Marathon, forming the centre of the army, admits the inference that the wings were other troops, but the statement itself may be only inference. He observes that Datis, when he sailed from Rhenea took with him Ionians and Aeolians. The Barbarians had impressed Islanders into their service, but the Aeolians seem to imply that these were contingents (no doubt naval) from Asia, who may have joined at Rheneia. A Phoenician vessel appears incidentally at Myconus on the retirement of the Persians. One may conjecture that the Phoenician fleet which fought at Lade had never quitted the Aegean, but awaited at Samos the arrival of Datis from Cilicia, and formed the sole escort and fighting naval force of the expedition. It may be put at 140 ships (p. 274 *sq.*).

From Samos the whole fleet sailed out to sea to Naxos. The Naxians took to the hills and abandoned their city to sack. The other southern Cyclades were visited, and a contingent was exacted or enlisted from Paros. Datis then steered for Delos. The Delians fled to Tenos, but he treated their sacred isle with a politic consideration in which we may divine the inspiration of Hippias. He anchored his ships on the opposite shore of Rheneia, and made a munificent offering of incense on the altar of the Delian God. A golden torque preserved in the sanctuary two centuries later was registered as a dedication from Datis. Herodotus reports on the authority of the Delians that the departure of Datis was marked by an earthquake, the first and last in the history of the island. Thucydides throws some doubt on the statement by ascribing the same uniqueness to an earthquake at Delos just before the outbreak of the Peloponnesian war.

After leaving Delos the expedition moved forward on its deliberate course, and made a tour of the northern Cyclades, levying contingents of troops, and taking hostages—an almost excessive precaution, had these Islanders submitted the year before. The summer was far spent when Datis and Artaphernes reached Carystus on the south coast of Euboea. The Carystians refused to give hostages, or furnish forces against their friends and neighbours, Eretria and Athens. The Persians besieged their city and laid waste their territory, until they reduced them to obedience. How long the siege lasted is not recorded, but it was probably very brief.

III. ERETRIA AND MILTIADES' DECREE

The resistance of Carystus was the first encountered by the invaders. It is here that the active campaign opens, and the serious historical difficulties begin. Let the simple read Herodotus and be content. The critical reader will soon discover in the narrative omissions which can be supplied only by conjecture, obscurities

to be illuminated only by imagination, and questions to which no
certain answer can be found. He must again and again go beyond
and behind the positive evidence. History is always interpretation,
and different interpreters will lay stress on different points. There
are innumerable theories about the battle of Marathon. Some deal
with each particular difficulty separately, and accumulate a dozen
disconnected hypotheses to meet them in detail. But the real
problem is: what is the simplest single hypothesis which will solve
at once the most and most important questions, and best explain
the best tradition? 'One point,' as a modern critic observes[1],
'must be conceded before each and every fresh attempt at a final
synthesis; there never has been, and there never can be, a theory
which shall reconcile all the elements, even all the plausible
elements, in the traditions, and hypotheses of antiquity upon this
subject.' The present writer more than twenty years ago published a theory which was perhaps drastic, but had the merits of
simplicity and comprehensiveness. That he now puts forward
another is due to further experience of Herodotus, deeper insight
into his methods, and more sympathetic appreciation of the per-
plexities of his task. The worst trouble to Herodotus was not the
lack of materials, nor the errors or prejudices of his informants,
bad as that may have been, but the difficulty of piecing the bits
together, how to string or twine the loose strands and ends of
yarn into a continuous narrative, in fact the sequences and syn-
chronisms of his history; and it is here first and foremost that his
mistakes are to be sought. The following reconstruction substitutes, for the suggestion that an essential factor in the story
has been suppressed by a tacit conspiracy of Herodotus' sources,
the hypothesis of a maladjustment of the chronology of the
several parts.

The attack on Carystus, an inoffensive Dryopian city, may
seem to have been a waste of time. The motive is to be found in
the geographical position of the little town and its fine bay, which
offered easy communication with Asia and a convenient base at
once against Attica and Eretria. The Athenians and Eretrians
must have had ample notice of the enemy's outset and his progress
across the Aegean, and have taken their measures for defence.
The support of the Spartans had no doubt been promised, and
the allies had probably arranged plans not only for the mobilization but also for a concentration of their forces to oppose the
invaders. But even when the hostile fleet lay at Carystus, it was
still quite uncertain where the blow might fall, and this un-

---

[1] Macan, *op. cit.* vol. II, p. 234.

certainty must have paralyzed and disconcerted their schemes. The Persian generals knew their business.

Not until the enemy's ships began to move up the Euboean channel and passed the bay of Marathon, was his first objective revealed. Eretria in her prime could parade 3000 hoplites and 600 horse, but of what avail were they to take the field against the Persian host? So her citizens, rejecting pusillanimous counsels of flight to the hills or surrender, rested their salvation on their strong walls and the speedy help of their allies. An urgent message called the Athenians to the rescue. They responded to the call, but they never came; and Herodotus at this critical juncture deviates into an apology devised to excuse this apparent desertion, which at a later day, when the victory of Marathon, stark, solitary, and imposing, dwarfed all other features of the situation, appeared flagrant and inexplicable. The Athenians did vote to go to the aid of their allies—that fact was admitted, and credited to them —but they did also, it is pretended, give them substantial assistance, for they assigned (or at all events left) to them for their defence the Athenian settlers at the neighbouring Chalcis. Why these colonists did not join the Eretrians, but saved themselves by way of Oropus, is explained by the irresolute and treacherous attitude of the Eretrians themselves, which rendered their defence hopeless and was revealed to the Athenians by a leading citizen.

Herodotus' whole elaborate and controversial exculpation conveys the impression of afterthought. Calumniators of Athens in a later generation can hardly have missed the point that she did eventually profit by the destruction of Miletus and Eretria. They may have charged her with a deliberate sacrifice of her allies for her own advantage. Moreover, the number 4000 for the Chalcidian settlers, whether a calculation from the Periclean cleruchy or from the 20 triremes at Artemisium, points to a date long after the Persian War. But incidentally one hint emerges which may enlighten us on the operations of 491 B.C. The settlers escaped to Oropus. How? The Athenians had resolved to go to the help of the Eretrians. How were they to get across to Euboea? We hear nothing of the Athenian fleet, but is it not more than probable that it had been already sent in advance to Oropus (or Chalcis) in order to keep up communications between the allies and be ready to ferry the Athenians to Euboea, or the Eretrians to Attica, as the enemy's attack might direct?

Pursuing the apology Herodotus loses sight of the Athenian response to the appeal. It is to be recovered in 'the decree of Miltiades.' This resolution was extant in the fourth century B.C.

and Plutarch (*Qu. Conv.* I, 10, 3) can still date it to the Prytany of the Tribe Aeantis. Demosthenes describes (XIX, 303) how Aeschines exploited it to stimulate the patriotic pride of the Athenian people. The Scholiasts on the passage can tell no more of the purport of the decree than might be inferred from such casual references as the above, and from current notions of the situation on the eve of the battle of Marathon. But fortunately Aristotle in his *Rhetoric* (III, 10, p. 1411 *a* 10) quotes, not indeed the decree itself, but an allusion to it which throws a flood of light upon it, and puts it in its true setting. 'Cephisodotus once,' he tells us, 'impelling the Athenians to Euboea, said that they must *do Miltiades' decree* and find their commissariat there.' Cephisodotus needs no introduction, and the occasion can be determined beyond all doubt. The emergency which evoked the apt reference of Cephisodotus must have been the expedition to Euboea improvised in the year 357/6 B.C. It is narrated by Diodorus, is often mentioned by Demosthenes and Aeschines, and has been further elucidated by two important inscriptions. Its main purpose was to save Eretria from the Thebans. In this context the obvious and almost irresistible conclusion, which gives Cephisodotus his real point, is that to save Eretria was to effect or execute Miltiades' decree, that the object of the decree was to rescue Eretria. Cephisodotus in fact quoted the precedent of Miltiades' decree because it was entirely appropriate and applicable to the occasion; he demanded the same instant action to rescue the same Eretria. It is characteristic for the evolution of the story of Marathon that whereas Herodotus has to excuse the loss of Eretria, and omits the decree intended to save it, the orators of the fourth century can parade that resolution as a signal proof of promptitude and dash.

It was probably on the 5th of the lunar month (corresponding to the Julian 10th of September 491 B.C.) that the Persian general Artaphernes disembarked the troops of his division and the whole of the cavalry at Tamynae and other places east of Eretria. The Eretrian appeal would be received at Athens on the same day, and Miltiades' decree in response to it be passed on the next, the 6th. The Athenian army was of course already mobilized. The generals dispatched a courier, Philippides (or, less probably, Pheidippides), to acquaint their Spartan allies of their plans, and to solicit their support. Another messenger must have been sent to summon the Plataeans. Philippides, starting from Athens on the evening of the 6th, or, as the Greeks (whose day began at sunset) would reckon, with the first hour of the 7th, achieved a memorable feat in reaching Sparta in 48 hours. The distance (if Argos be avoided) is, as closely as can be computed on modern maps, about 134 miles, or in practice say nearly 150; but there is no cogent reason to discredit the record, and we cannot be sure that Philippides did not get a lift on boat, horse, or cart, over part of the way. He delivered his message to the government on the 9th of the month, but not in the eloquent words put into his mouth by Herodotus—'Lacedaemonians, the Athenians beg you to come to their aid and not let a city oldest in Greece be reduced to servitude by Barbarous men; for already Eretria has been enslaved and Hellas has lost no mean city'—that appeal is obviously literature not authentic history, Herodotus not the generals' dispatch. Unfortunately the moon had now passed her first quarter, and the month was (in all probability) that of the Carneian festival, which culminated at the full moon[1]. The Spartans did not venture to violate the sacred ordinance which forbade them to go forth to war before the moon was full. Possibly the objection was pressed by the party opposed to Cleomenes, and indicates a conflict of policy.

IV. THE ARMIES AT MARATHON

The Athenian army marched out from Athens no doubt on the morning after Miltiades' decree had been passed. It consisted entirely of infantry, for Athens had as yet no regular cavalry corps. Herodotus tells us nothing of its number. Later writers— Pompeius Trogus in Justin, Cornelius Nepos, Plutarch—give 10,000 or 9,000; to which are to be added at Marathon the Plataeans, whom they reckon at 1000. One may assume that their authority (Ephorus) had no precise information, but estimated each of the ten Athenian tribal regiments at 1000, and the Plataeans at 1000; then *more suo* suppressed his calculation, and spoke of 10,000 at Marathon, without making it clear whether he referred to the Athenian or the whole allied army. The figures are of course to be interpreted to mean only the fully equipped men at arms (hoplites), but a tomb shown to Pausanias attests a supplement of light-armed attendants. They would be unusual in an Athenian force, at all events in Thucydides' time, but may indicate the urgency of this occasion. The thousand Plataeans may

---

[1] The moon would be full on the night 19th to 20th Sept. 491 B.C. Plutarch, *Nicias*, 28, seems to prove that, at all events in the Syracusan calendar, the Carneian full moon might fall even so late as the 27th.

be questioned, for at the battle a dozen years later at their gates, where they were of course present to the last man, they muster on Herodotus' list only 600; but a fair case can be made out for allowing them 1000, or at least 900, at that battle. The myriad of Athenian hoplites, however conjectural, is plausible enough. Athens sent 8000 to the battle of Plataea, when her much larger fleet was on active service (pp. 324, 341).

Herodotus incidentally recognizes the tribal regiments, but does not distribute the ten generals to them, and falls into vagueness and anachronism over the office of the Polemarch and his relation to the generals. Here the corrections offered by Aristotle's *Constitution of Athens* may be allowed, although it may be doubted whether they are based on any positive evidence. The Polemarch was still elected, not (as Herodotus has it) appointed by lot, and was still the constitutional commander-in-chief of the whole army. The ten generals commanded each his own tribe. Herodotus is no doubt right in representing them as forming collectively a staff or council of war, and as such they may have encroached upon, or practically superseded, the authority of the Polemarch. But that is not all. Herodotus may not have intended to invest Miltiades with an official superiority or primacy over his colleagues, such as later statesmen enjoyed, although his language in two passages may suggest it to scholars interested in that constitutional development. At all events, if he did, the position attributed to Miltiades would be incompatible with the Polemarch's supremacy, just admitted, and would have to be rejected. But he certainly does postulate a daily rotating presidency in the college of generals. This diurnal precedence is flatly inconsistent with the annual primacy of one general, but is also difficult to reconcile with the supreme command of the Polemarch. No wonder that critics have disputed the representation of Herodotus, and supposed that this presidency, which appears to carry with it the control of the army, has been transported into the story of Marathon from the practice of a later time.

Their argument would be strengthened, if it could be shown that the practice was usual in the Athenian army of the Periclean age. The fact, or probability, that the battle fought on Miltiades' day followed ten days after the decree carried by Miltiades, may be thought to reveal the source of error; but it may also be quoted in support of Herodotus. A probable solution may be found in the suggestion that Herodotus has preserved a trace of a transitional stage in the evolution of the military command. The Polemarchy, since the institution of the generals, had sunk into

MAP 6

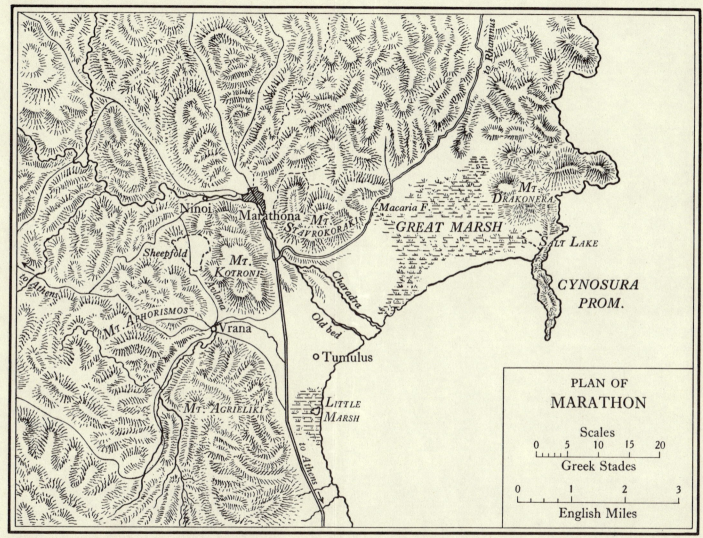

Ninoi
Marathona
Mt Stavrokoraki
Macaria F.
Mt Drakonera
GREAT MARSH
Salt Lake
Sheepfold
Mt Kotroni
Charadra
CYNOSURA PROM.
Mt Aphorismos
Vrana
Avlona
Old bed
to Athens
to Athens
to Rhamnus
Tumulus
Little Marsh
Mt Agrieliki

PLAN OF
MARATHON

Scales

| 0 | 5 | 10 | 15 | 20 |

Greek Stades

| 0 | 1 | 2 | 3 |

English Miles

INDEX TO NAMES

Agrieliki, Mt
Aphorismos, Mt
Avlona

Charadra
Charadra, Old bed of the
Cynosura Prom.

Drakonera, Mt

Kotroni, Mt

Macaria, F.
Marathona
Marsh, Great
Marsh, Little

Ninoi

Salt Lake
Sheepfold
Stavrokoraki, Mt

Tumulus

Vrana

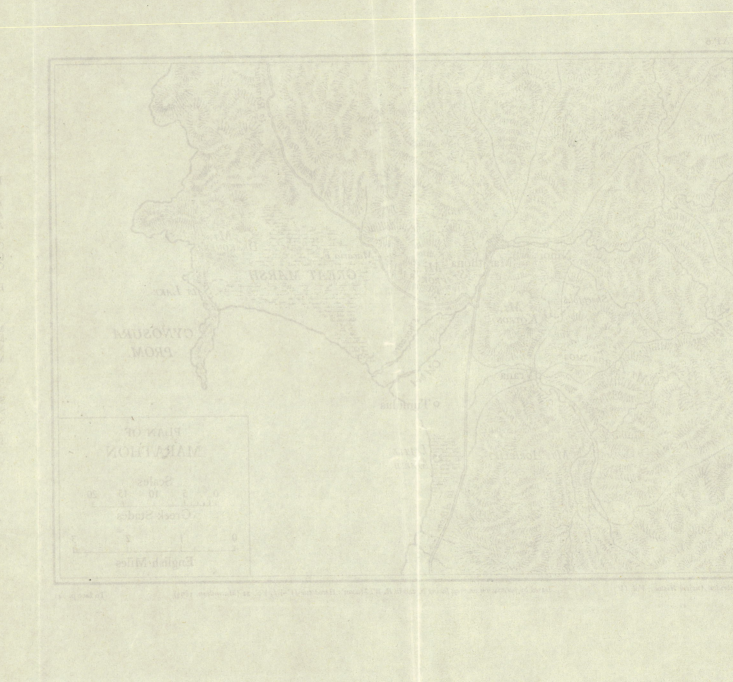

a titular or honorary dignity. The college of generals had usurped
the real direction of military affairs. But, inasmuch as the college
was not in perpetual session, it was soon found advisable, we may
suppose, to entrust the control of the army and the responsibility
for its operations to one of the generals, each day by day in turn.
The action of the presiding general would be nominally subject
to the sanction of the Polemarch, more effectively to that of his
colleagues, but in practice he would enjoy a wide discretion and a
largely free hand. The system was not, to be sure, efficient for
war; but it might serve for administration in peace-time, and it
did not last long (p. 155). If Miltiades' colleagues tendered their
days to him, their offer was a criticism on present usage and an
anticipation of future reform.

It was, of course, the Polemarch himself, Callimachus of
Aphidna, who led the march out from the city. The object was to
save Eretria, and we must assume that the Athenians took the
shortest and easiest route for Chalcis, by Decelea and Oropus.
(Chalcis was probably to be the point of crossing, for the Athenian
fleet could hold the Euripus against Artaphernes' squadron, which
would by the 7th be already in possession of the channel between
Oropus and Eretria.) But the column had not yet quitted the
plain of the Cephisus, when news reached the Polemarch which
arrested its northward march and diverted it at full speed to the
east, along the hill roads that skirt the foot of Mount Pentelicus,
towards Marathon. The Persian generals, doubtless well informed
from Eretria as well as from Athens, had anticipated the movement to rescue Eretria, and countered it by a thrust on the right
flank, which was designed to intercept it and keep the Athenian
army busy in Attica. Datis, having wound up the settlement of
Carystus, and guided by Hippias, was landing his division at
Marathon.

The Athenian commander instantly wheeled to the right, and
gained the valley of Vrana, south of the hill Kotroni, which stands
between the modern villages of Marathona and Vrana. The valley
is an inlet of the seaboard plain of Marathon running up straight
westwards between Kotroni and Agrieliki, a high bastion of
Mount Pentelicus, to Vrana at its head. North of Vrana the tributary valley of Avlona joins it, coming down at the back or landward side of Kotroni from the low ridge which divides the valleys
of Vrana and of Marathona. Several roads or tracks converge on
this neighbourhood from the west—two through Stamata, one
to the north of these through Spata, and one through the ancient
Icaria. They are not such as a general would select for his com-

munications and supply, but the Athenians were not encumbered with baggage or commissariat, and in the emergency had no choice. On the other hand, fortune or skill had led them into an excellent strategical position. The precise site of their camp or headquarters would be fixed, if we could determine the precinct of Heracles, where Herodotus places it. The enclosure known as 'the sheepfold of the old lady' at the head of the valley of Avlona has been suggested, but is rather remote and waterless and is not certified by any epigraphical or archaeological evidence. The Athenian army may have mustered there on its first arrival, but its real camping ground must be sought lower down near Vrana and its little burn. No other possible site so well suits Pindar's description of the sanctuary 'in Marathon's recess.' The valley of Vrana, about a mile wide at its mouth, offered a position which was defended on both sides by impassable rocky slopes, sufficiently covered or guarded the outlets from the plain towards the west, and flanked the main road to Athens between Pentelicus and the sea.

The Persians, one gathers from Herodotus, fought in the subsequent battle with their backs to the sea, and pursued the Athenian centre 'inland,' an expression which would naturally indicate up the valley, towards its encampment and its exits of escape. Their position would appear to have faced the mouth of the valley, and to have extended from the little marsh of Vrexisa on the left to the Charadra, or brook of Marathona, on the right, which perhaps reached the sea about half-a-mile to the south-west of its present issue. At about the middle of this position, and about a mile from the mouth of the valley and half-a-mile from the shore of the bay, stands the mound, which both Pausanias and the archaeological results of excavation identify with the tomb of the Athenian dead. It has been conjectured that, for the sake of a convenient supply of water and for security, the Persians were encamped along the left bank of the Charadra, between that rivulet and the great marsh which occupies the north-east corner of the plain. However that may be, their station in the battle appears to be clearly established. Both the Persian position and the Athenian, let it be observed, equally commanded in flank the main road southwards towards Athens, and interdicted the use of that road to the enemy.

Herodotus gives no estimate of the Persian force at Marathon, and the figures furnished by later writers are worthless. If we may suppose that the total infantry shipped from Asia was 25,000, and that 10,000 of them, with the whole of the cavalry[1], were in Euboea—surely enough to deal with Eretria—Datis would have 15,000 infantry at Marathon. Herodotus puts the Persian dead at 6400. On the assumption that the army of Datis fought in three approximately equal divisions, and the centre was practically annihilated, whereas the two wings were let off lightly, these numbers agree sufficiently well.

If the Athenians reached Marathon on the 7th of the lunar month and the battle was fought on the 16th, as appears from the movements of Philippides and the Spartans, the armies must have confronted one another for eight days without an engagement. Datis had no motive to attack the enemy in their strong position. He had attained his object. The Athenians had been diverted to Marathon, and could not withdraw except by laying open the road to Athens, or defeating him on his own ground. Eretria, deprived of their succour, must fall in a few days, and its fall would free Artaphernes to transfer his forces to Phalerum. Athens, denuded of her defenders and divided between the partisans of Hippias and Miltiades, a Persian and a Spartan alliance, the democratic constitution and the *ancien régime*, would offer little or no resistance. If the Athenian commander could extricate his army without fighting, and get back to the city before the Persians, yet the moral effect of the retreat would decide the issue in favour of Hippias, who of course knew that fact as well as Miltiades. It was, however, desirable to make sure that the Athenians should not slip away to molest the landing at Phalerum, and Datis had doubtless occupied the position opposite to the valley of Vrana, if it was not indeed his original position, before the critical day.

The Athenian generals on their part had to think twice before attacking the superior force opposed to them. The risk gave them pause, and the enemy's archers inspired dread. The arrival of the Plataeans, probably a couple of days after the Athenians, brought little to redress the disparity. It was obviously prudent to await the help of the Spartans, and some, to whom the foreign foe seemed more formidable than the domestic, might advise a retirement to the shelter of the city walls, until they should appear.

---

[1] Herodotus notes the disembarkation of cavalry in Euboea. Although he says that Hippias chose Marathon for the landing in Attica partly because it was suitable for cavalry, no trace of cavalry appears there. It may have been destined for Marathon after the fall of Eretria, but never arrived. Suidas preserves a story that 'the Ionians' signalled its absence to Miltiades, who accordingly attacked.

At all events the decision could be deferred so long as Eretria held out and detained Artaphernes.

The Eretrians meanwhile were making a stout defence. For six days they repulsed all assaults. On the seventh, or rather, probably, on what we should call the night of the sixth, two prominent citizens treacherously admitted the enemy. The city was given to fire and pillage, the Eretrians were embarked for transportation to Asia. Hippias, who had presumably come from Marathon to assist in the intrigues and triumphs, present and prospective, of Artaphernes, took charge of the prisoners. He sailed with them, apparently in advance of the armament, to Aeglea, a small island off the Euboean coast opposite Styra, and deposited them there to be called for at leisure.

The first assault on Eretria may be dated to the 6th of the lunar month, and the surrender accordingly to the night of the 11th. The fall of the city would be known to the Athenian generals at Marathon within a few hours. Their decision could no longer be delayed. The momentous Council of War at which Miltiades pressed his proposal to fight at Marathon, and his appeal to the Polemarch, are to be placed on the morning of the 12th. The story, as told by Herodotus, may have been elaborated. The generals, it is said, were divided on the question whether to join battle or not. Five were against Miltiades, and four with him. He went to the Polemarch, made a powerful appeal to him, and secured his vote, which settled the matter. Thereupon his four colleagues who had supported him gave up their days to Miltiades. He accepted them, but nevertheless waited for his own day before delivering his attack. There are obvious difficulties in this account. The Polemarch is not present at the meeting. He seems to be called in as an external authority, independent or superior, to solve a deadlock; yet the language of Herodotus seems to describe him as an ordinary member of the Council. But let that pass—Herodotus has never faced that problem, and he has a confidential communication to put into the mouth of Miltiades for the Polemarch's private ear. Further, the story seems to imply that the four generals who voted for Miltiades' motion are the next four on the rota for the 'Presidency'—a singular coincidence. Finally, Miltiades after all his urgency does not use the four days resigned to him, but waits for his own. The simplest explanation is as follows. Miltiades was 'President' on the 6th of the month, when he carried his decree in the Assembly at Athens. During the next five days the question of fighting at Marathon did not become acute, because Eretria was holding out. On the 12th the news of the fall of Eretria made it urgent. It was decided, possibly by the odd vote or intervention of the Polemarch, but possibly even unanimously with his concurrence or sanction, to engage battle and to give Miltiades a free hand. All the other generals surrendered their days to him, but the battle did not come at once on the 12th, nor on the next three days, but on the 16th. He was in authority for four days without fighting, and then fought on his own day. The decision was not to fight immediately, but to fight before returning to Athens. As long as Artaphernes stayed at Eretria, the Athenians could still wait for the Spartans. As soon as he moved southwards, they must drive the Persians at Marathon into the sea in order to get back to Athens to meet him. Herodotus tells us that the Persians remained at Eretria for several days after its surrender. It was the sailing of the Persian ships from Eretria that determined the day of the battle. That it happened to be also the day of Miltiades' own 'Presidency' was accidental.

V. THE BATTLE AND AFTER

It was probably on the 21st of September, 491 B.C., which may be equated with the 16th of Boedromion[1] according to the later reformed or 'Metonic' calendar, and more speculatively with the 11th of Thargelion on the archaic Attic calendar, that the Athenian commander, be he the Polemarch Callimachus or the general of the day Miltiades, drew out his army to attack. News had arrived that Artaphernes was moving, and no doubt that his cavalry was embarked, for either Marathon or Phalerum. At Marathon the cavalry would heavily weight the scale against the Athenians, at Phalerum it could make a dash for Athens, or rout

[1] Plutarch thrice puts the battle of Marathon on the 6th Boedromion, but that date cannot reasonably be reconciled with Herodotus' full moon. The suggestion that it was the day of the celebration only, and the battle was really fought just after the full moon of Metageitnion three weeks earlier, is not convincing. But perhaps the festival of the Boedromia celebrated to Artemis on the 6th took a Marathonian colour from Miltiades' decree to 'run to the rescue' of Eretria and from his, or Callimachus', vow of a sacrifice of goats to the Goddess, and misled Plutarch into substituting the date of the decree for the date of the battle.

In the year 490 B.C., to which the battle is commonly assigned, the full moon of Boedromion was on the 8th Oct.; in that year the ('Metonic') 6th Boedromion would fall on the 30th Sept., and the 16th on the 10th Oct. Dates so late in the season are improbable and constitute an additional argument against that year.

the Spartans, if it met them on the plain, as the Thessalian horsemen of Cineas had broken the hoplites of Anchimolius (see p. 81). The critical moment had come; the Athenians must strike instantly, now or never.

From Herodotus and Plutarch one may perhaps reconstruct the manœuvre of their deployment. The valley of Vrana is about a mile long and about a mile wide at its mouth. About a mile in front of its mouth stands the Tumulus, which probably marks approximately the centre of the Persian front, where fell most of the Athenian dead. We may assume that the tribe Aeantis led the van out from the Athenian encampment. It was the tribe of the Polemarch himself, and was fighting on its own territory, and in its own 'Prytany.' After the Aeantis followed the other tribal regiments, presumably in their regular official order—the natural interpretation of Herodotus' words, although they are ambiguous. The deployment into line was doubtless designed to be made at the mouth of the valley, where the rocky slopes on either side would protect the two flanks. But an army of, say, 10,000 men in column of eights would occupy about a mile in length. The rear of the column would be as far behind the point of deployment as the enemy's front in advance of that point. That disposition would be a tactical blunder. It was obviously better to march down the middle of the valley in two parallel columns, and wheel them outwards, right and left, into line. Let us suppose that the Pole-march divided the column into two, and himself led the right column, consisting of the Aeantis and the first four tribes (Erechtheis, Aegeis, Pandionis, Leontis), while the Plataean com-mander, Aeimnestus (or Arimnestus), led the left column, con-sisting of his own contingent and the other five tribes (Acamantis, Oeneis, Cecropis, Hippothontis, Antiochis). Then on wheeling into line the Aeantis would form the extreme right, as Aeschylus' elegy vouches[1]; the Plataeans would form the extreme left, as Herodotus describes; and the two rearmost tribes, the Leontis and the Antiochis, would find themselves side by side in the centre, as Plutarch indicates[2]. It is true that Herodotus, assigning to the Polemarch the post of honour on the right, places all the tribes in the line of battle from right to left in their customary order. But his unnatural divorce of the Polemarch from his tribe, and the testimony of Aeschylus, prove that he is speaking at random, and may be ascribing to the tribes in line an order which applied only to their stations at the camp before the march began. The sequel entirely confirms the above reconstruction.

[1] Plutarch, *Qu. Conv.* I, 10, 3   [2] *Arist.* 5.

There happened exactly what might be expected from such a manœuvre over unsurveyed ground. The line in close order of course occupied less space than the column. The leaders were anxious to secure the protection of the walls of the valley on their flank, and overshot their proper distances. A gap opened in the centre of the line. The two middle tribes were therefore compelled to extend into (say) four deep instead of eight deep.

The Persians on their part were of course prepared for the attack. The meanest intelligence could have anticipated it under the circumstances, and Datis was no fool. The Persian front, drawn between the Little Marsh on its left and the nearest bed of the Charadra on its right, would occupy about the same space as the Greek. If Datis had, as we have supposed, 15,000 men on the field, he would presumably form them ten deep, a formation quite appropriate to an army organized, like the Persian, on a decimal system.

The hostile armies now confronted one another in battle array. The Athenian commander had no time to waste, but must attack at once. He could trust his panoplied infantry to rout the enemy in equal combat at close quarters. But he had two difficulties to meet. In the first place the Persian archers would shower arrows upon his men as soon as they got within range, and might disintegrate their phalanx. His object, therefore, was to shorten the passage through the zone of danger, and traverse the last two hundred yards, when his troops came within bowshot, at the double. Herodotus, indeed, understood that the Athenians doubled over the whole mile's interval between the two armies. But that famous charge, if barely possible, would at least be senseless, and is to be regarded as a misapprehension. The second danger was the weakness of the Athenian centre, which was also opposed to the best troops of the enemy. Herodotus accounts for the slender formation of the centre by the need of extending the smaller force to equal the larger's front. Another reason was suggested above, but it comes to much the same thing, for the Athenian position was about as long as the Persian. No doubt it is tempting to conjecture a deeper design in the distribution, a strategical purpose to draw the enemy to his ruin. But this interpretation is over-subtle. We can hardly impute so hazardous a plan to a general in command of a half-trained Greek militia. The attenuated centre was the unwelcome result of a miscalculation rather than a deliberate stratagem. The genius of the commander really shows itself in turning the miscarriage into an opportunity of victory.

As soon as the front was formed and the sacrifices proved favourable the Athenians and Plataeans advanced. Rushing in through the arrows they closed with the enemy, and there ensued a long and obstinate struggle. At last the Persians and Sacae broke the thin line of the Athenian centre and pursued it inland, presumably up the valley towards its camp. But the Greek right and left routed the Persian wings. Letting the fugitives flee to their ships, the victorious Athenians and Plataeans turned upon the victorious Persians, who had to run the gauntlet between them, and defeated them. They chased them into the sea, and essayed to haul back and burn their ships. The bulk of Datis' army made good its escape, and only seven ships were taken. But the victory was complete. The Persians were swept out of Attica, with the loss of about 6400 dead. Herodotus notices no prisoners, and Plutarch's casual mention of them hardly guarantees any. Only 192 Athenian citizens fell, but they included the gallant Polemarch, Callimachus; Stesilaus, one of the generals; and Cynegirus, the brother of Aeschylus, whose hand, grasping the stern of a ship, was severed by an axe. The losses of the Plataeans, and among the 'servants,' who probably defended the camp against the Persian centre, are not recorded, but Pausanias was shown their common grave. One would like to know who were these 'slaves,' deemed worthy of burial with the freemen of Plataea.

The story of Marathon, as has been shrewdly observed, would hardly be authentic without some touches of the supernatural. But the exaggerations of the legend took a matter-of-fact and pedestrian turn—numbers and persons, times and distances. The supernatural is abnormally scanty and credible. The Athenian people so completely appropriated the victory that little was left to the gods. The sudden blindness and last vision of Epizelus, who beheld a monstrous bearded man-at-arms smite down his neighbour and saw no more, is not beyond the possible. The mysterious ploughman, who laid about him so effectively with his share, only afterwards received the name or dignity of the hero Echetlus. The presence of the eponymous hero Marathon, of Theseus, Athena, and Heracles, was a convention as much artistic as spiritual, which was canonized or originated by the famous picture of the battle by Micon or Panaenus in the Painted Portico at Athens. Whether the artist, when he represented the barbarians butting headlong into the marsh in their flight, preserved a genuine tradition or was merely making the best pictorial use of his topographical data; which marsh he may have intended;

whether the marsh is not a mistake of the later critics for the sea—these are idle questions.

The battle from first to last was a brief affair, a morning's work before luncheon. The 'long time' of conflict described by Herodotus applies only to the hand-to-hand fighting, and must be interpreted according to the context. It is to be measured in minutes, not in hours. The vanguard of Artaphernes' fleet may have passed the headland of Cynosura by noon and already met the retreating vessels of Datis. At this juncture, 'when the Persians were already aboard their ships,' somebody signalled to them with a shield, presumably from some conspicuous height overlooking the bay. Whereupon they incontinently made off in the direction of Cape Sunium, intending to get to Athens before the Athenian army.

It is clear that the Athenian public connected the signal with the movement of the fleet. It is surely a gratuitous perversity to invent pretexts for dissociating the two. On the other hand, the popular version may have read into the signal more than a shield could convey. The expressions of Herodotus, when he first mentions the incident, waver between two inconsistent interpretations—first, that the signal originally suggested the plan, which would therefore be a happy thought to retrieve the defeat at Marathon; second, that the signal was part of a preconcerted plot. The second is of course the only possible meaning. Whoever may have proposed the very obvious scheme of sending a force round Sunium to seize Athens in the absence of her defenders, a contingency which must have preoccupied the mind of every responsible person concerned in the campaign for at least a week past, the shield was no doubt the index of organized co-operation between the Persians and the friends of Hippias in the city. But further, was it an invitation or a response? did it mean, 'We are ready, Come,' or rather 'We note your coming, and shall be ready'? At all events, on the general interpretation here adopted of the campaign, the signal was addressed primarily, not to the retiring defeated Datis, but to the advancing victorious Artaphernes. It came too late because Artaphernes had come too late. Thanks to Miltiades and Callimachus, he was bound to be too late, whenever he came. But there was still a bare hope that the Athenians would rest too long at Marathon, and let their city go by default.

The Athenians subsequently imputed the signal, and the plot which it revealed, to the Alcmaeonidae. The charge was more than probably just, although the proofs of it are not likely to

have emerged at the time, for the Alcmaeonidae remained strong
enough to take their revenge on Miltiades, and their leaders were
not ostracized for several years. Herodotus gives us what we may
assume to be their own defence, which had perhaps figured in
the courts or in public debates. The burden of the plea is that
the Alcmaeonidae were ever anti-tyrannic, and that their position
at Athens was so high that they had nothing to gain, but everything to lose, by compounding with Hippias and the Barbarian.
Neither of these hardy assertions will bear the slightest scrutiny.
The Athenians knew their Alcmaeonidae, and readily believed
the accusation which Herodotus treats as incredible. Nobody else
than the Alcmaeonidae seems ever to have been held responsible
for the signal, and the fact that Herodotus so long afterwards has
still to defend them tells against them. The action ascribed to
them agrees very well with its context, the political situation and
position of parties at the moment, the attitude of the Alcmaeonidae
in the recent past and in the subsequent future, the warning to
Callimachus put by Herodotus into the mouth of Miltiades and
the reticent allusion by Pindar in his Pythian ode for Megacles
to the odium under which he lay. Their conduct, however shortsighted and reprehensible in the light of later history and in the
broader view of Hellenic or even Athenian interests, was not in-
excusable on the narrow ground of domestic politics, and neither
Pericles nor even Themistocles could have afforded to reprobate
it without reserve.

Herodotus duly notes that the Barbarians on quitting Marathon
picked up the Eretrian prisoners from the island Aeglea. They
transported them to Susa; and Darius planted them not far
away at a place Ardericca near a famous oil well, where they still
remained, Herodotus adds, and still spoke Greek. He does not
tell their number, but it is not likely that it was more than a few
hundreds. Artaphernes might have detached a score of ships to
embark them without delaying his course. But it is more probable, and indicated by Herodotus (although the point cannot be
pressed), that they were taken off by the squadron of Datis, which
now became a mere rearguard.

The Athenian generals had no time to lose. The Persian fleet
would be arriving off Phalerum on the morning after the battle.
Plutarch[1] is doubtless right in putting the march back to Athens

---

[1] Plutarch also tells that Aristides and his regiment, the Antiochis, were
left at Marathon in charge of the prisoners and spoils. The story is suspicious, for it is directed, like other questionable stories, against Callias, and
Herodotus gives no hint to confirm it. But it is probable that a rearguard

on the same day as the battle, and Herodotus implies as much. The army marched from the precinct of Heracles at Marathon to the precinct of Heracles in Cynosarges, a coincidence which appeals to Herodotus. The situation of Cynosarges is not determined. It is usually placed to the east of Athens under Lycabettus, but the references in Herodotus distinctly point to the south or south-west of the city. After a battle it was a long tramp, even by the easier road now open, but the battle had been a victory, the troops would be in good heart, and the need was urgent.

The Persians showed themselves off Phalerum, where, if anywhere, they might look for a welcome from their Alcmaeonid partisans. But no signal invited them to land. Not only was the Athenian army in position to defend the city, but the victory of Marathon had destroyed all hope of a revolution in favour of Hippias. The game was up. They put about, and steered their course for Asia.

On the evening of the same day the Spartans, or their vanguard, two thousand strong, reached Attica. The rapidity of their march is remarkable, and the statement that they arrived in three days has been doubted. But just as historians have exaggerated by assuming that they reached not only Attica, but Athens, so Herodotus (or his informant) may have exaggerated by assuming that they started from Sparta. It would be characteristic of the Spartans, if the force was already mustered on the Laconian frontier before the full moon. The distance from frontier to frontier, by a route which avoids Argos, may be about 108 miles. Thirty-six miles a day is hard marching, but not unparalleled, and the arms and accoutrements might be carried by helots or on waggons. Plato states positively that the Spartans arrived on the day after the battle, but does not say where. Presumably he means at Athens, but in Attica might be enough for his purpose. That they arrived very soon after the battle is indicated by their visit to the field, where they viewed the Persian dead still unburied. Having paid to the Athenians a doubtless very gratifying tribute of praise for their achievement, they set out homewards.

Looking back on the little campaign we must acknowledge the skilful strategy of the generals of Darius. The attack on Eretria drew the Athenians out. The descent on Marathon

was left, if only to bury the dead and tend the wounded, and that the Antiochis, the last in the official order of the tribes, was detailed for the duty. One might conjecturally add to the Antiochis the Plataeans, whose homeward way would naturally lie through Aphidna and Tanagra.

arrested them, and pinned them there. The movement to occupy Athens in their absence was well conceived. The initiative remained throughout with the Persians. The one miscalculation was that the Asiatic troops could withstand the Greek charge; and even so, the battle might have had a different issue, if Datis had been able to restrain his successful centre. On the other side, the Athenian commander, Miltiades or Callimachus, was equal to every emergency, and improvised a counter to every stroke. He penetrated the enemy's design, recognized his own strength and weakness, waited for and never missed the right opportunity for action. Surprised by the landing at Marathon, he seized the very best position that could have been chosen; put on the defensive, he knew the precise moment to take the offensive, and how to bring his hoplites to close quarters with the least risk; driven to attenuate his centre, he snatched victory out of its defeat. Marathon was a triumph of the intelligent use of tactics, discipline and armament.

The Athenians were proud of their own singlehanded victory, and in after times were prone to magnify it. A decisive battle in the military sense it obviously was not. So far from finishing the war, it only began it, or precipitated a greater. But it did make a definite breach between Athens and Persia, and so prepared the way for Themistocles. It was the brilliant prologue to a grander drama, for which it set the scene and disposed the parts. For that reason posterity will always see in Marathon, not Artemisium, the sacred spot 'where sons of Athenians laid the resplendent foundation of freedom.'

VI. THE PARIAN EXPEDITION AND THE DEATH OF MILTIADES

The story of the Parian Expedition as told by Herodotus (vi, 132–6) is one which no sober critic could accept as it stands. Miltiades asked the Athenians for a fleet of 70 vessels, promising to lead them to a land from which they might obtain as much gold as they wished. The fleet is voted, and is employed by him for the reduction of the island of Paros in order to gratify a grudge against one of the Parian citizens. An indemnity of 100 talents is demanded for the help given to Datis and Artaphernes, and when this ultimatum was refused the town was besieged without success. At the end of 26 days the siege was abandoned, and Miltiades returned home with a wounded thigh.

There are three questions here which call for an answer. What was the date of the expedition? What was its object, and what was the cause of its return? 489 B.C.[1] is the date usually assigned for the expedition, but the narrative in Herodotus suggests that the fleet set sail soon after the Battle of Marathon, and there are strong reasons in favour of the autumn of 490 B.C. rather than the summer of the following year. The object of the expedition may be surmised to have been the organization of an outer line of defence against the Persians, and, if this were to be effected, the work must be taken in hand before the opening of the next campaigning season. There was plenty of time[2] before the winter began, even if Marathon was fought as late as September. Paros was to be taken by a *coup de main*, and the submission of the other islands would quickly follow. The stronghold of the anti-Persian cause in the Cyclades was Naxos, which some ten years earlier had successfully resisted the expedition sent under Aristagoras and Megabates and had been sacked by Datis and Artaphernes on their way to Marathon. Paros, on the other hand, had made its submission to Persia. The two islands were separated by a narrow channel, and the reduction of Paros was indispensable to the security of her neighbour. With these two islands on his side, Miltiades might hope to bring all the Cyclades into alliance with Athens before the Persian invasion. The unexpected resistance at Paros wrecked the scheme. The bad weather was approaching and there was nothing left but to return home.

Miltiades was at once brought to trial for his failure to fulfil his promise. The trial took place in the assembly, instead of in one of the courts of law, and the procedure may have been by Eisangelia, although this is not certain. The charge was that of having deceived the sovereign people; the prosecutor was Xanthippus, who probably had played the same part in the former trial; the penalty demanded was that of death. Miltiades was brought into court a dying man, for his wound had gangrened. His friends appealed to the memory of his great services to the state, and the appeal was so far successful that the penalty was reduced to a fine of 50 talents. Soon after the trial he died, and the fine was ultimately paid by his son Cimon.

[1] In this and the following sections of the chapter the usually accepted date of the Battle of Marathon (490 B.C.) is adopted, see above, p. 233.

[2] If the Athenians entered on the siege of Sestos after Mycale (p. 345), in spite of the stormy character of the Dardanelles, they could certainly have risked an expedition to Paros, near at hand, and in comparatively calm seas.

VII. ATHENS AND AEGINA

For the relations of Athens and Aegina down to the Great Persian War Herodotus is our main and almost our sole authority, and it is hardly too much to say that the history of these relations presents some of the most difficult problems which historical criticism can be called upon to solve.

Three stages are to be distinguished in the events narrated by Herodotus: firstly, the 'Ancient Feud' between the two states; secondly, the πόλεμος ἀκήρυκτος (the 'Unheralded War'), which is alleged to have broken out about 506 B.C. in response to the appeal of Thebes to Aegina, the motive of which is found in the 'Ancient Feud'; and finally, the war which resulted from the refusal of Athens to restore to Aegina the hostages deposited by Cleomenes. If Herodotus' statements are correct, there had been a war between Athens and Aegina at some remote period long before 506 B.C., and in this year a second war broke out, the duration of which is left undetermined. That the two states were at war in the interval between the first and second Persian invasions, all critics are agreed. The two questions which have to be answered are these; in the first place, is the 'Ancient Feud' of which Herodotus speaks historical or imaginary; and in the second, is Herodotus correct in connecting the outbreak of the 'Unheralded War' with the appeal of Thebes to Aegina c. 506 B.C., or is the outbreak of this war to be connected with the refusal of Athens to restore the hostages after the death of Cleomenes? In other words, was Athens at war with Aegina continuously from 506 B.C. to 481 B.C., or did hostilities between the two states first begin after the death of Cleomenes? It is to these questions that we propose to address ourselves.

As to the 'Ancient Feud,' opinions differ. There are some who maintain that the alleged 'feud' between Athens and Aegina is historical, and that its date is to be put in the earlier half of the sixth century B.C., or even in the seventh century (see above, vol. III, p. 540 and *ibid.* n. 1), although they are compelled to admit that the details of the story as told by Herodotus (v, 82–8) are in the main mythical. There are others who agree with Wilamowitz-Moellendorff[1] in regarding the whole story as unhistorical. It is difficult, indeed, not to accept Wilamowitz's conclusions that Herodotus' narrative presents us with a series of aetiological myths, explanatory of ritual usages.

Secondly, as to the 'Unheralded War.' In a previous chapter

[1] *Aristoteles und Athen*, vol. II, pp. 280 *sqq.*

(p. 162) it has been pointed out that Herodotus connects the outbreak of the 'Unheralded War' with the appeal addressed by Thebes to Aegina for an alliance between the two states against Athens. He further states that when the Aeginetans in response to this appeal sent the statues of the Aeacidae, the tutelary heroes of the island, by way of assistance to the Thebans, the latter sent back the statues, and asked for aid of a more material kind. Thereupon the Aeginetans began an 'Unheralded War' on the Athenians, and ravaged several of the demes on the coast. The Athenians were about to retaliate, when they were prevented from taking action by the news that Sparta had summoned a congress of her allies, in order to secure their support for the restoration of Hippias. At this point the narrative breaks off, and we hear nothing more of the relations between the two states until we come, in the middle of the Sixth Book, to the embassy from Athens to Sparta to demand the punishment of the Aeginetans for their action in giving earth and water to the heralds of King Darius, in the spring of the year 491 B.C. We are subsequently told that on the death of Cleomenes the Spartans sent Leotychidas to Athens, to demand the restoration of the Aeginetan hostages who had been deposited with the Athenians by his fellow-king. The refusal of the Athenians to restore the hostages led to the seizure by the Aeginetans of an Athenian sacred vessel, which lay off Cape Sunium with a number of leading citizens on board. The Athenians retaliated, and a war broke out which was brought to an end in 481 B.C. through the mediation of the Congress of the Greeks (p. 278).

It is beyond dispute that Herodotus connects the outbreak of the 'Unheralded War' with the appeal of Thebes to Aegina, and that he puts the ravaging of the Athenian coast by the Aeginetans before the Peloponnesian Congress at Sparta, c. 504 B.C. If the war in question did not break out until after the death of Cleomenes, Herodotus is convicted of error, and that of the gravest order. If the case against Herodotus is to be proved, it must be proved up to the hilt. The improbability of such an error is so great that we may fairly demand arguments that are conclusive. What then are these arguments?

To begin with, it may be pointed out that, while Herodotus asserts the outbreak of a war c. 506 B.C. and mentions the termination of a war between the two states in 481 B.C., he nowhere either states, or implies, that war between Athens and Aegina was waged continuously from the returning of the Aeacidae to the meeting of the Congress. That war went on continuously between these two states is not the assertion of the historian, but the hypothesis of his critics. If Herodotus had conceived the state of war to have been continuous, we should have looked for some reference to it at the time of the appeal of Aristagoras in the Ionic Revolt, and if the two states were really at war Aegina would hardly have failed to avail herself of the opportunity offered by the absence of the twenty Athenian vessels in Ionian waters. But neither on the occasions of the appeal, nor on that of the withdrawal of the Athenian squadron from Ionia, does Herodotus even hint that Athens was at the time engaged in hostilities with Aegina. Nor, if the language of Herodotus is examined when he is dealing with the embassy of Athens to Sparta in 491 B.C. (VI, 49), does it suggest that Athens was already at war with Aegina at the time of her appeal to Sparta. It implies merely a hostile sentiment, but not a state of war. Further, no details are given of the war alleged to have broken out *c.* 506 B.C.; it is only when we come to the events that followed the seizure of the sacred vessel at Sunium that we find particulars given. Finally, a phrase employed in a passage in the Seventh Book (*c.* 144), in which the building of 200 additional vessels at the instance of Themistocles is mentioned, seems definitely to exclude the hypothesis that Herodotus regarded the hostilities in which the two states were engaged *c.* 482 B.C., as part of a war which had begun as far back as 506 B.C. In the passage in question he states that it was the outbreak of the war between Athens and Aegina (οὗτος ὁ πόλεμος συστάς) that saved Greece from the Persian peril by compelling Athens to become a naval power. Surely it would be little short of ludicrous to maintain that the outbreak of the war between the two states a quarter of a century before the Persian invasion saved Greece, because it compelled the Athenians to build a great fleet some twenty-two years later. When Herodotus wrote the passage, he certainly conceived the outbreak of the war as recent, not remote. These considerations, when taken together, are at least sufficient to prove that Herodotus did not regard the war waged during the period between the two Persian invasions as forming part and parcel of the 'Unheralded War.' The most that can be contended is that he believed that war broke out *c.* 506 B.C. Of that war, however, he has nothing further to tell us. It began, but how or when it ended, he knows not.

Such considerations, it may be urged, are sufficient to disprove the hypothesis of a continuous war, but insufficient to refute the historian's assertion that the outbreak of the 'Unheralded War' is to be connected with the appeal of Thebes to Aegina. To prove

Herodotus in error on this point; to prove that there was but one war and that it belongs to the period between the two Persian Invasions; to prove, in other words, that 'the outbreak of this war' (οὗτος ὁ πόλεμος συστάς) is none other than that of the 'Unheralded War', three arguments can be adduced, the cumulative effect of which may not improperly be called conclusive. The first of these arguments has been indicated in a previous chapter (p. 162). The sending of the Aeacidae by the Aeginetans in answer to the Theban appeal was clearly equivalent to a diplomatic refusal to join in hostilities against Athens. There could be no question that Herodotus is right in connecting the appeal of Thebes to Aegina with the defeat of the Theban forces by Athens *c.* 506 B.C., and it may be assumed that his narrative of the events down to the return of these images by the Thebans is correct. His error lay in connecting the outbreak of the 'Unheralded War' with the return of the Aeacidae. If the motive of the Aeginetans in sending these statues to Thebes has been correctly interpreted, *cadit quaestio*; the Aeginetans did not attack Athens when the statues were sent back by the Thebans.

The second argument is based on the term, the 'Unheralded War'; a term which in itself means no more than a war in which heralds are not employed, and thus might cover both a war without quarter given, a relentless war, and an irregular or guerilla war. In the context in Herodotus it can only denote a war without formal notice, and this has been generally recognized by commentators and critics. The charge made by the Athenians against the Aeginetans, that the latter had ravaged their territory without the customary declaration of war by means of a herald, was analogous to Mr Asquith's declaration in 1914 that Germany by her invasion of Belgium had violated the public law of Europe. We are impelled to ask where in the narrative of Herodotus can we find any event or incident that explains this charge, and to this question only one answer can be given. The seizure of the sacred vessel off Sunium must have constituted, according to the sentiment of the age, a violation of the public law of Greece; it was an act of hostility without due notice, and it was directed against a sacred vessel. Clearly then, the term ἀκήρυκτος ('Unheralded), would find an adequate explanation in the seizure of this vessel. The capture of the sacred vessel, however, occurred not in the interval between the appeal of the Thebans to Aegina and the convening of the congress at Sparta to restore Hippias, but after the death of Cleomenes, and some considerable time after that event. It will be shown presently that the death of

Cleomenes cannot be put earlier than 489 B.C.; the earliest date therefore for the seizure of the sacred vessel will be 488 B.C.

The third and the most conclusive argument is based on an oracle which Herodotus (v, 89) connects with the outbreak of the 'Unheralded War.' He tells us that when the Athenians were meditating reprisals on the Aeginetans for their unprovoked attack on Attic territory they received an oracle from Delphi which commanded them to desist from hostilities against the Aeginetans for a period of thirty years, and in the thirty-first year they were to dedicate a precinct to Aeacus, and then they might attack their enemy with good hope of success.

Instead of obeying the oracle, the Athenians proceeded at once to dedicate a precinct to Aeacus, and they were about to begin reprisals when they heard of the summoning of the congress at Sparta to discuss the restoration of Hippias. It is commonly assumed that the oracle is a *vaticinium post eventum*[1], but it is over-looked that what Herodotus gives us is not the text or the sub-stance of the oracle, but the gloss put upon it by those who claimed that the prophecy had been fulfilled. No oracle, whether genuine or forged, would have indulged in a date so precise as the thirty-first year. It may be surmised that the term used in the oracle was a generation, of which thirty years was one of the conventional equivalents. The advice given by the oracle was merest common-sense. The Aeginetans were superior at sea to the Athenians; war, therefore, at that moment could only result in the discomfiture of Athens. The dedication of a precinct to Aeacus implied a claim to the possession of his island; it was an invitation to quit the barren rock of Aegina and make his abode among the pleasant things of Attica. 'Leave,' said the oracle, 'the prosecution of the feud to your children; let the next generation dedicate the precinct, and enter on the *guerre de revanche*.' It was in the year 458 B.C. that the Athenians inflicted a decisive defeat at sea on the Aeginetans, and all but annihilated their navy. It was then that the success promised by the oracle was attained. If we reckon back 30 years from 458 B.C., we arrive at the year 488 B.C., the true date of the seizure of the sacred vessel. When in the year

---

[1] It has been the practice of modern critics to explain away most of the oracles recorded in Herodotus and other writers as *vaticinia post eventum*. Such a method is singularly unscientific. The oracles were carefully pre-served in the archives of the states, and although it was easy enough to forge an oracle, it was not so easy to secure its general acceptance. At any rate, the *onus probandi* rests with those who impugn the genuineness of any given oracle.

458 B.C. the devout claimed the fulfilment of the oracle, they could point, in support of their contention, to the date of the dedication of the precinct of Aeacus, just 30 years before, the name of the archon on whose term of office the dedication was made being either inscribed on the walls of the precinct itself, or else to be read in the decree ordering its erection. 'If only we had listened to the wisdom of the oracle, we should have been saved the sufferings and humiliations of the former war.' This reasoning was only possible if the true date of the dedication of the precinct was 488 B.C. Thus the third argument leads us, although by a different route, to the same conclusion as the second.

VIII. CLEOMENES AND AEGINA

If we may trust the indications of date afforded by Herodotus[1], it was in the spring of 491 B.C. that Darius sent heralds to the mainland of Greece and the islands, to demand earth and water. Among those who gave these symbols of submission were the Aeginetans. Their action need not be judged too harshly, nor is it probable that it was prompted solely by hostility to Athens. Aegina depended for her existence on her commerce, and her commerce was with the East rather than with the West; for the most part, with ports in the Persian empire, or at least along the routes which lay at the mercy of the Persian fleet. One of the earliest facts known to us in the history of Aegina is her war with Samos in the reign of King Amphicrates[2], perhaps about the beginning of the seventh century B.C. In the middle of the next century Aegina was the only state of European Greece that had a share in the Egyptian trade at Naucratis[3]. It is clear from a passage in Herodotus (VII, 147) that in the early years of the fifth century she was the entrepôt of the Pontic corn trade. Hence it might well seem to Aeginetan statesmen that a good understanding with Persia was indispensable for their trade. At Athens, on the other hand, it must have been evident to every responsible statesman that the medism of Aegina must involve momentous consequences for their city. A Persian invasion of Attica was not likely to be long delayed, and with a hostile Aegina on her flank Athens was doomed. But one course lay open to Athens if this danger was to be averted; to appeal to Sparta to coerce her ally. Although Herodotus does not expressly state that the Athenian appeal was addressed to Cleomenes, the subsequent course of events renders

---

[1] Cf. VI, 48 with VI, 95.
[2] Herodotus III, 59.   [3] *Ibid.* II, 178.

it certain that it was on the support of the Spartan king, rather than on that of the ephors, that the Athenians relied.

It is hard to say which is the more remarkable, the appeal or the response to the appeal. When the previous relations of Athens and Sparta since the fall of the Tyranny are borne in mind, it may well appear astonishing that Athens should have conceded to Sparta all, or more than all, that Sparta had ever claimed for herself. Aegina was accused of treason to Greece[1]. The charge is that a Panhellenic obligation has been contravened, and the implication is that Sparta is the appointed guardian of Panhellenic interests. Grote shows his accustomed insight in claiming that this appeal is one of the turning points of Greek history. We may be certain that but for the victory of Sepeia the appeal would never have been made. It was the crushing defeat inflicted on Argos by King Cleomenes that gave Sparta such a supremacy in the Greek world as can alone explain the action of Athens. The response of Sparta to the appeal is not less surprising. Sparta was bound to Aegina by almost every conceivable tie. Aegina was Dorian; she was a leading member of the Peloponnesian League; and she was more consistently oligarchic in her policy than almost any other Greek state. Only three or four years before she had lent her fleet for the transport of the Spartan forces from Thyrea to Nauplia in the Argive War (p. 165 sq.). It was asking much of Sparta to demand that she should sacrifice the interests of Aegina to those of Athens. That, in spite of this, the appeal met with a favourable response was due entirely to the far-reaching vision of the Spartan king. He saw as clearly as the statesmen at Athens the imminence of the Persian peril; he realized that, at all costs, Aegina must be coerced. He crossed over to the island in order to arrest those who were chiefly responsible for the giving of earth and water, but he met with a resistance on which he had not counted. His colleague, Demaratus, who years before this had thwarted his attempt to restore Isagoras, had again played him false. He was now acting in concert with Crius, one of the leading statesmen in Aegina, and had instructed him to dispute the authority of Cleomenes, on the ground that he was acting without the approval or support of his colleague.

Cleomenes was compelled to return to Sparta without effecting his purpose, but he saw that the moment had come for a trial of strength between him and his fellow-king. There had long been gossip at Sparta about the birth of Demaratus, whose legitimacy had been called in question. Cleomenes set to work to secure his

---

[1] Herodotus VI, 49.

deposition on the ground of his birth, and with this end in view he entered into a compact with a kinsman of Demaratus, Leotychidas by name, to whom the succession would pass in the event of the deposition being decreed. It was resolved to refer the question of legitimacy to the arbitrament of the Delphic oracle, which gave its decision against Demaratus. Leotychidas was thereupon elevated to the throne. Cleomenes now saw the last obstacle to his policy removed, and with his subservient colleague crossed over to Aegina and arrested ten of the leading members of the oligarchical government, and deposited them as hostages in the hands of the Athenians.

Meanwhile Demaratus, whose deposition had not involved his exile from Sparta, had fled to Persia in consequence of an affront put upon him by Leotychidas, and had met with a warm welcome from King Darius, who bestowed on him estates in the Troad which in the time of Xenophon, a century later, were still in the occupation of his descendants (*Hell.* iii, 1, 6). Demaratus had disappeared from the scene, but the party of which he had been the leader, or possibly the tool, was as active as ever in its opposition to Cleomenes and his policy. Cleomenes was charged with having procured the decision of the oracle by means of an intrigue with Cobon, a leading Delphian, who, it was alleged, had brought undue influence to bear upon the priestess Perialla. The charge may have been well founded, for Cleomenes was none too scrupulous in his choice of means. However that may be, he thought it prudent to withdraw from Sparta, while his enemies secured the exile of Cobon and the deposition of Perialla. Cleomenes at first took refuge in Thessaly, but before long he returned to the Peloponnese, and attempted to effect his restoration to Sparta by the aid of the Arcadians, among whom disaffection was rife. So great was the alarm at Sparta that he was recalled and reinstated. According to the story told to Herodotus on his visit to Sparta some fifty years later, Cleomenes went mad immediately after his recall and his relations put him under restraint. He succeeded, however, in procuring a knife from the helot who was his keeper, and mutilated himself so horribly that he died.

Herodotus' narrative of these events is lacking in precision, and presents some obvious difficulties. He does not tell us whether Cleomenes was formally deposed when he quitted Sparta, nor whether it was a successor or regent who acted in his place. It seems improbable that one who was sane enough to organize an Arcadian revolt should so soon afterwards have gone raving mad. It has often been suggested that he met his end by foul play, and that the story told to Herodotus was invented to conceal the true facts. In a state so well disciplined as the Spartan, it is not incredible that the version which had the *imprimatur* of the ephors should come to be accepted without question a generation or so later. On the other hand, there had always been a strain of violence in his nature, and it may be that this developed into insanity. It may be granted that the character of Cleomenes is not calculated to attract; certainly it had none of that charm which makes Brasidas, as we see him in the pages of Thucydides, the hero of the Archidamian war. Cleomenes was unscrupulous, violent, and cruel; although it may be pleaded in extenuation that their training did not make Spartans humane, and that few Greek statesmen of that or any other generation were scrupulous in their methods.

But, whatever the character of the man, the importance of his career cannot be mistaken. His victory over Argos had two results, a direct and an indirect one. Its direct result was to cripple Argos at the time of Xerxes' invasion, and its indirect result was the hegemony of Sparta. It was his victory at Sepeia that rendered possible that unity of command without which the Greek army would have had no chance against Persia. His intervention in Aegina forced her into patriotism in spite of herself. Had Aegina been on the Persian side in 480 B.C., the Battle of Salamis could never have been fought. If Argos had been able to support the Persian cause with her military forces unimpaired, Pausanias would never have ventured beyond the lines of the Isthmus in 479 B.C.

One point remains to be determined in connection with the career of Cleomenes—the date of his death. Herodotus appears to put between the spring of 491 B.C. and the summer of the next year the whole series of events which starts with the appeal of Athens to Sparta against the medism of Aegina and ends with the earlier stages of the Aeginetan War. Everyone is agreed that all these events cannot by any ingenuity be squeezed into a space of twelve or fifteen months. Two things are certain; firstly, that Cleomenes' death cannot be put before 489 B.C., and secondly, that he cannot have been at Sparta at the time of Marathon. It is probable that he was in Thessaly or Arcadia when the battle was fought. The passage, however, in Herodotus (VI, 94 *ad init.*) in which he appears to put the death of Cleomenes and the outbreak of the Aeginetan War before the summer of the year of Marathon is no real note of time. It is a mere literary device for ending a digression and returning to the main subject[1].

[1] Cf. v, 90, where again we have a mere device for passing from one digression to another.

IX. THE AEGINETAN WAR

The opposition lost no time in setting to work to reverse the policy of the dead king. Leotychidas must be offered up as a victim to appease the wrath of the Aeginetans. Party passion ran so high that Leotychidas was sentenced to be delivered up as a hostage to the Aeginetans, to be set against their own hostages in the hands of the Athenians. The Aeginetans were at first disposed to accept the offer, but wiser counsels in the end prevailed. They could hardly fail to recognize that the Spartan king would be more useful to them as an agent in negotiations with the Athenians than as a hostage. He was sent to Athens to demand the return of the hostages, but, as might have been expected, he met with a refusal. It was now clear to the Aeginetans that there was no prospect of recovering their hostages by diplomatic means, and that, so long as the Athenians held hostages and they held none, their hands were tied. It was not long before an opportunity offered of getting possession of the persons of Athenians of rank corresponding to that of their own hostages. A sacred vessel had been dispatched from Athens to Cape Sunium to convey a number of Athenians of the highest rank, who had been commissioned to represent the state at a festival held at the neighbouring temple. By a surprise attack the Aeginetans succeeded in capturing the vessel and all on board. At length their hands were free. Either the Athenian hostages could be exchanged for their own countrymen, or at least, so long as they held hostages from Athens, their own were safe.

At Athens, the act of the Aeginetans aroused the utmost indignation. It was denounced as a violation of the public law of Greece. But it was recognized that their own navy was no match for that of the enemy. Hence, if there was to be war between the two states, it was a war that could only be won by political weapons. Consequently, we find Athens attempting to play in Aegina at this moment the game which she played with such conspicuous success in Boeotia thirty years later. She entered into negotiations with Nicodromus, the leader of the democratic opposition in the island. There was to be a rising of the democrats under his leadership against the ruling oligarchy, and the Athenians were to land a large force in support of the insurgents. The plot miscarried, partly because the conditions were less favourable than those of Boeotia in 457 b.c., and partly because the Athenians arrived on the scene a day too late[1]. In Aegina there was at one

[1] Cf. the failure, for the same reason, of a similar scheme for the betrayal of Boeotia at the time of the Battle of Delium, 424 b.c.

end of the social scale an aristocracy of merchant princes and at
the other an immense servile population[1], and these are the conditions which are least likely to afford a congenial soil for the
growth of democracy. The Athenian excuse for their delay in
arriving on the scene was that they were waiting for a reinforcement of twenty vessels which the Corinthians had agreed to
transfer to them. The Aeginetan government suppressed the
rising with ease, although they could not prevent the escape of
Nicodromus and some of his followers, who were established by
the Athenians at Cape Sunium whence they carried on a guerilla
warfare against their native island. The day after the flight of
Nicodromus, an Athenian fleet, raised with the aid of the 20
Corinthian vessels to the number of 70 sail, appeared off the
island. The Aeginetans put out against them with the same
number of vessels, and in the action which followed the Athenians
claimed the advantage. It was not, however, long before the
Aeginetans inflicted a defeat on the Athenians, and captured four
of their vessels with their crews.

At this point the narrative of Herodotus breaks off. Evidently,
Athenian tradition had no further successes to recount. This
silence as to the subsequent course of the operations is eloquent;
but there are two facts which may help in the reconstruction of
the story of the war. The first of these facts is the assignment of
the thalassocracy of the Aeginetans to the period between the
first and second Persian invasions[2]. It is clear that the claim was
advanced that during these years Aegina ruled the waves, and
equally clear that the claim went unchallenged. The second fact
is the magnitude of the effort made by Athens to wrest this naval
supremacy from her rival. We hear nothing further about the
war until we come to the year 482 b.c., when Themistocles induced the assembly to devote the surplus funds in the treasury,
arising out of the proceeds of the silver mines at Laurium, to the
building of a fleet of 200 triremes of a new type, instead of distributing the money among the people. Herodotus is once again
less precise in statement than might be wished. He leaves it uncertain how large the surplus was, or whether such distribution of
surplus funds had been customary. The mines at Laurium had
long been worked, and they continued to be worked till the
middle of the fourth century b.c., but it would appear that shortly
before 482 b.c. a new deposit of peculiar richness had been dis-

[1] Aristotle (*ap.* Athenaeum, vi, p. 272 D) put the number of the slave
population at 470,000, an incredible figure.
[2] Cf. Eusebius, *Chron. Can.* p. 337.

covered at a place called Maroneia, somewhere in this district[1]. The mines were the property of the state, and they were leased for a short term of years for an initial payment, usually of one talent, and for an annual payment of $\frac{1}{24}$ of the gross produce. We need not suppose, either that the whole surplus in the treasury was marked for distribution, or that the surplus had resulted from the proceeds of a single year. Later writers reduced the number of vessels to be built to 100, but Thucydides (I, 14) seems to imply that the vessels that formed the Athenian contingent at Salamis were those which were built in accordance with the measure carried by Themistocles. If this view is correct, his statement supports that of Herodotus, and we can hardly go wrong in accepting the testimony of these two witnesses. It may also be inferred from Thucydides that Themistocles appealed to the danger from Persia, as well as to the war with Aegina, but there can be little doubt that the constraining motive that induced the Athenians to forego the distribution of the money was the nearer danger rather than the more remote. A navy of 200 vessels was an effort out of all proportion to anything that Athens had yet attempted. In the greatness of the effort we may find some measure of the success of Aegina and the humiliation of Athens. By the spring of 481 B.C. vessels of the new model were ready for use, but it was not against Aegina that they were employed[2].

X. POLITICAL PARTIES AT ATHENS

In a former chapter (pp. 138, 170 *sq.*) it was argued that the evidence available points to the conclusion that at the time of the Battle of Marathon four parties can be distinguished in the political arena at Athens, and that on more than one critical occasion two of these parties, that of the Alcmaeonidae and the adherents of the exiled tyrants, were acting in concert, while the aristocratic party under the leadership of Miltiades made common cause with the radical party under Themistocles on all questions of foreign policy. If our explanation (p. 252) of the Parian Expedition is to be accepted, the scheme was one which, if not inspired by Themistocles, must have received his approval. Its failure was a blow to

---

[1] Arist. *Const. of Athens,* XXII.

[2] It may well be doubted whether it was within the capacity of Athens at this period to build 200 vessels in the space of a twelvemonth. It is probable, therefore, that the whole number were not completed until the beginning of the next year, 480 B.C.

the cause which he had at heart, and he must have used his influence to secure the acquittal of Miltiades, or at least the mitigation of the sentence. The conviction and the death of Miltiades meant the triumph of the party which had brought him to trial. A few months afterwards, in the spring of 489 B.C., Aristides was elected to the Archonship, which was still an office of high administrative importance. He had been an intimate associate of Cleisthenes[1], and that he remained a member of the Alcmaeonid party may be inferred, not only from his opposition to Themistocles but from the fact that the supreme command in 479 B.C. is shared between him and Xanthippus after the fall of Themistocles from power.

Themistocles was not the man tamely to accept defeat. During the next few years his energies are devoted to securing for himself the leading position in the state. In order to accomplish his purpose he had recourse to two weapons, ostracism and legislation. Early in 487 B.C. he secured the ostracism of Hipparchus the leader of the Peisistratid party, and in the following year that of Megacles, to whom the signal of the shield at the Battle of Marathon was popularly attributed. The ostracism of the head of the great Alcmaeonid clan must have been a serious blow to the influence of the party led by Xanthippus and Aristides, and it is not surprising to find that both of these statesmen followed Megacles into exile, Xanthippus in 484 and Aristides in 482 B.C. It may be surmised that the ill-success of this party in the conduct of the Aeginetan War may have contributed to the unpopularity of its leading members.

Themistocles had thus disposed of all his rivals. Meanwhile, he had succeeded by means of legislation in transforming the character of the Athenian executive, and in creating for himself an office which would render possible One Man Power ($\dot{\eta}$ τοῦ πρώτου ἀνδρὸς ἀρχή). In the year 487–486 B.C. sortition was substituted for election in the appointment of the archons; a change which implied that the archonship was reduced to insignificance, and that the strategia took its place as the chief executive office in the state (see above, p. 155). Before long a further step was taken in the creation of the new office of *strategos autocrator* (commander-in-chief), a position which we find him holding in 480 B.C. In his final triumph, that over Aristides, a question of momentous importance for Athens and for Greece was involved. Was Athens

---

[1] Plutarch, *Aristides*, 2, *ad init.* Κλεισθένους...ἑταῖρος γενόμενος. There may be a reference to the ἑταιρεία in Arist. *Const. of Athens*, XX, I.

to rely, as in the past, mainly on her army, or was she to aspire
to be the greatest naval power in the Greek world? It was in the
same year in which Aristides was ostracized that Themistocles
carried his proposal to build 200 vessels of an improved type.
When the decisive moment came, and Xerxes was on his march
towards Greece, the office and the man to fill it and the weapon
which he had forged were there.

CHAPTER IX

XERXES' INVASION OF GREECE

I. XERXES' MARCH AND FORCES

KING Darius was bound to avenge the rebuff at Marathon, which impaired the prestige of Persia in the Aegean. Moreover, the scope of the war had now been enlarged, for behind Athens stood the paramount power, Sparta. The annexation of Greece could no longer be shirked or postponed. The preparations, put in hand at once, were on a scale which showed that Darius was determined to settle the business, and the organization of the expedition was worthy of his reputation. But a providential respite was granted to the Hellenes first by the revolt of Egypt, and then the king's death in the autumn of 486 B.C.[1] His son Xerxes, who inherited his throne and project, was for a while fully occupied with the Egyptian, and perhaps also Babylonian, rebels. His apparent slowness to resume the enterprise may have been mistaken in Greece for vacillation in his purpose[2]. It was not until the year 481 B.C. that Xerxes put his forces in movement towards the west and himself set out, presumably from Susa.

Of the king's route as far as Celaenae in Phrygia, at the source of the Maeander, Herodotus has nothing to tell but that he picked up his army, or the portion of it which was to journey with him, at Critalla in Cappadocia, and crossed the Halys. The site of Critalla is not fixed; and the passage of the Halys is probably no more than an inference by Herodotus from his misconception of the course of that river. His knowledge of the march extends in fact no farther eastwards than the point where Greek information may be supposed to have begun. We may assume that the king traversed Mount Taurus by the Cilician Gates, and that Critalla lay not far from the exit from the pass, perhaps near Tyana or Cybistra. A probable route onwards to Celaenae, passing between

---

[1] On the date see J. K. Fotheringham's *Note on the Regnal Years in the Elephantine papyri* in the Monthly Notices of the Royal Astronomical Society, LXIX (1909), pp. 446 *sqq.* and 542.

[2] This misinterpretation may have given occasion for the drama presented by Herodotus in the early chapters of his Seventh Book.

the great lakes and the Sultan Dagh range, has been recently suggested[1]. Thenceforward, although questions may arise in detail, the line of march is on the whole clearly marked by Herodotus and by nature.

Elaborate preparations had been made along the road. Two bridges of ships were built across the Hellespont from Abydos to a point near Sestos. When the first pair was destroyed by a storm, they were rebuilt under the direction of a Greek engineer, Harpalus. The bridges of Darius over the Bosphorus and the Danube were of course useful precedents. Another bridge was thrown across the Strymon, no doubt another across the Hebrus, and possibly others over big rivers. A canal was cut through the low isthmus which joins the promontory of Mount Athos to the mainland. Its use is problematic; and its existence has been questioned in ancient as well as modern times, but is guaranteed by Thucydides and by vestiges still visible. The road was doubtless put in order. The 'king's way' in Thrace remained an object of veneration to the natives for generations to come. When the army reached the frontier of the empire in Macedonia, one-third was sent forward to clear a route through the forests of the Pierian highlands. Great stores of corn were accumulated at suitable intervals—Herodotus notes five such magazines on the road through Thrace and Macedonia; and the cities on the king's itinerary had notice to provide for his entertainment. The bridges over the straits and the canal through the isthmus most impressed the imagination of the Greeks. Xerxes with Titanic might ignored the divinely ordered constitution of the world; his army marched across the sea, and his navy sailed through the dry land. But the organization of the supplies for the expedition, although we hear less of it, was probably a greater feat.

The king spent the winter 481–480 B.C. at Sardes. Thence he dispatched heralds to invite the Greek states, except Sparta and Athens and possibly their allies with whom he deemed himself to be already at war, to recognize his sovereignty and furnish food for him on his coming. With the advent of spring he set out for the Hellespont. Herodotus in his description of Xerxes' route not infrequently gives only one, and not always the most obvious, of several roads probably used. It may be doubted whether he is right in sending the whole army from the plain of Thebe to Ilium by the toilsome and unnecessary route round the eastern flank of Mount Ida. Surely the mass of the forces took the easier road along the coast; but here as elsewhere Herodotus' information

[1] By Sir W. M. Ramsay, *J H.S.* XL, p. 89.

follows only one division. Another statement in this context is indisputably false. No eclipse of the sun marked the departure of Xerxes from Sardes. The real foundation of the story may be found in the annular eclipse of the 17th of February 478 B.C. The conjunction of the phenomenon with the king's march is commonly ascribed to popular superstition, but the same difference of two years occurs so often in dates of this period that one may suspect that the myth originated in chronology.

The passage of the Hellespont is variously stated by Herodotus to have occupied two days, a week, a month. Perhaps the combatant forces crossed in two days, the baggage train in a week, and the total pause from beginning to end from the arrival of the first vanguard to the departure of the last rearguard lasted a month. The fleet first appears at Abydos. It seems unlikely that the whole of it was brought so far up the straits. But the two bridges demanded respectively 360 and 314 vessels, and most or all of these may have been drawn from the expeditionary fleet of transports or ships of burden, and have been released to resume their voyage when the army had passed over. The Greeks were surprised to find after the battle of Mycale that the bridges were gone. The explanation, that a storm had wrecked them, may be mere inference. It is hardly probable that they were intended to be kept up continuously after the crossing, although the cables were ready at Sestos for their reconstruction on the return of the troops.

From Sestos the army marched round the head of the Black Gulf to Doriscus, near the mouth of the Hebrus, whither the fleet had directed its course. Here the vast motley host was finally organized for the campaign. It is implied that Doriscus was the point at which the last Asiatic contingents joined and the concentration was completed. The force which journeyed from Critalla with the king was not the whole. No doubt it was furnished only by the central and eastern provinces of the empire. Divisions from the western provinces may have joined at Sardes or Abydos, or even come by sea to Doriscus. If Tyrodiza, one of the depôts, was really in the territory of Perinthus, it may indicate that some of them crossed the Bosphorus. Herodotus pictures the multitude assembled at Doriscus as a mere confused mob, a mixed inarticulate crowd. That conception is absurd, and incompatible with his own description of the king's march from Sardes. We have rather to imagine the local or provincial levies coming in day by day at haphazard perhaps, but already regimented and probably brigaded in myriads. All that was now needed was to distribute them to the higher units or army corps.

Herodotus gives a ludicrous account of the numbering of the infantry. Ten thousand men were packed tightly together; a line was drawn round them, and a wall built on the line; the troops were then herded in batches into this pen, which measured their number. Possibly there may have been a standing camp, designed to accommodate 10,000 men, which successive myriads occupied for a night on their arrival until they could pitch their own, and Greek wit may have amused itself with the idea of Xerxes counting his millions like corn by the bushel. The important points are that the unit is the myriad and the total 170 myriads, to which Herodotus adds ten more myriads for the mounted troops (80,000 cavalry, and 20,000 chariot and camel corps), making a grand total of 1,800,000 men for the entire army. By computing in addition to these the crews of the fleet and the reinforcements gathered in Europe on the march, and by doubling the figures to include the non-combatant attendants, Herodotus (still omitting the camp-followers, male and female) succeeds in reaching 5,283,220, a truly prodigious number. It is easy to discount his conjectural estimates of the attendants and the European recruits, and his figures for the service ships and light vessels and their crews. But his total of 180 myriads for the army requires explanation and invites criticism.

Let us start from his 'Homeric catalogue' of the 46 nations marshalled under 29 archontes or brigadier-generals. Stripped of its descriptive embroidery, its details of armature and dress, for which Herodotus may be partly indebted to Mandrocles' picture in the Heraeum at Samos (see above, p. 104), and marginal notes of history or biography, this list is clearly an official document. Without the personal names of the commanders it might almost be called an abstract of a *Notitia Dignitatum militarium in partibus Orientis*. But, like the Notitiae, it gives no numbers. We must look to the organization of the army for light on Herodotus' figures. The system is decimal up to the myriad, which is evidently the divisional unit. There are decarchs, hecatontarchs, chiliarchs, and myriarchs. Above the myriarchs Herodotus puts his archontes or brigadiers, and above these six generals-in-chief. But the number of the archontes, 29, is quite incongruous with all the other numbers, which obviously demand 30. The name of Hydarnes, the commander of the king's guard, the 'Immortals,' almost obtrudes itself as the thirtieth. Hydarnes commands only 10,000 men, and we should certainly expect the archontes to be the divisional commanders or myriarchs. But Herodotus' total 1,800,000 divided by 30 gives 60,000 to each archon. The solution of the problem seems to be that by some confusion he has promoted the myriarchs (archontes) a step too high, and assigned to them the command of army corps of 60,000 which really belongs to the six generals-in-chief. If so, the total number of the army is at once reduced to 360,000. But 30 myriarchs give only 300,000. We must assume six more myriarchs; and the obvious suggestion is that they are hipparchs. Herodotus appears to have merely estimated the mounted contingents on an average rate of 10,000 for each of the eight nations which furnished the cavalry, and to have made up the round 100,000 with the chariot and camel corps. Six hipparchs, each in command of 10,000 horse, would supply the required 60,000, one myriad to each army corps.

Herodotus sends only three hipparchs on the campaign[1], but implies that there were others, or at all events other cavalry, not present. This fact suggests that perhaps only three of the six army corps actually took part in the expedition. It is significant that the army leaves Doriscus in three separate columns. Certainly only three distinct commands (those of Mardonius, Artabazus, and Tigranes) can be detected in the subsequent operations. It is obvious that Herodotus, but for his reservation or revoke on the cavalry, included in his catalogue of Xerxes' host the whole military forces of the Persian empire, probably as organized by Darius. Any complete list of the Persian army of the period would pass as an accurate enumeration of Xerxes' army on this campaign, for Herodotus, and the Greeks at large, believed that Xerxes led against Hellas the entire forces of his empire. But it is incredible that Xerxes can have denuded that empire, hardly yet pacified, of practically all its garrison, in order to settle accounts with a few troublesome but petty tribes beyond its western frontier; and our suspicion that Herodotus' catalogue is no true record of the muster at Doriscus, but a general 'Army list,' and not even an up-to-date list, is confirmed when we find that several Persian officers hold quite different rank or posts in the catalogue and in the narrative of the war[2]. In particular Artabazus and

---

[1] Pharnuches, who was left behind at Sardes disabled by a fall from his horse, was no doubt replaced by Masistius, who appears later in the story as a hipparch.

[2] It is singular that outside VII, 121, a passage which refers back to the army at Doriscus and repeats the names of all the six generals-in-chief, not one of them except Mardonius can be shown to have taken any part in the invasion. In VIII, 26 all the best MSS. read Tigranes, not Tritantaechmes. Masistes, IX, 107, 'happened to be present' at Mycale, coming presumably from Sardes.

Tigranes are mere archontes or myriarchs at Doriscus, but reappear in command of army corps. These two instances may
preserve a clue to the origin of the confusion between myriarchs
and generals-in-chief. However that may be, the above considerations justify us in concluding that Xerxes took with him
only three of the six corps, and his expeditionary army numbered
180,000 combatants.

One might expect Herodotus to have had better information
about Xerxes' navy than about his army. He does indeed give
numbers for the several contingents of ships. But this precision
proves fallacious. His total at Doriscus is 1207 triremes. To them
he adds afterwards 120 from the Greeks of Thrace and the
Thracian islands; but he admits that this is a conjectural estimate,
and it is certainly too large for the year 480 B.C. He pays no
further heed to it, and we may here ignore it. The 1207 agrees
with the figures ascribed to Xerxes' fleet by Aeschylus in the
Persae (341–3)—a thousand ships, with 207 pre-eminent for
speed. Aeschylus, to be sure, writes of the battle of Salamis, not
of the review at Doriscus, but the distinction is negligible. Herodotus knew the *Persae*, and could half quote a line (l. 728) from
it on occasion (VIII, 68). He appears to have taken his total, 1207
triremes, from Aeschylus, and to have estimated the contingents
to fit that sum. Many of his estimates, particularly those of contingents from regions south of the Aegean, are improbably high,
the 17 from the Islands are too obviously a residue to balance
the account, and the total itself is monstrous and fantastic,
challenging and outdoing the legendary armada of Agamemnon.
Never before or after is there any authentic Mediterranean fleet
which remotely approximates to these 1207 triremes.

Whether Aeschylus meant the total sum to be 1207, and not
rather 1000, may be disputed; his words are ambiguous, and do
not make it clear whether the 207 are to be added to the 1000
or included in it. But whatever he may have intended, there can
be little doubt that the latter alternative must be the better
interpretation of his figures; for without the inclusion of the 207
the 1000 can hardly be explained. The thousand is of course a
round number. That fact does not discredit it, for Xerxes' fleet,
like his army, was organized on decimal numbers; but it does not
carry much conviction. We can, however, make out how the
thousand was reached. Herodotus describes the navy on a geographical scheme from south to north, save that the Phoenician
contingent is put first on the list. This precedence is one mark of
its primacy and superiority, which is recognized throughout his

history. Clearly the admiral of the Phoenician fleet held the highest rank in the Persian navy. Now Herodotus names four admirals; and two of them are sons of Darius. Achaemenes, full brother of Xerxes, is in command of the Egyptian fleet; Ariabignes, Xerxes' half-brother, commands the Ionian and Carian fleet (to which must be reckoned also the Dorian contingent); Prexaspes and Megabazus are of inferior rank and less account. From these and other indications it has been acutely inferred[1] that the King himself must have been the admiral of the Phoenician fleet. The remaining two territorial divisions, southern Asia Minor (including Cyprus) and the Hellespontine region (with Aeolis), separated by Ariabignes' command, may be assigned to Prexaspes and Megabazus. Thus we have five distinct commands—(1) the Phoenician, (2) the Egyptian, (3) the Cilician or Cypriote, (4) the Ionian, (5) the Hellespontine or Pontic[2]—which we may surely assume to have been a permanent system in the Persian organization. Now further, Herodotus reckons the Egyptian fleet at 200 sail; and the Ionian fleet, if the Dorians be included, at 200; and again, in spite of his own assessment of its contingents, the Cilician at 200, if (as will be argued below) that was the fleet sent round Euboea before the battles at Artemisium. Bringing the other two fleets into line with these three, we get five fleets of 200 ships apiece, or the same total as the thousand in the *Persae*.

But 1000 and 200 cannot be regarded as the normal numbers of ships in the Persian navy and in a division of it respectively. Herodotus has an almost stereotyped number for a Persian fleet, 600. He applies it to the fleets on the Scythian expedition, at Lade, and on the Marathon campaign. He 'writes down' Xerxes' fleet itself towards this normal number before it reaches Attica. A total of 600 would give 120 ships to each of the five fleets. Sure enough, Herodotus, left to his own devices to raise a Thracian fleet, puts it at 120 triremes. Ephorus, if Diodorus reproduces his figures, reckoned the Hellespontine fleet at 120. Possibly he corrected Herodotus' 160 by some local record at Cyme. Further, reasons have been shown[3] for believing that the Persian navy was organized on the model of the Phoenician and the Phoenician was organized in units of 60 ships. Carthaginian fleets normally consist of 60 ships of the line, or multiples of 60, with 10 additional cruisers or scouts. Even the cruisers recur in

[1] By Tarn, *J.H.S.* xxviii, p. 207.
[2] The Euxine seems to demand a fleet. Perhaps this fleet was normally stationed at Byzantium and was rather Pontic than Aegean in its service.
[3] By Tarn, *ibid.* p. 229.

the Phoenician fleet of Xerxes, in the 10 Sidonian ships which reconnoitre the Greek position at Artemisium. On the whole evidence there is at least a very strong presumption that 600 ships were the official and generally recognized total Persian navy, and 120 the number in each of its component fleets[1].

But 1000 and 200 might be not normal but exceptional numbers, including a special increase of the navy for the purpose of this war. Each fleet of 120 ships postulates two squadrons of 60. Supported by the Phoenician and Carthaginian parallels we may conjecture that each squadron had its 10 cruisers (which may or may not have been triremes). A third squadron of 60 ships of the line would raise each fleet to 200, or, if we credit the third squadron with 10 cruisers, to 210, which might in round numbers be counted as 200. (The Carthaginian examples show that our authorities sometimes reckon, sometimes omit, the cruisers, and usually calculate a three squadron fleet at 200 ships.) Five fleets of 200 ships give the Aeschylean thousand; and we may suppose that the Greeks arrived at that figure by imputing to each fleet a third squadron.

But is the 1000 much more credible than the 1207? Darius and Xerxes had no doubt made great preparations for the invasion of Greece; there had been much shipbuilding for several years. But most of it must have been, not 'fresh construction,' additions to the navy, but replacement of old vessels, especially obsolete penteconters by new triremes, the latest type of warships just then being introduced. (Hence, of course, the abundance of vessels available for bridges, transport and supply services.) It is most improbable that even the Persian king not only rebuilt his fleet, but also increased it by half as much again, to a figure far beyond all other record, in order to defeat an enemy who could not muster a third of as many ships to meet him. He must have fancied that he had before him a task easy in comparison with his recent victory over the Ionians, when half his navy had been on the wrong side. The hypothesis that there had been a general increase is therefore inacceptable. But we have positive evidence to prove that one fleet, the Phoenician, the King's own command, had been reinforced by a third squadron, cruisers and all. Herodotus repeatedly notes that the Phoenician ships were the best and fastest of the Persian navy. Aeschylus' 207 ships pre-eminent for speed can be none other than the Phoenician fleet. The exact figure is reached by deducting from the original 210 the three

[1] It may also be noted that the naval numbers, 60 and 600, stand in a certain harmony with the organization of the army in six corps of 60,000 men.

Sidonian cruisers lost on the rock Myrmēx. Herodotus often implies that the Sidonian contingent was a distinct squadron. He may indicate the three squadrons in his mention of the three most notable Phoenician leaders, one from Sidon, one from Tyre, and one from Aradus. It is also significant that he puts the Phoenician contingent at 300 ships, just 50 per cent. above the conventional 200 ascribed to other fleets. The Phoenician fleet, their hereditary foe and rival on the sea, so completely occupied the attention and dominated the imagination of the Greeks, that we may readily believe that they took it for the type and measure of the rest, and computed them all on that standard. But that computation does not bind us, and our estimate of Xerxes' entire fleet will be 660 ships of the line with not more than 110 nor less than 30 cruisers. Perhaps a total of 730 ships, allowing 30 cruisers to the Phoenician fleet and 10 to each of the other four, would be a reasonable calculation. A few more may have come in after Doriscus (*e.g.* the Island contingents at Phalerum), but, on the other hand, the Abydene contingent, Herodotus tells us, was left in the Hellespont to guard the bridges (or cables?), and it is at least extremely probable that the whole Hellespontine fleet, of which there is no clear trace in the operations, remained there until the king was in Attica.

The concentration and final organization of the forces at Doriscus must have taken some time, hardly less than three weeks, but no doubt at least half of the time overlaps the month at Abydos. The army, when it set out for Therma, moved in three columns, each, as Herodotus would have us to believe, under its own *two* generals. Herodotus conceives the three columns marching on a single front by three parallel roads, one along the coast, one inland, and the third between these two. The configuration of the country from Doriscus to Therma offers in parts two alternative routes, but nowhere three, except perhaps for a short distance east and west of the Strymon; and only occasionally does any road touch the sea. If we are to insist upon three parallel routes, we must either push the right-hand column far into the interior on an immense détour, up the Hebrus and across the upper Strymon and down the Axius, or thrust the left-hand column out to sea on the ships. It is more probable that the parallel advance is a figment of Herodotus' fancy, and that the three Persian army corps marched much of their way by a single road, but where there are two (notably from the Symbolum Pass onwards) used both roads. Herodotus notes the tripartite division of the army only on the section between Doriscus and Acanthus, but he drops a hint of it on the approach to Thessaly, and it may be assumed throughout the campaign. He can, however, hardly be right in bringing any large force to Acanthus, south of the hog's back ridge of Chalcidice. On the contrary, the bulk of the army must certainly have taken the shortest and easiest road to Therma along the shores of Lake Bolbe, although Herodotus does not clearly recognize that route. But no doubt Xerxes himself came to Acanthus to inspect the new canal. There he celebrated the obsequies of Artachaeës, the commandant in charge of the work, and seems to have spent some time. Meanwhile his army was presumably marching to Therma, whence one-third of it was sent forward into Pieria to prepare the road through the passes into Thessaly. Herodotus obviously confuses the king's movements with his army's, and more than once Therma with Pieria. It would ease his narrative if we might suppose that Xerxes parted not from his fleet, but from his army, sailed in fact from Eion first to Acanthus, then to Tempe and Pieria, and finally to Therma.

The fleet at all events, which since leaving Doriscus had been in frequent touch with the army, turned away southwards from about the mouth of the Strymon to Acanthus, and passed through the canal, perhaps under the eyes of the king. Thereafter Herodotus ascribes to it an absurd itinerary. He takes occasion to present a detailed '*periplus*' of the coasts of Chalcidice, exploring every inlet and omitting scarcely a seaside village. Having sent the whole royal navy on a cruise round the Toronaic gulf, although it had just cut across its entrance from point to point, he finally dispatches it on a futile voyage up to Therma, where it cannot have been wanted[1]. Perhaps ever since the expedition of Mardonius in 492 B.C., certainly since the inception of the canal, Acanthus had been the naval arsenal of the Thracian station. It probably remained so; and the advanced base of the fleet and starting-point of its subsequent operations may be placed on the southern coast of Pallene, in line with the Pass of Tempe. But no doubt the Phoenician fleet, Xerxes' own guard of honour, conveyed him to Therma. In Pieria Xerxes received the heralds sent forth from Sardes, who brought the tokens of submission from most of the peoples north of Mount Oeta and even (could we trust Herodotus) others farther south. There he 'tarried many days'; but probably the days are reckoned from the arrival of the Persian vanguard and include some of the king's stay at Acanthus.

[1] The army had a depôt of provisions there. Even the supply ships were not needed, and the warships were worse than useless. For defence the mouth of the gulf was their proper post.

II. THE GREEK DEFENCE

The Persian forces had now reached the Thessalian frontier without hindrance. What measures had the Greeks taken to meet the invasion? They had long warning of the king's preparations and ample notice of his approach. The attack was aimed primarily at Athens and Sparta, and they doubtless took the initiative in organizing the defence. A league was formed, and a Congress representative of its members met at the isthmus of Corinth in the autumn of 481 B.C., of course under the presidency of Sparta. Efforts were made to compose quarrels and feuds among the allies or other Greek states. In particular Athens and Aegina were reconciled. An oath of vengeance, vowing to confiscate the property of any Greek people which voluntarily joined the Persian, and dedicate a tenth of it to the Delphic god, is best put here, and may be interpreted mainly as a threat against states which might refuse to enter the alliance. Nevertheless there remained lamentable gaps in the confederacy. North-western Greece was scantily represented, the Achaean cities of the Peloponnese not at all, and Argos stood aloof, sullen and sinister. The adhesion of the Boeotians and the Thessalians was a relief almost too good to be true, and few of them could be implicitly trusted. It was indeed too much to expect of them that they should be enthusiastic for a policy which might lead to a Spartan domination over the whole of Greece. The Congress however, conscious of the magnitude of its task, attempted to enroll even Argos in the league, and endeavoured to get help from the still independent Greek states of the east and the west.

The results were small. The Cretans, who took little interest in the affairs of Greece and were exposed to Persian attack, sheltered themselves under pretext of an oracle from Delphi; but possibly the Greek envoys did some fruitful propaganda on their way through the Cyclades. In the west the main object was to secure the support of Gelon Tyrant of Syracuse, the strongest Hellenic power at that time in the world. But Gelon, whether by an unlucky coincidence or by Persian diplomacy, had his hands full with a no less formidable struggle against the Carthaginians (see further below, pp. 375 *sqq.*). The embassy perhaps enlisted one volunteer in Magna Graecia, for Phayllus of Croton brought his own ship to fight at Salamis. At all events the Corcyraeans promised assistance, and in due course sent 60 ships as far as Cape Malea. The plea that they could get no farther owing to contrary winds is refuted by the presence at Salamis of small

MAP 7

CENTRAL GREECE

Scale – English miles

0 5 10 15 20

0 10 20 30

Kilometres

INDEX TO NAMES

contingents from Leucas and Ambracia. But the charge that they waited in order to claim favour from Xerxes, if he had won, may be suspected of afterthought; at least they may have hesitated between, not Greek and Barbarian, but the allies and Gelon. The Argives could never forget their ancient supremacy in the Peloponnese nor forgive the Spartans for having usurped it. They were still sore from their defeat by Cleomenes (p. 165). They were not without reason accused afterwards of intriguing with the national enemy, and their guilt is no less credible because Herodotus will not assert it outright. They produced a rather obsolete oracle from Delphi to justify them in remaining neutral, but professed themselves willing to join the league, if the Spartans would concede to them a peace for 30 years and the command, or at least an equal share in the command, of the allied forces. This impudent attempt to extort a recognition of their old pretensions can only have been intended to throw the odium of their refusal on their successful rivals.

Besides these diplomatic missions the Congress had to deal with military and strategical matters. Xerxes was now at Sardes. Three spies were dispatched thither to report on his forces. The story runs that they were arrested, but that the king, with superb confidence and politic calculation, let them inspect his troops and go home to warn the Greeks of the futility of resistance. The command of the allied army was of course committed to Sparta. The Athenians put forward a claim to the command of the navy, but did not press it against the wishes of the majority. Thus on both land and sea the conduct of the war was formally assigned to the Spartans. But Themistocles, who at this critical juncture directed the policy and led the forces of Athens, knew that he would carry weight second to none in the counsels of the allies. In the strategical plans, presumably then discussed at the Congress and afterwards carried out, we may clearly recognize his influence.

The scheme of defence was dictated by the method of the attack, the relative forces on either side, and the configuration of the Greek peninsula. The Persian army was too large to be shipped across the Aegean. It was bound to follow the land route through Thrace and enter Greece from the north. The allies could furnish a considerable army, but when every contingent was mobilized, they could not muster more than half the troops brought against them by Xerxes. Outnumbered by two to one they could not face the enemy in the open field but must look for strong narrow positions. The Greek mainland presented several such positions on the road southwards. Not to mention Thaumaci and Dryoscephalae, which are too easily evaded, there are the defile of Tempe, the pass of Thermopylae, and the isthmus of Corinth. But, of course, all of them could be turned by sea, and the allies had to reckon with the Persian fleet, which was not tied to the army and might land troops in their rear. Apart from any distrust of the Thessalians and Boeotians, this importunate danger was aggravated by the attitude of Argos, which offered to the enemy a foothold and a valuable ally in the Peloponnese. Through half a generation's rest Argos had recruited her forces, not only by natural increase of population, but probably also by admission of fresh citizens. She was perhaps stronger than before Cleomenes' massacre, more democratic, and more hostile to Sparta. And if the Argives with Persian aid made a flank attack on Laconia and raised the Helots in revolt, could the Mantineans and Eleans be trusted to remain loyal? Hints in Herodotus suggest that they were not whole-hearted for the league (p. 340). In short nothing but a fleet strong enough to dispute the command of the sea with the Persian, or a garrison large enough to crush any invasion or rising south of the Isthmus, could safeguard the Peloponnese, the very citadel of Greek independence. Themistocles, to be sure, had already provided Athens with a fleet evidently designed to be equal in number and quality to the Phoenician. But the total allied navy was as heavily outnumbered by the Persian as the army on land, and could not confront it on the open sea. At all costs, therefore, the bulk of the allied army must be retained in the Peloponnese; and consequently the Isthmus must be the main line of defence by land. This fundamental necessity was obviously the first axiom in all the discussions.

But a defence confined only to the Peloponnese was open to grave objections. It would abandon to the enemy the whole of northern and central Greece, and sacrifice all hope of support from states north of Cithaeron. It would put severe strain upon the loyalty of the Athenians. Above all it would imperil the safety of the Peloponnese itself. The Peloponnesians might confidently meet Xerxes at the Isthmus, or suppress any hostile landing or movement in their rear; but if he reached the Saronic gulf with his army and his navy intact and together, they had to reckon with both attacks simultaneously, and that would be an almost desperate emergency. Even had they the forces, could they retain their troops at the Isthmus when the Barbarian was threatening their homes? It was impossible to advance the main line of defence on land farther northwards; but if the Greek fleet, taking advantage of narrow waters, could inflict on the enemy, before he approached the Isthmus, such losses as to impair his command of the sea or render him incapable of detaching a squadron against the Peloponnese, the situation was at once relieved. A naval victory as far north as possible was clearly the best solution; and a complete naval victory would probably be decisive of the war, for it would free the allies to threaten the Persian communications and excite a rebellion in Ionia, which would compel Xerxes to send back a large part of his army. The channel inside Euboea or the sound of Salamis offered admirable positions, where the enemy could not use his superior number for a frontal attack, but might be tempted to divide his fleet in order to take the defenders in the rear, and so give a chance of defeating his main force before the other division came into action. The problem was to get the Persians to attack in the narrows. Here the immense advantage of the Euboean position appears. The sound of Salamis was a forlorn hope; it was too far south—actually in the Saronic gulf—and presented little inducement to the enemy. But the strait between the north end of Euboea and the south cape of Magnesia covers the only practicable landing-places on the east coast of Greece from Tempe to Marathon; for the seaboard of Thessaly is fenced by the range of Ossa and Pelion, and the long island of Euboea protects the shores of central Greece. (Marathon was of course too far distant for a turning movement, and a force landed there would be intercepted by the Greeks from the Isthmus.) If, therefore, Xerxes (who must arrive at the Isthmus and occupy the allied army there before he could invade the Peloponnese by sea) were blocked at Tempe or Thermopylae, he would be compelled to use his fleet to turn the obstruction to his progress on land, or, in other words, his fleet must attack the Greek naval position. Now the pass of Tempe or the pass of Thermopylae could be defended, for the short time needed to give the Greek fleet its opportunity of fighting, by a small detachment, which would not seriously weaken the garrison of the Peloponnese. Should the fleet succeed in crippling the enemy's, the Peloponnesian army would be set free to advance and confirm the defence, and Greece from that point southwards might be saved from invasion. The farther north the stand were made, the more allies would be gained or retained.

Accordingly, and in response to a call from 'the Thessalians,' when Xerxes was at Abydos a Greek fleet conveying 10,000 hoplites was dispatched through the Euripus to Halus on the gulf of Pagasae under Evaenetus (a Spartan polemarch) and Themistocles. The fleet may have been entirely Athenian and

Themistocles, who was no doubt the sponsor of the scheme, in command of it, while Evaenetus was leader on land. If so, the other contingents were to follow; for the main object must have been the naval battle at the entry to the straits. The army included, if we may trust Aristophanes of Boeotia (*ap.* Plut. *de malignitate Herodoti,* 31), 500 Thebans, who would naturally be picked up at Aulis. It marched from Halus to Tempe, but did not stay there many days. Tempe is not the only gate into Thessaly from the north. Apart from the mountain path by Gonnus, which is not of much account, there are in chief the passes of Petra and Volustana. They were too distant to be comprehended in the defence of Tempe, and required to hold them a much larger force than could be spared from the Peloponnese. The Thessalians had promised to co-operate in the defence. Presumably they had undertaken to guard the other passes, if the allies would hold Tempe. But only the cavalry, the Thessalian aristocracy, presented itself, and it was of little use for the purpose. The mass of the Thessalians, perhaps intimidated by Macedonian reports of Xerxes' irresistible strength, perhaps seduced by his envoys, more probably suspicious of Sparta and inclined to the party of the Aleuadae, who were said to have invited the Persian invasion, stood aloof. The appeal of the Thessalians to the allies proved to have been a far from unanimous summons. Evaenetus marched back to the ships and withdrew the whole forces to the Isthmus.

This ominous opening to the campaign evidently discredited Themistocles' strategy. He had to overcome opposition both among his colleagues at the Isthmus and among his own fellow-countrymen. The linked positions of Thermopylae and Artemisium provided a line of defence stronger, more compact, than Tempe and Artemisium, but not altogether free from the same defects—the pass could be turned by another, and the peoples behind it could not be entirely trusted. Some of the Peloponnesians, shortsighted in their caution and their confidence, were reluctant to try again at Thermopylae the plan which had failed at Tempe. They relied upon the Isthmus alone and would occupy no outpost beyond it. On the other hand, a party at Athens, especially the Agrarians, very naturally but unreasonably insisted that the whole allied army should march out and give battle in defence of Attica, if not at Thermopylae, at all events in Boeotia.

It was probably at this crisis, when the defence seemed for the moment to have fallen back to the Isthmus and Salamis, that the oracles were delivered to the Athenians at Delphi which Herodotus records rather than places at an earlier date, at the inauguration of the league. The character of the responses is incompatible with that date, and they have commonly been put after the disaster at Thermopylae. But there is no room for the mission to Delphi in the four or five days between the fall of Thermopylae and the Persian occupation of Phocis; and by that time there was no doubt to be solved or question to be asked. The interval between the retreat from Thessaly and the decision to hold Thermopylae presents the most suitable occasion. In the two envoys deputed to consult the god we may perhaps see representatives of the Themistoclean and the Agrarian parties respectively. Neither got any encouragement for their immediate purpose, although Themistocles could extract some for future use. The Pythia Aristonice bade them 'begone to the ends of the earth' and 'school their hearts in woe.' Even when at the suggestion of Timon, a man of influence in Delphi, they returned in guise of suppliants and begged for a kinder answer, the god was obdurate against any resistance on land, conceded salvation only in 'a wooden wall,' and pointed to Salamis as the site for a battle. The Delphians in fact pretty accurately gauged the probabilities. The Peloponnesians would not, could not, come out in full force to fight north of the Isthmus; to hold Thermopylae and Artemisium was to incur a double hazard; the issue would ultimately be decided on the last line of defence. The Delphians, anxious for the interests of the great institution under their charge, the 'Bank of Hellas,' would not invite the risk of being involved in an unsuccessful or merely temporary stand against the invader, and had a more secure protection in reserve. At least six, possibly nine, of the twelve 'nations' represented on the Amphictyonic Board, which nominally directed the affairs of the sanctuary, were already hastening, probably on instructions from Delphi, to give their submission to Xerxes. The policy of *la haute finance* is seldom heroic.

Nevertheless the Athenians decreed to meet the invader in full force in their ships with the assistance of what other Greeks would join them, and the allies decided by a majority of votes to occupy Thermopylae. Leonidas, the Agid king of Sparta, led forth 4000 Peloponnesian hoplites including his royal guard of 300 Spartiates. He picked up 700 Thespians and 400 Thebans in Boeotia, and found 1000 Phocians and the whole levy of the Opuntian Locrians mustered in response to a message in advance at Trachis. We may reasonably add the Trachinians, who appear in Diodorus as 1000 Malians. With Helots and light-armed troops, who are not reckoned, the total force may have amounted to 10,000 men.

The fleet took up its station at Artemisium on the north coast of Euboea flanking the entrance to the straits. It consisted (if we may here add the 53 ships which Herodotus brings up later) of 324 triremes and nine penteconters. The Athenians contributed their entire navy, 180 triremes manned by themselves and 20 by their Chalcidian cleruchs. They were led by Themistocles; but the supreme command was vested in the Spartan admiral Eurybiades, whose contingent numbered only ten ships. The disproportion between the land and the sea forces plainly indicates that a naval battle was the primary object and the defence of Thermopylae was in the first instance only subordinate to that end. But naturally the chiefs emphasized their intention of bringing up the main army in support after the Olympian and Carneian festivals, without dwelling upon the proviso that the fleet should first have won its victory.

The Greeks were only just in time. The vanguard of the leading Persian column had already entered Pieria and Xerxes had doubtless reached Acanthus. The failure in Thessaly and the opposition which delayed the occupation of Artemisium and Thermopylae may have had this fortunate result, that the Persian generals believed that the enemy had definitely abandoned all hope of resistance north of the Isthmus. Otherwise one cannot see why they omitted to seize in advance those cardinal positions.

III. ARTEMISIUM

The account given by Herodotus of the naval operations which followed is a tangled tale, and the fumbling expedients of Ephorus or Diodorus only involve it in worse confusion. The solution here offered may appear drastic, but endeavours, while unravelling the threads, to retain whatever can be reasonably accepted and can be fitted into a coherent whole. The clue is to be found in a recognition of the several separate narratives combined in the story of Herodotus. His ultimate sources may be reduced to three—(1) Pytheas (supplemented by Phormus), (2) Scyllias, who sailed with Sandoces, (3) an Athenian on board of one of the 53 ships. Each of the three narratives naturally covered only particular portions of the whole series of events; but they have been imperfectly adjusted and their information has been misapplied outside their proper limits in the attempt to extract from them a complete account of what happened.

The Persian navy having traversed the canal proceeded to establish an advanced base on or near the southern coast of the

peninsula of Pallene, probably at Scione. Leaving the rest there,
the Phoenician fleet set out to reconnoitre the passages through
the islands which extend eastwards from the extremity of Magnesia. Led by the Sidonian squadron with its ten cruisers in front,
it struck straight across the open sea to Sciathus[1]. There three
Greek scoutships were stationed, a Troezenian, an Aeginetan, and
an Athenian. It is not clear why they did not escape to Artemisium;
probably the enemy approached under cover of night, entered
the channel between Sciathus and Peparethus at daybreak, and
surprised them in the harbour of Sciathus. They fled from the
harbour, which opens southwards, but the swift Sidonian cruisers
must have headed them off from the Euboean channel and driven
them northwards through the strait between Sciathus and the
point of Magnesia. Here three of the pursuers ran upon 'the
Ant,' a reef off the Magnesian side of the entrance, and were lost.
But the Troezenian and Aeginetan ships were soon overtaken
and captured, the latter after a stout resistance of which a valiant
Pytheas was the hero. He lived to be released at Salamis from
his Sidonian captors; and that is doubtless how we know the tale.
The delay rescued the Athenians, but not their ship. After a long
chase their captain Phormus ran his vessel ashore at the mouth
of the Peneus and brought his crew safely home through Thessaly
—evidently the Persians had not yet occupied Tempe.

The seven Sidonian cruisers with their prizes would rejoin at the
naval base. Before returning thither the Phoenician fleet, having
presumably suppressed the Greek signal station on Sciathus,
appears to have proceeded to Scyrus. At all events it was a
Scyrian, Pammon, who explained the mystery of the sunken
reef. So before the advance of the whole armada a monolith was
provided to mark the dangerous spot and, no doubt for the
purpose of its erection, the professional services of the diver
Scyllias of Scione were commandeered. This duty however

---

[1] Herodotus VII, 179, ὁ δὲ ναυτικὸς Ξέρξεω στρατὸς ὁρμώμενος ἐκ
Θέρμης πόλιος παρέβαλε νηυσὶ τῇσι ἄριστα πλεούσῃσι δέκα ἰθὺ Σκιάθου.
But (1) παρέβαλε ἰθὺ Σκιάθου never meant a voyage from Therma;
(2) Herodotus has confused three distinct movements—the reconnaissance,
the marking of the reef, and the sailing of the navy on the 12th day after
Xerxes' departure—and the escape of Phormus and his crew indicates that
there was an appreciable interval between the first and the last; (3) it is
very unlikely that the ten ships were not supported by a fleet, and the
effect of the signal (or, if it be preferred, the confusion of two signals) to
the Greeks from Sciathus suggests a fleet of 200 ships. One may suspect
that Herodotus wrote in his rough notes, although not in his text, πλεούσῃσι
σι ἰθύ.

devolved upon another division; the Phoenician fleet had to convey the king to Tempe and to Therma.

The advent of the 200 Phoenician ships had been signalled by beacons from Sciathus to the Greek admirals at Artemisium, who must have foreseen the probability of a turning movement round Euboea to circumvent their position. They dispatched 53 Attic ships[1] (a squadron of 50 with three scouts) to defend the Euripus at Chalcis, where it narrows to little over 200 feet. In order to observe and report to the squadron at Chalcis the progress of the enemy southwards, coastguards were posted along the hills which overlook the east shore of Euboea. The Athenians had to wait at Chalcis for some time, and it was not the Phoenician fleet that eventually came.

Xerxes at length resumed his advance[2]. On the 12th day after he had marched from Therma the armada began to move southwards. Although Herodotus lets him first hear of the defence of Thermopylae on his way through Thessaly, the king must have known the distribution of the Greek forces from the naval captives and his allies on land. The Persian plan of operations was that the army and the main part of the fleet should arrive simultaneously before Thermopylae and the entrance to the channel north of Euboea and engage the Greeks there, while a squadron sent round the island should attack or threaten both positions from the rear. The bare threat might make the enemy retire; and if he evacuated either position, the other became useless and the road to the south would be cleared. Obviously the turning squadron, which had a long way to go, would move first; and to it would be assigned the incidental task of marking the reef between Sciathus and Magnesia. We argue from indications which will appear that it was the 'Cilician' fleet. Let us suppose that it sailed at daybreak from Scione, whence it took the diver Scyllias, and that it had twelve hours' start of the main fleet (except the Phoenicians, who had an extra day's voyage and would sail at the same

[1] Herodotus refers the signal to the capture of the three guardships and sends the whole Greek fleet to Chalcis—a strategical absurdity which he seeks to explain by panic. His information here comes from the 53 ships and is limited to their movement. Having sent away the whole fleet, he has to bring it back. It is improbable, although barely possible, that even the 53 went back to Artemisium before their return on the eve of the last battle. The astonishment attributed to the Greeks on their return at finding the enemy in such great force in spite of the ravages of the storm is much more appropriate to the crews of the 53 ships than to those of the main fleet.

[2] A diary of the land and sea operations which follow will be found at the end of the chapter.

time from Therma). In the afternoon it will have approached
Sciathus and, passing perhaps out of sight from it, shed a detachment of Cypriote ships to set the mark upon 'the Ant.' This
detachment, having planted the obelisk on the reef about sunset,
would prudently retire round the heel of Magnesia (Cape Sepias)
towards its supports and after nightfall put in at one of the little
anchorages along the coast, there to await the passing of the main
Persian fleet. With the dawn came the fleet, but with it came a
north-easterly gale, the dreaded 'Hellespontias' which afflicts
those inhospitable shores. The great bulk of the fleet no doubt
slipped safely round the corner into shelter at Aphetae, which is
best placed at Platania between the cape and Olizon, but the
rear-guard may have been caught too far north and have sustained
some losses; certainly the ships of burden strung out far behind
must have fallen under the full blast of the storm. Many were
dashed to pieces on the precipitous Magnesian coast; others
escaped only by running ashore on the rare beaches. The Cypriote
squadron, anchored in a 'quincunx' formation eight deep pro-
jecting like an equilateral triangle from the strand, suffered
heavily; 11 of the 12 Paphian vessels perished; and out of the
36 ships, which the formation would suggest, only 15 reappear.
Isolated and distrustful of the native tribes, the survivors of the
crews fortified their camp with a fence of wreckage.

The storm raged for 24 hours. Herodotus makes it last for
three days and three nights, but he has preserved evidence for
his own refutation: (1) in the parallel narrative derived from the
53 ships there is no hint of more than a one day's storm;
(2) Xerxes enters Malis on his twelfth day[1] out from Therma and
that day is two days before 'the fleet' reached Aphetae after the
storm—by 'the fleet' we must here understand the hindmost part
of it (mostly supply ships) which was caught and driven ashore
by the storm and was all that Scyllias could observe. The storm
therefore lasted only from dawn of the 13th to dawn of the
14th days of the diary. Why did Herodotus prolong it? Because
the Cypriote squadron in which Scyllias was sailing, 'having put
to sea long after the rest' (from its Magnesian anchorage) arrived

---

[1] Not the 11th, for the fleet sails on the 12th, and obviously the arrival
of the fleet at the entrance to the Euboic sound and of the army in front
of Trachis were intended to be simultaneous. Xerxes waits four days for
the Greek army to run away, but these four days include the day of his
arrival, for Herodotus is clearly right in making the three days of fighting
at Thermopylae and at Artemisium coincide, for the capture of the pass
ends both fights.

two days later, on the 16th. No doubt the salvage operations of Scyllias, which were extensive and profitable, needed time and calm water, and there were repairs to be done. But Herodotus has assumed that the delay was due to the storm, that it involved the whole fleet, and that the whole fleet reached the Euboean channel on the same day. By reducing the storm to one day we both relieve the congestion of events on the 16th, the day of the first battle, and get rid of the discrepancy of two days between the diaries of the army and the fleet, which has vexed every student of Herodotus.

On the morrow, then, the barbarians who had weathered the storm launched their ships and followed the coast round to Aphetae, where the admirals held a review to take stock of the damage. The Cypriote squadron however, now reduced to 15 vessels, under Sandoces the governor of Cyme (who may or may not have been its original commander) came up two days later. Never expecting to find the Greeks still maintaining their position, and sighting them before he saw the Persians in the bay of Aphetae, Sandoces steered straight for them and delivered his squadron an easy prey into their hands. Herodotus surmises that Scyllias came across the strait in a boat. We go further and suppose that he was on board one of the 15 ships. The prisoners, doubtless including Scyllias, who now makes his exit from the narrative, were closely questioned and forwarded under guard to the head-quarters of the allies at the Isthmus. The Greek admirals learnt from them, or by his own story from Scyllias himself, of the Persian losses in the storm and of the dispatch of the ships to sail round Euboea, which appears to have been news to them. They held a council of war, which must have decided to attack the enemy at once[1] in the absence of the 'Cilician' fleet.

The Greeks accordingly made a brusque attack late in the afternoon, trusting to the darkness to cover their retreat should they come off badly. The description given by Herodotus of this action reads suspiciously like a varnished replica of the final battle

---

[1] Herodotus ascribes to this council the incredible decision to stay at Artemisium till midnight and then sail off to meet the ships sent round. It is true that the defence of Thermopylae was subordinate to the naval strategy, and Leonidas could easily have been warned. But that decision is incompatible with the naval strategy and with what the fleet actually did. It might be more intelligible on the next day, when its abandonment might be accounted for by the arrival of the 53 ships (and the protest of the Euboeans, if it may be put there), but probably it is transferred in error (with adaptation to the circumstances) from the council after the final battle two days later.

two days later, and suggests that he had little or no information on what happened between the arrival of Scyllias and that of the 53 ships, but, bewildered by his interpolated two days, has inadvertently used the same material twice. Even the postscripts are questionable. Plutarch[1], who supplements Herodotus from some monumental source, places the exploit of the Athenian Lycomedes in taking the first ship from the enemy not at Artemisium but at Salamis. The capture of 30 prizes 'would be more intelligible,' a critic observes[2], 'if these 30 ships were cut off in some way from the main fleet'; and we venture to conjecture that, as the prisoners included Philaon, brother of the king of the Cypriote Salamis, the 30 ships were really part of the Cilician division destroyed, according to Herodotus, on the next day.

Thus, if Herodotus' account of this first engagement be discredited, there seems to be a clear field for the alternative version drawn from the recently discovered fragment of Sosylus[3], which cannot otherwise be fitted into the story of the battles at Artemisium. Sosylus tells that the Massaliotes fighting against the Carthaginians in the second Punic War bethought themselves of the scheme of a second line of ships in reserve behind the front, whereby Heraclides of Mylasa had long before at Artemisium countered the Phoenician *diecplus* (breaking the line) and had won the victory. A Heraclides of Mylasa figures in Herodotus' narrative of the Ionian revolt, in which he destroyed a Persian army in Caria by an ambush. No naval battle in the Ionian revolt nor any in the Persian wars other than these battles in 480 B.C. is recorded to have been fought at an Artemisium. Herodotus himself ascribes to the Greeks in this first attack the wish to test the enemy's method of fighting and in particular his *diecplus*. Nevertheless Heraclides certainly cannot have been in command here, the result of the action was, if by courtesy a victory, hardly a conspicuous advertisement to his stratagem, and it is extremely improbable that the Massaliotes (or Sosylus either) knew more than Herodotus about the operations. It is easier to suppose that Heraclides emigrated, like Dionysius of Phocaea, to the west in order to escape Darius, and assisted the Massaliotes in a battle against the Carthaginians off the Iberian Artemisium (Dianium), which seems to become the boundary between their respective spheres of influence in Spain. Sosylus therefore cannot be used with any confidence to fill the gap in Herodotus.

Night ended the brief engagement. The Greeks were not en-

[1] *Themistocles*, 15.　　　[2] Macan, *Herodotus*, VII–IX, vol. I, ii, p. 373.
[3] Bilabel, *Die kleineren Historikerfragmente auf Papyrus*, No. 10.

couraged to renew it and the Persian admirals still hoped that the
ships sent round Euboea would draw them off. What had become
of those ships? Herodotus here derives his information from the
53 Attic ships on guard at Chalcis, but misapplies much of it to
the combatants at Artemisium. The scouts posted on the hills
ran down to Chalcis on the day after the storm and announced
that a large squadron of the enemy had been caught by the
tempest out on the open sea east of Euboea and been wrecked or
driven ashore. The Athenians praised Poseidon; but had more
to do before they rejoined their comrades than Herodotus appre-
hended. Not all the enemy's ships had perished on the east coast.
The recorded scene of their destruction is the Hollows of Euboea,
the south-western coast of the island, where the north-easterly
gale could not have hurt them, in fact the best refuge whither
they could have run. The key to the puzzle is to be found in
Herodotus' notice (VIII, 14) of the coming, or rather return, of
the 53 ships to Artemisium. In his story they came (out of the
void) to help the Greeks; with them came the news of the wreck
of the enemy's division sent round Euboea; so having waited for
the same hour they (the Greeks?) on their voyage ($\pi\lambda\acute{\epsilon}o\nu\tau\epsilon\varsigma$,
present tense) fell upon a force of Cilician ships; having destroyed
the Cilicians they set off when night was coming on to sail back
to Artemisium. It is fairly obvious that the news of the wreck
was brought by the 53 ships. Is it not obviously probable, and
suggested by the curious expressions of Herodotus, that the rest
of the statement was also news brought by them and gives an
account of their doings, which Herodotus has inadvertently transferred from *oratio obliqua* into *oratio recta*, from the place (the
Hollows) and time (the previous day) of their enactment to the
place and time of their announcement at Artemisium, from the
53 ships to the main Greek fleet? This solution explains why
the 53 ships did not return to Artemisium immediately after the
news of the wreck reached them; why the Hollows are brought
into the story of the destruction of the ships sent round Euboea—
the survivors rallied there under the lee of the island and fell a
prey to the 53 ships, which swooped down upon them from
Chalcis; why the Cilician division was caught far apart from the
main Persian fleet; and (may we not add?) how the capture of
the 30 ships, including Cypriote, although rightly dated is mis-
placed to Artemisium. The news of the wreck reached Chalcis
on the day after the storm; the 53 ships would sail southwards
on the next day; and the action at the Hollows would be fought
on the following day, the day of the first battle at Artemisium, a

coincidence which would be remarked; the 30 ships may have been all of the Cilician fleet that had survived the storm.

The 53 ships arrived at Artemisium, probably in the evening, on the day after the first battle. Their crews may have been disappointed at the formidable array of the enemy in spite of the storm, but their succour and their news cheered the Greeks there, who, if ever they had meditated a retreat during the night, were now encouraged to hold on and fight again. This time it was the Barbarians who attacked; they had doubtless heard of the failure of the turning movement or inferred it from the arrival of the 53 ships. Having awaited through the forenoon in the vain hope, we may suppose, of news of the fall of Thermopylae, which would have absolved them from another action, they advanced about midday, and pushing forward their wings in a crescent enveloped the Greek flanks. The Greeks, ranged in a semicircle with their backs to the land, presented their prows to the enemy, and at a signal charged stem to stem. There was no room for manœuvres. The battle became an obstinate struggle at close quarters. The Greeks, striking out from the centre, maintained better order than their assailants, who pressed inwards and fell foul of one another; but neither gave way and neither gained a decisive advantage. Of the Barbarians the Egyptians with their heavy armour most distinguished themselves, of the Hellenes the Athenians, and of these Cleinias, son of Alcibiades (presumably a great-uncle of the famous Alcibiades), who commanded a ship built and manned at his own cost. The Greeks were left in possession of their station and of the wreckage, but had suffered severe losses[1]. Themistocles had had his day, but had not won his victory. If Herodotus may be trusted, the council of admirals had already determined to withdraw when a boat detailed for the purpose brought news from Thermopylae and announced the disaster there, which left them no choice. Having lighted fires to deceive the enemy, and roasted the cattle of the Euboeans driven down for removal, they retired under cover of the darkness, making for the Euripus and the Saronic gulf.

IV. THERMOPYLAE

In contrast with the composite patchwork of the naval narrative Herodotus' account of the operations on land is simple and suggests a single source or the smooth ground of an orthodox tradition. Criticism by cross-examination and impertinent ques-

[1] They appear to have lost, from first to last, 70 triremes. (See below, p. 302.)

tions may reveal omissions, inadvertent or deliberate, and smould-
ering controversies beneath the surface, but Herodotus ignores
them as far as he can, and declines to spoil his story.

The Persian army still moving in three columns, as is indi-
cated by the pioneer work of one-third of it, may have entered
Thessaly by the three main passes, Tempe, Petra, and Volustana.
Knowing of the path by Gonnus, a mere by-pass to Tempe,
Herodotus insists on sending the whole army over it; but that
is doubtless no more than misapplied geography. The three main
passes converge upon Larissa. Thence Xerxes followed the route
by the gulf of Pagasae to Halus and round the east end of Othrys.
But it is probable, and supported by the mention of the river
Apidanus, that the bulk of his army used the direct road through
Thaumaci. On the 12th day after quitting Therma he entered
Malis and camped 'in the Trachinian territory,' presumably
between the rivers Melas and Asopus, in the plain below Trachis.

The descriptions given by Herodotus of the defile of Thermopylae and the approach to it fit the topography on the whole very
well, if allowance be made for the retirement of the sea due to the
silting up of the gulf, and for the erroneous orientation which
represents the pass lying north and south instead of west and
east. But it is obvious that, although he appears to have made
some enquiry about the path Anopaea, he has only a vague idea
of the mountainous country above and behind the heights which
overhang the plain and pass, 'the Anopaea' in the broad sense
of the name. And there is one astonishing omission. The pass of
Thermopylae is not the only practicable route from the Malian
plain to the south. A not really difficult hill road runs up the ravine
of the Asopus and over the comparatively low ridge between Oeta
and Callidromus into the valley of the Cephisus. Herodotus
almost calls attention to this road later, for he sends the whole
Persian army by it into Doris after the fall of Thermopylae and
perhaps brings Artabazus and his corps back by it after the battle
of Plataea. Thus he himself proves the strategic importance and
military use of this road; but in his account of the defence of
Thermopylae he barely hints at its existence. Yet it is not too
much to say that, had this road been open, there would have
been no defence of Thermopylae at all, no attack, no turning
movement. Xerxes would simply have dispatched a column up
the Asopus into Phocis and unlocked the gates without a blow.
The fact must be, in spite of the silence of Herodotus, that this
road was held. The obvious and regularly adopted method of
barring it was to put a garrison into the citadel of Trachis, which

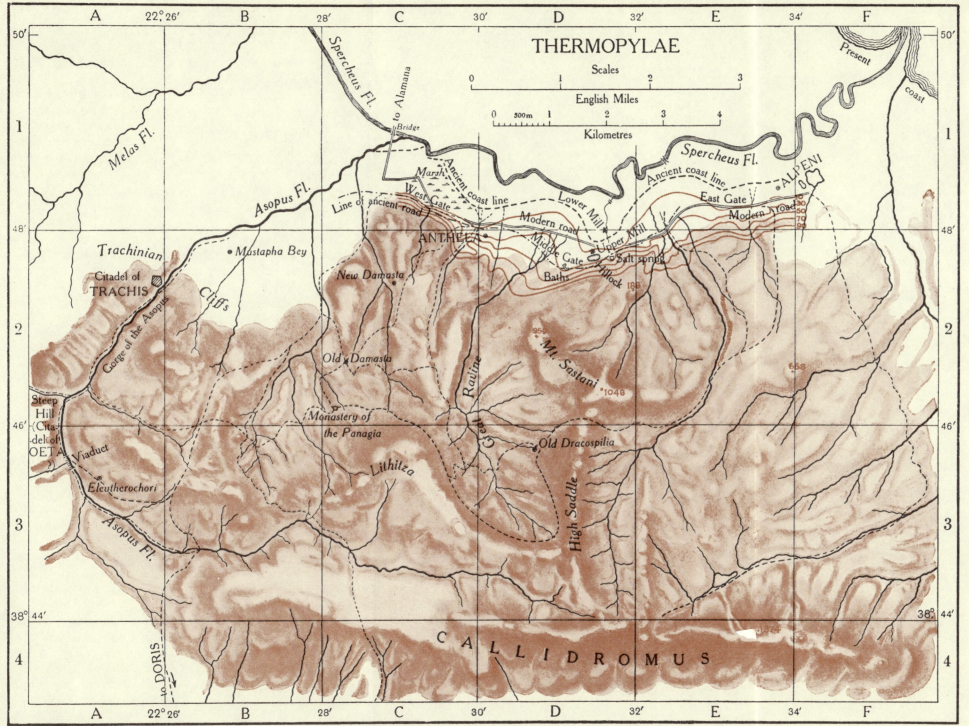

MAP 8

THERMOPYLAE

Scales

English Miles

Kilometres

INDEX TO NAMES

Alpeni, E 1
Anthela, D 2
Asopus Fl., A 3
Asopus Fl., A–C 1, 2
Asopus, Gorge of the, A 2

Baths, D 2
Bridge, C 1

Callidromus, C–E 4
Cliffs, B 2
Coast, Present, F 1
Coast line, Ancient, C–F 1

Damasta, New, C 2
Damasta, Old, C 2
Dracospilia, Old, D 3

East Gate, E 1
Eleutherochori, A 3

High Saddle, D 3
Hillock, D 2

Lithitza, C 3

Marsh, C 1
Melas Fl., A 1
Middle Gate, D 2
Mill, Lower, D 1
Mill, Upper, D 2
Mustapha Bey, B 2

Oeta, Citadel of, A 3

Panagia, Monastery of, C 2

Ravine, Great, CD 2, 3
Road, Line of ancient, C 1
Road, Modern, DE 1, 2

Salt spring, D 2
Sastani, Mt, D 2
Spercheus Fl., B–F 1
Steep Hill, A 2

Trachinian, A 2
Trachis, Citadel of, A 2

Viaduct, A 3

West Gate, C 1

stood near the angle between the Trachinian cliffs and the *cañon*
of the Asopus and commanded the gorge. Trachis, according to
Herodotus, marks the Greek front line against the Persian on the
eve of the fighting, and it was there that the Locrians and the
Phocians had assembled. Assuredly they did not entirely evacuate
it. A parallel omission in Herodotus' distribution of the defenders
confirms the inference. The Peloponnesians and Boeotians are
with Leonidas at Thermopylae, the Phocians are guarding the
Anopaea, but the Locrians are missing. The Locrians must have
been the garrison of Trachis. To them may be added the Trachinians themselves, who figure in Diodorus as 1000 Malians.

Xerxes therefore found both the coast road and the hill road
blocked. He waited three days after the day of his arrival expecting, Herodotus says, that the Greeks would run away, but
more probably in hope that the fleet sent round Euboea would
compel them to abandon Thermopylae. The Persian generals
evidently appreciated the strength of the Greek positions and
wished to avoid frontal assaults on them. It is not surprising that
they appear to have made no attempt on Trachis, a very formidable task. But even their first attack at Thermopylae on the fourth
day, when it had become clear that the naval stratagem had somehow miscarried, may have been no more than a reconnaissance
in force to test the Greek defence, or possibly to divert attention
from the turning movement, which may have been originally
planned for the night of that day. Leonidas had no difficulty in
repelling the attack, but probably did not seriously defend the
west gate of the defile. This gate is not protected by inaccessible
heights on the landward side; and presumably it remained in the
enemy's hands. Herodotus' description of the combat reads like
a fancy picture and can hardly be trusted in detail; in particular
the employment of the Immortals is questionable, at least they
ought to have learnt to distinguish Lacedaemonian 'red coats'
from Phocians two days later. The Persians, however, no doubt
ascertained how costly an undertaking it would be to force their
way through the pass.

Several Greeks were afterwards charged with the betrayal of
the path Anopaea to the enemy. Herodotus fixes the guilt upon
Ephialtes, a Malian of Trachis, for the sufficient reason that the
Amphictyones set a price upon his head. The path starts from
the Asopus above Trachis, runs over rough partially wooded
country, crosses near its upper end the great ravine which issues
inside the west gate of Thermopylae, climbs to a high saddle
between Callidromus and the mountain which dominates the

middle gate, descends an upland valley clothed with dense pine forest, and finally drops down over clearer slopes to Alpeni beyond the east gate. For the most part the course of the path is certainly determined by natural features, but its exact starting point in the valley of the Asopus may be disputed. A recent explorer scrambled up a very steep and rugged track through a gully which enters the deep gorge a couple of miles above Trachis[1]. But an easier, more practicable route, preferable also for its more serviceable communications southwards, may be found near the modern hamlet of Eleutherochori a mile or two higher up the valley, here fairly broad and open. The total distance from the Asopus to Alpeni, which, measured on the map[2], is not less than ten miles, may well be half as much again on foot. Throughout its length the path is difficult, and it attains a height of 3000 feet. Herodotus reveals a false idea of it when he says that it 'stretches along the spine of the range,' but his precision in placing the two extremities and his mention of 'the culminating ridge' below 'the apex of the mountain' may indicate local information. Arduous as the Anopaea is, it has time after time been traversed by large forces of armed men, and the king's Immortals, who were now detailed for the enterprise, were not the first.

The night following the preliminary fight at Thermopylae, if one may judge by the weather at Aphetae, was sombre with thunderclouds and heavy showers. If the march, which needed all the light of the full moon, had been designed for that night, it must have been postponed till the next. At all events the second day's fighting in the pass was probably as perfunctory as the record of it and had no other purpose than to distract attention from the movement. It was 'about the hour of lighting lamps' that Hydarnes set out from the Persian camp under the guidance of Ephialtes. The way up the gorge of the Asopus was closed to him by the fortress of Trachis and its garrison. He must have struck the Anopaea path by some other route which circumvented the obstacle. Herodotus tells how the Persians, taking the Anopaea path after crossing the Asopus, marched all night, having on their right the mountains of the Oetaeans and on their left those of the Trachinians. Did they pass to the east or west of Trachis? did they cross the Asopus in the plain or above the gorge? were the mountains on their right the long comb of Callidromus or the main mass of Oeta? It is a nice question. Two fairly easy paths (and only fairly easy paths could be attempted at night) lead up from the plain to join the Asopus road, the one from the eastern,

---

[1] G. B. Grundy, *The Great Persian War*, p. 301.   [2] See map 8.

the other from the western, end of the Trachinian cliffs. The eastern is the old mule-track now engineered into the carriage road from Lamia. The western begins by ascending the Melas and works round behind Trachis to the wide valley of the Asopus above the gorge[1]. Both routes would strike the Anopaea path near its western extremity in the neighbourhood of Eleutherochori. The balance of evidence inclines to the western route. If the eastern is the shorter, it is also steeper; if the eastern is to-day more frequented, twenty-four centuries ago, when the centre of the Malian plain was sea and marsh, the western was no doubt in more general use; the Oetaean mountains can hardly mean any other than the *massif* of Oeta; Herodotus appears to have jumped to his conclusion and inverted the order of his description—he starts the Persians on the Anopaea path, then explains how they got there, by crossing the Asopus, and finally harks back to their nightlong march which brought them to the river; Pausanias, who had been at Thermopylae and was interested in its history, recognizes both routes and expressly sends Hydarnes by the western, extending, to be sure, its circuit too widely by carrying it through Aenianian territory; the western path lying beyond the Greek left flank might be expected to be unguarded, whereas the eastern would presumably be occupied or at least patrolled by light troops; other considerations to be noted below tend in the same direction.

The Phocians, 1000 strong, had volunteered to defend the Anopaea. Most historians have placed them at the summit of the path on the saddle above the site of Old Dracospilia. There is much to be said for this station. It is strategically correct, for, wherever the invaders might ascend, they must inevitably pass that point on their way towards Alpeni. It is an excellent position, near the eastern edge of the great ravine which cuts into the mountains above Thermopylae. It fits the descriptive notes of Herodotus, who puts the Phocians 'on the gable of the mountain ' below a yet higher peak or crest off the path, and states that the descent from the mountain is much shorter and more direct than the circuitous ascent. Nevertheless there are objections to this argument, and there are other indications which lead us to put the Phocians farther to the west. In the first place Hydarnes started at dusk, encountered the Phocians at daybreak, and arrived

---

[1] The writer owes his information on this western path to Mr Jerome Farrell, who has traversed it. He estimates that it is three hours' easy walking by this route from Mustapha Bey round to the Asopus under the nameless high-perched fortress (which may be Oeta) near the railway viaduct below Eleutherochori. West of the river the maps are of little value.

at the east gate of Thermopylae about noon; that is to say, he took about nine hours of darkness to reach the Phocian station and about seven hours of daylight to complete his march. Is it credible that he took seven hours to descend from the summit above Old Dracospilia to Alpeni? If that was his rate of progress by day and downhill, what becomes of the much longer ascent in the dark? Next, the Phocians learn the approach of the Persians by the rustle of their feet in the fallen oak-leaves of the forest in the stillness of the dawn. Can we doubt that this touch goes back ultimately to an ear-witness? But whereas there are deciduous oaks enough in the Asopus valley and as far east as the prominent crags known as Lithitza or 'the Great Gable,' there are none beyond that point, two good miles (as the crow flies) from the summit of the path. Further, a hint dropped by Herodotus throws a flood of light on the instructions, or rather undertaking, of the Phocians. They were not only guarding the Anopaea path, but also defending their own country. This expression must mean that they were covering a way into Phocis; and that way can be no other than the hill road over the ridge into Doris. Herodotus, looking back on the tragedy of Thermopylae after the event, has been too exclusively preoccupied with the Anopaea path. To Leonidas the road into Doris was hardly less important than that path; to the Phocians it was more important. Strategically regarded, the defence was dual; Leonidas held 'the pass' with a base at Alpeni and communications through Elatea; 'the mountain' was committed to the Phocians, with their own country as base and communications through Doris. We may be sure that what the Phocians volunteered to defend was 'the Anopaea' in the broader sense of the name, and that they never understood their pledge to mean solely, or even primarily, the path. Herodotus' descriptive phrases which seem to place them above Old Dracospilia we may surmise to be derived from a topographical rather than a historical source.

We put the Phocians therefore near Eleutherochori, let us suppose about a mile to the east of it, in the dip between the steep hill which stands north-east of the hamlet and the westernmost outlying height of the Lithitza range. There they would command the junctions of the main routes, the Asopus road (which had already absorbed the path from the west of Trachis), the path from the eastern end of the Trachinian cliffs, and the Anopaea path. The unexpected approach of the Immortals from the west confronted the Phocian general with a strategical problem; was he to defend the road to the south or the path to the east? He

might argue from the advance of the Persians up the Asopus
that they were making for the Cephisus valley; perhaps they knew
nothing of the Anopaea path; a defence of it, if successful, would
turn them upon Phocis; if unsuccessful, would draw them down
upon the rear of Thermopylae. Care for his communications, for
his line of retreat homewards, for the sentiments of his men, the
appeal of city and country in jeopardy, the narrow patriotic
instinct of the Greek, called him southwards; it was almost a
foregone conclusion that he took the road for 'the summit of the
ridge' towards Phocis. We may however credit him with ordinary
observance of military usage and his duty to his allies, and assume
that before relinquishing the eastward path he dispatched runners
to tell Leonidas that he was retiring on Phocis followed by the
enemy, whom he would hold in check to the best of his power[1]. But
Hydarnes, well pleased to be rid of what might have been a serious
obstruction, did not pause to pursue. If we have rightly determined
the spot, he had marched all night at the rate of about one mile to the
hour, but he had still some 14 miles to cover. Having dismissed the
Phocians with a few volleys of arrows and presumably detached a
force to protect his rear, he turned along the Anopaea path.

Apart from the prognostications of his seer Megistias, the first
warning of Hydarnes' march was brought to Leonidas during
the night by deserters from the enemy's camp. They could
announce no more than an expected movement against which
provision had already been made. The next news came from
scouts who ran down from the hills. Herodotus says that they
arrived 'at dawn'; but that is the precise time at which Hydarnes
came upon the Phocians by surprise. Either they could tell no
more than that the Immortals had gone up by the path west of
Trachis, or Herodotus has put their arrival too early. We assume
that these 'scouts' were in fact sent by the Phocian general and
reported his first impression, that the Persians were bound for
the valley of the Cephisus. Here was official intelligence of a
fresh development in the situation; and a council of war met to
consider it. Opinions differed whether to hold the pass or to
evacuate it. No decision is recorded; but after the meeting most

---

[1] We have put the best face on the conduct of the Phocians. Their
subsequent medism, and in particular the appearance of 1000 of them in
the Persian camp, might suggest that they came to terms with Hydarnes
then and there; and one might suspect that Delphic interests and Delphic
influence played a part in their surrender. But the number 1000 may be a
coincidence or convention, and although Herodotus is clearly primed with
apologies for them, their treachery is not proven.

of the allied forces marched away and eventually went home, while Leonidas with his Spartiates and (probably) his other Lacedaemonian troops and the Boeotians remained at Thermopylae. It was afterwards contended that out of regard for their lives he had dismissed those who went, but that it was unseemly for him and the Spartiates to desert the post which they had been sent to hold. It was also said that an oracle from Delphi had declared when the war was about to begin that either Sparta or a Spartan king must perish, and that Leonidas therefore devoted himself in order to save his country. Further it was asserted that whereas the Thespians, 700 in number at the opening of the campaign, volunteered to stay with Leonidas, the Thebans, 400 hoplites, were retained by him under compulsion as hostages.

These several allegations will not bear scrutiny, and betray their origin out of later controversies. It cannot be maintained that the military code of honour of his country forbade a Spartan general to retire in face of the enemy, if he deemed it expedient; in this very war Eurybiades retreats from Artemisium, and Pausanias from his advanced position at Plataea. It is generally recognized that the oracle was invented, or at least resuscitated, in order to counteract the dismay caused in Greece by the news that the Spartan king had been defeated and slain. It is a crude example of the familiar bulletin issued after a disaster—'Our strategical scheme is working out according to plan'; it is not a factor in the events, but a product of them. Why the self-sacrifice of Leonidas must have involved his comrades was not explained; but the more was his heroic death glorified, the more invidious became by contrast the withdrawal of his allies, which saved their lives but exposed them, like Aristodemus, the sole survivor of the 300, to ignominy. The story of their deliberate dismissal to their homes is no doubt their answer to criticism. The reproaches against the Thebans, that they stayed under compulsion, embraced the opportunity of the catastrophe to surrender, and after all suffered the infamy of branding by Xerxes like slaves, are obviously spiteful slanders and have been sufficiently refuted by Plutarch in the *De malignitate Herodoti* (31–3). Thebes had not yet declared for the invader, and however disloyal may have been the intentions of her politicians, there is no reason to implicate her soldiers in their guilt. The mention of Leontiades, father of the Eurymachus who organized the attack on Plataea in 431 B.C., suggests that Herodotus has too easily accepted a story distorted by later prejudices. Moreover, he makes Leontiades the commander of the Thebans at Thermopylae and Eurymachus their commander in the attack on Plataea; but Thucydides implies that Eurymachus was not in command on that occasion, and Plutarch (see above, p. 282) quotes Aristophanes of Boeotia, who seems to have had documentary evidence, to prove that the Theban general at Thermopylae was not Leontiades but Anaxander.

Putting aside the retrospective interpretations imported by subsequent controversies, and endeavouring to envisage the situation as it may have presented itself to Leonidas at his last council of war, we find a fairly simple explanation of the facts. Leonidas never expected the Immortals by the Anopaea, but did expect them by the much longer route round the southern side of Mount Callidromus, which would have taken them at least another day's march. Accordingly he dispatched most of his forces, not up the Anopaea, where they would have met and probably stopped the Persians, and so (especially in view of the recriminations afterwards) we should have heard of the fighting, but towards Tithronium and Elatea in order to keep Hydarnes in check and his own line of retreat open. He retained his best troops, the Lacedaemonians and Boeotians, for the defence of Thermopylae. But why, instead of withdrawing his whole army at once into safety, did he incur so great a risk for the sake of delaying Xerxes' march by one day or at best two days? Leonidas, we have argued, had come to Thermopylae with the instruction, or undertaking, to hold the pass in order that the Greek fleet might compel the Persians to a naval engagement which they would of course decline if the land road were clear. It was his duty to defend his post so long as he could hold it, or so long as the fleet could still challenge the enemy's to battle at Artemisium. He had seen the 53 Attic ships pass up the channel on the day before, and had doubtless heard their good news and their too sanguine hopes. Could he but keep the pass for one day more, the decisive naval battle might be fought and won. From his last two days' experience he believed that with 2000 men he could do it, and to his eternal honour he made the gallant attempt. But at the moment it was no forlorn hope, no desperate sacrifice, but a well-calculated scheme which offered fair promise of success. The descent of Hydarnes by the Anopaea was a complete surprise.

Xerxes, by arrangement with Ephialtes, attacked at 'the hour when the market is fullest,' that is to say, about the middle of the forenoon, soon after which it was expected that the Immortals would appear upon the scene. But Ephialtes had not reckoned the delays introduced by the Phocians and by the number of the troops employed. He came evidently several hours too late, and the heaviest fighting was over before the attack from the rear developed. Leonidas had already fallen, and on the Persian side two sons of Darius. Thereupon, except the Thebans, the survivors of the Greeks, or at any rate of the Lacedaemonians, retired to a hillock afterwards crowned with the sculptured Lion of Leonidas, probably the knoll about the centre of the pass, near the upper mill, midway between the baths and the salt-spring. There they made their last stand and sank, overwhelmed with missiles, fighting to the bitter end.

The part of the Boeotians in the final struggle is not very clear. The Spartan tradition took little heed of them. Herodotus parenthetically lets the Thespians die to a man with the Spartans on the hillock, and he recounts at full length the discreditable story of the Thebans' surrender. If the hillock is rightly identified, it is tempting to suppose that, when the approach of the Immortals was announced, the Boeotians were told off to defend the rear, the Thespians at the east gate, the Thebans on the steep track which descends to a point a little west of that gate; Hydarnes then, having detached a force to contain the Thebans, came down to Alpeni and drove the Thespians in upon the Spartans; thus the Thebans were left isolated and surrendered at discretion.

The fighting at Thermopylae and Artemisium coincided, according to Herodotus, with the Olympian festival (480 B.C.)—that same meeting which witnessed the epic contest between Theogenes and Euthymus, the greatest of Greek boxers. With the Olympian Herodotus couples the Carneian celebration; and as the two festivals ended at the full moon, both must have finished on either the 21st July or the 19th August, for no other full moons of this year are possible. Although the seasonal notes in Herodotus favour the former, other considerations lead us to prefer the latter date[1].

---

[1] Xerxes starts from Sardes 'with the spring.' He spends a month in crossing the Hellespont. His ships are caught by the storm off the Magnesian coast 'in the season of mid summer.' He marches from Trachinia on the third day after his victory, and his fleet reaches Phalerum on the ninth. He arrives in Attica within three months of quitting the Hellespont. If the fighting at Thermopylae and Artemisium was about the 21st July, he entered Attica about the end of July or beginning of August. If the fighting was about the 19th August, he entered Attica about the end of August or beginning of September. The battle of Salamis is to be put on the 23rd September. It is hard to believe he had been in Attica about seven weeks before the battle. Moreover, Mardonius occupied Athens in the tenth month after Xerxes, i.e. in either May or June 479 B.C., and the battle of Plataea followed on the 27th August. It is difficult to fill up even two months between the occupation and that battle.

V. THE WOODEN WALLS OF ATHENS

The retreat of the Greek fleet was announced to the Persians at Aphetae during the night. At sunrise they crossed over to Artemisium, and proceeded after noon to occupy Histiaea. On Xerxes' invitation all who could procure a boat spent the next day in a visit to Thermopylae to view the Greek dead. They returned on the following day to Histiaea. On this same day the army began its march from Trachinia; but the fleet stayed three more days before starting down the channel and through the Euripus for Phalerum, where it arrived on the third day from Histiaea or ninth after the last battles on sea and land. No doubt the army or its vanguard was timed to reach Athens by that day. The distance from Trachis could quite well be covered in a week, and the operations on the way need not have detained the leading column.

Trachis must have surrendered on the fall of Thermopylae. Herodotus accordingly adds the Malians and Locrians to Xerxes' forces. He sends the whole Persian army by the hill road into Doris, but probably the bulk of it with the king himself marched by the coast road. The Dorians saved themselves by 'medism,' the Phocians by flight to Parnassus. The invaders, we are told, instigated by the Thessalians, laid waste the Phocian towns with fire and sword. But it is likely that the Phocians, 1000 of whom figure subsequently in the enemy's ranks, have made the most of the devastation. The king appears to have disapproved of the pillage, for it ceases when the routes unite at Panopeus, and Macedonian officers are sent forward to protect the cities of Boeotia. The expedition dispatched from Panopeus to Delphi may be interpreted as a similar protective measure, although it was afterwards represented as hostile. Delphi must have owed its immunity to an arrangement with the Persians. The fantastic story of its salvation is clearly an apologetic figment; words dropped by Herodotus admit the suggestion that an inventory was made for the king of the treasures of the temple, which were presumably guaranteed by his seal. Except the Plataeans and Thespians, whose cities he burnt, the Boeotians declared for the invader, and proved staunch auxiliaries. Xerxes entered Attica within three months of his departure from the Hellespont.

Meanwhile the Greek fleet had taken up its station in the sound of Salamis, and the main strength of the Peloponnesian army under Cleombrotus, brother of Leonidas and regent for his son Pleistarchus, had rushed on the news of the fall of Thermopylae to occupy the Isthmus, where probably everything had been prepared beforehand whether for an advance or for defence. Now in all haste the road from Megara was broken up and blocked at the Scironian cliffs, and the Isthmus was fortified with a wall. The fleet had presumably pressed its pace and may well have reached Salamis on the third morning of its voyage. Reinforced by ships collected at Pogon it numbered, according to Aeschylus, 310 triremes, to which we may add from Herodotus seven penteconters. The detailed figures given by Herodotus, amounting in all to 380 triremes, are best explained[1] as 'campaign totals' representing the whole number of ships contributed by each state during the entire year.

The positions at the Isthmus and Salamis had without doubt been determined from the first discussions of the plans of campaign. Herodotus' account would suggest that the fleet was bound for the Isthmus and put into Salamis merely to enable the Athenians to transport their families across the water, and that the army was pledged to march out and give battle in Boeotia in defence of Attica. These crude and incompatible schemes are not likely to have been proposed by responsible commanders in the navy or the camp, least of all after the lessons of Thermopylae and Artemisium. They emanate from the strategists of the lower deck, and are perhaps not uncoloured by subsequent events, Themistocles' message to Xerxes, the Athenian misinterpretation of the westward movement of the Corinthians before the battle, the army's advance north of Cithaeron under the very different conditions of the next year. Herodotus here and in his stories of the councils of war, drawing possibly on literary sources, reproduces the surmises and recriminations of the rank and file, the rumours and feelings which agitated the outside public, the murmurs of the opposition, the criticism and prejudices of a later day, rather than the authentic debates and decisions of the generals. He reflects the current impressions of the situation and uses the councils

---

[1] With Tarn, *J.H.S.* xxviii, p. 219. Herodotus gives the total as 378, afterwards raised to 380 by adding the Tenian ship which deserted from the enemy and the Lemnian which had come over at Artemisium. But his items make only 366. The missing 12 are generally taken to be the 'other ships,' which the Aeginetans had in commission guarding their island, reckoned rather loosely to the fleet at Salamis. If so, the accessions (including the Tenian) above the several contingents at Artemisium add up to 55, which with the 325 at Artemisium make the same total, 380. The difference between Herodotus' 380 and Aeschylus' 310 gives us the Greek losses at Artemisium.

as a dramatic vehicle to convey them[1]. We cannot believe that Herodotus reveals to us the secrets of the leaders, but need not doubt that he preserves a picture on the whole truthful, in spite of all contaminations, of the environment in which their deliberations were conducted, and enables us to estimate their difficulties at this crisis.

Probably at least as stubborn as any from his colleagues on the council was the opposition which Themistocles had to overcome in persuading the Athenians to abandon their country and city to the enemy. He worked upon their superstition by announcing that Athena's serpent had left his cake uneaten, and exploited for his purpose what dubious encouragement could be extracted from the Delphic response of a few months before. Cimon loyally seconded his efforts, ostentatiously hung up his bridle on the Acropolis, and embarked to fight afloat. The Council of Areopagus smoothed obstacles by a grant of 8 drachmae a head to the crews. A decree committed the city to the care of her goddess and ordered the evacuation of Attica. The ten generals proclaimed that the citizens should save their families as best they could. The mass of the population was accordingly transported to Troezen or Aegina or Salamis. But the evacuation was not complete; 500 prisoners (afterwards released by the Samians) were captured in Attica by the Persians, and, probably a concession to the die-hards of the opposition, possibly a scheme to prolong the campaign into the season of storms, a garrison was left in the Acropolis. The defence was subsequently represented as the attempt of a few paupers and fanatics who were too poor to migrate or too obstinate to give up their own opinion that the 'wooden wall' of the oracle meant the stockade or barricades behind which they took refuge.

Xerxes naturally made for Athens rather than the Isthmus. The punishment of Athens was the prime object of his expedition; he could not prudently leave Attica on his flank in the enemy's hands; he could not freely use his navy against the Peloponnese until it had disposed of the Greek fleet; he was anxious to concert his next operations with his admirals. He occupied Athens about the beginning of September and besieged the Acropolis. The

---

[1] One of his *personae*, Mnesiphilus, who prompts Themistocles to upset an alleged decision to retire from Salamis, seems to have been (or become) first a supposititious claimant put forward by Themistocles' calumniators to rob him of his best stratagem, and then an argument used by the educators in support of their theory that Virtue is Knowledge and every stroke of genius the product of instruction.

Persians established themselves on the Areopagus and attacked the gates and fortifications on the ascent to the citadel from the west, shooting arrows bound with burning tow into the wooden palisade. The defenders rolled blocks of stone upon them and for a long time repulsed all their assaults. Although hard pressed they rejected the terms of surrender offered to them through the Peisistratidae, and the king was at his wits' end to overcome their resistance. At last some of the enemy succeeded in climbing up by the chapel of Aglaurus behind the defence and opened the gates from within. The garrison was put to the sword and the temple of Athena to the flames. Xerxes had attained his first objective and dispatched a courier to announce his achievement to Artabanus at Susa. Herodotus implies that the Acropolis was taken two days before the battle of Salamis, that is to say, on the 21st of September. The siege therefore had lasted about three weeks. On the next day Xerxes invited the Athenian exiles to ascend to the Acropolis and do sacrifice according to their own ritual. They are said to have reported that the burnt stump of Athena s olive had already put forth a shoot a cubit long. No doubt they returned with Mardonius next year and their report has been antedated. It was probably on this same day (22nd September), although the day cannot be precisely determined from Herodotus, that Dicaeus, one of the exiles, with Demaratus, the former king of Sparta, witnessed in the Thriasian plain a phenomenon which he interpreted to be a portent of disaster to the Persian fleet. He saw a cloud of dust, as from the passage of 30,000 men, sweep across from Eleusis to the Greek station at Salamis, and heard the mystic invocation with which the Athenians were wont to conduct Iacchus in procession to Eleusis on the eve of the great day of the Mysteries. It was the season of the Mysteries, and (at all events in the later Attic calendar) the day of the procession was also the eve of the date of the battle of Salamis. Herodotus tells that on that same evening Xerxes' army began to move towards the Peloponnese. Was it his vanguard that raised the dust and the chant?

VI. SALAMIS

The Persian fleet since its arrival from Histiaea had lain at Phalerum. If we may assume that the Hellespontine or Pontic division had been left at Abydos, and that some 250 ships had been lost by storm and battle, it numbered about 350 triremes. With so narrow a majority the admirals did not attempt to force an entry into the sound of Salamis. The enemy's strategic position there was extremely strong, but sooner or later starvation would drive him out to fight at a disadvantage in the open. Nevertheless, if the Greek provision of bread was running low, so also was the Persian. Day by day the summer waned, but the Greeks did not move. Even could Xerxes have maintained his huge forces in Greece over the winter, a second campaign was an unwelcome prospect. Under these circumstances the Persian commanders appear to have decided to blockade the Greeks at Salamis and proceed against the Peloponnese. They prepared to close one, no doubt the easternmost, of the exits from the straits by a mole and barricades of vessels lashed together, preparations afterwards mistaken by the Greeks for an attempt to construct a bridge from Attica to Salamis. But recognizing that they had not ships enough to contain the enemy's and at the same time to detach a division for operations elsewhere, they beat up contingents from the Islands, and above all, summoned the Pontic fleet from the Hellespont[1]. The reinforcements from the Islands (17 ships, if we could trust the catalogue at Doriscus) arrived at Phalerum, one gathers from Herodotus, on the day of the capture of the Acropolis. The Pontic fleet was not far behind, for we find it on the evening of the next day on the east side of Attica, its first squadron at Ceos, its second at Cynosura near Marathon. That next day Xerxes, advised, of course, of its coming and now free for an advance on land, held a council of war at Phalerum. It was presumably to that meeting that a man from the Greek head-quarters at Salamis was introduced who had a momentous message to deliver. Perhaps his advent was the reason for the meeting.

The fall of the Acropolis deeply stirred the Greeks at Salamis, whether Athenians or not. It portended that the attack on the

---

[1] This hypothesis not only explains better than any other the subsequent course of events but also solves several difficult problems in Herodotus' narrative—(1) the complete disappearance of this fleet from the active operations of the campaign; (2) the pause in the naval war before the battle of Salamis; (3) the computation introduced at this point that the accessions to Xerxes' forces balanced the losses, a computation which Herodotus has endeavoured to interpret by applying it to the *personnel*; it would be more appropriate if it originally meant that the Pontic fleet replaced the lost Cilician; (4) the obscure reference, preserved but not understood by Herodotus, to the Persians 'stationed around Ceos and Cynosura'; could any explanation be more hazardous than (what has often been done) to conjecture an unknown Ceos and an unknown Cynosura in order to bring them within the strategic horizon of Herodotus, and to construe a past participle ('stationed') in a future sense?

Isthmus was imminent. But still graver must have been the news, known of course to the higher officers, that the Persian naval reserves had been called up and were now near at hand, indeed beginning to arrive. The risk of being shut up in the sound of Salamis and slowly reduced by hunger, while the enemy launched an expedition against the Peloponnese, became an urgent danger. Was it not better to escape while escape was still possible, sacrifice the advantage of the position, and, as the Corinthians clamoured, fight a desperate battle at the Isthmus, covered in rear by the allied army? The answer from the other side was simple and conclusive. No Mnesiphilus was needed to demonstrate that, if it quitted Salamis, the fleet would break up. Eurybiades might order it to the Isthmus, but not a third of it would obey. Neither he nor Themistocles could compel the Athenians, the Aeginetans, the allies from the Argolic peninsula, to abandon their families to the enemy. If, as Herodotus represents, Themistocles threatened that the Athenians would embark their wives and children and sail off to Italy, he spoke the brutal truth. But he had his better alternative solution ready. The enemy, instead of concentrating his forces, might be encouraged to disperse them still further, and then be drawn into a battle before his reserves could come up and give him a decisive superiority at the critical point. Xerxes was flushed with success and the now assured hope of capturing the entire Greek fleet. Let him be told that it was about to run away, and he would try to prevent its escape, divide his forces in order to block both ends of the channel, and give a chance of defeating them in detail. This bold scheme was accepted by Eurybiades and the council. The version of Herodotus, that it was a ruse practised by Themistocles not only on the enemy but also on his own colleagues, receives no countenance from Aeschylus and may be relegated to the cycle of legends which clustered about Themistocles.

So Sicinnus, 'pedagogue' to Themistocles' boys, was sent on the 22nd September, the day after the fall of the Acropolis, to the Persian headquarters at Phalerum to tell the king (or his admirals) that the Greeks meant to slip away out of the straits under cover of the coming night. Their destination, to judge from the silence of our best authorities, was left vague; Pogon might seem to the enemy as plausible a guess as the Isthmus. Herodotus professes to add a second clause to the message, that the Greeks were quarrelling among themselves and some of them (the Athenians, it is implied) were prepared to join the Persians and turn their arms against their allies. Is this another accretion on

MAP 9

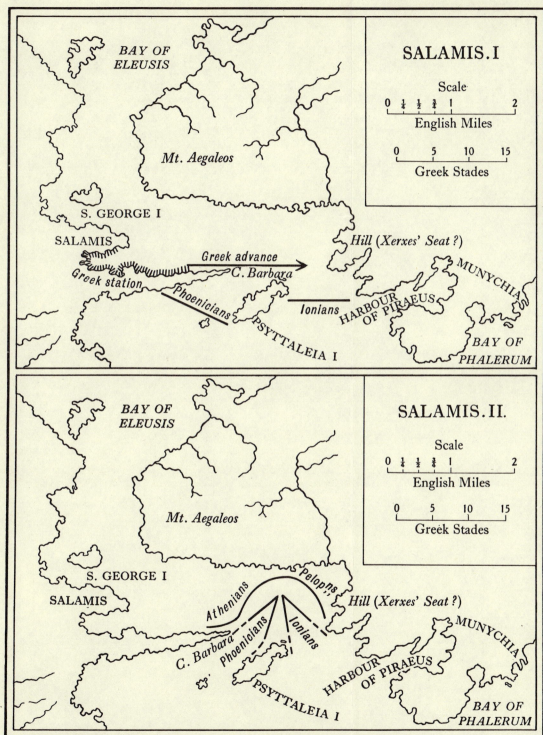

INDEX TO NAMES

Aegaleos, Mt, I and II
Athenians, II

Barbara, C., I and II

Eleusis, Bay of, I and II

Greek advance, I
Greek station, I

Hill (Xerxes' Seat?), I and II

Ionians, I and II

Munychia, I and II

Peloponnesians, II
Phalerum, Bay of, I and II
Phoenicians, I and II
Piraeus, Harbour of, I and II
Psyttaleia I., I and II

S. George I., I and II
Salamis, I and II

Xerxes' Seat?, I and II

the story? Herodotus is the sole authority for it. It is barely consistent with the main purport of the message. It matches the tissue
of legends which were spun about Themistocles; and if it also
harmonizes with the context of the particular situation, that very
fact may betray the motive for its insertion. It may be defended,
hardly as an authentic part of the official message, but possibly
as a private instruction to Sicinnus from Themistocles, who may
well have been intent upon the strategic problem of the future
battle and anxious to coax the enemy into relieving the Greeks of
the formidable task of forcing the gates of the sound, or even to
reserve to the Athenians a last expedient at the expense of their
allies, if the worst came to the worst. This explanation, however,
is a little too subtle to be altogether convincing, and provokes the
questions how Herodotus got the information, and why he alone?
At all events it is unsafe to build anything on so dubious a
foundation.

Herodotus differs again from Aeschylus on the time and circumstances of the mission of Sicinnus. He fetches the Persian fleet
from Phalerum into the sound (not a mile broad) and arrays it
for combat parallel to the Greek line on the afternoon before the
battle, which is postponed only by the dark; after nightfall
Themistocles dispatches Sicinnus with his message, whereupon
the Persians occupy the island of Psyttaleia, and after midnight
close the straits on both wings. The absurdities of this account
need no demonstration. It is refuted by its own incongruities, by
Aeschylus, by the topography, and by common sense. Herodotus
has started with an entirely wrong preconception of the battle
and has tried in vain to adjust or force his information into conformity with it. We may dismiss it and base our interpretation
of the story on Aeschylus, whose *Persae*, written by a combatant
for the ears of his comrades within eight years of the event, imposes
a limit to every controversy.

It is clear from Aeschylus that Sicinnus arrived at Phalerum
by daylight on the day before the battle. He arrived probably
early in the day, for time must be allowed for the Persian deliberations and preparations, and he would start presumably not later
than the ship which the Greeks now dispatched to Aegina to
fetch the Aeacidae—indeed it is a plausible conjecture that both
he and that ship were sent out under cover of the previous night
in accordance with a decision taken on the day before, and that
he arrived therefore soon after sunrise. Perhaps it was on the news
of his arrival that Xerxes, leaving the Athenian exiles to perform
their sacrifice, came down to Phalerum to preside at a council of

war, at which we may assume that the message of Sicinnus was
the main business for discussion. The result was the king's order
to his admirals of which Aeschylus gives the substance. As soon
as the sun had set and darkness overspread the sky, the bulk of
the fleet was to be posted in three lines to guard the channels of
exit from the sound, and other ships were to be stationed round
about the isle of Salamis; should the Greeks steal out and escape,
the king's captains would forfeit their heads. The intention of
this order is plain enough. The Greeks were to be enclosed in
the straits, not a man of them was to be let slip through the
blockade. The three lines of ships obviously correspond to the
three channels—(1) between the Attic coast (north of the
mouth of the Piraeus) and the island of Psyttaleia (Lipsokutali),
(2) between Psyttaleia and the long eastern promontory of the
island of Salamis, (3) between the western extremity of Salamis
and the Megarian headland which stretches out towards it. What
else, in the names of all the Muses, could have been in this context
the sense and point of Aeschylus' insistence on the three lines?
The 'other ships' were no doubt placed to catch any boats which
might be launched from the outer shores of the island of Salamis.
To these dispositions we may add, what Aeschylus reserves for
a pendant to his naval picture but Herodotus puts in its right
order at the beginning of the operations, the occupation of the
island of Psyttaleia. Its purpose was afterwards inferred from its
part in the subsequent battle, to help friends and slay foes who
might be driven to land there, but was originally (we may rather
suppose) to facilitate the blockade of the eastern channels. We
assume that Psyttaleia is to be identified with the modern Lipsokutali or Lipsokutala. A recent attempt[1] to transfer the name to
the island of St George rests on insufficient evidence and in-
admissible premises.

The king's armada lying in the bay of Phalerum had its front
to the south and west. Of its three component fleets the Phoenician of course held the centre, the royal post of honour in every
Persian array, the Egyptian no doubt formed the right or western
wing, and the Ionian the left. After supper the crews embarked,
and at nightfall the fleets moved out in succession, by the right,
to take up their several stations to guard the three channels.
Naturally the stations were assigned to the three fleets in the
order of their sailing, the farthest westernmost channel to the
leading (right) wing, the middle channel to the centre, and the
nearest (easternmost) channel to the rear (left) wing. If we may

---

[1] Beloch, *Gr. Gesch.* II², 2, pp. 107 *sqq.*

trust Herodotus and our interpretation of him, the king's order was also communicated to the Pontic fleet at Ceos and Cynosura, which weighed anchor, but does not appear to have arrived in time to take part in the battle. Its failure is not surprising. The order would be sent overland to Marathon; the squadron at Cynosura would have to embark its crews and clear; the squadron at Ceos had to be picked up, involving more delay; and it may well have been after sunrise when the fleet left Ceos on its 50 miles' voyage to the scene of action.

The closure of the channels was announced to the Greek commanders by Aristides, who narrowly escaped capture on his way in from Aegina. Herodotus (or his authority) has not missed the opportunity for a dramatic episode between him and his rival Themistocles, and conveys the impression that Aristides was only now arriving from his banishment. But this story cannot impugn the statement of the *Constitution of Athens* (xxii) that all the exiles were recalled in the previous archontic year; and, on Herodotus' own showing, Aristides appears next day in command of Athenian hoplites, presumably as one of the ten generals in office[1]. He must have gone to Aegina on some mission, perhaps to concert for the co-operation of the Aeginetan squadron there in the coming engagement. It is a probable conjecture that he went and returned on the (Aeginetan) ship sent to fetch the Aeacidae. His report of the enemy's movement was soon confirmed by a Tenian vessel which came over from the king's fleet. The Greek admirals accordingly made their final preparations for action. These included, we may assume, the dispatch of the Corinthian squadron (with possibly the Ambraciote and Leucadian contingents) to hold the Megarian channel against the Egyptians. Its mission figures in Herodotus only as an Athenian allegation against the Corinthian Adeimantus and his crews, that, when the fleets were about to engage, they fled away and were turned back by a mysterious barque, which met them off the temple of Athena Sciras with the news of the Greek victory. This scandal, which did not impose upon Herodotus and hardly needed Plutarch's elaborate refutation[2], originated no doubt from an ignorant misinterpretation of the movement at the time, and has been afterwards sharpened by Athenian malice. One point that has been whetted is the hour

---

[1] Tarn (*op. cit.* p. 220, n. 66) neatly suggests that the 20 Athenian triremes manned by the Chalcidians represent the command of Aristides, who was, with his men, serving ashore. Compare the 'fatigue duty' of the tribe Antiochis after the battle of Marathon.

[2] *de malignitate Herodoti*, 39.

of the Corinthians' departure, which is held back until it appears to be a flight in the very face of the enemy. They acted, we may be sure, upon orders and started long before the engagement. The duty assigned to them, as to the 53 ships sent back from Artemisium to Chalcis, was to protect the rear of the Allies. Plutarch's evidence proves that they took part in the fighting, although not in the main battle.

At daybreak, after the customary exhortations, the other combatants embarked. The fleet lay fringing the Salaminian shore, facing north. The commander-in-chief, Eurybiades, with his 16 Lacedaemonian triremes, of course held the post of honour on the extreme right; the Athenians, more than half the force present, occupied the left. As they pushed out the crews raised the measured chant of the paean; a trumpet called; with a quick turn to starboard the long line of ships moved off in column due eastward down the coast, the right wing leading in orderly array. The men were in good heart and full of resolute courage, but Eurybiades and his colleagues may well have felt qualms of anxiety. A short mile or half mile of water to traverse, a few minutes' row, and the head of the column would shoot out beyond Cape Barbara into full view of the enemy. That was the critical moment. Themistocles had doubtless provided a plan for every contingency. Were the Greeks prepared to rush the channels and attack the blockaders outside? Probably, but only in the last resort. It would have been a hazardous enterprise, although we cannot bind the genius of Themistocles, who may have had his stratagem ready. That contingency never arose. Themistocles staked first upon the chance that the enemy could be drawn into the straits, and used every artifice to invite them in. The Greek fleet had noisily advertised its start from its anchorage behind the screen of the long eastern promontory of Salamis. It emerged past Cape Barbara and trailed its train across the Phoenicians' bows within a bare mile of their beaks. It hesitated as though caught unawares and faltering at sight of its foe. It edged off, formed front, to be sure, towards the enemy, but only to back water away from him towards the Attic shore in its rear. The Persian admirals were in a reckless mood, stimulated by Sicinnus' message, the nearness of their reserves, the presence of the King, who was arriving by land, presumably to receive the expected surrender of the Hellenic navy. They could not resist the tempting opportunity of cutting through the Greek column as it filed out from behind the cape. With a cheer the Barbarians dashed forward, pressed through the channels, and flung themselves in a tumultuous torrent at the centre of the Allies' line, which steadily sagged away from them. This manœuvre of the Greeks drew the enemy farther into the net and enabled the Athenian rear to deploy into very effective action against the Phoenician left flank. It will be noted that both fleets had changed front since quitting their respective anchorages; in the battle the Phoenicians fight on the Persian left, the Ionians on the right, the Athenians on the Greek right, the Lacedaemonians and other Allies on the left. Themistocles doubtless saw to it that the formidable Phoenicians should be opposed by his own new navy.

There was of course a limit to the sagging of the Greek line. Themistocles could not allow a gap, through which the enemy might pour, between his extreme right and Cape Barbara. It was when that limit was reached, we may suppose, that the very natural cry of protest arose, which was afterwards deemed supernatural, 'Madmen, how much farther are you going to back?' The point was no doubt crowded with Athenian spectators, not to mention Aristides' hoplites, who were horrified at being cut off from their protectors. At all events the retrograde movement was arrested and the Greeks took the offensive, probably on both wings at once, for it was disputed whether an Athenian trierarch, Ameinias (brother of Aeschylus?), or the Aeginetan vessel which had brought the Aeacidae struck the first blow. The Barbarians, already disordered from the crush through the channels and assailed on both flanks, soon fell foul of one another and lapsed into worse and worse confusion as more ships pressed in from behind. The Greek captains thrust at them in well-timed charges and herded them together, like dogs about a troop of oxen. The welter was complete when the foremost ships turned back to escape and collided with those which were still pushing on. It may be conjectured that the Athenians, who may have had a certain surplus of ships on their right wing, and more of them as the ambit of the line contracted, succeeded as the day wore on in shutting the channel between Salamis and Psyttaleia. At the opposite extremity of the arc the Greek left wing, where the Aeginetans appear to have been posted and to have eclipsed all rivals, was working down to seize the eastern channel.

As the claws of the pincers closed the combatants encountered unexpected adversaries or allies. Thus a Samothracian trireme, attached no doubt to the Ionian division, sank an Athenian, and was then rammed by an Aeginetan; Polycritus, son of Crius, in command of an Aeginetan ship, captured the Sidonian cruiser on which his compatriot Pytheas (taken off Magnesia) was a prisoner, and then

fell foul of Themistocles; Artemisia, queen of Halicarnassus, chased
by the Athenian Ameinias, deluded both her pursuer and her
sovereign by sinking Damasithymus, dynast of Calydna, her own
vassal, who stood in her way (perhaps politically as well as
physically), and secured at one blow her escape and great praise
from Xerxes. The king watched the battle from a neighbouring
hill[1], and his secretaries noted the exploits of his captains. Most
of them, even the Ionians, fought stoutly. The Samothracians, for
example, not only sank an Attic ship but also boarded and took
the Aeginetan which rammed their own; Herodotus knew the
names of many trierarchs who captured Greek ships, although he
gives only two, Theomestor and Phylacus, both Samian. The
Greeks could not achieve the closure of the eastern channel.
Whether the Aeginetans, who according to Herodotus' information waylaid the fugitives sailing out to Phalerum, were inside,
in, or outside the channel, and whether they were the 30 ships
contributed to the allied fleet or the squadron on guard at Aegina,
are open questions[2]; but if they were the squadron from Aegina,
it must surely have numbered more than 12. On the other hand,
the Athenians by their advance eastwards gained possession of
the more westerly of the two channels and enabled Aristides to
get his troops transported across it to Psyttaleia, where he shot
down or hacked to pieces the entire Persian garrison.

Perhaps the approach of the Pontic fleet balked the Greeks of
the full exploitation of their victory. At all events the Persians
managed to extricate a large proportion, at least a half, of their
ships from Themistocles' trap. They abandoned the scene of
battle strewn with wrecks and floating men, whom the victors
clubbed with oars or spitted like tunny. The slaughter, but
probably not the fighting, went on till nightfall. Among the dead
was Ariabignes, Xerxes' brother, the admiral of the Ionian fleet.
The fugitives fled to Phalerum to the protection of the troops
there, and were doubtless joined by the Egyptian and Pontic
divisions. The Greeks, who must have suffered considerably,

---

[1] The site is variously conjectured. One would naturally place it on the
headland half-way between the mouth of the harbour of Piraeus and the
Bay of Keratzini, overlooking the channel between Attica and Psyttaleia.
Herodotus, in conformity with his conception of the battle, plants Xerxes
at the foot of Mount Aegaleos. Later writers set him near 'the Heracleum,'
but its position is not determined, and they may have been guided by the
same theory.

[2] Herodotus, VIII, 91, puts them ἐν τῷ πορθμῷ. In VIII, 76 he uses the
same word of the water outside the channels. Aeschylus (*Agam.* 307) applies
it to the whole Saronic gulf. Strabo regularly calls that gulf πόρος.

made no attack on their still superior enemy, but returned to Salamis and prepared for another conflict. The king however had lost confidence in his navy now defeated, demoralized, disorganized, and dangerously Hellenic in composition. The winter was at hand; his supplies were running low; there was no longer any hope of a speedy solution to the strategical problem; perhaps news of trouble in Babylon disquieted him; he had accomplished enough to make a good show, and Mardonius could complete the conquest in a second campaign. So the order went forth that the fleet should return to the Hellespont to guard that vital spot in the line of communications, and the army should evacuate Attica and seek winter quarters farther north.

The battle of Salamis was fought on the 23rd of September 480 B.C. Plutarch in one passage gives the date the 20th Boedromion, in two others the 16th Munychion. If we may assume that down to the publication of Meton's cycle the Attic calendar was of the primitive type indicated by Herodotus (I, 32 and II, 4); that Meton determined the solstice on the 13th Scirophorion 432 B.C.; that before that date an extraordinary Hecatombaeon had been intercalated, as provided in a well-known inscription[1]; that in 480 B.C. the Eleusinian Mysteries had no constant relation to the civil calendar; then Plutarch's two dates are reconciled, for they coincide on the 22nd/23rd of September 480 B.C., the 16th Munychion being the 'Old Style' date and the 20th Boedromion being a reduction of it to the 'Metonic' or 'Metonicized' calendar.

The forces actually engaged in the main battle on the two sides may have been about equal in number; or if the Persians had a surplus, it was quite small. Diodorus (Ephorus) gives the losses as 40 Greek ships and over 200 Persian. These figures are not likely to be better than estimates or calculations, but they agree fairly well with Herodotus' statement that the Persians had 300 ships at Samos in the next summer, and would be plausible enough, had not Diodorus reckoned the ships at Samos at over 400 without the Phoenician. What put the king's navy out of action for the rest of the war was not so much the numerical loss as its incidence. The Phoenician fleet had shrunk almost to a squadron, the Egyptian had probably suffered heavily, and the Hellenic divisions could no longer be trusted. Thus, Xerxes, although he still had the larger number of ships, lost the command of the sea, and with it eventually the war. In the first place, one of the three army corps had to be sent back to hold Ionia and

---

[1] *I.G.* I. Suppl. p. 59 *n.*, 27 *b*. Cf. R. H. Tanner, *Class. Philol.* XI, p. 65.

another to guard the communications in Thrace; in the second place, this reduction of the land forces became in any case inevitable when supplies could no longer be sent by sea. The good fight put up by Mardonius and his corps, the best troops of the empire, may obscure but cannot invalidate the truth of Aeschylus' verdict, that the defeat of the fleet involved the destruction of the army.

VII. XERXES' WITHDRAWAL

Herodotus, if we strictly demand of him an account of every day that passed, is committed to the statements that the Persian fleet fled from Phalerum in the night after the battle, and that the Greeks, apprised at last of its departure, started next day in pursuit, and followed it as far as Andros. His narrative does not convey the impression of such haste, and whether intended or not, this rapid development of the situation can hardly be accepted. The Persian fleet was surely in no condition to sail a few hours after the battle; time must be allowed for the king's deliberations with his counsellors; the Greeks would not quit Salamis before they were certain that the enemy either had evacuated Attica or had at his disposal no vessels in which he might cross the straits. Neither the Persian flight nor the Greek pursuit was so precipitate. It was at Andros, according to Herodotus, that a council was held at which the admirals debated whether to push on to the Hellespont and cut the invader's communications by destroying the bridges, or to leave him every facility for retirement. We may well believe that Themistocles urged the advance and that the Peloponnesians, ever anxious to restrict their liabilities abroad, outvoted him. But the story that, with an eye to future needs, he made capital out of his discomfiture by sending Sicinnus back to Attica to tell Xerxes that he had frustrated the project, is obviously a figment evolved out of his own pretence to Artaxerxes' gratitude[1]. Attacks next made on Andros and Carystus are a logical sequel to the council's decision. These two strongholds kept the straits between them open for the enemy, should he return. The Allies seem to have aimed at securing the Cyclades and pushing forward their naval front to their eastern margin, where Leotychidas next spring takes up his station at Delos. They appear to have imposed a fine or levy upon the Islanders who had furnished ships to Xerxes. The charge that Themistocles exacted these monies for his own pocket (while the Allies enforced

---

[1] Thucydides I, 137.

his demands) is plainly a malicious scandal. The Parians, whose attitude had been ambiguous, were perhaps let off, and Themistocles may have been suspected of appropriating their payment. The Andrians and Carystians resisted, successfully for the nonce. The Allies were unwilling to spend time in reducing them and returned to Salamis, where they vowed thank-offerings to the gods and awarded the prizes of valour to the victors. The award of the first prize to the Aeginetans suggests that our tradition does scant justice to their part in the battle.

It was some days after the battle that Xerxes began to withdraw his army by the same route whereby he had come, through Boeotia. On the 2nd October Cleombrotus was deterred by the solar eclipse of that day from taking the offensive from the Isthmus against presumably his rear-guard still south of Cithaeron. Mardonius and his corps were left in winter quarters in Thessaly, where most food and fodder were to be found. There he held a safe strategical position, secure from naval raids, and neither too far forward to risk his communications nor too far back to support his Boeotian allies. The king pushed on through Siris (Seres) and Abdera to the Hellespont. (Herodotus refutes a story that he took ship from Eion to Asia.) The bridges, *pace Aeschyli*, no longer stretched across the straits, but his fleet put him and his army over to Abydos, whence he regained Sardes. The fleet then went part to Cyme and part to Samos for the winter.

The homeward journey of the haughty invader offered a fine theme for Greek rhetoric, which has embroidered it with every circumstance of horror and ignominy. Possibly some details (*e.g.* the collapse of the ice on the Strymon) may be referred to the retreat of the remnant of the Persian army in the next winter, but even so the exaggeration is patent. The superfluous numbers attributed to Xerxes' host had to be disposed of somehow. Three facts in particular discount the accounts of panic and starvation. First, Xerxes, if we may believe Herodotus, spent 45 days on the march to the Hellespont, no record speed, even if reckoned from Attica. Second, Artabazus accompanied him, we are told, to the Hellespont, at all events to Thrace, with 60,000 men, and then returned to Chalcidice. He seems to have had no difficulty in maintaining his troops during the winter; probably a supply service had been organized by land or sea. Third, the force in Ionia next year is still computed at six myriads. It appears clear that of the three army corps one was left with Mardonius in Thessaly, a second was retained under Artabazus in Thrace and Macedonia, and the third crossed with Xerxes into Asia.

There was work for Artabazus and his command. The Potidaeates and the inhabitants of Pallene rose in rebellion in the
king's rear, and the Bottiaeans of Olynthus were implicated in
the revolt. Artabazus besieged and took Olynthus, put the
Bottiaeans to death, and handed over their city to their neighbours, the Chalcidians. He laid siege to Potidaea for three months,
but failed to capture it in spite of treachery within the city. His
final attempt to circumvent the (north?) wall through the sea on
occasion of a very low ebb tide proved disastrous, for the attacking
column was caught by the returning flood and perished. The
revolt was near enough to the line of the Persian communications
to be dangerous, but it was still more serious as a token of what
the Greek victory at Salamis might elsewhere provoke.

Diary of operations at Thermopylae and Artemisium.

To face p. 316

Days from start from Therma	12th	13th	14th	15th	16th	17th	18th
Xerxes' army	Enters Malis and camps over against Trachis	Inactive	Inactive	Inactive	First battle at Thermopylae	Second battle at Thermopylae	Last battle at Thermopylae
The 'Cilician' fleet (the '200' ships)	Sails from Scione at daybreak, and passes outside Sciathus in the afternoon	Caught by the storm and wrecked on the east coast of Euboea	Survivors make for the rendezvous at the Hollows	Survivors rally at the Hollows	Annihilated by the 53 Attic ships	—	—
The 53 Attic ships	Probably at Chalcis since at least a fortnight	At Chalcis	At Chalcis receive news of the wreck of the Cilician fleet	Sail for the Hollows	Capture and destroy (30?) 'Cilician' ships at the Hollows. Start back at nightfall for Artemisium	Arrive at Artemisium in the evening	—
Sandoces' squadron	Detached from the Cilician fleet off Sciathus. Marks reef. Retires round Cape Sepias	Caught by the storm at anchor on the Magnesian coast	Engaged in salvage operations	Salvage	Rounds Cape Sepias (before noon) and falls into the Greek fleet	—	—
The main Persian fleet	Awaits Phoenician fleet from Therma, and sails late in the day from Pallene	Reaches Aphetae (about sunrise), but rear divisions (mostly supply ships) are caught by the storm and driven on the Magnesian coast	Survivors of rear divisions join at Aphetae in the afternoon	Numbering	First battle at Artemisium (late afternoon)	—	Last battle at Artemisium, after noon

CHAPTER X

THE DELIVERANCE OF GREECE

I. MARDONIUS AND THE ALLIES

MARDONIUS had undertaken a difficult task. It is true that he retained the best of Xerxes' troops, and by calling up Artabazus' corps and the king's Greek allies could muster a force larger than the enemy's. We have argued that his own command was one army corps, 60,000 men (p. 272 *sq.* and p. 315). Herodotus gives him 300,000 (one-sixth of the total ascribed to Xerxes), or in detail five national divisions and cavalry. It may be doubted whether two divisions were Persian, for the Immortals would surely have escorted the king with their commander Hydarnes, but, on the other hand, the Bactrians and Sacae may have formed one, as at Doriscus. We may suppose that each division was a myriad and the whole cavalry a myriad. The small drafts incorporated from other nations may have replaced losses in the ranks. Artabazus can bring from Potidaea 40,000 out of his original 60,000 men (whom Herodotus reckons in Mardonius' 300,000). The medizing Greeks are estimated by Herodotus at 50,000, but cannot reasonably be put at more than 20,000. Thus Mardonius might concentrate a total force of 120,000 men to complete the conquest of Greece. But the wall at the Isthmus defended by a Peloponnesian army had in the former campaign deterred Xerxes himself with his 200,000, and Herodotus insists that it was still being strengthened. This impregnable position could not be turned by land, and the Persians no longer commanded the sea.

The Thebans therefore and subsequently Artabazus, unless the advice attributed to him on the Asopus be not indeed his criticism *post eventum*, recommended patience and bribery to make a breach in the Greek defence. But Mardonius had other ideas. If he could induce the Athenians to come over with their navy to his side, no wall could keep him out of the Peloponnese. The political situation at Athens seemed favourable to the attempt. Themistocles had, presumably at the beginning of the new year (on the old Attic calendar 5th December 480 B.C.), handed over the direction of military affairs to his former opponents, Aristides and Xanthippus. Their action in the past, their political traditions and connections, might suggest that they would prefer a reconciliation with Persia to the alliance with Sparta. How else could Athens in her present plight reassert her independence and preserve her democratic constitution? At all events the Agrarians, Aristides' own party, had a growing grievance against their Peloponnesian allies, and it is clear from Herodotus and Plutarch that a section of the Athenians was ready to entertain proposals for a change of policy. It was not without good hope of success that Mardonius in the spring or early summer of 479 B.C. dispatched Alexander of Macedon, a *persona grata* to the Athenians, to negotiate. Alexander on behalf of Mardonius and in the name of Xerxes offered to them remission of all penalties for their offences against the king, restitution of their territory, as much more land as they might ask, autonomy, restoration of their burnt temples, and alliance with Persia on free and equal terms. The story of the Spartan counter-embassy and the replies of the Athenians, rejecting with a *beau geste* the Persian proposal and the Peloponnesian charity, may be suspected of dramatic and rhetorical embellishment. But the Spartans may well have been alarmed and have sought to allay Athenian impatience by assurances that they and their allies would provide (or continue to provide) for the refugees from Attica during the war. One point may be noted which here emerges. Herodotus conceives that the Athenians returned to Attica after the battle of Salamis and on the advice of Themistocles set to work at tilling their farms and rebuilding their city. That notion is incredible. So long as Mardonius commanded the mainland down to the Isthmus, no sane Athenian would have sown a crop or repaired his house. The Persian offer, to give back their land to the Athenians, proves that they had not reoccupied it. The Spartans condole with them on the loss of two harvests. Herodotus does, to be sure, bring Alexander to Athens, but he afterwards implies that he had to cross the straits to Salamis[1].

The Athenians then in spite of all temptations rejected the handsome terms conveyed by Alexander; but at the same time they claimed of their allies a prompt advance to deliver their country which lay defenceless at the mercy of the invaders. Their refusal of the Persian offer must be pronounced to have been not only patriotic but also prudent. Whatever immediate advantages they might have gained by accepting it, their independence under the protection of Persia would have been hollow and short-lived.

[1] IX, 4, διεπόρθμευσε.

The final argument of the Spartans may have been more convincingly developed than appears from the bald aphorism to which Herodotus has reduced it. Long views however were not likely to appeal to distressed refugees impatient to get home. The promise of maintenance for their families was more pertinent to the occasion, but did not go far enough. The Athenian demand for an immediate offensive was natural and urgent. It could not without peril be long ignored.

Mardonius, disappointed in his first plan, seems to have tried a second of which there are fragmentary and dislocated indications in Herodotus. Persia had friends, or at least Sparta had enemies, within the Peloponnese. Mardonius could reckon on the Argives; and to judge from their subsequent behaviour the Mantineans and the Eleans might have joined him on a favourable opportunity (p. 340). He concerted a scheme whereby he should suddenly appear at the Isthmus and carry its wall by a *coup de main*, while the Argives detained the Spartans at home or interrupted them on their way to defend it. So he abruptly broke up his camp in Thessaly and pressed southwards in hot haste, picking up his Greek auxiliaries as he went. It was surely before he crossed Cithaeron, and not at Athens as Herodotus says, that a courier from Argos met him with the message that 'the youth has marched out from Lacedaemon and the Argives cannot stop it; take your measures accordingly.' We may understand by 'the youth' the first five years of the Spartan levy and identify it with the vanguard of 1000 Lacedaemonians who (afterwards, according to Herodotus) pushed forward to Megara in advance of the main army. They must have reached the Isthmus in time to be ready to repel, with the allied troops there stationed and busy on the wall or within call, any possible attack by Mardonius. Similarly one may suspect that the signal sent by Mardonius to Xerxes by beacons through the (north) Aegean islands[1] is to be put earlier in the story and means that he was calling for the Persian fleet from Samos. The Argives could hardly have been expected to act alone, and Mardonius, calculating that his approach would keep the Athenian fleet at Salamis and unaware of the demoralization of the Persian navy, may reasonably have reckoned that the 300 ships at Samos could get across to Argolis in spite of Leotychidas and his attenuated squadron. The Argives however were not supported and made no attempt to arrest the Spartan march. Mardonius had to devise a fresh plan of operations.

---

[1] Herodotus IX, 3.

His third idea was to use the Athenians as a lever to prise the Peloponnesians out from their stronghold. Alexander's report must have told him of the rising indignation of the Athenians at the delay in rescuing their land, and of the apprehensions of the Spartans lest they should medize. By fomenting these feelings he might bring the Peloponnesian army out into the open. So far there had been no hint of its taking the offensive, and the main Spartan force had not stirred from Laconia. Accordingly on receipt of the Argive message Mardonius changed his course and marched into Attica. Probably he left the bulk of his army behind to prepare his fortified camp on the Asopus, but he took with him his cavalry, which was perhaps all he had yet in Boeotia. He reoccupied Athens, Herodotus notes, in the tenth month after Xerxes, that is to say, in June 479 B.C. Thence he sent a Helles- pontine Greek, Morychides, to Salamis to repeat his former offer to the Athenians, not so much, we may surmise, in the hope of converting them as of alarming the Spartans. The Council of the Five Hundred refused to entertain the offer, and with the by- standers promptly lynched one of its members, Cyrsilus (or Lycides, as Herodotus names him), who proposed to submit it to the Assembly of the citizens. The women went beyond official instigation by stoning to death the wife and children of the offender. From a reference by the orator Lycurgus it appears that the executions were retrospectively legalized by a decree, perhaps the same whereby Aristides, according to Plutarch, put a curse upon anyone who opened negotiations with the enemy or renounced the alliance of the Greek states.

Evidently the government had a firm hand on the situation and was resolute to crush any attempt to treat with Persia, but the incident was ominous. Mardonius by reoccupying Attica had raised a dangerous ferment among the Athenians. Something must be done at once to vindicate the government's policy and above all to expedite the long-expected offensive campaign. By the same or another decree proposed by Aristides, either now or while Mardonius was still in Boeotia (Herodotus has inextricably confounded the alternative occasions), Cimon, Xanthippus, and Myronides, men of weight and probably representative of the three parties, were sent to Sparta to urge the necessity of im- mediate action if the loyalty of the Athenians was to be guaranteed. With them went envoys from the Megarians and the Plataeans. The Spartans were busy celebrating (or preparing for) the Hya- cinthia, a festival to which they attached great importance. Its date cannot be precisely determined, but may be inferred from

the latest evidence to have been about midsummer. The Ephors
put off their answer to the embassy from day to day for ten days.
Meanwhile the wall at the Isthmus was completed with battle-
ments. At last, warned by a trusted Tegeate, Chileus, that the
defection of the Athenians would open wide doors into the
Peloponnese, in the night before the day appointed for the final
interview with the envoys they dispatched 5000 Spartiates with
35,000 Helots for the Isthmus. The envoys were prepared to set
off homewards next day. They reproached the Ephors with the
Spartans' betrayal of their allies and announced that the Athenians
would now make terms with the Persian king and join his forces.
They were now told that the Lacedaemonian troops were already
at Orestheum on their march to the front.

Clearly the story of the embassy has been cooked and served
up with Attic salt. Neither the Isthmian wall, defensible ten months
before, nor the neat but very obvious criticism of Chileus, nor
the parody of Spartan methods, now rudely swift now obstinately
slow, are much to the point. Probably the envoys conceded a
postponement until after the Hyacinthia and the Ephors promised
the mobilization within ten days after the festival and kept their
word. We have no sufficient reason to suppose that there was
serious antagonism between the Spartan and Athenian governments. They understood one another's difficulties and maintained
a fundamental accord. The impatience of the Athenian populace
was directed against both. The Athenian government had to bear
the brunt of it and humour it; but its diplomatic representations
at Sparta were probably less truculent than its attitude at Salamis.
The Spartans, however anxious to expel the Persians from Greece
and gratify their ally by an immediate offensive, could not ignore
the need of gathering the year's harvest, if supplies were to be
provided for a big army or the Peloponnesians induced to take
the field; the military advantage of letting Mardonius come as
far south as he would, and perhaps break his head against the
Isthmian wall, instead of seeking him in the north; the risk of
denuding the Peloponnese of its garrison while there was a Persian
fleet in being and the Argives lay in wait to deliver a stab in the
back. This cool strategic argument may have irritated the indigent
and irresponsible refugees at Salamis, but have been better appreciated by the Athenian generals.

The forbearance, however, was not all on the one side. The
Spartan government had a legitimate grievance against Athens,
although it scarcely appears in the mainly Attic tradition. King
Leotychidas had assembled the allied fleet at Aegina at the be-

ginning of the spring, 110 ships. The number, 200 less than at Salamis, plainly indicates that the Athenian navy was absent[1]. Leotychidas, therefore, could not venture across the Aegean in response to a pressing invitation from certain Chians, but was restricted to a defensive station at Delos. The Spartans would have felt more secure if the Athenian contingent had been there, and the situation in Greece would have been greatly relieved by a Mycale four months before it was actually achieved (p. 341). The Athenians, at all events if protected by 20 triremes and 2000 hoplites, would really have been as safe at Salamis as behind the Isthmus, and can hardly have needed their whole fleet to ferry their army across the straits. But they appear to have kept their ships on guard until Mardonius had withdrawn beyond Cithaeron; and the Spartans respected their fears. Some friction there probably was between the two allies; the Spartans would not stake too much on the fleet's defence of the flank of Greece, nor the Athenians on a Spartan victory over Mardonius. But their differences were not beyond compromise, and we may see in the simultaneous offensive by land and sea after midsummer a plan of campaign agreed upon in advance.

II. PAUSANIAS' ADVANCE BEYOND CITHAERON

Cleombrotus was now dead. His son Pausanias, who had succeeded him as regent for the young king Pleistarchus, was appointed to the command of the Spartan and allied army. Why Euryanax, son of Dorieus, was passed over, is not clear; but Pausanias, for reasons which may be variously conjectured, associated him with himself in the command. The Spartiates and Helots, followed next day by 5000 picked Perioecic hoplites, marched, as Herodotus implies, by way of Orestheum. It is not easy to see why they took this roundabout route to the Isthmus unless to avoid skirting the Argive frontier and passing by Mantinea. But that explanation would be far more appropriately applied to the 1000 'forerunners,' whom we have supposed to have preceded Pausanias two or three weeks before, than to the imposing force which he brought with him. Herodotus has failed to distinguish that advance-guard from the main body and still reckons the Spartiates with Pausanias at 5000. The

---

[1] Herodotus (VIII, 131), to be sure, mentions that Xanthippus was the Athenian admiral, implying that he was present; but Xanthippus was still available as envoy to Sparta about midsummer.

route by Orestheum may have been the former's, not the latter's.

Pausanias and his Lacedaemonians may have arrived at the Isthmus in the first half of July, but several weeks may have elapsed before the allied army was assembled—indeed, if Herodotus be trusted, some contingents joined only on the Asopus. It is there in the Plataean land, when all were gathered, that Herodotus first gives a catalogue and enumeration of the army, in battle order. His list of the states represented closely agrees with the names on the 'serpent column' from Delphi (p. 339), although naturally he arranges them in a different order and omits solely maritime states. Did he derive the names (directly or indirectly) from the Delphian list (or some similar record, such as the inscription on the parallel monument at Olympia of which Pausanias the Periegetes has preserved an imperfect copy), or had he any independent information? The very test which might seem to vindicate his independence has become the strongest evidence against it. He alone includes the Paleans, and he omits the Eleans, who appear in the Delphian and Olympian lists. But the suggestion that both these discrepancies are due to a misreading of the name Ϝαλεῖοι (Eleans) is almost irresistible. More important is the question of the numbers. The inscriptions give none. Had Herodotus any authentic record of them, or are they mere estimates? He puts the 'Paleans' at 200, which might be a plausible figure for the little Cephallenian town, but not for Elis, if we are to substitute Eleans for Paleans. Has he invented a contingent to suit the mistaken name? But this argument is not conclusive. He states in another passage, and there is no reason to doubt it, that the Eleans and the Mantineans came too late for the battle at Plataea. Yet the Eleans, but not the Mantineans, are inscribed at Delphi and Olympia among the states which fought and won the war. The presence of 200 Elean hoplites at the battle of Plataea would best account for the entries on the trophies without invalidating the general statement that the Eleans as a whole were absent. The 400 Thebans at Thermopylae did not exculpate their city at large from the charge of medism, but if Xerxes had been repulsed there, they would have sufficed to enrol her name among the saviours of Hellas. But, again, it may be questioned whether any Potidaeates fought at Plataea, and whether the numbers assigned to several of the contingents are credible in the light of later history. Did Sparta really send 10,000 hoplites, Corinth 5000, Sicyon and Megara 3000 each?—although, to be sure, the future historian may find it hard to accept the figures for the British army in 1916 to 1919[1].

The 35,000 Helots 'trained for war,' seven to each Spartiate, are beyond all parallels; but Herodotus repeats the number several times, and his insistence may indicate that they were a novel and peculiar feature in the campaign. There is no trace of them in the fighting, but possibly the Spartans had organized them as a special Service Corps for the supplies and commissariat of the whole army. If so, it was a remarkable achievement, which no other state could have done, and deserves more explicit recognition; but all the less acceptable is the (confessed) estimate of a light armed man for every hoplite beyond the 5000 Spartiates, a reckoning which holds good in Lacedaemonian and Boeotian armies but certainly not in the Athenian, nor probably in those of other naval and democratic states. Athens had however (at all events in the Peloponnesian war) 1600 archers, and Athenian archers are prominent in the campaign; 800 of them may be implied by the surplus of 800 in Herodotus' calculation of the light troops, and the other 800 be assigned to the fleet in accordance with Plutarch's quota of four to each trireme. To sum up, the numbers given by Herodotus in each category are 38,700 hoplites, 35,000 Helots, 34,500 other light armed men, making a total of 108,200 troops, to whom he adds 1800 Thespians (without heavy armour) to complete the round 11 myriads. None of these figures are above suspicion, and it would be rash to accept them as authentic records; but none are wildly impossible, and even as conjectured estimates, superficial may be and uncritical, they are still Greek and almost contemporary estimates of a Greek force. After all allowances for error and exaggeration we may put the total at about 80,000 men, of whom about two-fifths were hoplites.

The strategic movements which led to the battle of Plataea are a lost chapter of history. Herodotus has little to tell of them and imperfectly understands what he tells. We are left to reconstruct an intelligible account out of very inadequate materials. It may have been early in August when Pausanias marched out from the Isthmus to Eleusis, where Aristides joined him with 8000

[1] On the other side of the account Herodotus puts the Plataeans at only 600, brigaded with the Athenians, but his notice (IX, 64) of the death of their general Aeimnestus in the third Messenian war combined with an allusion in Thucydides (III, 54) indicates that at that date they could muster 900, and the Boeotarch of Plataea ought to imply 1000 hoplites at some time. Were some Plataeans with the Spartans on the right wing? Aeimnestus kills Mardonius and talks with the mortally wounded Spartan Callicrates.

MAP 10

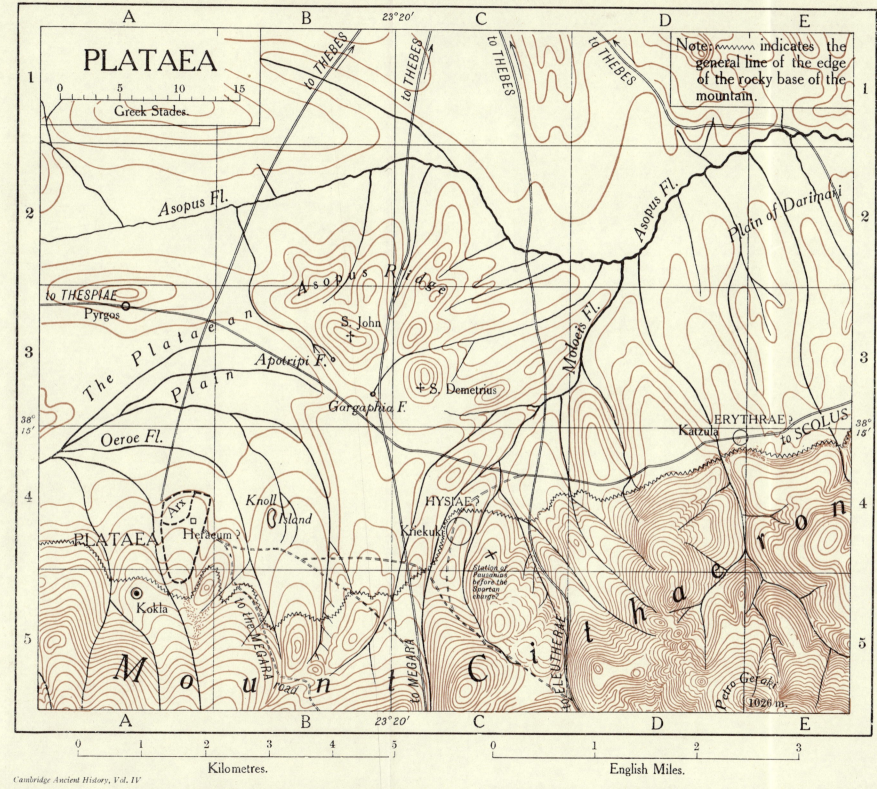

INDEX TO NAMES

Apotripi, F., B 3
Arx, A 4
Asopus Fl., A–E 1, 2
Asopus Ridge, BC 2, 3

Cithaeron, Mt, A–E 5

Darimari, Plain of, DE 2
Demetrius, S., C 3

Erythrae?, D 4

Gargaphia, F., BC 3

Heraeum?, A 4
Hysiae?, C 4

John, S., B 3

Katzula, D 4
Knoll Island, B 4
Kokla, A 5
Kriekuki, C 4

Moloeis Fl., CD 2, 3

Oeroe Fl., AB 4, 5

Pausanias, Station of, C 4
Petro Geraki, DE 5
Plataea, A 4
Plataean Plain, The, AB 3
Pyrgos, A 3

Based upon Captain Tribert's survey (1834). A more modern and detailed survey of part of this area will be found in G. B. Grundy's *The Topography of the Battle of Plataea* and *The Great Persian Wars*. Some details have been added from the former book by permission of the Royal Geographical Society.

To face p. 325

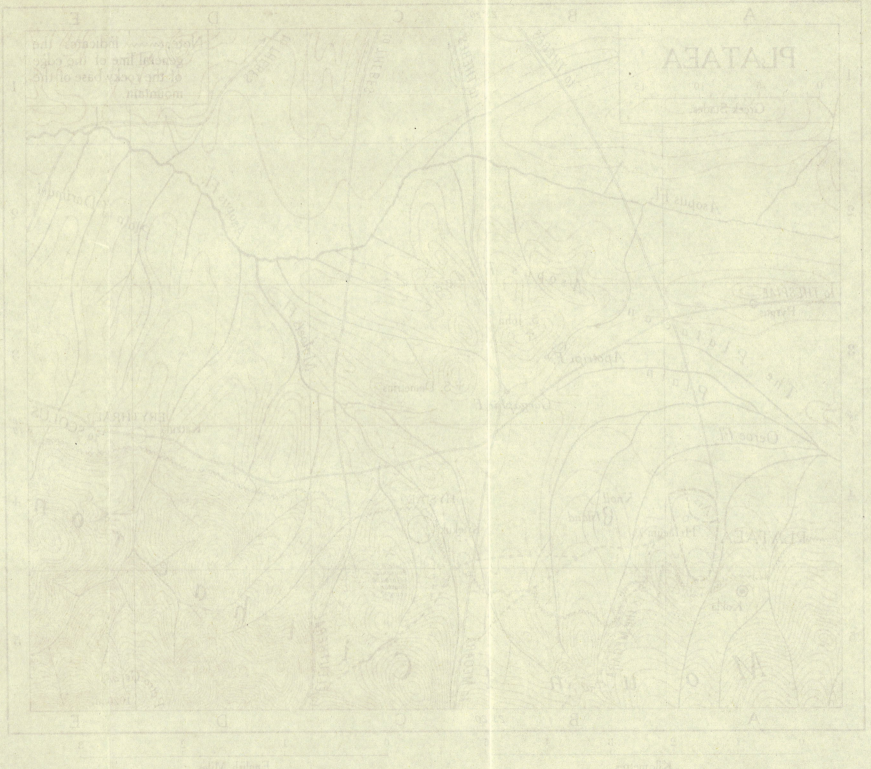

Athenian hoplites. Mardonius, according to Herodotus, had burnt Athens and begun to evacuate Attica on receipt of the Argive message before Pausanias had reached the Isthmus, but, hearing that 1000 Lacedaemonians had pushed on to Megara in advance of the rest, he turned back in order to catch them and overran the Megarid with his cavalry. He seems, however, to have returned to the plain of Athens, whence on arrival of a third message, that the Greeks were assembled at the Isthmus, he retired to Theban territory by way of Decelea, Sphendale, and Tanagra. It is unlikely that he withdrew from Athens twice, and we have already connected the Argive message with the march of the 1000 Lacedaemonians from Sparta before midsummer. The raid into the Megarid is best explained if referred back to that date, when Mardonius was not quitting but entering Attica. Presumably the 1000 Lacedaemonians pressed forward to save Megara and succeeded. The Persian horsemen were useless against a walled city and could only ravage the country. Mardonius did not burn and evacuate Athens before the Greek army was in Attica. His route to Boeotia round the eastern end of Parnes indicates that the roads to Cithaeron were already in the enemy's hands and even the road to Thebes by Phyle was cut or threatened, no doubt in the neighbourhood of Panactum. With his nimble cavalry he could afford to take risks in face of an adversary on foot, and probably he wished to draw the Greeks away from the Isthmus by offering a chance of intercepting him from his main force and base. Herodotus, believing that he had his whole army with him, ascribes to him some superfluous reasons for quitting Attica, which may reproduce Greek reflections on the campaign.

From Tanagra Mardonius turned to Scolus, where he was in Theban territory. Although now on friendly soil, he set about felling the trees of his allies in order to build a 'wooden wall' which should serve as a protection to his camp beside the Asopus and, in case of defeat, a refuge for his army. The one clear fact about this fortification is that Herodotus has no clear ideas about it. He does not expressly say where it was, but we might naturally infer that it was at or near Scolus, and the inference is supported by Xenophon's mention of a stockade (*Hellen.* v, 4, 49) just there, one of the palisades erected by the Thebans more than a century later to keep Agesilaus out of their country. Scolus lay[1] at the

---

[1] The 40 stades of Pausanias, IX, 4, 3, must be reckoned from the passage of the Asopus, not on the direct Plataea-Thebes road, but (as the mention of Gargaphia and the Electran gate suggests) on the Megara-Thebes road or the Eleusis-Thebes road.

foot of Cithaeron near the point where the road from Phyle issues
from the hills and crosses the Asopus. The work might be on
either or both of the banks of the river and still be near Scolus,
but (1) it is afterwards said to have been constructed 'in the
portion of Thebes,' which favours the left (north) bank, and
(2) the whole narrative of the campaign conveys the impression
that at all events the camp was on that bank. When, therefore,
Herodotus here hastens to explain that the camp stretched from
Erythrae past Hysiae into the territory of Plataea, all towns on
the right of the river, we must suppose that he has not clearly
distinguished between the army and its camp—the army was
posted on the south side of the river, in front of the camp, the
camp lay behind on the north side. But the camp must have been
at least coextensive with the position across the river. The
'wooden wall' on the contrary had, according to Herodotus, a
frontage of only 10 stades, and seems to have stood near Scolus,
where it could cover nothing but one flank of the long lines, which
began at Erythrae. How could it (put it where you please) be
a 'bulwark' or 'fence' to the camp and render it too a refuge?
Has Herodotus misconceived its character? He imagines it to
have been an elaborate square fortress provided with towers. Has
he perhaps confused it, as a comparison of his descriptions of the
two works suggests, with the Persian stronghold at Mycale (see
p. 342). Was the wooden wall of Mardonius after all a stockade,
or rather a series of four stockades, like the Theban palisades
against Agesilaus, guarding the four roads to Thebes from the
south, and has Herodotus pictured to himself the four frontages
on the river bank as a single quadrilateral fort? This answer to
the puzzle appears to be the most satisfactory, and is not without
precedent, for Plutarch having at first accepted from Herodotus
the square single fort is constrained at last to resolve it into a
number of distinct fortifications.

Hardly less difficult, owing to its brevity, is Herodotus'
account of the advance of the Greeks into Boeotia. He notes only
that they moved forward from Eleusis and, when they arrived at
Erythrae[1] and observed the enemy encamped on the Asopus,
took up a position facing him on the base of Cithaeron. It appears
further, that this position was unassailable by cavalry except in
one limited part, where the Megarians were stationed. Two main
roads crossed Cithaeron—(1) the Great North road from the

[1] The Persian position began from Erythrae. But probably neither army
held the town itself, which would lie between them. The term Erythrae
can include its territory.

Isthmus and Megara by the Vilia pass[1]; it threw off two branches to Plataea, the one a rough track starting from a point south of the crest and passing through another pass[2] about a mile west of the Vilia pass, the other diverging from the road near the northern end of the Vilia pass; but neither of these branches is of much account in the operations; (2) the road from Eleusis by Eleutherae and the pass commonly but erroneously called the 'Dryoscephalae' pass. On or hard by this latter road stood Hysiae, at or near the modern Kriekuki, perhaps three-quarters of a mile to the east of that village, but certainly not to the west of it, for the upper waters of the Oeroe must be assigned to Plataea. Erythrae was east of Hysiae on the road from Thespiae and Plataea to Scolus. Pausanias (the Periegetes) mentions it with Hysiae as lying 'a little' off his direct route from Eleutherae to Plataea, which no doubt branched from the Eleusis-Thebes road at a point above Hysiae. Could Erythrae be placed between Hysiae and the high shoulder of Cithaeron which rises a mile and a half east of Kriekuki, we might assume that the Greeks crossed the ridge by their most obvious road, through the Eleutherae pass. But that site for Erythrae is impossible for two reasons: because water, which is abundant there, was, according to Herodotus, scanty at Erythrae; and because Hysiae, which furnished a Boeotarch (implying 1000 hoplites and 100 horse), demands a big territory. We are driven therefore to put Erythrae farther east, probably at Katzula about midway between Hysiae and Scolus, and to suppose that Pausanias, who seems not to have visited it, accommodated his 'little' distance to the propinquity of Hysiae.

Neither, then, the Eleusis-Thebes road nor still less the Megara-Thebes road (which passed to the west of Hysiae) led to Erythrae, and it is inconceivable that the regent Pausanias, having once reached Hysiae, abandoned it for a position where water was scarce and supplies precarious. But a glance at the strategic situation suggests another route to Erythrae. Mardonius was in Attica tempting the Greeks eastwards. It is fairly obvious that in order to safeguard his camp during his absence, and to enable him to fall upon their western wing and cut them off from the Isthmus should they be drawn so far to their right as to endanger their left, he must have thrown forward his own right wing over the Asopus and occupied the Vilia and Eleutherae passes. Pau-

[1] Grundy's 'Pass 2' in *Topography of the battle of Plataea* (map) or 'Plataea-Athens Pass' in *The Great Persian War* (map).

[2] Grundy's 'Pass 3' or 'Plataea-Megara Pass' (*ibid.*).

sanias, we may suppose, had no mind to force those passes by a frontal attack, but having now extended his right to the gap between Cithaeron and Parnes, where Mardonius might have escaped into Boeotia by the Phyle road, he may naturally have conceived the idea of advancing through the gap and intercepting him between Tanagra and Scolus, and at the same time turning the Persian left, perhaps weakened by reinforcement of the right. He would, of course, leave his left wing and centre to hold the southern exits of the western passes, and to advance through them if, as might be expected, the enemy fell back in consequence of the threat to his left flank. Some such hypothesis would explain the strategy. The arrival of Mardonius, and the stockade at Scolus, frustrated the full success of the movement. Pausanias, not venturing on to the plain in face of the cavalry, turned westward along the skirts of the mountain to Erythrae, where he formed his troops (the Lacedaemonians and Tegeates) fronting the enemy. He thus did at least compel Mardonius to withdraw his forces from the passes to the north bank of the Asopus. It was a result achieved by manœuvre without fighting, and so left no clear trace in the tradition. The theory that Mardonius invited the Greeks across Cithaeron to a battle on ground of his own choice is inconsistent with his stand on the Asopus. His proper ground would have been nearer Thebes with the open plain in front of him. He is on the defensive, probably awaiting his supports from Thrace, and although he will strike if he finds an opportunity, he contests each successive position, the line of Cithaeron as well as of the river. Pausanias, on the other hand, presses forward for a decisive battle before Artabazus should arrive (p. 338).

It was probably in order to cover the withdrawal of his right wing by the Megara-Thebes road that Mardonius launched his cavalry led by Masistius against the Greeks who were following his retreating troops from the passes. Masistius arrested them on the edge of the rocky slope of the mountain, where they no doubt deployed to the right so as to get into touch and line with Pausanias and his division. We may assume that the Athenians and Plataeans were the centre and advanced by the Eleutherae road, while the Megarians headed the left column debouching from the Vilia pass down the Megara road. The rocky mantle of the mountain swings sharply southwards along the western border of the village of Kriekuki admitting a wide bay of cultivated land over which the Megara-Thebes road runs. The Megarians may have pushed on down the road into this re-entrant angle in order to keep their alignment with their comrades on the right. Accordingly, they found themselves in the one weak spot in the Greek line and had to bear the full brunt of the cavalry's attack. Hard pressed, they dispatched an urgent message to Pausanias begging to be relieved. The Athenians alone, in the Attic story retailed by Herodotus, volunteered for the duty. As they alone had a regular corps of archers, they would in any case have been the first to be deputed. Aristides at once sent forward a company of 300 select hoplites under Olympiodorus, son of Lampon, along with the bowmen, and followed with his entire division. The Athenians were to occupy the left flank of the army; the left wing, including the Megarians, were to close to the right and become the centre. The Persian cavalry continuing its attacks charged by squadrons (thousands?), until Masistius, thrown by his horse which was wounded by an arrow, was overwhelmed, and was killed by a stab in the eye. His men by a combined assault essayed to recover his corpse, but were repulsed by the main body of the Athenians arriving at the critical moment. The Persians then abandoned the attempt, and the dead Masistius was placed on a cart and paraded along the Greek line, on the Erythrae road, no doubt, which ran just in front of the position. His corselet of gilt scale armour afterwards hung in the temple of Athena Polias on the Athenian Acropolis.

III. THE GREEK REBUFF AT THE ASOPUS

The repulse of the dreaded cavalry encouraged Pausanias to advance beyond the rocky base of Cithaeron into the Plataean land. Herodotus says that the reason was to get a more convenient site for the camp and in particular a better supply of water than at Erythrae. He describes the new position as beyond Hysiae, and near the spring Gargaphia and the precinct of the hero Androcrates, and extending over hills of no great height and flat ground. The hills can be no other than the ridges which rise between the foot of Cithaeron and the Asopus. Separated from the mountain by a trough of lower ground they stretch north-westwards from the rivulet[1] which may with some confidence be named the Moloeis (p. 333) to within a short distance of the Asopus, and culminate near their south-western verge in three summits, on two of which, just one mile apart, stand churches, on the north-western the church of St John, on the south-eastern the church of St Demetrius. The direct road from Plataea to

---

[1] Stream A. 6 on Grundy's map, *op. cit.*

Thebes runs half a mile west of the hills over the level Plataean plain to the Asopus. This plain must be the flat ground on to which the Greek lines extended. The spring Gargaphia is best identified with the fount half a mile west of the church of St Demetrius, near the probable intersection of the Megara-Thebes and Thespiae-Erythrae roads. Of the Androcrateum nothing certain can be said except that it was a well-known landmark on the right of the direct road from Plataea to Thebes. It may have stood at the church of St John or near the Apotripi spring below that church.

Details may be obscure, but the general lie of the Greek position is clear. If all the hoplites were deployed eight deep, their front must have been at least three miles long. If its right flank be placed at the church of St Demetrius, its left falls west of the direct Plataea-Thebes road and quite near to the Asopus. Herodotus is primarily concerned with the movement of the right wing. It is Pausanias and his division who were stationed at Erythrae and felt the lack of water there; it is they in particular who descended from the higher slopes of the mountain and marched past Hysiae; it is they, as afterwards appears, who are posted at the spring Gargaphia. The prominence of Gargaphia in the story and its use as a fixed point whence measurements are reckoned show that Herodotus derives information from the right wing. Probably 'the reinforcements arriving' are no other than the centre and left wing coming on to the scene through the passes. But in later references, derived no doubt from Attic sources, Herodotus does recognize, although confusedly, the wide extent of the position. The Greeks encamped 'on the Asopus'; they drew water from it; the nearer to the river were their respective stations, the farther were they from Gargaphia. When he states that 'the island' (p. 333) was ten stades from the Asopus and from Gargaphia, the bewildered historian attempts to apply a single measurement to the standpoints of two informants at different distances, one in each wing.

This broader view of the position shows that the aim of the movement was not merely to secure the supply of water and food but also to execute on the enemy's right flank the offensive which had been foiled on his left. It was no well-considered station to be occupied for an indefinite period, but a temporary foothold whence to launch an attack. The left wing in particular must have been intended to take instant action. The general idea appears to have been that, while the right wing and centre occupied the enemy opposite, the left wing should force the passage of the

Asopus (in August probably almost dry) and turning sharply to the east should sweep down the left bank crumpling up the hostile line already engaged in front. Perhaps it was hoped that the Greek allies of Mardonius on his right would offer only half-hearted resistance—the story of a nocturnal visit from Alexander of Macedon to the Athenian camp suggests collusion, and in the subsequent battle only the Boeotians put up a fight. There was, however, the cavalry to be reckoned with; and the success of the Athenians against Masistius marked them out for the post of honour and danger on the left wing rather than the Tegeates, who are said to have claimed it[1]. If, as surmised above, a stockade on the river bank barred the direct road from Plataea to Thebes, the Athenians' reputation in siege-warfare may also have recommended them. How the Greek army moved to its new position is not recorded; but we may conjecture that the Athenians stood fast at the Megara-Thebes road while first the right wing and then the centre marched behind them along the base of Cithaeron to the left flank, the Athenians next passing behind them resumed their place on the left, and finally all advanced together in line. This hypothesis would suit the catalogue of the army in battle array here inserted by Herodotus and account for the strange story, which he gives a little later, of the double exchange of wings between the Lacedaemonians and the Athenians.

Mardonius on the opposite bank conformed his movements to those of the Greeks and followed them up the river. Yet for eight days, as Herodotus appears to mean, the two armies confronted one another without an engagement or any action whatsoever. No reason is assigned for their inaction except that the omens on both sides forbade them to cross the Asopus. Why should Pausanias, if he intended no more, have abandoned a strong for an untenable position? Why should Mardonius, who is represented as eager for the fray in spite of all omens, have refused battle? If, as is more likely, he had no wish to move out from his fortifications for a general attack, why did he not use his cavalry at once, instead of a week later, to cut the enemy's communications? Did he really need to be prompted by a Theban, Timagenidas? The delay is so improbable that it is better to suppose that the eight days ought to be counted from the arrival of Pausanias north of Cithaeron. We may even go

---

[1] In Herodotus the dispute lapses into an academic discussion of the usual logographic type. Perhaps both peoples afterwards claimed (rightly enough) to have held the left wing in the battle, and their rival pretensions may have given rise to a general comparison of their achievements in history.

further and conjecture that the next two days (the 9th and 10th of Herodotus' diary) are to be identified with the following two (the 11th and 12th) which immediately preceded the battle. Herodotus, who has already invoked the soothsayers with their past careers to provide an interlude between the scenes of his drama, here seems to call up the whole chorus of his supernumerary reserves to beguile an interval in the action. In Plutarch's manner he throws into a void in his story a miscellaneous stock of unemployed anecdotes. We are treated to (1) a conference on the plan of operations between the headstrong Mardonius and the prudent Artabazus, (2) an argument, incongruous with Herodotus' account of the Persian attempt on Delphi, drawn by Mardonius from an oracle in order to silence the misgivings of his subordinates, (3) Alexander's nocturnal visit to the Athenian generals, warning them of an impending attack, (4) the exchange of the Greek wings, already anticipated above, (5) a challenge from Mardonius to the Spartans inviting them to a duel with the Persians.

These stories serve a double purpose; they fill a gap not only in time but also in the record of the Greek operations. Something has dropped out, or his informants have kept it from Herodotus. The allied forces, when they emerge again into view, are no longer in the same position as that to which they had advanced from the base of Cithaeron. The Athenians are no longer in the plain, but on a hill whence they have to descend into the plain on their way to their next intended station at 'the island'; the contingents of the centre on the contrary are presumably on the flat ground, for they have borne the brunt of the attacks of the enemy's cavalry and been harassed to the verge of demoralization; the Lacedaemonians on the right wing are so far west that they have relaxed their hold not only on the Eleutherae road, but also on the much more vitally important Megara road and Gargaphia. The simplest explanation of this situation is that the Greek offensive had failed; the Athenians, who led it, either did not press their attack with resolution or were repulsed, and were driven off the Plataean plain; they took refuge from the enemy's cavalry on higher ground, evidently at the western edge of the plain; Pausanias, in order to fill the gap caused in his line, shifted his centre down into the plain and his right wing westwards into the place of the centre. We may suppose that the Greeks had moved forward from the foot of Cithaeron on the evening of the seventh day, that the Athenian failure was on the eighth, and that the Theban Timagenidas at once reported the breach in the

Greek line to Mardonius, who on the night of the eighth day, as
Herodotus records, sent his cavalry to the passes which issue from
Cithaeron towards Plataea. The cavalry, advancing no doubt
through the gap, captured a train of 500 pack animals bringing
provisions from the Peloponnese, as it was emerging on to the
plain. Pausanias of course hastened to close the breach next
morning, but he thereby lost his hold on the Megara-Thebes
road and his main source of water, the spring Gargaphia, which
the Persian horsemen choked on the following, if not the same,
day. They now raided freely round his right flank and cut off
all supplies through the passes.

On the 10th (Herodotus' 12th) day the situation of the Greek
army had become critical. It was short of water and food, it was
harassed by constant attacks from an enemy who could not be
brought to close quarters, the centre in particular was tried
beyond endurance. The advanced station was clearly no longer
tenable, and a council of war decided to retreat during the night
to a position at the base of Cithaeron better protected against
cavalry, well provided with water, and covering the passes. This
position is described as 'the island,' a strip of land between two
of the head streams of the river Oeroe. The exact spot is no doubt
rightly recognized[1] in a prominent knoll about a mile east of the
citadel (or north-west corner) of Plataea. But evidently the island,
which Herodotus himself puts at only three stades broad, could
not be more than a small fraction of the new line. The full extent
of the position must be gathered from the movements of the
army. In the second watch of the night the centre began to retire,
and halted in front of the Heraeum, which stood in front of the city
(acropolis) of Plataea. The front of the temple is, of course, the east,
and the front of the city is naturally also the east, the direction
from which most travellers, especially Athenians, would approach
Plataea. The site of the large building probably to be identified
with the Heraeum supports this interpretation, and agrees approximately with Herodotus' estimate of 20 stades from Gargaphia. The centre therefore appears to have taken up its post
between the island and the no doubt ruined but still defensible
citadel of Plataea, which covered its left flank. The right wing,
the Lacedaemonians and Tegeates, waited until the peep of dawn
and then marched 10 stades, reckoned evidently from Gargaphia,
to a station near the river Moloeis and a place named Argiopius,
where was a temple of Demeter Eleusinia. Argiopius gives us no
clue, but the Kriekuki brook, much the largest and most copious

---

[1] Grundy, *op. cit.* pp. 480 *sqq.*

hereabouts of the affluents of the Asopus, may plausibly claim to have been the Moloeis. Plutarch, a good witness, gives some further evidence on the site of the temple. He describes it as near Hysiae, under Cithaeron, at the fringe of the rocky base of the mountain, which rendered the ground impracticable for cavalry. Two inscriptions assigned to the early part of the fifth century B.C. and referring to the worship of Demeter have been discovered close under the rocky slope a few yards west of the Eleutherae road. They may have been carried, but prove the neighbourhood of a temple of the goddess. If the temple be put at the north end of the village of Kriekuki, it would be a little over 10 stades from Gargaphia, a couple of hundred yards from the conjectured Moloeis, and just where Plutarch indicates. The right wing accordingly appears to have been drawn up along the edge of the base of the mountain, between the Megara-Thebes road and the Eleutherae road, and no doubt commanding both.

The account given by Herodotus of these movements is obviously influenced by Attic sources and reflects Athenian recriminations against the Allies. The Athenians presumably were blamed for the failure of the advance to the Asopus and its disastrous consequences, which made the retreat necessary, and for the miscarriage of the plan of withdrawal, which nearly involved the whole army in an overwhelming catastrophe. They retort by obscuring their own share in the operations and throwing the blame back upon their confederates. They represent the centre as having fled in panic to a point twice as far from Gargaphia as the island, and the Lacedaemonians as having been delayed by the contumacious obstinacy of a subordinate officer and surprised by the enemy on their march. Both, we are given to understand, were making for the island, but neither got there. Inconsistently enough, the divergent course taken by the right wing is explained by anxiety to avoid the plain, where the cavalry could attack it, or by a project to rescue the convoys blocked up in the passes— no doubt a main motive for the retirement, but easily attainable without dividing the army.

These Athenian misrepresentations cannot be allowed. It is pretty clear that the centre arrived in good order at its proper destination, and that the right wing occupied its intended station before the enemy attacked it. Both positions were well selected and formed parts of a single strategic design. Only the Athenians (with the Plataeans) failed to reach their appointed place. It was they alone who were directed to the island, and their absence there left a yawning gap in the Greek line. By their own account they

waited 'at the post assigned to them' for the Lacedaemonians to
move, 'knowing that their words could not be trusted to reveal
their intentions.' This bold diversion merely seeks to distract
attention from their own default. Were they unwilling to re-
linquish the coveted left wing to the centre? or to exchange the
comparative security of a station opposed to the compliant Greek
troops of the enemy for the risks of another less remote from
the redoubtable Persian cavalry? or have they in their anxiety
to incriminate their allies overreached themselves, and by imputing
to the centre a precipitate flight spoilt their own best plea, that
the slow procession of the centre across their path prevented their
reaching the island? They pretend to have waited for the Lacedaemonians to move, but it may be surmised that really the Lacedaemonians waited for them.

The Athenian story of the obstinacy of Amompharetus is suspicious, and the facts suggest a different and simpler explanation.
Amompharetus, the story says, the commander of the Pitanate
battalion, which according to Thucydides never existed, had not
been present at the council when the retreat was settled, and now
refused to disgrace Sparta by 'running away from the foreigners.'
In vain Pausanias and Euryanax argued with him all night. A nameless Athenian horseman, sent to headquarters for news and instructions, arrived to witness (in the dark? three days after the new
moon) Amompharetus plant a boulder at his general's feet and
tell him that this was his vote for staying[1]. Pausanias then turning
to the messenger besought the Athenians to close up to the right
wing and conform to its movements. At dawn of day he left
Amompharetus and his Pitanates behind; but, hoping that they
would follow and unwilling to abandon them beyond all rescue,
he halted his troops near the Moloeis and the temple of Demeter.
The Pitanates presently rejoined, retiring slowly with the Persian
cavalry on their heels. Cleared of Athenian misconstruction and
jugglery, the narrative indicates that Pausanias deferred his start
in order to cover the flank of the Athenian march to the island,
and that Amompharetus was detailed to hold the Megara road
to the last moment at the valley between Gargaphia and the church
of St. Demetrius—a duty which he admirably performed.

It has become clear that the general position designed for the

---

[1] It is a tempting conjecture that the monument shown to Pausanias the
Periegetes on the right of his road into Plataea as the tomb of Mardonius
represented a warrior uplifting a rock in front of an august person, and was
alternatively interpreted as Aeimnestus braining Mardonius, who was killed
according to Plutarch by a stone, or Amompharetus recording his vote.

Greek army extended from the walls of Plataea, which covered the west flank, to the high bastions of Cithaeron, which covered the east flank. This position was practically the same as that which the army had occupied on the eve of its advance towards the Asopus. It is further evident that the former centre, which was now to be the left wing, and the Lacedaemonians and Tegeates, who were still to be the right wing, duly took up their appointed stations, but the Athenians, who ought to have formed the new centre, never reached their post at the island. Sunrise found the Athenians still trailing across the Plataean plain and the army split up into three widely separate divisions. Mardonius naturally seized so obvious an opportunity. He crossed the Asopus and attacked.

IV. PLATAEA

The first impact came from the Persian cavalry, who had resumed at daybreak their incursions on the Greek lines. Finding the forward position void they pushed on, drove in Amompharetus, and set to harassing the Lacedaemonians and Tegeates at the foot of Cithaeron. The rocky ground, except perhaps at the extremities of the front, precluded cavalry charges, but the troopers were also archers and javelin-men, and always relied more on their 'artillery' than on shock tactics. Pausanias, we are told, dispatched a mounted man to beg the Athenians to come to his aid or at least to send their bowmen. They were, of course, the acknowledged masters in this warfare and had saved the Megarians a few days before on almost the same spot, but this flattering appeal may be received with a grain of scepticism. The Athenians at all events, although they responded with alacrity, never arrived, for they were engaged on their way across the plain by the medizing Greeks, and Pausanias managed to do without them. Mardonius was presumably from the first informed of the situation by the cavalry. He pressed forward with the Persian infantry at the double and was followed by the other Asiatic troops in haste and disorder. He led his whole Barbarian forces against the Greek right wing, leaving his auxiliaries to deal with the Athenians. Herodotus states that he crossed the Asopus in pursuit of the Greeks believing them to be in full flight, but directed his attack upon the Lacedaemonians and Tegeates alone, because he could not see the Athenians in the plain owing to the intervening hills. The point of the remark seems to be that, had he seen the Athenians, he either would have realized that they at all events were not running away or would have deemed them a foe more worthy of single combat. No great stress can in such a context be laid on the mention of the hills, but it confirms the general implication that Mardonius' attack was developed through, and round the eastern end of, the ridges between Cithaeron and the Asopus, that is to say, along the Megara and the Eleutherae roads. The attack on the Athenians naturally followed the direct Thebes-Plataea road over the plain.

The Persian infantry took over from the cavalry the attack on the Lacedaemonians and Tegeates. Planting their wicker shields upright in front of them, they poured arrows on the Greeks. The line of shields presented the aspect of a fence, but afforded no protection against a charge of hoplites and probably had no practical purpose beyond freeing the hands of the archers. The Greek men-at-arms on their side, each crouching behind his shield, opposed to the wicker a hedge of steel, and endured the hail of shafts without movement. Some were shot dead and many wounded, but the omens from the sacrifices remained adverse. Probably the soothsayers kept one eye on Pausanias, and he on the massing enemy. The other Asiatic troops now arriving behind the Persians would block their rear, leaving them no room for their tactics of touch and go, the elastic front which yields and returns, and so would compel them to a combat at close quarters. At last, looking away to Hera's temple, the white façade of which full in the morning sunlight must have shown up sharply against the mud buildings of Plataea, Pausanias lifted his voice and prayed to the goddess 'that we be not disappointed of our hope.' Instantly, as he spoke, the Tegeates sprang up and rushed upon the enemy. The Lacedaemonians, better disciplined, waited for the sanction of the sacrifices, which immediately followed. The Persians dropped their bows and met them with their dirks and javelins at the fence of shields. This frail shelter soon collapsed, but they maintained a stubborn fight by the Demetrium, gripping and trying to snap the hoplites' spears, dashing forward against the Spartans singly or by tens or in little groups to their own destruction. Mardonius, mounted on a white charger and accompanied by his special corps, 1000 strong, rallied his troops now here now there and pressed the foemen hard. But when he fell by the hands of Aeimnestus, and with him the best of his followers, the rest gave in and took to flight, carrying with them their Asiatic auxiliaries. Pausanias had won 'the finest victory ever recorded in Greek history.'

Meanwhile the Athenians were engaged on the plain with the Boeotians, who alone of Mardonius' Hellenic allies showed any appetite for battle. The Greek centre now posted near the Heraeum appears to have been unmolested. The elevated 'Asopus ridge' in front of it diverted the enemy's attacks along the roads on the east and west and protected its position. That it bestirred itself only on news of Pausanias' victory may be rejected as a malicious slander. Probably Pausanias sent an order that it should hasten to the aid of the two wings. Accordingly the larger right brigade turned eastwards by the upper road, over the spurs of Cithaeron, towards the temple of Demeter. Whether it arrived in time to take part in the fighting there, or ever got there at all, is left uncertain in the perfunctory mention of it by Herodotus. The left brigade moved in loose order down on to the plain. There the Theban cavalry under Asopodorus caught and routed it and drove it on to the slope of Cithaeron, leaving 600 men dead on the field. This diversion and the flight of the Asiatics on the other wing may have relieved the pressure on the Athenians and enabled them to beat off the Boeotians, who retired straight for Thebes, having lost 300 of the foremost and noblest of the Thebans. The destination of the other medizing Greeks is not recorded. The Barbarians fled to their 'wooden wall.' The cavalry intervened on both wings to protect the fugitives. Artabazus, Herodotus tells, was marching forward with 40,000 men as though to battle, but filled with misgivings and disapproval of Mardonius' conduct of the campaign and determined to act independently on his own judgment. He had already advanced far on his way when he saw the Persians in full retreat. Immediately he wheeled about and made off with all speed by the quickest route neither for the wooden wall nor for the fortress of Thebes, but for Phocis and the Hellespont.

Where was he when he met the routed Persians? He has figured in Herodotus' story of the Plataean campaign never as an actor but only as the critic and monitor of Mardonius. Has Herodotus perhaps reproduced in dramatic form the subsequent animadversions of Artabazus on the strategy of Mardonius, and his vindication of his own? Did Artabazus ever arrive on the field of Plataea? The very words used, or preserved, by Herodotus suggest that he did not, but was still far in the rear of the fighting line. If so, one might conjecture that he was summoned from Macedonia only when the Peloponnesians were already mustering at the Isthmus.

The Asiatic troops of Mardonius rallied behind their 'wooden wall' and defended it obstinately. The Athenians, who prided themselves on their skill in siege warfare, claimed to have effected

the breach, but it was the Tegeates who entered first and plun-
dered the tent of Mardonius. The brazen manger of his horses
afterwards adorned the temple of Athena Alea at Tegea. The
victorious Greeks fell upon the huddling barbarians and slaughtered them like sheep. Only 3000, it is said, escaped. According
to Herodotus, 91 Spartiates, 16 Tegeates, and 52 Athenians fell
in the battle. Plutarch, who repeats these figures, states on the
authority of Cleidemus that the 52 Athenians were all of the
tribe Aeantis, and gives the total Greek losses at 1360. It is
probable that the numbers are authentic but refer to particular
'units' in the several forces, and that the total is incomplete.
Herodotus is hard to reconcile with Pausanias on the subject of
the graves of the dead, and some of the cenotaphs which he
mentions may not have been so fraudulent as he was told. If
Plutarch may be trusted, the award of the prize of valour was a
compromise. The Athenians disputed the claim of the Spartans,
but both agreed to the Corinthian suggestion that the Plataeans
should have the prize. Herodotus gives his personal verdict for
the Lacedaemonians and among them for Aristodemus, the survivor of Leonidas' 300, whom his fellow-Spartiates rejected
because he had sought death to end his shame. They did however
honour (among others) Amompharetus, an argument against the
story of his insubordination. Of the Athenians Sophanes of
Decelea most distinguished himself. The famous anchor with
which, it was said, he held his ground may have been an offensive
grapnel. Among the offerings made out of the spoils in commemoration of the victory was a gold tripod dedicated to the
Delphian god. It rested on a brazen column formed of three
entwined serpents (not, as Herodotus says, a single serpent with
three heads) which now stands in the Hippodrome at Constantinople engraved with the names of the states which took
part in the war. The allies guaranteed by oath to the Plataeans,
who on their part undertook the tending of the dead, their independence and the security of their land. An altar was erected to
Zeus the Liberator, and a festival, the Eleutheria, ascribed to the
initiative of Aristides, was instituted, which was still celebrated
in the time of Plutarch, although its continuous observance can
hardly be credited.

In his *Life of Aristides* (c. 19) Plutarch puts the battle on the
day on which it was commemorated in his own time, the 4th
of the Attic month Boedromion, which he equates with the 27th
of the Boeotian month Panemus. It is not clear how the dates
are to be reconciled, nor whether he means that they coincided

in 479 B.C., or in the year when he was writing, or in both, or, if they sometimes differed, whether the Attic or the Boeotian date was the day of the commemoration. But in two other passages in his works[1] Plutarch gives the 3rd of Boedromion as the day of the battle, and this may be regarded as the accepted date. It may be assumed to be a 'Metonic' reduction of the original date in the old Attic calendar and may be identified with the 27th of August 479 B.C.

Plataea, like Marathon, was a tactical victory wrung from a strategic failure. Mardonius had frustrated the advance of the Greeks, and rightly used his opportunity of attacking them when they had fallen apart into three isolated divisions. Theoretically he ought to have driven them back over Cithaeron in headlong rout. What saved the day were the steady discipline of the Lacedaemonians and the cool judgment of Pausanias in launching his charge at the precise moment when the Persian infantry could no longer evade it. At close quarters the hoplites' armour and 'the Dorian spear' soon decided the issue.

The Mantineans and at any rate the main force of the Eleans arrived too late for the battle. They professed their regret and offered (or afterwards pretended to have offered) to pursue Artabazus and his corps, a ludicrous proposal which Pausanias of course vetoed. When they got home, they banished their generals. Probably the delay was not involuntary but political and indicates that the party in power was not wholehearted for the cause of Hellas.

The Allies had still to reckon with Thebes, the chief stronghold of medism in Greece. Ten days after the battle they invested the city and demanded the surrender of the partisans of Persia and in particular their leaders, Timagenidas and Attaginus. On the refusal of the demand they began to lay waste the territory of the Thebans and to assault the walls. On the 20th day Timagenidas and his friends offered to give themselves up and stand their trial. The Thebans negotiated a surrender on that condition and handed the medizers over to Pausanias, all except Attaginus, who made his escape. The prisoners expected, and seem to have had a right to claim, a trial, and relied upon bribery to pull them through. But Pausanias, having dismissed the allied army, took them to Corinth, and there, anticipating their design, put them to death. It is possible however that his action was less arbitrary than appears in the brief narrative of Herodotus. How summary and incomplete that narrative is, may be judged from

---

[1] *Camillus*, 19; *de gloria Ath.* 7.

a consideration of the terms imposed on the Thebans, which must have included far more than the extradition of the medizers, and altered the whole status of Thebes in Boeotia. But we can only infer this change from incidental notices in later writers and from the subsequent history.

V. MYCALE

On the same day, it is told, as the battle of Plataea the Greeks won another victory on the Ionian coast at Mycale, the promontory east of Samos. Leotychidas and his fleet had lain at Delos on guard throughout the summer. Xanthippus and the Athenians, who joined him probably when Mardonius evacuated Attica and Pausanias crossed Cithaeron, may have raised the total of ships to about 250[1]. The time had come for offensive action on sea as well as on land. Accordingly, when three envoys arrived from the Samians inviting the fleet to Samos, promising an immediate revolt in Ionia, and assuring the admirals of the unseaworthy and helpless plight of the enemy's navy, Leotychidas took an omen from the name of their spokesman, Hegesistratus[2], accepted their proposal, and concluded a treaty of alliance with them. On the morrow the sacrifices proved favourable and the fleet sailed for Samos, where they anchored off the Heraeum and prepared for battle.

For Xerxes' admirals had on the advent of spring concentrated the remnants of his armada at Samos, where they kept ward over the Ionians. According to Herodotus, they had still 300 ships, but deemed them unequal to coping with the Greek force, and therefore on news of its advance sent the Phoenicians away and withdrew the rest to the mainland to be under the protection of the army. There are three new admirals in command, Mardontes, Artaÿntes and Ithamitres, and the number might suggest that the Phoenicians went earlier in the winter or even, as Diodorus says, straight from Salamis. But the Phoenicians hitherto had no admiral other than the King; they are to be reckoned in the 300 ships at Samos. Whither they were sent we are not told. It has been conjectured that they were dispatched to the Hellespont or north Aegean, but at all events there is no trace of them there, and Artabazus crosses the Bosphorus in 'boats' not 'ships.' Herodotus presumably means that they went home. The problem involves more than the Phoenician division, for Mardontes is an admiral, but has no fleet. Probably he commanded the Egyptian

---

[1] So Diodorus XI, 34.   [2] *I.e.* 'leader of the army.'

contingent and sent away his ships with the Phoenician, but retained the marines, apparently Egyptians, of whom Mardonius had already picked out the best individual fighters. What remained then at Mycale of the navy was only the intact Pontic fleet and the residue of the Ionian, both almost wholly Hellenic and probably less than 200 ships in all.

There could be no question of a naval battle. In order to save the ships they were beached at a place named (perhaps afterwards) Scolopoeis, by a river Gaeson (to be identified with the Eski Menderes, 'old Maeander'), under the south slopes of Mount Mycale a few miles south-west of Priene. The Maeander has long since silted up the Latmian gulf and pushed its plain far westwards past the probable site, nearly due north of the island of Lade. There, within view of the scene of the last struggle of the Ionian revolt 15 years before, the Persians built a fort of stones and stakes to protect their stranded fleet. The general Tigranes was present with no doubt a considerable force, but surely not, as Herodotus believed, his entire army of 60,000 men, the bulk of which would be at Sardes with the King. The naval commanders might muster about 5000 marines, but the Ionian and Aeolian crews were a positive danger. The Samians, whose city was already suspected owing to the release of the prisoners taken in Attica and was now in open rebellion, were disarmed. The Milesians were sent away to the rear on the pretence of securing the passes over the mountain.

Herodotus places the Persian decision and preparations after the Greeks had departed from Delos, puts the precautions against the disaffected Ionians after an appeal addressed to them by Leotychidas through a herald from his ship, and represents the Allies as disappointed of a battle at Samos and in doubt whether to go back or to sail to the Hellespont. It is more likely that the Persian admirals formed their plan as soon as they heard that the Athenians had joined Leotychidas, and withdrew from Samos before Hegesistratus and his colleagues started for Delos. This hypothesis would give them time to secure the co-operation of Tigranes and to build their elaborate fort, and would explain the Samian mission, Leotychidas' prompt response to it, and the release of the Athenian prisoners. The debate of the Greek commanders at the Heraeum would be more intelligible at their council on their return to Samos from Mycale, and their preparations for battle before and after that debate might well coalesce. Among other things they provided landing bridges, which imply that they were aware that the enemy was no longer afloat.

Having accomplished the voyage of about 20 miles in the morning, the Greeks rowed past the enemy's position and disembarked, probably at a long distance from it, for they were not opposed, and to the east or south-east of it, for the Lacedaemonians, who presumably held the right wing, approached it over a gully and hills, while the Athenians marched on level ground and along the shore. Their number is as vague as their enemy's. Leotychidas could easily have landed 25 or 30 thousand men, but only the marines, at most 5000, would be regular troops. As they moved forward a rumour spread through the ranks, that their brethren were victorious over Mardonius in Boeotia, and heightened their courage. The left wing or Athenians, Corinthians, Sicyonians, and Troezenians, who had the easier and perhaps shorter route, came into action first. The Persians awaited the attack in front of their fortification behind their wicker shields and for a time held their ground. The approach of the Lacedaemonians spurred the Athenians and their consorts by a spirit of rivalry to fresh efforts, and perhaps enfeebled or distracted the defence. They pushed through the hedge of shields, fell upon the Persians, drove them after a stubborn fight into their stockade, and pressed in with them. Thereupon the other Barbarians fled, but the Persians grouped in small bands kept up their obstinate resistance until the Lacedaemonians with the rest of the right wing arrived and took a hand in disposing of them. In this combat Mardontes and Tigranes fell and not a few of the Greeks. The Sicyonians in particular lost many lives including their general, Perilaus. Of the Hellenes in Xerxes' service the Samians claimed to have been the first to turn against the Barbarians. Their example was followed by the other Ionians and doubtless the more numerous Aeolians and others, whom Ephorus did not forget, although Herodotus omits them. As the Samians had been disarmed and Herodotus can say no more of their achievements than that they did what they could to aid the Greeks, one may surmise that their claim was rather political than military and referred to the mission of Hegesistratus rather than daring deeds at Mycale. The Milesians, whose turn came last, have a better title to a share in the honours of the day. They so shepherded the fugitives escaping up the mountain that they delivered them over to their pursuers, or finally slaughtered them outright. When the Greeks had made an end of killing they set fire to the Persian fort and fleet (or did not the enemy rather burn them on abandoning them?) and sailed back to Samos. The prize of valour went to the Athenians and individually to Hermolycus, son of Euthoenus.

The description given by Herodotus of the battle of Mycale so closely reproduces some of the incidents and language of his narrative of the operations at Plataea that it raises the suspicion that the two have somehow been contaminated. Had the synchronism of the battles, the emulation of the services naval and military, and the rivalry of the protagonists Athenian and Lacedaemonian provoked a forced assimilation of the stories, which was further developed by the Greek love of parallels and coincidences? Was the preliminary fight at Mycale approximated to the Spartan victory on the Moloeis? was there ever a temple of Demeter Eleusinia at Scolopoeis? was the wooden wall by the Asopus modelled on the fort by the Gaeson? and was the tale of its capture adapted from the Athenian drama enacted in the other theatre of war? Diodorus drew from Ephorus a different version of the battle of Mycale, which ascribes a more prominent part to the Asiatic Greeks, but it is hardly consistent with Herodotus and is of dubious authority. Both accounts leave uncomfortable doubts. How and where between sea and river did the Greeks land unopposed? What was the number engaged on either side, 5000 or 25,000? Was Mycale a big battle or a hasty raid? designed to liberate the Hellenes of the eastern continent at large or merely to destroy the enemy's last fleet in the Aegean before his army could come down from Sardes? The Islands and the Hellespont were the prizes at stake, says Herodotus, but the result, he notes, is a second Ionian revolt.

VI. THE CAPTURE OF SESTOS

On their return to Samos the Greeks (no doubt the council of admirals) debated the transplantation of the Ionians from their country. But that was not the primary question discussed. It appears that the real business of the meeting was to determine whether the fleet should now go home or to the Hellespont, the question in fact which, according to Herodotus, had been considered on their first arrival at Samos. The Peloponnesians were anxious to go home and to limit their liabilities overseas by leaving Asia to the Persians. The Athenians would not abandon to the enemy their Ionian kinsfolk and other Greeks who were now committed to their cause. The proposal to transfer the Ionians to Greece and settle them on the territories of the medizers, who would be exported to Ionia, was the Peloponnesian answer to the Athenian objection. This drastic solution has its humorous side, but, however crude, it had a show of rough

justice and expediency and may have been put forward as an
argument or debating point in the controversy. A national migration was an idea familiar to the Greeks and had been suggested
to the Ionians long ago by Bias and to the Athenians only the
year before by Themistocles. In A.D. 1923 it has become an
accepted method of solving the Eastern question. But obviously
under the circumstances the point could not be pressed against
the will of the Ionians and of the Athenians, who disputed the
right of the Peloponnesians to dispose of their 'colonies.' If
Herodotus may be trusted, the Samians, Chians, Lesbians, and
other Islanders were now formally admitted to the alliance. The
fleet, in which Thucydides subsequently includes Ionians and
Hellespontines, then sailed for Abydos.

Herodotus believed that the object of the move to the Hellespont was to destroy the bridges, but on his own showing they
were already gone at the time of Xerxes' return. Whatever the
rank and file might expect, the Greek generals must have known
that fact. It was, however, important to secure the Hellespont and
to impound the cables, and the Athenians, who constituted the
larger part of the expedition and more and more plainly asserted
themselves in its direction, had interests of their own to promote
in that region. The fleet, which was delayed at Cape Lectum by
contrary winds, can hardly have reached Abydos before the middle
of September. The Persians in the neighbourhood had time to
concentrate their forces at Sestos under Artaÿctes, the governor
of the district. Sestos was strongly fortified and was the key of the
Straits. Thither Oeobazus, commandant of Cardia, had conveyed
the cables for safety. The autumn was beginning. The Spartans
disliked sieges. Neither they nor the other Peloponnesians had
any enthusiasm for a transmarine war mainly for the benefit of
Athens. They had no mind to sit down to a prolonged blockade.
Leotychidas was not sorry to leave the task to the Athenians and
the new confederates. He took the Peloponnesian contingents
back to Greece, and thereby manifested that rift between the
allies which soon grew into an open breach.

The Athenians with their associates invested Sestos, but met
with a resolute resistance. As the autumn waned the crews began
to murmur and demanded to be led home; but Xanthippus and
his colleagues refused to retire before the fortress was taken,
unless on express orders from the Athenian people—which they
had doubtless made sure would be withheld. At length one night,
when the garrison had been reduced to eating their bed-straps,
the Persians climbed down the wall on the landward side and

abandoned the town. At daybreak the citizens opened the gates
to the besiegers. Artaÿctes was overtaken at Aegospotami; and
at the instance of the Elaeusians, who accused him of offences
against the hero Protesilaus, was crucified by the Athenians.
Oeobazus fell into the hands of the Apsinthians, who sacrificed
him to their god Pleistorus. This indication of his course suggests
that Artabazus on his way from Greece with his army corps was
perhaps expected when the Persians broke out and they hoped
to meet him. The siege had trenched upon the winter—Thucydides' word[1] need not mean that it lasted all through the winter,
but would imply that it continued at least into the second half
of November. Artabazus travelled within three days' march of
Sestos, and proceeded to Byzantium. He made no attempt to
save Sestos, nor did the Athenians molest his passage of the
Bosphorus. Sestos must have already fallen and the fleet been
dispersed. But if Artabazus reached Byzantium only about the
end of November, three months after the battle of Plataea, his
'flight' cannot have been so precipitate as Herodotus represents.

The Greeks, when they crossed Cithaeron and the Aegean, had
already passed beyond a strictly defensive attitude to an offensive
defence. The capture of Sestos concludes at once the campaign
and Herodotus' history and this phase of the war. Xanthippus,
when he took the Athenian fleet home, brought with him the
cables of the invader's bridges to be dedicated in the temples of
the gods.

[1] I, 89, ἐπιχειμάσαντες.

CHAPTER XI

CARTHAGE AND SICILY

I. THE PHOENICIANS IN THE WESTERN MEDITERRANEAN

WHEN Greek settlers began in the latter half of the eighth century B.C. to descend upon the coasts of Sicily, they found the greater part of the island inhabited by the people to whom it owes its name, the Sicels. According to Thucydides this people had entered Sicily from Italy some three hundred years before the Greek colonization, and had displaced and confined to the western part of the island an earlier population, the Sicans. This latter people, the earliest inhabitants of Sicily that we hear of, claimed to be autochthonous, but Thucydides believed them to be Iberians who had been driven out of Spain by the Ligurians (see vol. II, p. 24 and below, p. 438). Whatever be the truth as to their origin, the two peoples were racially distinct, and the similarity of their names is merely accidental. The Sicans maintained a separate existence in a number of towns, of which the chief was Hyccara, but they play little part in Sicilian history. In the same quarter we find the Elymians, whom a tradition of dubious value describes as fugitives from Troy: their towns were Eryx, Entella and Segesta. Of far greater importance than any of these three peoples, who may be regarded as the native population of the island, and from whom the Greeks had little to fear, were the Phoenician settlers; for the early history of Sicily is largely that of the conflict between Phoenicians and Greeks.

The chronology of the Phoenician settlements in the western Mediterranean is a matter of some uncertainty. It is possible that the adventurous traders of Tyre and Sidon had established posts on the north African coast as early as 1100 B.C.: it is certain that they had passed the Straits of Gibraltar and entered into commercial relations with Tartessus (Tarshish) before 1000 B.C. The chief motive for the Phoenician penetration of the western sea was the prospect of profitable trade with this important city at the mouth of the Baetis (Guadalquivir). The Tartessians, who had developed a civilization far in advance of other Iberian peoples, owed their prosperity mainly to the rich mineral deposits of Andalusia, silver, copper and lead, partly also to the enterprise of

their seamen in the quest for tin in Ireland and the islands off the
coast of Brittany, and for amber in the lands of the North Sea.
These were the precious metals for which the Phoenicians exchanged their own wares, and the good value that they received
is suggested by the story that the first Tyrian traders returned
from Tartessus with so much silver that some of it had to be used
as anchors for their ships. The earliest Phoenician settlement in
Spain was at Gades (Cadiz) in the near neighbourhood of Tartessus: the date assigned to its foundation, 1100 B.C., may well
be approximately correct, and it was probably established with the
goodwill of Tartessus[1]. Gradually, however, relations grew worse;
the south and south-east coasts of Spain became dotted with Punic
factories, such as Malaca, Sexi, Abdera; peaceful penetration
changed into the lust for possession, and Tartessus came to feel
in danger of being cut off from the sea. Ultimately it must have
come to fighting, in which the Phoenicians prevailed; for before
800 B.C. we find that Tartessus has become a tributary of Tyre.

Meanwhile a number of Phoenician settlements had sprung up
on the north African coast, including Hadrumetum, Utica, and
the two towns known later as Hippo Regius and Hippo Diar-
rhytus; while outside the Straits Gades in the north was matched
by Lixus (El-Arish) in the south. The only importance of these
towns is that they came to form the nucleus of the empire of
Carthage (*kart-ḥadasht*, the 'New Town'), the last and greatest
of the colonies of Tyre, founded probably towards the end of the
ninth century B.C. It is indeed doubtful whether we are justified
in speaking of the pre-Carthaginian settlements in Spain and
Africa as towns: they were perhaps no more than trading-stations
or factories, which would explain the lack of archaeological evidence for the presence of Phoenicians in the western Mediterranean
until as late as the middle of the eighth century B.C. (vol. II, p. 581;
III, p. 642). It is, however, difficult to believe that Gades and
Utica were not real colonies; for the subjugation of Tartessus
implies a military establishment based on Gades, while Utica was
powerful or venerable enough to maintain a position of quasi-
equality with Carthage down to the time of the second Punic War[2].

In addition to their settlements in Spain and Africa the islands
of Sardinia and Malta also furnished sites for Phoenician occupation. With regard to Sicily, there is no sufficient reason to doubt
the statement of Thucydides (VI, 2) that its promontories and

---

[1] See vol. II, p. 379. The present writer accepts the main conclusion of
A. Schulten's *Tartessos*. See however vol. III, p. 642.
[2] Polybius VII, 9.

the small islands round its coasts were occupied by Phoenicians before the coming of the Greeks, though here again archaeological evidence is wanting. We have no means of dating these settlements, but we may take them to be pre-Carthaginian, for it is unlikely that the Sicel trade, which Thucydides expressly assigns as the motive of their establishment, would have been neglected down to the time when Carthage herself began to colonize.

Just as the Sicans had retreated into the west of Sicily before the Sicel advance, so now the Phoenicians retreated before the Greeks to the three towns of Motya, Panormus and Solus; possibly these towns only came into existence at this date, though no doubt their sites had been in Phoenician occupation before.

It is significant that the motive assigned by Thucydides for the Phoenician withdrawal to this corner of the island is its proximity to Carthage. The older Phoenician colonies were as early as 735 B.C. beginning to look for support to the city founded less than a hundred years before. But Carthage was as yet not strong enough to oppose the Greek occupation of Sicily, nor probably did she feel it necessary to do so. The first clash of Carthaginian with Greek was not destined to come about until Carthage had become an imperial state, mistress of the Phoenician possessions in Africa and the islands, nor until Phoenician commercial interests were more vitally threatened than they were by the presence of the Greeks in Sicily. It was not until the sixth century B.C. that these two conditions were both fulfilled. In the history of the western Mediterranean the two hundred years (735–535 B.C.) between the foundation of Naxos and the battle of Alalia witness on the one hand the growth of Carthage into a powerful sea and land empire, on the other the ever-encroaching advance of Greek colonists and traders into the regions which the Phoenicians claimed as their preserve.

II. THE ADVANCE OF CARTHAGE

At the moment when Greeks were beginning to colonize Sicily, the cities of old Phoenicia had fallen upon evil days. Tyre, the most famous of them, had been thrice besieged by Assyrian kings in the eighth and early seventh centuries; and although each time she proved impregnable upon her island, yet she was so exhausted that soon after the siege by Esarhaddon she submitted in 669 B.C. to Assyrian control (vol. III, p. 115). When Babylon succeeded in 611 B.C. to the power of Nineveh, the Phoenician cities recovered some degree of independence: but in 588 B.C. they were attacked by Apries of Egypt in the course of his revolt from his Chaldaean masters: for a few years they remained under Egyptian control, but in 586 B.C. Nebuchadrezzar defeated Apries and began yet another siege of Tyre which lasted thirteen years (see vol. III, p. 302). After her capitulation Tyre became further exhausted by a period of civil disorder, until she passed without a struggle under Persian control *c.* 539 B.C. The place of Tyre as leading state of Phoenicia was taken by Sidon, but although as subjects of the Persian Empire they entered upon a new period of commerical prosperity and constituted the main part of the Persian navy, neither city was now powerful enough to influence the course of events in the western Mediterranean.

But powerless as Tyre had become, there still subsisted between her and her colonies the ties of religion and of sentiment. Though Carthage had long since freed herself from all political dependence she continued for several centuries to show her respect by the annual despatch of sacred envoys to the festival of Tyrian Melkart. As we learn from Herodotus (III, 19) Tyre showed herself, on one occasion at least, ready to brave the displeasure of her Persian rulers in the interest of her daughter-city. Cambyses, after his conquest of Egypt, is said to have intended to subjugate Carthage, which he probably affected to regard as rightfully subject to Tyre and therefore to himself: the refusal of the Phoenicians in his fleet to proceed against a Phoenician colony led him to abandon his project (p. 20).

It was to Carthage that the western Phoenicians must now look. The rapid growth of Carthage in power and prosperity was due partly to her geographical situation; an excellent harbour favoured her commerce, a fertile hinterland her agriculture; even more perhaps was it due to the superior energy and genius, military and political, which raised her above her Phoenician fellows. It is a probable suggestion that with the decay of Tyre and Sidon the best elements in their population were attracted to Carthage; in any case it was her fortune, now as in later days, to produce statesmen and soldiers who realized her task and had strength to lead her on in the path marked out for her by destiny. That she was moved by the desire of power and wealth for their own sake we need not deny; but the same is surely true of all conquering peoples, and praise and censure in such matters are equally idle.

Little is known of the stages by which Carthage won her empire. It is probable that she began by gradually asserting a hegemony over the Phoenician towns in Africa, adding to their number by colonies of her own. We may suppose that she was not slow to maintain and develop the Phoenician trade with

Tartessus; her occupation of Ebusus (Iviça), an island off the south-east coast of Spain, assigned by Diodorus (v, 16) to as early a date as 654/3 B.C., was probably designed to safeguard and facilitate the passage of her vessels to and from the peninsula. We have no certain evidence of any Carthaginian settlement in Spain itself earlier than the fourth century B.C., but the first treaty with Rome (508/7 B.C.[1]) appears to shut off Roman enterprise from Spanish waters, and we may believe that before that date Carthage controlled the old Phoenician settlements in Spain. But we have no ground for assuming a date much earlier than this; for the Carthaginian conquest of southern Spain was more than an assumption of hegemony over Phoenician settlements, which might be readily enough conceded; it necessitated in all likelihood a conflict both with Tartessus and with the Greek colonists in Spain.

We have seen that at some time before 800 B.C. Tartessus had become tributary to Tyre. About a century later she appears to have regained her independence, probably in consequence of the weakening of Tyre by the Assyrian siege, and in the early part of the sixth century we find her apparently mistress of the Tyrian colonies in Spain. These were the flourishing days of Tartessus, which have left their mark in Herodotus' story of her wealthy and phil-Hellene King Arganthonius ('Silver-man'); it has been suggested that the lifetime of 120 or 150 years assigned to him by Greek legend may symbolize the period of Tartessus' greatest wealth and prosperity, from about 700 to 550 B.C. It is possible no doubt to exaggerate the importance of Tartessus and the extent of her dominion; but the point that is important and significant for the record of Carthaginian development is that after the middle of the sixth century B.C. Tartessus completely vanishes from history. The most probable explanation is that it was destroyed by the Carthaginians about the same time that the Greeks were driven by them out of southern Spain, and that the expulsion of both Greeks and Tartessians was rendered possible by the battle of Alalia (535 B.C.), in which the victory of Carthage, aided by the Etruscans, over the Phocaeans secured for her the command of the western sea together with the ability to close the Straits of Gibraltar to the merchantmen of Tartessus[2].

---

[1] See for the date Tenney Frank, *An Economic History of Rome*, pp. 30 *sqq* and n. 29.

[2] Schulten (*op. cit.* p. 45) suggests that Tartessus vanished so completely as to be confused by later historians with the neighbouring Gades, and that the account in Athenaeus περὶ μηχανημάτων *ap.* Vitruvium, x, 9 of the destruction of Gades really refers to Tartessus.

In tracing the steps by which Carthage acquired her Spanish dominion it has been necessary to anticipate the account of Greek colonization in the peninsula; this is part of the general westward expansion of Greece in the seventh and sixth centuries B.C., and to that we must now turn.

III. GREEK EXPANSION IN THE WESTERN MEDITERRANEAN

It has been seen (vol. III, pp. 669–683) that the Greek colonization of Sicily, begun in 735 B.C., went on steadily for one hundred years. By the time of the foundation of Selinus (c. 630 B.C.) the best sites in the island with the exception of Acragas (founded in 580 B.C.) had been occupied, and the energies of adventurers began to be turned elsewhere. In Africa, where the Theraeans had planted about 630 B.C. their colony of Cyrene, whose territory expanded rapidly westwards, Greeks became near neighbours of the Carthaginians who were simultaneously advancing eastwards. The African coast west of Carthage shows no trace of any attempt at Greek settlement, a fact which may perhaps be taken as confirming the early supremacy of Carthage in that region. Spain was reached by Greek mariners at least as early as 620 B.C., when Colaeus of Samos was driven out of his course by an east wind beyond the Pillars of Heracles to the kingdom of Tartessus(p. 89). This chance introduction of the Greeks to a region which, as we have seen, had been long since exploited by Phoenician traders was shortly afterwards followed up by some adventurers from that most enterprising commercial state of seventh-century Hellas, Phocaea.

It is to Phocaeans that the distinction belongs of penetrating farther west than any other Greeks, and of first occupying a site which has ever since been one of the world's greatest ports, Massilia. The date assigned to this Phocaean colony is 600 B.C. More important, however, for our present story is another Phocaean colony, less famous and immeasurably less permanent, Maenaca, a little east of Malaca (Malaga) on the southern Spanish coast. It was founded probably rather earlier than Massilia, and may be regarded as the Greek counterpart to the Phoenician Gades, both being established for the sake of trade with Tartessus. It is probable that the Phocaeans came at a favourable time, for with the lessening prosperity of Tyre the Tartessian trade with Phoenicia would suffer and their market be open to newcomers. Of the history of Maenaca nothing is known, but it must have disappeared at some time in the sixth century B.C.: and the most likely explanation of its disappearance is that the Carthaginians destroyed it, as they probably destroyed Tartessus, soon after the battle of Alalia. Just as Tartessus was afterwards confused with Gades, so was Maenaca with Malaca.

The Carthaginians were thus without a rival in southern Spain, but Greeks still maintained a footing on the northern part of the east coast, at Emporiae and Rhode, two colonies founded by Massilia after the fall of the Phocaeans.

In Corsica the Phocaean settlement of Alalia (Aleria) on the east coast was established about 560 B.C.: while the neighbouring island of Sardinia appears to have exercised a perennial attraction for homeless and exiled Greeks: a Messenian settlement was projected after the second Messenian war towards the end of the seventh century (see vol. III, p. 557) and about 545 B.C. a suggestion was made by Bias of Priene that the Ionians should migrate to Sardinia *en masse* to escape the rule of Persia: later still an enterprising adventurer, Histiaeus of Miletus, proposed to Darius that he should acquire the island for the Persians themselves (p. 222).

It is plain that the Greeks were becoming an increasing menace to Phoenician supremacy, political and commercial, in the western Mediterranean. During the seventh century however no hostilities occurred, for both Greeks and Phoenicians seem to have deliberately avoided those regions where their rivals were actually settled. Thus Greek settlements are not found on the north African coast west of Carthage, nor Phoenician settlements in Magna Graecia. But in Sicily the peril of the Greek advance was brought home more vividly to the Semites. Their presence in the north-west corner was obviously endangered by the later Hellenic colonies of Himera, Selinus and Acragas. These three states were destined to play each a prominent part—two of them were to make common cause with the barbarian—in the first episode of the struggle between western Greece and Carthage, the episode which ended with the battle of Himera: though the leading rôle was played by none of them, but by a city of the east coast which in 600 B.C. can hardly have seemed very dangerous to Phoenician interests, the city of Syracuse.

IV   EARLIEST CONFLICTS BETWEEN PHOENICIANS AND SICILIAN GREEKS[1]

We have now to trace, so far as the scanty evidence permits, the events which lead up to the predominance of Syracuse in the early fifth century and to the crowning mercy of Himera.

[1] A map of Sicily and Magna Graecia will be found facing p. 113.

The earliest conflict of which we know between Phoenicians and Greeks upon Sicilian soil may be dated about 580 B.C.; that is to say simultaneously with, or very little later than, the foundation of Acragas. The Sicilian Greeks had hitherto respected the retirement of the Phoenicians to their three towns in the north-west corner of the island: but the enterprise of Pentathlus which we have now to relate was undertaken by Greeks from the Aegean, Cnidians and Rhodians, and was directed towards the 'barbarian corner' itself. It would be interesting to know the true motive of this expedition. Was it a deliberate attempt at the complete domination of Sicily by the Greeks, to be secured by driving the Phoenicians from their sole remaining portion of the coast line? We do not hear of any such motive, and if it had existed, one would have expected the initiative to have come from Greeks of Sicily, in particular from Selinus. But this does not seem to have been the case.

Whatever the motives of Pentathlus and his comrades, they met with utter failure. On their landing they found a struggle going on between the people of Selinus, Dorians like themselves, and the Elymians of Segesta. As might be expected, the new-comers made common cause with the Selinuntines: we are tempted to conjecture that their arrival was not so unexpected by Selinus as our accounts imply. This co-operation however called forth Phoenician help for the Elymians. In any case Pentathlus would have had to fight the Phoenicians for a footing on the promontory of Lilybaeum: for its occupation by Greeks was obviously not to be tolerated by the men of Motya. Pentathlus was defeated, and according to one story killed: a number of his followers however made good their escape to the Aeolian Islands where they settled in Lipara, the largest of that group. It is of no moment whether a Greek colony was actually established at this time on Lilybaeum or not: if it was, its life was exceedingly brief. The 'barbarian corner' was to remain barbarian for well-nigh two centuries more; but they were content, it seems, with the repulse of Pentathlus and his allies of Selinus, for we hear of no injury inflicted on the Selinuntines as a sequel of their defeat[1].

For the next thirty years the history of Sicily is almost a blank. One name alone stands out, that of Phalaris, tyrant of Acragas.

---

[1] The story of Pentathlus is preserved in two versions, that of Pausanias (x, 11, 3–4), whose source is Antiochus of Syracuse, and that of Diodorus (v, 9) which is probably based on Timaeus. It has been argued with much probability that the account in Diodorus has been amplified with details belonging to the later enterprise of Dorieus in this same region.

To sift out the residuum of fact from the mass of legends that grew up around this notable figure is a task of much difficulty. Rising to power, some ten years after the city's foundation, by a trick of a type ascribed to many other usurpers, he ruled Acragas for sixteen years with a rigour and cruelty unexampled even among Sicilian tyrants. The story of the brazen bull, in which he roasted his victims to death, must be accepted as literal fact: for it rests on far too good and too early authority to be explained away as a misunderstanding of some religious practice of Semitic origin. But we may well believe that it was from Phoenician models that Phalaris learnt to practise a form of torture so repugnant to Greek sentiment.

With regard to the extent of his dominion, it is possible that it embraced other Siceliote cities: we hear of him as ruling at Himera and at Leontini, and a very late reference makes him tyrant of all Sicily. It would however be most unsafe to take any of these stories as facts. One scrap of information about his exploits has an air of probability, namely that he was engaged in warfare with the Sican tribes of the interior: it is reasonable to assume that he came into contact with this early stratum of native population in the course of extending the territory of his city, which as we know from a casual notice embraced the hill of Ecnomus beside the southern Himera river. About 554 B.C. he fell as the result of a popular movement; we know the name of the liberator of Acragas, Telemachus, the ancestor of Theron, who was destined to rule and bring great glory to his city three generations later. We know also the names of two intervening rulers, Alcamenes and Alcander; but they are mere names, and Acragas like other Siceliote cities has for us no history for some seventy years after the fall of Phalaris.

There were tyrants, less famous or infamous than Phalaris, in other Sicilian cities in the early part of the sixth century, such as Panaetius of Leontini and Theron of Selinus. But it is only with the beginning of the fifth century that we find tyrants simultaneously in almost all the cities. At Catana it would seem that the citizens forestalled the appearance of a tyrant by the wiser course of appointing a lawgiver. To Charondas, whose date cannot be determined with any exactness, there was ascribed a mass of political and social legislation comparable to that of Lycurgus or Solon. It is said that he was the pupil of another famous lawgiver, Zaleucus of the Italian Locri (see p. 116), and that his laws were observed in other cities of Sicily and Italy. Although we have no trustworthy information as to the details of his life and work, yet he was certainly a real personage: and the reputation which is attached to him by numerous Greek writers from Plato onwards attests the excellence of his work and the permanence which it secured[1].

Towards the middle of the sixth century we get another glimpse of the conflict between Greek and Phoenician in Sicily: and by this time it is not the resistance of the isolated barbarians of the north-west corner that the Greek has to meet, but the aggressive power of Carthage. With the figure of Malchus, whose campaigns in Sicily may be put about 550 B.C., Carthage emerges into the light, though it can hardly yet be called the full light, of history. Our information is no more than this, that Malchus waged a long and successful war and subdued a part of Sicily. It is generally, and not unreasonably, assumed that his opponents were Greeks; but if so we have no means of saying what Greeks; that they were the troops of Phalaris is a mere guess based on the fact that Phalaris and Malchus are roughly contemporary; it is surely to be expected that the numerous stories of Phalaris' exploits would contain some reference to such warfare if it had occurred. It is perhaps more likely that Selinus was amongst the foes of Malchus, as being the Greek colony nearest to the Phoenician corner, from which we may suppose any Carthaginian army would operate. On the other hand it has been suggested that the enemy was not Greek, but Phoenician, that Carthage had to assert her supremacy over Panormus, Motya and Solus by force of arms. No certainty is attainable: we can only say with assurance that the middle years of the century witnessed the presence of a Carthaginian army on Sicilian soil, and the subjection of the Phoenicians on the island to Carthaginian dominion or hegemony whether by agreement or by the sword.

The first certain instance of conflict between Carthage and Sicilian Greeks belongs to the last decade of the century. Between 550 and 510 B.C. we chance to know more of Carthaginian than of Sicilian affairs. Malchus after his successes in Sicily met with some disaster at the hands of native tribes in Sardinia. The islanders were able to withstand the Carthaginian armies for many years, until their resistance was finally broken about 520 by the commanders who succeeded Malchus, Mago and his sons Hasdrubal and Hamilcar[2]. Under their leadership Carthage secured

---

[1] Strabo (XII, p. 539) records that in his day the laws of Charondas were in force in Mazaca, a town of Cappadocia.

[2] The first treaty with Rome (508/7) implies that Carthage was then in effective possession of Sardinia.

a firm grasp of the coast regions, the natives being driven back into the mountainous interior. Meanwhile the failure of Malchus had important consequences in the Carthaginian state. Condemned to exile together with the survivors of his defeated army Malchus defied the ruling oligarchy and by a successful *coup d'état* made himself master of the state. He did not however, as might be expected, attempt to convert the constitution into a military monarchy: contenting himself with the execution of ten members of the Council he left the oligarchy in control, with the result that after no long interval he found himself again at their mercy: accused of aiming at monarchical power he was condemned and executed.

In this story of Malchus, preserved to us in a late authority with a surprising amount of circumstantial detail, we see Carthage passing through a critical stage of her development. Experience had shown that the maintenance and extension of her commerce demanded a strong, and if need were, an aggressive army. So long as that army was content to be the obedient instrument of the commercial oligarchy no troubles ensued: but as soon as it aspired to a voice of its own in the destinies of the state it became dangerous to the oligarchy. We may suppose that the latter seized upon the defeat of Malchus in Sardinia as a favourable occasion for a trial of strength; but if it lost in the first round, it would seem to have recovered in the second, since Malchus was either unwilling or unable to secure his position permanently. Happily for Carthage a compromise was found which saved her from the disasters of prolonged internecine conflict. To Mago, the successor of Malchus as general, belongs the credit of a bold and sweeping reform, which, though not without its dangers, as later centuries were to prove, was at this time salutary and essential. Henceforth the ranks of the Carthaginian army were to be recruited no longer from her own citizens, but from subject peoples, allies and mercenaries: in practice from the battle of Himera to that of Zama her troops were largely mercenary, though officered by Carthaginian citizens. The danger thus removed, it was felt to be safe for the chief command to be held by one of the two Suffetes, or heads of the civil administration for the year: in fact such a combination of offices seems to have been normal for the remainder of the period with which we are now concerned[1].

These years witnessed great military activity on the part of Carthage, activity crowned in the main with success. In addition

[1] Hence it is that we find our authorities using the terms βασιλεύς, *imperator*, *dictator* and *dux*, when referring to Mago and his successors.

to the long warfare in Sardinia against natives, the neighbouring island of Corsica was the scene, in 535 B.C., of the encounter, already referred to, between the allied fleets of Carthage and Etruria and that of Greeks from Phocaea. The colony of Alalia founded some twenty-five years earlier had just received an accession from its metropolis, abandoned by its citizens by reason of the aggression of Persia. The original establishment of the colony had been resisted by the ships of Carthage, which had then fought without an ally and suffered defeat. But on the present occasion her sixty vessels were supported by an equal number of Etruscan ships. The battle of Alalia was the most outstanding result—and indeed the only result, of which we have a detailed record—of an alliance between the two powers interested in preventing the expansion of the Greeks in the western Mediterranean. When the treaty was drawn we are not told, perhaps early in the sixth century: it was both a military and a commercial treaty containing clauses dealing with the trade between the two contracting parties and with the redress of grievances.

The victory was claimed by the Phocaeans: but it was a victory in which the victors lost more than the vanquished, and it resulted in the abandonment of Alalia. Corsica was now lost to the Greeks, but it fell to the share not of Carthage but of Etruria. It is probable that we should assign to a date not much later than the battle of Alalia the naval victory of Massilia over Carthage which brought an end to a war of some duration. The Phocaean colony would naturally feel it incumbent on her to champion the cause of Greek against barbarian after the defeat of her mother-city. The battle was followed by a definitive treaty, which probably fixed the Cape de la Nao as the boundary between Massiliote and Carthaginian 'spheres of influence.' Neither the Etruscan nor the Massiliote treaty has been preserved, but we may suppose that they followed the lines of the first treaty with Rome (508/7) which is quoted by Polybius. We can thus see that in the latter half of the sixth century Carthage was employing both military and diplomatic means in the steady pursuit of a forward policy and rapidly becoming a strong naval power.

V. THE ENTERPRISE OF DORIEUS

After the defeat of the Phocaeans and the settlement with Massilia, Carthage might reasonably expect that the tide of Greek expansion in her waters would rise no higher; but it was not to be so. Rather more than twenty years after the battle of Alalia she received yet another provocation, this time from a city that had hitherto founded but few colonies in West or East. A man of Sparta now appeared to trouble the peace of the same Phoenician 'reserve' in north-west Sicily that other Dorians had troubled seventy years before. But it was the enterprise rather of an individual Spartan prince than of the Spartan state[1]. The wife of King Anaxandridas had borne him no child: he therefore took another wife who bore him a son, Cleomenes. Soon afterwards, however, another son was born to the king by his first wife. His name was Dorieus. On the death of Anaxandridas the succession was decided in favour of Cleomenes as the firstborn. But the young prince Dorieus, high-spirited, enterprising, encouraged by popular esteem, deemed it intolerable to abide at Sparta under the rule of his brother. His first design was to found a colony in Libya, at the mouth of the river Cinyps, a point between the Greater and the Lesser Syrtis. Thither he was guided by men of Thera, and it is to be supposed that the scheme had the support —it may even have been the suggestion—of the neighbouring Theraean colony of Cyrene. The spot selected was attractive from its fertility, and the new settlement endured for two years. But Carthage proved as vigilant and jealous on her eastern land-frontier as in the waters of her sea: in the third year (c. 510 B.C.) Dorieus and his fellow-adventurers were expelled by a force of Libyan natives acting with Punic troops. In the action of Carthage we may see the assertion of a claim to control the coast as far as the southernmost point of the Great Syrtis.

The failure of Dorieus was ascribed by pious Greek sentiment to his omission to seek religious guidance for his enterprise—he had neglected to enquire of Apollo what land was destined for his new home. Returning to the Peloponnese he resolved to make good his omission. The share of Apollo in this second enterprise was limited to an oracular blessing upon a suggestion that came from another source. Dorieus had chanced to fall in with a certain Antichares, a Boeotian skilled in prophecies, from whom he learnt that he must make his way to Sicily and recover for the descendants of Heracles their rights to that region of Eryx which was the scene of one of the hero's most famous exploits. So romantic an adventure, so plain a duty of filial piety doubtless seemed to the mind of the Heraclid prince certain of heaven's favour; though to one of a more prudent and less idealistic temperament it might have occurred that the fact of human opposition was one to be reckoned with. If the Phoenicians of Motya and her sister-towns

---

[1] For this latter view see vol. III, pp. 684 *sq.* and above, p. 112.

had viewed with disfavour a settlement by Pentathlus on the promontory of Lilybaeum, they had as good reason to oppose that of Dorieus upon Eryx: while the Elymians of Segesta would hardly submit to a Greek settlement on Elymian ground.

But Dorieus had an enemy to face far more serious than had Pentathlus, an enemy stronger than the Elymian of Segesta or the Phoenician of Motya: Carthage had now beyond all doubt the controlling voice in the affairs of Phoenician Sicily, and she was no less alive to Greek encroachment in the island than she had just shown herself on her land frontier in Africa. And so it was that Dorieus like his predecessor fell in battle against the united forces of Phoenicians and their subjects or allies—we know not which—of Segesta. These latter paid their conquered foe a curious tribute of admiration. Amongst the companions of Dorieus was a certain Philip of Croton, famed as the most beautiful of all Greeks. The barbarians built for him a tomb and over it a chapel where they might honour the fallen warrior with sacrifice as a hero. The Spartan prince himself gained no such memorial: the land which the oracular voice of Delphi had pro- phesied would be his was no more than the soil of a nameless grave.

Whether Dorieus did or did not found a short-lived colony on the chosen site cannot be certainly decided. Herodotus, our principal and by far our earliest authority for this episode, clearly had heard nothing of such a foundation: if he had, he could not have omitted it from his narrative. On the other hand we are told by Diodorus (IV, 23), presumably on the authority of Timaeus, that Dorieus did found a city of Heraclea, which quickly grew to prosperity, to such an extent indeed that the Cartha- ginians became fearful of losing their hegemony in Sicily, attacked it with large forces and razed it to the ground. The attempts that have been made to harmonize the two accounts are ingenious but unsuccessful: Herodotus clearly believed that Dorieus was de- feated and slain very soon after landing in Sicily, Diodorus that he lived long enough at least to see his projected colony in being for a period which can hardly be reckoned as less than a year. For the credit of the oracle of Antichares we may perhaps suppose that the colony did get as far as a technical existence, but was wiped out almost before it was born, and that its rapid growth and prosperity were the product of imaginative Siceliote historians.

As to the voice of Delphi, Apollo could justify himself for giving his prophecy so grim a manner of fulfilment. Dorieus had sinned in that he did not go direct to the accomplishment of the task assigned him: he had tarried on the way. On his voyage from Peloponnese he had passed along the coast of southern Italy, following the usual course. He came at the moment when Sybaris, once the wealthiest, perhaps even the most famous of all Greek cities in East or West, was engaged in her death-struggle with the neighbouring city of Croton. With the aid of Dorieus and his followers Croton was victorious over her rival: so at least Herodotus was told in later days by the descendants of the conquered Sybarites who still survived on a soil which they no longer ruled. The men of Croton denied the story, and each side endeavoured to prove its case to the curious enquirer. The arguments of neither are convincing: but the balance of probability is in favour of the intervention of Dorieus having actually occurred: for it is more likely that Croton should have denied a true account that seemed to lessen the glory of her victory than that Sybaris should have invented an account that had no foundation in fact. The question is of no great moment for us: what is certain is that the Sicilian enterprise of Dorieus took place at the time of the fall of Sybaris, that is to say about 510 B.C. The doubts that have been cast upon this date cannot be sustained.

The surviving followers of Dorieus, like those of Pentathlus, were resolved to do at least something to rescue their names from oblivion. If they could not found a new Heraclea they could at least confer the name upon an existing city. Farther south along the coast lay the town of Minoa, an outpost of Selinus designed perhaps to guard against aggression on the part of her nearest neighbour Acragas. This place, we are told, the Spartan company led by Euryleon occupied, and Herodotus adds that they helped the Selinuntines to get free from their tyrant Peithagoras. What the exact connection between these two exploits was is not clear: it may be that the occupation of Minoa was really, or nominally, part of the joint operations against Peithagoras. At all events Euryleon soon dropped the rôle of liberator, proclaimed himself ruler of Selinus and her territory, and maintained his rule for a short while. His end which came soon as the result of a popular uprising can hardly excite our pity or surprise. It is curious that the memory of this usurper was preserved in the name of the town that he had seized: Minoa in after days was known as Heraclea Minoa, and the name must be a record of the Spartan who had been disappointed of his share in the glory of the true Heraclea on Mount Eryx.

If we may believe a vague and doubtful scrap of information given us by a late authority[1], the fight between Siceliotes and

[1] Justin xix, 1.

Carthaginians did not begin with the attack on Dorieus, nor cease with his fall. It would appear—the very text is corrupt—that Dorieus had received the aid of Sicilian allies provoked by Carthaginian aggression, and that a heavy and protracted war was waged with varying success. The most natural ally of Dorieus would be Selinus, the city that had given aid to Pentathlus.

VI. THE RISE OF SYRACUSE

But the story of Sicily for the next thirty years, that is to say in the interval between the enterprise of Dorieus and the campaign of Himera, so far as it has come down to us, is that of the struggle not of Greek with Carthaginian but of Greek with fellow-Greek. It is moreover a new phase in the development of the Sicilian colonies upon which we are now entering. Hitherto the affairs of one city had been little, if at all, affected by the affairs of another: they had lived side by side in amity, or at least without conflict, except in isolated cases and in exceptional circumstances, such as the war between Syracuse and her semi-independent out-settlement of Camarina, presently to be recorded. There had been mistrust, a feeling that the more distant and vulnerable parts of a city's territory must be guarded against aggression: thus Camarina was planted as an outpost of Syracuse against Gela, and Minoa barred the encroachment of Acragas upon the land of Selinus (p. 375). But, generally speaking, it had been possible for the most flourishing cities to expand without threat or damage to any but the pre-Greek inhabitants of the island. With the opening of the fifth century this was no longer the case. The tyrants who are found in many cities, some rising to power in their native places and by their own enterprise, others set in control by a foreign overlord, tend to look beyond the confines of their own territories; it is an age of alliances and combinations, and of the rise of one great power which finally attains a supremacy hardly less than the lordship of Sicily. But before we come to those great and memorable events which culminate in the battle of Himera and the glory brought to Syracuse by the ruler who forsook his own city to dwell there, it is necessary to record what can be recorded of that city's growth since her foundation.

From the days of Archias to the days of Gelon the city proper was confined to the island of Ortygia. This was not indeed the only inhabited quarter; the adjoining mainland soon became dotted with fortified posts and temples and other buildings. Amongst these were Polichna, the hill commanding the road

which led south to Helorum, crowned with the temple of Olympian
Zeus; Temenites, the quarter which took its name from the sanctuary of Apollo, likewise commanding the inland road leading
westward; and Achradina to the north, where a line of stone
quarries provided the hill with a natural defence that could easily
be adapted to military ends by simply cutting out the rock. The
lowland between this hill and Ortygia was afterwards included
in Achradina, but was for the present left unfortified and un-
inhabited, with the result that upper Achradina remained an
isolated outpost.

The geographical situation of Syracuse, on the east coast but
not far from its southern extremity, and the fact that to the north
her way was soon blocked by Megara, pointed her naturally to
expansion southward and westward. Her citizens would aspire
to stretch across the south-east corner of the island from the
eastern to the western sea: and the record of her early settlement
marks the fulfilment of that purpose. It is probable that two sites
away from the immediate vicinity of Ortygia were early occupied,
Neëtum amongst the hills to the south-west, and Helorum on the
coast to the south. But the first settlement actually recorded is
that of Acrae in 664, situated, as its name implies, on high ground
about twenty-four miles west: and the next is Casmenae in 644,
due south of Acrae a few miles from the southern sea. We may
thus suppose that within a century of her foundation Syracuse
had secured control of the whole district enclosed between the
coast and a line drawn north from below Casmenae to Acrae and
eastward thence to Ortygia. Although these two places are included by Thucydides, to whom we owe the dates, in his list of
Sicilian colonies, they were certainly not colonies in the ordinary
sense: their inhabitants were citizens of Syracuse, and their coins
the coins of Syracuse: they were in fact in the same position as
the nearer outpost of Achradina in the period before it was connected with Ortygia.

In 599 B.C. a settlement of a different character was planted,
Camarina on the south-west coast, which possessed seemingly
from the first some measure of independence. Her relation to
the mother-city was not that of the normal Greek colony, which
was bound only by ties of sentiment and religion: it was rather
analogous to that subsisting between Corcyra or Potidaea and
their metropolis of Corinth: the degree of control retained by
Syracuse is not known to us, but it was such that when Camarina
attempted to shake it off some forty-five years later, the attempt
was held to be that of a rebellious subject.

By the time of the foundation of Camarina Syracuse had realized her ambition of extending her sway over south-eastern Sicily from sea to sea, and possessed a territory far larger than any other Sicilian city. There is some evidence that in the earliest times she was ruled by kings: for several writers, one as early as the days of Gelon, speak of a king Pollis, who if he is a historical personage must have been a constitutional monarch, not a usurping tyrant. But apart from this shadowy figure the earliest glimpse we get shows us an oligarchical type of government. In accordance with the normal course of development in Greek colonies political power remained in the hands of the descendants of the original settlers, while later comers remained unenfranchised. Thus as the population of Syracuse grew by successive additions from without, the government, originally democratic, approximated more and more to oligarchy. Long before the end of the sixth century the unenfranchised and landless Demos must have far outnumbered the citizens who became known as the *Gamori* or landowners. A third class of the population were known as Kyllyrioi, a name of uncertain derivation: these were the natives who remained on the lands of their conquerors in the condition of serfs or villeins bound to till the lands of their masters: Herodotus, not without some exaggeration, speaks of them as slaves of the Gamori, but a more exact comparison, save for the fact that they were of a different race, is that drawn between the Kyllyrioi and the Helots of Laconia or the Penestae of Thessaly.

The first recorded act of war between Greeks in Sicily is that War of Independence waged by Camarina in 554 B.C. to which reference has been made. It was evidently a war of some magnitude, for both sides called in allies, Syracuse winning the aid of Megara and of the Sicels of Enna, Camarina that of other Sicels and of Greeks unnamed. It appears that Gela was at this time in some sense an ally of Camarina, but she refused to fight against Syracuse. It is not easy to conjecture the motives which inspired the readiness of Megara, or the unreadiness of Gela: it may have been fear of a powerful neighbour operating with different results. That the Sicels should in the main fight on the side of the weaker city against the stronger, which was continually advancing at their own cost, was only to be expected. Somewhere east of the river Hyrminus the battle was fought. It was a day of disaster for Camarina and she paid dearly for her struggle for independence. Her land was devastated, her existence blotted out; we may conjecture that the victors felt they could dispense with the outpost against Gela, for that city which had been unwilling to join the enemies of Syracuse would hardly attack her unaided. It was many years yet before a tyrant of Gela was destined to bring her beneath his sway.

But it is with the record of Gela that the story of this second phase of Sicilian history begins. One characteristic feature thereof we have already noted, the interaction of one Sicilian city upon another: but it is marked by a second and even more important characteristic, the interaction of Sicily with Hellas proper, and with Magna Graecia across the narrow strait. The island had of course never been cut off from connection with Old Greece, but the connection had hitherto been fitful and intermittent: in the main the development of the Sicilian colonies had been independent. But henceforth Sicilian history becomes an integral part of the history of Greece: we are drawing near to the time of the Persian invasions, to the time when eastern and western Hellas are to meet and repel not indeed the same barbarian foe but two barbarian foes aiming independently at the same object, the extinction of Greek civilization in its two most famous seats. It is with the year 499 B.C.—about ten years after the destruction of Sybaris and the discomfiture of Dorieus—that we resume our story. In that year the oligarchy at Gela, doubtless of the same origin as that of the Gamori at Syracuse, was overthrown by Cleander who established himself as tyrant. He ruled the city for seven years but of the nature of his rule we know nothing.

In 492 B.C. he was slain by one of his subjects, but the tyranny was not overthrown. It passed to his brother Hippocrates, destined to exalt Gela for some years to the pride of place amongst her sister-cities. With the exception perhaps of Phalaris, whose title to fame is at least dubious, Hippocrates is the first great name in Sicilian history. Energetic, ambitious and unscrupulous, not content with rising to supreme power in his own city but aiming at the dominion over the whole or, if that might not be, over a great part of the island, he has been justly called a precursor of the great Dionysius and of Agathocles. We possess but the barest summary of his exploits: we know that he employed Sicel mercenaries to supplement the troops of Gela, that he sometimes employed them even against Sicel towns. It was to the east coast that he directed his main energies, a fact which suggests that he, like his successor Gelon, had an understanding with Acragas, his nearest western neighbour, which debarred him from advance along the western coast. He conquered in turn Naxos, her colony Callipolis, Zancle, and Leontini, all of which, in the words of Herodotus, he reduced to slavery. What this implies in the cases of Naxos and Callipolis we do not know, but in the latter two cities he either found or set up tyrants to be answerable to himself as overlord. One city he marched against but did not enslave: the prize of Syracuse was to fall not to him but to his successor.

In the year in which Hippocrates succeeded his brother at Gela, the city of Rhegium, on the other side of the Strait of Messina facing Zancle, passed under the control of a tyrant, Anaxilas, whose character and ambitions were very similar to those of Hippocrates, though he preferred the path of diplomacy and fraud where possible to that of warfare. Acting on the favourite principle of usurpers, that their best chance of maintaining the goodwill of their subjects is a successful foreign war, Anaxilas, at the very outset of his reign, looked about for a favourable opportunity of attacking Zancle. This project however was destined to remain unrealized for the present: for a situation arose which seemed to offer the tyrant of Rhegium a chance of securing the control of Zancle in another way. The year of his accession (493) witnessed the final collapse of the revolt of the Ionians against Persia. The battle of Lade and the fall of Miletus had extinguished the last hopes of the Greeks of Asia Minor and the Aegaean islands. In their extremity it seemed to some better to quit their homes than to endure the rule of tyrants of their own race acting as the vicegerents of the Persian.

Even before the end had come, the eyes of some had been turned westwards: many years before, when the struggle with Persia was only beginning, there had been talk of a migration of Ionian Greeks *en masse* to Sardinia: now it was Sicily that seemed to offer them a refuge. Dionysius of Phocaea, true to the enterprising spirit of his people, had gone off with the ships under his command, together with three others captured from the foe, to Sicilian waters, where he proceeded to combine patriotism with profit by piratical descents upon the merchantmen of Carthage and Etruria. It is a plausible suggestion that this refugee from Phocaea came in the course of his voyaging to Zancle and there suggested a project for the succour of the distressed Ionians. However this may be, an invitation was sent from Zancle proposing that the Ionians should come and establish a settlement at a spot on the north Sicilian coast midway between Himera and the Zanclaean settlement at Mylae, named Cale Acte, to be taken from its Sicel possessors.

We can hardly suppose that this proposal was inspired by pure compassion or friendliness. Zancle was not free to act in matters

of foreign policy at her own caprice: she was under the rule of
a tyrant, Scythes, who was in alliance with Hippocrates of Gela:
but, as the sequel shows, the relation between Scythes and Hippocrates was by no means one of equal alliance. The lord of Gela
was overlord of Zancle, most probably by inheritance from his
brother Cleander. We may be certain that the invitation to the
Ionians was given with the consent, if not at the behest, of
Hippocrates, and that it was part of a policy which aimed at
securing the control of that stretch of coast between Mylae,
already controlled by him as overlord of Zancle, and Himera—
a coast hitherto empty of Greek settlements. The Ionian refugees
might be counted upon to offer no opposition to the suzerainty
of one already recognized as the overlord of the generous city
that had stretched out the hand of friendliness to them; and
anyhow they would prefer the mild rule of an independent Greek
tyrant at a distance to that of a Greek tyrant acting under the
orders of Persia close at hand. And if it be asked why Hippocrates preferred this indirect method of securing the hegemony
of northern Sicily instead of the more obvious course of a campaign
against the Sicels of Cale Acte, we may reply that he had other
work on hand for his troops in the reduction of the Greeks of the
east coast, and that he would probably have found it difficult to
collect from Gela a sufficient number of willing colonists for the
projected settlement.

The invitation met with less response perhaps than Scythes
and Hippocrates had anticipated: the only Ionians that sailed to
Sicily were some Samians—how many we are not told—and a few
Milesians, who after the fall of their city had managed to escape
the fate of their fellow-citizens whom Darius had carried off to
Mesopotamia. These came, but they did not come to Cale Acte.
They were diverted by Anaxilas of Rhegium, who was minded
to show that he could turn the situation to his own advantage.
He knew well that if he stood by and permitted Hippocrates to
realize his project there was an end to his own ambitions in north
Sicily. Why should not the Samians accept him as their protector
and overlord instead of Hippocrates? It was merely a question,
he felt, of offering them a more tempting bait. Instead of a mere
site which they would have to wrest from Sicels, he would offer
them Zancle itself, which at the moment was providentially destitute of a garrison, the Zanclaean troops being away on a campaign
against the Sicels. He could turn them out again later on, if it
appeared desirable. And if, as might be expected, the Zanclaeans
resisted this simple plan, and the Samians proved too weak to

hold the city, it would leave Anaxilas no worse off than before. True, there was Hippocrates to reckon with: but what could he do without a fleet to Anaxilas across the Strait? We must suppose that Anaxilas had good reason to think that the Samians, once in possession of Zancle, would be able to hold it: at the very least it was worth trying, for the risk was not his.

The sequel however was other than he had expected. At the cry of Zancle her overlord came at the head of an army, which besieged and captured Zancle: but it was not to restore the city to its rightful owners that he came. Instead he seized and imprisoned Scythes, affecting to regard him as responsible for the loss of the city, and came to terms with the Samians. The Zanclaeans were enslaved, and 300 of their chief men were given over to the Samians for execution, a privilege which they declined to use. From the moral standpoint, the conduct of Anaxilas, of Hippocrates and of the Samians alike falls short of the highest standards.

For some years the Samians remained in occupation of the city of the Straits, but they were not their own rulers. The tyrant of Gela determined to retain his control by the same means as before the coming of the Samians, by an inferior tyrant owing him allegiance. The man whom he now set in authority at Zancle was Cadmus the son of the former tyrant. Father and son had both had experience of ruling elsewhere before they came to Sicily— Scythes had been tyrant of Cos, and had abdicated, for reasons unknown to us, in favour of his son. Later the son in his turn abandoned the reins of government at Cos, an act which Herodotus insists was entirely voluntary, and followed his father to Sicily, where the turn of events which he certainly cannot have foreseen was ultimately to place him in his father's seat.

The affair of Zancle thus settled, Hippocrates was free to stretch out his hands for the greatest prize the island had to offer. There is no reason to suppose that his attack on Syracuse was anything but unprovoked, and indeed it was not the habit of tyrants, in Sicily or elsewhere, to waste time in diplomatic niceties. Whether Syracuse expected an attack or made any special preparations to withstand it we cannot say; we are simply told that the opposing armies met on the banks of the Helorus, and that the Syracusans were defeated. After the battle the victor marched on and encamped on the hill of Polichna, hard by the Olympieum. If possible he would avoid assault or siege. He knew that all was not well within the city that he looked down upon: the commons were murmuring against their rulers, and it is likely that the recent disaster on the Helorus had exaggerated grievances that had long been growing up. An opportunity of posing as the people's friend lay ready to the hand of the invader. Alarmed for the safety of the rich treasures of the temple, its custodians were seeking to remove them out of Hippocrates' immediate reach: he promptly denounced them as sacrilegious robbers, at the same time ostentatiously refraining himself from laying hands on any of the sacred emblems: thus he would gain favour at once with heaven and with the Syracusan Demos.

The prize indeed seemed within his grasp without further fighting, when it slipped from his hands. Syracuse was saved for the present by the intervention, not in arms but in the guise of peacemakers, of her mother-city Corinth and her sister-colony Corcyra. It is strange that these two secular enemies should for once unite to effect such a purpose: and it is to be regretted that we are told nothing either of the motives that prompted the intervention, or of the nature of the pressure brought to bear upon Hippocrates to submit. Was there perhaps a threat that the ports of Corcyra and of Corinth might be closed to the merchantmen of an enslaved Syracuse? However that may be, it was agreed that the Syracusan prisoners should be restored and that Hippocrates should receive the territory of devastated Camarina as ransom. With this acquisition of territory he was perforce to rest content for the time: Camarina he rebuilt, but we can hardly believe that he permanently relinquished his ambition of reigning as lord of Syracuse.

The precise dates of the events above recorded are in doubt: but it is probable that the battle of the Helorus was fought in 491 B.C. and that the re-population of Camarina was effected in 489 B.C. The remainder of Hippocrates' life seems to have been spent in warring against Sicel towns: we hear of one town, Ergetium, captured by a dishonourable trick, and of another, Hybla, in the assault on which the tyrant fell. He had lived long enough to incorporate in his army—presumably as mercenaries—citizens of the restored Camarina, and his death probably occurred in 485 B.C.

VII. GELON

Hippocrates is a notable figure in the history of Syracuse and indeed of Sicily: but for Herodotus, and consequently for us, he is memorable chiefly as the forerunner of one far more notable; for his successor in the seat of authority at Gela was Gelon, destined to preserve the liberties of western Hellas on the day of

Himera. Belonging to a family of some distinction, Gelon adopted a military career and attracted the favourable attention of Hippocrates soon after that tyrant's accession to power: he had indeed held some position of trust under Cleander. It is probably to the time of Cleander that we must attribute the earliest recorded exploit of Gelon. If we may believe the story[1], he was at one time the supreme magistrate at Himera, combining the civil and military powers under a title with which we shall meet again in Sicilian history, that of 'general with supreme power' ($\sigma\tau\rho\alpha\tau\eta\gamma\grave{o}s$ $\alpha\grave{v}\tau o\kappa\rho\acute{a}\tau\omega\rho$). How a man of Gela came to win this position at Himera we cannot tell; it must have been a purely individual enterprise implying no relations between the two cities. It is to be supposed that Gelon must have given the Himeraeans proof of his capacity in the field, and it may be that Himera had been amongst those allies of Dorieus with whom the Carthaginians had carried on the fight after the Spartan's death. In that case we may picture Gelon as having been chosen in early life to do battle against the same enemy that he was to meet later, beside that same city of Himera, when it had passed into the hands of a tyrant who looked to its former enemy for help against fellow-Greeks.

But whatever the situation was that had occasioned Gelon's election at Himera he was not minded to rest content with an office which, wide though its powers were, was yet hampered by constitutional restrictions. He would become tyrant, and sought sanction for the appointment of a personal bodyguard, a regular step in the career of aspirants to tyranny in Greek cities west and east alike. And it seems that he was likely to have gained his end but for the intervention of the poet Stesichorus, who opened the eyes of his countrymen to the danger in which they stood. Gelon did not become tyrant of Himera, nor, to all seeming, did he retain his magistracy there; but it was no great loss, for a path to fame lay open to him in the service of his native city, or as we should perhaps rather say, in the service of that city's ruler Hippocrates. Distinguishing himself beyond all others in one campaign after another, he was appointed commander of the cavalry, a post in which he continued, with the full trust and confidence of Hippocrates, until the latter's death in 485 B.C. It is evident that by that time Gelon stood out as the most prominent son of Gela: it was not likely that he would be content to remain in a private station nor to serve a lesser man. The people of Gela however had had enough of tyrants and of military adventure. Hippo-

---

[1] There are two versions, one of which substitutes Phalaris for Gelon; Aristotle, *Rhet.* 1393 b 10, and Conon *ap.* Westermann, *Mythogr.* p. 144.

crates had contemplated the succession of his sons, Eucleides and
Cleander, though of course there could be no question of a constitutional succession to an unconstitutional power. But these
sons were minors or weaklings, and the Geloans would have none
of them. In the troubles which ensued, during which we may
suppose that Gela experimented in democracy, Gelon came forward as the champion of Eucleides and Cleander: by force of
arms he overthrew the opponents of tyranny, and then without
more ado threw off the mask of champion, and established himself
as tyrant of Gela and successor to all the conquests of Hippocrates.

It would be idle to speculate whether we should condole with
Gela on the failure of her attempt to recover her freedom or rather
congratulate her on finding a strong and powerful protector. For
Gelon the fortunes of his native city were not the paramount
consideration: his accession to power there was but a necessary
step in the path he had marked out for himself. He had determined to accomplish the great project of which his predecessor
had been baulked, to become master of Syracuse, master of that
city whose situation marked her out in his eyes as fitted above all
others to become the seat of government, the capital of a ruler
who hoped to bring all Sicily under one united sway. It may be
that Gelon cherished another and a nobler ambition, to lead the
armies of a united Greek Sicily against that Phoenician foe with
whom he had perhaps in earlier life engaged on the field of battle.
One thing at least we may confidently affirm, that he did not
spend seven years of inactivity at Gela, as the received chronology
implies: the words of Herodotus, apart from considerations of
probability, make that certain[1].

Hippocrates, as we saw, had found Syracuse divided against
herself: and at some point in the six years that had elapsed since
he encamped beside the Olympieum the conflict had come to a
head. The commons had risen, and with the aid of the Sicel serfs,
whom we must suppose to have won some recompense, perhaps
a restricted measure of citizenship, had expelled the oligarchy,
who had taken refuge at Casmenae. Whether it was Gelon that
made overtures to them, or they to Gelon, we are not told; but
merely that he brought them back to Syracuse, where the Demos
surrendered to his invading army without resistance. Why the
banished oligarchs should set their hopes on Gelon, or why he
should expect them to do so, is not easy to understand; they
must surely have known that if he once gained entry into Syracuse

[1] This account follows the chronology of Pareti, *Studi siciliani e italioti*,
pp. 28–63.

he would be master of oligarchs and democrats alike. We can only suppose that their existence at Casmenae was so distasteful and their longing for a return home so keen that they were prepared to pay the price of submission to foreign rule. Equally difficult is it to see Gelon's object in taking them back; for we are not told that they did anything to facilitate his capture of Syracuse, though of course it is possible that some intrigues were set on foot by them which made resistance on the part of the democrats impossible or ineffective. Gelon was now tyrant of Syracuse, but it must be remembered that, although the term tyrant is commonly applied by Greek writers to those who had seized power in an unconstitutional fashion, it was never formally recognized as a title; for the essential meaning of the word is an unconstitutional ruler, and no tyrant would emphasize the character of his power by claiming recognition. It is probable that Gelon, like Dionysius in later days, was formally invested with the office of 'general with full powers,' that same office which he is said to have held at Himera: a prouder title was to come to him five years later, after his great triumph over Carthage.

Leaving Gela under the control of his brother Hiero, Gelon now established himself at Syracuse; and without loss of time he set about strengthening and enlarging the city in such a fashion that it might permanently maintain its position as the capital of an island empire. As we have seen, Ortygia had always been the heart of the city, and it did not cease to be so now: it was always the stronghold, to which the name Acropolis was inaccurately but intelligibly applied; and it was doubtless there that Gelon and his successors established themselves. But Ortygia was no longer in the strict sense an island; for some sixty years before this time it had been connected with the mainland by a mole of stone. To compensate for the loss of security which this involved Gelon resolved to unite Ortygia with the fortified outpost of Achradina, and this was effected by continuing the western wall of Achradina down to the Great Harbour. It is probable that the docks in this harbour were now constructed, for under Gelon Syracuse became a strong naval power, which five years after his accession was able to offer no less than 200 triremes to fight for Greece against the Persian invader.

The city thus enlarged to a size many times greater than the original settlement on Ortygia required additional inhabitants, and it was the tyrant's next duty to provide for this need. This was effected by wholesale transplantations. Four cities were forced to give up a greater or less proportion of their men to swell the population of the new Syracuse. Of these one was Gela, the tyrant's own native city, who lost more than half her men; we can hardly suppose that most of these went willingly, but sentimental considerations did not greatly weigh with Gelon. Another was the ill-starred Camarina, and in this case there was more excuse; for Camarina had provoked the wrath of the lord of Syracuse by inflicting the death sentence on the tyrant, one Glaucus of Carystus, imposed upon her by Gelon shortly after his accession. As a punishment for this Camarina had a second time been destroyed, and her whole population transferred to Syracuse. The third was Megara, whose nearness to Syracuse was enough to doom her to the loss of independent political existence. The demands of Gelon caused a division of opinion amongst the Megarians, the commons counselling submission, the oligarchs resistance. Of the condition of Megara in these years we know nothing[1], but it may be inferred from the words of Herodotus that the city was under an oligarchical government, against which, however, the commons were able at least to make themselves heard, though on this occasion ineffectually. The fate of the resisting oligarchs was assuredly contrary to what they expected. On the subjugation of Megara they were transported to Syracuse with full Syracusan citizenship, while the Demos, who had given no cause of offence to Gelon, were sold as slaves, their purchasers being prohibited from keeping them in Sicily. Precisely the same differential treatment was accorded to the Leontine colony of Euboea, the fourth city that was forced to give up its sons to fulfil the purposes of the lord of Syracuse.

Gelon's own comment upon his action in this matter is preserved to us: the common people, he said, were a 'most unthankful neighbour': that is to say he relied on the support not of the masses, as did the ordinary Greek tyrant who normally rose to power as their champion against the oligarchy, but of the wealthy, the men of substance. He preferred, it would seem, the adherence of a select few, attached to him by personal ties of service and friendship: some of these adherents came from Old Greece and are known to us by name, such as Phormis of Maenalus in Arcadia, and Agesias of Stymphalus, an Olympic victor celebrated by Pindar. We seem to see the picture of a great prince surrounded by nobles and courtiers rather than that of a typical

---

[1] It may be said with certainty that the political conditions described in the poems of Theognis are not those of the Sicilian Megara. The city of which he writes was not in the control of a strong government which could declare war upon a foreign power in the teeth of popular resistance.

Greek tyrant, solitary and inaccessible, fearing and feared by all his subjects. Yet Gelon was not slow to reward the humbler amongst those that had served him well: some ten thousand of his mercenaries, of whom the majority were probably non-Greek, received Syracusan citizenship. It is possible, however, that this last action belongs to a later date, when the victory at Himera had won him a popularity that removed all danger from the side of the multitude.

Before we pass to the greatest event of Gelon's life, we are bound to take account of a problem for which it seems difficult to find a wholly satisfactory solution. Was Gelon ever engaged in warfare against the Carthaginians before the Himera campaign? Herodotus[1], when reporting Gelon's reply to the envoys sent by Sparta and Athens to Syracuse in the spring of 480, makes him refer to a refusal on the part of those states to render help 'at the time of my quarrel with the Carthaginians.' Whether these words imply an actual outbreak of hostilities must remain uncertain; but there is one point on which we can pronounce with some assurance, namely that Gelon is referring to a time when he was already in a position to lead the forces of Greek Sicily against the barbarian, or rather to lead those Greeks that were still willing to make common cause against the barbarian. For, as we shall see, there were some Siceliote cities which in the years immediately preceding Himera had come to be in friendly relations with Carthage, and to look for support against their rivals to those that should surely have been deemed the common foe. If there was any Carthaginian war waged by Gelon before 480, it must then have been within the preceding five years, that is to say after his accession to power at Syracuse. The fighting was evidently in Sicily, but it is well-nigh impossible to believe that any large-scale expedition was sent from Carthage: it is more likely, and it is not inconsistent with the words of Herodotus, that the force opposing Gelon consisted of the 'phoenicizing' Greeks of Sicily supported by the Phoenicians of the north-west corner, stiffened by a small contingent from Carthage herself. If there had been a Carthaginian invasion comparable to that of 480 B.C. it would surely have left some trace in our extant records beyond this vague allusion in Herodotus. In any case, the danger had been great enough to induce Gelon to seek the assistance of Greeks from the mother-country, assistance which was refused: but the barbarian menace was for the time being repelled.

[1] vii, 158.

VIII. THE ANTECEDENTS OF THE CARTHAGINIAN INVASION

If we are to appreciate the full significance of the Himera campaign it is essential to gain as clear a conception as we can of the somewhat complicated situation existing in Sicily in the years preceding 480 B.C. The key to that situation is to be found in the growing opposition to the predominance of Gela, or, as it ultimately became, the predominance of Syracuse. It is *a priori* likely that the rapid advance of Hippocrates and of Gelon would arouse the jealousy of other Sicilian powers; and there were particular causes which tended to stimulate such jealousy. One action of Gelon's we may interpret as being at once the effect of the opposition of which he was becoming ever more conscious and the cause of strengthening it. This was his alliance with Theron, tyrant of Acragas, formed probably about 485 B.C. and clinched by Gelon's marriage to Theron's daughter Demarete and by Theron's own marriage to the daughter of Gelon's brother Polyzelus. The natural result of this alliance was to draw together into what may almost be called a coalition against Syracuse and Acragas all those states which had reason to fear or to hate either.

The clearest case is perhaps that of Selinus. From earliest times there had been enmity between her and Acragas, and the Selinuntine outpost of Minoa seems to have been more than once the bone of contention and the scene of conflict. By good fortune an inscription[1] has recently been brought to light commemorating the spoils taken by Acragas from Minoa, and the reference is probably to a capture of Minoa from Selinus at some date between 530 and 490: but whether before or after the exploit of Euryleon (see p. 361) we cannot say: it is conceivable that Euryleon won it back for Selinus. At some time during the reign of Theron, probably earlier than 480, it again appears as part of Acragantine territory. Selinus may well have feared that the aggressive ambitions of her neighbour, which had been in evidence ever since the days of her first tyrant Phalaris, would not rest content with the possession of Minoa. Moreover the treatment meted out in 483 B.C. by Theron's new ally to Megara, the mother-city of Selinus, was not calculated to reassure her. In short, evidence is not lacking to explain why Selinus was ranged beside the enemies of Syracuse and Acragas on the day of Himera.

But Selinus was not the only city that 'phoenicized.' It was from a city of the northern coast—from Himera itself—that the

[1] See Blinkenberg, *Die Lindische Tempelchronik*, Bonn, 1915.

invitation which brought the Carthaginians to Sicily was actually sent: and it was sent at the instigation of one whom we have already met as the determined opponent of the ambitions of the tyrant of Gela, Anaxilas of Rhegium. It seems clear that Anaxilas was deliberately working to bring about a coalition of the enemies of Syracuse and Acragas, and that by co-operation with the Carthaginians he hoped to overthrow the power of Gelon and Theron, and win for himself a hegemony over northern Sicily as a philo-Phoenician power. How the conflicting interests of Greeks and Phoenicians in Sicily were to be harmonized we cannot conjecture, but we must suppose that some agreement as to partition of the island, or recognition of different spheres of influence, had been devised between Anaxilas and the rulers of Carthage.

Anaxilas was undoubtedly a skilful diplomatist, who played his cards to the best advantage and was, as we have seen, untroubled by moral scruples. In his original design upon Zancle he had been foiled by the equally unscrupulous Hippocrates. In the mixed game of fraud and force in which Zancle figured as a pawn the first success had gone to the tyrant of Gela: but Anaxilas was biding his time. He certainly did not intend the Samians to live on for ever at Zancle under the suzerainty of his great rival: and when a favourable moment occurred he expelled them by force. The date of this incident is unfortunately not preserved, but it has been argued with some probability that a likely moment was that immediately after the death of Hippocrates, when his successor was too fully occupied with affairs in Gela to interfere with Anaxilas' designs. The tyrant of Rhegium was now firmly established as tyrant of Zancle, re-named by him Messana in memory of his own original home in Greece: though it would appear that the old name was not wholly ousted for the present.

The next city to engage the attention of Anaxilas was naturally Himera. If we accept the story of Gelon's attempt to secure the tyranny of that city we may suppose her to have been none too well-disposed towards him after his failure. From the fact that it was at Himera that Scythes of Zancle took refuge after escaping from his imprisonment by Hippocrates—an incident which, we are told, occurred before the death of Darius—we may infer that by 486 B.C. the city had declared herself opposed to the tyrant of Gela. It cannot have been much later—it may indeed have been earlier—that Himera came under the rule of a tyrant Terillus, whose daughter became the wife of Anaxilas. This could not be tolerated, for it was plain evidence that Himera had been won for the philo-Phoenician cause: it was answered promptly by Theron, acting doubtless in agreement with his ally. Terillus was expelled from Himera by force of arms, and the city came under the control of Acragas and Syracuse. The time was now ripe for Anaxilas to call upon Carthage; the expulsion of Terillus was made a *casus belli*, and Anaxilas gave his children as hostages to Hamilcar, the Suffete and commander-in-chief of the Carthaginian armies.

Our lack of precise chronology becomes at this point more than usually regrettable. We have no means of determining the exact date of the expulsion of Terillus, nor of the appeal to Carthage. It was probably in March 480 B.C. that representatives of Athens and Sparta came to Syracuse asking for help to repel the imminent invasion of Xerxes. That help was refused by Gelon owing to the impossibility of reaching a satisfactory agreement on the question of the command against Persia. In his description of the tone and attitude of the speakers at this famous conference Herodotus no doubt indulges his *flair* for a dramatic situation: but we cannot doubt that Gelon did make a conditional offer of assistance, both military and naval, on a large scale. Not a word was said by him of the danger of denuding Sicily of troops in view of an imminent expedition from Carthage, a fact which can only be explained by supposing that Gelon was not aware of any immediate danger. He became aware of it two or three months later. For Herodotus, after his account of the embassy, goes on to say, on the authority of Sicilian records which there is no reason to disbelieve, that Gelon would after all have sent assistance to Greece, had it not been for the action of Terillus and Anaxilas in calling upon Carthage. In consequence of this he sent not an expeditionary force but an agent, Cadmus, the ex-tyrant of Cos and of Zancle, to Delphi to watch events, taking with him a large sum of money to be paid to the Great King, together with the customary tokens of formal submission, in the event of a Persian victory. The mission of Cadmus occurred when Gelon had received the news that Xerxes had crossed the Hellespont, that is to say probably in April or May. It follows that it was not until the late spring that Gelon became conscious of the danger threatening him[1].

This is the natural interpretation of the straightforward account given by Herodotus (VII, 157–165) who has drawn upon both Greek and Sicilian sources of information. For him the simultaneous occurrence of the two barbarian attacks upon eastern and

---

[1] It is impossible to determine how long before this the appeal of Terillus to Carthage had been made.

western Hellas was quite fortuitous: for him the expedition of Hamilcar was sudden and unexpected, and moreover fully explicable by reference to the situation in Sicily. He knows nothing of any order or request from Persia to Carthage, he knows nothing of any concerted action or communication of plans between the barbarians of east and of west. And we must surely believe him. It was not until more than a century after the event that the attractive hypothesis of a concerted Perso-Carthaginian plan was advanced, only to be implicitly rejected by Aristotle, who knew at least as much of the history of Carthage as Ephorus, the historian whose testimony he repudiates.

It appears that the chief reason why the account of Herodotus has been doubted is the supposition that Gelon must have known, at least as early as the time of the Greek embassy, that Carthage was making her preparations. But this is a purely arbitrary assumption, resting on nothing but the mention by Diodorus of a three-years preparation by Carthage: that period is merely an outcome of the belief in co-operation with Persia. Herodotus had assigned four years to the preparations of Xerxes: the smaller armament of Carthage could not require quite so long, and was therefore given three. It is true of course that Carthage was always a potential enemy, and her troops had perhaps actually been encountered by Gelon on Sicilian soil in the very recent past; but it does not follow that another attack was to be immediately anticipated: it is rather likely that Gelon imagined himself to have got rid of the menace for the moment.

The battle of Salamis was fought on the 23rd September 480 B.C. (see above, p. 313); and the Siceliote tradition which was later communicated to Herodotus reflected men's sense of the coincidence in time of the twin Greek triumphs in east and west, by assigning to the battle of Himera the selfsame day. This exact synchronism has doubtless a symbolic value for the historian, but it has had a misleading effect in so far as it has been taken to support the erroneous belief in Perso-Carthaginian co-operation. We can hardly believe in the exact coincidence; but we may well believe that the two battles were separated by but a few days. That Herodotus believed this much is a justifiable inference from the fact that he does not explicitly accept or reject the synchronism which he records as the Sicilian belief. It was enough for him, as it must be for us, that Salamis and Himera were roughly simultaneous, and the attempts of modern writers to set Himera in 481 or 479 B.C. must be decisively rejected.

IX. THE BATTLE OF HIMERA

In the late summer of 480 B.C. the great expedition sailed from
Carthage. We have no trustworthy information as to its size: the
figures given—300,000 fighting men, more than 2000 warships
and more than 3000 transports—are plainly impossible. But it
was a great host, composed like later Carthaginian armies of mercenaries enlisted from lands near and distant, from Africa, Italy,
Spain and Gaul. The objective was not Syracuse, but Himera
whence the appeal for help had issued; and as might be expected
the fleet set sail first for Panormus, the chief Phoenician city of
the island. Its voyage thither was unmolested, save by the forces
of nature: a storm arose and the vessels conveying the horses and
war-chariots were lost. We are told that, on gaining the safe
waters of the harbour at Panormus, Hamilcar exclaimed that the
war was over, implying that he had escaped, though not without
loss, from the only enemy that he feared. It is surprising that
we hear of no attempt on the part of Gelon to use his fleet to
intercept the Carthaginians on their voyage; he could hardly have
failed to know of their coming before they reached Panormus.
It may well be that his fleet was engaged in immobilizing that of
Anaxilas, or that the latter was playing his part in the campaign
by immobilizing that of Gelon. It was of course an immense
advantage to the Carthaginians that Anaxilas' control of the Straits
prevented the Syracusan fleet from hastening to the succour of
Himera by the short route of the east coast.

Our authorities however are completely silent as to the action
of the lord of Rhegium and Zancle throughout the campaign. At
Panormus the troops were disembarked and given three days'
rest, after which the march to Himera was begun, the fleet
coasting along in touch with the army. Still no opposition was
offered by Gelon or his ally. It would seem that the defence
against the barbarian had been allotted to Theron alone in the
first instance: it was of course his territory that was being attacked,
and he may have thought his own resources adequate. We can
hardly suppose that Gelon could not, if he had wished, have acted
sooner than he did. When Hamilcar reached Himera he found
the town occupied by Theron with a considerable force; he was
permitted however, still unmolested, to beach his triremes and
fortify a naval camp and to dispose his troops so as to cut off the
town on two sides, north and west. Having completed his preparations Hamilcar with a picked body of men led an assault upon
the city in person. A sally was made against him but it was beaten

back with heavy losses. Theron realized at once that he could not hope to defend himself unaided, and a messenger was despatched in hot haste to Syracuse. Meanwhile Gelon, anticipating the call for help, had been collecting an army, with which he promptly marched across country to Himera. The numbers assigned to his force, 50,000 infantry and 5000 cavalry, may be somewhere near the truth: indeed the tendency to magnify the exploits of Gelon, which is manifest in the account of Diodorus, would work rather towards underestimating than exaggerating the size of the victorious army. The appearance of Gelon and the aggressive action which he at once adopted on reaching the neighbourhood of Himera had a prompt effect in raising the spirits of its faint-hearted defenders. Marauding parties of the enemy, hitherto left to ravage the country at their will, were surprised and more than 10,000 prisoners are said to have been taken. The city gates which Theron had blocked up were re-opened and fresh openings in the walls constructed through which sallies might be made.

Thus far we may follow the account of Diodorus without much hesitation. But of the description of the actual battle which follows it is doubtful how much we may accept. The inclination, mentioned above, to magnify the exploits of Gelon seems to involve on the one hand a depreciation of the part played by the forces of Acragas, and on the other the invention of fictitious parallels with the contemporary struggle in Greece.

The writer followed by Diodorus, whether Ephorus or Timaeus or some other, is clearly seeking to suggest a parallel between Gelon and Themistocles, to the advantage of the Sicilian: and, as he does not scruple to doctor facts by making Gelon live on in the enjoyment of power to a good old age in order to contrast him with the exiled Themistocles, we are naturally chary of belief in other points in his story which we cannot so easily check. His moving back of the date of Himera by some two months, so as to make it synchronize not with the victory of Salamis but with the defeat of Thermopylae was perhaps designed to suggest that Athens profited by the example and the result of the victory of Syracuse: if the Carthaginians had been successful they were, it was said, to have gone on to co-operate with the Persians directly against the eastern Greeks. Still, after making deductions for falsifications of this nature, there seems no good reason to doubt the most important point in the story of Diodorus, namely the stratagem to which the victory was mainly due. Hamilcar, it is said, was seeking to propitiate the gods of his enemies by a great sacrifice to Poseidon in the naval camp. For the performance of the proper ritual he needed the guidance of Greeks, and had therefore arranged for the presence of a body of horsemen from his ally Selinus. A letter from the Selinuntines revealing on which day they were to appear was intercepted by Gelon, a piece of good fortune which he was prompt to turn to account. A troop of horse duly presented itself, but they were Syracusans instead of Selinuntines; Hamilcar was surprised and slain and his warships, intended as we may suppose to attack Syracuse after the capture of Himera, were burnt. In the later stages of the battle the troops of Acragas under Theron played an important part.

From Herodotus we get another picture of the battle, or rather of the part played by the Punic commander himself. The story came to Herodotus from a Carthaginian source, and told how Hamilcar sacrificed whole carcases of beasts from morning till evening to the gods of his people, and how at last, finding all other sacrifice unavailing, he threw himself into the flames. All that need be said of this story is that it is not impossible, and that the grandeur of its telling makes us wish it may be true.

The magnitude of the victory and its results have undoubtedly been exaggerated by patriotic Sicilian historians, just as Herodotus exaggerated the results of Salamis. We are told that so many prisoners were taken that the whole population of Libya seemed to have become captives, and that many of the citizens of Acragas, into which territory most of the refugees had fled, had 500 slaves apiece. Those who managed to escape on the Punic warships were wrecked, and only one small boat with a handful of survivors got back home to tell the tale. The panic at Carthage was extreme, and the walls were manned night and day in the expectation of an immediate invasion by Gelon. In sober fact the result of Himera was that Greek Sicily gained immunity from Carthaginian attack for seventy years. Gelon had never any thought of invading Africa, nor did he even disturb the peace of the Phoenician territory in Sicily. The terms of peace arranged were moderate, amounting to little more than an indemnity of 2000 talents. But the position of Gelon in Sicily itself was immensely strengthened by the victory. His treatment of Anaxilas and of Selinus seems to have been magnanimous, for we are told that envoys from the cities and rulers who had opposed him were graciously received and granted alliance. Directly or indirectly the lord of Syracuse, with Acragas as his willing but less powerful ally, controlled virtually the whole of Greek Sicily. It is possible that Catana, of which we hear nothing throughout the story of

Hippocrates and Gelon, still retained her independence, but we can hardly doubt that she was in actual, if not formal, dependence upon Syracuse after 480 B.C.

The political and commercial power of Syracuse and Acragas is attested by a significant change, which took place during the first two decades of the fifth century, in the coinage of the island. The earliest coins struck in Sicily had been those of the Chalcidian cities, Naxos, Himera and Zancle, which adopted the Corcyraean standard of weight[1]: the Dorian cities soon afterwards began to strike coins on the Euboic-Attic standard; but by 480 B.C. the latter had displaced the former throughout the island. In this connection mention must be made of the splendid decadrachms known as 'Demareteia'[2] issued by Syracuse to commemorate the victory of Himera. It is said that they were struck out of a present made by the Carthaginians to Gelon's queen, Demarete, who had pleaded for their lenient treatment. In his own capital Gelon was for the remaining two years of his life an unchallenged ruler, welcomed by all classes alike. At a great assembly convened soon after the day of triumph he was saluted by the enthusiastic Syracusans as 'Saviour, benefactor and king,' and it is highly probable that the royal title was adopted by him thenceforward, though we have no record of an official vote conferring it. If he did now become king, that does not imply that he relinquished the former basis of power expressed by the title of General; a title continued by his brother and successor, Hiero. In regard to the succession one account, based on Timaeus, says that the generalship was bequeathed to a younger brother, Polyzelus; and this may imply a division of power, the civil authority going to Hiero and the military to Polyzelus. This however seems impossible to reconcile with the account of Diodorus; and we should perhaps accept a recent suggestion that the generalship in question is the lordship of Gela, where Polyzelus was to step into the position that Hiero had occupied during the eldest brother's lifetime.

---

[1] See Volume of Plates i, 308, *b, c.*   [2] *Ib.* 308, *g.*

CHAPTER XII

ITALY IN THE ETRUSCAN AGE

A. THE ETRUSCANS

I. SOURCES OF KNOWLEDGE AND METHOD OF ENQUIRY

THE period which may be roughly described as the Etruscan age is that which ends at the beginning of recorded history in Italy. This limit is marked by several well-known events of which the chief was the establishment of republican government at Rome after the expulsion of the Tarquins who belonged to an Etruscan dynasty. With the fall of this dynasty what may be called the Etruscan hegemony in Italy was broken, and the period of the greatest Etruscan influence brought to an end. But the beginning of the age is by no means so easy to define. Such evidence as there is for determining when this peculiar people arrived in Italy and whence they came, we must examine in due course; but in any case the movements and conditions which it is the purpose of this chapter to describe belong, roughly speaking, to the first half of the last millennium B.C.

The chief difficulty before us is the almost complete absence of absolute dates. The linguistic evidence by which we shall mainly be guided will provide us with many points of interest that have a chronological bearing; and from them we may take some steps towards a relative system of chronology. Exactly the same reservation applies to dating based on the successive strata of remains which archaeological science observes; and it is only fair to warn the reader of the probability that there may still be a real gap in our information between the questions raised in connection with the Bronze Age in a previous chapter (vol. II, chap. XXI) and those which we may hope to frame in this. Yet it should at least be possible to indicate the questions which mark the present limits of knowledge. Our enterprise is not unlike that of adding piece by piece to the ends of two arms of a cantilever bridge, intended to meet at the centre; until they have met and are firmly and finally riveted, the bridge cannot offer a safe passage. It may well prove, when further evidence comes to light, that the conclusions reached in prospect in vol. II, p. 573 *sq.*, and those suggested in retrospect from the facts we have now to consider, do in fact over-lap or at least touch one another, in point of time; but until the evidence that we possess for identifying the speakers of particular languages with the users of particular forms of culture, represented by particular sets of material remains, has become far more definite than it is, the ends of our two structures may still, for all we know, be facing one another in the air.

One danger in particular should be clearly understood. Many, if not all, of the names which tradition gives to the different tribes of early Italy are used in one sense by students of archaeology and in quite a different sense, that is, to connote quite different sets of facts, by students of language. Ligurian, Umbrian, Oscan, Sabine, Siculan, and even Latin have all (at least) two meanings. To the linguist these names represent the tribes or peoples who at the beginning of the historical period in Italy, *i.e.* in the fifth century B.C., were speaking certain languages of which we have knowledge by direct or indirect records. But the archaeologist, when he uses any one of these terms, means by it some tribe whose existence and character he deduces from a particular group or stratum of remains, and which he has labelled by what seems to him the most likely title chosen from those offered by ancient tradition. Even where his choice has been approved by a preponderant weight of archaeological opinion, it has still to be shown whether the tribe in question, at the epoch in question, was speaking the language called by its name in the fifth century. For example, we know that the pre-Tuscan people of Etruria were called *Ombroi*, but this gives us only a *prima facie* presumption that the language they spoke was the same, or closely related to, the dialect which is commonly called Umbrian, in which the famous *Tables of Iguvium* (a town in the Umbria of Augustus) are written (p. 452 *sq.* below). In this chapter therefore we shall do well to speak of the *Ombroi* on the one hand and the Iguvine dialect on the other. Similar distinctions will be drawn as we approach different parts of our enquiry; but the whole study of early Italy has suffered so much from these hasty and often quite unconscious identifications that it is well to put the reader on his guard.

The present stage of our enquiry will be complete on the day, which at present seems remote, when we can name with confidence the language or languages spoken by each of the nine groups of communities in the Early Iron Civilization which were distinguished at the close of the sections dealing with Italy in vol. II, p. 572, and when we can also attach to them some definite chronology.

The procedure necessary in view of the fragmentary state of our knowledge is dictated, in the main, by geography; that is, we must be content to ask what can be known of the different communities of Italy, during this period, tribe by tribe. In each case our story, such as it is, can find no definite ending short of the point when the fortunes of the particular tribe or area are merged in the general history of Rome; so that in the later periods which this chapter touches, there must be some overlapping with what will follow. This local method will not shut the door upon further progress towards a more general view; but at present we may well be content with it, all the more because the majority of historical students, remote from philological and even epigraphic studies, are still hardly conscious of the many barriers of language by which Italy was divided when the Tarquins fell.

Since the period that we are considering is most conveniently named after the people who in the course of it certainly held the largest share of political power in the peninsula, we must begin with a brief account of what is known of them, in particular of: (*a*) the geographical area over which we can trace their occupation; (*b*) the traditional data for their history; (*c*) the archaeological evidence of their arrival and subsequent movements; supplemented by (*d*) the varieties of alphabet used by them and the other tribes of Italy during this period; (*e*) the nature of their language, and their probable origin; (*f*) their manner of life in Italy.

We can then survey, proceeding generally from north to south, what is known of the other tribes of Italy at the earliest stages to which our records of them take us; and conclude by asking how far we are justified in grouping them under any ethnographical scheme, and what influence the facts which we have arrived at, dry and impersonal as of necessity they must be, have nevertheless exercised upon the subsequent course of history in Italy and therefore in Europe.

II. THE GEOGRAPHICAL DISTRIBUTION OF THE ETRUSCANS

These people were called *Etrusci* and, more commonly, *Tusci* by their Roman neighbours, *Turskum numen* (which would be in Latin *Tuscum nomen*) by their eastern neighbours, the people of Iguvium, and Τυρσανοί, Τυρρανοί (in Doric), Τυρσηνοί, Τυρρηνοί (in Ionic-Attic) by the Greeks. The two forms *Turs-co-* and *Turs-āno-* look like parallel[1] stems; but we know nothing at present

---

[1] Cf. *e.g. Volusus, Volusius, Vol(u)sci, Volusenus; Pontius, Ponteius, Pontanus,* Etr. *Puntna; Velanius, Velasius,* Etr. *Vela.*

of the first syllable of the word *Etrusci*, which may be merely due to some peculiar thickness of pronunciation given by the Etruscans to an initial *t*, so that to Roman ears it sounded like a separate syllable. Some late Greek writers, like Strabo, write Ἐτροῦσκοι[1]. *Etruria* is merely a later Latin form of an older **Etrusia[2].

Of the Etruscan inscriptions which we possess, and of which nearly 6000 have already[3] been collected, the great majority have come from Tuscan soil, that is from the region of the peninsula which the Romans recognized as Etruria proper. We have inscriptions and remains, both numerous and ancient, from the table-land which covers the south-west triangle between the coast and the Tiber (Caere, Veii, Falerii, Tarquinii, Volcii) with the range of hills running north not far from the coast (Cosa, Vetulonia, Volaterrae); a multitude more of rather later date come from spots farther inland, like Clusium (Chiusi) and Perusia (Perugia).

Outside Tuscany we find Etruscan inscriptions in Latium, as at Praeneste and Tusculum, a name which is itself significant; in Campania, as at Capua, Suessula, Nola; and as far south at least as Surrentum and Salernum. In the eastern half of Italy we find them in Ravenna, Pisaurum and elsewhere in Umbria; one of especial importance from the modern Novilara which archaeologists refer to the sixth (or even some earlier) century B.C. has often been taken to show, not indeed normal Etruscan speech, but at least some Etruscan features. Farther north, the remains found on the south-west of Bologna (the Roman *Bononia* but Etruscan *Felsina*) have explained the tradition of the Etruscan origin of the town, by showing their predominance in it at a certain epoch (p. 394); especially a second group at a spot in the valley of the Reno, now called Pian di Misano (probably *Mesanum*[4] in antiquity) near Marzabotto. Tradition also vouches for Etruscan rule in Mantua. Farther west, at least one remarkable Etruscan inscription has been found at Piacenza, though upon an object easily transported; and at least one with Etruscan endings from Sondrio, near the north end of Lake

---

[1] The name Ῥασέννα, given by Dionysius Halic. (I, 30) as the name used by the Etruscans themselves, is by Schulze regarded as belonging merely to the *gens Rasinia* of Pisa; it is clear that the two forms are akin, but there is some evidence that *rasna* means 'Etruscan' or 'national'; see p. 412.

[2] ** marks a form which is not actually recorded but reconstructed from its later form (as **Etrusia from the later *Etruria*) or from some kindred word.

* marks an object illustrated in the volume of plates.

[3] In the *Corpus Inscriptionum Etruscarum*, now in its second volume

[4] Compare *Messanicus* the older name of the Padusa

Como, *i.e.* not far east of Chiavenna, the ancient *Clavenna*, whose termination may be of Etruscan origin[1].

A group of inscriptions found near the Brenner Pass, especially in the neighbourhood of Trent and Bozen, has been called Raetic; and it has been enlarged by an interesting find of brief dedications, written on fragments of split stagshorn found at Magrè about 20 miles north-west of Vicenza. The language of this group was formerly supposed to be a kind of Etruscan, because the script much resembles the Etruscan alphabet, but it has been recently shown that many of the forms are unmistakably Indo-European in origin; the language therefore, if it be Etruscan at all, cannot be classed as Etruscan pure and simple.

A document showing the existence of an Etruscan-speaking community (? colony) in Egypt[2] in late Ptolemaic or Caesarian times; and the close resemblance to Etruscan of an early inscription of Lemnos will be discussed later on (pp. 403 *sqq.*, 408).

III. TRADITIONAL DATA OF ETRUSCAN HISTORY

It is still impossible to write a history of the Etruscans. But there are some points well attested by tradition which we may use at least as a basis for enquiry.

Traditions preceding recorded history, when their chronology is explicit, derive it often from a count of generations, orally transmitted, or of the successive holders of some eponymous office (like the Consuls at Rome or the Priestesses of Hera at Argos); and it would be quite as foolish to treat them with contempt as to accept them without comparison with other evidence.

---

[1] The ending is certainly Etruscan in τήβεννα, the Etruscan name for the toga, and in personal names *Porsenna, Rasenna* (p. 386, n. 1 above), *Sisenna* as in other masculine names in -*a* (p. 407). The forms Τρασυμέννα, *Fescennia, Ravenna* (p. 386 above) and the *Porta Ratumenna* on the north-west side of Rome, considered in the light of the frequent Etruscan use (like the English) of place-names for nomina (*e.g.* Etr. *Tarchna*, Lat. *Tarquinii*), give some ground for this view of it in place-names also. Yet the place-names may have been there before the Etruscans (cf. *e.g.* the Ligurian *Bagienni* and *Ucenni* and the river *Scultenna* at Mutina).

[2] It is impossible to do anything but guess whether the appearance of this document in this place and epoch can be brought into any connection with a mysterious people called *Tursha* (see vol. II, pp. 24, 167, 282) "about 1200 B.C." in Egyptian sources and spoken of as "allied with Libyans and Achaeans and in conflict with Egypt in the Ramessid period." What is certain is that its script belongs to the latest form of the Etruscan alphabet which was developed in Italy

Tradition, both Greek and Roman, which clearly reflects what the Etruscans themselves believed, and which is confirmed by a mass of other evidence now at our service, is wholly agreed in representing them as invaders of the northern half of Italy (then occupied by the *Ombroi* or *Ombrikoi*), not as natives to its soil. They believed that they came from Lydia (see above, vol. II, p. 24); Roman writers continually call the Tiber *Lydius amnis*; Catullus applies the same epithet to the *Lacus Benacus* (the modern Garda) because of Etruscan settlements in that region, as at *Mantua* (a name connected with that of an Etruscan minor deity) on the *Mincius*, the outlet of the lake.

In Etruria a good number of well-recorded local names are akin to words familiar in Latin and kindred languages, such as *Graviscae, Vetulonium, Populonium, Rusellae, Luca, Luna* and the river *Minio*, to mention only some whose etymology is most obvious; and there are some, like that of the river *Umbro* and *Camars* (the older name of Clusium; cp. *Camerinum* near Nuceria), which definitely point to the people of the region east of the Tiber which the Romans later on called Umbria.

The epoch to which the general tenor of these traditions would lead us to refer the immigration of the Etruscans is that which followed the Trojan War, the end of which was dated by the best Alexandrine computations some four centuries before the First Olympiad. Preceded, it may be, or accompanied by similar adventurous expeditions from their Pelasgian neighbours, the Etruscans came to Italy as pirates; and their successive settlements were no doubt, like those of the Danes and Saxons in England in a later age, spread over a considerable period. Ten generations after the Trojan War, according to Ephorus, was the earliest date at which Greek sailors acquired skill and courage enough to found settlements or even to trade on the east coast of Sicily in defiance of the 'Tyrrhenian pirates.' This implies that these Tyrrhenians had been long powerful in Italian waters before the earliest Greek colony in Sicily was founded (see vol. III, p. 671).

The era implied in the Alexandrine dating receives some confirmation from a note of Augustus (recorded by Servius), who quoted the declaration of Volcatius, an Etruscan augur, to the effect that the appearance of the comet in 44 B.C. had marked the end of the ninth Etruscan *saeculum*. This measure of time was variously computed at different epochs; sometimes it is made as brief as 100 years, sometimes as long as 123; Varro's account would put the beginning of the first *saeculum* into the eleventh century B.C. On the other hand Plutarch mentions 667 A.U.C.

(87 B.C.) as the end of the eighth *saeculum* according to Sulla (whose name betokens Etruscan connections, p. 407), and this would not take us back beyond the tenth century B.C.

The origin and development of the alphabets of early Italy, which we must shortly examine (pp. 395 *sqq.*), link the earliest Etruscan inscriptions with the Greeks who were founding (or were to found) Cumae. Greek traditions represent this as a colony from Chalcis in Euboea in the eleventh century B.C.; and according to the account which Strabo followed, possibly depending on Ephorus, a native of the Aeolian Cyme, that town joined in the enterprise (see vol. III, p. 676). The old objections to this date based on the limitations of sea-transport at so early an epoch have lost some of their force in view of our knowledge of the maritime resources of Minoan Crete; and whether it was the Cyme of Aeolis (the town which Strabo certainly meant by Κύμη), next neighbour to Phocaea, or a small community in Euboea of that name (mentioned only by Stephanus of Byzantium) that was the partner of Chalcis, as some scholars suppose, seems a small matter, since in any case the Cyme of Aeolis would be in touch with the community which shared its name in Euboea (being presumably its parent town); and Aeolian colonists would also be interested in the adventures of the Phocaeans who must have been familiar with Western waters long before they founded Massilia at the end of the seventh century.

The rate of discount to which the figures given by tradition should in this case be subject depends wholly on the archaeological evidence; and the archaeologists are not yet agreed in their deductions from it, though the site of Cumae has been deeply explored. It is universally admitted that no Greek settlement in the West has left remains of an earlier character; and until an upper limit of date can be safely assigned to the Greek vases with geometrical ornament (Dipylon-style) with the earliest of which the earliest type of vase at Cumae, the lecythus of Tataie, is contemporaneous, we must be content with a figure like 800 B.C., which even the most sceptical of modern authorities[1] are not prepared to dispute.

The tradition of the Etruscans' invasion of the Po valley gives us no date beyond the fact that they were settled there before the coming of the Gauls—since we are told that some of the Etruscans, driven out by these new invaders, fled northwards into certain Alpine valleys—and the same traditions would lead us to

---

[1] Ridgeway and Montelius are prepared to follow the traditional dating more closely.

refer the first arrival of Gauls in Italy to the sixth century B.C.
'Two hundred years before they were destined to take Rome,'
is Livy's account.

The zenith of the Etruscans' land-power was marked by their
becoming masters of Rome and Capua. The orthodox tradition
ascribed the establishment of the Tarquin-dynasty in Rome to
616 B.C. Cato, quoted by Velleius, tells us that Capua was founded
by the Etruscans 260 years before it was taken by the Romans.
The most likely interpretation of this statement refers it to the
alliance with Rome in 338 B.C. when from the town-lands
the *ager Falernus et Stellas* was ceded to the Romans; so that the
foundation would be in 598 B.C. Velleius, however, understood
Cato to be thinking of its destruction by the Romans in 211 B.C.,
which, as he wisely says, would allow too little time for all its
known history (see below); and he mentions another view by
which the 'foundation' (by whom?) would be dated about
800 B.C.; but the reckoning which places the Etruscan conquest
of Capua nearer to the Tarquinian era in Rome is clearly more
probable.

At the naval battle near Alalia in Corsica about 535 B.C.
the Etruscans in alliance with the Carthaginians defeated
the Ionian (Phocaean) colonists; but in 524 B.C. the Etruscans
were defeated on land by Aristodemus of Cumae; and a detachment of King Porsenna's forces, after his attack on Rome, were
repulsed from Aricia by the help of the same able despot. Later,
in a great naval battle off Cumae in 474 B.C., the Etruscans were
defeated by Hiero of Syracuse who offered to Zeus at Olympia,
with other spoil, an Etruscan helmet which he took in the battle.
These dates indicate probably the period of the greatest naval
power ever held by the Etruscans; though some of their towns
were still able to send three large ships to aid the Athenians in
besieging Syracuse in 414 B.C.

Within the same period falls the expulsion of the dynasty of
the Tarquins from Rome (510 B.C.), of which Livy's account gives
the main traditions in a perfectly credible form. Especially noteworthy is the alliance between the Tarquins and an Etruscan
potentate, Lars Porsenna, from so far north as Clusium.

The decline of the Etruscan power appears further in their
expulsion from Capua by the invading Samnites somewhere between 445 and 425 B.C. But many of them still spoke and wrote
Etruscan in different parts of Campania at least until the next
century, as they did in Praeneste and Tusculum till the third
century or later. In Etruria itself the Romans had become every-

where dominant early in the third century. The last stages of the Etruscan resistance are marked by their two defeats at Lake Vadimo in 309 and 283 B.C.; and the last triumph over Etruscans recorded in the Capitoline Fasti is in the year 281 B.C.

IV THE EVIDENCE OF ETRUSCAN REMAINS

We have now to combine this meagre chronicle with the un-dated record of the material remains found upon Etruscan soil. The quarry is rich, and in the last forty years archaeological study led by explorers like Brizio and Ghirardini, and illumined by the learning of Helbig, Montelius and Ridgeway, has advanced far towards an agreed system of relative dating for the different types of graves and their ornament. Provided therefore that we re-cognize frankly the inherent limitations of the method, we may look to it for valuable guidance.

When once Etruscan inscriptions begin to be found, we are on fairly safe ground, because we have a double or treble clue, by combining, as we then can, the evidence of both the alphabet and the linguistic forms which the inscriptions show, with that of the character and style of the objects around them, including the shape of the tomb and the method of disposing of the dead. For other tombs we have to trust to the likenesses and differences which they show in these latter characteristics when we compare them with those marked as Etruscan by the explicit testimony of inscriptions. As we go backwards in the series, so soon as these non-inscriptional characteristics become fewer in number and less definitely related in type to those in tombs which are explicitly Etruscan, the task of identifying the makers of any particular tomb or group of tombs becomes more difficult. At this stage our chief criterion is the presence or absence of Greek vases belonging to well-known epochs, with occasional help from Egyptian objects bearing some name for which Egyptology can provide a date. In periods where both are absent our chronology becomes, or should become, merely relative. The historical results of the present position of knowledge can be briefly expressed if a more or less dogmatic statement be pardoned. The sources which will be cited in the Bibliography provide ample room for further study.

At some time in the troubled epoch that followed the Trojan War, known to modern historians as the Age of Migrations, bands of Lydian pirates, long associated in the intercourse and rivalries of trade with their neighbours on the west coast of Asia Minor— by whatever name those neighbours may then have been known—

began to land and settle on the west coast of Italy. Naturally
enough they chose the less rocky and less stormy half of it,
that is to say, the shores that stretch north of the mouth of
the Tiber. There they found in possession a people known in
tradition as *Ombroi* who dwelt in villages of round huts and
already enjoyed the advantages of the early Iron Age, with
weapons and ornaments of the types (from the earliest onwards)
found at Villanova (vol. ii, p. 571 *sq.*). These *Ombroi* cremated
their dead and placed the bones and ashes in earthenware receptacles which they then buried in pits (*tombe a pozzo, Schacht-
gräber*); these pits were not isolated but in groups.

The civilization, such as it was, of the whole region developed
steadily, without any sudden appearance of new types of ornament
or utensils, or any sudden disappearance of the older types. Pit-
graves were succeeded by trench-graves (*tombe a fossa*); then both
began to be grouped inside a low fence of flat stones set on end
(*tombe a circolo*); and to some of the groups thus enclosed a large
tumulus was added above the surface. Later came the corridor-
graves (*t. a corridoio*), and finally the chamber-graves (*t. a camera*)
of more than one shape in different localities. All through this
succession, the development of the ornaments, such as *fibulae*, and
other possessions placed in the graves seems to be unbroken.
Even the appearance of inhumation cannot be referred to any one
point in the series; for the oldest cemeteries show some cases of
inhumation side by side with the prevailing practice of cremation;
while even in the latest group some cases of cremation survive.
But it is apparently in the period of the *tombe a circolo* that the
scale begins to turn in favour of inhumation.

What is perhaps the earliest Etruscan epitaph yet known (...*leś
feluskeś*) is on a stele[1] with an incised portrait of a warrior which
stood upon a tumulus over a *tomba a circolo* at Vetulonia. The
warrior wears a metal helmet with an enormous crest and carries
a double axe which is neither a Greek nor an Italian weapon, but
a regular offering to Zeus Labraÿndos in Asia Minor, and to some
deity or deities of the Minoan Age in Crete. In Homer we
find it used by the Trojan Pisander and all its associations are
oriental. The circular shield has a six-rayed geometric star, a
pattern which recurs on two shield-like rosettes carved on a gold
plaque from Tralles in Lydia[2] (now in the Louvre) and on a sarcophagus from Idrias in Caria. The shape of the stele itself recalls
that of Lemnos[3] (see p. 408).

The tomb, like others of the same type, contained painted
Greek vases belonging to the oldest products of insular Greek

[1] See Volume of Plates i, 326, *a*.   [2] *Ib.* 326, *b*.   [3] *Ib.* 326, *c*.

ceramic art, and dating from 650 to 600 B.C. These, however, are not the earliest importations into Tuscany from Greece, for in the younger (and the older) groups of pit-graves (*e.g.* at Corneto and Vulcii) there are found numerous examples of the well-known Dipylon type of vase with geometric ornament which are at least as early as the eighth century B.C. and may be much earlier. At Corneto also was found a Phoenician vase of Egyptian porcelain with the name of King Bocchoris (*c.* 718–712 B.C.); whereas in the chamber-grave known as the Grotto of Isis at Volcii there was a scarab of Psammetichus I (663–609 B.C.).

Is there any point in this long development at which it is reasonable to conjecture that the Etruscans rather than their subjects began to build the tombs? Two suggestions have been made, both of which appear reasonable. One is that the chamber-tombs should be regarded as definitely introduced by the Etruscan invaders[1]. The evidence for associating this form of tomb with a race from Lydia is quite overwhelming; few who compare the pictures of the chamber-tombs in Etruria with those in Asia Minor will find it easy to doubt the oriental origin of this quite non-Italian practice; the lions at the door of some tombs are particularly convincing.

We must however reckon with the fact that Etruscan inscriptions appear in tombs which the archaeological evidence shows to be somewhat earlier than the chambers, *e.g.* that from Vetulonia with the portrait of the Etruscan warrior just described. This was found, not in a chamber, but above one of the groups of trench-graves (*tombe a fossa*) covered by a tumulus. Hence it has been proposed to find in the type of graves to which this last belongs the first evidence of the presence of Etruscans, since it is these graves which show for the first time anything like a profusion of ornament buried with the dead or (as in the Vetulonia tumulus) with his ashes[2].

It is hardly necessary to point out that these two suggestions are not really in conflict. In order to be able to excavate a site for one of the chamber-tombs and to build it in the elaborate and costly fashion which many of them show, the Etruscans must have been not merely safely landed but firmly established in authority and with command of abundant labour. Before that time it is natural that they should have contented themselves with something less stately than what their native Lydian customs prescribed for a wealthy family. In any case it is difficult to conceive

---

[1] B. Modestov, *Introduction à l'histoire romaine.*
[2] Körte, in *P.W.*, *s.v.* Etrusker.

of any human community as a whole confining its burials to such costly tombs. Family vaults are common in England; but in no churchyard are they so numerous as the humbler graves. It seems reasonable therefore to adopt the view that it is in the stone-ringed groups of graves, rather than in the chamber-tombs, that we must look for the first certain traces of the Etruscan invaders; though we shall further recognize in the appearance of the chamber-tombs the sign of their complete domination. This must, in view of all the indications, have been established some time in the seventh century B.C.; their first settlements not later than the first half of the eighth; how much earlier, *i.e.* at what point between 1000 and 800 B.C., the first Lydian pirate beached his ship on the Italian coast, we must await more precise evidence to determine.

But archaeological research has borne definite fruit also in a later part of Etruscan history, their invasion of the valley of the Po. The tradition connecting them with Bononia (the modern Bologna) which they called *Felsina* has received complete confirmation from the ancient cemeteries uncovered in recent years. The Bologna Museum exhibits in a wonderful series the whole development of the tools, ornaments and pottery of the Early Iron Age from finds, representing successive epochs, on the estates known as Benacci (I and II), Arnoaldi and La Certosa, all lying on the western side of the modern town. In the last two, in the cemeteries near the bank of the Reno, and farther up the same stream at Marzabotto, there were found remains definitely marked as Etruscan by the presence of tombstones and other objects marked with Etruscan inscriptions as well as by resemblances in the graves and their contents generally to those of Etruria; they all belong to the class of *tombe a fossa*, and both incineration and inhumation appear side by side, in the proportion roughly of 1 : 3. The most distinctive single characteristic of the material remains of La Certosa is a new type of fibula*, which has been named from the site because it appears there for the first time. It is developed from earlier forms* known in the 'Benacci' and 'Arnoaldi' periods, and its peculiarity is that the catch (*agrafe*) in which the pin of the fibula is secured is not merely prolonged and often crowned with a knob, but has its end bent upwards and backwards, so as to cover completely the point of the pin. These fibulae however have their spring still only on one side. The earliest Attic vases found in these Etruscan tombs are black-figured, but show the features of the latest of that type, contemporaneous with the earliest of the red-figured (which also occur

in this cemetery), and are referred therefore to the epoch of the
Peisistratidae, that is to the second half of the sixth century B.C.
From the same kind of evidence it appears that the most brilliant
period of Etruscan prosperity in Bononia was from 450–400 B.C.,
and that the importation of Greek vases continued well into the
next century, until the Gallic invaders did away with all the
Etruscan wealth and probably with most of its owners.

V. THE ANCIENT ALPHABETS OF ITALY

Less interesting but in some ways more cogent evidence of
the relations of the Etruscans to the peoples around them
appears in the form and growth of the earliest alphabets used in
various parts of Italy. Most of them were in use by the end of
the fifth century B.C., and some of them probably some centuries
earlier. In many cases the signs are known to us from abecedaria
(ancient records of an alphabet as such, cf. p. 420 below) as well
as from inscriptions; and the word *script* will be used instead of
alphabet wherever it is important to indicate that our information
is drawn merely from inscriptions with no abecedarium to
guide us.

It is desirable, even though it may be superfluous for most of
the readers of this volume, to remind them that the history of an
alphabet is altogether distinct from that of the languages which
it is employed to represent; the Russian alphabet, for instance, is
derived from the Greek alphabet, but the Russian language is not
derived from, nor even closely akin to, Greek. On the other hand,
when one community borrows a system of writing from another,
the transfer is clear evidence that the two communities were in
some kind of contact, direct or indirect, at the time; and that at
least a certain number of people among the borrowers or intro-
ducers understood the language, spoken and written, of the folk
from whom they borrowed. Again, although we shall find reason
for tracing most of the varieties of script with which we are
concerned to a definite 'source' or 'basis,' recent study makes it
more and more clear that no one of such varieties can be wholly
explained until it is recognized that in the difficult, often prolonged,
and always disappointing quest of symbols to spell the sounds of
their own speech, early spellers were wont to look for help from
any available source, and not always and only from the source to
which they owed most. This fact (which has been often over-
looked at great cost of time and paper) complicates our study; but
it often suggests historical considerations of some value.

The table at the end of this section provides a concrete basis for the history of writing (and of the civilization of which writing is the measure) in Italy in this period; and also some faint indication of the intercourse which existed between different tribes.

It has seemed desirable to make the table as complete as our knowledge allows, in order that it may serve as an instrument for further study. But comments upon it have been restricted to matters which are of importance from the historical point of view.

Enumerated in what seems to be the chronological order of the earliest known monuments of each, the alphabets under consideration are those best known as (a) East-Italic ('Sabellic'), (b) Etruscan, (c) Latin, (d) Venetic, (e) Oscan, (f) Umbrian, (g) Messapic, (h) Faliscan and (i) Raetic and other Alpine varieties of the Etruscan; but this order is by no means certain and in any case it is to some extent accidental, i.e., it may be disturbed at any moment by the discovery of an inscription hitherto unknown.

It is clear at the outset that all these belong to the great family of alphabets ultimately derived from a source in the east of the Mediterranean: this source used to be called Phoenician[1] and to it at all events the Phoenician alphabet is closely akin. And it is not less certain that they all came into the hands of their different users in Italy mainly through Greek channels, and especially from those Greeks who used what is known as the Western Alphabet (see below, p. 397).

From this ascription to the Western Greek type we must except at once the Tarentine-Ionic and its close congener the Messapic, which show characteristics of 'Ionic,' i.e. Eastern Greek writing (X meaning χ and Ψ meaning ψ). But we must separate also that named first in the list above (third in the table) which appears in a few very ancient and still obscure inscriptions from spots on or near the east coast of Italy, such as Grecchio in Marrucine territory and Bellante in Picentine. This script offers too many uncertainties and peculiarities[2] to be at present safely connected with any one variety of Greek alphabet. Again, at the lower end of the period (at least 600 years) which the Table covers, we must

---

[1] See below, p. 469 and n. 1.

[2] Especially the number of signs for vowels (⋏ as well as V and Ⅴ, ◇ and ◈, Λ and Δ and perhaps P, and of course ⌐) and for sibilants or (at all events) fricatives of some kind (Ⓧ, ᔑ, ᔑ, I(?), ❢, ⋈, ⊠ and perhaps M); but on the other hand there is (as yet) no sign corresponding to φ or χ or ψ. The symbol ⋏ appears in the Lycian alphabet where it denotes some kind of e-sound beside E (= i) and P (= a).

put on one side the Raetic script, of which that from Magrè is given as a type, with its North-Etruscan congeners like that from Sondrio (there are varieties from Lugano and Bolzano) until earlier and fuller records enable us to judge how far the differences[1] from the common Western type which appear in the few inscriptions we at present possess are due to accident or to lateness of date. But of all the rest, groups (*b*)—(*f*) and (*h*) on p. 396, it may be said without a shadow of doubt that they are based on one or more varieties of the Western Greek alphabet. The outstanding features of this 'Western' family are the use of X with the value of *x* (Ionic *ξ*) not of *χ* (*chi*); its place before, not after, *φ* in the abecedaria; and the use of Y with the value of *χ* not of *ψ*[2].

By a rare kindness of fortune there has been preserved on a vase of the sixth (if not an earlier) century B.C., found at Formello, near the site of the ancient Veii, two slightly variant copies of an alphabet which may safely be called the mother-alphabet of all the six varieties we are now considering. The vase contains also an Etruscan inscription, and a 'syllabary' containing the letters *a*, *z*, *r*, *s* and *u* in various combinations. The forms and order of the letters here are very precisely confirmed by those on another vase (likewise containing an Etruscan alphabet, syllabary and inscription) found at Caere in a chamber-tomb (p. 392 above), though the writing here is less careful and the whole has suffered some slight damage. Much the same appears on a small ivory plaque, found twelve miles from Orbetello[3], now at Florence.

Whether this Formello-alphabet be called the daughter or the sister of the alphabet used at Cumae in the earliest periods of the existence of that Chalcidian colony is a matter of some interest for the history of Mediterranean civilization, though it is of minor importance for the history of Italy itself. If we acknowledge our uncertainty (see below) on this point by calling the Formello-alphabet *Chalcid-Etruscan*, and if we recognize frankly that all its descendants show, both at once and later, changes and additions drawn from other sources (p. 395), then the following

---

[1] Especially the interesting 𝔖 from Magrè (representing some dental fricative); ⋔ for *z*; the absence of *φ* and *χ*; W for *m*, Y for *u*, and Λ for *l*. The last three peculiarities may perhaps point to Corcyra and Corinth (whose alphabets are drawn from the Eastern type).

[2] Notice further, as a feature especially characteristic of Boeotia and Chalcis and its colonies including Cumae (p. 389 and below), the sign L for *l* (not Λ), as in the inscription of the fifth-century coins of Chalcis YAL, whereas the script of Phocis has ⌐.

[3] At Marsiliana d'Albegna, which has ⌐ instead of < (see Bibliography).

stemma may be taken to represent the most important facts of their descent.

Western Greek
(Chalcis, Boeotia, Phocis)
|
Chalcid-Etruscan
|
Latin (Praeneste, seventh cent.) — Campano-Etruscan — Etruscan (sixth cent.) — Umbrian

Campano-Etruscan → Oscan

Etruscan (sixth cent.) → Faliscan, Venetic

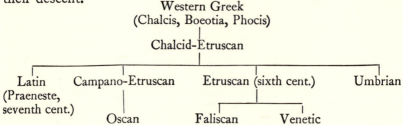

The historical value of this stemma would be increased if we could fix with certainty the epoch of the foundation of Cumae (p. 389). But that colony was certainly not the only point at which the Etruscans were in contact with people[1] who used a Western Greek alphabet. For while, on the one hand, the Etruscan alphabet resembles the Cumaean in the position of the sign for *l* (⅃ not Λ) and in the position and rounding of that for γ (>, Ɔ, not ˥ nor ⅂), yet it shows other features which link it rather to the congeners of Chalcidian script in Phocis (though this has ↾ for *l*) and Boeotia (which has ⅃), *e.g.*, the preservation of M (the letter known as *san* which appears in the abecedaria between π and Ϙ) in living use beside and distinct from ≀ or ϟ; the retention, at Formello and Caere, of the central dot of the vowel sign ⊙; the two forms of Koppa Ϙ and ϙ, and the regular ⅂ (or ˥, not ϙ) for *p*. The derived Venetic alphabet has the Phocian (not the Chalcidian) form of *l* (⅂). It may be observed also that to the script of Phocis is closely akin that of the seventh-century inscriptions of Lemnos which undoubtedly contain a language closely resembling (if not identical with) Etruscan (p. 408). This script is the same as that of the oldest group of Phrygian inscriptions; these mention King Midas and are therefore older than the Lydian conquest of Phrygia in *c.* 600 B.C. All these scripts use Ψ to mean χ, not ψ. The spread of the Phocian forms has been very happily explained by Sommer as probably due to the far-reaching influence of the Delphic oracle, which we know, for instance, to have been consulted by the Etruscans of Caere soon after the battle of Alalia, *c.* 535 B.C.

For one sound, however, of the Etruscan language, that which when Etruscan came to be transliterated into Latin characters was always written *f*, no symbol existed in any Greek alphabet. From the outset, therefore, the Etruscans had either to draw help from some non-Greek source, or to devise some modification of

[1] On the Thessalian origin of Caere see Sir W. Ridgeway, *Early Age of Greece* (1901), pp. 244–6.

a symbol used for some not wholly dissimilar Greek sound. In fact they did both, but in different places, and perhaps at different times.

(*a*) The oldest Etruscan inscription we possess—not counting the Lemnian just mentioned, where the sound does not seem to occur—is of a man called (in the 'genitive') ...*leś feluskeś* on the warrior-tomb of Vetulonia (p. 392); and the symbol for *f* seems to be 𐌚 (which appears also in a Raetic (?) inscription on a bronze helmet from Negau), the forerunner of the later 8 which existed in the Etruscan script whence (ultimately) both the Oscan and the Umbrian were derived and which passed into general use in all Etruscan communities.

(*b*) But another means of representing the sound was current in many districts where Etruscan was spoken and written, down to, at least, 400 B.C., namely (written from right to left) the combination 𐌅𐌇, *vh*, properly denoting a purely labial breathed fricative, the true sound of *wh* in English (which may still be heard in the dialect of Edinburgh). This appears in very ancient inscriptions, *i.e.*, probably of the fifth (or possibly sixth) century B.C. from Caere and Volsinii, in the *Manios* inscription of Praeneste (Latin, probably of the seventh century, see p. 455) and on Campano-Etruscan vases of the fourth (or fifth ?). Further, it must have been in use in the form of Etruscan script from which the Venetic alphabet was taken, since it maintained itself in that alphabet till the alphabet itself died out in the last century before Christ; and it was of course from this conjoint symbol (FH in later writing) that there arose by simplification the Latin use of F alone.

(*c*) A third method was to use a different sign, namely ↑, which we find in Campania (on coins of Nuceria Alfaterna about 300 B.C.); and in regular use in the Faliscan alphabet, known to us from about the same period.

The nearest parallels to all these three methods come from Asia Minor. The symbol 𐌚 appears on Lydian inscriptions of Sardes with the value of *f*; the combination 𐌅𐌇 appears in Pamphylia (and also at Tanagra in Boeotia) to denote a breathed *w*-sound in the pronominal acc. form 𐌅*he* (Attic ἕ, Sanskr. *sva*, cf. Lat. *sē*, *suus*); and the symbol ↑ has been convincingly derived (by Sir William Ramsay) from Ϙ used in Phrygia in combination with κ to denote the sound of *qu-*, first in the form Ⴔ and then in the form ↑, in the same name, so that the letter properly denotes a *w*-sound, as it does in the Iberian alphabet, where ↑ stands for *w* as well as for *u*. No doubt in Italy it came to denote *f* first in combination with *h* and then alone, just as F did.

It has been conjectured that the symbol 𐌚 was introduced from

Asia Minor through intercourse in the sixth century B.C. with the Phocaeans of Massilia, or with those of Alalia in Corsica, whom the Etruscan fleet defeated; but there seems no need to suppose that the Etruscans were dependent on the Greeks, often their enemies, for their communications with Lydia—though no doubt that avenue may also have contributed something from time to time—since from at least the sixth century B.C. onwards Greek imports abound in all Etruscan cemeteries.

On the history of the other alphabets in the table only one or two remarks need be added to what has been already said, in order to explain and supplement the stemma constructed on p. 398.

We observe first that Etruscan speech knew no distinction between the voiced and breathed sounds—*b* and *p*, *g* and *k*, *d* and *t*; to an Etruscan ear the two sounds in each pair were one and the same[1]. Hence for writing Etruscan one of the corresponding symbols in each pair in the Chalcid-Etruscan alphabet was superfluous in its original meaning. 𐌁 and ◁ never appear in any pure Etruscan inscription; and ⟩ or Ɔ, after existing side by side with ⋈ and ꟼ for some centuries (see below), ultimately drove them out of use altogether for writing Etruscan[2].

We should note, however, that from the seventh century down to the fourth, or later, we find a difference in the use of the signs in South Etruscan, ⋈ being used only before *a*, Ɔ only before *e* and *i* and (so long as it remained in use) ꟼ only before *u*. The same practice has influenced, though not wholly controlled, the spelling of the Latin Forum-inscription probably of the fifth century B.C. (p. 455), and of the *Duenos* inscription in the fourth (*pakari, qoi,* and *feked* altered into *feced*). And there can be no doubt, after Hammarström's careful analysis of the evidence, that the names of these letters in the Latin alphabet, CE, KA, QU, which have descended into English, must be derived from the Etruscan names. And it is, further, a reasonable conclusion that all the other Latin letter-names (though it would be out of place to discuss them here) were either taken over directly from the Etruscans, or at least

---

[1] 'Αγαμέμνων, 'Αλέξανδρος and Φοίβη appear on Etruscan mirrors as *acmemeno* (and *aχmemrun*), *alixentros* (also *elχsntre*) and *φuipa*.

[2] Except in the north, where ⋈ drove out Ɔ at a very early date; that is, in inscriptions from Vetulonia, the district of Saena, Clusium, Cortona, Perusia, and the Po valley. In the abecedaria from Clusium (*C.I.E.* 1372 f., *c.* 500 B.C.) the sign for Ɔ is wanting. Hence in the derived Umbrian and Venetic alphabets we have only ⋈, but in the Faliscan alphabet only Ɔ (Fal. *cuando, cupa* beside Lat. *quando, cubat*). These observations are due to Hammarström.

shaped largely on the Etruscan practice. The date of either event would probably fall between 500 and 300 B.C.

The changes in the Latin alphabet made about 300 B.C. hardly concern us here. But it is well to add that, whereas down to that date the third letter, thanks to Etruscan influence, had to serve for both *c* and *g* (as in *recei = regi* on the Forum-inscription and in the familiar abbreviations c. for Gaius, cn. for Gnaeus), by a change probably to be attributed to Appius Claudius Censor (312 B.C.) the sign ᴄ—of which the earliest form on inscriptions is ⊂—was adopted to denote the voiced sound[1].

The points just discussed show how closely in the most vital of all the arts of civilization the Roman community was linked with its Etruscan neighbours and temporary masters. Many obvious features of the Oscan and Umbrian and Venetic alphabets, especially their retrograde[2] direction, make their Chalcid-Etruscan origin not less clear; the complete absence of the signs for *g* and *d* and the uncertain use of that for *b* (which alternates with *p*) in the Umbrian alphabet, and the complete absence[3] of all three from the Venetic alphabet, make a direct dependence on a northern form (p. 400, n. 2) of the Etruscan alphabet certain for these two. The Oscan alphabet also is clearly derived from or greatly influenced by a script which had no sign for *d*, since its users had to adopt a special symbol ٩ (an occasional form of ٩ *r*) from the Chalcidian store to express the sound. But since ᴤ and ⟩ (*b* and *g*) seem to have been always present in their alphabet, just as в and ᴅ were in the Latin alphabet, we cannot suppose that in these two communities the influence which established the new art was wholly Etruscan. Since we have no Oscan inscriptions before the end of the fifth century, and since during all that century the chief speakers of Oscan, the Samnites (p. 449), were in contact with both the Etruscans of Capua and the Greeks of Cumae and Naples, nothing is more natural than that early writers of Oscan should draw help from both sources[4]. The Romans of the sixth

---

[1] It has been conjectured with some probability that this symbol was nothing but Ϝ, the seventh symbol (*sade* or *ζῆτα*) of the Chalcid-Etruscan alphabet put to us for the first time in writing Latin, the use being suggested by the resemblance which this form of it had to the third letter ⟨ (later C).

[2] But see below, p. 402.

[3] On the nature of the sounds in Venetic represented by ⅄, ⊕, and ⋎ respectively see below, p. 443, n. 2.

[4] It is impossible to discuss here all the points in the Oscan and Latin alphabets which illustrate this double origin, but the reader may discover some of them by a study of the Table of Alphabets.

century, and perhaps of the seventh, at least its latter part, were
more nearly enclosed in the Etruscan net; but even that did not
exclude all Greek influences. We need not, indeed we cannot,
now doubt that the art of writing was known in Rome at least
as early as 600 B.C. But the expulsion of the Tarquins was
soon followed by a conspicuous break with Etruscan fashions at
Rome. For the Latins, like the Greeks (but unlike the Etrusci,
Osci, Umbri and Veneti), adopted the left-to-right direction of
writing in the course of the fifth century. We have no hint that
the Twelve Tables, ascribed to 449 B.C., differed in this respect
from later Latin writing.

It remains only to mention briefly the special features of Venetic
writing. One is that the Venetic inscriptions we possess, both
votive and epitaphic, show the old fashion of '*boustrophēdon*' (see
p. 470), in which the direction of the letters was reversed in
every alternate line. This is used in the Latin Forum-inscription,
and it is regular in Greek inscriptions of the sixth century, and
appears in the earliest from Cumae. But in the East Italic group
(p. 445) and in Venetic (as well as in two places, perhaps by
accident, in the Forum-inscription), not merely the direction but
the erection of the letters is reversed, the feet of the letters in one
line touching the feet of those in the next.

Secondly the Venetic inscriptions show a system of 'pointing,'
as to the meaning of which complete agreement has not been
reached, though the theory advanced and still maintained by the
present writer, that the dots indicate the accent, may be said to
hold the field. In all carefully written inscriptions one syllable in
every word (sometimes more than one, especially in long words)
is distinguished by a pair of dots placed in the middle of the line
on either side of the last sound of the syllable, as in, e.g., ·e·χo
'ego,' zona·s·to 'dedit,' lehvo·s· 'Laevus,' Gr. λαιϝός. There are
some regular exceptions (as meχo 'me') which may be enclitics
or proclitics; and the puncts are regularly omitted when they
would have occupied the same place as (either or both of) the dots
which are part of the sign for h (·|·); see below, p. 442 *sq.* It would
seem that such puncts occasionally appear in Etruscan (*e.g.* in
C.I.E. 8412 a·i·ta twice, interpreted no doubt rightly as = Gr.
Ἀίδης, Att. ᾁδης) and possibly at Magrè and in the East Italic
group. For the linguistic aspect of the question the reader must
be referred to the articles cited in the Bibliography; but if the
accentual theory is correct, the close resemblance of this Venetic
fashion to the method of denoting accent used in Sanskrit writing,
in the grammarians' text (*Pada* text) of the Rig-Veda, raises

the same interesting question of transmission as does the earlier method of denoting accent in Greek papyri.

The general result of the evidence examined in this section may be stated almost in a single sentence. Between 800 and 200 B.C. the art of writing spread over the whole of Italy between the Alps and the Mediterranean, with the exception of Liguria where we have no pre-Roman evidence; and if we except the two peninsulas of Messapia and Bruttium, the Greek colonies like Cumae and Ancona, and a few scattered points on the coast of Picenum, there was no community in the whole area which did not learn the art, directly or indirectly, from the Etruscans, and which was not burdened, temporarily or permanently, by anomalies due to the way in which the Etruscans had curtailed the resources of the Greek alphabet to suit their own comparatively barbarous observation of the elements of language. The paucity of vowel symbols and the redundancy of *c*, *k* and *q*, the two chief weaknesses of the Latin alphabet, still survive to plague every child who uses that alphabet to spell his own language; and they are part of humanity's debt to the Etruscans.

VI. THE ETRUSCAN LANGUAGE

Substantial progress has been made in recent years in our knowledge of Etruscan, thanks to the more sober method of enquiry which has at last prevailed of interpreting the inscriptions in their own light, that is, by comparison with one another, and by a study of all the material surroundings in which they were found; no longer by the wild-goose chase after resemblances to individual words in other languages. The statement of Dionysius of Halicarnassus in the time of Augustus that the language was like no other is even yet hardly superseded; but fortune has rewarded the efforts of enquirers in the last thirty years by bringing into our hands two or three much longer documents than had before been known. The Stele of Capua written during the period of Etruscan dominion in that town, and therefore in the sixth or fifth century B.C., which was first published in 1900, is complete in itself and contains some 200 words of continuous text, divided into paragraphs. Somewhat earlier there was noticed in the Museum at Agram a quantity of Etruscan writing on a Mummy-band, amounting to 1500 words, which make a continuous text in each of the half columns remaining—the upper half of each column was on a corresponding strip of linen which has perished. The material and ink used are referred by Egyptologists to the

last two centuries B.C. It has been reckoned that there are some
40 words common to these two documents; and from the fairly
frequent repetition of words and phrases it is clear that both are
of a liturgical or formulary nature, such as we know to have
constituted a large part of the *disciplina Etrusca* (see below,
p. 415). The names of the gods *tinś* 'Iuppiter' and *mariś*
'Mars' with *aiseras* ('gods') itself recur on the leaden Tablet of
Magliano (*C.I.Etr.* 5237) now in the Florence Museum. This is
certainly a *defixio*, *i.e.* a curse, like others from Volaterrae (*ib.* 52)
and Populonia (*ib.* 5211).

Only a few of the interpretations so far reached are certain
enough to be mentioned here. The only verbal inflexions that
are clear appear in a few past tenses—(i) *-ce* in *amce* 'was,' *svalce*
and *lupuce* both meaning '*vixit*,' *tece* 'set up,' *turce* 'gave,' *zilacnuce*
'held a magistracy'; (ii) *-ne* in *leine* or *line* and *mulune* 'dedicated,'
'built' or 'set up' applied to the person or persons who made the
tomb or placed the urn. These inflexions, however, seem to be
sometimes omitted, like the Greek augment, so that e.g., *lupu*
appears instead of *lupuce*, as in *avils* XXXVI *lupu* 'vixit annos XXXVI,'
and *mulu* instead of *mulune*. These words illustrate the character
of the mass of the inscriptions which are either sepulchral or
votive. In both, the pronominal *mi* 'this (is the monument or
the offering) of' preceding a proper name in the 'genitive' is
common. The meanings of *alpan* (used of several kinds of
votive) 'offering,' *śuθi* 'grave,' *flereś* 'statue,' *zamaθiman* 'brooch'
appear from the objects to which they are attached; so *hinθial
terasiaś*, the name on a figure on the back of a mirror picturing
the scene of Homer, *Od.* XI, 90, clearly means ψυχὴ Τειρεσίαο
'the soul of Teiresias'; *lautn* 'familia,' *lautni* 'libertus'[1], *naper*
'limit' or 'measure,' *ril* and *avil* both meaning either 'year' or
'aged' (Germ. 'bejahrt'), each regularly accompanied by numbers:
and the enclitics (*u*)*m* and *-c* 'and' are not less clear from their use.

The names *puia* 'wife,' *sec* or *seχ* 'daughter,' *clan* 'son' (*clens*
'of the son,' *clenśi* 'for[2] the son,' *clenar* 'sons') are very common;
ati 'mother,' θ*ura* 'brother,' *nefts* 'grandson' (clearly connected
with Lat. *nepos*), *prumaθs* (Lat. *pronepos*) 'great grandson' are less

---

[1] This word is so rendered on the bilingual insc. *C.I.L.* XI, 1990 =
C.I.E. 3692.

[2] As in the dedication of the famous statue of the orator (arringatore)
at Florence (*C.I.E.* 4196) which begins: *auleśi meteliś ve vesial clenśi cen
flereś tece* (followed by the names of the person or persons presenting it),
i.e. 'To Aule Meteli (Aulus Metellus) the son of Vel (and) of Vesia,
(so and so) erected this statue.'

frequent but still beyond doubt. This illustrates the care with which epitaphs were composed, the family of the deceased being carefully recorded, often for two or more generations back; sometimes only the father's name (*i.e.* his praenomen) is given, sometimes only the mother's, sometimes both[1]. This aristocratic habit is further illustrated by a characteristic peculiarity of the language which is known as the *genetiuus genetiui*—which shows that what we call a 'genitive' was felt rather as a descriptive adjective which could itself give rise in its turn to a further descriptive. Thus *velθuruś* means 'of Velthur,' *arnθial* and *arnθal* 'of Arruns' and often appear after the names of their respective sons and daughters; but forms like *velθuruśla, arnθalisa, arnθialiśla* appear attached to those of their grandchildren. Similarly the 'agnomen' *hanusa* describes the wife or a son of Hanu (*hanunia* seems to be proper to daughters); but *hanuslisa* describes the wife or son of a son or descendant[2].

The genitive *neθunsl* from *neθuns* (borrowed from Lat. *Neptunus*) appearing on a mirror as the name of a person armed with a trident gives an instructive example of the way in which the Etruscans 'inflected' borrowed words; the Lat. *-s* of the nom. has become a part of the 'stem' in Etruscan. It must be further pointed out that these same inflexions (*-s, -ś, -al*) which have borne the meaning of a genitive in the examples just given serve also with a datival meaning, *e.g.* in such a sentence as

(*mi*) *θuplθaś alpan turce*
'(hoc) Thupelthae (deae) donum dedit.'

The words for many of the numbers are preserved, but not yet completely identified. Those of the first six, recorded on the three pairs of opposite faces of two dice, are *maχ, zal; θu, huθ; ci, śa.* Of these it is certain that *maχ* means 'one'[3] and that *zal* is either

---

[1] Examples are: (*a*) *C.I.E.* 1710 (from Clusium) *arnθ anie carcu anieś* 'Arruns Annius Gargo Annii (filius)'; (*b*) *ib.* 4353 (from Perusia) *la vipi venu vipinal clan* 'Lars Vibius Venno Vibinia natus'; (*c*) *ib.* 455 (from Cortona) *lθ. tite lθ. alfnal saχu, i.e.* 'Lars Titius Lartis (filius) Alfia natus Sacco.' *A. Ancarius A. f. Tolmaca natus (C.I.L.* xi, 2267) may be given as a Latinized parallel.

[2] So we have: *C.I.E.* 4882 *θania titi latinial śec hanuslisa* 'Thania Titia, daughter of Latinia, wife of a Hanusa' (*i.e.* 'of a descendant of Hanu'); *ib.* 1853 *hastia cainei leusla* 'Hastia Gaia, wife of a son of (someone called) Leo.'

[3] Besides other evidence (the fact that it never occurs with plurals like *clenar*, as *ci, zal* and *śa* do, nor to denote the number of times a man has held a magistracy, as *ci, zal* and *θu* do), its position on the two dice is decisive: only

'six' or 'two'; the corresponding *zaθrum* will be either 'sixty' or 'twenty'; 'seven,' 'eight' and 'nine' are *cezp, semφ* and *muv*, but it is not clear yet which is which. The syllable *-alχ* denotes at least some of the tens, as in *cealχ* or *celχ* beside *ci*, and in *cezpalχ*, *semφalχ, muvalχ*. Questions of especial interest, which must be regarded as still open, are whether the language had ever any distinct forms for Nominative and Accusative, for Singular and Plural in Verbs, and for Gender in Adjectives (if there were such things); so far at all events as study has yet progressed no affirmative answer to any of them can be supported by evidence. For a negative answer to the first two there seems already to be much that, *prima facie*, could be adduced.

One other feature in the history of the language is of historical importance, and it happens to be one which stood for a long while in the way of a true method of interpretation. A large number of Etruscan names are based on pure Latin or Sabine words such as *vespa, nero, āter*, though their derivatives show a number of suffixes which are characteristically Etruscan and not Latin, cf. Etr.-Lat. *Vesprius* (from Asisium and Ostia), *Vespronius* (from Mantua); Etr. *neru, nerina*; Etr. *atre, atru, atrunia*. This is only the natural reflexion in language of the fact that the Etruscans were a race of pirates who made themselves, in virtue of their larger acquaintance with the material arts of civilization, the ruling class among the Italic peoples whom they subdued but spared to act as their servants and subjects; and these subjects provided certainly all the nurses and many if not most of the mothers of Etruscan children.

Conversely, the intercourse between the Italic and Etruscan races which lasted for so many centuries left traces on the language of the Romans. Many are names of things, persons or customs which the Romans adopted from (or through) the Etruscans such as *histrio*, which Livy derives from Etr. *ister*, 'actor'; *lanista* 'a gladiator' ('carnifex lingua Tusca' Isidorus); *persōna*, Etr. *φersu* (from Gr. πρόσωπον) 'mask'; *haruspices*, 'diviners' (where the second element but not the first is Latin). Since the lictors and their bundles of rods and axes came from Etruria (p. 413) it is quite likely that the curious word *lictor* goes back to some Etruscan form. A number of borrowed words are marked by the change of what in Greek was a voiced plosive (*b, d*, or *g*) into the breathed sound (*p, t, c*) in Etruscan and hence

when the dice are so placed that the word *maχ* stands written in parallel direction on the top surface of each, do the words on the other five sides of each die occupy the same side in each.

in Latin; *sporta* 'basket,' ultimately from Gr. (acc.) σπυρίδα; the triumph, an institution whose pomp (κόσμος), as we know from Strabo[1] was taken from the Etruscans, probably owed to them the changes of sound by which its name in pre-Ciceronian Latin (*triumpus*) differed from its Greek original (θρίαμβος)[2]; *catamitus*, which we know to have been first used in Italy as the name of Γανυμήδης 'Ganymede, a boy favourite,' no doubt owes its *c-* for *g-* and the second *-t-* (for *-d-*) to the same influence.

Besides these and other less significant examples we have a curious class of masculine names ending in *a* (e.g. *Sulla, Perperna, Catilina, Cinna, Pera, Ruga*), which, like *Porsenna* (see above, p. 387, n. 1), are all of Etruscan origin. Many of their owners exhibited the marked Etruscan characteristics of licentiousness, aristocratic pride and a quite Turkish love of cruelty and torture, such as we find, for instance, portrayed by Vergil in the Etruscan king Mezentius.

It concerns us further to notice the close connections which have been traced between many Etruscan family names and some of the earliest names in Roman history, such as the *Porta Ratumenna* (cf. Etr. *ratumsna*, a derived name, like Etr. *percumsna* beside Etr.-Lat. *Pergonius*); the *Porta Capena* (cf. the Etr. gentile name *capna*). The old tribal names *Ramnes, Tities, Luceres*, and even *Romulus* and *Roma* itself have their respective parallels in Etruscan[3]. With these names it is natural to link the large part taken, according to tradition, by the Etruscan dynasty of the Tarquins in the fortification of Rome, especially the building of the Capitol; and much of the early political organization ascribed to Servius Tullius was no doubt shaped by Etruscan influence. All this however hardly justifies the somewhat hasty inference that the earliest founders of the city were Etruscan. In view of the continual derivation of personal names from place names (e.g. *Coriolanus, Norbanus, Gallus, Sabinus, Aufidius, Camerius, Pompeius, Tiburtius, Umbrius, Umbricius*)—though the opposite development occurs (*Appii forum; Tylorstown* and, more simply, *Nelson*)—it seems more likely that the *rumate* took their name from *Roma* than that they gave their own to the city.

---

[1] v, p. 220.

[2] The explanation given in Conway, *Italic Dialects*, p. 230, of the *-ph-* in *triumphus* may still be maintained.

[3] Etr.-Lat. *Ramennius, Ramnius* (cf. the augur *Rhamnes* associated by Vergil, *Aen.* IX, 327, with Turnus the devoted ally of Mezentius); Etr. gentil. *titie*, also *luχre* (cf. Etr.-Lat. *Lucretius*), and *rumulna* and *rumate,* Etr.-Lat. *Romatius, Romaeus* (*Sex. Romaeus Tuscus* of Telesia).

With these ascertained characteristics of the language as it existed in Italy we can now, though with due caution, combine what scanty evidence has come to light of languages spoken farther East which present parallel features. In 1885 there was discovered in the island of Lemnos an epitaph or pair of epitaphs in a language which (whether or not it be identical with the Etruscan of Tuscany) must at least be closely akin. The stone shows on its flat surface a roughly outlined figure of a warrior, and one inscription runs round it, just as in the Warrior-tomb of Vetulonia which belongs to the seventh or eighth century (p. 392); the other is on the side of the stone. In the first inscription occurs the phrase *sialχveiz aviz*, in the second *aviz sialχviz*. It is impossible to demur to the conclusion that *aviz* corresponds to Etr. *avils* 'years' and that the syllable *-alχ-* denotes some one of the tens, corresponding most probably to the Etr. simple numeral *śa* (p. 405) which must have given *śalχ-* or the like as the base of the corresponding numeral in the series of tens. The alphabet has ϒ with the value χ, and is identical with that of some Phrygian inscriptions, the latest of those in which King Midas is mentioned, which are therefore assigned to the seventh century B.C.; the date of the use of the script in Lemnos may of course be somewhat later. The appearance of Etruscan in Lemnos is by no means surprising, since we know from Thucydides that there were once Tyrrhenians in Lemnos (whom he counts as part of 'the Pelasgic element'), and from Herodotus that there were Pelasgians in the neighbouring islands of Samothrace and Imbros as well as Lemnos. One of the words on the inscription, *morinail*, has been reasonably referred to the town of Myrina on Lemnos; another, *φokasiale*[1], to the people of the by no means distant city of Phocaea with whom, as we have already seen (pp. 388, 400), the Etruscans were closely associated.

Some fairly close connection in point of language between Etruria and Asia Minor in the pre-classical period has been made exceedingly probable, if not absolutely demonstrated, by the evidence of a large number of family names recorded in both areas, and by the coincidences in the methods of extension by which derivative names are formed. A systematic enquiry over a large field of inscriptional evidence[2] places the connection beyond all

---

[1] For the formation cf. Etr. *truial-* 'Troianus.'

[2] By Herbig, *Kleinasiatisch-etruskische Namengleichungen*, Bay. S.B. 1914, Abh. 2. Many of the likenesses were first pointed out by Pauli, *Alt-ital Forschungen*, vol. II, and some of the methods of formation by Kretschmer, *Einleitung in die Geschichte der griechischen Sprache* (1896), p. 334.

doubt, however much we allow for the possibility of the intrusion of Italian names into Asia Minor in Roman times. On the Asiatic side the names are taken as recorded in Lycian sources, which happen to be abundant from the fifth century B.C. onwards; and if there were any reason for connecting the Etruscan and Lycian languages, this name-evidence would need to be carefully weighed from the linguistic point of view. In the absence of such reasons, the parallel features must be judged as attesting some actual historical connection, of a fairly direct kind, between the populations of Asia Minor and Etruria long before the fifth century B.C.; for such marked peculiarities are not developed in one or two generations merely. From a ten-page list of parallels we note first a few of the simplest: names in Etruscan alphabet are printed without capitals, those from Latinized sources with capitals.

Asia Minor	Etruria	Asia Minor	Etruria
Αβιναση	*Abenna*	Σασας	*Sasaius, Sas(s)ina, Saserna*
Αρυα(city and river)	*Arnus* (river), *arna*, *arnθ* (*Arruns*), *arnθi* (*Arruntia*)	Σατας, Σαδας	*satira, Satanas, Satanus*
Κωκας	*Cocceius, Coccius, Cocius, Cocidius*	Σολλασος	*Sulla*
		Σισινα, -ινης	*Sisenna, -ennius*
Ουαλας	*Vala* (whence *Valesius, Valerius*)	Ταλας	*Talasius, Talanius*
		Ταργυηνος	*Tarquinius*
Πισ(σ)ας, Pisidia	*Pisae* (city) (whence *Pisius, Piso, Pisenius, Pisinius, Pisurius, Pisentius*)	Ουετουσσα	*vetu, vetusa, vetsnei, Vetusius, Veturius*

Even more striking are the methods of forming new names from more simple ones by extensions with various elements: (i) *-a-*, (ii) *-e-*, (iii) *-i-* and *-ie-*, (iv) *-u-*, (v) *-l-*, (vi) *-r-*, (vii) *-n-*, (viii) *-s-*, (ix) *-t-*. Herbig gives a table showing derivatives by means of these formants from five different stems or 'roots' (*caθ-, cuθ-, cur-, saθ-, trq-*) in parallel series, of which one may be quoted (*-e-* and *-t-* extensions are absent in this series). *Asia Minor*[1]: (i) Κοττας, (iii) Κουτι, (iv) Κοτυς, (v) Κοτυλων and Κωδαλος, (vi) Κοδρος, (vii) Κυδνα (with Κοτουνης, Κοτανα, Κοτεννα, Κοδδινουπέτρα), (viii) Κυδισσος (with Κοτυσις, Κοτασις). *Etruria*: (i) *Cotta*, (iii) *Cottius*, (iv) *cutus*, (v) *Cotlus*, (vi) *Cotrius*, (vii) *cuθna, cutna*,

---

[1] It may be noted in passing that the great variety of spelling, which appears in these and a host of the other examples in Lycian alphabet, is a tolerably clear indication that the names themselves were in origin foreign to the Lycian tongue.

cutuna, Cotonia, cutana, cutanasa, Cotena, Cutennius, Cotinius,
(viii) *Cotisius.*

At the same time various other likenesses have been pointed
out in the name-systems of both regions of which the most important is the practice of forming family names from words
denoting relationship. In Asia Minor many of the 'Infantine'
appellations ('Lallnamen') of 'father'; 'mother'; 'dad' or 'gran-
dad'; 'mother' or 'grandma' or 'nurse' such as *papa, mama,
ap(p)a, nanne* are used both as common nouns and as proper
names: in Etruria *papa, mama, ap(p)a,* and *Nanneius* all appear
as proper names. Similarly in Etruscan from the words *clan, sec,
ati, puia* (p. 404) we have the proper names *clanin, clante; secu,
secne; ate, atei;* and *puina.*

By this time it will have been realized that for the student
of Etruscan origins all roads lead to Asia Minor; but can we
point to any record of any one Anatolian language in which any
features are discernible in the least resembling Etruscan? As the
exploration of Asia Minor and the study of the documents already
in hand proceeds, this question will no doubt receive a definite
answer. At the present moment the hunter can afford to neglect
no line of search that offers even a faint scent of his fox; and it
is therefore right to mention briefly here, though with much
reserve, two recent attempts. In 1899 it was pointed out[1] that
many of the languages spoken in the Caucasus (*a*) form their
noun-plurals[2] with *-r-*; (*b*) form their genitives in some dialects
with *-l-*[3]; (*c*) and that in some the genitive form can itself be
declined (in the singular) as an adjective; thus from Hyrcanian
(north-east Caucasian) is quoted *kivala* the genitive of *kiva* 'sheep'
declined as an adjective to mean 'ovine.' In Kazi-Kumukh
the commonest adjectival suffix *-ssa* can be added at will to any
word, even a case of a noun or pronoun, as *ttulsa* 'mine' from
ttul 'of me.' Of these apparently striking resemblances the third
at least may deserve further enquiry, if it be conducted with due
consciousness of the risk—not indeed prohibitive, but sobering—
of conducting such comparisons across a gulf of more than two
millennia.

Even more promising, and therefore calling for even more

---

[1] By Prof. V. Thomsen of Copenhagen.

[2] Thus in Svanetian (a dialect of Georgian; south Caucasian) *čaž* 'horse,'
čažar 'horses'; in Kazi-Kumukh (also called Lakh; north-east Caucasian)
maz 'tongue,' *mazru* 'tongues.'

[3] Kazik. *max* 'iron,' *muxal* 'of iron,' in some with *-sa* and *-s* (Georg.),
in some with *-š* (Svan.)

prolonged scrutiny, is the identification[1] of the genitival and adjectival suffix -*l*- in Lydian, a language of which we now know enough from the inscriptions found at Sardes to be certain that it does not belong to the Indo-European group, in spite of some borrowings from its (Phrygian) neighbours and invaders. In Lydian beside genitives like *atal'*, *katoval'*, there appear adjectives *atalis*, *katovalis*; and beside the name *Mane*, the derived name *Manelis*, exactly as Etr. *mane*, Etr.-Lat. *Manius* gave rise to *Manilius*, Etr. *ate* and *Atius* to *Atilius*, Etr. *caθa* and *Catius* to *Catellius*, *Catilina*, and a host of others. As Fraser points out, there can be no doubt that the much greater frequency of the -*li*-suffix in Latin than in any other Indo-European language is due directly to the influence of this Etruscan -*l*-, which was certainly a widespread element in the formation of names in ancient Anatolia, and for which a Lydian origin seems now to be at least not improbable.

VII. ETRUSCAN CUSTOM AND RELIGION

Only the briefest account of Etruscan institutions can here be attempted. Our information comes mainly from Hellenistic and Roman sources, but the customs to which it relates go back into far earlier periods. The political organization of the Etruscans was based on a number of self-governing cities joined in an alliance, mainly for military purposes, though sometimes interfering in the strictly political concerns of the separate communities. The number of the allied towns is regularly given as twelve in Etruria; and it is probable that this was the actual total in the third century B.C. From several trustworthy accounts in our traditional sources, combined with the evidence of what is left of the list of the members on a handsome monument dedicated at Caere, almost certainly to the Emperor Claudius, the names of these twelve have been identified with very great probability as Arretium, Caere, Clusium, Cortona, Perusia, Populonia, Rusellae, Tarquinii, Vetulonia, Volaterrae, Volcii, Volsinii. At an earlier period Falerii and Veii belonged to the League; Faesulae and Pisae may have done so later. But it is not possible to identify the twelve cities which the Etruscans were said to have ruled east and north of the Appennines, though Atria, the modern Adri at the mouth of the Po, was one. There seems to have been an annual festival, probably in the spring, at which all the allied towns were represented at a temple of Voltumna, the site of which,

[1] By Prof. J. Fraser in 1923 (following Danielsson and others).

however, has not yet been identified. The chief business here
seems to have been the election of a High Priest of the Alliance,
known as *praetor* or *sacerdos Etruriae* in Latin writers, *zilaθ meχl
rasnal* ('magistratus societatis Etruscae' or 'societatis publicae')
in Etruscan inscriptions. The *zilaθ* was attended by twelve lictors,
and he had beside him an inferior magistrate known as *mar(u)nuχ*;
praetor and *aedilis* were their titles respectively in Latin.

We hear more than once in the fifth and fourth centuries of
individual cities refusing to join with the rest in some particular
campaign; and sometimes of their being excused. They were
always at liberty to make war on their own account if they wished.

The evidence of Etruscan inscriptions, especially epitaphs
which enumerate the offices held by the dead man in his lifetime,
have thrown a good deal of light on the constitution of this league.
As a religious body it survived till after the time of Constantine,
having been re-organized for that end very early in the Empire
and probably by Augustus, under whom it would seem its language was changed from Etruscan into Latin, and the number of
its cities increased from twelve to fifteen; the dignity which still
attached to its highest office is shown by the fact that it was once
held by the Emperor Hadrian. Every one of the communities
belonging to the League had its own chief magistrate called *zilaχ
tenθas*, and it is no doubt these magistrates (not the whole body
of nobles) whom Livy calls *principes populorum*. In the fifth
century B.C. they seem to have been elected annually in most of
the towns; Livy tells us that the revival of the monarchy at Veii,
instead of annually elected magistrates, was resented by the
other towns. But in earlier times the ruler of each town, like
Lars Porsenna of Clusium, had been called a king (Etr. *lucumo*)
and held power for life, though like Tarquinius Priscus at Rome,
he was probably 'elected' to his throne.

Beside the *zilaχ tenθas* stood two lower officers called[1] *marniu*
and *purθne*, roughly corresponding to aedile and quaestor at
Rome. The offices were all annual and stood in a fixed order of
precedence; and all but the headship of the League could be repeated several times. The details of the system are preserved best
for us in the inscriptions of Caere where the Etruscan constitution
lost its political meaning earliest and therefore, for religious
purposes, survived in its primitive form to the latest date. The
most striking feature of the Etruscan system, as compared with
the Roman, was the absence of any collegiality; each magistrate

[1] The precise form of the words seems to vary in different places and
periods.

exercised his powers alone, though, no doubt, he was limited by the powers of any higher magistrate.

It should be added that Vergil's picture of the Etruscan host which was arrayed against Aeneas probably reflects the conditions of the period with which we are concerned in this chapter at least as nearly as the state of things in the third century B.C. In this picture we find the whole army under command of Tarchon (the eponymous hero of Tarquinii and the ancestor of the latest Tarquins); but divided into four sections, each of a group of communities; one, that led by Messapus, included folk from Latium; another was led by Osinius, King of Clusium. Even in the Augustan period we find the pontifices in some social eminence at the mainly Etruscan town of Mantua, since their college was then appointed trustee for a public endowment.

The rank and file of the army of course consisted of the humbler classes of society, namely the conquered inhabitants who were of Italian not Etruscan blood. But its military capacity seems to have been considerable, at all events in the sixth century. Of the arms used by the army we know little except what the monuments show, a long pike (*hasta*) and a short sword. The round shield also appears on early monuments like the tomb of the warrior of Tarquinii, which is ascribed to the seventh century B.C., and that of Vetulonia, already discussed (p. 392). Greek writers ascribe the invention of the trumpet to the Tyrrhenians (*Tyrsenoi*), by which name, however, they meant not the inhabitants of Etruria but their forefathers in Asia Minor and the Aegean. Characteristically Etruscan features in Roman life were the rods and axes of the lictors who attended praetors and consuls, the ivory chair and purple-hemmed robe of the higher magistrates, and all the insignia of the triumph in which the victorious commander proceeded to the temple of Jove.

The Coinage of the Etruscan towns is almost wholly later than the period with which this chapter is concerned, but its beginnings are instructive[1].Till the end of the sixth century their only currency was the *Aes Rude* or rough lumps of copper. The oldest foreign coins found on Etruscan sites come from Phocaea and other towns of Asia Minor. When their own coinage begins (about 500 B.C.) the oldest among its types seems to be a lion-head with open jaws (on gold coins with the reverse plain) which appears also in Asia Minor and in some Phocaean colonies. The town of Populonia seems to have been the most active in striking coins in all three metals from the fifth to the third century; its oldest silver coins show what may be a Perso-Babylonic standard of 11·3 gms.

[1] See Volume of Plates i, 310, *b–d, e–k.*

which had been in use in Lydia in the sixth century; the later
show the Euboic of 8·4 gms., also used in Lydia (see above,
pp. 131 *sq.*) and Syracuse. These two systems appear also side by
side in Cyprus by the fourth century; and in Cyprus too we find
many coins with one side blank, which was the regular practice
in Etruria. A noteworthy feature of the types is the frequency
of those representing mythical creatures, especially from the
Underworld, all cruel, the Gorgon, Griffin, Chimaera, Cerberus,
and Sphinx. The influence of Syracuse becomes quite clear in
the fourth century. (See further below, p. 428.)

Since the Etruscans themselves came into Italy by sea, it is not
surprising that from the beginning we find them buying wares
from abroad. Even in the pit-graves (p. 392) Phoenician imports are found, and they continue until at least 550 B.C. in graves
of all kinds; objects of ivory, Phoenician cups, Egyptian scarabs
are typical examples. But from the beginning of the sixth century,
if not earlier, the Phocaeans were formidable rivals of the Carthaginians, and at one time we find the Carthaginian and Etruscan
fleets allied against them.

The trade with and through Cumae, which had Phocaean connections (p. 389), began, as we learn from the same kind of
evidence, not later than 700 B.C., and all through the seventh
century Cumae, and (by the end of that century) Syracuse, seem
to have been points from which Greek wares reached Etruria.
In the sixth century, probably, began the direct trade of Etruscan
vessels with Athens which became regular in the fifth. The most
striking feature was the importation into Etruria of Greek vases;
at Vulcii alone over 20,000 vases have been unearthed, of which
the greater part are recognized as Greek. Geometric, 'Proto-
Corinthian,' Corinthian and Attic vases in all their successive
varieties appear in Etruscan tombs. The chief exports from
Etruria, and probably the chief basis of its wealth, were native
copper from the mountains, especially those south of the Arno
round Volaterrae, and iron, especially from Populonia and the
rich island-mines of Ilva.

As early as the beginning of the sixth century, this trade, aided
by piracy, the national pursuit, had produced great material
wealth among the governing class, displayed in the luxury attested
by tradition and by scenes represented in Etruscan works of art
and not less clearly attested by their actual remains (p. 393).
Their dress was the loose, flowing attire of the Ionians; their
tombs and no doubt their houses were adorned with wall-paintings,
largely of stories from Greek mythology (though these seem not

to have been taken from Greek writers, but merely copied from Greek works of art and often misunderstood). The corpulent type of figure (*pinguis Tyrrhenus*), still common in Tuscany, was regarded with contempt by the Romans, but seems to have been counted for beauty among the Etruscans themselves; at least if we may judge from its frequent appearance on sepulchral monuments the execution of which shows accomplished craftsmanship. Nor were Greeks and Romans less outspoken in their contempt for the effeminate licence which was characteristic of the wealthy Etruscans. Without taking too literally the somewhat lurid account of their banquets given by the third-century Sicilian historian Timaeus, we are nevertheless led by other evidence to regard them as a nation which, before they came under the powerful influence of Rome, had hardly risen above matrilinear ideas. This appears in their epitaphs in which often a man's mother is the only parent mentioned, though more often, perhaps[1], she is mentioned side by side with his father; and also in works of art where the mother appears at table beside her husband. This is good evidence of her importance in the family, but has little bearing on the question how strictly or loosely the tie of marriage was itself interpreted. The looseness which Timaeus observed, and its sharp contrast with the conceptions of the Patricians of Rome, appears in the typical but no doubt historical tragedy of Sextus Tarquinius and Lucretia. Another side of it is condemned not less clearly by Plautus, a shrewd observer and a native of Umbria, as 'the shameful Tuscan fashion'

ubi ex Tusco modo
Tute tibi indigne dotem quaeras corpore.

Precisely this institution was practised by the Lydians and other communities of Asia Minor, especially in the worship of Anaitis; but it was abhorrent to every one of the peoples among whom the Etruscans lived in Italy.

In Roman tradition we have much information as to the ritual included in what was known as the *disciplina Etrusca*, of which a great part was taken into Roman use. Of their religion at earlier periods, from the documents already mentioned, like the Stele of Capua (p. 403), we have learnt the names of many deities, and something of the various offerings paid to them respectively. From Etruscan works of art, especially the *paterae* and the backs of metal mirrors, we learn the attributes of many deities who are there portrayed and labelled with their names. All our information

---

[1] No statistics are available; cf. the examples cited on p. 405, nn. 1 and 2.

substantiates Livy's description: *gens ante omnes alias eo magis dedita religionibus quod excelleret arte colendi eas*, 'a race above all others devoted to religious beliefs and ceremonies, all the more because it excelled in the art of their observance.'

Some of the Etruscan gods have names remote from both Greek and Latin; others have clearly taken their names from those used by the Italic tribes. *tinia*, *tina* or *tinś* (the Roman Iuppiter), who is mentioned ten times in the Mummy-band (p. 403), has a purely Etruscan name; but he is closely associated in ritual with *uni* (Iuno) and *menrva* (Minerva). This trinity was connected with the foundation of every Etruscan town, as it was with the temple which the Etruscan kings built upon the Capitol of Rome. *mariś* (Mars) and *usil* the sun (from Sabine *Ausel* 'born at dawn,' whence in Latin the name of the *gens Aurelia*) have also Italian names; *vesuna* too, who was also worshipped in Umbria and among the Marsi, and who, etymologically, ought to be nearly akin to the Roman *Vesta*; and *neθuns*, the Roman Neptunus, a water-god (cf. the place-name *Nepete*, from a root meaning 'to flood' which appears in the language of Iguvium[1]). But *śeθlans* (Hephaestus), *turan* (Aphrodite), *turms* (Hermes) and *θesan* (Aurora) have purely Etruscan names; so has a frequent figure with unmistakable characteristics, the wine-god *fufluns*; but that of his bride *areaθa* has suffered something in coming over with her Greek story (Ariadne).

Among minor deities we have several taken from the Greeks: Etr. *aita* ('Αΐδης), Etr. *hercle* ('Ηρακλῆς), Etr. *φersipnei* (Persephone), Etr. *χaru* (Charon), who has however a companion in the purely Etruscan winged demon *tuχulχa*, and two feminine companions Etr. *vanθ* and *culśu*, equally associated with death. There appear however in the documents many other names of which we can say hardly more at present than that they denote objects of worship; *eθauśva*, a winged and diadem-wearing goddess, may be seen on a Praenestine mirror in the British Museum (along with another figure labelled *θanr*) rendering some service to Tinia at the difficult moment of the birth of Minerva from his head. Of others, *θuplθa(s)*, *cvlalp*[2], *leθam(s)*—all three named on the Piacenza-templum—and many more, we know even less.

That some deities had special relations with families (and pre-

---

[1] *ninctu nepitu* 'snow upon them, rain upon them,' one of many curses on the enemies of the Iguvines.

[2] In Etruscan writing letters (especially *l*, *r*, *m*, *n*) often represent the syllables used for their names; the word *cvlalp* in Latin spelling probably would be *Quelalp* (cf. the *n* in *lautn* or the *l* in *θuplθas*).

sumably with localities also) appears from the frequent addition to their names of a gentile epithet, *culśu leprnei* 'death goddess of the gens Leprinia,' *uni ursmnei* 'Iuno Orsminnia.' It should be added that according to Varro the chief deity of the Etruscans was Vertumnus; but neither of him nor of Nortia or Voltumna has any mention or delineation yet been identified in the Etruscan monuments which we possess; nor of the *fatidica Manto* whom Vergil connects with the name of his native city. Even this list of names is enough to show that Etruscan polytheism was no less hospitable than Greek or Roman, and the high position assigned to the Capitoline triad, two of which had Italian names, shows clearly that the official system of the Etruscans was not merely developed in Italy itself, but owed much to the beliefs of the Italian peoples, among whom the Etruscans were for so long predominant.

The Etruscan ritual was a considerable body of doctrine ascribed to an inspired prophet named Tages and also to a nymph Vegoe, bearing the name of a gens from Clusium (*Vegoia* and *Vegonia*), Etr. *vecui, vecunia*, whose 'book' was preserved beside the Sibylline in the temple of Apollo at Rome. The compilation of these volumes, which must in origin have been a collection of practices common in different Etruscan towns, seems from some indications, especially a statement of Varro's, to have been made in the second century B.C. (*octavo eorum saeculo*) and to have been translated into Latin by Tarquitius Priscus not later (and perhaps not earlier) than the time of Cicero.

Cicero tells us that there were three main divisions of this sacred law, the rules of (1) Hepatoscopy (*libri haruspicini*), that is divination from *exta*, the livers of sacrificed victims; (2) the Doctrine of Lightning (*libri fulgurales*), that is to say the directions for procuring, averting, and 'expiating' strokes of lightning. (It was this part of the doctrine that was attributed to Vegoe and it was probably more recent than the rest.) (3) The *libri rituales* dealt with *ostenta* ('portents') and contained directions for the foundation of cities and the consecration of temples and other buildings, and religious introductions to many public acts, such as the holding of elections or the beginning of a war.

One important part of these Books dealt with the measurement of land; the word *acnua*, meaning a portion of land, is certainly Etruscan and the curious substantive *iugerum* was probably equally alien to pure Latin. The word *gruma* or *groma* which sometimes denotes a surveyor's typical instrument, the circular level table crossed by diameters at right angles and by strings with weights, and sometimes its place of erection in a camp or other enclosure, is a typically Etruscan modification (like *Aχmemrun* from 'Αγα-μέμνων) of a Greek word γνῶμα (Attic γνώμων). There is preserved a Latin version of an 'oracle' of Vegoe given to the practitioners of this sacred profession, bidding each man cherish the rules (*disciplina*) and be *neque fallax neque bilinguis*, excellent advice (for land-agents and others) in a country where differences of language were common. This geometrical lore, derived no doubt from Egypt or Chaldaea, and applied to such excellent purposes by Roman engineers, was the solitary item that can be called whole-some in what we know of Etruscan ritual.

From the somewhat voluminous details of the rest only one or two points especially characteristic and likely to be primitive can be noted here. The professional *haruspex* was expected always to answer four questions: From what deity did the portent on which he was consulted proceed? Why had it been sent? What did it portend? How was it to be 'expiated'—that is, how was the contingent evil to be averted? Readers of Livy will realize how large an influence on Roman politics and even on the course of history was exerted by this oriental superstition, unknown to Homer, which the Etruscans first transplanted to the West. A curious monument of it has survived in what is known as the Bronze Liver of Piacenza—a neatly conventionalized model of a sheep's liver, marked out into sections each bearing an Etruscan label, those on the right-hand half of the object's upper surface corresponding in number to the Etruscan divisions of the sky, the whole serving as a kind of catechetical index for the proper training of the *haruspex*. Similar clay models with cuneiform in-scriptions have been found in Hittite and in Babylonian sites (cf. vol. I, p. 409). The two halves of the Piacenza model are labelled on their underside *usils* ('of the sun') and *tivs* ('of the moon') re-spectively. Among the gods who do not receive mention are *Menrva*, *Šeθlans*, *Turan* and *Turms*.

But the great mass of Etruscan ritual and belief was exercised with one thing only, namely Death, and what it was expected to involve of future ill. The favourite subjects of Etruscan artists were either the most tragic stories of the Greeks, such as the death of Actaeon, and the sacrifice of Iphigenia, or the sufferings of the dead at the hands of Charon and *tuχulχa* and their feminine satellites *vanθ* and *culśu*. Vergil's life-long interest in conceptions of the Underworld is no doubt connected with the Etruscan traditions of Mantua; and a glance at some of the Etruscan pictures of hell (see p. 429 *sq.*) will show how deeply ingrained in

the race was the instinct of cruelty which in a later age starved
Ugolino and his sons and inspired the torturing demons of Dante's
Inferno.

The longest fragment of Etruscan literature that we possess,
written as we have seen on the linen wrapped round an Egyptian
mummy, although its torn condition leaves some doubt whether
it has a real or merely accidental connection with the particular
interment to which its material was applied, has been nevertheless
reasonably compared with what is known as the *pulena*-roll held
in the hand of a figure which is sculptured above the lid of one
of the series of sarcophagi found at Tarquinii and probably belonging (like the Scipionic sarcophagi) to the third century B.C.
The roll is partly unfolded and shows an inscription of about
60 words, no less than 22 of which also occur on the Band. The
phrase *aisna hinθu,* which occurs repeatedly on the Band and whose
first word is connected with *aisar* 'gods,' is reasonably interpreted
to mean the deified soul of the dead man, *deus animalis,* owing its
divinity to the performance of special sacrifices as Servius and
others describe. It is still doubtful whether the prescriptions of
this one surviving example of a *liber linteus* were meant for the
use of the dead woman herself, as those of the *pulena*-roll would
seem to be for that of the man whose effigy holds it, or had been
composed for living persons, possibly the friends of some other
dead man. In either case it seems clear that in this system of
ritual we have at least one source of the burdens connected with
the mediaeval doctrine of Purgatory.

These grim pre-occupations left their mark on everyday life.
We have several long inscriptions, like the Tablet of Magliano
(p. 404), scratched on lead and entrusted to the keeping of dead
persons in tombs for transmission to the infernal authorities, in
the belief that on its receipt they will execute the Curse which
it records. Analogous documents in Oscan from Campania—a
region long under Etruscan control—show us the kind of matter
we may expect when we attain the privilege of understanding
more fully the Etruscan texts: Pakis Kluvatiis, who was cursed
at Capua in rather illiterate Oscan in the fourth or third century
B.C., was to be suffered neither to eat nor drink nor beget children
nor find favour in heaven or hell; but was to be haled away by
the infernal gods to be roasted, frozen, and chopped (?) up like
turf—if we may trust the apparent meaning of many bad words.

To one method of protection against curses and evil deities,
a method greatly in favour, it would seem, in Etruria in the sixth
and fifth centuries B.C., we probably owe most of our knowledge

of the Etruscan alphabet (p. 397); viz. the practice of writing out all its letters, and as many likely combinations of them as your bronze tablet or clay vase could be made to hold, all in good order, and dedicating it to some friendly goddess—for feminine deities[1] seem to have had preponderant authority in these personal matters. She was then expected to prevent your enemies from using any of these dangerous symbols or sounds in concocting a spell against you; or even she herself, being provided with so much useful material, might succeed in framing a blessing for you and yours. From such ancient practice came the '*ab-ra-ca-da-b-ra*' formulae of later witchcraft; just as to our pagan forefathers in Jutland the verb *to spell* seems to have meant originally to construct a magic charm by means of the written symbols of the alphabet[2].

Finally must be mentioned a practice, rooted in primitive savagery and no doubt brought by the Etruscans with other miseries from the East, but destined in its Roman form to darken the life of Western Europe for many centuries. That the Etruscans introduced human sacrifice into Italy we cannot be sure. It was mentioned in the XII Tables, as Pliny tells us; but it must be remembered that these were not composed till after the period of Etruscan supremacy in Rome. But Vergil ascribes to Aeneas (with a certain parsimony in number, if we compare his practice, as we are meant to do, with that of Achilles at the funeral pyre of Hector) the sacrifice of captives to honour the funeral of Pallas; and in, or round, a few tombs of the early Iron Age at Villanova, which are earlier than the appearance of Etruscans in that region, besides the remains of the proper tenant which in many cases at least had been burnt and enclosed in urns, there were found skeletons from bodies (most, if not all, of them female) which had been nakedly interred in the ground; one of them was actually holding the urn on its knees. These are plausibly explained as the bodies of human victims, slain in savage honour to the dead. But it is certain that the Etruscans loved to massacre their captives, and to watch the massacre. The hapless Phocaeans whom the Etruscans took at the naval battle of Alalia were conveyed to Caere and there stoned to death in the market-place; and in 358 B.C.

---

[1] This is an inference from the Venetic alphabetic tablets addressed to Rehtia and the Oscan curse addressed *Keri Arentikaí*. The Etruscan curses are not yet interpreted with any certainty, though *tinś* 'Iuppiter' seems to be mentioned in the Curse of Magliano.

[2] The magical use of the Greek and Latin alphabets survives in the Roman rite for the consecration of Cathedrals, of which the English Church retains a much modified form.

a body of 307 Roman captives were sacrificed at Tarquinii. The Etruscans seemed to have held that one could secure immortality for a dead friend by killing someone else. Sulla followed the Etruscan antecedents of his name when he butchered 6000 Samnites in the hearing of the Senate; and scenes of human sacrifice, like that of Iphigenia, had long been favourite themes of Etruscan art (see p. 428 *sq.*). In 216 B.C. at Rome in the panic after Cannae, the *libri fatales*, which were almost certainly Etruscan, commanded what Livy calls the *minime Romanum sacrum* by which a Gaulish man and woman were buried alive in the *forum Boarium*. A trace of the older superstition we have already (p. 419) seen in the *hostiae animales*, 'victims equivalent to a man's life' of the *disciplina* of Tages, reflecting far-off the substitution of a non-human for a human victim ascribed by Israelite tradition to the experience of Abraham.

But the most obvious effects at Rome of this Etruscan superstition were two. First the practice of slaughtering the prisoners who were led in procession in a Triumph—an institution which we have seen (p. 413) to be of Etruscan origin; until they had been slain, the triumphing general could not pay his vows to Iuppiter Capitolinus in the temple built by an Etruscan king. Secondly the institution of gladiatorial shows, which was first introduced in the year 264 B.C. from Etruria by the sons of D. Junius Pera at their father's funeral; their name, like Sulla's, vouches for their Etruscan connections (p. 407). It had long been in use in Etruria, as the representations of gladiatorial fights on their monuments testify, confirming the traditions; and when once it had become popular in Rome, it lasted in spite of the doubts or disapproval of humaner spirits like Cicero, Vergil and the mature Augustus, until more than four centuries later it was finally suppressed by Christian protests[1]. *Tantum potuit suadere malorum religio Etrusca*, drawn, like the rest of their mentality, from the lower stratum of the Eastern world.

VIII. ETRUSCAN ART

The art of the Etruscans is a phenomenon which has no parallel in the ancient world. It derives its whole vitality from the Greeks, a people alien in race, imagination and customs from the Etruscans.

[1] It was at Perusia in 40 B.C. that the young and hard-pressed Octavian 'sacrificed' to the shade of Julius the captive Republican 'die-hards.' The ceremonial side of the massacre would have been impossible in Rome itself.

and is developed without any contributions of national taste or feeling except those, such as extravagance or crudity, which, by inhibiting the full realization of the beauty and elegance of the prototype, definitely restricted the standard of achievement. There was besides no clear original basis of native inspiration upon which the Etruscan artist could build. The earliest known Etruscan painting or sculpture is the nearest to its Greek original; with decadence the Etruscan spirit of extravagance and distortion emerges more clearly and the original purity of the Greek inspiration is left behind.

Etruscan art thus differs profoundly from the art of other non-Hellenic peoples who absorbed the Hellenic spirit. The art of Bactria used its own modes and canons: under Greek influence these developed with an unexpected vigour and freshness. The art of Spain had a history of its own that was later moulded into Hellenic channels. The Scythians used Greek methods and motives upon a foundation of fine artistic feeling. Etruria alone of the artistically Hellenized peoples has no previous artistic repertoire of its own. All that can safely be said of the origin of Etruscan art is that the invaders (see p. 392) found themselves in an area where and near to which certain traditions of technique were firmly planted. The Iron Age stock of Villanova, Este and the other great Iron Age sites of northern Italy had introduced the customs of metal-working and pottery-making upon lines hitherto unknown in Italy. The innumerable bronze figures of men, animals, chariots and waggons and the bronze ornaments that are found in such large numbers in the north Italian necropoleis, gave to or stimulated in the Etruscans at least the methods and the technique of bronze work. The elaborate and varied pottery of the Iron Age afforded the Etruscans no excuse for neglecting their own pottery wares. But in the earliest known Etruscan works of art we see little direct inheritance from the Iron Age and nothing which suggests the oriental home which gave them birth. Some authorities assign to the Etruscans a series of crude bronze figures of the seventh or eighth century B.C. of a 'geometric' type (such as have been found in large numbers on the Aventine at Rome); but such figures are certainly the work of the Indo-European Iron Age stock. The earliest Etruscan vases of deep black polished clay (*bucchero*)[1] resemble not only the Iron Age pottery, but, particularly in their types of handle, the earlier terremare wares of the Bronze Age. Yet these Etruscan wares develop rapidly a type of their own which is based chiefly on Greek prototypes. The very *bucchero* itself, at least when it takes shapes

[1] See Volume of Plates i, 328, *c*.

such as the kylix and oenochoe, seems little more than a heavy copy of the black-glaze wares of Greece. What elements there are that can be labelled 'Etruscan' in the pottery defy analysis, and there seems to be no essentially Etruscan residuum, after all the extraneous contributions have been accounted for.

No Etruscan works of art can be assigned, as yet, to an earlier period than the seventh century B.C. At this time the intrusive influences of Greece first appear and, as might be expected, they are various. Corinth, Ionia and the Greek islands, whose record of colonization begins earlier than in the case of other Hellenic regions, are first upon the scene. In the 'Tomba Campana' at Veii the wall-paintings[1] represent wild and fabulous beasts, horsemen and grooms in a style which is all but identical with the large fresco-like panels of seventh-century Melian vases. In pottery black *bucchero* jars and goblets are decorated with zones in which chariots and warriors of Greek type and panoply appear. These zones are impressed by a cylinder which is run round the sides of the vessels when wet. This method of decoration was popular in Etruria where it lasted through the sixth and fifth centuries. In Greece, from which it is derived, it is rare and confined to Crete and the southern Sporades in the middle of the sixth century.

Contact with the mainland of Greece appears early in the sixth century in the paintings[2] of the 'Tomba dei Tori' at Corneto. Here Homeric legend is depicted, but the style is indisputably that of the Peloponnese. The formal border of the painted panels of this tomb is of a type found on contemporary Laconian pottery: the horsemen are familiar in Corinthian art or in the archaic sculptures of Crete at Prinia and other Doric sites. Tarentum may well be the intermediary.

By the middle of the sixth century Etruscans had begun to import Greek pottery in large quantities. The Ionian importations usually called Caeretan hydriae, which are numerous at this period, seem to have moulded the contemporary style of Etruscan tomb-painting. The faces and figures on the walls of the 'Tomba degli Auguri' at Corneto are essentially Ionian and by an Etruscan artist who has almost eliminated his native mannerism. To the middle and second half of the sixth century must be also assigned the earliest metal work of Etruria which is, without exception, under Ionian influence. From Perugia comes a group of bronze reliefs which served as attachments to chariots. They are now at Munich. In the British Museum are to be found some fine reliefs of the same type and style in parcel-gilt which come also from Perugia, perhaps from the same chariot. The Munich bronzes

[1] See Volume of Plates i, 330, *a*.   [2] *Ib.* 329, *b*.

represent hunting scenes and wild or legendary beasts in high
repoussé which is Ionian in flavour but essentially Etruscan in
character. The parcel-gilt reliefs are of a higher level of technical
excellence and constitute the earliest known examples of such
metal work in either Greek or Etruscan art. The scenes they
represent show a horse-race and lions attacking boars. Two
similar but more careful reliefs in bronze come from Monteleone
and are now in the Metropolitan Museum at New York: they
also are derived from chariots and represent, the one a charioteer
driving a team of two winged horses, the other a combat of two
warriors over a fallen body. The latter suggests comparison with
a fine terracotta relief of the same date or a little later in the
museum of the Villa Giulia at Rome.

To the last quarter of the century and to the same influence
may be assigned the elaborate paintings[1] of the 'Tomba delle
Iscrizioni' at Corneto. Here the Ionian influence is clear and
pronounced. About the same time arises the most vigorous growth
of Etruscan plastic art in clay. Sculpture in stone is rare and never
seriously rivals clay-modelling in Etruria where the plastic artist,
partly through lack of marble and partly owing to his predilection
for easy material, never achieved success in stone. Funeral altars
and cinerary urns decorated in very low relief, always in two
planes, are almost the only works of the stone-cutter that we know
in Etruria. A fine helmeted head of the mid-sixth century in the
Museo Archeologico at Florence is one of the few exceptions: it is
clearly inspired by small Corinthian vases (*aryballoi*) of the period
which represent warriors' heads. The reliefs on the funeral altars
and caskets are usually cut in coarse limestone and are invariably
in the Ionian style. They last only for a short while from the late
sixth to the beginning of the fifth century. Good examples are
to be seen in the British Museum, the Louvre, the Museo Archeologico at Florence and the Museo Baracco at Rome.

The *floruit* of Etruscan bronze work falls in the last half of the
sixth century. The small votive or ornamental figures which are
to be seen in large numbers in most of the European museums
represent, perhaps, the finest achievement of the Etruscan bronze
artist. The influence which underlies them is primarily Ionic but,
as the century closes, increasingly Attic. So successful is the
Etruscan at this work that it is almost impossible, in some cases,
to distinguish between Etruscan and Hellenic workmanship. To
the close of the century belong the remains of an admirable life-
size group in terracotta recently discovered at Veii[2]. It represents
Heracles and Apollo fighting for the body of a stag, flanked on

[1] See Volume of Plates i, 332, *a*.   [2] *Ib.* 334, *a, b.*

either side by Hermes and perhaps Artemis, the last-named being conjectural. Nearly the whole figure of Apollo, the head and knees of Hermes, the feet of Heracles and part of the stag survive and are in the museum of the Villa Giulia at Rome. The work is of the first order and shows a clear and decided Ionian influence, though their proportions and structure exhibit the fundamental inability of the Etruscan artist to understand Greek methods. We learn from Pliny that there was a famous Etruscan artist at Veii called Vulca who was employed at Rome by the Tarquins for the adornment of the Capitol and other buildings. Amongst other works he made a figure of Hercules called the 'clay Hercules.' Possibly he is the artist of this group from Veii, and the figures almost certainly come from an Etruscan temple in the ruins of which they were found. Large terracotta figures of the same type have been found at other Etruscan sites, and, according to Pliny, there were no less than two thousand statues of Etruscan work at Volsinii. Presumably these too were of terracotta. Sarcophagi[1] surmounted by life-size reclining figures of the deceased are common at this period and reflect the same influences as are seen in the Veii figures. There is a fine sarcophagus of this type, of the close of the sixth century, in the British Museum, and others at Rome and Florence. The group from Veii, however, remains our finest example of such work.

What may, perhaps, be a lingering survival of taste from the Villanova period is seen in the popularity of amber for small works of art at the close of the sixth century. Some fine archaic female heads from Canusium and a large group of Peleus and Thetis from Armento, now in the British Museum, show the Etruscan plastic artist working on a material which was rarely used by Greek artists until Roman times.

Gold work in the shape of brooches, pendants and earrings exhibits the fine quality of Etruscan craftsmanship in the sixth century and the Etruscan fondness for intricate metalwork. Throughout the sixth century a profusion of gold work exceeds in technical cunning and in actual beauty anything that the Hellenic artist could produce at this time. It is, in fact, in the precious metals alone that the Etruscan artist and goldsmith produce work that had no rival in the Mediterranean. Such work was known and appreciated in Athens in the fifth century B.C. Fibulae ornamented with couchant lions, earrings, necklaces and pendants decorated with admirable care and taste are profuse in Etruscan tombs. The particular method of gold decoration known as 'granulation' constitutes one of the most specialized

---

[1] See Volume of Plates i, 334, c.

forms of technique, if not an actual invention, of the Etruscan goldsmith. Not until the fifth century does Hellenic gold work approach that of Etruria in skill or merit. It is remarkable that the most characteristic oriental methods of gold work are not found in Etruria. Inlay work which uses paste or semi-precious stones, which was a fashion widespread over the Orient in the sixth and fifth centuries B.C., finds no favour with the Etruscan jeweller.

In gem-cutting the Etruscan artist has achieved a reputation which, for the sixth century, is almost equal to that of his Greek teacher. It is evident here, as in metal work, that the Etruscan was supreme at the minor arts. In the sixth century Etruscan gems are only to be distinguished from Hellenic by their greater conventionality in type and treatment, and even then the attribution is only indisputable where the presence of an inscription disposes of uncertainty, or where the subject chosen can only be Etruscan.

To the early part of the fifth century must be assigned the only large works in bronze which come from Etruscan hands—the famous wolf[1] in the Conservatori Museum at Rome, wrongly identified and restored as the foster-mother of Romulus and Remus, and the Chimaera[2] from Arezzo, now at Florence. Both exhibit a solidity of body and a surface treatment of hair which has no parallel in Greek art. Only in certain terracottas of Etruscan manufacture, such as a lion-rhyton in the British Museum, can we see the same technique.

Side by side with Etruscan gem-cutting and bronze work there grew up a wholly distinct Italian or Latin school of art. Local Italian artists seem to have copied Hellenic works of art without, perhaps, the benefit of Greek instruction. They achieved results, however, which are of a very high standard of excellence and Latin art deserves a place at the head of those non-Hellenic schools of art which owed their growth, but not their inspiration, to Greece. An Italian school of art was, in fact, known and clearly distinguished from that of Etruria in antiquity. Pliny expressly makes this distinction and mentions as characteristic of the Italian style a Hercules by Evander and a Janus dedicated by King Numa at Rome. In extant works the Italian style is clearly seen in a large series of archaic gems which exhibit an excessive use of the drill, rather in the way in which barbarian die-cutters made local imitations of Greek coins, and, perhaps more clearly, in a series of small bronze figures which runs parallel to the Etruscan series and reaches its finest achievement in the middle of the fifth

[1] See Volume of Plates i, 336, *b*   [2] *Ib.* 336, *a.*

century in works such as a fine warrior in helmet and corselet in
the British Museum. It is from this tradition of Italian art that
the later art of Republican Rome takes its origin in very large
measure.

The course of Etruscan art follows the course of Greek history.
With the beginning of the fifth century the inspiration of the
artist has changed. As the wares of Attica gradually ousted those
of Corinth in the cities of Magna Graecia and Sicily at the end
of the sixth century B.C., so the artistic influence that reached
Etruria was predominantly Attic. In the evidence of art one can
trace at an early date the beginnings of those changes which led
to the Peloponnesian war. In the beautiful panels[1] of the 'Tomba
del Triclinio' at Corneto we see the true inspiration from Attic
art of the early fifth century. The more serious faces, the full
chins and eyes in profile are those of Greek vase-painting as remodelled by artists such as Brygos. So, too, the panels of the
'Tomba delle Bighe' at Corneto recall the work of Euthymides
or Euphronius. The wave of Ionian influence has been succeeded
by a wave of Attic.

But the revival of art in Etruria is brief. The defeat of the
Etruscans (see p. 390) in 474 B.C. by Hiero of Syracuse marks
the beginning of the political collapse of the Etruscan empire.
The history of Etruscan art is henceforward one of rapid decline
until it becomes, in Roman times, little more than a provincial
mannerism.

Small bronze votive figures last well into the middle of the fifth
century but after this time the Etruscan bronze-worker seems to
have concentrated more on producing objects of practical use.
Candelabra and mirrors[2] are produced in very large numbers in the
middle and latter part of the fifth century. Boxes and caskets as
well as the majority of the mirrors produced at this time are, for
the most part, decorated with mythological subjects engraved on
the surface. In fact, as was so often the case with metal work in
Etruria, this method of engraved decoration is almost exclusively
confined to Etruscan art. Sometimes the standard of achievement is high, particularly in the earlier examples, but later the
mirrors and other bronze works become little more than objects
of commerce. Wall-painting is rare in the early part of the fifth
century and besides those already mentioned, which belong to the
opening years, we have nothing to show except the magnificent
panels of the 'Tomba del Triclinio' at Corneto.

In clay-modelling we see the old Etruscan tradition surviving
in the numerous antefixes[3] from Cervetri, Conca, Civita Lavinia

[1] See Volume of Plates i, 338, c.   [2] Ib. 340.   [3] Ib. 332, b.

and other towns (many of which are outside Etruria proper),
which exhibit every variation of style throughout the century. At
their best some of the female busts, which are the most common
type of antefix, achieve a beauty that is almost indistinguishable
from that of similar antefixes from the Greek cities of Magna
Graecia and Sicily. There is, in fact, the possibility that terracotta work of this type for temple adornment is derived by Greece
from Etruria through the medium of Greek artists working in
Italy. Certainly it has no early history in Greece before the sixth
century and, in fact, never finally ousts similar work in marble.

The Etruscan potter of the fifth century seems to have continued the manufacture of the typical black *bucchero* wares of the
sixth century but in the second half of the fifth he openly copied
Greek importations[1]. Etruscan painted pottery, however, is uniformly unsuccessful. Lack of delicacy in outline or style in
drawing stamp the Etruscan vase-painter as an uninspired copyist.
A kylix in the British Museum of the close of the century represents the best that the Etruscan potter could achieve: it is
clearly from the hand of a painter who had studied in a Greek
workshop. Sometimes, as in the tomb-paintings, the Etruscan
artist adds to a Greek scene the monsters of the Etruscan Underworld: one such vase shows the farewell of Admetus and Alcestis[2].
The tragic scene is made the more realistically terrible by the
addition of the threatening figures of the Etruscan hammer-god
and the winged demon who, in the 'Tomba dell' Orco,' is named
Tuchulcha.

As with pottery so in his scanty coinage the Etruscan slavishly
copies Greek types and styles without achieving anything approaching the success that he achieved in wall-painting. Coinage
issues cover the period from 500 B.C. down to Roman times. The
standard used at first appears to be the Persic (see p. 413 above),
but early in the fifth century that of Syracuse comes in as a
rival. Throughout the whole period of issue the reverse of the
coins is rarely given a type: usually it is quite plain and flat, one
die only being used in the striking. With the appearance of the
Syracusan standard the Etruscan mints initiate a relationship
which is never abandoned. Small gold *hectae* with a male head
on the obverse and a plain reverse, and silver coins with Sicilian
types such as the hare or the squid, all indicate the source from
which Etruscans derived their ideas. Two curious coin-types[3],
a chimaera and an Athenian owl, appear on the obverse sides of

---

[1] See Volume of Plates i, 342.   [2] *Ib.* 338, *a.*
[3] Sambon, A., *Les Monnaies antiques de l'Italie*, Pl. I. 18 and p. 48.

two silver coins. Bronze issues appear about the end of the third century B.C. Populonia seems to have been the principal mint and has a numerous issue, often inscribed, which bears a gorgon's head and, on the reverse, a crescent and trident. Inscriptions on other bronze coins show that there were mints at Cosa Volcientium, Vetulonia (in Etruscan, Vate or Vatlun) and at a place called Peithesa. Almost all Etruscan coins bear marks of value and are based on the Sicilian silver litra of ·87 gm.

The close of the fifth century shows how much Attic influence has finally permeated the main streams of Etruscan art. Painting in tombs has invented a new technique for itself in which outlines and inner lines in black emphasize the detail in a way which recalls the later Athenian white-ground lecythi. The 'Tomba degli Scudi'[1] at Corneto is a good example of this technique and in the 'Tomba dell' Orco' at the same place we see a further advance in the addition of shading and contrasts of light and shade and in a more careful and conscious treatment of drapery. In the 'Tomba del Tifone' at Corneto the same characteristic is found with a further advance—the chief break with the archaic tradition— in which groups of people in perspective appear. This marks the final supremacy of the 'Polygnotan' tradition of vase-painting.

The gradual decay of Etruscan power and the increasing inability of the Etruscans to hold their own against encroachment is evident in their art. Unlike the Greeks the Etruscans felt that war and adversity were harbingers of ruin rather than stern taskmasters. The whole aspect of the people seems to have changed during their years of decline, if we can judge the people by their art. The boisterous vitality and good humour of the sixth century and the earlier years of the fifth has changed into a macabre absorption in the terrors of the after-life. In the place of satyrs and nymphs, dancers, flute-players and singers we find a hierarchy of demons and devils. The horrific Tuchulcha, the winged-demon with the hammer, a grisly Polyphemus and other malignant creatures are reminders of the Underworld, who, although, no doubt, old and feared members of the Etruscan pantheon, yet now appear for the first time from the brush of the artist. With the Etruscans, as has so often happened with modern oriental peoples, defeat brought despair and collapse beyond control or limit. Moral and with it artistic recuperation becomes increasingly difficult. What had in an earlier age been immorality or licence is now altered to cruelty and vice. The 'Tomba del Cardinale' at Corneto, which belongs to the middle of the fourth century, is an artistic nightmare. It represents the translation to

[1] See Volume of Plates i, 338, b.

Hell of Ramtha, wife of Larth, a girl of nineteen. Black demons
and the already familiar hammer-devil rush hellwards sweeping
the white-garbed souls of the dead along with them. It is an
epitome of the last phase of Etruscan civilization.

After the fourth century, Etruscan art seems to have assimilated
itself so closely to Hellenistic art that the two are with difficulty
distinguished. At the same time many, if not most, of the artistic
activities of the Etruscan artist have ceased. Bronze work, gold
and silver work, vase-painting, gem-cutting and wall-painting are
hardly represented by anything that can recall the excellence of
the fifth century. The sphere of art is confined almost exclusively
to the cutting in stone or modelling in clay of funeral cists. Small
boxes with lids made for holding ashes are the sole vehicle of the
last phase of Etruscan art. Scenes, usually from the more savage
incidents of Homeric legend, form the bulk of the subjects dealt
with and the lids are either plain or adorned with small figures
of the deceased. Some of these superincumbent figures are ugly
and grotesque, but it often becomes possible to see in their faces
the beginnings of that systematic portraiture of ancestors which
reached such distinction in the hands of Republican artists of
Rome. Larger sarcophagi also exist at this period with the usual
life-size reclining figures, but they are rarer. The style in which
such figures are rendered seems to be half-way between Hellenistic and Roman work.

The smaller cists and urns were usually placed round the inside
walls of the dome-shaped tombs which now supersede the square
chambers of the sixth and fifth centuries. Reconstructions of such
tombs complete with their contents are to be seen in the gardens
of the Museo Archeologico at Florence. The portraits, whether
full length or merely busts, which adorn the lids of these cists
and sarcophagi are themselves derived from the funeral urns with
caps shaped like human heads which constituted the earliest
Etruscan receptacles for the ashes of the dead. The Roman
ancestral bust thus has a long history. So numerous were these
Etruscan funeral cists in the last three centuries before Christ
that they must have been used very largely as articles of commerce, and have been exported to Roman officials or to Roman
citizens of Etruscan origin resident in distant parts of the Roman
empire. One such, of perhaps the first century B.C., has been
found as far afield as Meroë in the Sudan: it is now in the museum
at Liverpool. This last flicker of Etruscan art seems to have had
most vigour at Volaterrae where enormous numbers of such cists
have been found.

After the time of the Roman Republic Etruria is little more than a memory and Etruscan art has faded into obscurity. The artificial political revival of Etruria in the reign of Claudius has no artistic equivalent. The influence of Etruscan art upon the arts of later periods is confined to a few accidental debts which artists of the Renaissance owe to the tomb-paintings which then for the first time, in the popularity of the search for 'grottos,' began to be discovered. Possibly the Renaissance conceptions of Satan may in part be derived from the paintings of Tuchulcha and similar demons.

There remains the problem of the means by which Greek art first reached the Etruscans. Unfortunately research, which might well have thrown light upon this problem, is silent. Tradition, on the other hand, tells that before the Etruscans arrived from the East there were certain Greek cities in Etruria. Caere near Rome (Cervetri) had what purported to be an earlier and Greek name Agylla. As such it seems to have corresponded in type and wealth with a sister-city Spina on the opposite shore of Italy in the Po valley. Both were said to have dedicated treasuries at Delphi. Spina, however, except for a passing mention in Strabo, vanishes from history and its exact site is unknown. Caere was occupied by the incoming Etruscans and its name in popular etymology was derived from the Greek word of welcome which greeted the Etruscans. However worthless this story may be it is interesting as indicating certain friendly relations between Greeks and Etruscans. Spina seems to have been ruined or abandoned. The alleged dedication of treasuries at Delphi suggests that as late as the sixth century both towns were independent, since no treasuries or foundations that could be so identified are recorded at Delphi before that century. If, however, the Greeks of Caere were on friendly terms with their conquerors they might still have been in a position some time after their absorption to make such a dedication.

Besides Caere the towns of Falerii and Pisae were said to have Hellenic origins, the former being by some writers given an Argive and the latter an Elean origin. So too in Latium towns such as Praeneste were attributed to Hellenic founders. There was, in fact, throughout Italy a Hellenic penetration independent of the larger and more stable settlements of Magna Graecia. In addition to the direct artistic influence of the resident Greeks in Etruria itinerant artists must have contributed largely to the Greek moulding of Etruscan art. Pliny's story of the arrival of the three potters Eucheir, Diopus and Eugrammus tells us as much. Lastly there is the indirect influence of the Greek cities of Magna Graecia which must have been considerable. The influence of the coin standards of Sicily upon those of Etruria indicates still another connection. See above, p. 122 *sq.*, p. 428.

It is difficult to pronounce finally upon the essential qualities of Etruscan art which distinguish it from Hellenic art. Disregarding the frequent and, in some branches, complete lack of success in the attempt of the Etruscan artist to achieve his end, we find that there are some qualities which are quite peculiar to Etruscan art. Thus, for instance, there is a disjointed quality in wall-paintings which shows a certain lack of coherence such as is seldom met with in Greek work. Figures acting in wholly different ways are bunched closely together in groups which, in fact, have no cohesion. This is particularly evident in the 'Tomba degli Auguri.' Etruscan life and habits, moreover, were so fundamentally different from those of Greece that the full value and meaning of Greek art was never fully appreciated by the Etruscan. We have no record of Etruscan intellectual life and it seems doubtful if there was much to record. From their remains, however, and from literary references we can imagine the curious mixture of cruelty, superstition, immorality and luxury which occupied most of their time. Their fundamental cruelty does not really emerge until the end of the fifth century when it permeates all their art, but it is perceptible in the extreme brutality of the games depicted in the sixth and early fifth century, themselves the ancestors of the more brutal of the games of Rome. Entirely un-Greek are the immoral scenes in the paintings of the frieze in the 'Tomba delle Bighe.' But at times the artist's genius transcended his subject and there is, perhaps, no finer monument of Etruscan art than the brightly coloured paintings of the late fifth century which represent a battle of Greek warriors with Amazons, on the sides of a sarcophagus from Corneto, now at Florence.

The chief defects in Etruscan art might be summarized by saying that the artist as a general rule failed to understand to the full the underlying methods of balance, proportion and construction which were the essential qualities of his Greek prototypes. In consequence his work was deprived of the vigour of true artistic creation; it had no natural inspiration.

CHAPTER XIII

ITALY IN THE ETRUSCAN AGE
B. THE INDO-EUROPEAN COMMUNITIES

I. THE LIGURES AND SICULI

PASSING to a survey of the different Italian tribes at and before the beginning of recorded history, we may start in the north-west with the Ligurians (*Ligures*). The name Liguria in the time of Augustus was applied to the ninth region of Italy, bounded on the north by the river Po, on the south by the Gulf of Genoa and on the east and west by two small rivers running into it, the Macra and the Varius respectively. It is clear, however, that in earlier times the tribes recognized as Ligurian by our authorities occupied a much more extensive area, extending beyond the site of the Greek colony Massilia into Spain, and in Italy itself farther south, at least as far as Pisa and Arretium, in the time of Polybius. Part of the population of Corsica and that of Ilva (Elba) seems also to have been Ligurian; and a fairly strong tradition affirms the same of the Siculi. The same parentage was assigned to a shadowy people called the Aborigines who have a place in Cato's and Varro's traditions of central Italy, especially in towns with very ancient names like Tiora Matiene, Lista, both in the Aequian district, and Μηφύλα (?) in the Sabine.

The evidence as to the language of the Ligurians is clear. We happen to have a large number of place-names of the district preserved in early and eminently trustworthy records, such as the *Tabula Genuatium* of 117 B.C. A study of the evidence leaves no doubt that the language spoken in historical times by the people whom the Romans called Ligures belonged to the Indo-European family. Obvious Indo-European elements appear in such river-names as *Macra, Varius, Fertor, Merula, Vinelasca, Comberanea, Porcobera* (which Pliny calls by its Latin equivalent *Porcifera*); and river-names are generally among the most stable elements in local nomenclature. How many, for instance, are there in England which do not go back to pre-Roman days? Add to these such place-names as *Genua* and *Pedo*, and such tribal names as *Medulli, Statielli, Laevi, Marici*, to say nothing of their Latin name *Ligures*, compared with Greek λιγύς 'shrill-voiced' or Latin *lig-u-rire* 'to lick, be greedy.' In the latter case, and perhaps in the former, it would be the kind of title that is applied to a barbarous and thievish folk by their slightly more civilized neighbours; we could not safely regard it as belonging to the native Ligurian speech, but only as clear evidence of their having been in close contact with peoples who spoke an Indo-European tongue long before the time of Herodotus, who refers to them more than once. Other probably Indo-European and certainly Italic names in the district are *mons Ioventio, Cavaturini, Venascum*; and *mons Lemur-inus*, 'the ghost-mountain'; the name Ἐλίσυκοι, mentioned by Herodotus, looks very much like a Massilian Greek pronunciation of *Velesco-* or *Velesico-*, identical with Lat. *Volusci, Volsci*, from the stem appearing in Gr. ἕλος 'marsh'; see further, p. 458.

The solitary characteristic in many hundreds of names which, with any kind of reason, has been thought to show some non-Indo-European character is the first vowel of the very common suffixes *-asca, -ascum* (*e.g.* in the river-names *Vinelasca, Veraglasca*), since in other Indo-European languages the forms *-isco-* and *-usco-* are far commoner. But this solitary point might be equally explained by a dozen other conjectures, and is too narrow for a large ethnological inference. The frequency of the *-asca* element is certainly due to the influence of some one or more names in which the *-a-* was etymologically at home, *e.g.*, in such a word as *Venascum* if it is connected with Lat. *vena-ri* 'to hunt'; and such fashions may spring up at any time in any language[1]. Nor does this view exclude in the least the possibility of such a fashion having been ultimately based on something in the speech of some earlier stratum of population.

We may observe further that the tribal names *Soliceli, Stoniceli, Abicelus* seem to contain an element which appears also in the second half of Lat. (or Aequian) *Aequi-coli* 'dwellers in the plain,' from the I.-Eur. root *quel-* meaning properly 'to turn,' seen in Lat. *colo* 'I till,' *inquilinus* 'inhabitant,' Gr. πολεῖν 'to plough' and κύκλος almost identical with Sanskrit *cakra-* 'wheel' and English *wheel* itself. These words contain an Indo-European *q* which we should therefore infer to have been in Liguria preserved from the change into *p*. In any case, the preservation of Indo-European *q* as *q* or *k* (according to the vowel following) separates Ligurian from the Umbro-Safine group of dialects (Umb. *petur* 'four') and

---

[1] [Since the names of rivers in Liguria regularly ended in *-a*, *e.g. in flouium Neuiascam, ad riuom Vinelascam* and many more—*Macra, Trebia, Porcobera, Enesica, Comberanea, Rutuba, Merula, Stura, Vesubia*—the *-asco-* suffix may have started in the names of towns derived from rivers.—J Wh.]

also from the language of the Gauls (*petorritum* 'four wheeler') which greatly resembles Umbro-Safine, and this feature ranks Ligurian with Goidelic Celtic, with Latin, with Venetic and probably with Messapic also (see below, pp. 443, 451, 464).

It is further to be observed that in ancient historians we nowhere meet with any hint of linguistic demarcation in the intercourse between Latins and Ligurians, though such indications are clear in the case of Safine, Etruscan, Raetic, Gallic and Venetic; and the very speedy Latinization of Gallia Narbonensis (between 121 and 60 B.C.) suggests that the language of this region, which, as we have seen, had at least a considerable Ligurian element in its population, was not far removed from Latin. We shall see later on the special significance of the great frequency in this region of the *ethnica* formed in -*ci* and -*ates* (p. 456).

What differences existed between Ligurian and other dialects farther north and east, Lepontic and Raetic, it is difficult to say, until fuller records of all three are accessible; but it is probable that, like Ligurian, they belong to the Indo-European family. There has appeared recently an interesting inscription (dated by coins found with it to the third or second century B.C.) from San Bernardo near Ornavasso north of the Lago d' Orta and west of the Lago Maggiore, which should perhaps be called Lepontic, since the Lepontii are closely associated with the Salassi in the district round about Aosta and their kinsmen the Lepontii Uberi lived about the sources of the Rhone, north of the Simplon Pass.

The vase on which this inscription is written must have once contained a present of the costly 'Naxian wine' made to two persons, presumably man and wife, whose names appear in the dative *latumarui sapsutaipe*[1], the last syllable being clearly identical with the same particle in Safine, the equivalent of the Latin -*que*. The second half of the first name might well be Celtic (cf. *Indutiomarus*), but other points in the dialect, even in the records which we possess, are clearly non-Celtic[2]. Yet, on the other hand, the labialization which this inscription shows forbids us to ascribe it to the same tongue as the Ligurian forms just discussed.

[1] [Before -*pe* there is a double interpunct (:), whereas after every word the interpunct is triple (:).—J. WH.]

[2] [These Lepontic inscriptions all come from a limited area, roughly 50 miles by 35 miles; the language differs from that of the Gallic inscriptions (p. 440) in which final -*m* has become -*n* (as in *lokan*) and the dative of -*o*- stems end in -*u*. Further the particle -*pe* is wanting in Celtic; and Ligurian and Lepontic preserve original *p*- (as in Lig. *Porco-bera* 'salmon-bearing') which Celtic lost (Irish *orc* 'salmon'); cf. Irish *athir* = Lat *pater*, Gallic *are* = Gr. παρά.—J. WH.]

The Siculi. The early history of the tribe that gave its name to Sicily falls within the scope of this chapter only so far as that history is connected with that of the Ligures. For ancient historians speak of the Siculi, even more strongly than of the Ligures, as having once inhabited parts of central Italy. Thucydides says that they came into Sicily about 300 years before the Greeks; and Philistus of Syracuse, who is said to have begun his history in exile at Adria in 385 B.C., held that they crossed into Sicily eighty years after the Trojan War, which comes to much the same date (see above, p. 389). The name Segesta is familiar in Sicilian history, but it is recorded in several sources as that of a Ligurian town; and the Iemerii mentioned on the triumphal arch of Susa wear a suspicious likeness to the Sicilian Himera. Particularly strong traditions connect the Siculi with Latium, *e.g.*, at Tibur, and according to Pliny they were one of the thirty tribes regularly summoned to the festival on the Alban Mount[1].

The remains of the Sicel language, scanty as they are, are enough to put beyond all doubt the fact that it was Indo-European. In the Badisches Landesmuseum at Carlsruhe is a vase found at Centorbi, the ancient Sicel town of Centuripa, bearing an inscription which contains the words *hemitom esti durom*, repeated immediately in the form *durom hemitom esti*—so that the separation of them can admit of no reasonable doubt[2]. The linguistic character of these words, however we interpret them, cannot be doubted. It is also practically certain, since the inscription[3] runs round the body of an earthenware vase with a handle and spout, that this repetition is the jingle of a drinking song; and, that being so, it is difficult not to guess that it means 'half a cup is sorry cheer.' And though the meaning of these words must remain doubtful while the rest are obscure, yet the neuter singular endings, one of them the familiar participial *-tom*, the other the adjectival *-ro-m*, in concord with one another and with the word *esti*, and the fact that the text contains no conjunction of sounds

---

[1] In *Hist. Nat.* III, 69 Pliny writes *Sicani*; but in c. 56 he speaks of *Siculi* in Latium. Vergil uses the name *Sicāni* of a tribe in Latium (*Aen.* VII, 795; VIII, 328; XI, 317), and Servius (on VII, 631 and I, 2) took him to mean the Siculi. Vergil's support of Pliny's ascription of the Sicani to Latium and of their connection with the Siculi is decisive.

[2] The only doubt possible would be at the point between *hemitom* and *esti*; the epigraphic evidence, taken alone, does not compel us to separate them.

[3] The inscription is written *boustrophēdon* in what (the letters χ, φ, ψ being wanting) seems to be a western Greek alphabet of the fifth century not unlike the Phocian (p. 397, n. 2) with Λ for *l*, Γ for *p*, but Λ for *u*.

that cannot be paralleled in Greek or Latin make a group of characteristics which it is difficult to call anything but certainly Indo-European. In the Sicel district, too, place-names are numerous like *Camarina* and *Messana*, *Gela*, *Neēton* ('freshly ploughed land'?), to mention no others, for which it is very easy to find Italic etymologies; and none (so far as the present writer has observed) which the most fastidious ear could reject as showing non-Indo-European sounds.

From all this we need not, indeed, proceed at once to conclude that the Siculi were of pure Indo-European blood—if there ever was such a fluid—but it is clear that if they were not, at least they had lived long enough among communities speaking some western dialect (*i.e.*, a non-sibilizing, and probably non-labializing dialect, with *centum*, not *satem*, for 'hundred') of the Indo-European family of tongues to have acquired that dialect themselves. This would not prevent us from acknowledging, if good evidence seemed to point in that direction, that they may have retained or accepted some strange elements in vocabulary. And is there any known language whose vocabulary does not include many words which are inexplicable by any comparison with other words in the same or in kindred languages, and which therefore must have been drawn in from some other source?

The archaeological record derived from the material remains of the eastern half of Sicily (see vol. II, pp. 570, 572), though at present it cannot be said directly to confirm the evidence of language and of tradition, nevertheless appears to present no difficulty such as would lead us to doubt the conclusions to which this evidence has led us. No remains found in Italy have been at present connected with the Siculi; but the civilization of Sicily itself, in what are known as the Sican and First Sicel Periods, assigned to the 'Eneolithic' Age, is described as having, on the whole, the same character as that of South Italy. The Second and Third Sicel Periods belong to the Bronze Age and the Early Iron Age respectively, and it is these two periods that are expressly assigned by archaeologists to the people whom the earliest Greek settlers found in the eastern part of the island. The Third Sicel Period is followed immediately by the Siculo-Greek Period; and the development of types in pottery and ornament in the island appears to have been continuous and unbroken through all these five.

But the Periods Sicel II and III are marked by Aegean, not Italic, influence. In Sicel II there are many types of pottery clearly recognized as Mycenaean, and geometric decoration is just beginning to make its appearance. In Sicel III there appears painted geometrical ware in the style resembling that of the Dipylon vases. Thus the date given by Thucydides (VI, 2) for the passage of the Sicels into Sicily is well confirmed by this archaeological evidence, from which the Second Sicel Period would be assigned to the latter half, or the end, of the second millennium B.C. But the reader must not infer that the people of the earlier ('Sican' and 'First Sicel') Periods were necessarily different from those that followed. Vergil clearly, and Pliny hardly less clearly, identify the Sicani with the Siculi, so that in the traditions known to them the two tribes, if they were two, must have appeared, at all events, as completely amalgamated. The preponderance of recent archaeological opinion is to regard the Sicani as an earlier wave of the same people, even at the cost of having to reconcile with this view, in one way or another, the assertion of Thucydides that the Sicani came from Iberia, which is generally understood to mean Spain.

Hence from the point of view of language there is no difficulty in the assumption that the Ligures (and Siculi) were substantially identical with the main population of Italy of the period preceding the Etruscan invasion, that is, roughly speaking, the end of the Bronze Age. The archaeological evidence described in a previous volume pointed to a parallel identity (see vol. II, p. 574 and cf. *ibid.* p. 571). If the archaeologists could prove, as they seem to imply, that no change in population in Liguria proper (vol. II, p. 564) occurred from the Neolithic Age until the Roman period, it would follow that the earliest stratum of population which we could identify in Italy must have spoken an Indo-European language, and we should obtain a solid basis for the ethnology of Italy (see further, pp. 459 *sqq.*).

But it must be realized that the linguistic evidence, however clear, can give us, if it be taken alone, no more complete information than that of archaeology, taken alone. Whether the Ligures, who were speaking an Indo-European tongue at the beginning of traditional history, *i.e.* in the Early Iron Age, are to be identified with the invaders (if such they were) who built the Terremare in North Italy (the 'Italici' of many archaeologists) and not rather with the people who dwelt in the region of the rivers beside which the Terremare were built and who had presumably carved the pictograms (which show, *inter alia*, some bronze implements) on the rocks of the Val d'Inferno and other valleys north of Ventimille, or, again, with some intervening stratum—is a question to which the linguistic evidence just discussed can contribute nothing. The nature and extent of the gap which separates the *Ligures* of Greek and Roman tradition from the Neolithic (or early Bronze Age) cave-dwellers (whom archaeologists call Liguri or Ibero-Liguri), if gap there was, cannot be finally determined by any evidence of language. Even the oldest river-name can give only a relative date.

Here it may be added that the Ligurian tribes appear first to have come into contact with the Romans in 238 B.C., and that the chief point in their unwilling and broken submission is marked by the establishment of the colony at Luna in 177 B.C.

II. THE GALLIC INVASION

The order of geography brings us now to the Gauls, who established themselves in the north of Italy in the fifth and fourth centuries B.C., and whose inroads hastened the fall of the Etruscan power (p. 389). Their advance followed the line of easiest progress into the peninsula, a line afterwards marked by the Aemilian and Flaminian roads. The result was that both the Italian and the Etruscan inhabitants of the districts which this line traversed were sharply cut into separate divisions; the Ligurians in the west were cut off from all close intercourse with the Veneti in the east, and the Etruscans in the Po valley were cut off from their kinsmen south of the Appennines, and those of them that survived were mainly driven north into one or two Alpine valleys where their speech lasted on for some time and their alphabet still longer (see vol. II, p. 34 *sq.*).

These movements definitely marked the end of the period with which this chapter is concerned; but it is well to indicate briefly here what little we know of the invaders. These Gauls planted their name upon the whole district that lies between the Alps and the Appennines and west and south of the river Adige; and in most of the sites that have been excavated, especially at Bologna, the Gallic remains form a well-marked stratum, super-imposed on the Etruscan, and, in its turn, covered by the records of Romanized life.

We have seen that the beginning of the Etruscan settlements in the Po valley belongs to the sixth century B.C. (p. 394). The first advent of the Gauls is ascribed by tradition to the age of the first Tarquin, but their arrival in such numbers as to oust the Etruscans from Bologna and to change the character of the local civilization belongs to the following century, and to the latest part of it. We hear of them as pressing hard upon the Etruscans about that date, and, according to Nepos, they took the Etruscan town of Melpum in the Transpadane country on the same day as Camillus took Veii in 396 B.C. Ancient authorities attribute to the Gauls the towns of Mediolanum, Novara, Comum, Brixia and Verona, and count as Gallic the Insubres, the Cenomani, the Lingŏnes and Senŏnes, to mention only the most important.

With the exception of one or two points of surviving Etruscan culture, like the all-but-island Mantua, the Gauls in successive invasions spread themselves over the whole region all the way to the Adriatic coast, where the latest of them, the Senones, marked the north-eastern strip of Umbria by the specific name of *Ager Gallicus*, in which the colony of Ariminum was later on founded by the Romans (in 268 B.C.) to keep them in check, with that of Firmum not far south in Picenum in 264 B.C. The culminating point of the invasion of the Gauls was their transitory capture of Rome itself circa 390 B.C.; when they scattered from Rome, some reached South Italy and even Sicily where we find them allied with Dionysius of Syracuse in 385 B.C. In Umbria they fought in alliance with the Samnites against the Romans even as late as 295 B.C.

The Gauls brought with them the well-marked type of culture, then spreading rapidly over Central Europe, known as that of La Tène, from the discoveries at that point of the shore at the east end of the Lake of Neuchâtel, laid bare by a readjustment of the water-supplies of the Jura-district in 1874–1881 (see vol. II, p. 593). In the Bologna area the stratum of their remains is clearly distinct from the Etruscan; among its most characteristic features are the abundance of iron swords and lances, displacing the old Etruscan hatchet as weapons of offence, and the La Tène types of fibulae, marking an advance on those of Certosa (p. 394) chiefly by doubling the spring, so that it appears on both sides of the root of the pin; the characteristic Certosa knob or nose, on the bent back end of the catch, often receives decoration, as of a human face. But the details of this culture belong to the history of the period subsequent to that with which this chapter is concerned.

The linguistic remains of these people leave no doubt that their language was essentially the same as that of the Gauls north and west of the Alps. They have left very few inscriptions, and as these are in a script (or scripts) derived directly or indirectly from the Etruscan alphabet (p. 396 *sq.*), it is conceivable, indeed probable, that they first learnt to write in Italy. The two epitaphs which are most certainly Gallic come respectively from Novara and from Todi in Umbria, and it is difficult to assign either to any date earlier than the third century B.C. That from Todi obligingly gives us a Latin version as well as the Gallic. Both contain the

formula *lokan karnitu* (plural *karnitus*), which Celtic scholars agree
to render '*sepulchrum condidit*' (or '*condidere*'), though the nature
of the verbal forms is uncertain. But words like *petorritum* which
is recorded as Gallic for 'four-wheeled chariot,' place-names like
Eporedia, properly 'place of horse-chariots,' and personal names
like *Eppo Boius* (contrast the Venetic *Ecco*), all show the change
of *q* to *p* which marks the Brythonic Celts. These and other
resemblances of their language to that of the Safine tribes, if they
are not accidental, must, as we shall see (pp. 449 *sqq*.), go back
to a period earlier, though perhaps not remotely earlier, than
the century (namely the fourth) to which our records agree in
ascribing the arrival of the Gauls in Central Italy. It is noteworthy that in the list of enemies soundly cursed by the Iguvine
people—in a document which can hardly be later than the third
century B.C., and was probably a good deal older in its original
form—the Gauls are not mentioned.

III. THE VENETI

We have seen that the Etruscans had many settlements north
of the Appennines as at Mantua and Bononia (Etr. *Felsina*), and
that in certain valleys farther north, as at Sondrio near Chiavenna
and perhaps at Trent (*Tridentum*) in the valley of the Upper Adige,
their settlements survived even the Gallic invasion. But the
people, among whom they planted such groups of overlords,
appear, so far back as our evidence extends, to have been homogeneous and to have developed a civilization which was continuous
at all events from the beginning of what is known as the Early
Iron Age, and which is represented by the second of the nine
groups of remains enumerated in vol. II, p. 572. The beginning
of their culture, closely akin to that represented at Villanova, is
placed on archaeologist evidence later than the fall of Minoan
power in the Mediterranean, but earlier than the importation of
Greek vases showing the earliest geometric style; the date commonly assigned on these grounds to the earliest remains of the
Veneti is about 1000 B.C. Their area included at least all the
region north of the Padus and east of Lake Benacus and the
valleys running into it; and the Histrian peninsula. They even
founded a city (perhaps to be identified with Ptolemy's *Idunum*)
beyond the first line of the Alps, north of the Plöken Pass[1]

[1] The modern names *Venediger* and *Venetberg* for mountains in this
region of the Tyrolese Alps were connected by Pauli with this ancient
outpost of the Veneti.

between the valleys of the Gail and the Drave on what is now called the Gurina-plateau. The earliest remains of the town seem to date from the fourth century B.C.

Inscriptions in what is clearly Venetic alphabet or language are known so far (1924) only at Este (*Ateste*); Padua (*Patavium*); Vicenza (*Veicetia*); Treviso (*Tarvisium*); Belluno (*Bellunum*); M. Pore above Agordo in a valley running into that of the upper Piave below Belluno; Pieve di Cadore; Idria (in the Isonzo valley), the Plöken Pass and the Gurina, with fragments from Oderzo (*Opitergium*). The writers of these inscriptions called themselves Veneti in the historical period; and there is no doubt whatever that they have continuously occupied this area and were the stock from which Venice was founded in the sixth century A.D. Their artistic powers, which were one day to produce the school of Titian, appear at least as early as the fifth century B.C. in a series of beautiful bronze vases from the Cadore valley as well as in other remains. Among these may be mentioned the traces of the practice of ornamenting doors with bronze panels worked in relief, a custom in which we may see the origin of some of the most beautiful monuments of mediaeval art, such as the doors of San Zeno at Verona or the Baptistery at Florence. At the stage with which we are now concerned their civilization is best represented by a long series of remains from Este showing a gradual evolution of beautiful forms both of vases and statuettes. Nor is it irrelevant to note that it was this same Venetic stock in the city of Patavium which produced Livy, the most humane of ancient historians, and which, joined with Celtic and Etruscan elements, gave birth in Mantua to the poet Vergil.

The earliest record that has yet been found of their speech is upon a vase at Padua, which has been assigned to the sixth century B.C. The inscription runs retrograde in the Venetic alphabet (see pp. 398, 402):

$$voθo\ Kluθiiari·s·\ vhaχ·s·θo$$
'Otho (?) Klutearius fecit.'

These words show some characteristic features of the language. The verbal form has the middle ending of the Greek aorist, but without anything corresponding to the Greek augment; and the same is true of the two common verbs (meaning 'gave') which appear in dedications, z·o·to and zona·s·to. The pairs of dots in these words are also a characteristic mark of Venetic writing. We have seen reason to believe (p. 402) that they are marks of accent, placed on either side of the last sound of the

accented syllable (or syllables), omitted however when they would
have coincided with the dots of the letter ·|· (*h*).

A few other inscriptions will serve to indicate what we know
of the language:

> *ka·n·ta ruma·n·na zona·s·to rehtiah* (Este).
> 'Canta Romana dedit Rectiae.'
> *meχo zona·s·to e·φ· vhaφahtśa porah ·o·posoφo·s·* (Este).
> 'me dedit Eb(ura) Fabatia (deae) Optimae (ex)[1] operibus.'

On a tombstone at Padua:

> *puponeh e·χo rakoh e·kupeθari·s·*
> 'I am the charioteer (lit. 'horse-driver,' or 'horse-flyer') of Pupo Racus.'

The last word appears on another stone at Padua which pictures
a charioteer driving a *biga*; and it is elsewhere spelt (in Latin
alphabet) *ecupetaris*, and shows, like the name *Ecco* (contrast the
Gallic *Eppo*), the Venetic treatment of an Italic -*q*- before an -*o*-
(cf. Lat. *equus*)[2].

Our record of the life of the Venetic people down to their
incorporation in the Roman alliance, which may be dated by the
establishment of the colony of Aquileia in 181 B.C., is scanty, but
enough to tell us something of their tastes and pursuits. From
the earliest times they seem to have been peacefully inclined to
commerce, carrying on, for example, an extensive trade in amber,
which reached them overland from the Baltic Coasts. Dionysius I
of Syracuse helped them to repel an attack of Liburnian pirates,
and is said to have kept a stud of horses in their country. For,
like their namesakes (and, by a not very improbable tradition,
their kinsmen) the Ἐνετοί of Paphlagonia[3], they were devoted

---

[1] A parallel insc. has ·u·zeroφo·s· (instead of ·o·posoφo·s·) which corresponds to Lat. *uberibus* exactly as Ven. *lo·u·zera* does to Lat. *libera* (cf. Gr.
οὖθαρ and ἐλεύθερος respectively).

[2] Before -*e*- and -*i*- we find -*qu*- in the river name *Liquentia*, and the
Misquilenses pagani (*C.I.L.* v, 2090). These examples show also φ, z, χ
where in Latin we have *b*, *d*, *g*. That the sounds which the Venetic signs
represented cannot have been very different from these Latin sounds is
shown by such spellings as Φohiio·s· = *Boius*; and -χnos in patronymics spelt
-*gnus* in Lat. alphabet (*e.g.* Ven. Lat. *Enignus*); for z in place of Lat. *d* we
have several etymological identities (as z·o·to = Gr. (ἔ-)δοτο), but at present
no transliterated words. We do not therefore know yet precisely the sound
of Ven. z; it may have been that of Eng. *th* in *then*, or it may have been
simply *d*. The reason why the Veneti had no proper signs for *b*, *g*, and *d*
was that these signs had long died out of the Etruscan alphabet which they
took over (pp. 398 *sqq.*).

[3] The name appears also (in a derivative form) in Latium (*Venetulani*)
and was borne by a Celtic tribe in Armorica (Bretagne). Its use at Rome

to horsemanship—at least to charioteering, as appears both in tradition and in some spirited sepulchral sculptures, still visible at Padua.

We learn from Herodotus (who calls them an Illyrian people) of a curious marriage custom which prevailed among them. Every year the marriageable maidens of a village were collected and prices put upon them according to their beauty. These sums were paid by the men who chose them as their brides, and the money was used by the authorities to provide dowries for the less beautiful girls and so afford them also the chance of marriage. From another source we learn that the Veneti were fond of dressing in black—a custom which they retained till the time of Titian, and indeed to the present day. Their uprightness and severe code of morals were proverbial, even more than their wealth.

Of one deity whom they worshipped, the goddess Rehtia, we know a good deal. Her temple at Este has furnished us with a wealth of votive offerings, among them three interesting varieties —alphabetic tablets, votive pillars which once bore statuettes of race-horses (and probably of chariots, long since overturned), and substantial bronze hairpins, fit to cope with an ample coiffure. Recent study of these remains has shown that the goddess was especially interested in women; and that she had many characteristics of the Spartan, Argive and Epidaurian Orthia. Her great function, as both names no less than her Venetic epithet Sanatis[1] imply, and the numerous votive images of many parts of the human body (of both sexes) found in her temple prove, was that of restoring health and vigour; and it seems likely that she is the goddess whom Livy and other writers of his time identify with the Roman Juno.

At the end of the period with which this chapter is concerned we find the Veneti, as might be expected, the enemies of the invading Gauls; indeed Polybius ascribes the retreat of the Gauls from Rome in 390 B.C. to an attack made upon the Gaulish settlements by the Veneti; and this attitude brought them naturally into friendship with Rome. By the fourth century B.C. they seem to have spread northwards up the Tagliamento valley, over the Plöken Pass, into the heart of the Alps. Livy records with pride

to denote the colour blue was probably late (cf. 'Prussian blue,' 'Magenta red'). But the same people who called their settlement Venetulum, may have been responsible for the formation of the names Praeneste and Laurentum (p. 445 sq.).

[1] If this be the nom. of šahnateh which (with porah) is the regular epithet of the dat.-gen. rehtiiah.

the repulse of some Greek pirates who attempted to land at Padua in the year 302 B.C., a victory which was celebrated by an annual regatta at Padua even in his day.

In the time of Polybius the Veneti still spoke a language different from both Latin and Gallic, and we can trace its gradual decay upon the series of votive offerings to Rehtia; for the latest of them exhibit mere scratches, counterfeiting rudely what had been Venetic dedications in the earlier period. The archaeological evidence shows that the temple of this goddess lasted down to at least Augustan times; and it seems likely that the language did not completely die out in ritual use until then, though in popular intercourse it was no doubt superseded by Latin a good deal earlier.

Some resemblances (*a*) in place-names, especially the ending -*ntum*, Πικούεντον, *Tridentum*, compared with Pannonian *Carnuntum*, Liburnian *Argyruntum*, Dalmatian *Salluntum*; (*b*) in religion, such as the worship of *Lo·u·zera* (Libera); (*c*) in custom, together with (*d*) the numerous resemblances in personal names, of which there are between 30 and 40 clear examples[1], link the Veneti with Illyria and Pannonia (as well as Messapia) and it will therefore be convenient at this point to mention what little is known of the speakers of other languages ('East Italic' and Messapic) on the east coast of Italy who appear to have come there in early times from the east of the Adriatic.

IV. THE 'EAST ITALIC' COMMUNITIES

None of the inscriptions yet found on Italian soil seem to be in so ancient a script as a small number (less than a dozen so far) found near the east coast, in Picenum or a little farther south (Bellante, Castignano, Cupra Maritima, Grecchio). Their alphabet has been described already (p. 396). It is clear that their language, if it is not Indo-European, certainly contains Indo-European elements, such as the phrase *paterefo materefo* (though the ending may be rather -*ſo* than -*fo*), and also at least one Illyrian name *Meitime*. Pliny tells us that Truentum in Picenum was the only town left in Italy of the Liburni, a well-known Illyrian tribe whose name became attached to a class of swift-sailing galleys; and we have just noted that the ending -(*e*)*ntum* is characteristic of the Veneti and of Illyria. Of the history of these settlers from Illyria

---

[1] *E.g.* Ven. *akutna* (fem.), Norican *Acutio*; Ven. ·*e·no*, Pannon. *Enno*; Ven. *kavaro*, Noric. *Cavru*, Dalmat. *Cavari* (gen.); Ven. *ka·n·ta* (fem.), Pannon. *Cantius*. See the list in Pauli, *Veneter*, pp. 359–378.

these inscriptions, which we cannot yet completely read, and are far from translating, are the only monument; but their alphabet is primitive enough to belong to the sixth or some earlier century B.C.

V. MESSAPII AND BRUTTII

The *Messapii* appear first in history in 477 B.C. when they inflicted a serious defeat on the Tarentine Greeks. But tradition represents them as having come by sea from the Illyrian coast, occupying their peninsula, the 'heel' of Italy, before the foundation of the Greek colony at Rhegium (which is ascribed to the eighth century B.C.). We learn further that they shared with the Cretans and 'Oenotrians' the custom of common meals for men (like the Spartan *phiditia*). The recurrence in Messapia of many Illyrian names of tribes and places, such as *Iapyges*, *Sallentini*, *Calabri*, *Genusia*, and the endings *-ntum* (p. 445) and *-estini* (in *Grumbestini*, *Apamestini*, cf. Venetic *Tergeste*, *Ateste*) abundantly confirms the tradition of their origin.

We have Messapic inscriptions from Monopoli, Fasano, Brindisi, Carovigno, Ceglie Messapico, the neighbourhood of Taranto, Oria, Rugge (*Rudiae*, the birthplace of Ennius), Lecce, Vaste (ancient Basta), Ugento, Capo S.M. di Leuca, Castrignano del Capo, and elsewhere. Their alphabet has been described in the preceding chapter (p. 396). Few if any of them can well be older than 400 B.C. or later than 150 B.C.; the most important, such as that of Brindisi, probably belong to the third century. As typical sentences of Messapic may be given:

> *klohizis θotoria marta pido vastei basta veinan aran.*
> 'Audiant (omnes)! Tutoria Marta donavit civitati
>   Bastae suam arationem[1].'
>
> *daxta moroana aprodita hipades.*
> 'Daxta Moroana Ἀφροδίτη votum solvit[2].'

The genitives *blatθihi* 'Blossii' and *kalatoras* 'calatoris' (on a herald's staff), *baledonas* 'Baledonis,' give further examples of the likeness and unlikeness of the language to both Greek and Latin;

---

[1] The first verb is parallel to Greek κλύω and its termination is of an aorist optative 3rd plur. (or possibly 2nd sing.); *pido* contains *pi-* (cf. Gr. ἐπί) and *dō* (for *dōt*) 3rd sing. of the root-aor. act. which, as in Venetic, has no augment. *veinan* is for *(s)veinan* an adj. formed from the pronominal stem of Gr. (σ)ϝέ, Lat. *suus*—for the extension cf. Germ. *sein*, Eng. *mine*, etc.

[2] The verb has lost a final *-t* and is 3rd sing. act. of an *-s-* aorist without augment, from the root *dhē-* (Gr. τίθημι), compounded with *hipa-* = Gr. ὑπό. For the meaning cf. the Greek ἀνέθηκε.

like Venetic, it may be said to stand midway between the two. It is to be noted further that like Venetic and Ligurian (pp. 434, 443), Messapic seems to have preserved the original Indo-European velars as pure gutturals without labialization as in the name *penkaheh[es]* (gen. sing.) (Osc. *Pompaiio-*, Osco-Lat. *Pompeius*) from Indo-European **penque ('five'). The change of short *-o-* to short *-a-* (*e.g.*, in the gen. sing. of consonantal stems *-as* from *-os*) has been reasonably regarded as a link with some of the more northerly and easterly branches of the Indo-European stock, such as Gothic, Albanian and Lithuanian.

The names of persons in the inscriptions follow the system established in Italy as early as any of all our records, *i.e.* a gentile nomen preceded by a personal prae-nomen; and it has been conjectured, though the evidence is very doubtful, that some of the inscriptions show the interesting custom which appears at Heraclea in the fourth century B.C. and also at Capua and Cumae in the fourth and third centuries, namely, the use of coats of arms, or heraldic symbols (such as a tripod or anchor) peculiar to particular families.

The tribe contributed something to European literature in the poet Ennius, who was a native of Rudiae, and boasted of having three souls, probably because he could speak Latin, Greek and Messapic. At Rudiae Messapic was pretty certainly spoken at the date of his birth (239 B.C.), though the final establishment by the Romans of a colony at Brundisium (244 B.C.) must have been a powerful influence in spreading Latin in the Calabrian peninsula.

The *Bruttii* in historical times occupied the south-western peninsula (or toe) of Italy, the region once called Oenotria, to which the name *Italia* was first applied, being the Greek form of the Oscan name *vitelliu* 'calf-land'[1] which is also recorded. This suggests that at the time when the Greeks first made acquaintance with them—say, in the ninth or eighth century B.C.—the Bruttii were speaking an Indo-European tongue. Of the character of their speech, however, we can judge only from this and other local names, such as *Nerulum, Medina, Terina*, and from such traditions as remain of their having been driven south before the advance of the Lucanians, a Samnite tribe, at some time not long before or not long after 400 B.C. Aristotle reports the custom of having public meals for the men, as being found among the Oenotrians, of whom he counted the Chōnes of Messapia as a

---

[1] This is the form known to us from coins of the Allies in the Social War of 90 B.C.; the doubled *-ll-* before the *-ia-* ending is a mark of late Oscan.

branch. In these traditions and in all the place-names there is nothing whatever to indicate that the Bruttians ever used anything but an Indo-European tongue. Their Lucanian conquerors spoke Oscan, and this the Bruttii appear to have adopted; we find two or three Oscan inscriptions from the district (one or two from Monteleone near Bivona, probably of the fourth century B.C.) in Greek characters, though one or two of the inscriptions are written from right to left.

There seems to be no linguistic or other direct evidence to identify the Bruttii with the Siculi, but none to suggest that they were distinct; their name, we are told, was given them by the Lucanians in whose speech it meant 'runaways'; this would imply, what is improbable, that before then they called themselves by a different name and that this name has been wholly lost. In the fourth century they revolted and established themselves in more or less barbarous independence, though the best points of their coasts were occupied by Greek colonists who taught them to write and to coin money. Their relations with Dionysius of Syracuse and other Greeks belong to a period later than that with which this chapter is concerned.

VI. THE ITALIC PEOPLES PROPER

We pass now to the peoples whose speech belongs in the strict sense to the Italic branch of the Indo-European family. The first step to a clear view of their history is to realize that their languages are sharply divided into two groups. The division was not so large as to make the language of one group wholly unintelligible to the speakers of the other; nevertheless it was deep enough to be a bar to easy and friendly intercourse, especially in the cases where the speakers of one group had become cut off by some alien barrier, such as the presence of the Etruscans, or by geographical distance. The two groups may be conveniently called (1) Latinian and (2) Safine or Osco-Umbrian. Each of these we find to have become again sub-divided by the fourth century B.C. and probably earlier.

Latinian in 500 B.C. included Latin, and the speech of the Falisci in the south of Etruria; also probably that of one or two other tribes, near neighbours of Rome, which was merged by about 250 B.C. in the *sermo rusticus* of Latium; and by that date these idioms differed little, if at all, from what was spoken in the district called Sabine. This word is only the Latin form of the name Safine, and denoted the language (which by 250 B.C. was almost completely Latinized) of the direct descendants of the Safine tribe from whom all the Samnite communities were off-shoots.

Two peculiarities however appear in certain place-names and glosses and in some of the numerous words taken into Latin from the country speech of Sabine farmers, which may be mentioned here: (*a*) the change of Indo-European *gh* initially to *f* (pure Latin *h*), as in Sab. *fedus*, Lat. *haedus*, Goth. *gait-*, Eng. *goat*; Sab.-Lat. *ferrum*; Gr. χέρσος 'hard ground' beside Lat.-Hernican *herna* 'stone'; and (*b*) the change of *d* to *l* initially and between vowels, as in Sab. *Nouensiles*, Lat. *Novensides* 'gods of the nine seats'; Sab.-Lat. *lacrima*, Gr. δάκρυ, Eng. *tear*, beside pure Lat. *dacruma*, still certainly used by Ennius (*nemo me dacrumis decoret*, where the alliteration is essential to the Ennian verse) and Plautus who puns upon *dacruma* and *drachuma* (*dacrumis argenteis*), though in both places our manuscripts naturally write the word with *l*-. To complete our picture of the language of the Sabine country before it began to be Latinized these peculiarities must be added to those common to all Safine dialects which, in 500 B.C., were no doubt shared by the speech of this area also. On Latin and Faliscan see p. 454 *sq.*

Safine is the best name for the language spoken, with little variety, by all the Samnite tribes—Paeligni, Vestini, Marrucini, Samnites (who seem to have called themselves *Safinos*[1] [nom. pl.] and perhaps also **Safellos*), Hirpini, Lucani, Frentani, Apuli; and spoken also in Campania after its conquest by the Samnites from 438 B.C. onwards (see p. 390). For this reason it was known to the Romans as *Osca lingua*, although the name *Opsci*, later *Osci* (Gr. Ὀπικοί), properly belongs to the pre-Tuscan inhabitants of that fertile section of the west coast.

According to a well-attested tradition this migration of the Safines into Samnium and later into Lucania was the result of a Sacred Spring. That was the old Italian name for a national vow dedicating to a deity all the creatures, of the home and the farm, born in a certain year; all the boys and girls included in this dedication were bound by their father's vow, as soon as they reached full age, to leave the land in which they were born and go out to win fresh territory elsewhere. A similar dedication (in this case to Apollo) lay behind the settlement of the Campanian Mamertini in Messana at the beginning of the third century B.C.

---

[1] The name by which the Romans called them was determined partly at least by that given to them by the Campanian Greeks (**Σαφνιται or **Σαμνιται later Σαυνῖται). It was through the Greeks that the Roman contact with them began in the fifth century B.C. according to tradition.

Of the language of the Paeligni, Samnites and Hirpini, as well as of the Oscan-speaking towns of Campania (especially Capua, Nola and Pompeii), we have a valuable record in inscriptions and coins beginning in the fourth (or even the fifth) century, and continuing in many places down to the Christian era. From the Vestini, Marrucini, Lucani, Frentani and Apuli, we have only a small number of inscriptions, but they are enough to show the genuine Safine character of the language spoken in the places from which they come. Speaking broadly, we have no reason to suppose that Oscan died out as a spoken language in the southern half of Italy much before the Christian era. The Romans, at all events, thought it worth while about 100 B.C. to make a long treaty, written in Oscan, with the little town of Bantia (Oscan *Bansā-*) in Apulia, and to have it engraved on a tablet of bronze, the other side of which had been used to hold a Roman law recently repealed. And the Oscan *graffiti* on the walls of Pompeii cannot have been scribbled many years before the town was buried in the ashes from Vesuvius in 79 A.D.

The following sentences may serve as a specimen of Oscan which is the purest representative of Safine; they come from the Cippus Abellanus, the boundary-stone between Nola and Abella, regulating the use of the building and lands of a temple of Hercules which stood exactly across the line between them, and set up probably in the latter half of the second century B.C.

inim iuk tribarakkiuf pam nuvlanus tribarakattuset inim uittiuf nuvlanum estud. ekkum svai pid abellanus tribarakattuset iuk tribarakkiuf inim uittiuf abellanum estud. avt pust feihuis pus fisnam amfret, eisei terei nep abellanus nep nuvlanus pidum tribarakkattins.

'Et ea aedificatio quam Nolani aedificaverint (*indic.*) et usus (eius) Nolanorum esto. Itidem si quid Abellani aedificaverint, ea aedificatio et usus Abellanorum esto. Post muros autem qui fanum circumeunt, in illa terra neve Abellani neve Nolani quidquam aedificaverint (*subjunc.*).'

Of the phonology of Safine the most striking characteristics are: (*a*) The conversion of the Indo-European velars into labials, *e.g.* Oscan and Umbrian *pis*, Lat. *quis*; Osc.-Umb. *pod*, Lat. *quod*; Osc. *kombened*, Lat. *convĕnit* (the Osc. form is a Perfect contracted for **combebened). (*b*) The appearance of medial *f* representing an original voiced aspirate, such as *bh* or *dh*, where in Latin (and Ligurian, cf. the river-names *Porco-bera*, *Comberanea*, p. 433) the fricative has been converted into a voiced plosive such as *b* or *d*; Osc. *mefio-*, Lat. *medius*, Sansk. *madhya-*; Osco-Lat.

rufus 'red-haired,' Ligurian *Roudelius*, Gr. ἐρυθρός. (*c*) The extrusion or syncope (i) of short vowels in the second syllable of a word, *e.g.* Osc. *ůpsā-*, Umb. *osā-* from an Italic stem *opesā-* 'to work, build,' cf. Lat. *opera* 'work'; Osc. *actud*, Umb. *aitu*, Lat. *agitō*; (ii) of short vowels before final *s*, *e.g.* Umb. *ikuvins*, Lat. *Iguuinus*; Osc. nom. pl. *humuns*, Old Lat. *homōnes*; Umb. abl. plur. *avis* for ****avifos*, Latin *avibus*. (*d*) The preservation of *s* between vowels, where in Latin (and Umbrian) it became -*r*- (Osc. *fusid*, Lat. *foret* and Sabine-Latin *caseus*, *carbasus*); and before *n*, *m*, and *l* (whereas in Latin it is lost, with lengthening of the previous vowel when the change is medial) as in Umb. *ahesnes* (abl. plur.), Lat. *ahēnīs*; Paelignian *prismu* (nom. sing. fem.), Lat. *prīma*. (*e*) Instead of Lat. -*nd*- we have in Osco-Umbrian -*nn*- which the Umbrian poet Plautus (*Miles Glor.* 1399) reproduces as a vulgarism in a well-known phrase (*distennite hominem et dispennite*); so in the gerundives, Osc. *ůpsannam*, Lat. *operandam*. (*f*) Final -*ā* became *o* (written *ů* or *u*); Osc. *viu*, Lat. *via*; Umb. *adro* (nom. pl. neut.), Lat. *atra*.

In the morphology of Safine several primitive forms are retained which have been obscured in Latin, for example, in the first two declensions we have the gen. sing. fem. in -*as*, Oscan *eituas* 'pecuniae'; gen. plur. masc. *nůvlanum* 'Nolanorum,' and the locative is still a living case in both declensions, *e.g.*, Oscan *viai* 'in via,' *terei* (neut.) 'in terra.' In verbs the infinitive is formed in -*um*, Oscan *ezum*, Umbrian *erom* 'esse.' The fut. indic. act. is formed with -*es*-, Oscan *didest* 'dabit.'

One feature is of especial interest, the passive forms in -*r*. Although the full development of this passive is peculiar to the Italic languages, yet the evidence which the Safine forms afford us of its origin links these languages closely to Celtic. In Oscan and Iguvine (Umbrian), as in Welsh and Irish, we find what are best called the rudimentary forms of this passive; and the Oscan examples still show their rise from an indefinite 3rd pers. plur. act. by governing an accusative case, *sakrafir ultiumam* 'sacraverint (*i.e.* 'consecrent,' or 'sacris celebrent') ultimam (imaginem).'

These peculiarities are common to the whole of the Safine group and distinguish it sharply from Latinian. For our present purpose the first, namely, the conversion of the velar consonants into full labials, is of particular importance since precisely the same change is the most marked distinction between the two halves of the Celtic family, namely that generally known as Goidelic—the language of the Gaels of Ireland and the Scottish Highlands, which preserved *q*, and Brythonic—the language of the Britons and of most of the Gauls, including the Gauls who settled in North Italy, which everywhere converted *q* into *p*.

From this Safine speech sprang two dialects, known as Volscian and Umbrian, marked by changes of their own. These dialects are in fact recorded only in inscriptions from four towns: Velitrae in Volscian territory, afterwards included in Latium, and Iguvium in Umbria, W. of the Via Flaminia, with Asisium and Fulginia. It would be prudent to call the two dialects simply Velitern and Iguvine; in any case observe that their language—for Volscian is almost identical with Umbrian as far as our evidence extends—clearly belongs to the Safine, not the Latinian group, and that in both the ethnicon (*Iguvinus, Veliternus*) is formed with the suffix -*no*- (see below, p. 456).

The Volscian or Velitern inscription which belongs to the first half of the third century B.C. is of only four lines, a bronze label of some offering, probably a statue, to a deity (*deve declune statom* 'divo Declono'—or 'divae Declonae'—'consecratum'); and enjoins an offering (*façia esaristrom* 'faciat sacrificium') in certain circumstances. The community is called (in the gen. plur.) *velestrom* which probably means 'marsh men.' The preservation of -*s*- between vowels in *esaristrom* is the only feature in which the dialect might seem more like Oscan than it is like Iguvine of the same date[1].

The language commonly called Umbrian is preserved for us in one or two brief inscriptions (from Fulginia and Asisium[2]) and by a group of monuments of considerable length, the so-called Iguvine Tables. What is left of these contains many parts of the liturgy of a sacred brotherhood (who in Latin would have been called *Fratres Atiedii*) of the city of Iguvium, the modern Gubbio. The following sentences from Table II *b* will serve as a specimen:

> *vitlu vufru pune heries façu, eruhu tiçlu sestu iuvepatre. pune seste, urfeta manuve habetu. estu iuku habetu: iupater saçe, tefe estu vitlu vufru sestu.*

'Vitulum votivum cum voles facere (*i.e.* sacrificare), illa dedicatione sistito (*i.e.* consecrato) Iovi patri. Cum sistis, orbitam (*i.e.* a round cake) in manu habeto. Istum sermonem habeto: "Iuppiter sancte[3], tibi istum vitulum votivum sisto".'

[1] But since we have seen that the word *aisar* 'gods' is Etruscan (pp. 404, 419) this derivative may not be a native Volscian word.

[2] One or two from Tuder show a difference, the preservation of -*d* between vowels (see p. 453).

[3] The Umbrian form corresponds to the Old Lat. adj. *sancus*.

The dialect is marked off from Oscan, which is more primitive, by several changes, of which the following are important. (*a*) The palatalization of *k* and *g* before a following *i* or *e*, or consonant *i*, as in Umb. *tiçit* (i.e. *diçit*), Lat. *decet*; Umb. *muieto* past partic. pass. (pronounced as though the *i* were an English [or French] *j*), beside the imperative *mugatu*, cf. Lat. *mugire*. This change antedates by many centuries the similar decay in Late Latin and Romance. (*b*) The change of -*s*- to -*r*- between vowels as in Latin; Umb. *erom* 'esse,' Osc. *ezum*; gen. plur. fem. ending in -*aru*, Osc. -*azum*, Lat. -*arum*. (*c*) The decay of all diphthongs: *ai, oi, ei* all become a monophthong variously written *e* and *i* (rarely *ei*), as in the dat. sing. fem. *tote* 'civitati'; dat. sing. masc. *pople*, 'populo'; loc. sing. masc. *onse* from ***om(e)sei* 'in umero.' So *au, eu, ou* all become *o*, as in Umb. *ote*, Osc. *auti*, Lat. *aut*. (*d*) The change of *d* between vowels to *ḍ*, a sound represented by -*rs*- in the Tables written in Latin alphabet, e.g., in *peturpursus* 'quadripedibus.' This change does not appear in 'Volscian' nor in the dialect of Tuder.

Apart from the consequences of these phonetic changes, Umbrian morphology and syntax exhibit no serious divergence from Oscan, except an interesting perfect formation with -*l*- as in *ampelust*, fut. perf. 'impenderit' 'will have paid.' This tense is formed from what in Latin is merely an adjective (*pendulus* 'hanging,' 'being weighed'), but which in Safine, as in Balto-Slavonic farther north, has assumed the functions of a participle.

As to the relative dates of the Iguvine Tables, at least four periods in the history of the dialect can be distinguished. (*a*) Tables I, II, III and IV, and the first two inscriptions of V, are in Umbrian script; whereas the third inscription of V and the whole of VI and VII are in Roman characters of about Sullan date. It is clear that the tables in Umbrian writing are the older. (*b*) The first two inscriptions of V show the latest form of the Umbrian alphabet and also the latest form of the language; *i.e.* its language is identical, so far as has yet been ascertained, with that which is written in Latin characters in VI and VII. But III and IV which form a single document are somewhat older, and II and I older still; II *b* would seem to be probably the oldest of all. It is the only one, in which, at present, no manifest signs of re-editing have been detected. (*c*) Tables I, II *a*, III and IV show inconsistencies due to the partial modernization of older documents, from which they must have been drawn. In V final -*s* has everywhere become -*r* (as in *totar*, earlier *totas* 'of the city'); but in I and II *a*, we find an occasional -*r* creeping in, though the

bulk of the forms are written with the older -*s*. Again in III
and IV we have here and there the most archaic forms of all, for
example, *kebu* (Latin *cibum* 'food') side by side with examples
(e.g. *śimu* 'backwards,' cf. Lat. *ci-tra*) which show that at the time
the document was engraved on this particular table *k* had become
ç before a following *i* or *e*, although a few old forms were copied
unaltered from some earlier document, the words themselves
having (quite possibly) died out of living use.

It is not easy to translate this relative chronology into actual
dates; but it seems likely that the closer relations between Rome
and Umbrian communities which ensued after the Social War
in 90 B.C. brought about the adoption of the Latin alphabet, so
that Tables VI and VII would not be earlier than the time of
Sulla. Table V, with the modern elements in I and II which show
the language in the same condition, need not be very much older.
On the other hand, for the date of the first composition of the
oldest parts of the tables we have only general considerations to
guide us. Since the Etruscans are cursed among the enemies of
the Iguvines, the curse was obviously written at a time when the
two communities were in hostile contact. Further, since the
alphabet is derived, as we have seen, from the Etruscan we
cannot date the tables earlier than the earliest Etruscan inscriptions, which belong to the eighth or seventh century B.C.; and it
would be perhaps imprudent to go back for Umbrian further
than the (early) fifth century B.C., which is the earliest period at
which as yet we have traces of written public documents either
in Rome or in Campania. On the other hand, since there is absolutely no mention of the Romans, one would be inclined to choose
the fifth rather than the fourth century. The absence of any
mention of the Gauls would point in the same direction but for
the fact that we find the Gauls in history allied with the Umbrians.
Finally, in view of the evidence to be discussed in what follows,
it is important to observe that the men of Iguvium, with whose
language we are primarily concerned (since the language of the
neighbouring town of Tuder was not wholly identical with theirs,
p. 452, n. 2), formed their ethnicon (*Iguvini*) with the suffix -*NO*-;
but that later on they came to be called *Iguvinates*, the added suffix
being proper, as we shall see, to an older stratum of population
in which they appear to have been absorbed.

To the Latinian group belong (besides Sabine, the Latinized
form of Safine, p. 448) the country Latin of Marsians, Aequians
and Hernicans to the east and south of Latium proper, and
Faliscan, spoken by a tribe of close kin to the Latins but under

Etruscan rule from an early period of their invasion[1] down to
241 B.C. when the town was conquered by Rome. The Falisci
lived in the region west of the Tiber and north of Rome, and their
only town whose name has come down to us was Falerii (now
Cività Castellana). We have a few inscriptions earlier than
241 B.C., of which one round an erotic scene on a glazed patera
of some beauty may serve as a specimen:

> *foied vino pipafo, cra carefo.*
> 'hodie vinum bibam, cras carebo,'
> 'to-day I will drink wine (for) to-morrow I shall be without it.'

This illustrates three of the chief phonetic characteristics of
the dialect. (1) The appearance of medial *f* representing an
original voiced aspirate (just as in Safine words like *rūfus*) in the
future ending (-*fo*, Lat. -*bo*); (2) the appearance of *f*- instead of *h*-
for initial Ind.-Eur. *gh*-, in *foied* from ****ghŏ-died*, just as in Sabine
(p. 449); (3) the change of -*dį*- to some fricative sound like Eng.
or Fr. *j* (or perhaps only Eng. *y*) written simply -*i*- in *foied*,
just as in N. Oscan *Petieḍu* from *Petiedia*. Note also (4) the
preservation of *q* (written *cu*-), Fal. *cuando*, Lat. *quando*.

The oldest monument of the Latini, the gold brooch of Praeneste, is referred by archaeologists, as we have seen, to the seventh
or early sixth century B.C. (p. 399). The next oldest is the fragmentary 'Forum-inscription'—cut, probably in the fifth century,
up and down the sides of a slender pyramid which stood on a
specially sacred portion of the forum of Rome, outside what was
then the senate-house. In a subsequent raising and repairing of
the forum (probably early in the fourth century B.C. to cleanse
away all traces of the Gallic occupation) this old monument was,
so to speak, beheaded, and its trunk left standing but covered
up by the rubble below the new pavement. Owing to the way
in which it was written only one sentence can be called complete:

> *iouxmenta niquis agat*
> 'let no one drive beasts of burden (here)'

but it suffices to indicate the nature of the monument.

The characteristics of Latin are too well known to call for
analysis here. It is, however, well to note the historical implications of some two or three points in Latin morphology which to
students of language seem strange, not to say, monstrous; namely,
the curious havoc which has been wrought in the verbal system

---

[1] Falerii was not far from the site of the modern *Narce* where the series
of remains described in chap. xii, p. 392 is fully represented.

by the creation of the inflexions of the passive and of the inflexions of the perfect active; also, though in a less degree, by
the fusion of the conjunctive and optative moods. Of the Latin
passive, it is not too much to say that such an extraordinary jumble
of forms and syntax (in the course of which the objective accusative was replaced by the nominative) could hardly have come
about save by the forcible introduction of an idiom foreign to the
bulk of the speakers of Latin; and further that the characteristics
of the new introduction are emphatically Celtic[1].

VII. THE -CO- FOLK AND THE -NO- FOLK

From our knowledge, of which a brief outline has now been
given, of the different languages in use in Italy at 400 B.C., it is
possible to construct roughly a linguistic map of the tribal conditions at that date. But beyond the chronology of the alphabets
and of the inscriptions from different localities, and the fact of
the Safine expansion southwards, we have so far found little to
guide us as to the movements or history of the different Italic
tribes at an earlier date, that is, in the period with which this
chapter is properly concerned. But we must now observe a clear
distinction: some tribes, like the Hirpini, formed their ethnic
adjectives (the plural of which was used for the tribal name)
with the suffix -NO-: others used for this purpose the suffix
-CO- or the suffix -TI- (see the Table at p. 460). By this means
we can show that the -NO- peoples became masters of the west
coast and of central Italy at a period later than that at which
the -CO- and -TI- people or peoples were predominant.

The evidence of this consists in a number of pairs of names
like *Marruci* and *Marrucini*, *Ardeates* and *Ardeatini*, *Picentes* and
Picentini, *Reate* and *Reatini*; these show that the -NO- suffix was
imposed at a later date on existing names. The name of Teate
(Apulorum) by an even more drastic change was made into

---

[1] In the perfect indicative active, four, if not five, different tenses have
been forced into one paradigm; the perfect active and middle (*dedit, dedī*),
the *s*- aorist (*dīxit, dīxī*) active and middle, and the *sis*- aorist middle or active
(*dīxistī, dīxēre?*). In the forms of the moods, pure optative forms like *siem*
[cf. Gr. ἐ-(σ)ιην], *sīmus, dederīmus* stand beside apparently pure conjunctive
forms like *regāmus* and (probably) *stēs, dēs, amēs* with precisely the same
functions so far as the modal meaning is concerned. The disappearance of
the proper form of the 1st pers. sing. of a kindred tense, *i.e.* of the 1st pers.
corresponding to *regēs, reget* (whatever it was), and its replacement by the
conjunctive form in -*am* are more easily understood if we regard the change
in the same light as the distortions just mentioned.

Teanum Apulum[1]. That this practice may be reasonably associated with the governing class at Rome is shown by the name
Romani (contrasted with the older *Quirites*) and by the way in
which the Romans treated provincial names in many parts of their
empire. The *Neapolitai* became *Neapolitani,* the *Syrakosioi* became
Syracusani, the *Spartiatai* became *Spartani,* the *Asiatikoi* became
Asiani.

How large a part in the political nomenclature of Italy, in the
historical period, was taken by this use of the -NO- suffix will be
seen at once from the Table at p. 460, based on what is believed
to be an exhaustive collection of the place-names of ancient Italy,
arranged according to their tribal areas.

Little is needed to make clear the significance of the statistics.
To form tribal names in ancient Italy we find only six suffixes in
use (or eight if the derivative suffixes -CINO- and -TINO- be added).
One of the six, the suffix -*IO*-, is distributed in small numbers
over the tribal areas and offers no clear indication of racial kinship
beyond the fact that it is of course an ancient Indo-European
formant (as for instance in *Rhodii, Ubii*). Another, the ending
-*uli,* we may dismiss at once, though its occurrence in three or
four ancient names—*Siculi, Rutuli, Apuli,* and possibly *Poedi-
culi*—is perhaps significant of some connection between the four;
and with these must be mentioned *Vituli* which would have been
the Latin form of the name which gave rise to the Greek Ἰταλοί.
The only other case in which the ending is certain is the small
village of *Casperuli* in a Sabine district.

The suffix -*ensi*- again had a perfectly clear political use, namely
to form the ethnica of municipal towns in alliance with Rome,
as in *Foroulienses,* 'the inhabitants of Forum Julii.' Its (Latin)
etymology is equally clear, for example in the form *Furfensis* from
Furfo, the name of a little town in Sabine country, whose genitive
appears on an inscription of 58 B.C. (*C.I.L.* ix, 3513) in the
primitive form *Furfens.* Similarly we have *Faleriensis* from the
town of *Falerio.* It would therefore serve no purpose here to
include the statistics of these three endings.

Five points are of especial interest in these -CO- names:
(1) that they are grouped in a comparatively small section of the
peninsula; (2) that they all belong to the peoples who were most

---

[1] A curious consequence of this is that in one chapter (ix, 20, 4 and 7)
Livy narrates the same event twice over, once of 'Teate' and once of
'Teanum.' The fact is undoubted, if only from the evidence of coins with
the legends *Tiiatium, Tiati,* found on the site of Teanum (cf. *Ital. Dial.*
p. 30 and Mommsen in *C.I.L.* ix, p. 67).

quickly subdued either by the Safines (p. 449) or by the Romans;
(3) that a considerable number of them lived in marshy places.
The name *Volsci*, older *Volusci*, clearly contains a noun ****volus*
identical with Gr. ἕλος 'marsh,' and they lived in or near the
Pomptine marshes; the *Aurunci*, with *Glanica* and M. *Massicus*,
at the mouth of the Liris; the *Hernici* lived in the valley of the
Trerus; *Ustica* Horace calls *cubans*; and *Graviscae* means a region
of malaria. It is hard to believe that all these circumstances are
accidental, though we need (for our present purpose at least) put
the cause no further back than to conclude that these names belonged to a defeated population who found refuge in places which
their conquerors could not inhabit.

This is confirmed by what we know of the history of the Osci,
who, according to Strabo, were the pre-Tuscan inhabitants of
Campania, the last remnants of whom he tells us lived in *Teanum
Sidicinum*—where the form of the adjective tells the same tale as
that of *Marrucini*. We know further that the older form of the
name was *Opsci*, which may well be derived from the stem of
opus in the sense of 'farmer's work,' just as *Volsci* was from ****volus*.
The modern name of the same district is Terra di Lavoro; no
doubt because of its great fruitfulness.

Again we observe (4) that the -*CO*- (and -*ca*) suffix was fairly
common in the Ligurian area; and we actually have the name of
the Ligurian tribe Ἐλίσυκοι inhabiting marshes near the sea,
which looks suspiciously like the original of *Volusci* put into Greek.
The goddess *Marica*, whom we found in the salt marshes of the
Aurunci, appears again at the mouth of the river now called
Foglia in Umbria, and the name *Marici* appears among the
Ligurians. And in the Venetic district (Venetia proper and Histria)
the suffix appears in 5 out of 29 ethnica.

(5) A large number of these names contain Indo-European
elements, *Volsci, Osci, Hernici* (from *herna* 'a stone' from the same
root as Sabine-Lat. *ferrum*, p. 449), *Graviscae, Marica, Satricum*
(if it be connected with *saturare*), and perhaps *Caedicii* (if it be
connected with *caedere*). *Aequicus* and *Marsicus* obviously contain
the stems of Latin *aequus* and *Mars*, and there is no difficulty in
deriving *Massicus* from *massa* (cf. the modern name *Massa Carrara*
for the marble heights of that Ligurian chain). The eponymous
hero of Falerii is known in Latin records as *Halaesus*, whereas
the Faliscan name with its Sabine-Faliscan *f*- and the weaker form
of the stem in the second syllable (-*is*- instead of -*aes*-) vouches at
all events for a parallel form older than the separation of Latin and
Faliscan, perhaps older than the separation of Latinian and Safine.

The Table at p. 460 includes the adjectives *Aequicus, Marsicus, Umbricus*, though so far as our record goes they were not in substantival use as ethnica, except in Greek writers.

The names formed with the suffix -*TI*- are more numerous and spread more widely; but their frequency in certain districts is very remarkable. In Umbria 35 out of 59 names are so formed. In the Volscian district 10 out of 40. In Etruria 9 out of 45, in Latium 8 out of 55. Nowhere else south and west of the Appennines is the number above 5, and that is in Picenum, out of 21. But the suffix is common (9 out of 29) in the Venetic area (Venetia and Histria) and quite preponderant in Liguria (20 out of 49; -*CO*- and -*TI*- together come to 25).

We have already noted the practice of the Romans of imposing the suffix -*NO*- upon the names of their allies and subjects; and in view of its great frequency in the most purely Safine district, that of the Hirpini (31 out of 34, besides -*TINO*- in two out of the remaining three), it is difficult not to connect this habit with the Safine element in Rome, especially in such cases as *Sidicinum, Aricini* and *Marrucini*[1].

Finally it is important to observe how common the -*NO*- suffix is among the names of Gallic tribes. In the footnotes to the table there are mentioned six in -*ni*, like the *Cenomani*, whom we know to have been Alpine or Gallic; there are five (out of a total of 14) in the Regio Transpadana, three (and three more in -*TINO*-) in the Regio Aemilia; and of those counted as belonging to the Veneti and Ligures, six at least are obviously Gallic—see the list of authorities in the Bibliography—and probably the bulk of the rest.

But lest the reader should mistake the argument it should be added that there can be no doubt that -*CO*- and -*NO*- and -*TI*- are all equally Indo-European; the difference here pointed out is in the prevailing choice made between them to express a particular political meaning at a particular epoch. This choice clearly differed; and where the same choice prevailed over large areas, as

---

[1] It is worth while to quote some of the cases (not yet mentioned) where we have actually the older form -*TI*- side by side with the later -*TINO*-.

Umbria	Camertes	Camertini
	Tudertes	Tudertini
Campania	ager Stellas	Stellatina tribus (Etruria)
Etruria	Visentes	Visentini
	(Volcentes	Volcentani)
Marsi	Anxates	Anxatini
Volsci	Antiates	Antiatini
Apuli and Marrucini	Teates	Teatini
Veneti and Sabini	Reate	Reatini

of *-tes* among Ligurians, Veneti, and the pre-Tuscan inhabitants of Umbria, Etruria and Latium, it is hard to doubt the identity of the influence under which the choice was made. The argument here drawn from the imposition of the *-NO-* suffix, which extended into historical times, is exactly the same. The Spartiatae did not become Romans because the Romans called them *Spartani*; but they would never have received that name if they had not fallen within the Roman sphere of control. So when we find in Umbria (*a*) the *-TI-* suffix outnumbering the *-NO-*, (*b*) the *-NO-* suffix added to *-TI-* (*Camertes, Camertini*) only in four cases, but (*c*) the *-(A)TI-* suffix added to the *-NO-* (as in *Iguvini*, later *Iguvinates*) in ten or eleven forms, we conclude that the ways of the folk who liked *-TI-* prevailed again there ultimately over those of the *-NO-* people, though, as we have seen, the *-TI-* folk were earlier on the soil.

VIII. ETHNOGRAPHIC QUESTIONS

The evidence considered in this chapter seems to leave us with the following questions, which we are bound to raise, even though a clear answer to some of them cannot yet be confidently given. (1) With which of the peoples whom we have studied should the founders of the Terremare be identified? (2) In the facts we have discussed is there any evidence to show whether the civilization of the Iron Age was introduced by a fresh set of immigrants from the north or developed spontaneously by the people of the Terremare? (3) Was the language of the Ligurians—which we have seen to possess Indo-European characteristics—native to the Ligurian people or introduced among them by some wave of northern invaders? (4) Is the recorded language of the Veneti to be regarded as one proper to newcomers into Italy, or one which belonged to an earlier population on the spot? (5) To what epoch must we assign the appearance of the Safines in central Italy? (6) What, if any, is the connection of the Safines with more northerly tribes such as the pre-Tuscan *Ombrikoi*, the Veneti, or the Gauls? (7) Does the evidence obtainable throw any light on the origin of the two orders of the Patricians and the Plebeians at Rome?

Before considering these questions even briefly, we must explicitly recognize one general fact which has been already implied: so far as the evidence of language extends, there is no trace in ancient Italy of any non-Indo-European speech except Etruscan. The speculations which are common in archaeological writings, to what race it was that 'introduced' Indo-European speech

TABLE to show the Distribution of the -CO-, -TI-, and -NO- Ethnica

	-CO-	-TI-	-CINO-	-TINO-	-NO-
Messapii	•	•	•	9	7
Peucetii	•	•	•	6	9
Daunii	•	3	•	3	5
Bruttii	•	2	•	2	9
Lucani	•	3	•	6	7
Hirpini	•	1	•	2	31
Frentani	•	4	•	4	3
Samnites	•	4	1	•	5
Campani	•	5	1	8	35
Aurunci	2	•	1	•	2
Volsci	1	10	•	4	25
Hernici	1	2	•	1	2
Marsi	1	4	•	1	2
Aequi	1	2	•	•	6
Latini	1	8	2	6	38
Early Rome	a•	•	•	3	16
Sabini	•	4	•	2	11
Etruria (including the Falisci)	2	9	•	5	29
Marrucini	•	1	1	1	1
Paeligni	•	•	•	•	5
Vestini	•	4	•	1	7
Piceni	•	5	1	5	10
Umbri	1	35	•	4	19
Regio Aemilia	1	4	•	3	3 d•
Histria	1	2	•	2	•
Veneti	b4	7	b•	4	e9
Veleiates	9	3	•	2	1
Regio Transpadana	2	7	•	•	f5
Ligures	e5	20?	•	2	g22?
Raeti	3	5	•	1	4
	35	154	7	87	328

a Not counting *Vāticānus*.   *b* Not counting *Farraticanus* (*pagus*).

c Not counting *Mons Prenicus* nor three rivers in *-asca*.

d Not counting two tribes which Pliny describes as *Alpini*, namely the *Subocrini* and *Menoncaleni*.

e Excluding three Gallic tribes *Cenomani, Anauni, Sinduni*, and the Pannonian *Carni*.

f Not counting *Lacus Sebinnus*, but reckoning *Taurini* here as well as under *Ligures*: the total should therefore be strictly 327.

g Not counting four tribes in *-nni, Bagienni, Camunni, Vergunni, Ucenni*; nor *Ticinus fl.*, nor *Mons Lemurinus*; but many tribes like *Seduni, Velauni* which are no doubt really Gallic.

Notes to the Table of Ethnica

The names in the peninsula (south of the rivers Rubico and Macra) to which these figures refer can be identified at once in the corresponding sections of the place-names in *The Italic Dialects*: the following are the forms from Cisalpine Gaul. They are all taken from Mrs S. Elizabeth Johnson's collection kindly put at the writer's service in manuscript, and shortly to be published in *The Prae-Italic Dialects*.

Regio Aemilia: Spineticus: Padinates, Aquinates, Urbanates, Vettiregiates: Fidentini, Placentini, Truentini: Brixillanus, Otesini, Tannetani (besides saltus Gallianus).

Histria: Polaticus (besides a deity Seixomnia Leucitica): Polates, Tergeste: Parentinus, Piquentini.

Veneti: Benacus lacus, Bedriacum, Meduacus fl., Carnicus (not counting Bodincus, the older name of the Padus, probably Ligurian): Ateste, Arusnates, Altinates, Laebactes, Atinates (recurring in Volscian territory), Nedinates, Rundiates: Atestini, Tergestini, Vicetini: Mantuani, Pátavini, Brixiani, Sabini, Altinum, Tarvisani, Opitergini, Bellunum, Edrani, Siagitani.

Of these we know that the Brixiani were Gallic.

Veleiates: fundi—Caturniacus, Irvaccus, Noniacus, Quintiacus, Pisuniacus, Pulleliacus (hortus), Saecuasiacus, Scantiniscus, Stantacus: Veleiates, Regiates, Lurate: Briagontinus, Placentinus: Appenninus (but a number of purely Latin forms like Propertianus and the like are not counted).

Regio Transpadana: Taurisci, Libici (Λεβέκιοι Ptol.): Bergomates, Ausuciates, Anesiates, Corogennates, Modiciates, Montunates, Boutes: Taurini, Segusini, Sebuini, Agamini, Ticinus fl. (besides Verban(n)us lacus).

Ligures: Liguscus (and Ligusticus), Belaci, Camactulici, Canalicum, Ἐλίσυκοι (not counting the rivers Neviasca, Tulelasca, Vinelasca, nor mons Prenicus); Iluates, Genuates, Deciates, Caburriates, Velleiates, Arelate, Langates, Odiates, Dripsinates, Brixenetes?, Edenates?, Nantuates?, Adanates, Savincates, Quadiates, Bardarate, Carburriates, Casmonates, Celeiates, Cerdiciates: Ligustinus, Iadatini: Ligurinus, Apuani, Ingauni, (Ligures) Montani, Nemoloni?, Veneni, Cavaturines, Mentonines, Ἐρναγῖνοι, Brigiani?, Ecdini?, Esubiani, Velauni, Seduni, Veamini (-nii)?, Venisani, Vesubiani, Memini, Verucini, Cuntini, Ligauni, Taurini.

Raeti: Raeticus, Isarci, Rugusci: Ambisontes, Focunates, Suanetes, Vennonetes, Venostes: Τριδεντῖνοι: Breuni, Stoeni (Στουῖνοι), Trumpilini, Genauni.

Many of those in *-ni* may be recognized at once as Gaulish, either from their ending in *-auni* (resembling the *Anauni* who are recorded as Gallic)—*Genauni, Ingauni, Velauni, Ligauni*; or by express record as the *Taurini*, and *Seduni*; and the *Breuni* in this region contrast with the *Breuci* of Pannonia. Compare also the deity of the Great St Bernard Alps, *Iuppiter Poeninus* or *Penninus*, of which *Appenninus* would seem to be a derivative.

Notes to the Table of Ethnica (continued)

In the Ligurian list, the names with ? come from the *Tropaea Augusti* (*C.I.L.* v, 7817) and are not necessarily Ligurian but only among the *gentes Alpinae quae a mari supero ad inferum pertinebant*, as the inscription states.

From this list it will be seen that the tribes whose names are formed in Central Italy with the suffix -CO- are comparatively few, and all fairly near together, *Osci, Aurunci, Volsci, Hernici, Falisci, Tusci*. The town of *Labici* was near to the district of the *Hernici*; *Arici(a)* not far off, and the *Caedici(i)* lived among the *Aurunci*. These are the only ethnica ending in *-ci* in the whole peninsula on the south-west side of the Appennines. We note of course that the names *Tusci* (Umb. *turskum numen*) and *Etrusci* must owe their final shape not to the Etruscans themselves but to one or other of their Italic neighbours. It is probably reasonable to add to these a few names formed with the suffixes *-ca* or *-cum*; there are three in Auruncan territory, *Glanica, Maricae palus, mons Massicus*, two more in Volscian territory, Satricum and Ἔρρουκα (also the *ager Luca-nus*); one (or two) in Latin territory outside Rome, *Pollusca*, (Mars) *Fica(-nus)* with the village *Ficolea* (and the river *Numicius* seems to be based on a similar stem); two in Rome itself, both very ancient, *Pectuscum Palati* and the *ager Vatica(nus)*; to the last the -NO- suffix has been added, as in *Ficanus* just noted. Besides these there are in the whole peninsula only the following forms: four in Umbria, *Matelica, Usidica(ni), Naharkum, Iapuzkum nume(n)*; three in the Sabine district, *Tetrica, Trebula Mutuesca, Ustica*; one in south Etruria, *Graviscae*; and the *Marruci(ni)* already mentioned at the mouth of the Aternus, who however, in a religious inscription of the third century B.C., still called their city *tota marouca*.

into the peninsula, may have their place in regard to some earlier period, but they are totally irrelevant to the matter discussed in this chapter. In the last millennium B.C., some variety of Indo-European was spoken from end to end of Italy, the only exceptions known to us being those places where the Etruscans were settled. The evidence of the antiquity of the Ligures and Veneti in the north and in Latium, and of Siculi in Latium and the south, which both archaeology and tradition afford, seems too clear to leave a serious probability of any non-Indo-European and non-Etruscan element having existed in Italy in that period. If there were such elements, they have perished, so far as we can yet find, without leaving any linguistic record whatever. That such a disappearance is possible even between 1000 and 500 B.C. it would be difficult, in the abstract, to deny; but it is important to point out that the assumption which seems to underlie the phraseology adopted by many archaeologists—whether it be true or not—that no Indo-European people could have been autochthonous in the Mediterranean area or even settled there before the last millennium B.C., has absolutely no warrant in the linguistic record as we have it. Even in our oldest linguistic sources, such as the names of places and rivers, there is no form in ancient Italy, from the Alps to its southernmost point, which cannot be counted justifiably as either Indo-European or Etruscan. History, it is true, did not begin in 1000 B.C., and our direct knowledge of language in Italy and in Greece does not reach back even so far; but it is at least desirable that archaeological distinctions, which in themselves may be valid and important, should not be expressed by the use of linguistic titles, which are at best purely conjectural and which therefore must, in the nature of the case, be misleading.

With this negative caution, we may proceed to the separate points. The reader should at least know, as clearly as may be, where our knowledge breaks off in each case.

(1) As regards the question with which of the peoples whom we have studied the founders of the Terremare should be identified, such progress as we have made at present towards an answer leaves us what may be called a choice between three possibilities. No one can say that there are no other possibilities; but it is certain that these three are the only possibilities for which any argument can be found in the linguistic evidence. If the people of the Terremare were represented among the stocks which inhabited Italy from 600 B.C. onwards, they may have been the kinsmen of either (a) the pre-Tuscan inhabitants of Latium and Campania and indeed of the west coast generally, whom we have

no great reason for separating from the Ligures; *or (b)* the Veneti, or the 'East Italic' people, both of whom we find to have connections with Pannonia and the Illyrian coast; *or (c)* the people whom we have here called Safine, who, at some date, certainly not later than the fifth century B.C., and probably not later than the sixth, were masters of at least some parts of Umbria proper and the district later called Sabine; and who, in the fifth century B.C., swarmed over the whole of Samnium, Campania, and Lucania, driving before them many of the people of the older stratum into the extreme south-west peninsula where these older folk at last asserted their independence and were known as Bruttii. That the Safines used the -*NO*- suffix to form the names of political units cannot be disputed; and it is equally clear that both the Veneti and the Ligures, when left to themselves, preferred -*CO*- and -*TI*-.

Whether any similar distinction of time, place or race could be based on a comparison of the use of these two suffixes themselves must remain at present doubtful; the names in -*CO*- (fem. -*CA*) have perhaps the more ancient look, and -*ca* has outlived -*ti*- on Ligurian soil. It is possible that more precise indications might be found from a separate study of the names in which one has been added to the other (as in *Ligus-ti-cus* on the one hand and *Matelica-tes* on the other), but this cannot be attempted here.

We must conclude, therefore, that of these three conceivable identifications with the Terremare people, the first and second, that is, roughly speaking, the Veneti or Ligures, seem to possess more probability than the third, the Safines, who seem to be comparatively late comers into central Italy. If the view adopted in vol. II, chap. XXI, namely that, on the one hand the Terremare people were not the same as the Ligures and that, on the other hand, the civilization of Villanova is the work mainly of the Terremare folk, be approved, then we should hail the slight traces of Venetic characteristics in the place-names of Latium which we have noted (p. 443, n. 3) as indicating invaders from the N.E., even though we may conjecture also that the stock of the Veneti received new contributions from Illyrian or Pannonian immigrants which may have helped to preserve, or introduce, in the language spoken in Venetia, certain features other than those which it had assumed, or kept, in the peninsula proper. And since we have found quite as many traces of Ligures as of Veneti in Latium, we should have to admit the possibility that the streams of immigrants from the north-west and the north-east portions of the Po valley respectively, even if they were distinct, had become united in districts where the barrier of the Appennines could be crossed.

The question therefore between Venetic and Ligurian[1] character for the pre-Tuscan inhabitants of central Italy, is one which there is not enough linguistic evidence to answer. Nor is it yet quite clear what linguistic meaning the question has. Of Ligurian speech we have not a single sentence recorded; but it is certain that it was Indo-European, and that in preserving Indo-European *q* and in its use of the ethnic suffixes -*CO*- and -*TI*- it resembled both Venetic and the language of pre-Tuscan Latium. It must further be observed that since on the one hand the speech of the Ligurians extended at the beginning of our record—say in the eighth century B.C.—to Gaul, and since on the other the Veneti are closely connected—say from at least the sixth century B.C.—with Illyria, it seems difficult to suppose that either tribe imposed its language upon the other by way of conquest.

(2) In the facts we have discussed is there any evidence bearing on the question whether the civilization of the Iron Age was introduced by a fresh set of immigrants from the north or developed spontaneously by the people of the Terremare? The only point which we have noticed that is here relevant is that Venetic speech, as we have it, cannot be regarded as a direct ancestor of either Latinian or Safine. Some of its characteristics, such as the retention of middle inflections and the place of the word-accent, seem merely more primitive than anything in Latin or Safine. But others, such as the terminations of the cases and such a form as *meχo* as the accusative of the first personal pronoun, show changes which are quite independent of those which happened farther south. If then we assumed that the Iron Age civilization was introduced into (*e.g.*) Latium by a Venetic stock, we should still note (*a*) that they were at that time speaking a more primitive form of Indo-European than we find prevailing in Venetia in (say) the third century B.C., to which the bulk of the Venetic inscriptions probably belong, and (*b*) that this primitive form underwent fairly drastic changes in the new abodes of its speakers on Latin soil. But that Latin did undergo some fairly vigorous re-shaping is in any case certain (p. 456), so that the second caveat offers no difficulty; nor indeed does the first, in view of the distance of time that separates 300 B.C. from the epoch of the foundation of the Terremare.

(3) Was the language of the Ligurians—which we have seen to possess Indo-European characteristics—native to the

---

[1] This is a purely modern name with no ancient warrant; *Ligustic* or *Ligustine* would be more correct (see p. 458 *sq.*).

Ligurian people or introduced among them by some wave of northern invaders? This question is one to which the facts of this chapter are too late in date to contribute much. It is a crucial case for the historical value of the archaeological evidence of 'continuous occupation,' such as appears to be found in the Ligurian sites. If the archaeological evidence (vol. II, p. 564) be held adequate to prove that no serious change of population took place in Liguria from the Neolithic to the historical period, then it would follow that the Neolithic Ligurians spoke what we should have called, had we heard it, an Indo-European language. In any case the facts which we have considered above (p. 434) warrant us in saying that if Ligurian was a language introduced from Gaul, it must at least have been brought in by a people who had not changed Indo-European q into p as the Gauls of the sixth and later centuries certainly had done before they used such forms as *petorritum*.

(4) Is the recorded language of the Veneti to be regarded as one proper to newcomers into Italy, or one which belonged to an earlier population on the spot? What linguistic facts there are which bear on this question have already been partly discussed in dealing with the first and second. The only points which need be added here, are (*a*) that the specifically Illyrian characteristics of the Veneti, so far as they are linguistic (such as the endings -*ntum* and -*ste*), might have been introduced by comparatively small bodies of immigrants—provided that the latter were allowed to settle in a peaceable way; (*b*) that both endings are found in Liguria (Τριδεντ[ῖνοι] and *Ligusti-cus*, besides *Arelate*); (*c*) that we have seen that in point of the use of -*CO*- and -*TI*- there is little to choose between Veneti and Ligures, since among both of them both suffixes flourished; whereas (*d*) among both of them the -*NO*- suffix is distinctly less frequent and under suspicion in many (perhaps most) of its occurrences of having been brought in by Gallic invaders.

(5) To what epoch must we assign the appearance of the Safines in central Italy? It is difficult not to connect the arrival or the rise to power of the Safines (that is the -*NO*- folk) in central Italy with the expulsion of the Etruscans from Rome (as from Capua nearly a century later), and with the amalgamation of the Roman stock with the people whom they called Sabines which may be said to have been continuous from the days of Numa Pompilius—whose Sabine name and religion are the only historical elements in his mythical personality—down to the end of the struggle between the orders at Rome. The two

things are closely linked by tradition. The use of the suffix -NO- for political purposes—which began when the people whom the Greeks called *Rōmaioi* (and the Etruscans perhaps *rumate*) came to call themselves *Romani* instead of (or as well as) *Quirites*, and when the people of Latium came to call themselves *Latini*, leaving an older title (*Latiaris*) for divine use alone—must have been due to some definite change in the nature of the body which exercised political control.

(6) What, if any, is the connection of the Safines with more northerly tribes such as the pre-Tuscan *Ombrikoi*, the Veneti, or the Gauls? To answer this question we must first face another. Are all the occupants of Umbria in the historical period to be regarded as belonging to exactly the same stock as the Umbri (Ὄμβροι, Ὀμβρικοί) whom well-attested traditions, as we have seen (p. 388), represented as living in Tuscany and Umbria before the Etruscan invasion? No evidence is known to the present writer which would show that the Umbro-Safines with their *p* for *q* had arrived in Italy before the Etruscan invasion; but the fact that the Etruscans are cursed among the enemies by the *p*-folk (who were also a -NO- folk) of Iguvium prove that the Etruscans were in hostile contact with them before that curse took its final shape. There is perhaps some slight evidence to show that the Indo-European language, spoken in the areas which were afterwards Etruscan or Umbrian, still possessed the sound of q^1. And on the other hand from the linguistic point of view there is an obvious presumption in favour of regarding the Umbro-Safines as an early wave of the *p*-folk, *i.e.* of the Brythonic Gauls, who by the fifth century B.C. had over-run the central portion of north Italy and whom we find regularly allied with the people whom, at that date, the Romans called the Umbri. A Gaulish grammarian quoted by Suetonius did indeed identify the Umbrians with the Gauls. The question concerns what to an archaeologist is a very late date with nothing mysterious about it, when the Iron Age was in full course; so that if the presumption set up by the evidence of language and tradition needs to be supplemented or corrected, it ought, one would think, to be a simple matter to determine it by archaeological evidence. Is there, or is there not, any such gulf in the course of the Iron Age development of Umbria as should make it difficult to regard the Iguvines of (say) the sixth and fifth centuries B.C. as belonging essentially to the same stock as the Gauls of the fifth and fourth

---

[1] Cf. *Tarquinii* and a spot called *Aquileia* in Tuscany; the preservation of *q* in Faliscan (p. 455); and the names *Nequinum* and *Prolaqueum* in Umbria.

centuries? As we have seen, there is such a break between the remains of these same fifth-century Gauls and those of the Etruscans whom they turned out of Bologna (p. 440). Or, conversely, can archaeological evidence be brought to show that the Umbrians of Iguvium in the fifth century B.C. are clearly to be identified as kinsmen rather of the -CO- folk who were in possession of the soil of Tuscany and Umbria before the arrival of the Etruscans, than of the invading Gauls of the fifth century? Or again, a complete exploration of the strata of remains in some characteristic centre of the Paelignians or Samnites—Corfinium (mod. Pentima) or Bovianum Vetus (Pietrabbondante)—could hardly fail to throw direct light on this question.

Meanwhile, to the linguist, the indications of what evidence we have are at least clear. The advance of the Samnite tribes farther south, to conquer Campania and Lucania and the northern half of Apulia, is all recorded within the fifth century and seems to be historically part of the same tribal expansion as helped to drive the Etruscans out of Rome. We have already seen (pp. 456, 459) that the spread of the -NO- ethnica over the whole Safine district (Samnium, Campania, Lucania) was a consequence of the downfall of the Etruscan power; and also that it is the -CO- folk whom we must identify with the pre-Tuscan inhabitants of Rome and Latium and the Campanian plain. Further we have seen reason (p. 435) to believe[1] that in point of their treatment of Indo-European *q*, the Ligures, the Siculi, the Veneti, the Messapii were all alike and resembled the folk we call Latins. Hence the presumption seems fairly strong that the Safine tribes with their *p* for Indo-European *q* did not belong to the pre-Tuscan stratum; or at least, if they did belong to that stratum, that there must have been some new and highly efficient cause which made them suddenly, about 600 B.C., begin to despise the old names in -TI- and -CO- and insist always and only upon -NO- wherever they had control.

(7) Does the evidence obtainable throw any light on the origin of the two orders of the Patricians and the Plebeians at Rome?

It is outside the scope of this chapter to discuss the important question of the origin of the Roman Patricians, as it is so bound up with the history of the Republican period. But, in the opinion of the present writer, the linguistic evidence of the period surveyed in this chapter supports the view that the gulf

[1] The probability mentioned on p. 437 rests on (*a*) the likeness of *Sicani*, *Siculi* to the Goidelic *Sequani* and (*b*) the complete absence of any indication of labialization in the place-names of Sicily.

between Patricians and Plebeians in social and religious life implies a difference of race and that the Patricians were Safine in origin[1].

Further it must be pointed out that the undated but very early family traditions which represent the whole Claudian gens as being cordially welcomed into Rome from Sabine country, and not merely into Rome but into the governing body of Patricians, are remarkably confirmed by the number of Sabine words which were adopted into Latin, sometimes at the expense of the pure Latin form—*bos* 'ox' (pure Latin ****vus*), *lupus* 'wolf' and his connected deity *Lupercus*[2]; *Di Novensiles* 'gods of the nine seats,' *caseus* 'cheese,' *carbasus* 'spun linen,' *filum* 'thread for spinning,' *ferrum* 'iron'—the sword and the distaff were the typical implements of a Roman Patrician and his women-folk—not to mention *consules* with *consilium* and humbler words like *lingua* and *lacrima*. All these show Safine or early Sabine characteristics. So does the name of Numa Pompilius, the reputed founder of the Roman religion; the corresponding name of pure Latin origin would have been *Quinctilius* (more exactly ****Quinquilius*). The violent changes in the grammatical system of Latin, some at least introduced quite certainly from a Safino-Celtic source, have already been pointed out (p. 455 *sq.*) and are hardly less valuable evidence; and some very ancient names in -*CO*- (Table, at p. 460) have been found on the site of Rome itself.

This transformation of Sabines into Patricians would be in many ways parallel to the settlement of the Normans in England, where, though they became the dominant caste, and for long held all political power, they nevertheless, in the end, learnt the language of their Saxon subjects, though they stamped on it many traces of their own idiom, especially (but not only) in the vocabulary of public affairs. The facts of the English language alone offer a complete answer to any doubts that might be raised as to the possibility of such a fusion of races as has been here suggested. The parallel is all the more complete because we are not supposing that the conquest was made by people of wholly alien language; for although Norman-French was very different from Anglo-Saxon, it was nevertheless an Indo-European speech; and probably there was a larger gulf between Norman and Saxon than between the -*NO*- folk with their northern *p* for *q* on the one hand and the people of Rome and the Latin plain on the other. The

---

[1] See Sir W. Ridgeway, 'Who were the Romans?' *Proc. Brit. Acad.* 1907.

[2] The pure Latin form *lucus* (earlier ****luquos*) is recorded with the meaning 'pike,' though the Sabine form *lupus* was in commoner use.

vigour, not to say brutality, with which the Safines handled the voices, moods and tenses of the tongue they had to learn is not in the least more striking than the short way taken in the Norman age with the niceties of Anglo-Saxon grammar.

Disappointed as the reader may be with the incompleteness of the conclusions to which our study of the languages of early Italy has led us, he will realize clearly at least one central fact which, for the subsequent history of Italy and still more for that of Europe, is of cardinal importance. The task which faced the statesmen of Rome from the date when they shook off the oriental tyranny of the Tarquins was above all things this, to harmonize and unite in some measure of co-operation elements which, to start with, were both alien and hostile. It has long ago been pointed out that the secret of Roman statesmanship, which ultimately achieved the government and the civilization of the world, was not so much the Roman virtues of courage and tenacity, as the other not less Roman virtue of elasticity and open-mindedness in dealing with different individuals and different communities. Set in a centre, on which five different roads could at any time bring down dangerous forays from hostile highlands (by Tiber, Anio and Trerus) or from the Tuscan or Campanian coast, the Romans early learnt to deal with their enemies one by one; and to make reasonable peace, rather than mere devastation, the purpose of their efforts. The complicated system of separate treaties by which Rome bound to herself, first the numerous communities of Italy and later on the almost innumerable communities of the world beyond, may be said, perhaps, to have been the feature which distinguished the Roman Empire from any that went before it or came after, down to the government of India by the British. It was certainly the feature that produced the most lasting effect in European custom and European history. Indeed, one great chapter of Roman usage, the *ius gentium* (really of Italian tribes)— which, as Maine eloquently pointed out, became, partly by a lucky accident, the foundation of International Law—was directly derived from the necessities under which the Romans lay in dealing with the multitude of their neighbours. The account attempted in this chapter of the picturesque variety of folk and language which covered Italian soil at the dawn of the Roman epoch, however many riddles it may leave unsolved, should at least have made clear the historical conditions that planted so new and fruitful an element among the political conceptions of the Roman people.

MAP 11

INDEX TO NAMES

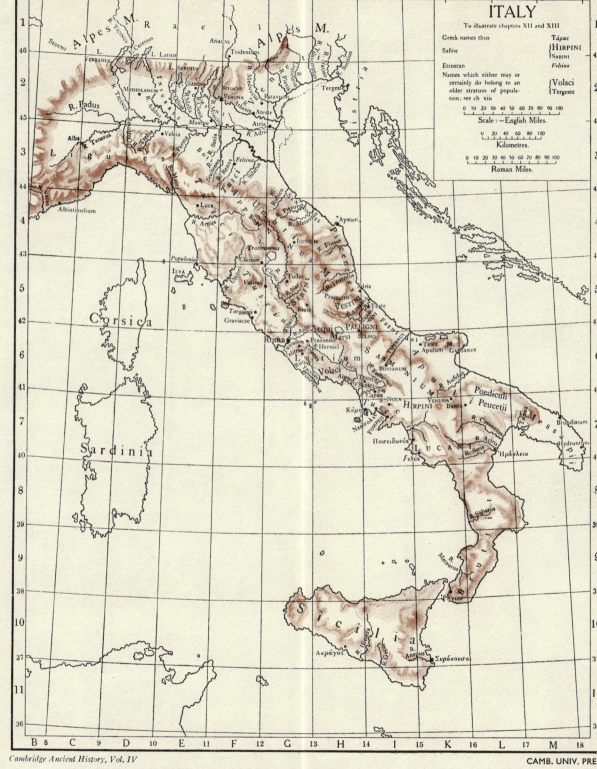

ITALY

To illustrate chapters XII and XIII

Greek names thus ... Τάρας

Safine ... Hirpini, Sabini

Etruscan ... *Felsina*

Names which either may or certainly do belong to an older stratum of population; see ch. xiii ... Volsci, Tergeste

Scale :— English Miles.

Kilometres.

Roman Miles.

Note.—The map of Italy above is based on what is known of the distribution of the various tribes about 400 B.C.; and although there is no particular reason for supposing that it was very different a century earlier, yet it is impossible to make any definite assertions about the different boundaries at that (or any earlier) date.

To face p. 468

CHAPTER XIV

GREEK LITERATURE FROM THE EIGHTH CENTURY TO THE PERSIAN WARS

I. THE ALPHABET

IT needs little reflection to see that European civilization could never have progressed as it has done if the alphabet had not been invented. That is a trivial truth, but it is in place to repeat it here, for it is right to emphasize what the world owes to the inventors of the alphabet and those who perfected it, bearers of forgotten and undiscoverable names. The three alphabets in use in Europe to-day, the Roman, the Slavonic, the Greek, all descend from the ancient Greek, and although the Greeks did not invent the alphabet, but received it from the east, their reception of it, possibly in the tenth century B.C., was an event. They did not invent it, but they improved it and fashioned it in such a way that it could become the easy instrument of thought that it has been proved to be through three thousand years.

When the Greeks first became acquainted with the Phoenician alphabet[1] (probably a form older than the earliest Phoenician alphabet we know) their problem was to adapt the signs to their own sounds which were not identical with the Semitic. The signs for consonants like *b*, *g*, *d*, *l*, *m*, *n*, *r* which were common to both could be taken over without change. But there were a number of sounds in Semitic which the Greeks did not possess, so that the signs of these must either be discarded or used in a different sense. The Phoenician alphabet being entirely consonantal, vowels had to be supplied by the reader. The original idea due to the Greeks was the representation of vowels by letters, and for this purpose they used some of the signs which the Phoenicians used for non-Greek sounds. Thus the first letter of the Phoenician alphabet, aleph, which represented a smooth breathing (*spiritus*

---

[1] R. Eisler, *The Cadmeian Alphabet* (*J.R.A.S.* 1923, pp. 35 and 169), deduces from the marks inscribed on new-discovered copper ingots from Hagia Triada in Crete, in a stratum just on the border-line between Middle Minoan III and Late Minoan II—*i.e.* in the middle of the 2nd millennium B.C.—new evidence in favour of the view that it was the Phoenicians who first introduced the art of writing into Greece.

lenis), was used for *a*, 'ain (a Semitic guttural) for *o*, hē for *e*.
A new symbol was invented for *u* (upsilon). Ḥēth (a guttural)
was employed to denote the rough breathing, *spiritus asper* (H).

We do not know where the Greek alphabet was first constructed; probably in Ionia or in one of the Aegean islands; but
in the reception of the Phoenician characters and their accommodation to Greek purposes, there was a clever brain at work which
imagined a new thing, the symbolizing of vowels.

Inscriptions of Melos, Thera, and Crete show the Greek letters
in the most primitive forms known to us, and the characters which
we find in these inscriptions closely resemble those of the Moabite
inscription of Mesa (ninth century; see above, vol. III, p. 372).
But as alphabetic writing made its way throughout Greece and
to the western colonies it underwent many modifications. Four
new letters were added to the alphabet (Φ, X, Ψ, Ω), but they were
not used everywhere as signs of the same sounds. For instance
in the greater part of European Greece as well as in Italy and
Sicily X was used for *xi* and Ψ for *chi*; in the Attic alphabet Ξ
and Ψ were not used and were represented by XΣ and ΦΣ; in
Paros Ω symbolized short *ŏ*, and O long *ō*[1]. In the oldest inscriptions the writing like Semitic was from right to left; then a
transitional system was sometimes used in which the lines ran
alternately from right to left and left to right (*boustrophēdon*, as in
ploughing); it was not till the fifth century that the left to right
direction became generally established.

Of all the varieties of the alphabet which were used in the early
Hellenic world, the Ionic proved the fittest and most convenient
and therefore survived. At an early period the Ionians gave up
the representation of the *spiritus asper* by H and used that symbol
to denote long *ē*; and they gave up pronouncing *v* (*w*), so that
the sign which stood for it (the digamma, *F*) was not needed and
was discarded. By the middle of the fourth century all the local
varieties of the alphabet disappeared in favour of the Ionic, which
had been adopted officially at Athens in 403 B.C. And so it has
come about that in our European (Roman) alphabet, which was
not derived from the Ionic, H has retained its original significa-
tion whereas in the Greek it is a vowel, and the digamma symbol

---

[1] We may distinguish two general groups of alphabets, (1) the eastern,
used in Asia Minor including the islands, (2) the western, used in Italy and
Sicily and in European Greece except Corinth, Megara, and Argos, while
Athens occupied an intermediate position. But within this general grouping
there were many local peculiarities. For the Latin and Etruscan alphabets
see above, pp. 399 *sqq.*

TABLE OF ALPHABETS II

	Hebrew name of letter	Apparent meaning	Greek name	Moabite	Cretan	Theraean	Ionic	Attic	Corinthian	Chalcidian	
1	āleph (alf)	ox	alpha								1
2	bēth (bēt)	house	bēta								2
3	gimel (gaml, giml)	camel	gamma								3
4	dāleth (delt)	(folding) door	delta								4
5	hē	lattice window (?)	ei								5
6	wāw	hook, nail	vau (digamma)								6
7	zayin	weapon (?), olive (?)	zēta								7
8	ḥēth (ḥēt)	fence or barrier (??)	(h)ēta								8
9	ṭēth (ṭēt)	a winding (??)	thēta								9
10	yōd	hand	iōta								10
11	kaph	bent hand	kappa								11
12	lāmed (lamd)	ox-goad	lambda								12
13	mēm	water	mu								13
14	nūn	fish	nu								14
15	sāmek (samk)	prop (?)	xei								15
16	ʿayin	eye	ou								16
17	pē	mouth	pei								17
18	ṣādē	fish-hook (?)	(see no. 7)								18
19	ḳōph	eye of needle (??)	koppa								19
20	rēsh	head	rhō								20
21	shin, sin	tooth	sigma, san								21
22	taw	mark	tau								22
23											23
24											24
25											25
26											26
27											27
28											28
29			u								29
30			phei								30
31			khei								31
32			psei								32
33			ō								33
	1	2	3	4	5	6	7	8	9	10	

• Forms with an asterisk come from a very early vase inscription and are found on no other Attic inscription.

For further notes on these alphabets see the Table facing p. 432 in Volume III.

UNIV. PRESS CAMB.

[Facing page 520

Hebrew name of letter	Apparent meaning	Greek name	Chalcis	Crete	Thera	Ionic	Attic	Corinthian	Chalcidian
aleph (אֶלֶף)	ox	alpha							
beth (בֵּת)	house	beta							
gimel (gaml, giml)	camel	gamma							
daleth (dāl)	(folding) door	delta							
hē	lattice window (?)	ei							
wāw	hook, nail	vau (digamma?)							
zayin	weapon (?), olive (?)	zeta							
ḥēth (ḥēt)	fence or barrier (?)	(h)ēta							
ṭēth (ṭēt)	a winding (?)	thēta							
yōd	hand	iōta							
kaph	bent hand	kappa							
lāmed (lāmd)	ox-goad	lambda							
mēm	water	mū							
nūn	fish	nū							
sāmek (sāmk)	prop (?)	xei							
ʿayin	eye	ou							
pē	mouth	pei							
ṣādē	fish hook (?)	(see note)							
qōph	eye of needle (?)	koppa							
rēsh	head	rhō							
shin, sin	tooth	sigma, san							
tāw	mark	tau							
		u							
		phei							
		khei							
		psei							
		ō							

(*F*) is preserved though in a different sense, representing not a spirant but a labial aspirate (*f*).

The alphabet must have made a great difference to Greece in the general growth and progress of her culture in the centuries after the Dorian invasion. It must have affected education, promoting the growth of a considerable reading public, and it must have helped the diffusion of ideas. Literature could not fail to react to these changes, and if the introduction of the alphabet had been postponed till half a thousand years later early Greek literature would certainly have been far different. Perhaps the alphabet affected it in another way too. That a script simpler than any of the older scripts facilitated composition can hardly be doubted. It is a nice question whether the notation does not exercise a subtle influence on forms of literary expression. To those who use alphabetic writing language cannot have the same aspect as that which it had for those who construed it by pictographs or syllabic signs. The alphabetic notation, resolving speech into its simplest elements, may have acted as a sort of 'transformer,' and it may not be unreasonable to speculate that if the Greeks had adopted, for instance, the syllabary which was used in Cyprus, their literature would in many ways have had a different character. In any case, it is a significant fact that the two most ancient literatures which have mattered, and still matter, to western civilization, the Hellenic and the Hebrew, were subsequent to the invention of the alphabet.

II. EPIC POETS (RHAPSODES)

Greek literature begins with Homer in the ninth century. But Homer came at the end of a long development of poetry, first in the Greek Motherland, then in Ionia, about which we have no direct information and can only say that a period in which narrative songs were sung to the accompaniment of the lyre was followed by a period in which epic tales were recited by rhapsodes and that by the ninth century epic (hexameter) verse had been refined and perfected, to be an instrument by which Homer's genius could express itself (see vol. II, p. 507).

The period between Homer's epics and the great age of Attic drama was longer than the period between Shakespeare and ourselves. The intellectual development which this period witnessed was no less striking than the political, and its details are veiled in similar obscurity. It found its expression in poetry. But we have to regret not only the disappearance of pre-Homeric poetry of which the Greeks themselves knew nothing, but also the far graver loss of most of the post-Homeric literature up to the time of the Persian wars.

The names of the great poets who lived and sang and illuminated the intellectual life of the Greeks during these centuries are very familiar; some of them are household words, and if their works had survived we should have a mirror of the thought and life of the Hellenes during the critical, formative centuries of their development. But nearly all their poetical literature, down to the end of the sixth century, which was accessible to Horace and to lovers of poetry for many generations after Horace, has perished, leaving us only fragments and a few short pieces; the exceptions being Hesiod and Theognis who, however interesting for many reasons, were not poets of the first rank. The corpus of fragments of some of the lyric poets prior to 500 B.C., which were preserved through being quoted by later writers, has been, during the last quarter of a century, considerably augmented by discoveries of Egyptian papyri, torn pieces of books which once contained the works of Sappho or of Alcaeus, generally badly mutilated and difficult to decipher. But, valuable though they are, they do not add a great deal to our knowledge.

We can discern a few general facts. We can see the influence of Ionia on the Motherland. We can see that the Asiatic Greeks originated most of the poetical *genres* which were practised in these centuries, and finally originated literary prose. We can see that the chief achievements of the European Greeks were the development of the lyric poetry which was sung by choruses, and afterwards the creation of tragedy and comedy. But for anything like a clear literary history of the period the data are wanting. The chronology is highly uncertain, as the Greeks found themselves, when, in the fourth and third centuries B.C., enquirers like Chamaeleon of Pontic Heraclea began to gather up all that could be discovered concerning the famous writers and artists of the distant past, and attempted to establish their dates.

Throughout this period, the influence of Homer was predominant in the Motherland as well as in Ionia. All who composed poetry, whether epic or elegiac or lyric, for recitation or for musical accompaniment, were brought up on the *Iliad* and the *Odyssey*. This indeed is true of later periods also, but in the earlier centuries his influence was particularly important because it set a high tone and established a standard of decency and refinement which was always maintained in Greek literary art (apart from comedy and satire).

The rhapsodes who composed epic poems on the Trojan war and Theban legends, in the eighth and seventh centuries, and who in late times were known as Cyclic poets, have been mentioned in vol. II, p. 500, where their principal works are named. They were imitators of Homer, but they did not attempt a long epic in his style and they had the tact not to re-handle the stories that he had made immortal.

> Nec tu diuinam Aeneida tenta,
> sed longe sequere et uestigia semper adora.

It was from very far off that they followed, so far as we can judge; we have not a single fragment of as much as twenty lines of any of these poets. They were uninspired and dull, and we shall hardly be doing them injustice if we surmise that none of them had mastered the Homeric technique in construction or introduced a new note of his own. The value of this body of poetry would ultimately become little more than that of a mythological handbook; supplying material to the lyric poets and the Attic tragedians, and to the vase-painters and sculptors of the sixth and fifth centuries.

The post-Homeric rhapsodes were however sometimes successful in short stories such as we possess in the 'Homeric Hymns,' a collection of preludes to recitations. Such a prelude was a hymn in praise of a deity and it might be quite short and formal, or might include a story of some episode in the divine career. The deity addressed would be chosen appropriately to the occasion and the place. For a recitation at Delos or Delphi Apollo would be the god invoked; at Eleusis, Demeter; at Sparta it might be the Dioscuri; in Arcadia, Pan. Several of the Hymns are of substantial length, and were composed in various parts of Greece, most of them perhaps in the seventh or eighth century. The Hymn to the Delian Apollo[1], one of the oldest, was the work of a blind rhapsode of Chios as the poet says himself, departing, as Hesiod and probably other rhapsodes did, from the impersonality of Homer; his name is not mentioned but it is supposed to have been Cynaethus[2]. Of all these poems the most interesting perhaps is the Hymn to Demeter which tells the story of the Rape of Persephone by Hades, the wanderings of the mother searching for the daughter, and the foundation of their worship at Eleusis.

---

[1] The Hymn to Apollo of our texts consists of two originally distinct poems (1) to the Delian, (2) to the Pythian Apollo, of which the second is considerably later. They were conjoined before the age of Thucydides.

[2] Inferred from a scholium on Pindar, *Nem.* II.

It is valued as the earliest document on the Eleusinian religion, and it is easy to divine that it was composed in the Motherland, perhaps in Attica, and that the poet had been initiated in the mysteries. But aside from this interest, it is the work of a poet of singular talent. The skill of Homer himself could hardly have surpassed the idyllic description of the coming of the sorrowing goddess, disguised as an old woman, to Eleusis, and the pleasure and excitement displayed by the four king's daughters in securing for her the post of nurse in their mother's palace.

HESIOD, who was revered by the Greeks as an epic poet second only to Homer and was by some considered his contemporary, lived not later than in the eighth century[1]. There is nothing in his works to give a definite clue to his date; he never refers to Hellenic politics. A native of Boeotia he was not of Boeotian stock. His father was a farmer who had come to the motherland across the sea from Aeolian Cyme; not having prospered at home he had migrated to Ascra, a small place not far from the town of Thespiae in the Boeotian highlands. It was a place of which Hesiod has no good thing to say, 'a miserable village near Helicon, bad in winter, distressful in summer, at no time good.'

Some verses of Hesiod enable us to guess the romance of his boyhood. As he fed his father's flocks on the slopes of the mountains, his day-dream was to be a poet. He must have heard the recitations of rhapsodes and Homer had captured his imagination. His dream was realized. He obtained the needful training and became a rhapsode by profession. He records incidentally that he won a tripod in a rhapsodic competition at Chalcis. His poems show that he was thoroughly saturated with the Homeric style and diction; he must have known the *Iliad* and *Odyssey* almost by heart. But he broke entirely new ground. He did not compete with the 'cyclic' poets. He was a thinker whose mind was busy with questions about religion and ethics, and the origin and history of the world; and, using the epic instrument supplied by Homer, he attempted to reduce to order the chaotic world of deities, and to systematize contemporary conceptions of life.

Abandoning the self-suppression of Homer, he comes forward in his own person, names himself and his home, and mentions some biographical details. We possess his two principal poems, the *Theogony* or book of the generations of the gods[2], and the

---

[1] On Hesiod; see also above, vol. II, p. 605 *sq.*; vol. III, p. 610 *sq.* and below, p. 535.

[2] Some think that the *Theogony* is not by Hesiod but by a disciple. This view was held by Welcker, and is held by T. W. Allen and M. Croiset.

Works and Days. Of a third, which there is no reason not to ascribe to him, the *Catalogue* of heroines, we have only fragments[1].

In those days to an enquiring mind seeking to make the universe intelligible for itself, the first step was to master the divine world, to know how the deities which controlled men's lives had come to be there. And this included nature, for earth and sky, sea, sun and moon, rivers, mountains were conceived as divine persons. In Hesiod's scheme Chaos is the first and original existence, after which appeared Earth and Love (Eros); then, as children of Chaos, Darkness (Erebos) and Night. The union of the two last produced Ether and Day; while Earth first, without sexual union, produced Heaven (Uranos) and Sea, and then, marrying her son Heaven, gave birth to a number of children including Rhea, Themis, and Memory, and, her youngest, Cronos. A thing to be noted in this attempt to explain the origins of the world is the position assigned to Eros at the very beginning— 'Eros who is fairest among the immortal gods, who subdueth the corporeal frame and the thoughts of all gods and of all men.' Hesiod's interest in Eros is probably due to the special cult of Eros at Thespiae. Eros is without parents, because he is necessary to the process of generation. When philosophical thinking begins, he will be transformed from a god into a principle.

It would be interesting to know what in this history of the gods, beyond arrangement and selection, was due to the poet's own invention. In personifying abstractions he goes much further than Homer. We may suspect that, for instance, in the progeny of Night and of her daughter Strife (Eris) a good many of the deities are of his own creation (211 *sqq.*). Night is the mother, not only of Death (Thanatos) and Sleep and Dreams, but also of abstractions like Mōmos (Blame), and Oïzys (Woe), Nemesis, Deceit, Old Age. Strife is the mother of Labour, Forgetfulness, Hunger, Pains, Battles, Murders and Manslayings, False Words, Disputes, Illegality, Aate (Ruin), Horcos (Oath). This is the spirit of classification on which Socrates, in the Platonic Dialogues,

---

The arguments are not sufficiently strong to force us to reject the general opinion of the Greeks. The belief of the Boeotian guardians of the shrine of the Muses on Helicon, as reported by the traveller Pausanias (IX, 31, 4), that Hesiod composed nothing but the *Works* (an ancient copy of which, engraved on a leaden tablet, they exhibited to visitors) seems to have been quite exceptional.

[1] This, or a portion of it, was also known as the *Eoeae* ('Hoῖαι), because each section, introducing a new heroine, began with ἦ οἵη 'or such as she who.' The *Shield of Heracles*, it is now agreed, is not by Hesiod.

insisted. But the *Theogony* is much more than lists; the relations of the deities to the world of mortals are described; the story of the struggle of the gods with the Titans is told at length.

If the *Theogony* is a history of the gods, the *Works and Days* contains a general history of mankind, of which the idea is that it is a course of decline. The first men were the Golden race whom the immortals of Olympus made in the time when Cronos was king in heaven. They lived like gods, without labour or woe or miserable old age, always equally strong in hands and feet; their souls had no cares, their lives were spent pleasantly in feasting, and their death was like sleep. They had all good things, the earth bare corn for them in abundance, of its own accord. Then the earth hid this race, but Zeus (who had meanwhile deposed and succeeded his father Cronos) willed that they should live on as good demons above ground, guardians of men and givers of wealth.

Then the gods made a new race, much inferior, the Silver race, unlike the Golden both in stature and in mind. Among them, the child remained with its mother for a hundred years before it reached manhood and then lived only for a short time. They suffered through their unwisdom, and refused to worship or offer sacrifices to the immortals. Zeus then hid them, in his anger because they did not honour the gods. Yet they were afterwards known to men as Underground Blessed; though only second in order, these too have honour.

Then Zeus made a third race out of ashtrees, the Bronze race, not at all like the Silver. They were stark and fearful, practising the woeful works of Ares; they did not eat food of corn; their hearts were hard as adamant; resistless hands grew from their shoulders; their arms were brazen, their houses brazen, and they wrought with bronze; there was as yet no black iron. The men of this race exterminated one another. Terrible though they were, black death seized them and they left the light of the sun.

After the extinction of the Bronze people, Zeus made another experiment. He created a fourth race, better than the third, the divine race of the heroes who are called demigods. They perished through wars, some of them at Seven-gated Thebes, others in ships which had crossed the great sea to fight at Troy for the sake of fair-haired Helen. Some of them were hidden away by death. To others Zeus, their father, gave life and habitations apart from men at the ends of the earth, and they live with unsorrowing minds in the islands of the blest by the deep eddying river Ocean, happy heroes for whom yonder the grain-giving earth bears honey-sweet fruit thrice a year.

Then came the fifth race.

I would (says the poet) that I were not living among the Fifth men, but that I had either (lived and) died before their time or were born later. For now we have the race of Iron. Never by day will they cease from toil and woe, nor by night, as they decline and perish; the gods will give them hard troubles. Fathers will not be as sons nor sons as fathers; guest will not be friendly to host nor comrade to comrade, nor brother to brother as formerly; soon they will dishonour their ageing parents and will blame them with bitter words, having no respect for the gods; and the observer of oaths and the just and good will have no favour in their eyes, but rather will the worker of wrong and the insolent be held in honour. Ugly of face and malicious, Zēlos (the spirit of rivalry and competition) will walk with them. And then from wide-wayed Earth to Olympus will depart Aidōs and Nemesis, veiling their fair flesh with white mantles, and enter the company of immortals, abandoning men. And sad sufferings will be left to mortals, and no help against evil (174–201).

This frame of the history of civilization was suggested by two facts and an old tradition. The first fact was that the modern age in which the poet lived had been preceded by the heroic age recorded in Homer's epics; the second that there had been an age in which there was no iron, and bronze was used for agricultural implements, domestic utensils, armour and weapons. The old tradition was that of an initial Golden age (dated before the celestial *coup d'état* by which Zeus made himself master of the world), when mortals had not to work and suffered no pains. As gold, in this tradition, was used symbolically to express excellence, so the inferior metals are used in Hesiod's scheme to express successive grades of decline but in the case of bronze and iron he has combined the literal with the symbolical significance of the metals. It is probable that his own imagination interpolated the age he named silver, to make the cycle of metals complete; we have no data enabling us to say that he had any traditional motive for inventing an age in which people hated religion or in which infancy was far longer than maturity.

His conception of the hard terrible Bronze men has forced him to separate them entirely from the heroic age which he designates by no metal. Such ogres could not be connected with the Homeric heroes, though from Homer's picture it would have been natural to identify the Bronze age with the heroic. Here in fact the poet had to face a difficulty. The heroes and their age were immensely superior to the Silver men, and therefore they could not be Bronze men living in a Bronze age, which would, by virtue of the symbolism of the metals, mean that they were inferior. To carry out that symbolism Hesiod had to invent a separate age of Bronze. Hesiod's conception of the successive ages of men has been often described as one of continuous degeneration. But this is an in-accurate summary of his history. The truth is that his history falls into two distinct parts, and only in the second of these is the word 'degeneration' to the point. The first section may be said to present a decline, but that decline is not a degeneration of the human race, for the Silver men are not descendants of the Golden, nor the Bronze men of the Silver. All three severally come straight from the creative hands of the gods. With the second section a new order of things sets in, and the men of the Iron age are not a fresh creation but are the lineal descendants of the men of the heroic age, and every year they are becoming worse. Here there is real degenera-tion. And here the awkwardness of the symbolical metals is glaring. The Iron men in the days of Homer and of Hesiod were evidently far superior to the ogres of the Bronze age whose hearts were as adamant. This contradiction with the symbolism is mitigated by the fact that the Bronze and Iron ages are not consecutive.

This short sketch of the past is introductory to a very gloomy picture of the present and to the main question of the poem which is the problem of how to live in an evil world and particularly how to live in the environment known to the poet, as a farmer in Boeotia. The poem is addressed to his brother Perses, against whom he had a grievance. It appears that on their father's death there was a dispute over the inheritance, and that the lawsuit went in favour of Perses, through the injustice and corruption of the judges as Hesiod believed.

In the ethical principles which Hesiod lays down and the general maxims which he imparts to his brother we find a great deal of the gnomic wisdom which elegiac and lyric poets of the following centuries were to make commonplace and rather tedious, the contrast between Justice (Dike) and Insolence (Hybris), the paths of Virtue and Vice. 'Wickedness can easily be had, as much as you like of her, for the way to her is smooth and she dwells near. But in front of Virtue the immortals have set sweat; for long and steep is the path to her and rough at first, yet difficult as she is, once the top is reached she is easy.' He has some characteristic apophthegms, like πλέον ἥμισυ παντός, 'half is more than the whole'; παθὼν δέ τε νήπιος ἔγνω, *experientia docet infantem*; χρήματα γὰρ πέλεται ψυχὴ δειλοῖσι βροτοῖσι, 'property is the life-breath of poor mortal men'; μελέτη δέ τε ἔργον ὀφέλλει, 'study improves work.' But we meet in Hesiod nothing so memorable or moving as Homer's

τλητὸν γὰρ Μοῖραι θυμὸν θέσαν ἀνθρώποισιν,

'the Moirai endowed men with a patient heart.'

The general note of Hesiod's theory of life is work; but work must be guided by the lessons of experience, and he composes for the benefit of the Boeotian farmer a regular handbook for agriculture which was afterwards to inspire Virgil. This is the most interesting part of the poem, not indeed on account of the precepts, but because it presents a realistic picture of country life in Boeotia. Here Hesiod has won free of the overmastering influence of Homer and displays his own original poetical powers. Take the following description of life in a severe winter:

Beware of the month of Lenaeon, of its bad kine-galling days and the frosts which prevail cruelly over the land under the blast of the North wind who, blowing through horse-rearing Thrace, excites the wide sea; and earth and wood bend before him; and high oaks and thick pines in the glades of the mountains are brought to earth by his onset; and all the multitudinous wood shouts and beasts shiver and put their tails between their legs; even those whose skin is covered with shag his chill penetrates; and he pierces the hide of the ox and blows through the long hair of the goat. But his force does not get through the fleeces of sheep, because their hairs are thick and full. The North wind makes the old man a runner, but he does not pierce the soft-skinned little maiden who sits in the house at her mother's side, not yet knowing the works of golden Aphrodite; her tender skin well washed and anointed with unguents, she will lie in the house on a winter day, when the boneless (polyp) is consuming his own foot in his fireless house and cheerless haunts. (*Works and Days*, 504–25.)

In metrical technique Hesiod did not possess a skill that can be compared to Homer's, but in a happy moment he could achieve a perfect verse, felicitous in its simplicity, like

$$\hat{\eta}\mu o\varsigma\ \kappa\acute{o}\kappa\kappa\upsilon\xi\ \kappa o\kappa\kappa\acute{\upsilon}\zeta\epsilon\iota\ \delta\rho\upsilon\grave{o}\varsigma\ \acute{\epsilon}\nu\ \pi\epsilon\tau\acute{a}\lambda o\iota\sigma\iota,$$

'when the cuckoo cuckoos amid the oak-leaves.'

The second-class kind of poetry which Hesiod created, didactic and expository, offers little room for artistic construction and invention. Neither of the two works which have come down to us can, regarded as a whole, be judged as a work of art, notwithstanding the merits of particular passages. The subjects he deals with in the *Works* are pedestrian, subjects for which afterwards when prose came to be written it would be decided that prose was a more appropriate vehicle. The minute directions which Hesiod prescribes for his brother the farmer, what clothes he should wear, how he should choose a wife, that he should keep and feed well a big dog to protect his home against the burglar whom he calls the 'day-sleeper,' and so on, and the farmer's calendar (the 'Days') with its trivial taboos, all this illustrates the poet's power to dignify commonplace things by his diction, but that is just about the average level of his attainment. The *Theogony* produces on us

much the same effect with its catalogues of names, decorated with
Homeric epithets. How different is the effect of the catalogue of
the sea-maidens who come with Thetis to the Trojan beach in
the *Iliad*, where the fifty lovely sea-names are recited, not because
the poet wishes to instruct his audience who the daughters of
Nereus were but for the aesthetic purpose of relieving the tension
in the story by a series of beautiful sounds which suggest coolness
and aloofness from the sufferings of mortals[1].

It does not seem probable that our judgment of Hesiod's art
would be much altered if we possessed the whole of his *Eoeae*, or
collection of the stories of mythical heroines. The idea of such a
collection was original, and was a part of his general idea of
bringing order into tradition and constructing a sort of encyclopaedia of the knowledge and wisdom of his day; but in its execution we may be sure that he was, like himself in the *Theogony* and
like the cyclic poets, an imitator of Homer. It is not probable
that his works were popular for recitation in Ionia and the Aegean
islands, and it was not for beauty or wonder that they were valued
and preserved. He succeeded, and was ultimately recognized
throughout the Greek world as authoritative, not as an artist and
great entertainer like Homer, but as a teacher. He supplied the
Greeks with things they appreciated, a mine of gnomic wisdom,
and a comprehensive, tolerably well-digested survey of mythology.
His authority came to be associated with that of Homer himself;
as time went on they were regarded as contemporaries, and a
story was invented that they contended against each other in a
recitative contest at Chalcis.

If we survey the body of post-Homeric rhapsodic poetry that
we possess—Hesiod, the Hymns, and the fragments of the Cyclic
poets—and compare it with the *Iliad* and *Odyssey*, we see that
many poets trained in Homeric tradition and with Homer's work
as a model reached a high standard of skill but that none of them
had learned his secret. None of them had his greatness of spirit,
none of them his power of telling a story; much less could any
of them create immortal figures, like Nestor and Odysseus and
Penelope and the witch Circe and, portrayed by a few touches,
Helen, so curiously attractive. Of such powers of artistic creation
we find indeed no trace in Greek poetry till we come to the great
Attic tragedians. None of the epic poets achieved that easy
loftiness which impressed and astonished later Greek critics and
of which they were fond of quoting as an example the description

[1] U. v. Wilamowitz-Möllendorff, *Die Ilias*, p. 165, well points out the
perversity of those who would reject the lines *Il.* xviii, 39–49 as Hesiodic

(in *Iliad*, XIII, 14 *sqq.*) of Poseidon driving over the sea in his chariot. 'The mountains trembled throughout all their length, and their woods and their peaks, and the towers of the Trojans, and the ships of the Greeks, under the immortal feet of Poseidon as he went. He drove over the waves, and rising from their caves the sea-beasts played all around beneath him and well they knew their lord; and in joy the sea parted asunder and his horses flew.' Hesiod, as Quintilian says (doubtless copying some Greek critic), *raro adsurgit*, and the remark would probably be true of all the late rhapsodes. Nor could they vie with Homer in the variety and charm of his similes, and here they seldom attempted to imitate him. Nor could any of them achieve wonderful verses like

$$\text{αἰνῶς ἀθανάτῃσι θεῇς εἰς ὦπα ἔοικεν}$$

(Helen 'is terribly like the immortal goddesses'), where αἰνῶς is the 'lonely word' that works the spell.

Homer was also supreme in his power of wielding the hexameter verse, in his sure ear for its modulations. His 'rapidity' has often been noticed, and it was a deliberate rapidity without signs of haste. He had an instinctive feeling for combining and varying dactyls and spondees; he knew how to make his spondees tell; his economy in their use heightens the effect of his rare *andante* movements as when he describes the approach of the ghost of Patroclus to the bedside of Achilles,

$$\text{ἦλθε δ' ἐπὶ ψυχὴ Πατροκλῆος δειλοῖο.}$$

The Epic measure was always used by the Greeks when they wished to treat in verse philosophical or scientific themes. They adopted it as the proper measure for expository poetry, and in such matters they had a sure instinct. The religious teachers who in the sixth century unfolded their doctrines about theology and cosmology in poems which were ascribed to Orpheus and Musaeus, wrote like Hesiod in hexameters. The Delphic priesthood adopted the metre for the oracles of the god (vol. III, p. 626 *sq.*). And some of the early philosophers preferred this form for explaining their systems to the vehicle of prose which had not yet been developed into a form satisfactory to their artistic sensibility. Three leading philosophers who are associated with south Italy and Sicily, Xenophanes, Parmenides, and Empedocles, wrote their treatises 'On nature' in epic verse (see below, chap. xv). Parmenides was ingenious and competent in handling his instrument in such a way as to make his abstruse exposition clear. But Empedocles of Acragas was a born poet as well as a

philosopher. His philosophy was to him more than knowledge;
it was an imaginative experience personal to himself. We can
hardly doubt that it was his poems that inspired Lucretius, who
so enthusiastically admired his genius, to attempt to win the world
to Epicureanism by arraying its doctrine in a poetical vesture.
In any case they are the only two poets who have ever handled
such themes in a way that appeals to the lover of poetry as well
as to the student of philosophy. They were both terribly in
earnest; impassioned, Lucretius for the saving truths taught by
his master, Empedocles for his own message to the world. But
enthusiast as Empedocles was, believing himself almost superhuman, professing incredible powers as a physician and as a
sorcerer, the note of his poetry was what an accomplished Greek
critic described as 'austere harmony.'

Empedocles did not conceal or minimize his high pretensions
to superhuman powers. He went about from city to city with
the airs of a god, in gorgeous array, his progress a continual
triumph. This is the opening of his poem entitled *Purifications*
(Καθαρμοί):

Friends, who dwell in the citadel of the great city on the banks of the
brown Acragas, ye who practise good works, august harbourers of strangers,
I greet you. I come among you now as an immortal god, mortal no more,
honoured among all men as is my due, with fillets on my head and festal
wreaths. When I enter, with my train of followers men and women, into
prosperous cities, I am worshipped; I am followed by thousands to enquire
where the path to profit lies, some in need of prophecies, and others, tortured
for long years by pains and diseases, seeking a remedial utterance (frag. 112).

III. IAMBIC AND ELEGIAC POETS

It would be a mistake to suppose that the epic hexameter was
the only form of metre used in the days of Homer. During the
age of the post-Homeric rhapsodes there appear in Ionia, alongside
of the hexameter, poetical forms, the iambic and the elegiac, but
they have reached such an advanced stage of perfection when we
first meet them early in the seventh century, that they must have
been in use long before. This conclusion is confirmed by their
antique unintelligible names—*iambus* and *elegy*. We have indeed
traces of the use of the iambic trimeter in the eighth century, if
we may ascribe to that age the burlesque poem, *Margites*, which
was produced at Colophon and was generally attributed to Homer
himself. Only a few lines of it are preserved, but we know that
its subject was the comic portrait of a feeble-minded person who
could not count above five and asked his mother whether his

father's womb had produced him. It was composed in hexameters, but iambic trimeters were occasionally introduced.

Early in the seventh century a great poet appeared whom in the judgment of the Greeks his genius placed on a pedestal not far off from Homer's[1], ARCHILOCHUS of Paros. The fragments of his vibrant poetry which have come down to us are short and scanty, yet his personality was so strong and so unreservedly revealed that we can form a definite idea of the man. His father was well-born but he started with the disadvantages of having a slave mother and of being very poor. Financial straits drove him to leave Paros and seek his fortunes abroad as a soldier. The Parians at this time had planted a settlement in the island of Thasos, and the southern coast of Thrace especially in the neighbourhood of the gold mines of Mt Pangaeus was attracting the enterprise of the Greeks as a field for colonization. To Thasos Archilochus betook himself and came in for fighting, not only against the Thracian tribes who were defending their soil, but also in collision with the Naxians who were attempting to share in the exploitation of the coast. At Thasos he probably composed the elegies and other poems, in which he described his military experiences. 'I am squire of the lord Enyalius (god of war) and skilled in the lovely gift of the Muses.' In one combat he threw away his shield and just escaped with his life. 'Some Saïan (Thracian)' he was not ashamed to sing 'is priding himself on my shield which I abandoned reluctantly near a bush; but I escaped death. Let that shield go to perdition, I will get another as good.' He was an adept in making enemies—self-assertive, truculent, ill-bred, and generally outrageous—and he made many in Thasos. He reminds us in some ways of Benvenuto Cellini, and particularly in his lack of reticence. A well-known Athenian noble of a later age, Critias, who was both a man of action and a man of letters, criticized Archilochus, not for what he did but for what he said:

If he had not himself told us, we should never have known that he was the son of the slave Enipo or that he left Paros on account of poverty or that having gone to Thasos he became the enemy of the people there, or that he spoke equally ill of his friends and his enemies. Nor should we have known that he was an adulterer and lustful and licentious, if we had not learned it from him, nor, worst of all, that he threw away his shield. He was not a good witness for himself[2]

[1] Cp. Aristotle, *Rhet.* III, 7. Heraclides of Pontus, in Diog. Laert. v, 7. 'Portraits' of the two poets are associated on a double herm.

[2] Aelian, *Var. Hist.* x, 13.

The Thasian period of his career did not bring Archilochus fair fame or wealth, and weary of the island of which he had no good to report he returned to Paros. It was after his return that there occurred the episode in his life which was best remembered by posterity, his deadly quarrel with his fellow-citizen Lycambes whose daughter Neobule he wished to marry. We do not know what precisely happened and cannot form an opinion on the rights and wrongs of the case. It would appear that Lycambes had accepted him as his future son-in-law, but he was not a very desirable match for a lady of the upper class at Paros; since his mother had been a slave, and he was poor. We do not know the feelings of Neobule herself for the man of genius who sought her hand, but the family seems to have been opposed to the marriage[1] and to have persuaded Lycambes to withdraw his consent. The infuriated poet avenged himself by pursuing the whole family, Lycambes, Neobule, and her sister, with lampoons so violent and effective that they could not hold up their heads in Paros; and in later times, through a misunderstanding of the word ($κύψαντες$, 'hanging their heads') which Archilochus used to describe their humiliation, it was believed that he drove them to suicide.

This was the most flagrant example of the poet's powers of invective, but he must have discharged the venom of his bitter censorious temper on many other victims. Animosities, quarrels, and abuse were, as Pindar said, the meat and drink which made Archilochus fat. A fragment, recovered some years ago from Egypt, illustrates the intemperance of his hatred:

May he be cast ashore, naked and stiff with cold, at Salmydessus and seized by Thracians (who will make him suffer, eating the bread of slavery), may he be covered over with shellfish in the surf, may his teeth chatter like a dog's, as he lies face downwards by the margin of the waves. That is what I should wish to happen to a man who wronged me, who was once my companion and trampled on his oaths[2].

There was just one luxury of hatred which in that age even an Archilochus did not permit himself, the jeers over a dead enemy in which the great heroes of Homer used to indulge.

We should know more about the details of the life of this

---

[1] *Frag.* 74 on a solar eclipse bears on the story. It has been generally supposed that the reference is to the total eclipse of April 6, 648 B.C., which was visible at Thasos. It is more probable that it is to the eclipse of April 15, 657 B.C., which was total in or near the island of Rhodes and of which the news would have reached Paros. Cp. Hauvette, *Archiloque*, 13–15.

[2] Diehl, *Supp. Lyr.* p. 4.

enfant terrible if inscribed stones in Paros had not been broken
and shivered (forming the base of a statue which was set up in
his honour about 100 B.C.) on which was written his biography
by Demeas (early third century), 'documented' by many extracts
from the poems[1].

It was characteristic of Archilochus that he resisted the influence of the Ionian epic. He could not escape the influence of
Homer altogether, but he struck out an original line for himself
which was as unlike the epic as possible in form as well as in tone.
He abandoned its conventions of dignity and decency, and he
avoided the use of the epic hexameter. He composed hymns to
gods, but they were in iambic metre. His hymn to Heracles was
to become more famous all over Greece than any of the hymns
of the rhapsodes. Everyone knew its refrain, τήνελλα καλλίνικε
('Io, the conquering hero comes'); it was 'vocal,' as Pindar says,
at Olympia—officially sung to greet the victors in the games.

There was good reason for setting the seat of Archilochus not
far from Homer's, on Parnassus, for the influence which he exerted
on the forms of subsequent poetry was immense. We may call
him the father of iambic poetry, and perhaps of elegiac, in the
same sense that Homer may be called the father of epic. This
does not mean that he created either, though in Greek traditions
he has been described as the inventor of both, but that he fashioned
them into perfect instruments for poetical expression. His elegiacs
are the earliest elegiacs we have. In his hands the technique of
the iambic trimeter, which was to be the metre of the Attic
dramatists, has reached perfection; and the trochaic tetrameter
was handled as skilfully by him as by any later poet. His experiments in combining different rhythms, the imitations of Horace
have made familiar. He appears to have made, though we must
speak diffidently because our knowledge is so imperfect, signal
contributions to what was one of the remarkable feats of the intelligence of the Greeks, the construction of their wonderful
system of poetical measures obedient to severe laws. Ancient
poetry depended entirely on quantity (the duration of syllables in
time); whereas in modern poetry stress has played the leading
part so that ancient theories of prosody have very little application to it and are more likely to mislead than to enlighten; yet so
imposing was the metrical analysis of the Greeks, and so much
have our notions of metre been based on it, that the subject is
seldom discussed without using Greek terms.

We possess much more considerable specimens of early iambic

[1] *I.G.* XII, 5, 445.

poems from a satirist who probably wrote not long after Archilochus, and also belonged to insular Greece, SEMONIDES of
Amorgos. His talent was immeasurably inferior to that of the
poet of Paros, but he could produce fluent iambics. He is chiefly
remembered for his mordant and rather brutal satire on the
characters of women, whom he classifies chiefly by their resemblances to animals—the sow, the vixen, the ass, the weasel, the
mare, the ape; and the existence of some good women whom he
praises highly and compares to bees does not lead him to qualify
the conclusion that women are the greatest evil that Zeus created.
Hesiod had set the example of the disparagement of women,
though we may guess it was a much older theme in popular verse,
but the poem of Semonides may give a true enough notion of
the types to be found in the society of most Greek towns. More
successful perhaps is a shorter poem on the vanity and disappointments of human life. He reflects that the issue of all things in the
world lies with thundering Zeus, who disposes as he likes; but we
men have no sense, and exist from day to day like animals, knowing
not how the god will bring each thing to accomplishment (i, 6 *sqq.*).

All men live on hope and faith in their ineffectual efforts, some waiting
for a day, others for the revolution of years, for the wanted thing to come;
and there is no mortal who does not believe that next year he will be better
off in wealth and good things. But before he reaches the goal he is overtaken by old age or miserable disease, or, killed in war, he is sent by Hades
beneath the black earth, or perishes in the stormy sea, or perhaps hangs
himself and by his own act leaves the light of the sun. So true it is that
no evil is spared us. Mortal men are doomed to suffer thousands of un-
imaginable woes and ills. If my counsel were followed we should not desire
evil things, nor, in addition to the ills we have of necessity, rack our spirits too

The scanty remains of these poets, who used iambic trimeters
for satirical and pedestrian subjects, show that this metre, which
was, two centuries later, to be the principal instrument of the
great Attic tragedians, had reached technical perfection by the
middle of the seventh century. Solon employed it for the purpose
of expounding his political ideas (see above, pp. 36, 49). Towards the end of the sixth century there walked about the streets
of Clazomenae a spiteful beggar named HIPPŌNAX, who used with
admirable facility in his scurrilous satires a modification of the
iambic trimeter, which by substituting a spondee for an iambus
as the last foot of the verse caricatured it and entirely altered its
effect. Later poets would realize the possibilities of these limping
iambics as they were called (choliambics), and use them for burlesque pictures and such subjects as beast fables. The most

famous remark of Hipponax was that the two happiest days in a woman's life were that of her marriage and that of her death. His verses were read by the later Greeks chiefly for the curiosities of his vocabulary for which he drew plentifully on the *patois* of beggars and the jargon of thieves.

The elegiac metre was not used for narrative poems. The early poets used it chiefly for subjects in which they could introduce their own personal experiences and reflections on life. Such were the elegiac poems of Archilochus and his younger contemporary Callinus of Ephesus (*c.* 650 B.C.). The Spartan Tyrtaeus (*c.* 630 B.C.) employed the metre for his exhortations, and we possess a notable example of its use by Solon in a philosophical poem which he addresses to himself.

The elegy was found to be an appropriate form for light amatory subjects, and MIMNERMUS of Colophon, an older contemporary of Solon, is the ancestor of the love poetry of Propertius, Tibullus, and Ovid. Mimnermus was haunted by the brevity of youth which passes 'like the dream of a moment,' and the horror of old age which is worse than death, and the sweetness of his cadences makes his melancholy moods attractive. An elegy is an occasional poem and it would be as wrong to infer from the few pieces of this poet that remain that he was always melancholy, as it would be to stigmatize him as a voluptuary, because in one poem he declared that the whole value of life depends on golden Aphrodite.

THEOGNIS of Megara is the most notable of the early elegiac poets. Born probably in the neighbourhood of 600 B.C., shortly after the tyranny of Theagenes, he lived through the period when his city was rent by violent struggles between the nobles and the democracy, of which the vicissitudes and the chronology are very obscure. Theognis, like Alcaeus, was a strong partisan who always regretted the happy days in which Megara was governed by its aristocracy and had a supreme contempt for democracy and the new men who were rising to the top. (For his political poems see above, vol. III, p. 569.)

A great many of his poems have been preserved in a collection (now usually known as the *Theognidea*), which included much of which Theognis was not the author. As it has come down, it falls into two sections or books, in the first of which probably most of the poems are by Theognis, in the second, which is entirely amorous, possibly only one. The poems of which he was certainly the author are those addressed to a favourite friend, Cyrnus son of Polypāus, but there are many others which there is no reason not to ascribe to him. The first book also contains short poems of known authorship (by Mimnermus, Tyrtaeus, and Solon) and, as it is reasonable to conjecture, others of which the writers are unknown but probably did not live later than in the sixth century.

None of the poems of Theognis is long; many of them are merely couplets, and their character is generally either didactic or reflective. Sometimes he criticizes life as a moralist, sometimes as a man of the world. The poem which is perhaps best known and which best deserved immortality is that which enshrines in sweet and sad verses a merciless expression of the sense of the worthlessness of life:

πάντων μὲν μὴ φῦναι ἐπιχθονίοισιν ἄριστον
μηδ' ἐσιδεῖν αὐγὰς ὀξέος ἠελίου,
φύντα δ' ὅπως ὤκιστα πύλας Ἀΐδαο περῆσαι
καὶ κεῖσθαι πολλὴν γῆν ἐπαμησάμενον.

'Not to be born is best of all lots for men upon earth, and not to see the rays of the piercing sun; but once born, the best a man can do is to make his tomb (lit. to lie, having heaped earth over himself) and pass as soon as he may through the gates of Hades.' The thought was to be echoed by Bacchylides, but without the suggestion of suicide; and was afterwards reset by Sophocles in sweeter glyconic cadences as a meditation on the life of Oedipus.

The wisdom of Theognis on such subjects as wealth and poverty, the evils of life, the caprices of fortune, the deceitfulness of friends is apt to become a little tedious, but he wrote some charming poems. His Σοὶ μὲν ἐγὼ πτέρ' ἔδωκα in which he predicts the immortality of his songs may be singled out[1]:

To you I have given wings, and by them uplifted you shall fly over the boundless sea, over the whole earth, Cyrnus, moving through the lands and the islands of Hellas, crossing over the unharvested fish-haunted sea. You shall not sit on the backs of horses, but the splendid gifts of the violet-crowned Muses shall escort you, easily. And you shall be present at all feasts and banquetings, your name set on the lips of many, and to the voices of flutes lovely youths will sing sweet songs of you, beautifully. And when you are dead and descend into the caves of the dark earth, to the wailing house of Hades, never shall you lose your glory, but always shall your deathless name be known to the world. And for all future men who esteem song you shall be a song, so long as there are earth and sun. Yet *from you I* do not get even a little honour but you deceive me with words, as you might a small child.

---

[1] 237 *sqq.* The convincing transposition of verses in this poem proposed by Mr Hudson Williams has been adopted.

One of the most interesting pieces in the collection is a re-
monstrance with Zeus for permitting a dispensation which treats
just men and unjust alike (373 *sqq.*):

Dear Zeus, you amaze me. You are lord of all, you possess honour and
great power. Well you know the mind and heart of every man, and your
sovranty, O king, is supreme over all. How is it then that your mind can
venture to put in the same class transgressors and the just man (indifferently)
whether their thought turns to moderation or to violence and injustice? The
Unjust get wealth secure, while they who keep their hearts far from evil
deeds may get poverty, the mother of helplessness.

Theognis had travelled a little. He mentions visits to Euboea,
Sparta, and Sicily, and evidently they were of some length, and
where he went he was well received as a notable poet. 'I went
once as far as Sicily, and I went to the vineclad plain of Euboea
(the Lelantine plain), and to Sparta, the splendid city of the reedy
Eurotas; and all men welcomed my coming and were kind to me.
But from those lands and hosts no pleasure came to my heart;
I proved that nought is dearer than one's native land.' In Sicily
he could not fail to visit the western Megara; and it is thought
that its citizenship was bestowed on him; Plato curiously imagined
that he was born there.

We do not know the date of his death. But he lived to share
in the perturbation which was felt in the motherland at the descent
of Cyrus to the coasts of the Aegean, the fall of Lydia, and the
subjugation of the Ionian cities. The feelings roused among
European Greeks by these events were not due merely to sympathy with the Greeks of Asia, but also to fear; they had a true
premonition that they were themselves menaced by the same peril.
Sparta had taken diplomatic action (vol. III, p. 524) and thoughtful
men like Theognis realized that there was cause for anxiety. We
have an echo of the rumours and fears which were abroad in
Hellas (about 545–4 B.C.) in his prayer to Apollo to protect
Megara (773 *sqq.*):

O lord Phoebus, as you yourself, in your favour to Alcathous son of
Pelops, built and made strong the acropolis, so now keep away from this
city the violent host of the Medes that the people in good cheer may send
you the famous hecatombs in the coming spring, taking their pleasure in
lovely feasts and harp-playing and the dances and the singing of paeans
around your altar. For in truth, I am afraid, when I regard the foolishness
and ruinous divisions of the Hellenes But be kind, Phoebus, and guard
this our city

The second book of the Theognidean collection may have
been compiled at a later date than the first; it contains pieces
which may be posterior to the sixth century, though this cannot

33

be proved. There is at least one piece by Theognis himself. The whole book is interesting because it illustrates an important side of Greek life which it is particularly difficult for modern people to appreciate, and some of the poems have great charm. They were intended to be sung at Symposia; and we have an illustration of their popularity in a picture on a red-figured bowl from Tanagra (which has been assigned to the early fifth century) where a man reclining at dinner is represented singing ὦ παίδων κάλλιστε[1], doubtless the same song which opens with these words (v. 1365) in the Theognidean collection: 'O fairest and most desirable of all boys, stand here and listen to a few words from me.'

There is a notable difference in tone between this older collection of amorous poems and the later collection, on the same subject, in which the authors of the pieces are chiefly of the Alexandrian or of a still later age[2]. Not only is the older book free from superficial indecencies but it is characterized by a moderation in expression which in amorous poetry may seem to a modern reader almost coldness. There are no outbursts of strong passion, and no erotic descriptions of the charms of the beloved. If the genders were altered and the poems addressed to maidens, we should criticize them as excessively sedate. In some the poet is wooing a beauty, in some he is reproaching a young friend for his unfaithfulness, in some exhorting him to be loyal, in others he is reflecting on the pleasures or the pains of *paedophilia*. But all are marked by an absence of passionate exaggeration.

O boy, having subdued my soul, hear me. I will say no word unpleasing or that could offend you. Only have patience to understand my pleading. Remember you are free not to do what is not to your mind (1235 *sqq.*).

Of such sort were the respectful overtures with which a man sought to gain the affection of a boy to whom he was attracted, perhaps in the gymnasium, and the liaison that followed was often the foundation of an enduring friendship. These relationships were on a much higher plane than relations with courtesans; for they could mean a moral and intellectual comradeship not to be found in the demi-monde, where Aspasias are always rare. No blame was attached to a boy who formed such a friendship, but the social code seems to have decreed that the amorous relation-

---

[1] Published by Köhler in *Ath. Mitt.* ix, 1 *sqq.*, 1844. Cp. E. Harrison, *Studies in Theognis*, 261.

[2] Collected by Strato in the reign of Hadrian, preserved in *Anthologia Palatina*, Book xii. Both collections have the same title, Μοῦσα παιδική (*Songs about boys*).

ship should cease when hair on his face began to appear. Like most human things, the custom of *paedophilia* had its drawbacks as well as its uses, as one of these poets observes; and perhaps the chief drawback was that many of the fair young folk were badly spoiled by the adoration and flatteries of their lovers. Many of them were finished coquettes and skilled in the art of plaguing the wooers who were competing for their favours, of exciting their jealousies, and of extorting gifts. But their caprices and tricks were tolerated; the privilege of beauty was recognized. 'I will not hurt you, not even if the immortal gods mean to bless my vengeance, O beautiful boy. For I do not sit to judge peccadillos, and for beautiful boys there is no punishment when they do wrong' (1279 *sqq.*).

This artificial social institution, as we may almost term it, generally offered the only way in which young men could satisfy the craving for what we call 'romantic' affection. We must remember that in many of the most highly civilized cities of Greece, no freedom or opportunity was allowed to women to display their attractions in public.

Among the elegiac writers of the sixth century XENOPHANES, who was born at Colophon but spent most of his life in the far west at Elea, must not be passed over. In expounding his metaphysical ideas he employed epic verse, which, as we have seen, was always recognized by philosophical poets as the appropriate vehicle; but he also composed elegies, and these poems seem to have been much longer than those of Theognis and very different in style. Particularly interesting to a modern reader is the following description of a festive gathering of serious-minded men— it might be the modest dinner of a philosophical club.

Now the floor is clean, and the hands of all are washed, and so are the cups. One slave is placing garlands on our heads, another is presenting fragrant oil in a phiale (flat bowl). The mixing bowl stands there full of good cheer; and there is another wine in jugs which vows that it will never fail us, mild, with bouquet of flowers. And in our midst frankincense sends up its sacred smell; and cold water is there, sweet and pure, and beside us are set brown loaves, and a noble table laden with cheese and rich honey. In the centre is an altar thickly covered with flowers, and song and festivity pervade the house. It is meet that men of good sense shall first of all praise the god with pure words and holy hymns; and when they have made libation and prayed for the power to do what is right (for to pray for this is our most obvious need), there is no wrong in drinking as much as you can hold without needing an attendant to escort you home if you are not extremely old. Praise that man who, having drunk, exhibits the power of his memory and the pitch of his soul on the subject of virtue. It is not good to tell of battles of Titans or giants, nor yet of the Centaurs—fictions of men of old time—or of violent civil wars, in which things there is no profit; but ever to consider the gods is good (frag. 1).

Besides the lighter uses of elegy, it was used for the graver purposes of dedication of offerings and of epitaphs on funeral monuments, and in the sixth and fifth centuries the art of composing epitaphs reached an austere perfection, never again to be equalled in their fine reserve and simplicity. Best known are those on soldiers who fell in the Persian wars. For instance that inscribed on the memorial set up at Thermopylae at the burying-place of the Lacedaemonian dead:

> ὦ ξένε, ἀγγέλλεν Λακεδαιμονίοις ὅτι τῆδε
> κείμεθα τοῖς κένων ῥέμασι πειθόμενοι.

('Stranger, tell the Lacedaemonians that we lie here, obeying their words'); or that which commemorated the Corinthians who perished at Salamis and were buried in the island where a fragment of the stone has been found:

> ὦ ξένε, εὔυδρόν ποκ᾽ ἐναίομες ἄστυ Ϙορίνθο,
> νῦν δ᾽ ἀμὲ Αἴαντος νᾶσος ἔχει Σαλαμίς.

('Stranger, we dwelled once in the city of Corinth rich in water, but now Salamis, the island of Ajax, possesses us.')

Of the epitaphs of this age, one of the most interesting is that on Archedice, daughter of Hippias tyrant of Athens, who married the son of Hippoclus the tyrant of Lampsacus:

> Ἀνδρὸς ἀριστεύσαντος ἐν Ἑλλάδι τῶν ἐφ᾽ ἑαυτοῦ
> Ἱππίου Ἀρχεδίκην ἥδε κέκευθε κόνις·
> ἣ πατρός τε καὶ ἀνδρὸς ἀδελφῶν τ᾽ οὖσα τυράννων
> παίδων τ᾽ οὐκ ἤρθη νοῦν ἐς ἀτασθαλίην.

('This dust hides the daughter of Hippias, who in Hellas was first of the men of his day, Archedice; who, daughter, wife, sister, and mother of tyrants, was not uplifted to presumptuousness.')

The most famous and most versatile poet of the age, Simonides of Ceos, was an adept in composing epitaphs and dedications, and in later times all the well-known 'epigrams' of the period came to pass for his. There is one which may safely be attributed to him (on the authority of Herodotus). It was inscribed on the tomb of the Acarnanian prophet Megistias, who was with the Greeks at Thermopylae, foretold the issue of the battle, and, though Leonidas urged him to leave the doomed army, remained to die. 'This is the tomb of glorious Megistias whom the Medes slew when they crossed the river Spercheus, the seer who then knowing well the approaching doom refused to leave the leaders of Sparta.'

IV. LYRIC POETRY (CITHAROEDIA)

As early Greek poetry (except that which was recited by a rhapsode) was accompanied by an instrument, its history was connected by the Greeks with the history of music. Here the untrustworthiness of Greek tradition is very clearly exhibited. The invention of the seven-stringed lyre was attributed to Terpander of Lesbos. The excavations in Crete have taught us that the seven-stringed lyre was in use there in the Late Minoan age. It can be seen depicted on a sarcophagus found in the palace of Hagia Triada. In the same way one might imagine from the musical tradition of the Greeks that flute-playing was almost a new art in the eighth century and was due to the introduction of a Phrygian instrument by the musician Olympus, who may have been a real person but is very shadowy. Here again archaeology shows that the double flute was known in Crete in Late Minoan times[1]. The art of music in Aegean lands was thus more advanced many centuries before Homer than the Greeks conceived. The truth is that there was an important development of music in the eighth century in Greek Asia, in consequence of the introduction of more richly toned instruments from Phrygia and Lydia, and the flute became more important than it had been as a rival to the lyre (the rivalry is reflected in the legend of the contest of Apollo the harp-player with the Phrygian flute-player Marsyas); and the later Greeks, according to their habit of turning improvers into inventors, ascribed to this movement inventions which really belonged to the distant past.

As Greek lyric poetry was always composed to be sung, music invariably accompanying it, the lyric poets were not only poets but musicians, and generally composed the melodies as well as the words. Melodies of early Greek poems have not been preserved, so that we cannot realize the total effect of these works which expressed the artist's experience by music and poetry combined—somewhat as the sculptor used colour as well as form to express his conceptions. In the sculptor's case the colour was quite subordinate to the form, and in the poet's case the music was strictly subordinate to the words. It seems probable, from

[1] See D. Mackenzie, *B.S.A.* xii, p. 249.

what we know generally about Greek music, that if we had the melody, say of a song of Alcaeus or of an ode of Pindar, it would not add to our enjoyment of it. Nor is it necessary to study the subject of Greek music in order to appreciate Greek lyric poetry as poetry. Of that subject it is sufficient to refer here to the difference of the 'modes' (ἁρμονίαι), to which the poets themselves sometimes refer. There were seven modes to which the strings could be tuned by varying the position of the semitones in the octave. There was the Dorian mode, in minor key; the Phrygian, also in minor; the Lydian, in major; and four other subordinate modes. The Dorian was considered bracing and spirited, suitable for serious and warlike themes; while a poet who was expressing passion would probably tune his instrument to the Phrygian scale; the Lydian was deprecated by moralists as enervating.

The name of TERPANDER of Lesbos, though his songs were not preserved and the inventions ascribed to him are extremely doubtful, does mean something in the history of Greek poetry. We know two facts about him. He founded a school of lyrical poetry in his native Lesbos, and his fame as a citharoedus or solo singer, accompanying himself on the harp, was such that he was invited to Sparta, at the suggestion of an oracle, to calm the passions of civil discord by his music. Probably he was contemporary with Archilochus, and probably he canonized some of the metres that were employed by the Lesbian singers of two generations later, who looked back to him as a master of the lyrical art. His name lives in the glory reflected backward from the two poets who made Lesbos a famous island.

That the names of these two Aeolian poets, Alcaeus and Sappho, are household words to-day, though only fragments of their poems have survived, is due to Horace. One of his imaginative pictures describes them in the lower world enchanting the shades by their singing:

utrumque sacro digna silentio
mirantur umbrae dicere.

Their lives were contemporary; they shared in the same exile; they were acquainted; it was believed that Alcaeus made proposals of love to Sappho which she rejected. In their poetry there was little in common beyond the Lesbian dialect, the employment of the same metres, and the strong personal note, of which the example had been set by Archilochus. Politics, war, his own exile, sea voyages were the leading themes of Alcaeus (*dura nauis, dura fugae mala, dura belli*), while Sappho confined her muse within a narrower circle of feminine interests. Horace, therefore, found much more to his purpose, for re-moulding and imitating, in Alcaeus than in Sappho; from Sappho he seems to have taken little or nothing. But she was the more accomplished poet. That was certainly the opinion of ancient Greek critics. Plato himself is said to have been the author of the couplet which procured her the name of the 'tenth Muse.' 'Some say the number of the Muses is nine. They have forgotten Sappho of Lesbos, the tenth.'

Alcaeus and Sappho were contemporaries of Solon of Athens. ALCAEUS was a soldier like Archilochus. He fought in the war against the Athenians for the possession of Sigeum (see vol. III, p. 516) and, like Archilochus, told in a poem how he lost his shield which the Athenians hung up there in a temple. As a soldier, his brother Antimenidas, one of the Greek mercenaries who took service under Nebuchadrezzar, the lord of Babylon, was more efficient and distinguished. The poet wrote a poem to him on his return to Lesbos 'from the ends of the earth' and mentioned the fame he had won by slaying in single combat a foe of gigantic stature. Alcaeus was a strong political partisan, prominent among the opponents of tyrants like Melanchrus and Myrsilus, and then resisting no less bitterly the rule of Pittacus whom Mitylene had accepted as a constitutional dictator, and whom Alcaeus despised as a man of the people[1]. This resistance led to his banishment (c. 596 B.C.). To conceive this Mitylenean aristocrat as a champion and poet of liberty, as Wordsworth has done, is a curious perversion of the truth:

> The spirit-stirring note
> When the live chords Alcaeus smote
> Inflamed by sense of wrong.
> Woe! Woe! to tyrants from the lyre
> Broke threateningly in sparkles dire
> Of fierce vindictive song.

Alcaeus was simply an oligarchical 'die-hard' and such vindictive verses as that in which he cried 'Now is the time to drink ourselves drunk; Myrsilus is dead' were hardly poems of liberty. Of his political poems one was always remembered, that in which he likened his city under the rule of tyrants to a storm-tost ship, and which may have contributed to making the phrase 'ship of state' a commonplace if it did not originate it.

[1] He speaks of the 'lowborn Pittacus who has been made tyrant of the discordant city amid the loud acclaim of all,' and heaps insults upon him (frags. 37 A, 37 B). See vol. III, p. 516, and above, p. 98.

But Alcaeus was above all a poet of wine and love, and if his songs had not been composed in the Lesbian dialect, they might have been as popular throughout Greece as those of Anacreon, a singer of the next generation. Anything is a sufficient reason for drinking, that is the burden of his wine songs. Is it winter, pour out wine without stint; do you hear spring coming, fill the mixing bowl; is it summer, drench your lungs with wine; πίνωμεν (let us drink) is his motto for every day in the calendar; in joy and in sorrow to get drunk is equally appropriate. Of his amatory poems nothing is preserved, but the name of his favourite boy is familiar from Horace, Lycus of the black eyes and black hair (*Lycum nigris oculis nigroque crine decorum*).

Alcaeus possessed a large collection of armour, of which he was very proud, and he described it in one of his poems. 'My halls gleam with bronze, the whole house has been decorated for Ares.' There are brightly polished helmets from which nod white horse-hair plumes; resplendent bronze greaves, hanging on the walls by concealed pegs; new linen breast-plates and bucklers, lying on the floor in heaps; Chalcidian swords; belts and military frocks. 'The most striking point about this fragment,' a modern critic has remarked, 'is its foppery. The poem seems to reveal a luxurious nature delighting in military millinery[1].'

SAPPHO belonged to a good Lesbian family, of which descendants were still living at the end of the fourth century. She was born (at Eresus) perhaps about 615 B.C., married young, had a daughter Cleïs to whom she was devoted; was involved like Alcaeus in the political troubles of Mitylene and banished from the island. We do not know who her husband was or what became of him, but on her return from exile—evidently a widow—she set up at Mitylene what we should now describe as an academy for training girls in music—she herself calls it a house of the Muses—and pupils of well-to-do families came to learn music and dancing. We gather from the remains of her poems that she took a deep personal interest in them. Her school was her world, and the motives of her most characteristic poems concern the life of this little society, revealing her feelings freely, when she was wounded by want of affection or ingratitude, expressing her grief at partings when girls she loved left her to marry, or recalling the simple pleasures they had together.

We have part of a poem, addressed to Atthis, one of her

[1] J. A. Symonds, *Studies of the Greek Poets*, 1st series, p. 142.

favourite pupils; it is dedicated to recollections of Arignōta who had married and gone to live at Sardes:

From Sardes still her thoughts come often hither. When we lived together Arignota sincerely adored you like a goddess and above all delighted in your singing. But now she shines amidst Lydian women, like the rosy-fingered moon when the sun has set, excelling all the stars, and she spreads her light over the salt sea, as well as over the flowery fields. The dew is shed beautifully, and the roses are luxuriant and soft anthruska and blooming melilote. And as she walks through the meadows, she is thinking of gentle Atthis, and her delicate mind is stirred with longing and her heart is heavy with distress. She calls aloud on us to come over there to her. And it is not Night, who has many ears, that bears to us across the sea the words we cannot hear (it is our own longing that tells us)[1].

We have a little bit of another song on the absent Anactoria, which may also be quoted:

The fairest thing on earth is some say an array of horsemen, some of footmen, others of black ships. I say it is that which one loves. It is easy to make this clear. Helen reviewed the beauty of the world and chose as best that man who destroyed the whole majesty of Troy; and she remembered not daughter or parents, but loved him and he seduced her. Now I bethought myself of Anactoria, who is far away; whose lovely gait and the bright glancing of her face I would rather see than the chariots of the Lydians or foot-soldiers in all their (glitter)[2].

The one complete ode we possess is an invocation of Aphrodite imploring the goddess not to break her heart with pains and languors, and recalling that once before she had come down from heaven on a bird-borne car and consoled her when she was pining through an unreturned affection—

You asked me what ailed me and what I desired so passionately. 'Whom would you that Peitho should draw into your friendship? Sappho, who doth you wrong? For if she flees from you, soon shall she pursue you, and, if she refuses gifts, shall offer them; if she loves you not, soon shall she love you though she would not.' Come to me now as then, deliver me from my distresses, fulfil that of which my heart desires fulfilment, and yourself be my auxiliary.

A Greek essay-writer of later times, who was well acquainted with Sappho's poetry, compared the beautiful young women who were her friends and pupils at Mitylene to the company of handsome youths who were disciples of Socrates at Athens. 'What Alcibiades and Charmides and Phaedrus were to Socrates, Gyrinna and Atthis and Anactoria were to Sappho. And to his opponents,

---

[1] *Berl. Klassikertexte*, p. 16. The interpretation of the last sentence is due to v. Wilamowitz-Möllendorff, *Sappho und Simonides*, p. 53 *sq.*

[2] *Pap. Oxyrh.* x, p. 23.

Prodicus, Gorgias, Protagoras, correspond her rivals, Gorgo and Andromeda; sometimes she censures them, sometimes she treats them ironically, just like Socrates[1].' But her pupils had no literary talent among them; none of them did for Sappho what Plato did for Socrates in his *Symposium*.

It is easy to divine that the highly-wrought emotional nature of the poetess caused her much suffering. 'Whomsoever I do well to,' she complains bitterly, 'they above all hate me.' The fragments bear out the impression that Horace, who had read all her poems, gives of them, when he describes her as

> querentem
> Sappho puellis de popularibus.

That was the dominant note of her most beautiful songs. Her affections were intense and jealous, and we may suspect that her sensitive nature made her difficult to live with. 'You forget me' she sings to some one, 'do you love some other better than me?' How passionate her feelings for her young friends could be she reveals without reserve in one of the most famous and poignant of her poems, that which Catullus translated and sadly spoiled. It expresses the suffering she endured in resigning herself to the loss of a girl who was about to be married. Here her art surpasses itself in the picture of her own physical collapse from the tortures she experienced at witnessing Agallis (if that was the girl's name, as has been guessed) talking and laughing with her godlike lover. 'And over all my body sweat is shed, a trembling layeth hold on me, yea I am paler than pale grass; little I lack of being wholly dead.'

This ode illustrates Horace's 'amorous ardours' (*calores*) and Byron's 'burning Sappho,' and perhaps more than any other evidence it is responsible for inducing many modern writers to listen to the scurrilities with which the Attic comic poets soiled her name and for prompting a talented French writer to his creation of Bilitis[2]. Whatever the intimacies of her life may have been—and it may be suggested that there are limits beyond which it is as impertinent to inquire into the private lives of eminent people of the past as of eminent people who are alive[3]—it is clear that in her own day in Lesbos her repute was unblemished. Alcaeus, as we know from his own words, thought her as pure as she was charming. There is no evidence against her good name

[1] Maximus of Tyre, xxiv, 8.
[2] Pierre Louis, *Chansons de Bilitis*.
[3] Mure, who was the leader in modern attacks on her character, would have liked to put her shade 'through the third degree.'

in any serious record of those who knew much more of her poems and life than we do, from Plato to Horace—and this fact remains, whatever a modern psychologist may make of the ode to 'Agallis.'

Sappho had a brother named Charaxus who was engaged in the wine trade, and at Naucratis he was ensnared by a courtesan, Doricha, whom Herodotus confuses with a more famous lady of the same profession, Rhodopis the fellow-slave of Aesop in Samos. Some centuries later a statue was set up at Naucratis in memory of Doricha simply for the distinction she had had of being mentioned by the great poetess. That mention was not very favourable, for Sappho was vexed by her brother's intrigue which probably cost him a great deal of money and created a scandal. A much mutilated poem, composed when Charaxus was expected back in Lesbos, has been recovered from Egypt[1]. Sappho prays to the Nereids for a safe voyage for him, refers to a disagreement between them, and hopes for a complete reconciliation. The disagreement is supposed to have arisen from the Doricha scandal, but the restoration of the poem is highly uncertain. It is a little amusing to see this incident naïvely used by some admirers of Sappho as an argument for her blameless life, as if either in ancient or in modern times the indignation of a well-born lady at the publicity and scandal caused by a brother's liaison with a notorious courtesan would prove that her own life was impeccable.

It was natural that the services of Sappho should often have been requested by her fellow-citizens for the composition of hymns for festive occasions. Some of her epithalamia were preserved in her collected works and a few fragments we have give us an inkling of their charm and originality. Two short pieces, which evidently belonged to the same nuptial hymn, may be quoted in the felicitous version of a great modern poet.

> Like the sweet apple which reddens upon the topmost bough,
> A'top on the topmost twig,—which the pluckers forgot somehow—
> Forgot it not, nay, but got it not, for none could get it till now.
>
>   *   *   *   *
>
> Like the wild hyacinth flower which on the hills is found,
> Which the passing feet of the shepherds for ever tear and wound,
> Until the purple blossom is trodden into the ground.

The name of the Ionian singer ANACREON of Teos is not less famous than those of the Lesbians. He was one of those agreeable songsters who do not take life very seriously, confine them-

---

[1] *Pap. Oxyrh.* I, p. 11.

selves chiefly to the themes of wine and love, and are most at home at the courts of kings and tyrants. Anacreon shone first at the court of Polycrates of Samos and on that tyrant's death (*c.* 522 B.C.) went to Athens to shine at the court of Hipparchus. He had seen military service, and says that he threw away his shield, as it seems to have been the fashion for soldier-poets to do. His songs were popular, being admirably suited for convivial occasions; and they immortalized the name of Bathyllus a handsome young flute-player, a minion of Polycrates, to whom he wrote amorous verses. Little of his poetry has survived, but one charming fragment may be quoted to illustrate the light grace of his style. 'Golden-haired Love, hitting me with a crimson ball, challenges me to play with a damsel shod with embroidered sandals. She comes from fair Lesbos, finds fault with my hair for being white, and yawns for some other prey.' He is not a bit serious when he laments the approach of old age; 'our temples are already grey, the hair white; gracious youth has gone; my teeth are old. Not much time of sweet life is left me. I often sob, in fear of Tartarus.' He was the model for many of the Odes of Horace.

But it is not the few fragments that we have of his songs, that have made his name familiar in modern ages. What Anacreontic poetry meant to the poets and classical scholars of the seventeenth and eighteenth centuries was a collection of songs which Anacreon never wrote and could not have written. These songs, which we now call the *Anacreontica*, were composed by imitators, probably five or six hundred years after his death, in the glyconic metres which he had used. They are very graceful, but they belong to an age of artificial poetry and to a different social atmosphere from that of the court of Polycrates. They were just what would take the fancy of cultivated readers in the eighteenth century, to whose taste we may suspect that the true Anacreon, had his songs been preserved, would have made much less appeal.

V. LYRIC POETRY (CHORAL)

The earliest piece of the choral poetry of the Greeks we have is from the later years of the seventh century. But this kind of poetry was very old. The paeans which were sung to Apollo, the processional hymns (*prosŏdia*) on solemn occasions of worship, hymeneal hymns, dirges for the dead (*thrēnoi*), all required poets and trained singers. Homer tells us of the paeans; and the dithyramb is assuredly, as its unexplained name suggests, also of great antiquity, though the Greeks pretended that it was invented at Corinth in the age of Periander by the Lesbian harp-player Arion, of whom the famous legend is recorded by Herodotus that he was cast into the sea by robbers and reached shore on the back of a dolphin. This is directly refuted by the fact that the dithyramb is mentioned, long before the age of Periander, by Archilochus.

The dithyramb became specially associated with the worship of Dionysus, but it is very doubtful whether it was originally Dionysiac.

The first glimpse we get of the organized choral poetry of the Greeks is at Sparta, whither in the middle of the seventh century the musician Thalētas was summoned from Crete, and some years later ALCMAN came from Asia Minor. Alcman was a Lydian who had fallen into slavery among the Greeks and had become quite Hellenized (see above, vol. III, p. 559). He is the earliest of the Nine canonical lyric poets, that is, of the nine whose works were collected and edited by the savants of Alexandria[1]. He was generously treated at Sparta and he made it his permanent home, and composed his poems in the Spartan dialect. His work had perhaps little influence on the future of Hellenic poetry; his ideas were too much circumscribed by the Laconian conditions in which he wrought to make a wide appeal; it was probably felt that he was rather provincial. But he had much charm.

One of Alcman's tasks was to train the Spartan maidens who sang and danced at religious festivals and to compose hymns for them—*partheneia* (virginals), as hymns sung by choirs of virgins were called. Of one of these we have a considerable piece, preserved on a papyrus found in Egypt in 1855.

This song consisted of ten strophes, and fell into two distinct parts. In the first five strophes stories from mythology were told to show how punishment awaits the presumptuous. 'Let no man fly to Olympus nor seek to wed Aphrodite.' Of this mythical part little has been preserved. The second part is concerned with the chorus itself, and the praise of its leader Hagesichŏra. The chorus seems to have consisted of ten singers, who are all named in the song, and to have been divided into semichoruses, one under Hagesichora who was the chorāgos, leader of the chorus as a whole, the other under Agĭdo, the second in command. The earlier stanzas may have been sung by the two sections alternately. But in the last five stanzas, the text of which has been almost com-

---

[1] The nine are: Alcman, Alcaeus, Sappho, Stesichorus, Ibycus, Anacreon, Simonides, Pindar, Bacchylides.

pletely recovered[1], this simple arrangement is impossible. It seems certain that each stanza was divided among more than one singer or group of singers. But the allotment of verses must be extremely conjectural, for there are some passages of which the meaning is uncertain, and there is no other work of a similar kind to help us to explain it.

It may be conjectured that the girls who sang this partheneion belonged to a female thiasus or club connected with the cult of a divinity, otherwise unknown, named Aōtis; and that they competed with another chorus, which was known as the 'Peleiads' (doves), and perhaps consisted of eleven choristers, on the occasion of presenting a robe or possibly a plough to Artemis Orthia. All this is conjecture, and there are various theories; yet notwithstanding the uncertainties, which will perhaps never be cleared up, we can enjoy the pretty banter of the chorus-maidens first disputing over the charms of Hagesichora and Agido as if there were a competition for a beauty-prize, and ending with unanimous praise of Hagesichora as a brilliantly skilful leader whom they all adore. Imperfectly understood as it is, it gives a unique tantalizing glimpse into a phase of Greek life of which it would be extremely interesting to know more. A few verses may be quoted, to show the manner of the composition.

> *Semichorus* 2 *(except Agido)*. I sing of the light of Agido. To my eyes she is like the sun on whom she calls to bear witness that she shines among us.
>
> *Semichorus* 1 *(except Hagesichora)*. I am forbidden either to praise her or to blame her by (the beauty of) our glorious[2] leader Hagesichora, who seems to be herself as surpassing fair among us as if a well knit prize-winning courser with ringing hooves, of a breed of winged dream-steeds, were set among common cattle.
>
> Strophe 7. See you not? The steed is Venetic; and the hair of my cousin Hagesichora blooms on her like pure gold, and her face silver-white—but why describe her in express words? There is Hagesichora.
>
> *Semichorus* 2 *(except Agido)*. She is second in beauty to Agido, and will run with her as a Scythian with a Lydian horse. For our contest is with the Pleiads, when we bear the robe to Orthia; and they rise up in the ambrosial night as bright as the star of Sirius.

---

[1] The establishment of the text has been mainly due to the labour of Blass. For the elucidation, the most important studies are those of H. Diels, U. v. Wilamowitz-Möllendorff, and J. T. Sheppard, of whom the last-named made it clear that some of the stanzas must have been divided among different singers. (For these essays see Bibliography.)

[2] So literally. But the word (κλεεννά) may possibly have implications which would be better rendered by 'adorable.'

The fact that it was in the motherland, and in Dorian states, that the art of choral poetry developed was reflected in the convention which prescribed language of Dorian-character—literary Doric, we might call it—for works of this kind, a convention preserved by the Attic tragedians. But although choral poetry thus received a Dorian stamp, it would be a mistake, in the opinion of the present writer, to suppose that it was a Dorian creation or that there was any breach of continuity between the choral performances of the heroic age and those of the seventh century. The continuity from Achaean days throughout what is called the 'Dark Age' is natural in itself and is strongly suggested by the 'Aeolisms' which are a marked literary convention in the songs of Pindar and Bacchylides. It seems more probable that these Aeolic forms are due to a tradition persisting from pre-Dorian days than that they are due to a later influence coming from Lesbos through lyrists like Terpander or Arion.

Alcman used the local Doric of Laconia, but in his age or possibly a generation later we find literary Doric used by a poet of Panhellenic significance who arose in the west and inaugurated a new period in the history of choral poetry. This was STESICHORUS of Himera, whose true name was said to be Teisias. There was always some mystery about his name, his date, and the place of his birth. There was a tendency to confuse him with a minor poet of the same name who lived in the fourth century, and there were some who wished to put him back to the age of Hesiod. One thing is certain; his life fell not later than in the first half of the sixth century. This follows from a verse in which Simonides (fr. 53) refers to him,

οὕτω γὰρ Ὅμηρος ἠδὲ Στασίχορος ἄεισε λαοῖς

('for thus did Homer and thus Stesichorus sing to the people'), and it rather gives the impression that he did not belong to the immediate past. The new idea of Stesichorus was that lyric chant should take the place of epic recitation, as a vehicle for narrative, and this fact is illustrated both by the conjunction of his name with Homer's in the verse just quoted from Simonides and by the names of his works like the *Helen*, the *Gēryonēis*, the *Oresteia* (a long poem which filled two books of his collected works). These poems were made to be chanted by standing choirs to the accompaniment of the lyre.

The effect of this idea of Stesichorus was to secure for the mythical stories the conspicuous place which they have in the later choral compositions of Pindar and Bacchylides.

It is clear that he was a very serious poet and was principally interested in heroic subjects. Horace, to whom his works were accessible, and who knew how to characterize in a word or two, sums his poetry up with *graues Camenae*. We may suspect that he did not enjoy great popularity among the Greeks and was little read except by professional men of letters. But his name was always well known on account of his treatment of Helen and the legend which was attached to it. The tale was that in an ode on Helen he had described her conduct so frankly that her brethren the Dioscuri were offended and afflicted him with blindness. Then he made amends by denying that Helen herself was ever at Troy; it was only an image of her. Appeased by this palinode the gods restored his sight. We know the opening lines of the palinode—

$$\text{Οὐκ ἐστ᾽ ἔτυμος λόγος οὗτος·}$$
$$\text{οὐδ᾽ ἔβας ἐν ναυσὶν εὐσέλμοις}$$
$$\text{οὐδ᾽ ἵκευ πέργαμα Τροίας.}$$

('This story is not true; you did not sail in benched ships, nor come to the citadel of Troy.') The first line became proverbial. Unfortunately that is all we have, and unfortunately the *Helen* itself is lost. For we should like to see how this poet took liberties with myths which he disliked.

It has been claimed for Stesichorus that he was the father of the Greek romance, to which in turn the ancestry of the modern novel can be traced. For his poems *Radine* and *Calyce* are love stories about fictitious men and women who had no connection with the heroic age or the beings of Olympus. Radine, who was beloved by her cousin, had fallen into the hands of a tyrant of Corinth. The tyrant killed them both and sent their bodies to Samos, their native land, and afterwards had them brought back to Corinth for burial. Calyce was a lady who was in love with Euathlus and, disdained by him, threw herself into the sea from the ubiquitous Leucadian rock. Plots, stated so briefly as that, do not sound very thrilling and they are referred to here only because they may possibly have had some actual significance in literary history.

The productive powers of Stesichorus were considerable, perhaps greater than those of any other lyric poet, if we may judge from the fact that in the Alexandrine edition his works were arranged in 26 books, while those of Pindar occupied only 17. Yet of none of these poets do we know less.

Another poet whose birthplace was in western Greece had a place among the canonical Nine, IBYCUS of Rhegium. We know his date, because he, like Anacreon, went to Samos to decorate the court of Polycrates. He composed poetry of two different kinds: erotic of which we have a couple of pleasing fragments exhibiting an elaborate style which contrasts sharply with Anacreon's simplicity. The impression he produced on the ancients was that he was the most erotic of all the Greek lyric poets[1], more susceptible than Anacreon or Alcaeus to the charms of beautiful youths. But he also wrote choral odes, and one of them, telling the story of the Trojan War, has recently been recovered from Egypt[2]. Here the style is extremely simple, and is, we may believe, modelled closely enough upon the style of Stesichorus. Ibycus was not one of the most brilliant lights among the nine classical lyric poets, and when, in one of his odes (IV, 9), Horace enumerates the early singers who are not obscure though their predecessor Homer is brighter than any, the two luminaries whom he omits out of the nine are Ibycus and Alcman[3].

With SIMONIDES, son of Leoprepes, we come to a time in which chronology is clearer. He was born at Iulis in Ceos in 557–6 B.C. He survived the Persian wars and in 476 B.C. we find him an octogenarian at Athens, and able to boast that he had won fifty-six victories in musical competitions, for dithyrambs performed with choruses. He lived seven years longer and, old as he was, visited Sicily and died at Acragas. Of his early life we know nothing, but he seems to have spent several years at Athens at the court of Hipparchus and from 509 to 490 B.C. he lived in Thessaly under the patronage of the Aleuadae.

Very few specimens of his poetry remain and they are fragmentary. In modern times his fame has partly rested on works which were not his, anonymous epitaphs on warriors who fell in the Persian invasions, and came to be ascribed to him (see above, p. 492). He did, however, commemorate events of that great struggle. He won a prize at Athens, defeating Aeschylus, for an elegy on those who fell at Marathon, and his epitaph on the prophet Megistias has been quoted already (above, p. 493). We have some verses of a hymn which he wrote in honour of the Spartans who fell at Thermopylae.

Renowned was their fortune and fair their fate. Their tomb is an altar; instead of laments they have remembrance, instead of pity, praise. Their

[1] See Cicero, *Tuscul. Disp.* IV, 33, 71.

[2] *Pap. Oxyrh.* XV, pp. 73 *sqq.*

[3] The omission of Bacchylides is doubtful, because the nephew may be included with his uncle Simonides in *Ceae*

shroud is such as neither decay nor the victory of time will touch, for they were brave men and their graveyard took the Glory of Hellas for its inmate. To this Leonidas the king of Sparta bears witness who has left a great memorial of valour and eternal glory.

For the age in which it was written, the style of these rather difficult verses is remarkable; one would almost think they were elaborated by a disciple of Gorgias. Simonides had a subtle mind which busied itself with questions which we associate with the later age of the sophists rather than with his own. This is illustrated by a *skolion* refining on a saying of Pittacus of Mitylene, 'It is hard to be a good man[1].' This *skolion* is addressed to Scopas the Thessalian prince who asked the poet what he thought of the wise man's dictum. In an argument, expressed without any poetical embellishment or metaphors, Simonides says in effect:

To be a 'good' man, in body and mind, square without fault or flaw, is not merely difficult, it is impossible. To be good is the privilege of gods. A man cannot help being bad, if circumstances are too much for him. Every man is good if he succeeds, bad if he fails; but success and failure lie with the gods. I will not search for the impossible, but when I find it, a blamelessly good man, I will tell you the news. Meanwhile I praise and love every man who voluntarily does nothing dishonourable; but under compulsion—well, the gods cannot fight with necessity.

He is groping towards a new definition of ethical merit.

Simonides wrote choral odes of many kinds, especially dithyrambs. The earliest recorded 'epinician' hymns, celebrating victories in games, were his, and it is possible that it was he who introduced *encomia*, songs sung at banquets or revels in praise of distinguished men, such songs as had hitherto been reserved for gods and heroes. Dirges were picked out by Horace as a kind of poetry in which he particularly excelled (*Cea nenia*) and Catullus speaks of 'Simonidean tears' as if he were a proverbial master of artistic laments. That he could sound sad and tender notes is shown by a beautiful piece preserved from one of his dithyrambs, in which Danae set afloat in a chest by Acrisius hushes her baby to sleep.

PINDAR was born about 522 B.C. at Cynoscephalae, a short mile from Thebes, in the country house of his father Daïphantus

---

[1] We know it from Plato's *Protagoras* 339 *sqq.* where it is discussed at length. U. v. Wilamowitz-Möllendorff has attempted a restoration of the text (*Sappho u. Simonides*, 159 *sqq.*). Pittacus was accounted one of the Seven Wise Men of the sixth century, to whom were ascribed short and pithy maxims of which the most famous were those set up in the temple at Delphi, *Know thyself* (γνῶθι σεαυτόν) and *Avoid Excess* (μηδὲν ἄγαν).

who had also a town house at Thebes. The family was noble and important, and seems to have been a branch of the stock of the Aegidae, whom we find in many places—Sparta, Thera, Cyrene. He went in his youth to Athens to be trained in music by Lasus of Hermione and Agathocles, but these experts in the lyric art did not form his style, which was entirely his own.

We are so fortunate as to be able to follow the development of Pindar's genius through a period of fifty years. For the first of his poems that we possess was composed in 498 B.C., and the latest in 446 B.C., a few years before his death. That earliest example of his skill is an ode celebrating the victory of Hippocleas of Thessalian Pelinna, in a boys' foot-race at the Pythian games, which he was commissioned to write by one of the Aleuad rulers of Thessaly. It is the Tenth Pythian Ode. Though the poet is not yet perfectly master of his art, this ode has the characteristics of the unique style which he had formed for himself and reveals the same ideas which pervade all his epinician hymns. The greatest happiness man can attain is to win victories by hands or feet in the great games of Hellas and to live to see a youthful son winning crowns like himself. 'The brazen heaven cannot be ascended by him, but of the splendours which we mortals can reach, he has accomplished the voyage to the furthermost mark. Travelling by ships nor yet by land could you find the wonderful road to the gathering-place of the Hyperboreans.' Then he goes on to describe the mythical visit of Perseus to the land of these favoured people who live beyond the north wind under the protection of Apollo, burdened by no labour, and spend their years in continual feasting and song and dances, and are never sick or sorry. It is not a great poem, but it shows the loftiness of his thought and diction, as well as the principal defect of his style, that abruptness, which makes an excessive demand on the mind of the reader or hearer, compelled to leap too quickly in following his rapid and sudden turns.

Eight years later we find him at Delphi in spring (490 B.C.) attending the feast of the Theoxenia, at which the gods were the guests and mortals their entertainers, a feast which had Panhellenic reputation and attracted many strangers. The Delphians had invited Pindar to compose the paean which was to be sung, and a large portion of it has been recovered from an Egyptian papyrus[1]. It was chanted by a chorus of Aeginetans. Having first told the story of the Trojan war, conceived as the unyielding

---

[1] Paean VI in *Pap. Oxyrh.* VIII. Diehl, *Supp. Lyr.* p. 64 *sq.*

strife of Apollo against Hera and Athena, Pindar takes the opportunity of singing the praises of Aegina:

ὀνομακλύτα γ᾽ ἔνεσσι Δωριεῖ
μεδέοισα πόντῳ
νᾶσος, ὦ Διὸς Ἑλ-
λανίου φαεννὸν ἄστρον.

'Your name is assuredly renowned, island set in the Dorian sea
as its mistress, bright star of Zeus Hellanius. Wherefore we
shall lay you in your couch not without a feast of paeans; but,
receiving surging streams of song, you shall declare how you came
by your destiny of being queen of ships, and won your fame for
respecting the rights of strangers.' This introduces the story of
Aegina's union with Zeus. It is an example of the way in which
Pindar his whole life long was wont to praise Aegina, a city to
which he was particularly devoted and where he had good friends.

The same year was a year of the Pythian games, and Pindar
was again at Delphi in the late summer. Xenocrates, younger
brother of Theron the tyrant of Acragas, won in the chariot-race,
and commissioned Simonides to write the official hymn of victory.
Thrasybulus, the son of Xenocrates, drove his father's horses.
Pindar made his acquaintance, and was so captivated by the
charm and sweet disposition of the youth that he spontaneously
addressed to him a short ode (preserved as *Pythian* vi) as a homage
to his skill as a charioteer and to the service he had rendered his
father. The opening verses strike a note which reveals the poet's
sensibility to the charm of attractive young men. 'Listen, for
assuredly we are ploughing a field of Aphrodite, the goddess with
the curving eyes, or of the Graces, as we come to the sanctuary
at the centre of the resonant earth.'

Thrasybulus would doubtless have this ode performed in Sicily;
and Pindar thus established friendly relations with the lords of
Acragas which would in later years bear fruit.

Delphi was within easy distance of Thebes and Pindar was
always on good terms with the Delphic priesthood. Of all the
Panhellenic games it must have been the Pythian that he most
often witnessed. And of all the places where Panhellenic festivals
were held, Delphi, in Pindar's age, probably offered the most
attractive surroundings. In its singularly striking position under
the Phaedriad cliffs, the precinct of the gods had not only the
temple which the generosity of the Alcmaeonidae had made a
wonder to see, but all the treasuries; at that time, Olympia hardly
approached Delphi in architectural beauties. It would not be

surprising if there were larger crowds of spectators gathered for
the Pythian than for the Olympian games from all parts of the
Greek world, because Delphi was in a more central position and
men could at the same time consult the Oracle or transact business
at the Panhellenic bank.

The Panhellenic festivals were unlike modern race meetings,
because they were religious festivals, there were no money prizes,
and betting was not one of their prominent features. But these
concourses were naturally occasions for a good deal of frivolous
gaiety, and sometimes there must have been stirring scenes between the partisans of the competitors. Among those who had
the time to spare and the money to frequent the games, there
were sure to be men belonging to a type which is to be found in
the cities of all ages—the type nowadays represented by those
whom the Americans call 'lounge-lizards'—and who in Greece
would have found no more agreeable occupation than ingratiating
themselves with youthful athletes, inspecting their charms, and
applauding their prowess. To Pindar these games were chief
among 'the delightful things in Hellas,' and victory the greatest
prize in life. He idealized and ennobled them.

The years of the invasion of Xerxes were the unhappiest of
Pindar's life. The part which Thebes played in that crisis of
Hellas was bitter to the patriotic pride of a Theban who aspired
to be a great Panhellenic poet. We can imagine what resonant
hymns of triumph he would have sung if his own city had helped
in the great deliverance; but when Thebes was covered with
shame and barely able to avoid the consequences of her Medism,
his voice was hushed. In an ode written in the year after Plataea to
celebrate the victory of an Aeginetan athlete at the Isthmian games
(*Isthmian* viii), he reveals his sorrow and his embarrassment:

My heart is afflicted, but I am asked to invoke the golden Muse. We have
been delivered from great woes, so let us not fall into lack of crowns nor
nurse cares, for some god has turned aside for us the stone of Tantalus
which hung above our heads, the trouble intolerable for Hellas. The dread
of things now past brought to a stop the powers of my art. It is right that
a man should have good hope, and that one reared in Thebes of the seven
gates should bring to Aegina, the fairest bloom of the Graces, for Aegina
and Thebe were twin daughters of Asopus.

The sympathies of Pindar are shown more clearly in an ode for
another Aeginetan athlete's victory on the Isthmus (*Isthmian* v) where
he praises the bravery of the Aeginetan fleet in the battle of Salamis:

Now too in war, Salamis, the city of Ajax, could bear witness that she
was kept safe by Aegina's sailors in the ruinous storm of Zeus, the hail-like

bloody death of innumerable men. Yet dip the boast in silence; Zeus dispenses this and that, Zeus the lord of all.

The date of the hymn may have been 476 B.C.; the poet went to Aegina for its performance. Had Thebes played a different part there would have been no word of silence.

In the autumn of this year (476), Pindar attended the Olympian games. The horses of Theron the tyrant of Acragas won the chariot-race and Pindar was invited to compose the choral ode to celebrate the victory. Hiero, tyrant of Syracuse, won the horse-race with his horse Pherenīcus which had a long triumphal career, for it had been the winner at the Pythian games in 482 B.C. and again in 478. There was another victor from western Greece, on this occasion, in whom Pindar was interested, Hagesidāmus of the Italian Locri, who won in the boys' boxing match, and Pindar was retained to celebrate the success. The young victor was beautiful and fascinated the poet. 'I have praised the lovely son of Archestratus whom I saw on that day, beside the Olympian altar, conquering by the might of his hands, with such beautiful form and bloom of youth as, by the favour of the Cyprus-born goddess, once saved Ganymede from a pitiless fate.'

After the games, Pindar sailed for Sicily, to visit Acragas and conduct the performance of the ode for Theron's victory. More striking than this ode (*Olympian* III) is the encomium on Theron (preserved as *Olympian* II) which must also have been performed while he was at Acragas and is one of his most beautiful poems.

It contains a wonderful description of a life, without tears or toil, enjoyed by the good after death. It is Orphic doctrine in which Theron, we must assume, believed. But it is not to be supposed that the passage reflects beliefs of the poet himself. In one of his Dirges (frags. 129–131) there was another picturesque description of the Elysian life of those who are redeemed. 'For them below the sun shines in his might while here it is night-time, and amid meadows crimson with roses their suburbs are shaded by trees of frankincense and laden with golden fruit. Their pleasures are horses and gymnastics or draughts or music, and among them blooms the flower of perfect happiness. And a fragrance pervades the lovely country, as they ever mix all kinds of incense with far-shining fire on the altars of the gods.' It has been conjectured that this dirge lamented an Athenian who was an initiate in the Eleusinian mysteries[1].

[1] U. v. Wilamowitz-Möllendorff has named the Alcmaeonid Hippocrates, father of the Megacles for whose victory in 486 at Delphi Pindar composed *Pyth.* VII.

From Acragas, Pindar went to Syracuse on Hiero's invitation. Another poet, Bacchylides, had been engaged to make the hymn in honour of the victory; but Pindar composed an extraordinary ode, which was not performed by a chorus, but was sung by the poet himself to the lyre in a hall of the tyrant's palace (*Olymp.* 1). Perhaps this year 476 B.C. may be said to mark the time at which his genius reached its fullness and the undisputed recognition of its greatness. He could now confidently speak of himself as shining in the front rank in the art of poetry among the Hellenes in all lands (πρόφαντον σοφίᾳ καθ᾽ Ἕλλανας ἐόντα παντᾷ). This first Olympian ode which begins with the familiar words ἄριστον μὲν ὕδωρ, 'water is best,' is one of his most characteristic poems, and a comparison with the ode of Bacchylides (Ode v) which was inspired by the same motive brings out the originality and inventiveness of Pindar's genius.

During the years after Pindar's visit to Sicily, Hiero, till his death in 467 B.C., was suffering from a painful malady, and Pindar indited to him a poetical epistle of sympathy and consolation (preserved as *Pythian* III), a simple and graceful example of the poet's imaginative art. He also celebrated a victory won by the king's chariot at Delphi in an ode (*Pythian* I) which is distinguished by a wonderful description of Mount Etna in eruption.

Pindar must have made large sums through the generosity of his rich patrons in Sicily and he returned to Thebes a rich man. But he was not miserly, and he devoted a considerable part of his wealth to building temples and setting up statues at Thebes. We have little information as to the scale on which cities or individuals rewarded poets for the songs they composed for festivals. Pindar, like Simonides, wrote dithyrambs for the Athenian Dionysia. In one of these (474 B.C.) he lauded the noble part played by Athens in the Persian wars. At Artemisium 'the sons of the Athenians laid a bright base of liberty' (ἐβάλλοντο φαεννὰν κρηπῖδ᾽ ἐλευθερίας) and the Athenians gave him 10,000 drachmae (£400) and made him their proxenus at Thebes. In this poem occurred the famous verses which Athens always cherished:

αἵ τε λιπαραὶ καὶ ἰοστέφανοι καὶ ἀοίδιμοι
Ἑλλάδος ἔρεισμα, κλειναὶ Ἀθᾶναι, δαιμόνιον πτολίεθρον.

'Renowned Athens, rich, violet-crowned, and songworthy, bulwark of Hellas, god-protected city.' Such praise was not likely to be agreeable to his Theban fellow-citizens, who could not rise to his ardent Panhellenism.

Pindar afterwards enjoyed the patronage of another wealthy ruler, Arcesilas IV, king of Cyrene, whose horses won the chariot-race at Delphi in 462 B.C. The official epinician ode (*Pythian* v) which the king charged him to compose opens with the significant words ὁ πλοῦτος εὐρυσθενής, 'the power of wealth is wide.' But just as the official ode for Theron's Olympian victory was outdone by the encomium which was an afterthought (see above, p. 511), so the official ode for Arcesilas was surpassed in amplitude and splendour by the song which Pindar subsequently despatched to be sung at a banquet in the king's palace. This ode (*Pythian* iv) which is the longest and most elaborate of all his epinicians had a special purpose. Damophilus, a noble of Cyrene, an accomplished harp-player, and a friend of Pindar, had been implicated in some rebellious movement against the king, and was living in exile at Thebes. The aim of this magnificent ode, which tells the story of the Argonauts, was to procure for Damophilus forgiveness and permission to return to his home. It closes with a tactful prayer for pardon.

The latest ode we have of Pindar was for the victory of an Aeginetan wrestler won at Delphi in 446 B.C. (*Pyth*. VIII). Tradition says that he died at the age of 80 (442 B.C.) at Argos, and that his friend Theoxenus of Tenedos was with him at the end, the Theoxenus of whose beauty as a boy he had once written an amorous poem (fr. 123). 'He who looks upon the beams that flash from the eyes of Theoxenus and does not surge with longing has a black heart forged of adamant or steel in a cold flame.'

Pindar had lived into an age with the spirit and ideas of which he was out of touch and out of sympathy. Simonides would easily have found himself at home in Periclean Athens; Pindar could never have been at ease there. He had not a curious or speculative mind. Like all Greek artists he looked facts in the face, he did not seek to minimize evils, death, old age, disease, care, disappointment, but such facts did not make his general outlook gloomy. He believed that a life thoroughly worth living could be lived on earth, through wealth, fame, and song, and it is on these things, constituent of a life of pleasure (τερπνὸς αἰών), that his thoughts and his poetry most dwelled. He was a simple believer in orthodox piety; and in the reflections on the vicissitudes of human existence, which the conventions of his odes required, there is nothing that goes beyond the ideas of earlier poets, though their gnomic wisdom may be strikingly reset. The attitude to life, expressed in his poetry, is on the whole cheerful acquiescence. He would not have sympathized with, as he could

not have created, the great rebel Prometheus imagined so sympa-
thetically by his coeval Aeschylus. The pitiless lapse of a fine
period of Hellenic development (a period which he expressed and
idealized with sincerity and amazing skill) had given the counter-
sign to a new age before his death. From the very nature of his
themes he could not be a 'universal' poet as Homer and
Sophocles were. His epinician odes were carefully built and the
parts connected by an intellectual argument; he thought of himself as an architect, comparing his poems to stately halls, and he
made a particular feature of imposing façades. 'Having set
golden pillars beneath the fair portals of our chamber, we will
build a sightly hall, and we must begin by making a far-shining
front.' In these fronts, he would usually place some resonant
word or arresting phrase.

These Odes conform to a pattern which had become conventional and had perhaps been fixed by Simonides (we shall find it
also in Bacchylides); that is, they contain three themes or elements,
praises of the victor, a myth, and sententious reflexions. In his
treatment of all these, Pindar's Muse gives the impression of
impatience. He disdains the leisurely pace at which other lyric
poets told their stories. It may be that his method in this respect
was partly due to a conscious reaction against the prolixity and
diffuseness which seem to have been characteristic of Stesichorus[1].
He picks out of the legends and emphasizes what is to his purpose;
his story of Jason and the Argonauts (in *Pythian* IV) is a brilliant
masterpiece of compression. The charm of his 'myths' depends
on the power he possessed of conceiving vivid pictures, such as
the birth of Iamus (in *Ol.* VI), or the throttling of the two snakes
by the infant Heracles (*Nem.* I), and conveying them in a few
words. No one who has read the First Olympian can forget the
picture of Pelops going 'near to the grey sea, alone in the dark'
and calling on his old lover Poseidon to aid him to win Hippo-
dameia. Pindar thought in metaphors and they are always vivid.
He makes us see, for instance, the city of the Epeans 'sinking
down into a ditch of ruin' beneath the force of fire and sword
(*Ol.* x, 36).

The skill with which he could ennoble subjects which other
singers might easily have left somewhat vulgar is illustrated by
the ode which he wrote (frag. 122) when Xenophon of Corinth,
having won an Olympic victory, bestowed, in fulfilment of a vow,
a hundred courtesans on the temple of Aphrodite in his native
city.

---

[1] *Redundat atque effunditur*, Quintilian x, 1, 62.

Girls that are hostesses of many! handmaids of Persuasion in rich Corinth! who burn yellow tears of fresh frankincense and in your minds often fly up to Aphrodite, heavenly mother of Loves, she granted to you, O children, to gather on lovely couches the fruit of the soft bloom of your youth without blame or reproach. Necessity makes all things fair.... But I wonder what the lords of Isthmus will say of me for inventing such a beginning of a honey-sweet glee-song to be married to much-married women.... O queen of Cyprus, hither into thy grove to graze, has Xenophon, gladdened by his vows fulfilled, brought a herd of a hundred girls.

The last of the nine lyric poets[1] was BACCHYLIDES of Ceos, son of the sister of Simonides. Till 1897, he was a very subordinate figure in our view of Greek literature, though his poetical gift was shown in a few vivid and memorable verses on the effect of wine in making the drinker happy by stimulating his imagination.

When cups speed round, and their sweet constraint warms the heart, and the hope of the Cyprian goddess mingling with the gifts of Dionysus thrills it; then a man's thoughts soar to great heights, strong citadels fall before him in an instant, he dreams that he shall be monarch of the world, his palace halls are gleaming with gold and ivory, and cornships are bringing him vast wealth from Egypt over the shining seas. With such feelings is a drinker stirred[2].

That is a classical expression of this common human experience.

But the fortunate recovery of large fragments of his works from Egypt has elevated him to a position of considerable importance for us. By the ancients he seems to have been estimated as a good singer of the second class who, just because he was not a poet of genius, avoided artistic faults which may be alleged against Simonides or Pindar. He was born towards the end of the sixth century (perhaps between the limits 512 and 505 B.C.). We have already seen him at the court of Hiero, for whose epinician victories he composed three odes, which we have virtually complete. Some time after 452 B.C. he was banished from Ceos and is believed to have lived for the rest of his life in the Peloponnese.

[1] In the age of Simonides and Pindar there were a number of minor poets, like Lasus of Hermione, a teacher of Pindar; Telesilla of Argos; Myrtis of Anthedon; Corinna of Tanagra. All perhaps stood near the gates of Fame, but their works were not preserved and collected, with the exception of Corinna's. Short pieces from two of her poems have been recovered from Egypt. She composed in the Boeotian dialect, and her themes were taken from local Boeotian legends.

[2] Frag. 27. A song of Pindar, addressed to Thrasybulus of Acragas (frag. 124), has some verses on the same subject, the voyage of the intoxicated imagination to a deceptive shore (ψευδῆ πρὸς ἀκτάν) on a sea of golden wealth.

The epinician Odes of Bacchylides resemble in general plan those of Pindar, but the treatment is different. There are the same three elements, the praises of the victor, a myth, and gnomic reflexions. Bacchylides is more diffuse and abundant in details than Pindar on the subject of the victory and often describes incidents of the event. He relates the myth in a leisurely way and with fullness, as if he enjoyed relating it for its own sake, whereas Pindar, as we saw, hastens, condenses, and concentrates on the points that tell. And, while Pindar introduces his gnomic wisdom in short sentences at different points of his composition and makes them serviceable for the purpose of transition, Bacchylides is more inclined to pack his reflexions together (cf. for instance *Odes*, i, xii, xiii). He was a master of easy and pleasing narrative in which he did not disdain simple and conventional ornament, and we can understand that his stories gave more pleasure to many than the sustained brilliance of Pindar, always impatient of anything that might sound commonplace, always conscious of his altitudes.

In the hymn which celebrated the long coveted and long de-layed triumph of Hiero in the chariot-race at Olympia (468 B.C.) he chose for his 'myth' a story not of the heroic age but of recent history, the fate of Croesus (see above, vol. iii, p. 524). The Lydian and the Syracusan kings resembled each other in two respects, in their wealth and splendour, and in their munificent gifts to Delphi. The story shows how Croesus was rewarded by Apollo, and it may have been invented in order to save the countenance of the god. The king and his family were already on the funeral pyre, when a violent shower of rain extinguished the flames (iii, 57 *sqq.*).

Nought that the gods take heed to do is beyond belief. Then Delos-born Apollo bore the old king with his shapely-footed daughters to the land of the Hyperboreans and gave him an abode there, for his piety, because he sent up to holy Pytho gifts greater than all men's gifts.

None of the poems of Bacchylides is more charming than the paean in which he tells the story of the voyage of Minos and Theseus from Attica to Crete with the tribute of boys and girls, culminating in the plunge of Theseus into the waves to visit the halls of the sea-gods to recover the ring which Minos had flung into the sea, and his return to the ship, unwet and with the wreath of his gracious step-mother Amphitrite on his hair.

Bacchylides speaks of himself modestly enough as the 'Cean nightingale,' or compares himself to a bee. He did not aspire to rival Pindar; he knew that he had not Pindar's eagle wings;

and there is no good reason to suppose that there was any bitter-
ness or jealousy between the two, though some ancient commentators on Pindar suggested it. On the contrary, Bacchylides has
in one or two places paid Pindar the compliment of echoing him
(a compliment which he also paid to Aeschylus[1]); and there is
one passage which is almost Pindaric in its phrasing.

I utter words which carry meaning to the wise. The depths of aether
suffer no defilement; ocean-water corrupts not; gold is gladness. To a man
it is not given, when he has seen old age pass, to bring back again the bloom
of manhood. Yet the light of a man's virtue wastes not with his body, but
Song keeps it alive.

We have seen what the early Greek poets did for the art of
poetry, in elaborating and regulating measures and in fixing genres.
Their works have another interest, for they indicate certain lines
on which the intellectual development of the Hellenes would
move. In this early literature there is revealed very clearly a
fundamental characteristic of the Greek mind which always distinguished both their art and their views of conduct. Perhaps
this may best be described as a sense of measure. 'Measure is
best' ($\mu\acute{\epsilon}\tau\rho\text{o}\nu$ $\ddot{\alpha}\rho\iota\sigma\tau\text{o}\nu$) is a saying ascribed to one of the Seven
Wise Men. It appears in their art as restraint in expression and
distaste for hyperbole; in their ideal of conduct, as moderation,
the moderation which was enjoined by the two maxims consecrated by Delphi 'Know thyself' and 'Avoid excess.' The passion
for order, the value set on classification, the love of clarity, and
horror of the vague, all these leading characteristics of Greek
thought can be related to the sense of measure. We find them
in the early poets and we find there too speculations already
pointing to doctrines which in later times the great authoritative
masters of thought would formulate precisely and impress upon
the world. Aristotle's theory that every virtue is a mean between
two vices was stated in a general way, without being justified in
detail, by Theognis, who wrote (v. 325) 'Avoid excess; the mean
course is best; and thus, Cyrnus, you will possess virtue, a hard
thing to get.' This view implies that however much the good
man and the bad may be contrasted, yet the difference between
them or between their actions is not regarded as a radical difference of kind, but as depending on the measure in which they do
things of the same kind. That was a view which could logically
lead to the theory of Socrates that virtue is knowledge. It excluded the conception which we mean by 'sin.'

[1] See Jebb, Introd. to edition of *Bacchylides*, p. 67.

The idea that justice is the chief of the virtues and that a just man, whatever his other qualities may be, must be pronounced a virtuous man appears in Theognis. 'All virtue' he observes 'is, in a word, contained in justice' (ἐν δὲ δικαιοσύνῃ συλλήβδην πᾶσ' ἀρετή 'στι, v. 147). This points from afar to the discussion of justice in the *Republic* of Plato.

Division and apportionment, which are implied in the notion of measure, underlie the general Greek conception of the circumstances of life and the relation of the human and the divine. A man's lot or destiny is his portion, and the birth-goddess Eileithyia has her seat beside the Moirai who regulate the conditions and events of his life. Moirai is conventionally rendered by Fates. That is a bad translation. *Fata* was the nearest equivalent the Romans had. But if you change the word, you change the idea. The Moirai were the Apportioners or Allotters. A principal feature in the order over which the Moirai presided was the sharp delimitation between the divine and human, within the common physical world to which they both belonged. 'One is the race of men, and one the race of the gods.' They are both sprung from one mother, the Earth, but their portions and powers are utterly different; for men there is no security, while the gods have 'the brazen heaven a sure seat for ever.'[1] The gods do not know the meaning of 'alas!'[2] Between these two provinces there is a frontier which man shall attempt to cross at his peril. The supreme folly of the presumptuous is to attempt to usurp privileges or powers that are reserved for the gods. 'Let no man fly to Olympus nor seek to wed Aphrodite.' This is the principle which underlies the Greek idea of the jealousy of the gods towards a mortal who has attained to super-eminent fortune. Felicity does not belong to the portion of men, and when *any* man exceptionally seems to have realized it, the gods feel resentment and ruin or abase him. The Greek sought to envisage the vicissitudes of life as participant in a general necessary Order, and they managed this by the conception of Moira, which is sharply distinct from that of blind Fate, although both conceptions have necessity in common.

It is not surprising that a race which possessed this instinctive appreciation of measure and proportion should have produced the original builders of a new world in which everything is exact and precise, in which there is no part not governed by scrupulous logic, and in which chance has no rôle or place, the world of pure mathematics.

[1] Pindar, *Nem.* vi, 1 *sqq.*   [2] See Aeschylus, *Prometheus*, 980.

VI. THE BEGINNINGS OF PROSE LITERATURE

In the latter half of the sixth century, advanced Greek minds in Ionia were beginning to pass from the age of theology and mythology into an age of philosophy and inquiry ('history,' ἱστορίη). Reason is beginning to question authority; there are signs of the dawn of rationalism; new knowledge is coming from the east and Egypt; the Greek intellect is discovering the field of mathematics; and Greek ideas of geography are being enlarged both eastward and westward.

An outward and formal sign of these new movements of thought was the rise of prose literature. Here as in the case of epic poetry, Ionia is the land of origin. The earliest prose book of which we definitely know was concerned with speculations about the cosmos and its origins, written about 550 B.C. by Anaximander of Miletus (see below, pp. 539 *sqq.*). It may have been no more than a text to explain the map which he had constructed and perhaps had no general circulation. The most influential of the Ionian prose writers was HECATAEUS of Miletus, the statesman and traveller whose historical *Inquiries* towards the end of the sixth century founded a whole school or series of writers who for nearly a century to come would devote themselves to sifting and co-ordinating the traditions contained in the old poets, particularly Hesiod and the Cyclics, about the early Greeks, reconciling discrepancies, working out genealogies, collecting local traditions and comparing or correlating them with the records contained in the poets, and seeking to establish a consistent and chronologically ordered account of the ancient history of Greece. The list of these Antiquarian historians, as we may call them (the Greeks called them λογοποιοί), is a long one, from Hecataeus to Hellanicus of Lesbos[1]. Their works had little literary interest, they were purely antiquarian.

One result of the Colonial movement had been to make communications among the cities of the Hellenic world more constant and travelling more frequent, and consequently commerce in ideas more rapid. In the sixth century, in most Greek cities from Ionia to South Italy and Sicily, there was much the same level

---

[1] It was supposed by some that the oldest of these writers was Cadmus of Miletus, to whom a book on the origins of Ionia was attributed and that he wrote before Hecataeus; but he is a very shadowy figure. Some of these logographers touched on the history of their own time, *e.g.* Dionysius of Miletus contemporary of the Persian Wars, and Hellanicus contemporary of Herodotus and Thucydides.

of education and literary culture. We should therefore expect to find that the example of writing in prose travelled very quickly from Ionia throughout Hellas—more quickly than rhapsody had spread three or four centuries before. It is unnecessary to enumerate by name the Antiquarians, of whose works many short fragments are preserved, but it is instructive to note their homes (*e.g.* Rhegium, Athens, Argos, Lampsacus, Chalcedon, Lydia). Writing prose works of this kind was a Panhellenic practice by the middle of the fifth century.

Those early prose writers thought only of the matter, and did not seek to please the ear. Their style was simple, concise and artless, without any decoration; sentences of the simplest form were strung together like a chain, with few subordinate clauses. And they all wrote in just the same style. With the exception of Heracleitus, it could not be said of any of them ' *Le style, c'est l'homme.*' One of the greatest works in Greek literature would be written in this Ionian prose in the second half of the fifth century; but Herodotus has introduced a certain elaboration and picturesqueness which were absent in the writings of his predecessors. The books of the Antiquarians were still extant in the time of Augustus, and literary critics found a considerable charm in their bald colourless archaic prose.

The *Geography* (Περιήγησις) of Hecataeus laid the foundation of Greek geographical science. It was a very methodical survey of the known world, divided into two sections, *Europe*, and *Asia* (which included Africa), and it contained an account of the author's visit to Egypt. We may divine that it was to the stimulus of this book that Herodotus owed his love of travelling and his interest in strange lands. Not a few fragments remain both of this work and of the *Inquiries*, but they are very short. The most interesting of them is the opening sentence of the *Inquiries*, with its avowal of general scepticism about Greek traditions. 'This is the story of Hecataeus of Miletus. What I write here is what I consider true; for the tales of the Greeks appear to me to be many and ridiculous.' But we cannot judge how far he pushed this admirable scepticism when it came to details. His contemporary, the brilliant philosopher Heracleitus of Ephesus, named Hecataeus along with Hesiod and other men of his own age, Xenophanes and Pythagoras, as examples of the truth of his contention that much learning does not teach good sense (πολυμαθίη νόον ἔχειν οὐ διδάσκει). We do not know what Hecataeus thought of Heracleitus.

Nearly all the early books in prose of which we have any

definite knowledge were antiquarian, or geographical, or philosophical. One philological work is recorded, by Theagenes of
Rhegium, on the language of Homer. It is possible however that
others existed of a more popular kind. This is suggested by the
literary problem of Aesop's fables.

The part which Ionia played in the origination of Greek science
and inquiry was conditioned by its geographical position and the
opportunities Ionian Greeks had for intercourse with orientals
and Egyptians. The visit of Hecataeus to Egypt was probably
the decisive intellectual experience of his life. Nothing is more
difficult to find or trace than the obscure channels through which
knowledge and ideas travel from one country to another; but it is
possible that the professional story-teller Aesop, a slave of Phrygian
birth, who used to tell his beast-fables in Samos, in the age of
Croesus, owed his material to oriental sources. Some of his fables
are found in the book called the *Sayings of the wise Ahikar*[1], of
which there are versions in several oriental languages. It used to be
thought that the author of this work derived them from a western
source, as no manuscripts had been found older than the second
century B.C.; but the discovery of an Aramaic copy (at Elephantine
in Egypt)[2] dating from the fifth century B.C. has shown that this
cannot be the true account of the relationship. It is uncertain
how the fables, as told by Aesop, were collected and when they
were first written down; probably early in the fifth century, for
they were well known at Athens before its end[3]. There seems to
have been a Life of Aesop in the time of Herodotus, and it has
been suggested that it may have formed a setting for his fables,
just as the *Sayings of Ahikar* are framed by the sage's life. From
what we know about Aesop, which is congruous with the fact
that the influence of Babylonian science is at much the same
time making itself felt, the probability arises that by the sixth
century Asiatic Greeks had become usefully aware of the existence
of foreign literatures and were learning something about them.
This may supply an answer to a question which may fairly
be asked. To write in prose has seemed so natural and obvious
a thing to do, both to the Greeks of later ages and to modern
enquirers, that to historians of literature the origin of Greek prose

[1] Ahikar is, in the story, the chief minister of Sennacherib, but it is
unknown whether he really existed.

[2] See A. Cowley, *Aramaic Papyri* (1923), pp. 204 *sqq.*

[3] Demetrius of Phalerum made a collection of 100 Aesopic fables Our
knowledge of the fables comes from the versified renderings of Babrius and
Phaedrus.

has never appeared puzzling. Yet when we consider that hitherto a book had meant for a Greek a composition in metre, we may reasonably ask how it was that towards the middle of the sixth century some Ionian writer was moved to discard the usual metrical form. May it not be surmised that the idea came to him from the example of other literatures, and that it is more than a coincidence that Greek literary prose began much about the time at which the Ionians were becoming acquainted, at least indirectly, with literary works of the Orient?

CHAPTER XV

MYSTERY RELIGIONS AND
PRE-SOCRATIC PHILOSOPHY

I. INTRODUCTION

A HISTORY which seeks to trace the movement of the Greek mind, not only through its outward expression in political action, but through the inward activity of the reflective consciousness, is justified in including within the limits of one chapter two subjects usually kept apart—the Eleusinian and Orphic mysteries and the earliest systems of philosophy. The fragmentary records of the sixth century B.C. show that the Greek spirit was advancing along two apparently diverging lines and attaining to a fresh apprehension of the universe and of human life. In the one direction we find, associated with the legendary figure of Orpheus, what is universally recognized as a religious revival—a word well chosen to describe that reanimation of older forms of thought which seems to occur by a refluence and withdrawal of energy from later channels that have been silted up and dried. In the other we witness the birth of science, the application to the world of Nature of a rational habit of thought, seeking to disentangle a strand of plain and literal truth from the tissue of mythical fantasy. Whatever scope this logical, matter-of-fact, habit may previously have found in the operations of practical life, it seems here and now, for the first time in the history of mankind, to advance an unlimited claim upon the field of speculation, ignoring with astonishing boldness the prescriptive sanctities of religious representation. At first sight, and in the view of some historians, this looks like a phenomenon with no roots in the past, the portentous apparition of a full-grown and motherless Athena. But a closer study shows that the relation of philosophy or science to mythology is not one of purely negative exclusion: it may even appear that here too the mind draws back, the better to make its forward leap, and that the rise of science is in a sense, like Orphism, a revival. A fuller knowledge of social psychology may some day bring into clearer light the deeper springs of both movements; all that can be attempted here is to explain why both should be treated together.

While there must always be a relation of some kind between the religion and the philosophy of any race and time, there is, in the case of sixth-century Greece, a specially intimate connection between the mystery religions and one of the two main currents of philosophical speculation. That there were two currents, separate in origin and divergent in tendency, was recognized by ancient historians of thought from Aristotle onwards. They were known as the Ionian philosophy and the Italian, because the former, founded by Thales, had its centre at Ionian Miletus, while the latter was established by Pythagoras in the western colonies of southern Italy and Sicily. This western region was also the stronghold of Orphism, and it is generally recognized that the Pythagorean philosophy was closely akin to this form of mystical religion, just as the school of Pythagoras was a religious brotherhood similar in type to the mystical cult-society.

At the opposite extremity of the Greek world, the Milesian school shows a sharp contrast of tendency and temper: it is rationalist and sceptical, and it contains the germ of that materialism which came to its maturity in the atomism of Democritus and the hedonism of Epicurus. In this tradition the conscious attitude of the philosopher towards religion or mythology is, if not hostile, at least critical and detached. The vital nerve of religion, known to later antiquity as *gnōsis* and to the Christian world as faith, has snapped. On the other hand, even the most tough-minded rationalist is certainly deluded if he imagines that the severance of this link implies that he has torn up every root of racial tradition from the deeper levels of his mind. A system of philosophy is not an artificial fabric; it is a living growth. This is ultimately true even of the latest systems called eclectic; much more is it true of the great original systems here to be reviewed.

It will accordingly appear that, in spite of the difference of conscious attitude, the Ionian tradition, as well as the Italian, is continuous with those earlier forms of Greek thought that we call mythical. In order to make this plain, it will be convenient to begin with the mystery religions, in which the myth maintained itself, in conjunction with ritual, throughout antiquity.

II. THE NATURE OF A 'MYSTERY'

The essential significance of a 'mystery' is not exhausted by the superficial meaning of the word *mysterion*, which to the Greek ear distinguished from the ordinary public worship conducted on behalf of the state, or of some subordinate social unit, a class of

rites which were secret, in the sense that the privilege of witnessing them and of receiving the consequent benefits was reserved to those who had undergone a preliminary purification.

This definition is merely formal; the circumstance of secrecy
tells us nothing of the content of the rites. There is another and
deeper sense of the word in which, for example, the Christian
ceremonies of baptism, marriage, and communion, though conducted in public, may rightly be called mysteries. The central
idea common to these ceremonies and to the Eleusinian and
Orphic mysteries is the idea of a renewal of life. Such a rite is
not primarily a 'service' directed externally towards a divinity;
though it has that aspect, it has also an inherent efficacy, an
inward 'grace,' which causes a change in the participant and, in
some cases, affects by sympathy even the life of external nature.
The general conception of a renewal of life includes entrance upon
a new phase of social existence, as in baptism, puberty-initiations,
or marriage; the annual renewal both of tribal life in the birth of
children and of the fertility of animals and plants on which we
depend for food; the refreshment of sacramental intercourse with
the powers that govern life; and finally the assurance of a new
and better life beyond the grave. Symbols appropriate to any
mystery are those of the new birth, of marriage, of death and
resurrection. The new birth is a return to the sources of life to
draw fresh energy therefrom; alternatively, this re-entrance into
the womb can be figured as marriage with the Earth Mother, or
again as a death to the old life, the condition of resurrection to
the new. The preliminary rite of 'purification' represents the
negative aspect—the preparation for contact with the divine by
the mystical washing away, at first of any 'impurity,' later of 'sin.'
Lustration in itself is not confined to mysteries, but it acquires
in connection with them the fuller significance of regeneration.

A second characteristic of many mysteries is the ritual form in
which the assurance of renewed life is conveyed, namely, a symbolic representation of the similar experience of a divine being.
The mystic drama or passion play evolves naturally out of the
earlier procedure of sympathetic magic, whereby an effect which
it is desired to produce, either upon some person or upon the
course of life in external nature, is represented mimetically. If
the implied belief were formulated, it would appear as a quasi-
scientific principle that *like acts upon, or produces, like*, or that
there exists between like things or actions a mysterious bond of
sympathy, easily conceived as a *continuum* which may equally well
be called 'material' or 'spiritual.' From such performances, in-

volving the impersonation of the beings, real or imaginary, whose action is to be affected, arises the passion play. In this phase the old outward efficacy of the magical rite upon the course of nature or the divine beings who govern it, is perpetuated; but there is further added an inward psychological effect upon those participants who are not themselves performers, but have sunk into the contemplative attitude of the spectator. As the Homeric *Hymn to Demeter* says: 'Blessed is the man who has *seen* these things.' The blessing so conveyed may for a long while be conceived only as some special favour assured to the initiate in the world of the dead by the mere fact that he has seen the rites; but at least a door is opened to the belief that the grace might partly consist in a reformation of the moral life.

The vision of the 'sacred things,' whether symbolic emblems or dramatic representations, is accompanied by a peculiar emotional state, conceived as 'participation,' communion, or even identification with the divine. These names denote an enhanced form of the primitive consciousness of 'sympathy' implied in mimetic magic; when raised to the level of an idea, the implicit thought emerges as the pantheistic doctrine of the continuity of all life. Identification with the divine is the guarantee that the experience of the initiate shall be similar to the god's. The sense of union may be induced by orgiastic means—by impersonating the god, who is believed to take 'possession' of his group or *thiasos*; by assimilating his virtue through the sacramental eating of his flesh or drinking of his blood; or by passionate contemplation of the spectacle of his sufferings and triumph. The possibility of such identification is the distinguishing mark of a mystery god. Like other gods, he owes those properties which constitute his 'divinity' to an act of projection, not from any individual mind, but from the collective mind of the group that is united in his worship. But he differs from that other class of gods who are so completely projected that they attain the independence, exclusiveness, and impenetrability which belong to an *individual*. The projection of the mystery god is arrested at an earlier stage: he is like a bird still tied by a string to the hand from which it flew. Whatever the causal explanation may be, the secret of his peculiar power lies in the fact that he remains, not merely of like passions with the worshipper—that is true of the individualized Olympian—but, unlike the Olympian, subject to change and death. The god who is immortal in the sense that he can never die has broken the bond of sympathy with all actual life in man and nature. Only the god who is immortal in the sense that he dies and yet rises again can remain continuous with the life that moves on the wheel of time and change, and grant that assurance of renewed life which answers to the deepest hope of mankind.

The strength of a mystery cult is, in great measure, due to the symbolic character of its rites. In the ordinary public services of family or state religion the ritual bears its meaning on its face; the intention is expressed and exhausted in the action and the accompanying words. A mystic rite, on the other hand, is felt to contain an efficacy beyond the visible action and a significance that can be indicated but not explicitly uttered. All this would be hidden from an uninstructed witness, even were he admitted; and among the initiates themselves there are commonly degrees of illumination. The last secrets may be reserved to the highest order, or closed to all but the arch-priest or hierophant. Hence the enduring hold that mystery religions have maintained upon the human mind. The profane cult is doomed to extinction so soon as the beliefs it openly and fully expresses begin to be no longer credible. There is no reserve of profounder meaning that can be drawn upon to renew the sense of spiritual satisfaction. But the content of a mystic rite is never fully disclosed and therefore never exhausted. If the ceremonial begins to seem crude, it is, after all, only a symbol: it is possible to read into it, and to believe that it has always really symbolized, the deepest thoughts and largest hopes of which the worshipper at any time is capable. A consequence is that the rites and formulas may remain substantially unchanged for an indefinite time. Thus it has not been proved that any important change was made in the mysteries of Eleusis during the thousand years which ended in the destruction of the sanctuary by Alaric the Goth.

Another consequence is that it is not possible to construct any history of a development of Eleusinian doctrine, or indeed to make out that, once the mysteries were fully established, any development occurred. Comparison with the theology of the Christian Church would be totally misleading. The Eleusinian cult was on a different footing from an established church. In the first place it was independent of social structure. True, there is reason to believe that the mysteries were at first reserved to natives of Eleusis and even to the members of the sacred families which continued to fill the highest offices; but the *Hymn to Demeter* seems to imply that, at least by the end of the seventh century, strangers were admitted. This independence of social structure is a feature common to all the mystery religions: they were not, like the family and state cults, the birthright of any member of a certain social group. But among the mystery cults themselves there is a difference of still greater importance. Unlike the Orphics or the worshippers of Attis or of Mithras, the Eleusinian initiates were in no sense a secret society or fraternity. They had no continuous existence as a group, nothing in common except the experience of initiation, which did not lead to the maintenance of mutual relations at any other moment of their lives. Thus there was no congregation that could ever be assembled for a second time, and the only permanent nucleus was the sacred families who guarded the tradition of the rites. In such circumstances, whatever may have been the private thoughts, in any age, of the hierophant on the one side or of the initiate on the other, there could be no possibility of a progressive development of theological doctrine, and no consequent reaction upon the form of the ritual. The few formulas disclosed in the latest age by the Christian Fathers bear the stamp of high antiquity; and the nature of the rites was still such as to lay them open to charges of indecency, pointing to the persistence of the innocent sexual symbolism of a primitive age. Thus it is probable that the imperfect picture we can now construct of the Eleusinian cult is valid for any date within the historic period of paganism.

III. THE ELEUSINIAN MYSTERIES

The Great Mysteries at Eleusis belong to a group of festivals associated, not with harvest, but with the autumn season of ploughing and sowing, when the new corn is committed to the cold and dark womb of earth. This group is balanced, at the other end of winter, by the festivals of early spring, marking the re-birth of vegetation under the influence of returning warmth. One of these was the Little Mysteries, held at Agra just outside Athens. It was here that all candidates underwent the preliminary purification in the waters of the Ilissus. In the following Boedromion (September) they proceeded to the Great Mysteries, which constituted initiation proper. Most of the *mystae* went no further; but some, after at least one year's interval, presented themselves again at the Eleusinian festival to receive the revelation of the higher grade known as the *Epopteia*.

The proceedings at the autumn festival fell into two parts. The first part, which began on the 13th and ended on the 20th of Boedromion, centred round the sacred objects (*hiera*) which were taken from their chapel at Eleusis, concealed in baskets, and escorted by the ephebi to the Eleusinion at Athens. On the 14th

the candidates who had already been purified at the Little
Mysteries were assembled in the Painted Colonnade and addressed by the hierophant in a proclamation (*prorrhēsis*), which
warned away those who might not have access to the mysteries.
On the 16th they purified themselves and their sacrificial
pigs by bathing in the sea at Phalerum. The sacrifice probably
followed in the afternoon. The next two days (the 17th and 18th)
were occupied by the Epidauria, a festival which may have commemorated the introduction of the cult of Asclepius and not have
formed an integral part of the mysteries, though it seems to have
provided for late comers a second opportunity for sacrifice.
Finally, on the 19th a great procession, again escorted by the
ephebi and carrying the sacred things, set out for Eleusis, headed
by the image of Iacchus. The procession arrived after nightfall;
the sacred things were replaced in their chapel; and this part of
the festival terminated with the reception of Iacchus and with
dances and hymns at the well Callichorus.

The second part consisted of the mysteries proper, the secret
rites within the enclosure surrounding the Hall of Initiation. At
this point, where the interest culminates, our information naturally
fails. The ancients speak of three elements in the ceremonies:
the things enacted (*drōmena*), including the performance of one
or more liturgical dramas; the things shown (*deiknumena*), namely
the 'sacred things,' emblems and probably mysterious statues of
the divinities; and the things said (*legomena*) by the hierophant
and his assistants, which would include any words spoken by the
actors in the drama and explanations of the things seen and
enacted. All these elements were under the seal of inviolable
secrecy, though this applied, not to the benefits promised to the
initiates, but only to the ceremonial means by which they were
assured. Everyone knew that the mere fact of initiation was believed to enlist the favour of the deities of the underworld and
to secure for the participant a 'better lot' after death. It was
permissible to describe the habitation of the blest and the contrasted sufferings of the uninitiate; but even the most guarded
allusion to the actual rites was dangerous. Hence we are dependent upon a few denunciatory passages in the early Fathers of
the Church, who saw in the mystery cults of paganism the most
serious rivals to their own religion.

It appears that the *mystae* were subjected to a fast, which
assimilated them to the mourning Mother, who had fasted while
she sought the lost Persephone. Like her, they tasted food only
after nightfall, by drinking the *kykeon*, a mixture of meal and

water flavoured with pennyroyal, and eating sacred food, which may have consisted of cakes of emblematic form, taken from a basket. To what extent this meal was regarded as sacramental is unknown. At the least, it must have signified some bond of alliance with the goddess, some assurance of her grace. After this ceremony, the *mystae* were admitted to the revelations in the Hall of Initiation. On the strength of a fragment of Plutarch and some passages in Plato, it is believed by some that these included a journey through the underworld, whose terrors were represented, in darkness dimly lit by torches, by some simple scenic arrangements in the lower storey of the pillared Hall. Hence the initiates proceeded to the upper storey representing the abode of the blest, and were finally led to the shrine containing the sacred things. The doors of this shrine were thrown open, and the hierophant exhibited the contents in a strong light, the blaze of which escaped from a lantern in the roof. It is conjectured that the sacred things included ancient wooden statues of the two goddesses and of the other divinities of Eleusis.

We have the explicit statement of Bishop Hippolytus that the 'great, marvellous, and most perfect mystery' revealed in the second grade of initiation—the *epopteia*—was 'a reaped corn-stalk.' It is impossible to doubt that this symbol, with which the mysteries must have familiarized many of those Corinthians addressed by St Paul in his famous chapter, conveyed a promise of life after death. The corn-stalk probably represented a re-risen god or goddess, originally, perhaps, Persephone restored from the underworld.

It is plain that the renewal of life was expressed under the same symbolism in the passion-play which represented the Rape of Kore by Pluto, the wandering and mourning of the Mother, the joyful reunion of the two goddesses, and the mission of Triptolemus. Since these divine events were publicly described in the *Hymn to Demeter*, the secret drama must have included other scenes. References in Christian writers point to a sacred marriage of Zeus and Deo, impersonated by the hierophant and the priestess of Demeter. The pair retired into a dark chamber, and the symbolic marriage can hardly have remained unfruitful. If we accept the evidence of Hippolytus, it was followed by the announcement that 'Brimo, our Lady, has born a Holy Child, Brimos.' It may have been while the initiates were waiting before the chamber for this annunciation, that 'looking up to heaven they cried, "Rain!" and looking down to earth they cried, "Conceive!"' This simple formula illustrates the transparent nature of the ritual symbolism. Whatever may be the true derivation of the name Demeter, the ancients understood it to mean Earth-Mother. In the annual marriage of Heaven and Earth and the birth of the new corn they found the assurance of another and better life for themselves.

The renewal of life is inevitably conceived as birth, and birth implies a previous marriage. Natural conception is separated by nine months from the resulting birth—the interval observed in the Christian calendar between the Annunciation and Christmas. But where there is no continuously existing congregation, no church which can pass annually through an ordered sequence of interrelated festivals, the natural intervals tend to be obliterated, so that marriage and birth are brought within the limits of a single ceremony. At the Eleusinian festival in the sowing season, the virgin seed, the spirit of the new corn, passes into the darkness below the earth. The first association is with death, rather than life: the corn of wheat falls into the ground and dies. But it does not abide alone: this death, though attended by mourning, is also the condition of conception and rebirth; it is a marriage, albeit a marriage in the underworld with the Heavenly Father's dark and terrible counterpart. But the symbolism resists a too close compression. The figures of the Virgin and the Mother remain distinct, with the consequence that the birth of the holy child results from a duplicate marriage, the union of Zeus of the upper world and the Mother, Deo. By this device the cycle is rounded out to completeness. The birth, which should occur in Spring, is brought within the compass of the sowing festival[1].

This joyful conclusion must, however, have been felt as what it was—an anticipation: that which is sown in tears is not yet reaped in joy; the hope of rebirth is still overshadowed by the presence of death in the gathering darkness of the year's decline. The natural quality of this season, in contrast with the actual outburst of new life in Spring, is congenial to beliefs and hopes centred in the idea, not of a literal rebirth into this life, but of another life in the house of death.

It is clear that the concept of rebirth or *palingenesis* admits of more than one application and calls for some analysis. The fundamental frame of fact is the course of the agricultural year, wherein the life of vegetation, on which all other life depends, passes

---

[1] Another explanation of the duplication of the sacred marriage is that a marriage belonging to the Thracian cult of Dionysus, son of Zeus and Semele, has been superimposed on the indigenous marriage of Zeus and Demeter, whose offspring is Persephone.

through the seasonal round of birth, growth, maturity, decay, death, rebirth. The purpose of agricultural rites is to secure the preservation and renewal of this life, its safe passage through each critical phase. At that level of thought where the unity or continuity of all life is an unquestioned assumption, the same ritual may be conceived to promote the renewal of life in the human group. Just as the danger that the life of the corn should perish at harvest or at sowing and not return must be averted, so must the danger that human life should pass over to the world of dead ancestors and not be reborn. Thus Socrates in the *Phaedo* reasons in defence of *palingenesis*: 'If there were not this constant compensation in becoming (or birth, *genesis*), whereby things move round in a circle; if becoming took place only in one direction, in a straight line that never bent round or returned again to the opposite point, you perceive that in the end all things must pass into the same state and becoming must cease (p. 72 B).' At this stage the life of nature is conceived as a divine being which dies in the decline of every year to be reborn in Spring; its 'immortality' must consist, not in exemption from death, but in recurrent resurrection. Similarly for human life 'immortality' means a perpetual rebirth into this earthly life, not an escape from the wheel of becoming into a deathless eternity. It is reasonable to suppose that, in a primitive stage of Eleusinian belief, rebirth in this literal sense was assumed to be the destiny of all human souls. The promise to the initiate would then have meant no more than a 'better lot' in the underworld during the interval between death and reincarnation, just as the rites in their agricultural aspect secured the favour of the powers of earth for the seed sown in hope. The language of the Homeric hymn need not, in fact, mean more than this. On the other hand, reincarnation is not mentioned; and thus an opening is left, wide enough to admit the largest claims that human nature has ever made to a share in divine felicity.

This unrestricted freedom of interpretation accounts for the unfailing popularity of the mysteries. The initiate was offered a blank draft upon the unknown future, which he might complete in the terms of any belief that he brought with him, with the assurance that it would be honoured. Nothing, moreover, was demanded of him in return, save that he should submit to purification and witness the rites. So far as we know, it was at no time enjoined that, in a moral sense, he should thenceforth walk in newness of life. It cannot, indeed, be doubted that a ceremonial so impressive must often have produced a more or less enduring

moral effect; but the nature of that effect was left to the predis-
position of the initiate; it was not prescribed by the religion itself.
This absence of any positive doctrine representing future happiness as depending upon conduct may be regarded as a defect;
but it may well have operated as an attraction and helped to
perpetuate the cult. It had at least the advantage of not restricting
the religion to any code of morals that might embody the ideals
of one age and fail to satisfy the next.

IV. ORPHISM

In many respects the form of mystical belief associated with
the name of Orpheus stands in clear contrast with the religion of
Eleusis, and is more closely allied with Pythagoreanism. The
initiates of the Eleusinian goddesses were dispersed and reab-
sorbed in their several civic communities. The Orphic movement,
on the other hand, gave rise to cult societies which traversed the
boundaries of existing social groups and were permanently united
by peculiar beliefs and a peculiar manner of life, setting them
apart from their kinsmen and fellow-citizens. There was, indeed,
no hierarchy or ecclesiastical organization to connect one such
society with another; they were not even linked, like the earliest
Christian churches, by the ubiquitous energy of a great missionary.
We do not know how the movement spread, nor from what
quarter it came. Observers like Herodotus saw in the common
features of Orphic ritual and the mysteries of Osiris the evidence
of Egyptian origin. The name Zagreus, the specially Orphic title
of Dionysus or the young Zeus, has been derived from Mount
Zagros, between Assyria and Media. The undoubted affinities
with Anatolian, and especially Thraco-Phrygian, ritual and belief
may perhaps be connected with a general unsettlement of the
East occasioned by the westward advance of the Persian power.
In the same way later the advance of Alexander in the opposite
direction had the effect of setting free from their local attachments
many hitherto scattered religious elements, to gravitate together
into the theocrasia of the Alexandrine age. In the sixth century,
Orphism was already established at Croton in South Italy, and
it is believed to have come from that quarter to Attica in the time
of the Peisistratidae, at whose court an Orpheus of Croton was
associated in tradition with the more famous Onomacritus.

Orphism was a free religion. Not only was it, like the Eleusinian mysteries, independent of the social structure of the civic
community, but, unlike those mysteries, it was not localized at

any sanctuary. In consequence of this detachment, it could spread wherever the theological literature which it produced in considerable volume found willing readers; and further its tradition remained fluid and susceptible of new influences from oriental religions and from the schools of philosophy. As in the case of other universal religions, the interval between its highest and lowest manifestations covered the whole range of spiritual life. At the worst, it was degraded to a sordid traffic in redemption by travelling charlatans, who professed magical power over the gods, and sold absolution for a modest fee. At the best, its doctrines interpenetrate the whole mystical tradition of Greek philosophy, Pythagoreanism, Platonism, Stoicism, Neoplatonism, and Christianity. At every stage the influence may have been reciprocal, so that the content of Orphic belief was perpetually modified. No history of this development can now be traced. All that can be attempted is an outline based on documents of the fifth and fourth centuries.

From the standpoint of history, the figure of Orpheus is lost in complete obscurity. He is variously regarded by modern students as a god or as a man, as the fox-totem of a Thracian tribe, as a missionary martyred by the savage votaries of Dionysus, or as the personified ideal of his own followers. Whatever the relation he bears to temporal fact, it is at least clear that, in content, the Muse's enchanting son was more akin to Apollo than to Dionysus. His music was of the lyre; it did not excite to orgiastic excess, but tamed the beasts themselves to mildness. He also shared with Apollo the attributes of the seer and of the healer. On the other hand, the rites he was believed to have revealed included elements that are recognizably but little removed from the totem feasts of the savage. In other words, Orphism stands for a religious revival, one of those reformations which come, not by the rational contrivance of a political or ecclesiastical hierarchy, but by a spontaneous uprush from the perennial sources of religious feeling in the unconscious mind of a people. In such a case, when the official forms of religion have ceased to satisfy spiritual needs, the wind of the spirit may trouble to their depths the waters that had sunk to stillness. Out of these depths arise once more primeval images of thought and modes of feeling, which the rational mind had learnt to despise, as the grotesque and incredible play of mythical fantasy. Abandoned forms of ritual symbolism are resuscitated and invested with what presents itself as newly revealed significance. In this way the religious consciousness, bursting its too narrow confines, seems at once to soar upward and to plunge downward; and the onlooker is puzzled, and perhaps repelled, by the strange spectacle of a cult both more spiritual and less civilized than any within the range of established observance.

Social psychology may perhaps discover a connection between the rise of these cult-societies or non-social religious groups and the breaking up, in the sixth century, of the old social units based on the theory or fact of blood relationship. The social bond, the sense of solidarity (*philia*), had once extended to the limits of the group of blood-kin; beyond were 'strangers,' if not enemies. There had also been a co-extensive religious bond in the common worship of some peculiar set of divinities, heroes, or ancestors. The system was naturally polytheistic. Now the rise of new religious groups, transcending the limits and ignoring the ties of kinship, is attended by consequences of great importance. On the social side, at least the seed is sown of the doctrine that all men are brothers; the sense of solidarity, set free from its old limits, can spread to include all mankind, and even beyond that to embrace all living things. *Philia* ceases to mean kinship, and begins to mean love. This change well illustrates the double movement of a religious revival: the advance to a higher conception of universal kinship is achieved by a renewal of the ancient sense of continuity in all life. At the same time the social basis of polytheism is undermined. Either pantheism must take its place, or at least the belief—essentially true—that the mystery gods worshipped by different groups, whether called Dionysus or Adonis or Attis, are really the same god—one form with many names. Thus the unity of all life and the unity of God become cardinal doctrines of mystic faith.

On the other hand, there is a no less significant change in the psychology of the individual. The old solidarity of the blood group had entailed that diffusion of responsibility for the actions of any one member among all the other members which still survives in the vendetta. When collective responsibility goes, individual responsibility is left. The guilt of any action must now attach personally to its author. It cannot be expiated by another, or by the blood group as a whole. The punishment must fall upon the individual, if not in this life then in the next, or perhaps in a series of lives in this world. When the Pythagoreans reduced justice to the *lex talionis*, the effect was that it applied to the guilty person only, not to his family. The doctrine of transmigration completes the scheme of justice for the individual soul. The mere idea of reincarnation was nothing novel; on the contrary it was of immemorial antiquity. What is new in transmigration is the moral view that reincarnation expiates some original sin and that the individual soul persists, bearing its load of inalienable responsibility through a round of lives, till, purified by suffering, it escapes for ever.

Thus we arrive at certain axioms of faith which are characteristic of many forms of mystical religion in every age and country. God becomes one in the inclusive sense—in the language of personification the Lord, not of this clan or city, but of all mankind and of all living things; and his servants become, on their side, one all-inclusive group. Conversely, the soul acquires a unity in the exclusive sense. The individual becomes a unit, an isolated atom, with a personal sense of sin and a need of personal salvation, compensated, however, by a new consciousness of the dignity and value of the soul, expressed in the doctrine that by origin and nature it is divine. From God it came, and to God it will return.

Such are some of the essential tendencies of thought, the outcome of a long evolution whose stages cannot be traced, which recommend the doctrine of transmigration. In the fifth century it was believed that Pythagoras had learnt this doctrine in Egypt; and it is still disputed whether the absence of any traces of it in the scanty monuments of sixth-century Egypt is enough to outweigh the evidence of Herodotus. Some hold that the doctrine may even have travelled from India across the Persian Empire, which in that century stretched from the Punjab to Ionia. But the origin of the belief is of small importance as compared with its content, and the view of the nature and relations of God and man which it implies. This content is the expression of fresh religious experience; the form it assumed—the belief that the same soul can pass up or down the scale of life, through the bodies of men, animals, and plants—is inessential.

V. ORPHIC COSMOGONY AND ANTHROPOGONY

A religion of this type must needs possess a cosmology. This will be no mere legendary account of the origin of the world and of the generations of the gods, like the Theogony of Hesiod. The interest of Orphism centred in the destiny of the soul, and its cosmology was a vision of the universe conceived and felt in terms of good and evil and of that conflict between them which was the dominant fact of inner experience. To the chapter of cosmogony is added what is missing in Hesiod—the chapter of anthropogony, the explanation of the double nature of man, pointing forward to the means of redemption.

The Neoplatonists appear to have known, under the name of the 'Rhapsodic Theogony,' a great Orphic bible, into which the whole body of doctrine had in the course of centuries been gathered. It was a poem, probably in twenty-four cantos, the substance of which was drawn from earlier scriptures (*hieroi logoi*) current in the various communities. The essential features dated back to the sixth or seventh century and were known to Xenophanes, Aeschylus, Empedocles, Aristophanes, and Plato. The contents may be considered under three heads: (1) the origin of the world order; (2) the dynastic succession of the gods; (3) the myth of Zagreus, including the primal sin, the origin and nature of man, and the mystery of redemption.

(1) With regard to the origin of the cosmic order, the fundamental scheme of conception is one that is found independently in many parts of the world. In the beginning there was a primal undifferentiated unity, called by the Orphics 'Night.' Within this unity the World Egg was generated, or, according to some accounts, fashioned by Ageless Time (*Chronos*). The Egg divided into two halves, Heaven and Earth. Mythically, Heaven and Earth are the Father and Mother of all life. In physical terms, the upper half of the Egg forms the dome of the sky, the lower contains the moisture or slime from which the dry land (Earth) arose. Between earth and heaven appeared a winged spirit of light and life, known by many names, as Phanes, Eros, Metis, Ericapaeus, etc. The function of this spirit, in which sex was as yet undifferentiated, was to generate life either by the immediate projection of seed from itself, or by uniting the sundered parents, Heaven and Earth, in marriage. The offspring were successive pairs of supreme gods: Oceanus and Tethys, Cronos and Rhea, Zeus and Hera. The symbolism in which this scheme is clothed is primitive in the extreme. Thus Ageless Time is figured as a winged serpent with the face of a god, flanked by the heads of a bull and a lion. The native tendency of the Greek imagination was towards the expurgation of the more grotesque elements, but this was counteracted by syncretistic influxes from oriental quarters; and between the two it is impossible now to reconstruct the vision of the sixth-century Orphic.

(2) The ancient fable of the successive dynasties of gods is open to more than one historical interpretation. Some see in it the memory of cataclysmic moments in the development of religion; others, yet dimmer memories of a phase of social life when

the adult male head of the group, as father or as king, was ousted by his growing sons. Both these explanations, and perhaps others too, may be true. The notion of the supreme god attempting to destroy his children and being finally overthrown by them became a scandal to the unsympathetic and foolishness to the rationalist. The religious mind clung to it as an enigmatic symbol; Aeschylus seems to have read into it the truth that the lower or earlier expression of religious consciousness is never abrogated, but perpetually subsumed in the later or higher. In the Orphic myth the ancient symbolism is adapted so as to apply the characteristic motive of rebirth to the formation of the world. Zeus, the supreme god of our dispensation, is readily identified with the Father of life (*Zēn*), swallows Phanes and, helped by attendant Justice, creates within himself the world anew.

(3) The myth of the divine Son, Dionysus-Zagreus, who has been identified with Zeus himself reborn in infant form, leads up to the doctrine of the twofold nature of man, good and evil. The horned infant, Zagreus, born of the marriage of Zeus in serpent form with his daughter Persephone-Kore, was installed on his father's throne and received the sceptre and the powers of thunder, lightning, and rain. He was attacked and cut to pieces in his bovine form by the Titans, who boiled his limbs in a cauldron and devoured them. Zeus smote the Titans with his bolt and gave the limbs to Apollo for burial. The heart became the means of resurrection. According to the common view, Zeus made from it a potion, which Semele (the Earth goddess) drank, and from her Zagreus was reborn as Dionysus. From the ashes of the blasted Titans men were made. Since the Titans had eaten of the divine flesh, man contains a particle of the heavenly essence, imprisoned and entombed in a body of evil nature.

This anthropogony, under the grotesque traits which are the surest guarantee of its antiquity, contains conceptions charged with the deepest significance to the religious consciousness of the mystic. The double nature of man implies the perpetual war in our members, and a condemnation of the body and of the sense-world to which it belongs. Life on earth becomes part of a purgatorial round, continued through the intervals of successive reincarnations. In the language of the amulets found in Orphic graves, dating from the fourth century onwards, the cycle of births and deaths is a 'sorrowful weary wheel.' But the child of Earth is also the child of the starry Heaven. By ceremonial asceticism and moral purity during life, and by expiatory suffering in the underworld, the soul may hope for a final release and for reunion with its divine source. The alternative is the eternal damnation of the soul that cannot be healed. The supreme means of grace is the sacramental feast in which the soul feeds on the substance of the god who suffered, died, and rose again, and thereby is assured of ultimate deliverance from the cycle of re-birth. This central rite is the most awful of mysteries. It is a re-enactment of the primal sin committed by the powers of evil, and at the same time the sacrament of redemption and atonement.

VI. THE MILESIAN SCHOOL

To pass from mythical cosmogony, such as that of the Orphics, to the earliest philosophic systems of Ionia is to enter a new atmosphere in which the twilight mists seem to give place to the clarity of sceptical intellect. There is not, indeed, a sudden and complete abandonment of all existing modes of thought—such an occurrence is psychologically impossible—but rather that change of outlook which comes when the mind of a race, awakening from the dream world of mythical imagery, demands an account of the real world acceptable to acute and cultivated minds as literal, prosaic fact. The conditions necessary for such a change are rarely found. Among them may be named the absence of a politically powerful priesthood; the absence of a belief in a supreme creator God and of any sacred book comprising both a cosmogony and a moral law, so that the cosmogony cannot be questioned without impugning the basis of social life; an exceptional degree of native intelligence, and a high level of prosperity and conse-quent leisure. All these conditions were realized, at the opening of the sixth century, in the Ionian cities of Asia Minor, where an already long tradition of independent political life and com-mercial activity had enriched the heirs of the old Cretan civili-zation with intellectual culture and material wealth. At the same time quickening impulses from the East were penetrating to Ionia through more than one channel. In the previous century access to Egypt had been opened by Psammetichus I, who, in gratitude for military help, had established regular commercial relations with Miletus, which were continued by his successors (see above, p. 87). In Asia Minor itself, during the brief empire of Croesus, Sardes was, according to Herodotus, the resort of 'all the wise men of Hellas.' Finally, the westward thrust of the Persian power ended by uniting in one well-organized system a territory ex-tending from the Aegean to the borders of India.

This happy combination of circumstances attended the birth

of European philosophy and science. The first date in the Ionian tradition is given by the eclipse of the sun predicted by Thales in 585 B.C. In the next two generations at Miletus, the first great system of cosmology was projected by Anaximander and improved by Anaximenes. After the destruction of Miletus in 494 B.C., there is some reason to believe that the successors of Anaximenes carried on the tradition at the Milesian colony of Lampsacus. In the age of Pericles it was continued by Diogenes of Apollonia, and by Anaxagoras of Clazomenae and his Athenian pupil Archelaus, who is said to have taught Socrates.

The nature and extent of eastern influence on Greek speculation before Alexander have been alternately exaggerated by pan-babylonian fanaticism and undervalued by the prejudice of the hellenist. Jewish religion may be entirely excluded, and it has not been made out by what channel Indian ideas could have travelled so far. On the other hand, Thales learnt in Egypt some rules of land-measurement which were to develop on Greek soil into the science of geometry, and Aristotle attributes to the leisure of the Egyptian priesthood the foundation of 'the mathematical arts.' It has been shown, further, that all the essential features of Thales' cosmogony can be paralleled from earlier Egyptian documents. He must also have learnt, directly or indirectly, from Babylon of the cycle of lunations which enabled him to predict an eclipse of the sun (see vol. III, pp. 237 *sqq*.). Herodotus (II, 109) says that the Greeks learnt from Babylon 'the twelve parts of the day' and the use of the sun-clock (*polos*) and of the dial (*gnōmōn*), the first specimen of which Anaximander is said to have erected at Sparta. It is clear that the Greeks owed to the Orient some rudimentary astronomical and mathematical information, a few technical methods and instruments, and some hints of larger philosophical conceptions. Their naturally inquisitive intellects received a quickening shock, but, in their essential quality, the great systems from Anaximander onwards are unlike any product of priestly speculation in the East. In their groundwork and architecture, and still more in the free spirit that plays through them, there is nothing that betrays any clear break in the continuity of Greek thought about the world.

This continuity may be illustrated by a brief analysis of Anaximander's system, which is of cardinal importance as setting the pattern for the whole Ionian tradition. It represents a remarkable advance upon the crude cosmology which the first Milesian may have brought from Egypt. Thales had conceived the earth as a flat disk floating on the waters under the dome of the sky, across which the heavenly bodies, probably regarded as disks or bowls of fire, moved laterally round the earth, without passing under it. The sky itself was enveloped in the primordial element of water, the living source from which arose the world and all the life it contains. Of the process by which the world was formed we are told nothing; analogy points to the conjecture that the original mass of water was somehow divided, the sky being raised up to enclose the hemisphere of air above the plain of the waters supporting the earth. The entire image is not far removed from the World Egg of the Orphics.

Anaximander dealt with the two traditional problems of cosmogony: (1) How did the world come to be arranged as it is? (2) How did life, especially human life, arise?

(1) The genesis of the world order starts from a primordial stuff, negatively described as 'the Unlimited.' The formula of the cosmogonical process is the 'separating of opposites' out of this original mass. At some point within it a spherical nucleus appeared, in which the warmer stuff, 'the Hot,' moved outwards, while 'the Cold' sank towards the centre. Thus, we are told, 'a sphere of flame grew round the air encompassing the earth, like the bark round a tree.' Three of the popular elements[1]— fire, air, and earth—are here mentioned by our authority; the fourth, water, appears when the moist earth is partly dried by the fires of heaven and the seas shrink into their beds. The second pair of opposites, the Wet and the Dry, were thus separated, and the elements now occupied their appointed provinces. Finally, the sun, moon, and stars were formed when the sphere of flame was burst by the internal pressure of evaporation. Its parts were enclosed in circular tubes of 'air' (i.e. mist) dense enough to conceal the fire within, which is visible only at certain apertures. The sun-ring is outside; next comes the moon; and nearest the earth the stars, among which, apparently, the planets were not distinguished. The earth, unsupported at the centre, is a cylinder, 'like the drum of a column.' Such is the world order.

(2) Within this order the origin of individual living things and the explanation of meteoric phenomena are referred to a second type of process, which may be called the weather process. The elements, instead of confining themselves to their proper spheres, encroach and prey upon one another. The Hot draws

---

[1] The strict conception of 'elements' as primitive *immutable* substances is not older than Empedocles, who calls them 'roots.' The word is here used, for convenience, to cover the four great masses into which the world is divided.

up moisture to feed the heavenly fires, and the cold earth, in its
turn, claims warmth and rain. To this intercourse and mixture
of the elements the origin of all life is due. The first living things
were generated out of moisture evaporated by the sun. Man, like
the other animals, must have been a fish-like creature, which later
took to the land. This traffic of the elements was to Anaximander
a work of 'injustice,' of encroachment and self-assertion on the
part of the hostile 'opposites.' It must be paid for by the dissolution of every such temporary combination, and finally by the
relapse of the warring powers themselves into the primitive confusion of the Unlimited. This law of mortality is laid down in
the only surviving fragment of his work: 'Things perish into
those things from which they have their birth, as it is ordained;
they pay to one another the penalty of their injustice according
to the order of time.' From the Unlimited another world arises,
to perish in its turn, and so for ever.

If we disengage the abstract formula of this cosmogony, it will
be seen that it closely resembles the scheme of many mythical
cosmogonies, including that of the Orphics above mentioned.
There is (1) a primordial undifferentiated unity; (2) a separation
of opposites in pairs to form the world order; (3) a reunion of
these sundered opposites to generate life. The formula is stated
by Euripides' *Melanippe* (frag. 484): 'The tale is not mine; I had
it from my mother: that Heaven and Earth were once one form
(the primal unity), and when they had been sundered from one
another (the separation of the pair, Father Heaven and Mother
Earth), they gave birth to all things and brought them up into
the light (the reunion of the pair to generate life).'

Thus Anaximander unsuspectingly accepted from tradition
not only the problems of cosmogony but the framework of the
solution. The result is as if he had taken (say) the Orphic cosmogony and expurgated every element he could identify as
mythical or anthropomorphic—above all personification and the
language of sex—admitting only those indubitably real factors
which the mythical symbolism had, after all, but thinly veiled.
Not that he actually proceeded in this way; rather the traditional
thought, hitherto clothed in the imagery of myth, now rises clear
into the domain of rational thinking; the poetry is translated into
prose, which was, significantly, the medium consistently used
throughout the Ionian tradition. It is true that Anaximander,
though he rejects the imagery of sex, of Father Heaven and Mother
Earth united by Eros, retains the alternative symbolism of aggression and warfare between the elemental powers. The reunion

of the sundered opposites is to him a mixture that implies 'in-justice,' dooming the whole cosmos and all within it to dissolution and death.

To the philosopher, however, it seemed that he had pierced through the veil of fantasy to a clear sight of real, sensible things. It must be noted that the renunciation of sex-imagery left a gap in the scheme. The ambiguous word '*genesis*' could no longer screen the innocent confusion of 'becoming' with birth. The problem of motion begins to come into view. Anaximander was reaching out towards a mechanical conception; but he does not seem to have attained it. We hear only of an 'eternal motion,' whose nature was left obscure. The truth is that self-motion was an inherent attribute of the primordial stuff, which was not mere 'matter' (the word was not yet invented) but essentially alive, and directed or 'governed' other things which could not move themselves. This property of the Unlimited concealed from Anaximander the need to account more definitely for motion and becoming. On the other hand it spared him the problem that confronts other systems: how life could ever arise from the merely inanimate.

The term 'unlimited' applied to this living stuff probably does not imply, in the strict sense, spatial infinity; it is doubtful whether such a conception had been grasped at this date. It means pri-marily the absence of internal limits and distinctions, such as divide the elemental masses in the ordered world. It also implies 'imperishable.' The stuff does not begin or cease to exist when things arise out of it or relapse into it; it is not lost or used up in the forms that are separated out of it. Considered as matter, it persists as the stuff of which things consist. Considered as alive, it is 'ageless and deathless'—the one attribute of divinity, as conceived in the Olympian religion, which survives when all that is anthropomorphic is rejected. This image of the ultimate nature of things seems like a first approximation to the 'neutral stuff' which some philosophers now regard as the common matrix of matter and mind. Such an image was not given by Ionian tradition, nor was it deliberately fabricated by the Milesian philo-sophers. It may rather be thought of as the resuscitation, in a simplified form, of that representation of impersonal divine or magical energy which had preceded the development of personal gods. Thus the renunciation of mythical imagery takes philosophy back to the source from which mythology arose. Whether this living stuff is identified with water (as by Thales), or with air (as by Anaximenes), is a matter of secondary importance. In either case the vehicle of life is intermediate between the extremes, the fire of heaven and the earth; it has its place in that gap, filled by the series, water, mist, air, cloud, rain, between Father Heaven and Mother Earth, which was occupied by the Eros of mythical cosmogony.

The third Milesian, Anaximenes, introduced simplifications which disengaged the Milesian cosmology still further from the mythical atmosphere. He identified the substance of the Un-limited with the invisible and ever-moving air, out of which the visible forms arise by a process of 'thinning' and 'thickening.' Air is rarefied into fire, and condensed into wind, cloud, water, earth, stones. Thus differences of heat and cold are associated with differences of density in a continuous scale, and air, though still regarded as primary, takes its place in the same series with the other forms. The effect is to abolish Anaximander's conception of the cosmogonical process. The Unlimited is no longer a primeval fusion of opposite stuffs which are separated out into hostile pairs, conducting a perpetual warfare of aggression. Anaximenes applies his new conception of the weather process to the generation of the cosmos itself, and daringly refers to it the formation not only of the earth, a watery mass enveloped in clouds, but of the heavenly bodies, which were produced from moisture arising from the earth and rarefied into fire. Thus the cosmic order, the series of elemental forms, and the sun, moon, and stars, are all explained by the familiar every-day process of the exhalation and condensation of moisture.

But Anaximenes had not altogether shaken free of mythical preconceptions. Now that the unlimited air has taken its place in the series of forms ranging from fire at one end to earth and stones at the other, there remains no logical reason for calling it primary. The only ground for giving it an exceptional status is that it is the stuff of life—the breath (*pneuma*) or soul, not only of all living things within the world, but of the world itself. Outside the cosmos there is only air, which the living world respires. Inside the cosmos, this same air is the animating and moving principle which 'holds together' living things. It is on this account that it is held to be the primary form from which the rest are derived, and so pre-eminently the stuff of which all things consist. The distinction between soul and body substance is obliterated. According as the soul properties (consciousness and motion) or the bodily properties are emphasized, pantheism or materialism will result. The actual drift of the Ionian tradition was towards materialism—that tendency to reduce all the phenomena of life to mere motion of dead matter in space, which leads to Atomism.

VII. THE PHILOSOPHY OF PYTHAGORAS

In clear contrast with the Milesian scientific philosophy stands the Italian tradition founded by Pythagoras of Samos, who migrated to Croton in South Italy, perhaps to escape the tyranny of Polycrates (*c.* 530 B.C., see above, p. 93). The religious fraternity he there established lasted for nearly a century. When political troubles led to its dissolution, some of the leaders took refuge in central Greece, where Lysis, for example, taught Epaminondas at Thebes. Others returned to Italy later, and Pythagorean communities still existed in the latter half of the fourth century B.C.

Though we have little certain information about Pythagoras, he stands out in the history of thought as one of the world's greatest men. He was not only a great religious reformer and the prophet of a society united by reverence for his memory and the observance of a monastic rule; he was also a man of commanding intellectual powers, founder of the sciences of arithmetic and harmonics, and author of discoveries in geometry. In a man of this type, presenting an extremely rare combination of the highest spiritual and intellectual force, the religious motive, by its very nature, must be stronger than scientific curiosity; it must determine the direction of philosophic speculation because it demands that thought shall satisfy spiritual needs and aspirations. The world must have a certain character, if it is to respond to the claims of the soul. The Milesian philosophy, impelled by curiosity, had ignored these claims. Anaximander's God was an indeterminate mass of living stuff, still called divine because animate and immortal, but an object neither of love nor worship, and destitute of any value to the religious consciousness. By implication Anaximander had eliminated polytheism, as a system which had lost all hold on cultivated minds in the highly civilized, commercial, travelled community of Miletus, then the intellectual centre of the western world; but the monism he substituted was scientific; it was not monotheism. Of the destiny of the soul he had nothing to say, except, again by implication, that it was nothing but a temporarily separate portion of the one living stuff, of no more value or dignity than any other—a thing that could neither preserve its material identity after death, nor in any spiritual sense be 'saved.'

Pythagoreanism, on the contrary, begins, not with the elimination of factors that had once had a religious significance, but actually with a reconstruction of the religious life. To Pythagoras, who was said to have invented the word 'philosophy,' the love of wisdom was a way of life. He heralded and inspired all those systems—Socratic, Stoic, Neoplatonic—in which knowledge, no longer the child of wonder and of the unacknowledged desire for power over nature, became, if not a mere means to virtuous living, at least identified with the well-being and well-doing of the human soul. A tradition such as this is rooted in assumptions dictated by the hopes, fears, and loves of humanity; it is predetermined by certain axioms of faith. But faith was not yet opposed to knowledge. This philosophy seeks the satisfaction of faith and hope in the pursuit of knowledge itself, in the 'love of wisdom.' The earliest form of Pythagoreanism must have been a construction of the 'seen order' (ὁρατὸς κόσμος) capable of providing for the needs of the unseen.

Owing to the absence of any written documents before Philolaus (at the end of the fifth century B.C.) and to the pious tradition whereby the school ascribed all discoveries to the founder, any reconstruction of Pythagoras' system is largely conjectural. For reasons explained above, the surest method is to consider, first, what beliefs about the nature and relations of God, the soul, and the universe are implied in Pythagoras' known religious doctines and in the type of society he founded, and then how these beliefs can be connected with what we know of his cosmological principles—the theory of '*harmonia*' and numbers. The two sides of this philosophy, the religious and the scientific, apparently began to drift apart early in the fifth century. Tradition points to a split between the old believers who clung to the religious doctrine, and a modernist or intellectual wing who developed the number doctrine on scientific lines and dropped the mysticism. But in the original sixth-century system there cannot have been more than a latent, undetected inconsistency. It is incredible that the science of Pythagoras should have been in open disharmony with his faith.

The Pythagorean fraternity was modelled on the mystical cult-society, admission to which was gained by initiation, that is, by purification followed by the revelation of truth. The Pythagorean 'purification' partly consisted in the observance of ascetic rules of abstinence from certain kinds of food and dress, and partly was reinterpreted intellectually to mean the purification of the soul by *theoria*, the contemplation of the divine order of the world. 'Revelation' consisted in certain truths delivered by the prophet-founder (αὐτὸς ἔφα), and progressively elaborated by his followers under his inspiration.

In the analysis of Orphism, it has already been remarked that
the psychological experience which generates such societies leads
to two axioms. The first may be called the axiom of Monism:
All life is one and God is one. The second is the axiom of
Dualism: In the world, as in the soul, there is a real conflict of
two opposite powers—good and evil, light and darkness. Both
principles are implicit in the doctrine of transmigration, which
was certainly taught by Pythagoras. All souls come from one
divine source and circulate in a continuous series of all the forms
of life. Each soul, involved in the conflict of good and evil, seeks
escape from the purgatorial round of lives and deaths into a better
world of unity and rest. Any philosophy that emerges from a
religion of this type is threatened with internal inconsistency. On
the one hand, it will set the highest value upon the idea of unity,
and, at this stage and long afterwards, the notions of value and
of reality coincide. Unity is good; reality must be one. On the
other hand, Nature will be construed in terms of the inward
conflict of good and evil, appearing in the external world as light
and darkness. Light is the medium of truth and knowledge; it
reveals the knowable aspect of Nature—the forms, surfaces, limits
of objects that are confounded in the unlimited night. But it is
hard to deny reality to the antagonistic power of darkness and
evil. Hence the tendency to dualism—to recognize as real, not
the One only, but two opposite principles.

Aristoxenus says of the Pythagoreans that 'in all their defini-
tions of conduct, their aim is communion (or converse, *homilia*)
with the divine. This is their starting-point; their whole life is
ordered with a view to following God; and it is the governing
principle of their philosophy.' This 'following' or 'imitation'
(*mīmēsis*) of God was to end in a purification of the soul from the
taint of its bodily prison-house, so complete that there should be
no further need of reincarnation. Pythagoras was believed to
have attained this threshold of divinity. Empedocles later made
the same claim for himself in the words: 'I am an immortal god,
mortal no more,' echoed in the tablets found in Orphic graves,
where the dead man's soul is addressed: 'From a man thou hast
become a god.'

The means of rising to this condition was philosophy, the
contemplation of truth as revealed in the visible universe, and
especially in the order of the heavenly bodies. It is this order,
not the disposition of the Milesians' four elements, that constitutes
the 'cosmos,' an order whose beauty and goodness are implied
in this characteristically Pythagorean name. 'The wise tell us,'

says Socrates in Plato's *Gorgias* (507 ε), 'that heaven and earth, gods and men, are united by a bond of association and love and by justice and temperance or orderliness (*kosmiotes*); and that is why they call this universe an order (*kosmos*), not disorderliness (*akosmia*) or licence.' The universe, in fact, is informed by a moral order; and the fruit of contemplation is the reproduction of a corresponding order of beauty and goodness in the philosopher's soul. This is to become like God.

The formula of that structure which is manifest in the celestial order and can be reproduced in the microcosm, is *harmonia*. This conception is of central importance, since it forms the link between the religious and the physical aspects of Pythagoras' system, and leads on to the doctrine of Numbers. The word *harmonia* did not mean 'harmony,' the Greek for which is *symphonia*. The first meaning was the 'fitting together' or 'adjustment' of parts in a complex thing; then, specially, the 'tuning' of an instrument, and hence the 'musical scale' which results therefrom. There is from the first the implication of a right, or tuneful, adjustment. Pythagoras, probably by measuring on a monochord the lengths of string which gave the several notes, made the great discovery that the concordant intervals recognized in Greek music could be exactly expressed in terms of numerical ratios—the octave by the ratio 1 : 2, the fifth by 3 : 2, the fourth by 4 : 3. The lowest integers having these ratios to one another are 6 : 8 : 9 : 12, which may be taken to represent the four 'fixed' notes of the lyre with seven (or eight) strings. These notes were similarly related to one another in every variety of scale, the several scales being obtained by varying the pitch of the remaining three (or four) 'moveable' notes. Further, in this set of integers the internal terms, 8 and 9, are, respectively, the arithmetical and the harmonic means between the extremes, 6 and 12.

Thus the principle of *harmonia* was revealed as an unseen principle of order and concord, identical with a system of numbers bound together by interlocking ratios. The system moreover is limited, both externally by the octave (for the scale ends, as we say, 'on the same note' and begins again in endless recurrence), and internally by the means. The introduction of this system marks out the whole unlimited field of sound, which ranges indefinitely in opposite directions (high and low). The infinite variety of quality in sound is reduced to order by the exact and simple law of ratio in quantity. The system so defined still contains the unlimited element in the blank intervals between the notes; but the unlimited is no longer an orderless continuum; it is confined within an order, a *cosmos*, by the imposition of Limit or Measure.

The mathematical genius of Pythagoras was capable of abstracting this complex of conceptions from the particular case of sound. It must have been by a flash of inspired insight that he saw in it a formula of universal application. To the microcosm it was immediately applied in the doctrine that the good state of the body, health, is the proportioned 'mixture' (or 'temperament,' *krāsis*) of the physical qualities, hot and cold, wet and dry, etc. This conception was stated by Alcmaeon, a junior fellow-citizen of Pythagoras at Croton, and persists throughout ancient medical theory. Probably the application to virtue, the health or good condition of the soul, is equally old. The distinction between soul and body was not so sharply drawn as to prevent the Pythagoreans from practising psychotherapy. As they used charms for physical ailments, so they cured the sick soul by music and recitation of poetry. Protagoras in Plato's dialogue (*Protagoras*, p. 326) treats as a commonplace of educational theory the effect of music in producing a right attunement (*euharmostia* and *eurhythmia*) in the soul, with its result, virtuous conduct. The doctrine, indeed, only gave an exact and abstract expression to the popular notion that self-control (*sophrosyne, kosmiotes*) is moderation, the imposition of limit or measure upon passion that runs to excess—a notion that lay at the centre of Greek morality. The synonym 'temperance' enshrines the Pythagorean notion of the duly tempered mixture of opposites; and the mathematical conceptions, 'means' and 'extremes,' led on to Aristotle's famous theory of virtue as the mean between two extremes or opposite vices. Besides this view of moral virtue as the moderation of the lower nature, Pythagoreanism also contains in germ the other cardinal doctrine of Aristotelian ethics, that the highest activity in which the well-being of the soul consists is contemplation of truth (*theōria*).

The doctrine that the soul itself is an '*harmonia*,' which was certainly held by Philolaus, may go back to Pythagoras. It is possible that the soul, considered as a system of parts that might be related in consonance or discord, was conceived as an organizing principle, which (to use Anaximenes' phrase) 'held together' the body. Such a system could survive the dissolution of any particular bodily instrument, as a musical scale is not destroyed when a lyre is broken; and it could organize a series of bodies, consistently with transmigration. The reason for supposing that the doctrine is original is that it seems to follow from the correspondence of microcosm and macrocosm and to be required by the fundamental conception of the imitation of God, considered as the tuning of the soul into consonance with the celestial *harmonia*. The soul itself would be a system which might be well or ill-tuned, healthy and virtuous or the reverse. Virtue, like health, would be the right or good attunement (*euharmostia*).

The macrocosm, the organized visible world or 'Heaven,' is a living creature with a soul or principle of life and a body[1]. In Aristotle's phrase, 'the whole Heaven is a *harmonia* and number.' It is an easy inference that the life-principle or soul of the world is an *harmonia* or system of numbers (it is so described by the Pythagorean Timaeus in Plato)—that very *harmonia* which is manifest to sense in the order of the heavenly bodies, and is to be reproduced in the attunement of the individual soul.

A compendium of Pythagorean mysticism is contained in the symbol known as the *Tetractys* or *Tetrad*. This is itself a system of numbers, and it symbolizes the elements of number which are the elements of all things. In the Pythagorean oath (perhaps the oath of secrecy taken by the novice—only the two opening lines are preserved), the tetractys is described as 'containing the root and fountain of everflowing nature.' It was identified with the cosmic *harmonia*, and called *cosmos*, 'Heaven,' and the All.

The tetractys is also called the Decad, because it consists of the first four integers, represented in the old fashion by pebbles or dots arranged in an equilateral triangle .·. , and the sum of these numbers is 10. It 'represents all the consonances' in the sense that these four numbers are those which occur in the concordant ratios of the musical scale, discovered by Pythagoras. It 'embraces the whole nature of number,' because all nations count up to 10 and then revert to 1; all the other numbers are obtained by repetition of the decad. Further, the component numbers symbolize 'the elements of number.' These, says Aristotle (*Met.* I, 5), are 'the even, which is Unlimited, and the odd, which is Limited (or Limit). The One (or Monad) consists of both, for it is both even and odd. Number comes from the One, and numbers are the whole "Heaven".'

Later authorities throw light upon this obscure statement. The

---

[1] Zeller (*Philos. der Griechen*, I[5], 1892, p. 419) denies to the Pythagoreans the doctrine of a 'world-soul'; but by that he means 'die Annahme einer Weltseele, *als eines besondern, unkörperlich gedachten Wesens.*' He admits that the world was 'compared' to a living creature which breathed. His denial that this thought 'influenced' the system (p. 441) is arbitrary.

Dyad (to begin with that) is even and unlimited, an evil and female principle. 'In the division of numbers,' we are told, 'the even, when parted in any direction, leaves within itself a receptive principle or space,' 'an empty field, masterless and numberless, showing that it is defective and imperfect.' Thus the Dyad stands for the female receptive field, the void womb of unordered space, the Unlimited.

The Triad is its opposite, the good principle of Limit, the male whose union with the Unlimited produces the Limited. The numbers $5 (2 + 3)$ and $6 (2 \times 3)$ are both symbols of this marriage of odd and even.

The Monad is both odd and even, or, in mythical language, male and female, bisexed. It contains both the opposites, which are the 'elements of number' and proceed from it—a process following the same scheme of separation of two opposites out of a primordial undifferentiated unity that has already been noted in Anaximander and the mythical cosmogonies.

Finally, there is the number 4. If it is permissible to use, in the interpretation of the *Tetractys*, the identification of four, as the first square number, with Justice, the parallel with Anaximander will be complete. At the corresponding point in his system prominence was given to the notion of Justice, holding the balance of the sundered opposites and exacting 'the penalty of injustice according to the order of time.'

Such is the meaning of this extraordinary symbol, which both contains the elements of number and of all things, and, as 'the fountain of everflowing nature,' symbolizes also the evolution of the many out of the One, the cosmogonical process.

We have hardly any information about the earliest Pythagorean cosmogony. Pythagoras was the discoverer of the world of mathematics, which we conceive as a supersensible world of concepts related in an infinite system of eternal truths—a timeless world in which no change or process can occur, and which is unaffected by the existence, becoming, or perishing of any sensible thing. But Pythagoras was still far from realizing the nature of this new world of thought. To him, numbers and their relations were not only invested with a halo of divine and mystical properties, but were also implicated in the sensible world, serving as the substructure of reality within that world and occupying space. He could not yet distinguish between a purely logical 'process' such as the 'generation' of the series of numbers, and an actual process in time such as the generation of the visible Heaven, which 'is *harmonia* and number.' The cosmogonical process was thus confused with the generation of numbers from the One, and will appear to us as a translation of this, really logical, process into physical terms. The physical system will be determined by the way in which the generation of numbers is conceived. It was at this point that two distinct schools of Pythagoreans parted company. The original mystical doctrine of the founder and the more 'scientific' doctrine of the early fifth century started from quite different conceptions of the Monad. We are here concerned only with the original system.

In the primitive symbolism of the *Tetractys*, the Monad was the divine all-inclusive unity, containing both the opposites which are the elements of number and of things, the Unlimited and the Limit. The Monad was not itself a number; it was both odd and even, male and female, Limit and Unlimited. The evolution follows the old scheme. From the undifferentiated unity emerge the two opposite principles, and these are recombined to generate determinate ('limited') things, namely the series of numbers and the sensible objects which represent or embody numbers. Thus any determinate thing will, like the Orphic soul, contain both principles, the good and the evil, light and darkness.

How this process was construed in physical terms is obscure. The Unlimited was evidently the unmeasured field of space, which, though called 'the void,' was filled by 'air,' the circumambient envelope of the limited Heaven, the breath (*pneuma*) of the living world. It is the primeval 'Night' of the Orphics. The opposite principle of Limit is manifest to sense as light or fire. The product of the two principles is the cosmos or Heaven. As the unlimited range of sound is marked off by consonant numbers into the definite intervals of the musical scale, so the blank field of darkness is marked off by those boundary points of heavenly light, sun, moon, and planets, whose orbits (still conceived as material rings) are set at musical intervals to form the celestial *harmonia* or scale, bridging and binding together the visible order from earth at the centre to the outermost sphere of the fixed stars.

How was this majestic order evolved? Aristotle (*Metaphysics*, 1, 8) clearly states that the Pythagoreans did not distinguish between a mathematical solid and a physical body which has sensible properties and can move in space. If this is true, the task of cosmology—to generate a visible 'Heaven'—is reduced to the task of generating mathematical solids from numbers. The conception of numbers as occupying space is immediately suggested by the primitive practice of representing them by dots (or pebbles) arranged in geometrical patterns. Thus we hear of triangular, square, and oblong numbers. In the geometrical interpretation of the *Tetractys*, 1 symbolizes the point, 2 the minimum line (consisting of two points), 3 the first surface (a triangle formed by three points), 4 the first solid (the pyramid, such as might be constructed by poising a pebble on a base consisting of three others). In this and similar ways, the generation of solids from 'numbers' may be imagined, and bodies of any shape and size can be built up, representing numbers and their relations. If, as Aristotle says, these mathematical bodies were simply identified with the physical bodies which exist and move in space, the derivation of 'things' in the visible universe from numbers was achieved.

The Pythagorean philosophy, in contrast to the Milesian, is a philosophy of form as opposed to matter. In the sense world, which we have now reached, the principle of Limit is manifested as Light or Fire, the Unlimited as Air or Darkness. These are the equivalents of Anaximander's Hot and Cold. In the unlimited darkness of night all objects lose to the eye their colours and shapes; in the daily renewed creation of the dawning light they resume their distinct form, their surfaces and colours (the same word, *chroia*, was used by the Pythagoreans with both meanings). Thus, in the physical world, light, the vehicle of knowledge and truth, acts as a limiting principle, informing the blank darkness with bodies, bounded by measurable planes and distinguished by all the varieties of colour. A body is thus a limited thing in which two opposite principles meet—the Unlimited (darkness, air, 'void,' space) and Limit, identified with the coloured surface (*eidos, idea, morphē, schēma*).

We have no further information that seems relevant to the earliest Pythagorean cosmogony. But nothing more is needed. The world order, which it is the business of cosmogony to gene-rate, is to the Pythagorean the harmonious cosmos of the heavenly bodies in its changeless and divine perfection. When this has been deduced from Numbers, he possesses a frame of reality sufficient to provide an intellectual representation of the moral and religious truths from which he starts. All those processes and transformations of the elements, the atmospheric phenomena so interesting to Milesian science, were of no significance for what Pythagoras called philosophy. They belong to the sublunary region of mortality and change, from which the philosopher will turn away the eye of the soul.

VIII. HERACLEITUS

We have now reviewed the two great systems of Nature produced in the sixth century, the Ionian and the Italian, which confront one another with an unreconciled difference of inspiration and tendency. With the opening of the fifth century, philosophy begins to be a controversy. From opposite standpoints Heracleitus of Ephesus and Parmenides of Elea in South Italy assault and destroy the foundations of both the Milesian and the Pythagorean cosmology. The controversy is philosophical rather than scientific: it is confined within an extraordinarily small circle of ideas and concerned with the most abstract principles, such as the possibility of deriving a manifold world from a primitive unity, the conceptions of becoming, motion, and change, the harmony of opposites. It is very remarkable that, although the philosophers continued to dogmatize about the detail of natural phenomena, their interest is focussed upon ultimate principles. The progress that is made consists mainly in the clearer definition and distinction of concepts such as becoming, motion, and change, and of what they imply.

The controversy is opened by Heracleitus, whose work may be dated about 500 b.c. His haughty temperament acknowledged no master but the truth; he was the contemptuous critic and antagonist of all his predecessors. He spoke as a prophet, claiming to utter not merely his own opinions, but the eternal truth, in accordance with which all things come to pass. This truth, the *Logos*, was identical with the divine 'Thought (*gnōmē*) by which all things are steered through all things.' To know this is the whole of wisdom. It is both hidden in Nature and revealed to men whose souls can understand the language of their eyes and ears. It cannot be learnt by listening to poets and mythographers or to men like the Milesians and Pythagoras, whose science (*historiē*) is only a 'learning of many things.' Heracleitus describes his own method in the words: 'I searched myself.' The *Logos* is to be sought within, for man's nature is a microcosm and represents the nature of the whole. The wise will find it there, as well as everywhere else. Heracleitus was wise; in his own *logos* he reproduced, in the cryptic form of apparent contradictions which faithfully reflect its mysterious nature, the inmost truth of the world.

A philosopher who holds that the truth is within him will not be primarily a man of science. The astronomy of Heracleitus is reactionary and negligible. He had a general conception of the process that goes on in Nature, and this he held to be of the highest importance. He cared little for details, but much for a few great principles. These were: (1) All things change and flow; nothing remains the same; (2) the world is an ever-living fire; (3) there is a harmony of opposites. The key to his thought is to be found in the interpretation and connection of these propositions. Since he is destructive, the best approach is from a consideration of what he denounces and denies, rather than of what he affirms.

Both the sixth-century systems had postulated a primordial Unity—Anaximander's Unlimited, Pythagoras' Monad. This represented a beginning, from which the world order arose by some mysterious differentiation: the One became two, and then many; and yet, even after this cosmogonical process, the One remained one. Thus Anaximander's Unlimited continued to exist, outside the world which it enveloped, and also inside it as the one stuff of which all things were made. Even Anaximenes, though he simplified the scheme, still called his Air 'God.' It was immortal, exempt from decay and death, standing outside the wheel of time and change. It gave birth to things, and yet did not itself perish into those things. It was at once the soul of the world, the breath of its life, 'holding it together,' and the immutable stuff of the world's body, varying only in density.

Against such a conception Heracleitus rebelled. How can the life and soul of the changing world be itself exempt from change and mortality? There is no immortal being either outside the world or within it. There never was, nor will be, a primitive undifferentiated unity, abiding the same. *All* things move and flow. No undying substance can give birth to the things that die. Every birth is a death, and every death a birth. It follows that the world as we know it is unique, eternal, without beginning or end, always dying and always being born. There is no such thing as a cosmogony. 'This world was always, is now, and always will be an ever-living Fire'—ever-living (*aeizōon*), but not undying (*athanaton*). It is clear, too, that, whatever be the relation of this Fire to individual things, the principle of universal change precludes it from being a permanent stuff of which they are composed. Thus the Milesian scheme of cosmogony, with its original condition broken by the sundering of the opposite powers and its doctrine of an unchanging persistent form of matter, is swept away. The world is not first one, then many, then one again; but always both many and one. The world order is accepted as everlasting, and it is not so much an order as a process.

In his conception of this process which generates individual things, Heracleitus is again at issue with his predecessors. Anaximander's cosmogony had resulted in the separation of the four elements in their appointed regions, and he had implied that the mutual encroachment of these elements, whereby all living things come into being, was a work of 'injustice,' to be paid for in the final confusion of the elements and the dissolution of all the things they combined to produce. The right or just state of things, then, would be a static condition in which each element would remain within its province. Anaximander had not the notion of a harmony of opposites. The union of the opposite powers to produce life was a mere casual mixture; he saw it merely as a work of strife, not also of love. The Eros of earlier cosmogony had been banished with all the imagery of sex.

Heracleitus saw in this moral approval of a static condition a condemnation of the very life-process of the world. If the principle of justice, so conceived, were to be preserved inviolate, the world would be dead—a neat pattern of four forms of stuff arranged in concentric spheres, incapable of generating any living thing. To call this order 'justice' is to condemn the cyclic succession of the seasons, each prevailing in turn and bringing life, death, and rebirth in endless revolution. Heracleitus justifies the life of the world and that principle of strife which is the 'father of all things.' If Homer's prayer, 'O that strife might perish,' were heard, all things would pass away. 'War is common to all, and strife *is* justice.' Thus we are left only with the weather process, in which the whole life of the world, everything we call real, is involved.

The only thing that Heracleitus has in common with the Milesians is his recognition of this weather process—the 'way up and down,' as he calls it—as the significant process in Nature. It is a perpetual cyclic transformation of the elements into one another; but he cannot accept the notion of any persistent, really unchanging, stuff identified with any one of the opposite powers. The process must be re-interpreted so as to avoid this assumption. No one of the elements is 'immortal': 'Fire lives the death of air; air, the death of fire; water lives the death of earth; earth, the death of water.' What is constant in these transformations is not a persistent substance, but 'measures.' 'Earth becomes liquid sea, and is measured by the same tale (*logos*) as before it became earth.' 'All things are an exchange for Fire, and Fire for all things, as gold for wares and wares for gold': the substance changes; only the value is constant. The principle of Justice is satisfied by this

balance of 'measures kindling and measures being extinguished';
but the balance sways: there is an advance and retreat, which
explains the alternation of summer and winter, day and night.
Thus each encroachment or 'injustice' avenges a previous aggression, and the work of justice is thereby perpetually fulfilled.

The process of change is described, not as a mechanical condensation and rarefaction of unalterable stuff, but in terms of
living and dying. The transformation of the elements is paralleled
in the microcosm by the phases in the life of the soul. The soul,
on the downward way, sinks from its waking phase in which it is
fiery ('the dry soul is wisest and best'), through sleep, in which
moisture gains upon it, to death. 'It is death to souls to become
water, and death to water to become earth; but from earth comes
water, and from water soul.' Here are three phases of life, which
is not identical with any one of them, though at its best and purest
in the fiery phase. So in the macrocosm there is a divine life,
seen at its purest in fire, and therefore called Fire rather than
water or earth, but not simply identical with what is vulgarly
called fire. It is the 'thought' which 'steers all things through all
things.' It is 'willing and not willing to be called by the name
of Zeus' (*Zēn* = life)—willing, because it is life; unwilling, because life is also death. It is the 'one wise thing,' the *Logos* itself;
and it is Justice. It was precisely this complex of conceptions,
so difficult for the modern mind to hold together in a single
image, that the Stoics valued in Heracleitus. To them the *Logos*
was the all-pervading fiery breath of the living world, and also
Destiny, Law, Reason, Providence, God. It was not the same
thing as the fire they kindled on the hearth; nor was it so to
Heracleitus, though ordinary fire was the vehicle which best
revealed the nature of this hidden life.

To the Pythagoreans' moral dualism Heracleitus was even more
vehemently opposed. Aristotle has preserved their Table of
Opposites, in which ten pairs are arranged in a column of goods
and a column of evils. Limit, Unity, Rest, Light are among the
goods; the Unlimited, Plurality, Motion, Darkness are evil; and
this philosophy, like others, tends to assume that what it values
is real. Such propositions as these have no meaning for a scientific
man: why should anyone say, for instance, that motion is evil?
We find no such judgments in the Ionian tradition. They are the
utterance of desire, explicable only by religious preconceptions,
such as the longing of the exiled soul for reunion with God, for
an ultimate rest in some imagined haven of light. There are two
remarkable fragments in which Heracleitus seems to satirize this

ideal of unchanging rest in the service of our masters, the gods. 'The soul,' he says, 'finds refreshment in change'; 'to labour for the same (masters) and to be ruled by them is wearisome.' There is in fact no such thing as rest, nor any immortals that are not also mortal, 'the one living the others' death and dying the others' life.' Profoundly aristocratic, Heracleitus despised the notion that every one has a divine indestructible soul, of equal value and with an equal right to personal salvation—the spiritual basis of democracy. He spoke with contempt of the mystical sects, and of the ascetic ideal of purification, pursued in monastic retirement from the common life of the world.

Finally, alone among Greek thinkers, he rejected the whole conception of morality founded on the idea of 'Limit' or restraint, such a morality as the Pythagoreans elaborated in the doctrine of *harmonia*. There is a harmony of opposites; but it is not to be conceived as the imposition of fixed limits, arresting the natural movement of life. Limit, they said, was good; it quieted the troubled motions of the soul and put an end to conflict. In the physical world, as the principle of light, it ordered the dark void in a cosmic harmony. Light was good, darkness evil; they wanted a world which should be all light with no darkness; all summer with no winter; all peace with no war; all day with no night— a better world. Heracleitus answers: 'That men should get all they want is not a better thing: it is sickness that makes health pleasant; evil, good; hunger, plenty; weariness, rest.' 'God is day and night, summer and winter, war and peace, plenty and hunger.' Heracleitus rejects the notions that it is Limit that makes a harmony; that Limit is good; and that, in any pair of opposites, either can be called good, the other evil. The world consists of opposites, neither of which can exist without the other. 'They do not understand that what is at variance comes to terms with itself. It is a harmony of opposite tensions, like that of the bow or of the lyre.' It takes both hands, pulling opposite ways, to draw the bow: you cannot say that one pull is good, the other bad. The opposites check and balance one another; when one advances, the other gathers strength for the recoil. In this per- petual conflict justice is done by the combatants themselves. 'Good and Evil are one.' Nature, or God, knows nothing of human preferences and standards. 'To God all things are fair and good and right; but men hold some things wrong and some right.' Heracleitus does not mean that in God the opposition inherent in the world would finally be reconciled: that is pre- cisely the religious view which he combats. If the opposition should disappear, the life of the world would cease. His conception of what is meant by 'harmony' is totally different from the Pythagoreans', and is fatal to their whole philosophy of the cosmos.

Thus Heracleitus destroys every existing system of cosmology. He accepts the changing world we know, with its life-process, identified with the unceasing strife of opposite powers, revolving for ever in the wheel of time and change. There is no eternity beyond time; no immortal being over and above this ever-living and ever-dying world.

In Heracleitus, as in some others of the greatest thinkers, the historian is astonished and baffled by finding in his central thought what looks at first sight like an anticipation of the most modern views of physical reality, reached by intuition at one bound which overleaps all the painful process of observation, hypothesis, and experiment required to lead science to a similar standpoint. The appearance is in part illusory: the path of scientific progress is not circular, but more like a spiral. On the other hand, intuition plays a larger part in modern discovery than appears in the reasoned proof of its results; and it may be that the physicist to-day, like Heracleitus, is ultimately engaged sometimes in 'searching himself.' It is not surprising that what he finds should resemble the *logos*. In any case, nothing can lessen our admiration of Heracleitus' audacity in brushing aside the appearance of stability and rest and divining beyond it the unceasing flow of life itself.

IX. PARMENIDES

The criticism of Heracleitus does not appear to have had much effect in his own time. His influence is rather to be traced in the age of the Sophists, in Plato, and in the Stoics. It was left to his contemporary, Parmenides, to throw down a challenge that could not be ignored. The founder of the Eleatic school was bred in the Pythagorean tradition. He accepted the premises that Limit, Unity, Rest are good, and therefore attributes of the real. But, with a logic that seemed unanswerable, he exposed the latent contradiction in sixth-century Pythagoreanism, which had sought to combine these monistic premises with a dualistic system of Nature. If the real is indeed one, Nature cannot be a battle-ground of two opposite powers, good and evil, light and darkness, equally real. If the One is at rest, motionless, immutable, it cannot become two, and then many; it must always be one. Plurality, becoming, motion, change, and time itself must be in some way unreal. We must choose between monism and dualism.

Parmenides' own choice is not that of a man of science, prepared to accept and explain the obvious facts presented by the natural world. His preference for unity, rest, limitation, can be ultimately explained only by the value, and consequent reality, ascribed to these conceptions as divine attributes. The unity of God had been proclaimed by Xenophanes of Colophon, whose birth may be dated in the second quarter of the sixth century. As a satirist, he attacked both the religious movement as represented by Pythagoras and the traditional anthropomorphism of Homeric theology. On the positive side, he asserted the existence of 'one God, greater than any god or man, not like mortals either in form or thought, swaying all things without toil by the thought of his mind, and abiding ever in the same place, not moving at all.' Rather than surrender these attributes and what seemed to be their full logical consequences, Parmenides is prepared to set all common sense at defiance. Hence it is in the Eleatic school that the distrust of the senses, so immensely important in later thought, first emerges. This doctrine was indeed latent in the other-worldliness of the Pythagorean type of religion, in the condemnation of the body as a dark prison hiding the light of truth from the soul. Like the appetites, the senses were regarded as bodily and inseparably connected with pleasure, which ascetic religion suspects and denounces. But the philosophic conclusion that the senses are false witnesses to the external reality they profess to show us, was new. It was destined to lead, later on, to the scepticism of the Academy. The first parent of scepticism was not science, but religion.

Parmenides' work presents a blend, rarely to be met with, of prophecy and logic. Following the apocalyptic tradition, he cast his poem in the form of a revelation delivered to him by a goddess. Like the Orpheus and Pythagoras of legend, like the initiate in the mysteries, he visited the unseen world. But, if his premisses are dogmatic, he is also the first philosopher who argues; the very divinity who instructs him bids him 'judge by reasoning the much-disputed proof' she reveals. This proof is contained in the first of the two parts into which his poem is divided, the Way of Truth. It is a deduction of the nature of reality from certain premisses laid down as finally true. The conclusion is that the sense-world, since it exhibits plurality and change, which are inconsistent with that nature, cannot be wholly real. In spite of this conclusion, the second part, which may be called the Way of Seeming (*doxa*), contains a cosmology on the traditional dual-istic lines. Here the method of logical argument is dropped, and the cosmogony and anthropogony are narrated in the old dog-matic manner. What Parmenides can have meant by stating a cosmology apparently constructed on principles disproved in the first part, is a question that must be postponed until the Way of Truth has been examined.

The warning against the senses is given in the proem. The goddess tells Parmenides that he is to learn both 'ways of in-quiry'—both 'the unshaken heart of rounded truth' and 'what seems to mortals, in which there is no true belief.' From this second way he is to hold back his thought. 'Let not custom that has experience of many things force thee along this way, to cast an eye that wanders aimless, a hearing filled with murmuring sound, and a tongue; but judge by reasoning the much-disputed proof I utter.'

The premisses of the argument that follows in Part I are these: (1) What is, is and cannot not be; what is not, is not and cannot be. (2) What is, can be thought or known, and uttered or truly named; what is not, cannot. The second proposition seems to cover a number of meanings which Parmenides did not dis-tinguish. Thought must have an object, and that object must be something that is; it cannot be nothing. Only that which can be thought can be, and *vice versa*: the real must coincide with the conceivable, the logically coherent. The real is the only subject of true propositions, the only thing that, as Parmenides would say, can be 'truly named.' Two opposite predicates cannot both be true names of the real; one of them must be a false name, a name of nothing.

From the first premiss and from the axiom that 'what is,' or the real, is one, Parmenides deduces the impossibility, not only of absolute becoming out of nothing—that was common ground to all the philosophers—but of any kind of change or motion. This follows, if we understand the premiss to mean: what is not *now* cannot be *then*. He concludes that the real can neither be-come nor perish, change nor move. It is endless in time, though not in space, for it is not unlimited, but a perfect whole and 'in bulk like a well-rounded sphere.' Internally it is continuous (there is no Pythagorean 'void'), and homogeneous, for its unity excludes any distinction of parts.

This logical deduction disproves all previous systems. Both the Milesians and Pythagoras had believed in a cosmogony—an in-explicable becoming of many things out of one, by a motion or process which began, for no assignable reason, at some moment of time. The Pythagoreans taught the existence of a void ('what is not'), and a dualism of two real powers, light and darkness. Heracleitus, the worst offender, had denied all stable being and revelled in attributing opposite names to the real. All had fallen into hopeless error at the outset.

Some modern writers hold that Parmenides was trying to describe, in the extremely crude language at his disposal, an immaterial being. But the line between matter and mind was not yet drawn where Descartes drew it. The thinking substance was conceived universally as extended in space, and usually as consisting of the rarest form of body. On the other hand, it is equally a mistake to emphasize the 'material' properties, as if this substance were merely what we should call 'body.' Like the divine air of Anaximenes and the divine fire of Heracleitus, Parmenides' one Being overlaps the categories of modern thought.

In the earlier part of the poem, the goddess had denounced two ways of untruth, which appear to be the philosophy of Heracleitus and the false belief, common to all men, that becoming is possible—that 'what is not (at one time) can be (at another).' In the second part, she bids Parmenides 'learn what seems to mortals, hearkening to the deceitful fabric of my words.' She explains the causes of human error. 'Mortals have made up their minds to name two forms, one of which should not be named.' These forms are fire or light, and darkness, 'a dense and heavy form.' All the names ascribed to the latter are false and purely conventional; they are names of 'what is not.' Mortals believe them to be true because they are deceived by the senses, instead of following reason. Our conventional language follows the senses, which seem to show us a world composed of opposites, light and dark, hot and cold, and the rest. But if light is real, darkness must be unreal—a name of nothing, for there is no second thing beside the real. This ultimate error is shared by popular belief and all philosophic systems.

Nevertheless the goddess proceeds to state a cosmogony which starts by accepting this false appearance. The system has peculiar features, and there is no reason to doubt that it is Parmenides' own construction. The question of his motive for stating it has been much debated. Aristotle's view was that, though Parmenides' logic forced him to the conclusion that nothing existed except the one Being, he was 'compelled to fall in with appearances' and to admit a plurality of things according to the senses. The philosopher who founds a dissident school can hardly leave his disciples with no answer to the obvious criticism that the world does not look like an immovable plenum of evenly distributed homogeneous stuff. He would provide them with some account of 'appearances' which, though vitiated like every other by a false assumption, would at least be better than existing alternatives[1].

The details of this system may be passed over here. The importance of Parmenides lies in his advance towards the distinction between an intelligible and a sensible world, which becomes clear in Platonism. Some such distinction is already present in primitive thought, which observes a difference between ordinary tangible things and things that can be seen but not touched—reflections, dream-images, vapour, spirits, ghosts—and already wavers between regarding these intangibles as unsubstantial, less real than tangible objects, or as possessing supernatural power and in that way more real. In Greek philosophy the ways that part here diverge ever more widely. The Ionian tradition sets towards materialism, regarding body as more real than soul or mind, and ending in atomism, where all reality is reduced to the tangible. The mystical Italian tradition follows the other path, faithful to the religious estimate of the soul as more valuable and real than the body. It tends towards idealism which holds that the supersensible objects of thought are more real than the body and the objects of the bodily senses. This tendency was furthered by the preoccupation of the Pythagoreans with the world of mathematics. Parmenides takes a further step. His one Being is coming apart from the sensible world, whose appearances it refuses to support. It is the object of thought, not of sense, though these two modes of consciousness are not clearly distinguished. It is not tangible or properly a 'body,' though extended in space. Similarly a ghost, though extended and even visible, is 'bodiless,' because intangible. The only thing Parmenides calls a 'dense and heavy form' is Night—a false name for what is not. Parmenides is thus an ancestor of idealism, and for that reason spoken of by Plato with higher respect than he shows for any other predecessor.

[1] Other views of Parmenides' second part are: (1) that it contains 'the view of the world that would result from ordinary opinion' (Zeller)—but the system is not, so far as we know, any of the views that had in fact resulted; (2) that the cosmology is a Pythagorean system which Parmenides was renouncing. It is certainly on Pythagorean lines, in which Parmenides had been trained; but it is hard to believe that he would select out of a number of false systems the opinion of some Pythagoreans and call that 'the beliefs of mortals,' leaving his disciples with no account of the sense-world whatsoever.

X. EMPEDOCLES

The logic of Parmenides laid every physical system in ruins, and indeed denied *a priori* any possible cosmogony. The science of Nature, as then conceived, could not advance a step until some answer had been found, and the remaining pre-Socratic systems were contrived in order to restore to the real world plurality and motion. So this lofty debate upon first principles continued. Three solutions in the sense of pluralism were advanced. The pure Ionian tradition found, in the Periclean age, a leader in Anaxagoras, a typical man of science second in greatness only to Anaximander. The scientific wing of the Pythagorean school modified the doctrine of numbers into an inchoate form of atomism, which leads on to the atomism proper of Leucippus and Democritus. Between the two traditions Empedocles found a compromise. He reconstructed the system of Anaximander in such a way as, first, to accommodate the propositions Parmenides seemed to have established, and secondly to provide a scheme of the world's becoming and perishing in conformity with transmigration and all that it implies. The complications present in Empedocles' system and absent from that of Anaxagoras are traceable to the latter motive.

Born at Acragas in Sicily, probably in the first decade of the fifth century, Empedocles took a prominent part there in the democratic revolution. As the older associate of Gorgias, he was called by Aristotle the founder of rhetoric. He influenced profoundly the theory of the western medical school; he is one of the only two philosophers mentioned in the writings attributed to Hippocrates. Add to this that he was among those poets of whom Lucretius says that 'with divine inspiration they gave, from the inmost shrine of thought, oracles of greater sanctity and surer ground than any utterance of the Pythian priestess'—words which peculiarly fit the oracular style and temper of Empedocles' verse. The two poems of which fragments survive, *On Nature* and *Purifications*, contained respectively his physical system and his religious vision of the spiritual destiny of the soul.

The cosmology, though presented in the traditional apocalyptic manner, may be best understood by analytical treatment. Empedocles rejects Parmenides' wholesale condemnation of the senses: we are not to distrust any organ that gives 'a passage for understanding.' A theory of nature consistent with the appearances of sense is possible—especially a real conflict of opposite powers—even though some of Parmenides' conclusions be accepted. The theory offered is a remodelling of Anaximander's scheme of an undifferentiated unity, part of which remained in its original state enveloping the world, while part was differentiated by the separation of opposite powers out of the primal fusion. This process led to the world order, in which the four elementary masses occupied their concentric regions. Thus an ordered many arose from the one. Against this Parmenides had urged that the one real being must always be one, perfect, and at rest. All becoming, change, and motion, and all plurality were disproved by the principles that 'what is not (at one time) cannot be (at another),' 'what is one cannot be (or become) not one (many).' As directed against Anaximander's Unlimited stuff, this argument implies that if it is ever really one, a homogeneous continuum with no internal distinctions, there is no reason why at any moment of time it should depart from this condition, no reason why opposite qualities should begin to separate out of it, or why part of it should become denser, part rarer. An *eternal* motion does not explain how a world could 'arise later rather than sooner' (Parmenides 8, 9). The argument is unanswerable, if the unlimited One has the perfect homogeneity postulated by Parmenides; but not if it is a mixture of several eternally distinct elements. Empedocles saw here the way of escape. He begins by accepting two Parmenidean doctrines: the denial of a void (an existent nothing), and the denial of 'becoming and perishing,' with its corollary 'what is one cannot become many.' If the opposite powers, Hot, Cold, Wet, and Dry, came out of the One, they must previously have been in it; 'coming out' means only separation, not that what was not before begins to exist. The four powers, always conceived rather as things than 'qualities' (a later term), are ultimate, immutable 'elements' in the strict sense, for which Empedocles' term is 'roots.' They are originally mixed in the one mass; they separate out of it, and recombine to form, in infinite variety of compounds, all individual things. This simple amendment, hardly more than a clarification of the confusion in Anaximander's thought, rescues the Milesian scheme, so far, from the Eleatic criticism. By this curious route philosophy reached the fundamental conception of modern chemistry. In one other respect Empedocles, following Parmenides, modifies the Milesian 'Unlimited': the whole of the real is contained in a limited sphere, no part of the original mixture being left outside.

There remains the problem of motion. How could the primitive mixture be broken up and the elements sorted out into their proper regions? The cosmogonical process has to be restored.

Parmenides had spoken as if motion implied 'becoming,' and had denied motion in consequence: 'It is immovable...*because* becoming and perishing have been driven afar' (Parmenides 8, 26). Empedocles saw that his elements could move, without any becoming or perishing being involved, or any void, if one part of the mixture always replaced another. Motion, then, is not logically objectionable, given several things to move. But it needs a cause, to break up the primal mixture.

Empedocles provides two living and self-moving substances, which run through the elements and direct their motion. They are called Love and Strife. These are not new inventions. They represent the two forces, or opposite tensions, of the harmony of opposites as conceived by Heracleitus. Between opposite things such as the elementary pairs, Hot and Cold, Wet and Dry, there is both mutual repulsion, hatred, or strife, driving them apart, and also mutual attraction, a principle of love and union, drawing them together. The two principles are themselves opposed: Love is good, Strife evil. The Pythagorean dualism re-emerges in more explicit form. The good and evil principles, at war in the world and in the soul, are recognized as two distinct and irreducible factors in the composition of the universe.

The mythical traits of the combining principle, the Eros of Hesiod and the Orphics, who re-unites the sundered parents Heaven and Earth, had been suppressed by Anaximander, though he retained the symbolism of warfare and aggression; now, in the poet philosopher, both Love and Strife reappear in quasi-scientific form. Love, the cosmic force, is not only called Aphrodite, but explicitly identified with the power of attraction 'implanted in mortal limbs, whereby they have thoughts of love and accomplish the works of union.' The contrary power is Ares, the 'War' or strife of opposites which Heracleitus had called the 'father of all things.' Later, the same two powers, Venus and Mars, reassert themselves in a system which has no place for them, the otherwise arid atomism of Lucretius. In Empedocles Love and Strife belong at once to the world of mythical imagery and to the world of scientific concepts. Aphrodite and Ares are living and moving substances, existing in space and passing through the other four substances called 'roots,' from which they differ as being super-sensible—soul-substances rather than bodies. They are subject to the old law of *enantiodromia*: each prevails in turn and in turn gives way to the other. In this guise the life originally inherent in the Milesian world-stuff is detached from it and deposited in distinct substances which act, so to say, as fluid forces. Correspondingly, the bodily elements are depressed towards their final degradation as dead, inert 'matter.'

The factors of the Milesian scheme are thus clarified and rounded out; and we should expect that, impelled by Strife, the elements in the mixture should now move apart to their stations, and thus complete the world order. This does in fact happen; but at this point comes in the complication attributable to Empedocles' concern for the doctrine of transmigration. The life-history of the world runs parallel to the spiritual history of mankind and of the individual soul described in the *Purifications*. A comparison of the two, stage by stage, will show that the religious scheme set the pattern for the physical; for their common features are only explicable by theological pre-conceptions. The theme of the *Purifications* is the fall of man and of the individual soul from a blessed state of lovingkindness to a state of sin and misery, and the purification whereby paradise may be regained. The doctrine, Orphic in character, had already been outlined by Pindar in his second Olympian ode written for Theron, tyrant of Acragas, in 476 B.C. when Empedocles was a youth (see p. 510).

(1) In the primeval state of innocence Aphrodite held an undivided reign. This golden age knew nothing of war or bloodshed, animal sacrifice or flesh-eating. 'All creatures, beast and bird, were tame and gentle to man, and the flame of lovingkindness burned.' In language of extraordinary exaltation God is described as beyond the reach of our eyes or touch of our hands, and without bodily parts. 'He is a Mind, holy and ineffable, and that alone, flashing with swift thoughts through the whole order of the world' (frag. 134). The law which prohibits bloodshed 'extends everywhere, through the wide-ruling air and the infinite light' (frag. 135).

Now the condition of the universe before the evolution of our world is the physical counterpart of the moral condition above described. The 'Sphere' consisted of a complete mixture of the bodily elements, penetrated throughout and united by Love. Strife was excluded from the mass, of which it formed the envelope. 'There was no discord nor unseemly strife in its members' (frag. 27 a). In almost the same words that were used of God, the Sphere is described as 'without arms or feet, or knees, or parts of generation,' 'rejoicing in his encircled loneliness' (frags. 29, 27).

(2) The fall of man was caused by a violation of the universal law of lovingkindness, by bloodshed, the killing of animals and eating of flesh. Sextus observes: 'Pythagoras, Empedocles, and all the Italians say that there is bond of fellowship uniting us, not only to one another and to the gods, but also to the irrational

animals...Empedocles says: "Will ye not cease from ill-sounding slaughter? See ye not that in your unkindliness ye are devouring one another?"' 'O that the pitiless day of death did not destroy me, before ever I thought of the monstrous deed of devouring with my lips.' To the believer in transmigration all flesh-eating is cannibalism. The wages of this sin is the exile of the soul, which falls into the wheel of birth. The guilty spirit wanders for a great year of 'three myriad seasons' through a round of incarnations in the forms of man, animal, and plant.

Physically, the fall of the universe from the state of complete union animated by Love is caused by the incursion of Strife, which begins to pour into the Sphere and break it up by separating the elements, like to like. There begins a period of world-formation, to which our world belongs—or rather a half-period, for it is only half of the great year of the world, the wheel of time. Strife is now gaining on Love; our world is passing from the best state to the worst, the reign of Strife. In this latter state, at the opposite pole of the circle, the four elements, which meanwhile have combined with the moving substances to form all individual things as transitory compounds, will be separated completely in their concentric spheres. Love will be expelled from the world, now pervaded by Strife. This, be it noted, is the condition which Anaximander implied was 'just'—each element keeping within its bounds and not encroaching on the rest. But, as Heracleitus saw, it is a state of death; in it no individual thing can exist.

(3) The wanderings of the banished soul end when it is purified and returns to God. According to its deeds in each incarnation, it passes up or down the scale of life. 'At the last they appear among mortal men as seers, singers, physicians, and leaders of men' (Empedocles was all these), 'and then they spring up as gods highest in honour, sharing the hearth of the other immortals, free from human sorrows, from destiny, and from all harm' (frags. 146, 147). Empedocles had reached this threshold of divinity: 'In me you see an immortal god, mortal no more' (frag. 112).

To this return of the soul corresponds, in the physical system, the second half-period, in which, by a reverse process, Love gains on Strife and another world is formed that will end in the reign of Love and the perfect unity of the Sphere. Then the cycle begins again, in unending repetition of 'the twofold tale: at one time a One grows out of many to be alone; at another it parts asunder to be many out of One.'

In spite of this peculiar elaboration of the twofold tale, manifestly modelled upon the fate of the soul in the wheel of birth, modern critics almost unanimously declare that the system of nature excludes the possibility of the individual soul's persistence after the dissolution of the body. We are to explain this contradiction by assigning one or other of the poems to the philosopher's old age, or by supposing that he overlooked an inconsistency in the central field of interest, and never brought his religious beliefs and his scientific theories together in his mind. These desperate suppositions can be avoided by studying what Empedocles tells us of the second chapter of cosmogony—the formation of individual mortal things.

As in the old Milesian scheme, the origin of living creatures is referred to the 'weather process,' though this is no longer a transformation, but a mixing of eternally distinct elements. Plants arose (before animals) out of the ground where the fire contained in earth, moving upwards to seek its like—for the elements still retain self-motion in this form—combined with the moist earth tending downwards. Animals sprang from earth by the same process, in featureless shapes containing portions of moisture and heat. In our world, where Strife is gaining, they develop by differentiation. In the opposite half-period, where Love gains, the parts of animals arise separately, to be combined sometimes in monstrous abortive forms, sometimes in shapes fitted to survive. The organic tissues composing them—blood, flesh, bones, and sinews—consist of several elements united in definite proportions (ratios, *logoi*), expressible in numbers. Thus the formula for bone is: two parts water, two parts earth, four parts fire, 'fitted together by the cement of *Harmonia*' (*i.e.* Love). Of primary importance is the blood, for this is the vehicle of consciousness. As a physical body, this contains all the four bodily elements in about equal proportions (frag. 98); but, as a conscious substance, it also contains portions of Love and Strife, for, on the principle that like knows like, 'by earth we see Earth; by water, Water; by air, the bright Air; by fire, the destroying Fire; and *by Love we see Love; by Strife, grievous Strife*' (frag. 109). Death consists in the dissolution of the four bodily elements. If the living creature consisted only of these, there would be no soul to survive. But what becomes of the portions of Love and Strife?

It has already been shown that the two living things or forces, Love and Strife, hover on that still indistinct verge where the sensible merges in the supersensible, the physical concept in the mythical image. It is precisely here that we shall find notions that are certainly confused and will appear to us inconsistent. So they already appeared to Aristotle, who could not make out whether or not Empedocles intended to identify the soul with 'the proportion of the mixture' of bodily elements, and this again with Love, the 'cement of *Harmonia*.' Since Philolaus regarded the soul as an *harmonia*—a system of numbers regulating a 'mixture'—there is no difficulty in supposing the same complex of ideas in Empedocles, who influenced him. Philolaus, moreover, was not aware of any difficulty in combining this conception with survival and transmigration. It is possible, by an effort of imagination, to picture the soul as a portion of Love, contaminated, in the impure embodied state, with a portion of Strife, and to identify it with the numerical proportion, ratio, or *harmonia* of the elements, considered as an organizing principle capable of passing from one compound to another, and holding them together. To a mind which had not attained to conceiving anything as totally 'immaterial,' such a *logos* might present itself as an extremely rare substance or fluid force, pervading the bodily elements. Since Love and Strife are indestructible, the compound of both, which is the soul, can survive the dissolution of the body, retain its identity, and move into another bodily compound. It would lose its separate existence when the Love in it was finally purified from the taint of Strife and merged with the other portions of Love in the unity of the Sphere. This is the physical transcription of the spiritual reunion of the soul with God.

To the modern mind the confusion and inconsistency of such a complex image is so patent that we can only by a strong effort hold its components together. As concepts become clarified and distinct with the progress of reflection, it ceases to be possible to conceive a proportion as an extended substance; it passes irrevocably into the new category of relation. But to ascribe to Empedocles such a confusion of ideas is a different thing from accusing him of the kind of inconsistency that means the holding simultaneously two explicit and incompatible propositions, such as that the soul survives bodily death, and that the natural world contains no such thing as a soul that can survive. What is here denied is that Empedocles did clearly teach one of these propositions in his poem on Nature, the other in the *Purifications*.

XI. ANAXAGORAS

Anaxagoras of Clazomenae, born about 500 B.C., was some years older than Empedocles, but his work was later. He is said to have lived for about thirty years (480–450 B.C.?) at Athens. Then, after a prosecution which was part of a political attack upon his 'pupil' Pericles, the ostensible motive being his impious opinion that the heavenly bodies were nothing but incandescent rocks, he retired to Lampsacus, the Milesian colony, and became head of the school which continued the philosophy of Anaximenes, his reputed master[1]. Throughout his life he represented the scientific tradition of Ionia. He was celebrated for his discovery of the true causes of lunar and solar eclipses.

In cosmology Anaxagoras was concerned, like Empedocles, to remodel the Milesian system so as to meet Parmenides' objections; but being totally unconcerned with Empedocles' religious preoccupations, he was able to proceed on a simpler plan. We possess considerable fragments of his book; but the interpretation is difficult, because he had to express some very subtle conceptions in language exceedingly crude and ambiguous.

Unmoved by Parmenides' prejudice against infinity, Anaxagoras rejects the perfect sphere and reverts to Anaximander's conception of an unlimited mass enveloping any world that is formed within it. Like Empedocles, he accepts the denial of all becoming and perishing, and restores motion. He has also a distinct moving cause, no longer entangled, as in the Milesians and Heracleitus, with one of the opposites or elements, water, air, or fire. Empedocles, to whom the world was a battle-ground of good and evil, had required two moving substances. Anaxagoras, ignoring all notions of good and evil, strife and harmony, needs only one, to which he gives the unemotional name of 'Mind.' Mind, like the scientific intellect, neither loves nor hates, nor desires anything but order.

This Mind is endowed with just those qualities, and no others, that are required to cause motion and to produce an ordered world. It is a supersensible substance, conscious—for in order to have power over all things, it must know them—extended in space, rarer than all the bodily substances it moves, and so capable of penetrating everywhere. Portions of it form the living and moving principle in animate creatures. But it is unmixed with bodily substance, remaining always 'self-ruled' and distinct, perfectly pure, and homogeneous. Its cosmic function was to initiate, from some point in the mass, a revolution which spread, like an eddy, 'from a small beginning, and will spread farther still.' This revolution mechanically caused the 'separation' (in a peculiar sense) of the rarer portion of the matter involved in it from the denser, the hotter from the colder, and so on. The

[1] For the dates above given, see A. E. Taylor, *Classical Quarterly*, XI, (1917), 81; Burnet, *Early Greek Philosophy* (1920), 251.

primitive formula—separation of opposites out of an undifferentiated unity—still fits the cosmogonical process. Mind is nowhere described as aiming at goodness or perfection; it only sets
things in order. If the notion of design is suggested by the name,
it remains implicit; and Mind is called in only to impart a
mechanical impulsion. Hence the dissatisfaction of Socrates who
believed in Providence, of Plato whose Demiurge desired that
the world should be good, and of Aristotle whose God was actually
the end to which all creation aspires.

Anaxagoras' book opened with the description of the original
state of the material universe, in which 'all things were together.'
Like Empedocles, he sought to derive a manifold world out of a
unity without the assumption of 'becoming,' by pushing plurality
back into the unity. But he rejected the conception of a small
set of elementary substances, and succeeded in retaining the indeterminate character of the Milesian Unlimited.

The peculiar features of Anaxagoras' theory are traceable to
the fact that he construed the denial of all becoming and perishing
more strictly than either Empedocles or the Atomists. According
to Empedocles any organic substance was ultimately resolvable
into several distinct, immutable things; a piece of flesh, for
instance, was reducible to portions of the four elements combined
in nearly equal amounts. If these were sorted out into four
parcels, the flesh would vanish. If they were put together again,
the flesh would reappear; it would 'become' out of four things,
none of which was flesh before, and each of which must retain
immutably its characteristic properties. Anaxagoras took this
actual instance and asked, 'How can hair come out of what is
not hair, or flesh out of what is not flesh?' If the ultimate factors
were monads or indivisible magnitudes (atoms), the same problem
would arise. The Parmenidean canon 'what is, cannot come out
of what is not' would be violated. Flesh cannot come out of what
is 'not flesh' in the sense of atoms or Empedoclean elements. If
the canon is to be strictly observed, it is necessary to conclude
that every distinct substance to which we give a name is infinitely
divisible into similar parts. However far the division is carried,
you will never reach a point where flesh (or whatever it may be)
ceases to be flesh and is resolved either into fire, air, earth, and
water or into atoms. Infinite divisibility is clearly asserted: 'Of
the small there is no smallest, but always a smaller, for what is,
cannot cease to be by being cut[1].' There is no such thing as
an atom.

[1] Frag. 3, reading τομῇ with Zeller.

But, though flesh cannot come out of any alleged simpler and ultimately real atoms or elements, on the other hand not only flesh but all the organic substances in our bodies—hair, veins, sinews, bones—do come out of other substances on the same level with themselves, namely the food we eat and drink. Bread and water are not 'elements,' and flesh is not composed of portions of them added together; but bread and water can somehow *change* into flesh. Anaxagoras is the first philosopher to distinguish change not merely from sheer becoming out of nothing but also from motion or the rearrangement in space of immutable bodies.

His solution of the problem of change may be conjecturally reconstructed as follows. Every substance, *i.e.* every perceptible or imperceptible piece of matter, contains all the opposites or fundamental properties of matter. Anaxagoras may have recognized an indefinite number of such properties. Four pairs of opposites are mentioned: the hot and cold, wet and dry of the Milesians; the dense and rare of Anaximenes; the bright and dark of Parmenides. The statement that everything has a portion of all these 'things' might be expressed in modern terms as meaning that everything has some degree of temperature, of moisture, of resistance, and of colour. These are universal properties of matter. The only difference between two kinds of substance (flesh, bread, gold, etc.) is, as we should say, a difference of degree in one or more of these qualities; or, as Anaxagoras would put it, different things have larger or smaller 'portions' of these 'things[1].'

The essential novelty of his view is that he regards each pair of opposites as forming a continuum. Anaximander had thought of the hot and the cold as two distinct things, which, like wine and water, could be either completely fused in his Unlimited stuff or separated out. Similarly Empedocles' elements, grouped in pairs of opposites, remained eternally distinct, though they could be mixed together in the Sphere. Anaxagoras, on the contrary, substituted the conception of a continuum of hot and cold and of each of the other pairs of opposite qualities. 'The things (*i.e.* qualities) in the one world are not separated from one another or cut off with an axe—neither warm from cold nor cold from warm' (frag. 8). In the hottest thing there is some cold: even 'snow is black.' Since all the fundamental qualities are universal, any substance can change into any other by imper-

[1] Anaxagoras does not speak of 'qualities' (a term not yet invented), but of 'things.' The term 'quality' is used in the text only for the sake of distinguishing these 'things' from things in the ordinary sense.

ceptible changes of degree in one or more qualities. Thus the Parmenidean canon will not be violated. All the same qualities will be present after, as before, the change; no new 'thing' will have come into existence. To take an obvious illustration: steam, water, and ice differ in temperature and density. Each contains a 'portion' of heat and cold, of the dense and the rare. Transition from one form to another is effected by a change in the amount of these portions; but none of the 'things' or qualities involved will have begun or ceased to exist. In this view the transmutation of any substance into any other is theoretically possible. The notions of immutable elements and of atoms are abandoned.

With the aid of this conception the cosmogonical process can now be described. At the beginning 'all things were together': there was an unlimited mass, no part of which differed from any other in respect of any of the qualities. At some moment Mind initiated a revolution, which began to spread outwards, like an eddy, from some centre, and is still spreading. The first effect was that the matter towards the outside of the eddy became rarer, hotter, drier, brighter, while the matter towards the centre became denser, colder, wetter, darker. That is to say, the periphery began to assume the appearance of fire, the core that of air. As Theophrastus says, the original mixture resembled Anaximander's Unlimited, and might be regarded as 'a single nature indeterminate in quality and quantity[1].' But Theophrastus adds that it might also be conceived as an 'infinite number of material principles,' or (to use Anaxagoras' own expression) of 'seeds' of every kind. This term suggests that, as the differentiation proceeded, similar particles were formed at points where the same degrees of temperature, moisture, and density occurred. Such a set of particles would be the 'seeds' of some substance whose nature is determined by just these degrees of the various qualities. There would be an indefinite number of sets, one for each different kind of substance. Since there is no minimum size for a particle— no such thing as an atom—this process has strictly no beginning other than the first beginning of motion. Next, on the assumption (explicitly affirmed by Anaxagoras) that 'like moves towards like,' the similar particles forming any one set were attracted to one another, and so grew by aggregation until they became large enough to be perceived and recognized as different substances—

[1] This statement is historically true only if we take 'indeterminate in quality' to mean, not (with Theophrastus) the absence of any quality, but the absence of any limits between qualities, which, however, do exist in the original indiscriminate or unlimited mixture.

bread, flesh, gold, and all the rest. Thus Anaxagoras was able to represent the transition from the original indeterminate unity to an indefinite manifold as smooth and continuous. Proceeding in the reverse direction, you can resolve any perceptible piece of matter—say, a gold coin—into smaller and smaller pieces of gold. After a certain point they will cease to be perceptible, but they will still be gold, and thought can pursue them until they become mere points with a specific degree of all the universal qualities, somewhere in the mass. There is no moment of sudden 'becoming,' no catastrophic beginning, until you reach the beginning of motion. That was a catastrophe; and Anaxagoras seems to have left this unexplained intervention of Mind as a minimum postulate. Science cannot account for everything.

An important feature in this theory is the conception of the threshold of perceptibility, and the view of the senses it implies. Anaxagoras realized that thought can go beyond the senses and conceive the infrasensible. The senses 'because of their weakness are not able to discern the truth.' This weakness was illustrated by the inability of sight to follow the infinitesimal changes of colour when a black fluid is poured drop by drop into a white. But, within their limits, the senses are not discredited, as they had been by Parmenides. Objects actually have those qualities that we perceive, and continue to have them below the level of perceptibility. Qualities other than resistance are not dismissed, as they were by Atomism, as secondary or 'conventional.'

Thanks to the Socratics, the fame of Anaxagoras rested in later ages on his doctrine of Mind and the hint they took from it of a benevolent creator. Attention was thus distracted from his doctrine of matter, though this was the subtlest of all the pre-Socratic theories and deserved to rank with the most signal triumphs of scientific reasoning. Atomism, though cruder, had the advantage of being extremely clear and easy to conceive. It survived for this reason, and because it satisfied the requirements of the Epicurean school, who were antagonistic to the whole doctrine of divine providence constructed by the Socratics from the hint furnished by Anaxagoras' Mind.

XII   ATOMISM

In our account of the earliest Pythagorean system mention was made of the split which appears to have divided the school of Pythagoras in the fifth century into a conservative branch, who held to the religious and mystical doctrine, and a rationalist group, who turned from mysticism towards science (p. 545). The former tradition was represented in the time of Socrates by Philolaus, who adopted from Empedocles the conception of elements and built it into a remodelled Pythagoreanism. He clung to the theory of a world harmony and to the religious doctrine that the body is the tomb of the soul. In contrast with this religious branch of the school, there seems to have been a purely scientific re-interpretation of the doctrine of numbers, designed to obviate the criticisms of Parmenides and to avoid his monistic conclusion. This system was an inchoate form of atomism, from which atomism proper was developed by Leucippus about the middle of the fifth century, and by his more famous successor, Democritus of Abdera. Our knowledge of this earlier form is derived partly from Aris-totle, partly from the attacks made upon it by Zeno, the pupil of Parmenides. Zeno's criticism was not, like that of Parmenides, directed against the inconsistency of the monistic inspiration and the dualistic cosmology of the first Pythagoreans. As a faithful adherent of Parmenides, Zeno, with an amazingly subtle logic, attacked the view that the plurality and motion given in the sense-world and paradoxically denied by Parmenides can be restored by regarding the real as composed of an indefinite plurality of units or monads, set in empty space. This is not the hypothesis of primitive Pythagoreanism; nor is it the developed atomism of Leucippus, which belongs to a somewhat later time. It seems to represent the scientific Pythagoreans' answer to Parmenides. The system may be called 'number-atomism,' since it is a reinterpre-tation, in an atomistic sense, of the doctrine that all things are numbers.

Aristotle attributes to 'the Pythagoreans' the doctrine that sensible bodies are actually composed of 'numbers,' which are not abstract, but consist of indivisible units having spatial magnitude. These units are indistinguishable from one another (whereas the atoms of Leucippus differed in shape), and any one can be added to any other; they are identified with the units of number in the ordinary arithmetical sense. The theory is materialistic. What is composed of numbers is not the soul or intangible essence of a sensible object, not an *Harmonia* or ratio, but the visible, tangible body itself. A theory of this kind might be derived from the ancient practice of representing numbers by pebbles or counters arranged in geometrical patterns. The pebbles may stand, as it were, for magnified atoms; the space or 'field' between them is analogous to the void. By adding unit to unit, a solid body of any size and shape can be constructed. With this simple materialistic conception of an infinity of monads, the old mystical derivation of the world and its harmony from the divine Monad and the 'elements of number' disappears; and with it go all the religious notions of the harmony of warring opposites, good and evil, the correspondence of macrocosm and microcosm, and the ideal of the imitation of God. The real is reduced to discrete quantity, with the single purpose of restoring the possibility of plurality and motion. The theory amounts to an identification of the arithmetical unit with the geometrical point, and of both with the minimal indivisible pieces of which tangible bodies are built. A line is a row of these points or monads; a surface is a row of lines; a solid, or body, is made of surfaces superimposed in layers. Against this view Zeno forged those paradoxical arguments, including Achilles and the Tortoise and the Flying arrow, which were finally explained only within living memory, and which, incidentally, marked a great advance towards the mathematical conceptions of continuity and infinity.

The atomism of Leucippus, probably a native of Miletus who migrated to Elea about the middle of the fifth century, is a continuation of this inchoate number-atomism. It belongs, accordingly, to the Italian tradition, and is not, like the other two pluralist systems of Empedocles and Anaxagoras, a reconstruction of the Milesian scheme. Atomism has no primal unity, but an indefinite plurality of atoms which never were, nor will be, one. Its 'unlimited' is the Pythagorean void. The opposite qualities, hot, cold, etc., do not belong to the ultimately real atoms, but are described as merely 'conventional.'

Leucippus held that reality consisted of the atoms, which are 'compact' or 'full,' and the empty space in which they move. He defended the void against Parmenides by arguing that, though a void was 'nothing,' *i.e.* not real substance or body, there was no reason why it should not exist. The atoms, on their side, were material in a fuller sense than Parmenides' one Being. That Being was not strictly 'corporeal'; though extended in space, it was rather a soul-substance like Anaxagoras' Mind or Empedocles' Love and Strife, and was an object of thought, having no sensible qualities. The atom, on the contrary, is essentially corporeal; and, if it is imperceptible, it is so only because it is too small. In its nature it is the tangible, a solid offering impenetrable resistance. It is, moreover, lifeless. The system is materialistic in that it reduces soul to the level of body (for soul consists of atoms whose only peculiarity is spherical shape), and life to motion in space. By this simplification plurality and motion were once more restored. The controversy since Parmenides had turned on the question whether these were possible, and it had come to be thought that, once their reality was justified, the task of physics was almost done. The infinite variety of sensible qualities—colours, tastes, etc.—was disposed of by referring them to differences in the shape, arrangement, and position of the atoms. Thus the secondary qualities were transferred from the reality outside us to the subjective side; in a world containing no sentient creatures such things would not exist.

In this extreme pluralism anything that can be called God disappears out of the world, which must become the realm either of chance or of necessity. Leucippus chose necessity: 'Nothing,' he said, 'happens at random; everything happens on some account and by necessity.' The formation of any one of the innumerable worlds in space is due to an eddy or vortex, in which the smaller and smoother atoms are sifted out towards the circumference, while the larger and rougher congregate at the centre. Since there is no distinct soul-substance endowed with the power of moving itself, no special cause is left to account for motion. Leucippus took the scientific course of postulating that the motion of the atoms was an eternal fact.

The popularity of this cheerless philosophy in later antiquity is to be ascribed less to its intrinsic merits than to the anti-theological prejudices which it gratified. It was valued for its negative conclusions, for its banishment of God and the immortal soul, indeed of anything that can be recognized as life. It was, perhaps, necessary for the future progress of science that causes so inextricably involved in supernatural and mystical attributes should be totally excluded from physics in order to undergo the most rigid examination before being readmitted. Philosophy, however, proved unequal to this task. On the scientific side the first free impulse was already failing; and on the religious, Socrates was already preparing the reaction, in the interest of morals, against the materialistic denial of everything valued by the religious consciousness.

XIII. CONCLUSION

The alternative theories of Anaxagoras and Leucippus brought physical science to a point beyond which further advance was hardly possible in default of instruments of precision and of the methods of observation and experiment to which such instruments open up an immensely extended field. If some Archimedes had overcome the Greek prejudice against mechanical crafts and invented optical glass, the world would not have waited nearly two thousand years for a Copernicus to confirm the speculations of Aristarchus of Samos and deal the death-blow to geocentric astronomy. Such a discovery would have changed the whole course of history. As it was, the conflict of unverifiable hypotheses led to a reaction. The philosophers' controversy had become extremely abstract, beyond the reach of any but the greatest minds. In the latter half of the fifth century, lesser men, like Diogenes of Apollonia and Archelaus, the first Athenian physicist, were dropping behind and echoing the doctrine of Anaximenes. To the ordinary man—witness, the *Clouds* of Aristophanes—the philosopher was already a grotesque, unpractical figure, with a childish taste for logic-chopping and fantastic theories, which would have been merely contemptible, if they had not been suspected of threatening religion and morals. The influence of the sophists was diverting the ablest young men from the serious pursuit of what, till then, had been called wisdom, and substituting the pursuit of political success in the democratic state, where power was the reward of effective eloquence. Protests came even from the great exponent of the only practical art which had a scientific basis—the art of medicine. Hippocrates urged the claims of experience against the *a priori* hypotheses of metaphysics.

But the last word was with Socrates, who accomplished, in ancient thought, a Copernican revolution of another kind. Hitherto philosophy had been looking backward to find the beginning of things. Socrates turned it round and bade it look to the end—the good for which the world existed, not the source from which it came. The effect on physics was disastrous. For the first time in Greek thought there emerged the doctrine of a benevolent creator, the Mind of Anaxagoras, set to the task of designing a world upon a perfect model. This hypothesis cuts the heart out of physical speculation by providing a complete answer to every question. Why does this happen, rather than that? Because it is for the best. When the *why* is known, the *how* matters little. To Plato the 'science' which dealt with the sense-world was no science, but a plausible myth. Not even the genius of Aristotle could secure a permanent foothold for the study of truth, unprejudiced by the cult of virtue or the pursuit of happiness.

CHAPTER XVI

EARLY GREEK ART

I. INTRODUCTION

THE early story of Greek art is concerned with three phenomena: the reign of a primitive geometric art from the tenth
century to the eighth; the assimilation of Oriental influences
towards and after the close of that period; and the formation,
assisted at first by these Oriental models, of a new national style,
the Greek archaic, in the seventh and sixth centuries. The cul-
mination of this style, at the end of the sixth century and the
beginning of the fifth, is attended by the collapse, for the first
time in the world's history, of certain age-long conventions, and
the way is thus prepared for an art of unprecedented freedom,
the classical Greek art of the fifth and fourth centuries. The final
and most momentous period of archaic art will not be treated in
this chapter: the lower chronological limit will be about 520 B.C.

The literary sources for the history of sixth-century art are
extremely scanty, and for the art of the preceding centuries there
is hardly any direct literary testimony. Inscriptional evidence
begins in the seventh century. But most of our knowledge is
derived from the stylistic and other peculiarities of the objects
themselves, and from the circumstances of their discovery. Sometimes an object can be connected closely or loosely with a datable
person or event; and other objects can be dated relatively to the
first.

Of the vast number of objects produced in antiquity, some
had a better chance of surviving to our times than others. Some
substances are perishable (wood, plaster, textiles), others comparatively durable but convertible (marble, bronze), others comparatively durable and comparatively inconvertible (well-baked
clay, gem-stones). Thus painted clay vessels must take the place,
for us, of paintings on wood or wall; small bronzes, lost or discarded, for the most part, in antiquity, of the large bronze statues
which remained in place to be melted down; and only a small
proportion of marble statues have escaped utter defacement or
the lime-kiln. For these reasons, and for others, such as the lack

¹ The references in the footnotes of this chapter are to Volume of Plates i.

of exploration in many areas, there are great gaps in our monumental evidence. In the early period, however, our sources, though scanty, are untroubled: the objects to be dealt with are almost exclusively originals, and not, as in subsequent periods, largely later copies or imitations: unearthed but lately, they have suffered little at the restorer's hands: lastly we may feel confident that, on the whole, the best of them, whether sculptures or paintings, are equal in quality to the best of their time: for the archaic sculptures of the Acropolis were buried in an age which paid little respect to the work of the past, and were not disinterred until our own days; and it was not till well after the Persian Wars that painting took such a leap as to leave the decoration of vases far behind: 'the vases of the classical period are but a reflection of classical beauty; the vases of the archaic period are archaic beauty itself.'

II. GEOMETRIC ART

Between the flourishing of the Creto-Mycenaean civilization, and the geometric period proper, there lies a long period which has been named, not very happily, the proto-geometric: a period of cultural decay, doubtless of invasions and incessant conflict. The remains are chiefly ceramic. The shapes and decoration of the vessels are commonplace. The material which the painter uses is still that lustrous black glaze which was invented by Middle Minoan potters, but his repertory is limited to groups of semi-circles and circles, triangles, straight and wavy lines.

Somewhere about the end of the tenth century, a new style arose, the geometric style proper, which in the course of the ninth and eighth centuries conquered the Greek world. Its triumph was more complete in some districts than in others: in Crete and eastwards, proto-geometric and even late Aegean elements lingered; old shapes, and old ornaments, such as the concentric circle, persisted; and old principles of decoration.

The analogies between Greek geometric work and the products of the Northern Balkans and Central Europe point to the rudiments of the style having been brought to Greece by Northern invaders. When life in Greece became a little more settled, the seed ripened: and the rudiments were formed into a distinctive Greek style. That this Greek style originated in a single centre seems likely from the uniform character of early geometric decoration in places so far apart as Crete and Thessaly, Athens and Rhodes. Where the centre was is doubtful, but seeing that the development of the style is more consistent in Old Greece, especially in Attica, than elsewhere, its home probably lay in that quarter.

Geometric pottery reached its highest point in Attica, and the progress of the style can be traced better there than anywhere else. The earliest Attic geometric vases are decorated with horizontal bands, row over row, of simple rectilinear patterns—meander, lozenge, chain, zigzag; a broader band being set between narrower, and the narrower symmetrically disposed. New shapes of vase came in with the new style of decoration, and others were added later. These shapes differ widely from the harmonious forms of sixth- or fifth-century vases; but they please by their strength, clarity, and sedateness. The early geometric system of decoration was elaborated in two ways: first by a structural alteration in the ornamental scheme—the division of the main zone by means of verticals into rectangular fields; and secondly by the introduction of animal and human figures. A row of animals in single file is substituted for a pattern zone; the antithetic group, two animals facing, with or without a central object, is used to adorn a rectangular field; freer compositions appear, scenes of a general character from everyday life. The chief animals are birds, horses, deer: the scenes are mostly battles, often on the seashore, and funerals. The figures are schematized silhouettes. The men, for example, are very tall and thin, the trunk a triangle tapering to the waist, the head a knob with a mere excrescence for the face: towards the end of the style the head is lit up: the head-knob is drawn in outline, and a dot signifies the eye. The background of the picture is toned down by copious filling-ornaments[1].

The metalwork which has survived from the geometric period consists mainly of bronze bands, incised with patterns, which formed part of vessels; gold diadems with embossed designs; incised fibulae; further, of small bronze statuettes[2], some of them votive offerings each standing on its own base, others portions of larger objects, staves, pins, vessels, stands. The engraved and embossed decoration resembles that of the vases. On one class of engraved fibulae the adventures of Heracles are represented: mythical scenes are otherwise unknown in the geometric age, and these fibulae belong to the end of the period[3]. The statuettes are small figures of animals or of men, sometimes simple groups, mare and foal, rider, chariot. The best show artistic intention, decision, and some skill. The men are mainly arms and legs, but by the end of the period, the forms begin to round out a little and grow shapely; for instance in certain tripod figures from

[1] 344, 348, *a.*   [2] 346, *a.*   [3] 346, *b.*

Olympia: and in a small group of ivories found with geometric vases in an Attic grave, the greater corporeity, and the studied symmetry of the attitude, give a presage of Greek archaic sculpture.

This art of thin lines and sharp corners, this small, bleak, thrifty art, presents a strange contrast to the rich swell and swing of Mycenaean forms. But its achievement should not be underrated. Take one of those huge monumental vases which stood over Athenian graves[1]: we cannot fail to admire the simple firm lines of the shape; the careful arrangement of the decorative elements to suit their places; and the clear, compact composition of the main picture—a dead man lying in state, with mourners to left and mourners to right of him, and mourners seated and kneeling beside the bier.

III. ORIENTAL INFLUENCES: AND THE EARLIEST ARCHAIC ART

Even in the geometric period, the Greek world shows occasional signs of contact with the more ancient and far more highly developed art of the East: if more were known about early Ionia these signs would no doubt be more frequent. Towards the end of the eighth century foreign import and foreign influence increase greatly, and eventually lead to the transformation of the aspect of Greek art. Products of Hittite and Syrian art, and of the mixed art created out of Syrian, Mesopotamian and Egyptian elements by the Phoenicians, reached the Greeks of Asia Minor both overland and by sea, and penetrated farther west. Few of these products were of fine quality; but they served to place the artistic experience of ages at the disposal of the untutored Greek craftsman. The Homeric poems bear witness to a general admiration for the works of art made or peddled by the Phoenician: and the old belief that the shield of Achilles is based upon Eastern metalwork, though often assailed, holds the field. Side by side with this Oriental influence, there are traces, but much fainter traces, of another: Creto-Mycenaean traditions may have lingered in some districts after fading out elsewhere: and it is always possible that in various parts of Greece, Cretan or Mycenaean objects, remaining in view, or discovered from time to time, contributed at least the decayed nobleman's mite towards the formation not only of the Greek system of ornament but of the Greek figure style as well.

The phase of strong orientalization, which preceded the complete assimilation of the foreign elements and the formation of

[1] 348, a.

the new national style, the Greek archaic, may be illustrated on the one hand by the embossed bronze shields found in Crete, and on the other by the ivories found at Ephesus. The shields[1], with their cumbrous lions and sphinxes, deer and bulls, stand very close to the earlier and more Assyrian of a large class of metal bowls which have been found at Nimrud and in various parts of Greece: the shields are Greek imitations of such Oriental work; their date is probably the later part of the eighth century, for similar orientalizing bronzework is found in Italian tombs which can be dated, on external grounds, about 700 B.C. The Ephesian ivories belong to the same period and are closely related to a group of ivories found in the same room at Nimrud as the metal bowls. Like the shields, the Ephesian ivories may be called mixhellenic: but the ivory-worker, unlike the shield-maker, surpasses his models: the characterization of the radiant priest who toys with his beads[2]—a kind of small, Catholic counterpart to the Orthodox figure from Sargon's palace[3] (Place, *Ninive*, III, Pl. 31 *bis*, figs. 1–2)—is hardly equalled either in early Greek art or in the art of Hither Asia: and the hawk-priestess is a masterpiece of delicate finish[4]. Ruder ivories bearing the same relation to Nimrud as the Ephesian have been found at Camirus in Rhodes; and Sparta has yielded a long series of small ivory reliefs, mostly parts of fibulae, and ivory figurines[5]. The earliest of the Spartan ivories are older than the Ephesian: for the pottery of the stratum in which they were found is exclusively geometric. The earlier Spartan figurines recall the ivories from Camirus. A favourite subject in the reliefs is the Asiatic Lady of Wild Beasts, identified by the Greeks with their Artemis[6], and her male counterpart. Another collocation of man and animal is the old Asiatic type of a man grappling with two monsters: in the later plaques, this purely decorative type gives place to a mythical contest, Perseus and the Gorgon, Heracles and the Centaur. Lions appear, sometimes winged: sphinxes: griffins.

Oriental motives find their way into Attica, as into Sparta, before the end of the geometric period. Lion and griffin appear on diadems found with geometric vases: a man fights with a rampant lion; two lions devour a hunter: and from time to time an Oriental creature strays into pottery, like a prospector before the rush.

The geometric tripod bowls, with their engraved legs and accessory statuettes, give place, towards the end of the eighth century, to other types, in which the bowl is decorated with

---

[1] 346, *c*.   [2] 350, *b*.   [3] 350, *c*.   [4] 350, *a*.   [5] 278.   [6] 194, *c*.

winged human figures and heads of animals, all in the round.
The earlier examples, which are found not only in Greece, but
as far east as Armenia and as far west as Etruria, are not Greek
work: but many of the later, in which the animal heads are cast
hollow, are certainly Greek. Such is the vessel found at La
Garenne in the south of France[1], and such must have been the
bowl, ornamented with griffin's heads, which, according to Herodotus, the Samians dedicated to Hera on their return from
Tartessus (p. 89): the 'kneeling colossi' which supported the
Samian bowl can be imagined after a small bronze in the Louvre[2]
(*Bronzes du Louvre*, Plate 92). The chief seat of Greek metalwork in the seventh century was no doubt Greek Asia Minor
and the adjacent islands, and some of the bronze statuettes of this
period lead from the Ephesian ivories to later Ionian art. In the
Stockholm youth[3] the trunk is still strangely slight, the arms and
hands glued to the sides, the legs pressed together; but the head
foreshadows the Samian and Milesian heads of the sixth century.
Ionian bronzework, as well as Oriental, was imported into Old
Greece, and played a part in the shaping of the local style.

The pottery of the late eighth and the seventh century, from
its plentifulness and variety, throws more light upon the history
of Greek art during the period than any other class of object.
The technique of vase-painting changes towards the end of the
eighth century. The face, or parts of it, are now drawn in black
outline, with black lines for inner details. The 'reserved' spaces
(those contained by the black outline) are often uncoloured; but
female flesh is sometimes filled in with white, male with white or
brown. White and red are used for details as well as black. An
alternative process was to retain the old silhouette of the geometric period, but transformed by the use of incised lines for
inner markings: the black is usually enlivened by touches of red.
Both processes, 'outline' and 'black-figure,' may occur on the
same vase, even in the same picture; further, in the black-figured
pictures, the female flesh is regularly reserved, and the male
sometimes brown.

Geometric painting was monochrome: the new art contrasts
light with dark, and one colour with another. The geometric
painter divided his field into many small areas, and decorated
each with small oft-repeated units: the new art enlarges the areas
by reducing their number, decorates them with bigger and bolder
elements, connected by an ampler rhythm; lays more stress on
the chief area; achieves unity of design by subordination not by
diffusion.

[1] 352, *a.*   [2] 352, *b.*   [3] 352, *c.*

In patterns and in figures the straight line gives place to the curved. Lotus-flower, lotus-bud, and other motives floral and spiral were borrowed from the East, and out of these borrowed elements new and complex patterns were constituted, the ancestors of classical Greek ornament. For a long time animals are no less, even more, popular than before; but the choice changes; the favourites are now the ferocious or fantastic creatures of the East, lion, griffin, sphinx, and new monsters invented to keep these company. Turning to the human figure, we find the meagre schematic forms swelling out and acquiring volume. The arms are no longer match-like; thighs, buttocks and calves are big and strong: the joints are defined, breast, knee and ankle indicated, the facial features emphasized. In the geometric period legs and head were always in profile, breast always frontal: now the breast may be either frontal or in profile: frontal if the arms are extended to left and right of the body, in profile if the arms are close to the body or both stretched forward. The head can now look back. The movement of the legs is freer and truer: geometric figures are unsteady, specially when they would run: but seventh-century figures, standing, running or striding, have the steadiness of later Greek art. Symplegmas—one figure intertwined with another—are hardly representable in the simple silhouette style: if two geometric figures were in contact, they touched but gingerly: the seventh century, by its inner delineation and its colour contrasts, can demarcate one figure from another in an interlocked group: animal can close with animal, man with monster or man. 'Congruent' groups can also be formed, two figures side by side, one overlapping the other. The subjects alter: the battle pictures become more disciplined; hoplite faces hoplite in the prescribed attitude; in good order, a detachment advances at the double, or the victors follow up their success; the fallen are no longer ranged, one higher than the other, like specimens on a board, but lie grovelling or supine each on his own piece of groundline. The chariot-race supplants the slow funeral procession. Lastly, the Greek artist now sets himself to represent, on clay, metal or other material, the stories of the gods and the great men of old: and by the sixth century these 'myths' will have become his favourite theme. Old types are enriched and defined by a mythical content, new figures created to embody a particular story. The scenes are still confined to the barest necessaries: and the passions represented are the simplest: the desire to kill or to escape death, the delight at the sight of a friend. The 'Hesiodic' Shield of Heracles, in which mythical scenes are interspersed with scenes of a more general character and with animals fighting or in herds, reflects the graphic art of the seventh century.

The vases of this period divide themselves into two groups, an eastern, comprising the vases of Greek Asia Minor, of the adjacent islands, especially Rhodes, and of Naucratis; and a less homogeneous western. The contrast between the two groups is instructive. The east uses the outline technique, and long avoids incision: the black-figured technique arises in the west. The east is conservative, the west experimental. The east is content with the ancient monsters of the Orient, the west devises new: the east likes uniform rows of animals, a whole row of goats, another of deer, the west mixes its animals: the western patterns are now wilder, now more complex than the eastern: the west is narrative, the east decorative: the east, having no tale to tell, retains the filling ornaments, and needs no inscriptions: the west ends by clearing the ground for action and for word.

Geometric pottery, though exported, was not exported widely, and beyond the Greek world hardly at all: the potter worked mainly for local demand: but by the seventh century pottery was one of the principal articles of Greek export trade. Eastern Greek pottery was sent north to the Black Sea colonies, south to Egypt, west to Sicily and Etruria. The circulation of protocorinthian, and later of Corinthian pottery was even wider.

More eastern Greek vases of this period have been found at Rhodes than anywhere else: but the pottery found in other parts of eastern Greece shows that the same style prevailed throughout the area with local differences. The animals—predominantly wild goats and fallow-deer—and the pattern-bands, are inspired by the art of the Nimrud bowls, but the freshness and tartness of the drawing, and the contrast of white ground and black glaze, invest the vases with a peculiar brightness and charm[1]. The human figure, rare at first, becomes commoner in the later examples. The black-figured style of Corinth invaded the east late in the seventh century: the outline style survives, but its range is restricted, and the eastern Greek vases of the sixth century are chiefly black-figured.

It seems likely that Crete was one of the chief places in which Oriental and geometric elements were blended to form the style of the west. The Cretan figure style is best known from metalwork: bronze openwork plaques[2] (*J.H.S.* xxx, Pl. 12, 1 and p. 227: *Bronzes du Louvre*, Pl. 11, nos. 93–94) show figures of hunters, thin and angular, but full of a true feeling for line and for momentary action: these seem a little earlier than the bronze

[1] 348, *b, c.*   [2] 354, *a.*

mitra from Rethymno (*Ath. Mitt.* xxxi, Pl. 23) in which four youths
are arranged about a trophy, a development of the old group of
two figures about a central object, but vivified and hellenized.
One of the few examples of Cretan figure-work in painting is a
dish from Praesus, with a horseman on one side, and a symplegma,
Heracles grappling with a sea-monster, on the other[1]. The dish
resumes the technical devices of the new age—outline, added
colour, incision on black. The Cretan figure style is not confined
to Crete: it meets us, for example, on a jug, found in Aegina,
with a picture of Ulysses and his mates escaping from Polyphemus[2], and in the far west, oddly barbarized, on the walls of
the Tomba Campana at Veii[3].

The chief Peloponnesian fabric of the period is the so-called
protocorinthian, which is perhaps Sicyonian. The geometric
ware out of which it developed resembles the geometric of the
Cyclades: the mature style has Cretan affinities. Tiny, fine per-
fume vases were a speciality. The decoration is always clear and
well arranged: the filling ornament is discreet, and in some of
the later vases the background is left quite plain. The pattern-
work is often of great complexity and beauty; and the more
elaborate of the pictures rank among the masterpieces of the later
seventh century. It will be long before we re-encounter the light-
ness of movement, the varied and expressive attitudes, which we
find in the Berlin Centauromachy[4]. In the Chigi jug, now in the
Villa Giulia at Rome, the exquisite drawing is enhanced by an
unusually rich polychromy, which uses white and two shades of
red, of brown, of black[5].

The earliest products of the Corinthian fabric were imitations
of protocorinthian ware: then and thereafter shapes are usually
heavier, and drawing at least a little coarser or more conventional
than in good protocorinthian: the cheaper vases crowd the background with blot-like rosettes. We are not wholly dependent
upon vases for our knowledge of Corinthian painting: the painted
clay metopes of the temple of Apollo at Thermum in Aetolia are
probably Corinthian work: and a deposit of small votive plaques
in clay has been found near Corinth itself. The metopes are
painted in the outline technique, with details in black, white, and
three shades of red: the drawing is inferior to that of the best
seventh-century vases. Most of the plaques belong to the end of
the seventh and the early sixth century, and one of them is signed
by the vase-painter Timonidas: a few show a later stage of
Corinthian painting than any of the Corinthian vases. The
technique is now the black-figure, now the outline. Some of the

[1] 354, *b, c, d.*   [2] 356, *a.*   [3] 330, *a.*   [4] 356, *b.*   [5] 356, *c.*

representations are of a novel kind: scenes from the industrial life of the city: the clay-pit, the potter's oven, the potter's wheel[1].

Protocorinthian restraint finds a surprising contrast in the licence of the big Attic vases of the so-called Phaleron class. The Attic artist is at first intoxicated by the new wine. In the latest geometric vases, a strong wind seems to be blowing against the neat fabric and making it bend, totter and reel. Then comes the Analatos hydria (*Jahrbuch*, 2, Pl. 3) in which the men are still silhouettes, but the birds and the ornament are done in bold brush-outlines, and the vegetation is of tropical luxuriance. The next stage is represented by the remarkable amphora in New York (*J.H.S.* xxxii, Pls. 10–12)[2] with the crude vigour of its combatants, with its incredible animals, with its uncouth yet effective ornament. The Cynosarges vase (*J.H.S.* xxii, Pls. 2–4) is gayer in colour, soberer in drawing, and the wrestlers form a true symplegma, a triumph for the time. At the end of the seventh century, the black-figured takes the place of the outline technique in Attica: the exuberant ornament is reduced, the animals are powerfully stylized; the eccentricity disappears. The change is partly due to influence from protocorinthian art. The chief example of this stage is the Nessus amphora in Athens[3], where the group of Heracles and the Centaur yields to fine protocorinthian work in deftness, surpasses it in force. Other works by the same painter have been preserved: he is perhaps the earliest Greek artist whose personality we can grasp.

IV. THE SIXTH CENTURY, TO 520 B.C.: EARLY AND MIDDLE ARCHAIC ART

The figures and scenes with which we have hitherto been dealing were all small. In the later part of the seventh century large stone statues appear in Greece. The idea of making life-size or colossal statues came to Greece from Egypt, the home of grandeur, now open to the Greeks. There is no reason to suppose that the period of big stone figures was preceded by a period of big wooden figures: the material was probably stone from the beginning. Soft limestone could be shaped with the knife: marble needed hammer and chisel; but its clearness and brightness, and the high finish it would take, repaid the labour. Limestone is used freely by the sixth-century sculptor, but chiefly for the figures decorating buildings: free sculpture prefers marble. Large bronze statues could be constructed by attaching metal plaques

[1] 356, *d*.   [2] 358, *a, b*.   [3] 358, *c*.

to a wooden core: but in the second half of the sixth century improvements in the process of hollow casting enabled the Greek artist to *cast* large figures in bronze. Few such figures remain from antiquity: but from the late sixth century onwards, bronze was the favourite material for free statuary.

There was plenty of work for sculptors. The custom of giving representations of living things to the gods was a very old one. The new figures, so large, so life-like, so handsome, yet so durable, would be bound to delight the divinity and make him love the donor: and so the Greek sanctuaries became peopled with men, women and animals in marble or bronze. The image of the god himself is installed in his stone house. The effigy of the dead man is set over his grave. Moreover, the development of the stone temple leads to a great extension in the range of decorative sculpture. Certain parts of the building call for decoration: the frieze is adorned with figures in low relief: a new kind of work, high relief, enlivens pediment and metope: the pedimental figures tend to become detached in part or wholly from the background, and thus to approximate to the nature of free statuary. Besides this applied relief-work, there are substantive reliefs, funerary and votive. For work on a smaller scale there is great demand: for metal statuettes—parts of vessels and other furniture, or dedications each complete in itself; and for engraved seals and engraved dies to make coins with: the sixth century revived the old art of engraving in hard gem-stones, and the practice of issuing coins had already reached the Greek world.

Free sculpture long confines itself to a few simple types, and its repertory is very small compared with that of painting or relief. The chief types are the upright male figure, usually naked, one leg, the left, set well forward; the draped female figure, with legs close together, or the left slightly advanced; the draped seated figure. The statue is intended to be viewed directly from the front: two side views are also contemplated, and usually a back view. Each side view is a complete profile, corresponding to the complete profile in painting. The transition from side view to front view is more or less abrupt, and the stone figure retains a measure of the quadrature of the block from which it was hewn. The attitude of the statue is rigid: one leg may be set forward, the arms have a certain, limited, freedom of movement, and in draped statues the lines of the clothing may cut across the figure: but trunk does not twist or bend, legs are alike in posture, head looks straight forward, inclining neither up nor down nor sidewards. The main mass of the statue, now as before, is bilaterally symmetrical, the plane of symmetry being the median plane, that is the plane which passes through crown, nose, navel and fork.

The leading type is that of the naked upright man with left leg advanced, the 'Kouros.' The Kouros did not develop out of early Greek statuettes: it is something new in Greece, and the model was Egyptian. The hands may hold attributes, but the arms usually hang down along the sides, with the fists clenched. The figure is fully corporeal. The main divisions of the body are clearly marked: broad shoulders, big buttocks, big thighs, and muscular calves are emphasized by wasp waist and neat hard knees: the trunk remains summary. The figure becomes lighter with time, the limbs more refined, the facial features smaller and more vivacious.

The earlier female figures ('Korai') stand with legs pressed close together, the later take a little step forward with the left. In early western women, the drapery encloses the figure in a quasi-rectangular case, which may be diversified by patterns. The germs of a subtler system of drapery are observable in the Ephesian ivories, in which the lower part of the thin chiton is either covered with dense vertical lines, or divided by a plain central band or a group of central vertical folds in relief. In the sixth century, these devices were elaborated in eastern Greece and in the islands. In an Ionian bronze of the seventh century one of the hands grasps the central strip: the motive found favour; but a still more popular motive was that of the hand grasping the central strip and bearing it to the side of the body, thus drawing the chiton tight so that the legs show through, and setting up a system of long curving folds. For the upper part of the chiton we must turn once more to Ephesus: here the upper part is sometimes drawn down over the belt at the sides, so that the lower line of the chiton is an arc not a straight line. Later, the chiton is pulled farther down at one side of the belt than at the other, making the two sides of the garment asymmetrical: later still, the asymmetry is increased by the Ionic himation, the upper line of which cuts across the figure diagonally from shoulder to waist. Dense groups of rippled lines render the crinkling of the chiton, and both garments terminate below in series of step-like folds. The rendering of drapery thus developed is a complex one: it diversifies the surface by dividing it into a number of areas, each with its own system of curved or straight lines; and it vivifies the mass by revealing the bodily forms beneath.

Kouros and Kore, to give them their conventional names, remain the principal types of free statue throughout the archaic

period. It is not until about 480 B.C. that the two legs and the
two sides of the body come to be differentiated, the weight resting
on one leg, the axis of the trunk being thrown out of the straight,
and the head beginning to bend to one side. Then we shall no
longer be able to speak of Kouros and Kore: but that time is far
hence. The scheme of the Kouros is so simple, intelligible, and
compact, that no kouros will ever be quite ugly: οὔποτε πάγκα-
κον ἔσται. But we shall find great differences in quality as
well as in execution, and the later will not necessarily be better
than the earlier. Among the earlier kouroi, to which we are
confining ourselves for the present, two stand out: the huge and
very early Apollo of Sunium[1], in his rude majesty, like Otus, the
child giant who challenged the gods, or like Adam the first man;
and the Apollo of Tenea, spruce and fine[2].

The uniformity of substantive statuary does not extend to
relief-work. Here subjects and attitudes are far more varied. In
many of its uses, the relief is an alternative to the picture: the
chief theme is narrative, and the figures have nearly the same
rules as the figures of painting. In the decorations of metope and
pediment the relief is often very high indeed, and pedimental
figures are sometimes partly or wholly detached from the background: but however high the relief, it remains flattish: the artist
long hesitates to avail himself of the opportunity which the mass
affords of rendering the third dimension: the modelling is confined, for the most part, to the neighbourhood of the front plane,
and the effect is that of a drawing on stone with the contours
emphasized by being worked back from the surface. The same
slab-like character is observable in one of the few early statues
in the round which represent violent movement: the flying Nike
of Delos, with its frontal head and breast and profile legs. The
Nike is sometimes classed as a free statue, but it is really architectural decoration, for it was the lateral acroterion of a building;
and it makes one think of some pedimental figure, such as the
Corcyraean Gorgon, detached from its background.

The effect of the stone figure was completed by the application of colour, the predominant colours being a bright red and
a merry blue. In limestone figures, male flesh was painted red
or red-brown, and blue and red, occasionally other colours, used
for the garments; backgrounds were now plain, now coloured.
In marble the colouring was more discreet: the flesh was commonly left plain, with coloured details—hair, lips, eyes; part of
the drapery might be coloured, but most of it was plain, with
coloured borders or a sprinkling of little patterns: in reliefs the

[1] 362, a.   [2] 364.

background was dark, blue or red. Bronze was left in its natural tone; details sometimes inlaid in other material.

Our chief literary authorities for the history of early, as of later, sculpture are Pliny and Pausanias. Pliny had before him two accounts of the early history of sculpture in Greece: one, which probably goes back to a book by Xenocrates, a pupil of Lysippus, spoke of two Cretans, Dipoenus and Scyllis, who worked in Sicyon during the first quarter of the sixth century, as the first to win fame as sculptors in stone. Pausanias saw statues attributed to these artists, and, for all we know, signed by them, in several cities of the Peloponnese, and he mentions a number of works by Peloponnesians of the next generation, whom he describes as pupils of the two Cretans. The second account in Pliny, which has been traced back to Antigonus of Carystus, mentions a family of early Chian sculptors, the last generation of which came into conflict with the poet Hipponax. Finally Herodotus thinks of the Samian Theodorus as no mean artist: Theodorus, who worked both for Croesus and for Polycrates, was architect, sculptor, gem-engraver, author, and the first who cast statues, that is, presumably, large statues, in bronze. The names of other sixth-century sculptors are known from their signatures.

The signatures, and the literary record, show that artists, and works of art, often travelled far from their homes. But in spite of intercommunication and inter-influence, the sculptural style is not uniform over the Greek world. Stylistic areas or foci are distinguishable, each, naturally, with a more or less floating margin. We will speak first of Crete, then of the Peloponnese: then pass to Greek Asia Minor, and the islands adjacent to and remoter from the Asiatic coast; and conclude with Attica.

The early sculptural style of Greek Crete is known to us from works discovered on the island itself: the type of seated clothed figures is best represented by the statue found at Eleutherna; the type of standing woman is given by architectural reliefs from the temple of Prinia (*Annuario*, 1, p. 60), which still belong to the seventh century, and even better by a statue of unknown provenience, once in Auxerre and now in the Louvre[1]; the Kouros type by small bronzes (*A.J.A.* 1901, 396: *Mus. Ital.* 2, Pl. 12, 1). A few small bronzes from Crete, such as the Berlin ram-bearer and the warriors in the Louvre (*Bronzes du Louvre*, Pl. 12, 106 and 105), are somewhat later than most of the stonework: the style is peculiar, but akin to that of contemporary Peloponnesian bronzes.

[1] 360, *a*.

The earliest stone sculpture of the Peloponnese confirms the tradition that monumental sculpture was introduced into the country by Cretans. The Cretan figures already mentioned all find parallels in the Peloponnese. The Cretan Kouros reappears among the dedications at Delphi in the rude and forcible statues of the brothers Cleobis and Biton, known from Herodotus, which bear the signature of an Argive artist[1]: and greatly refined in a bronze statuette (*Fouilles de Delphes*, v, Pl. 3)[2] which recalls the plastic heads and painted figures on the latest protocorinthian vases. The number of sixth-century statues found in the Peloponnese is not great, and one of the most important, the Kouros from Tenea near Corinth[3], might be not local but island work. Reliefs and small bronzes are therefore our main source of information. Early Corinthian sculpture, we may take it, is represented by the earliest clay antefix heads of the Temple at Thermum in Aetolia (*Ath. Mitt.* xxxix, pp. 250 and 252), which are contemporary with the painted metopes: and by the pedimental decoration of the great temple in the Corinthian colony Corcyra, where the central gorgon is magnificent in its decorative effect[4], the other figures carved clearly and surely, but harsh in their lines and ill put together. With the work at Thermum and Corcyra we may connect the metopes from the early treasury-building at Delphi which is probably the Sicyonian. The art of the Dorian cities of Sicily is akin to that of the Peloponnese: here also, the principal monuments are reliefs, the metopes of the 'Salinas' temple at Selinus, and those of the Selinuntian Temple C (p. 603). The C metopes are later than they look at first sight, the work of a robust, old-fashioned sculptor living near the edge of the Greek world. Peloponnesian relief-work on a small scale is seen at its best in the so-called Argivo-Corinthian reliefs, a series of small bronze plaques, adjuncts of furniture, embossed with terse and expressive scenes from myth: the chief class of these, for there are earlier and later, bear Argive inscriptions: the style resembles that of Corinthian vases. Island influence reaches the Peloponnese in the second half of the century, showing itself for instance in Spartan tombstones: the style of these is a lifeless mixture of primitive and later elements: it would be unfair to count them characteristic specimens of the Peloponnesian art of their time.

An example of early Peloponnesian work in the round, not later than 600, is the head of Hera from Olympia[5], part of a colossal temple image: gaunt, flat-faced, flat-cheeked, the mouth bent up into a grimmish smile. This hardness of feature long

[1] 362, *b.*   [2] 360, *b.*   [3] 364.   [4] 366.   [5] 368, *a.*

persists in the Peloponnese, especially in the inner districts, and is a manifestation of a general tendency to reject a harmonious flow of line and surface. Witness, well on in the sixth century, such bronzes as the youth from Dodona in Berlin[1], the Zeus, signed by Hybristas, from Epidaurus, and the rider from near Megalopolis.

The monumental sculpture of eastern Greece is not derived from the Cretan, but from the older, semi-oriental art of the Ephesian ivories: quickened, it is true, in the sixth century by direct influence from Egypt. The marble woman, dedicated by Cheramyes, from the Samian Heraeum, shows the same general conception of form as the priestess with the hawk and her companions: a nearly cylindrical figure, contoured by long curves, spreading out towards the ankles, with the drapery rendered by long close-set parallel lines; new are the bigness and the grandeur.

The figure from the Heraeum belongs, on the one hand, to a small group of sculptures, all in Naxian marble, one of which is the colossal sphinx dedicated by the Naxians at Delphi[2]: on the other hand it has much in common with the art of Samos and Miletus.

The early sculpture of Miletus is known to us from a series of figures, mostly seated, found at Miletus itself and on the road from the coast to Didyma. Precisely the same style appears in the seated portrait[3] which Aeaces, father of Polycrates the tyrant of Samos, dedicated to the Samian Hera (see above, p. 90). With their sleek bodies, their joyous fleshy faces, and their soft rippling hair, these figures, though their bright colouring is lost, call up a vivid picture of the Ionian *eudaimōn anēr* and present a strong contrast to the harder, more angular figures of the Peloponnese. Egyptian influence is observable particularly in the quiet modelling and in the facial type. Another statue from Samos gives the corresponding standing figure (*Ath. Mitt.* xxxi, Pls. 10–12), and the statue dedicated by Leucius (*ibid.* xxv, Pl. 12), with statuettes from Egypt and Delphi (Deonna, *Les 'Apollons,'* p. 290; *Fouilles de Delphes,* v, Pl. 1, 6), supply the type of naked Kouros: and some of the stone kouroi found in old Greece belong to this type. A group of fine statuettes in clay helps to fill in the picture (*e.g. B.M. Cat. Terracottas,* Pl. 17, 2–4; and Pl. 18, 1–4 and 6–7): the clothed figures furnish exact parallels to the marbles: but the stock of types is not limited to these: there are kneeling and reclining figures, silens, dwarfs, animals, heads of Heracles, of negroes, of river-gods. The clay korai, and the marble korai which go with them, such as the Aphrodite in Lyons, the woman

[1] 360, *c.*   [2] 294, *a.*   [3] 368, *b.*

from Clazomenae in the Louvre, and the two new figures from Cyrene (*Notizie Archeologiche*, v, pp. 120–123), differ from the 'Island' and Attic korai by their greater massiveness, by the rotundity of their forms, and by their avoidance of deep cutting in the drapery. The most important examples of eastern relief-work are the sculptured columns from the Ephesian Artemisium, some of which were presented by Croesus: the style of such fragments of these as remain is closely related to the Samo-Milesian, but the modelling, more pronounced, speaks for island influence. A notion of eastern Greek metalwork may be formed from Etrusco-Ionian reliefs, such as those of the chariots from Monteleone and Perugia and of the Loeb tripods (Brunn-Bruckmann, Pls. 586–587; *ibid*. Pls. 588–589; *A.J.A.* 1908, Pls. 8–18) or from the golden horse-frontlet, in the shape of a fish, found at Vettersfelde in Prussia, and made by an Ionian artist for the Scythian market (Furtwängler, *Kleine Schriften*, 1, Pl. 18, 1). Many of the finest engraved gems are eastern Greek work, and the young reveller on the Ionides scarab[1] is worthy of a Theodorus. The coins of the eastern cities[2], and the vases presently to be mentioned, complete the impression of a vital if somewhat easy-going art and an alert and prosperous people.

Very little archaic sculpture has been so far found in Chios, the home of Micciades and his sons, and it is difficult to form a notion of Chian art as distinguished from the art of the more westerly islands. An early torso from Delos (Deonna, *Les 'Apollons,'* p. 202) differs from Samo-Milesian work in the shape of the head and in the bonier structure of the face, and leads the way to the marble Nike found in the same island. The Nike of Delos can no longer be connected with the signature of Archermus found near it, but it is no doubt the work of an island artist, whether from Chios or not one cannot say. The spareness and neatness of the bodily forms, the egg-shaped head, and the peaked features of the face, connect the Nike with a great number of naked youths found in the islands and elsewhere. The elaboration of the two leading types of archaic statue, the Kouros and the Kore, seems to have been in good part the work of island sculptors, not Chians exclusively, but Naxians, Parians and others. Island statues were exported to old Greece, and in the second half of the sixth century the skill and charm of these island marbles made a deep impression in the Peloponnese and at Athens. The decoration of the Siphnian treasury at Delphi offers a compendium of what the island sculptors had achieved by about 520 B.C. The Kouros is lacking; but the caryatids which take the

[1] 368, *c.*   [2] 300, *f*, *g*; 302, *b*, *c*, *d*, *h*, *i*.

place of columns are fine specimens of those draped female
figures which dazzled the Athenians. The pediment is disappointing, but the frieze brilliant, though coldly brilliant, in the
animation and variety of the attitudes, in the accuracy of the
execution, and in the skill and comparative complexity of the
grouping.

Attica, and above all the Acropolis of Athens, has yielded more
archaic sculpture than any other part of Greece: a fortunate
chance: for the quality of the yield is splendid. Attica was 'the
oldest land of Ionia,' but it was rooted in Old Greece: and the
Athenian people tempered together the virtues of both breeds of
Greek. But Attic sculpture does not present itself to the mind
as a mean between extremes: the impression which one receives
in the Acropolis Museum is a wholly positive one: the impression
of an art of vast health, strength and joyousness.

A whole series of limestone groups, which once decorated the
pediments of buildings on the Acropolis, have survived more or
less complete. The earliest of these represents a lioness devouring a bull, and belongs to about the same period as the
Corcyraean pediment. A second and grander animal group, a
bull devoured by a lion, is later than the earliest of the narrative
pediments, in which Heracles, the favourite hero of early Greek
art, is seen struggling with the Hydra. Much larger and much
more advanced than the Hydra group is the decoration of the
great temple of Athena, the Hecatompedon: Heracles wrestling
with Triton in the presence of a monster with three human heads.
The modelling in this as in the other limestone works is summary
but vigorous, and the monster, with his genial well-liking faces
and big wide-open eyes, is a wonderfully pleasant and attractive
monster[1]. The spirit which breathes in all these limestone works,
animal and narrative, earlier and later, we have met before: in
the Nessus vase and its companions.

Big marble statues were made in Attica very early. The oldest
of them are contemporary with the earliest limestone groups, and
there is no reason to suppose that the marble period was preceded
by a period in which the Attic sculptor's sole material was limestone. The colossal Apollo of Sunium, the grandest of kouroi, is
the first masterpiece of Attic sculpture[2]. The Calf-bearer from
the Acropolis, one of the most moving of archaic statues, is already
later[3]. Anyone can find fault with the anatomy both of man and of
calf: but the only fact that matters is this: a fine design carried
out with love and feeling. From the middle of the century signs
of island influence can be traced in Attica, and the signs multiply

[1] 370.   [2] 362, a.   [3] 372, a.

as the century wears on. Island statues were imported, islanders worked in Attica, and the Attic artists imitated them and learned from them. Yet the local tradition is not broken. The sculptor of the Kouros of Volomandra was affected by Ionian models, but his Kouros remains Attic, and placed beside his Ionian brothers looks like a decent bashful man in polished company. The development of native Attic art can be well followed in a fine series of male heads in marble ranging from the new Dipylon head[1] through the Rampin head[2] to late sixth-century works like the Jacobsen head and those of the metopes from the Athenian treasury at Delphi.

The favourite dedication to Athena was the Kore: and owing to the great number of Korai found in the excavations of the Acropolis, this type of statue has come to be regarded, commonly but unjustly, as the archaic statue par excellence. In the female figures from Attica, the island influence, though more pervasive than in the male, is not always dominant. The artist of the Kore who wears the Attic peplos over the Ionic chiton[3] is well acquainted with the new devices for representing drapery: he has rippled the chiton, and put bold step-like folds at the side of the peplos: but his art is not ostentatious: he has recurred to old Attic models, and the quiet stance, the unexpectedly simple costume, and the unaffected beauty of the head, make this lady more delightful than all her sisters. Most of the Acropolis Korai are later than 520 b.c., and we shall return to them later.

What were the materials of sixth-century painting? Clay slabs with pictures are found at Thermum, and votive pictures on clay tablets are common in the sixth century at Athens as well as at Corinth. A few paintings on marble slabs have survived from the later part of the century. Wooden panels we may take for granted, though no examples have reached us: but whether mural painting was already practised in Greece is an open question. It was practised in Etruria; moreover, the Etruscan tomb-paintings show overwhelming Greek influence, and some of them seem to have been actually executed by Greeks: but of archaic Greek wall-painting we have no fragment remaining, nor any mention in our scanty records. The black-figure method of vase-painting reached Attica, as we saw, at the end of the seventh century, and even penetrated into eastern Greece. During the greater part of the sixth century, the sway of the black-figure technique is almost undisputed: it is not till about 530 b.c. that a new method, the so-called red-figure, arises in Athens and gradually beats the old from the field. During the black-figure period, the outline

[1] 374, a.   [2] 374, c.   [3] 372, b.

method forms, as far as one can see, but a thin undercurrent:
but our impression would no doubt be different, if our non-
ceramic documents were more numerous.

The drawing of the earliest red-figure vases does not differ, in
essentials, from that of the black-figured work which preceded
them: and the style of the black-figured work changed but slowly.
New features appear between 600 and 525 B.C.: but what goes on
is mainly the fulfilment of ideas initiated in the seventh century,
and the refinement and systematization of older forms. Filling
ornaments, which declined in the seventh century, disappear by
the middle of the sixth. The friezes of animals fall into comparative neglect. Narrative engrosses the painters: mythical or
heroic pictures acquire greater volume and greater variety than
before. Simple compositions naturally predominate both now and
in the fifth century: Theseus grappling with the Minotaur, for
example, or the same flanked by a pair of spectators: but the
Corinthian painter of the Amphiaraus crater, the Attic painter of
the François vase, the Ionian painter of the Phineus cup, are able
to construct a many-figured narrative composition in which each
figure plays its own animated part. The emotions expressed by
the figures are more varied than in the seventh century: the tragic
dejection of the seer who knows that Amphiaraus will not return;
the joy of Theseus' crew at the sight of land and home; the
incorrigible impudence of the silens who form the bodyguard of
Dionysus and his bride. If there are more moods than there used
to be, there are also more kinds of people. The world no longer
consists of bearded men, beardless youths, women, animals and
a few monsters. The old man and the child become more frequent; the workman appears, and with him the capitalist; the
foreigner also, the eastern or northern barbarian in trousers and
quaint hat, the flimsy Egyptian, the hideous negro; the lover;
the man of pleasure; and most important of all, the wild man,
the silen, with horse's ears and horse's tail, the incarnation of our
less serious moods, and one of the chief vehicles of Greek humour
for many a day.

In the drawing of the figure, and even in the shapes of the vases,
there is a tendency to make the forms more precise, and usually,
to refine them: to proceed from the ideal expressed by Cleobis
and Biton to that of the Kouros of Tenea. The types of figure
are the same as before, full profile, or profile legs joined to frontal
breast; but a step is sometimes taken towards the three-quarter
view of the succeeding period: in a cup signed by the maker of
the François vase, to be dated, therefore, near the middle of the

sixth century, the off collarbone is drawn shorter than the other. Clitias marks the transverse lines on the chest; Execias and others try to render the 'inscriptions' between breast and groin; but as yet there is no consistent study of the surface markings. The garments, in the François vase, are still for the most part foldless: flat spaces covered with pattern, or plain black or red relieved by patterned bands or borders: but the mantle is sometimes divided into strip-like compartments by lines parallel to the edge of the garment. Later painters multiply the fold-lines, and emphasize them by colouring the stripes alternately black and red: presently the garment terminates below in the step-like folds which we found in sculpture.

Corinthian vase-painting reaches its highest point in the early part of the sixth century. The old technique is somewhat modified: the artist now places a layer of ruddled clay over the pale, cold surface of the vase; and paints his women white instead of reserving them. In the drawing of the figure there is little real change, and in the drapery none. The masterpiece of this period is the crater with the departure of Amphiaraus (Furtwängler-Reichhold, Pls. 121–2), which enables us to form a notion of another Corinthian work, famous in literature, the Chest of Cypselus at Olympia. Other vases, with less narrative interest, surpass the Amphiaraus crater in decorative effect: clean academic drawing, and a happy arrangement of clear, masculine colours, black, white, red, and the orange of the new ground[1].

The eastern custom of preparing a background for the painting by covering the vase with a white slip is adopted in the class of vases which used to be called Cyrenaic but are now usually assigned to Laconia. The slip, and the choice of patterns point to influence from east Greece: but the drawing is of pronounced Peloponnesian type, and akin, in the essentials, to Corinthian. It is a handsome ware, and the subjects are often rare and pretty, although the execution of the figure-work usually lacks finer quality. The best piece is perhaps the Berlin cup with soldiers carrying a dead comrade from the field[2]. The best known is the Arcesilas cup, which shows the wealthy king of Cyrene superintending the export of local products[3].

In eastern Greece, the white slip and the outline technique were abandoned in the course of the sixth century, and the vase-painters adopted the black-figure style of old Greece. The painted clay sarcophagi of Clazomenae preserve the traditional method after it has died out in vase-painting: but in many of the sarcophagi only part of the decoration is in the outline technique,

[1] 376, a.   [2] 378, a.   [3] 378, b.

the principal pictures being executed, sometimes in a modification of the black-figure method, with white lines instead of incisions, sometimes in a technique which, like the Athenian red-figure, reserves the figures and fills in the background. The vase-painters of Clazomenae sometimes use the white line, but the normal black-figure method is commoner: their drawing is often lively and amusing, but clay and varnish are apt to be poor, drawing ragged, and inner markings quite arbitrary: the fabric succumbs about the middle of the century.

The spectacle of a true blend of eastern Greek art and the art of old Greece is presented by the vases of Ionian Chalcis[1]. The excellence of the potter-work, the deep orange ground, and the mastery of the black-figure technique, all connect them with old Greece; and the subjects and motives have close analogies in Corinthian vases. But the figures, especially in the battle-scenes, have a passion and power unknown in Corinth, and the love of rich, swelling curves in figures and ornament points to eastern Greece. A somewhat later class of vases, the Phineus cup and its simpler companions, are also Chalcidian: the art of these is still more eastern in character, and finds its closest parallel in the coins and gems of Greek Asia Minor, and in the Loeb tripods.

The last important products of Ionian vase-painting are the so-called Caeretan hydriai. They were probably all painted by one man, a Greek of Asia Minor, somewhere about 530 B.C. This man was that rare thing, a great comic draughtsman. His chief piece is the Busiris hydria, with its wonderful group of Heracles, the huge sunburnt Greek, slaying ten puny foreigners at a blow: a brilliant parody of Egyptian representations of Pharaoh smiting his enemies[2].

In Attica, the so-called Vourvà vases, with their rows of animals, carry an earlier tradition on into the sixth century: the 'Tyrrhenian' group modernizes the Vourvà by using the principal frieze for narrative. Both kinds were produced in great numbers: Athens was by now competing with the Corinthians and the Ionians in foreign markets. Not long after 600 B.C., Attic vases appear in Naucratis, in south Russia and in Etruria: by the middle of the sixth century they have penetrated everywhere, and above all, the great Etrurian market is in the hands of the Athenians. Their monopoly of fine pottery remained almost unchallenged for over a hundred years. Signatures of artists and of potters and owners of fabrics, hitherto rare in Greece, now become common in Athens. The earliest Attic artist whose name we know is the vase-painter Sophilus. Sophilus was by no means

[1] 376, b.   [2] 382.

a dolt: but it was not such men as he who beat the Corinthians for ever from the field. It was men like Ergotimus and Clitias, the maker and the painter of the François vase, a nobly-shaped crater decorated with row upon row of pictures, chiefly scenes from myth, comprising hundreds of thin, angular, extraordinarily varied, elegant and expressive figures: a marvel of minute yet masculine work[1]. The François vase comes from the far west, from Chiusi in Etruria: a cup signed by Clitias has been found far in the east at Phrygian Gordium. It is on cups that the style and the spirit of Clitias continue: in the 'little master cups' with their tiny exquisite figures[2]. Larger pictures were painted side by side with these, and the black-figure technique may be said to culminate in the Vatican amphora signed by Execias[3]. The technique: for the style is already past its prime: the spirit which is able to express itself through silhouette and incision is departing, and the time has come for a new and freer means of expression, the red-figure style.

V. ARCHITECTURE[4]

The history of Greek architecture in the centuries following the Dorian conquests is obscure. Until stone began to replace wood and sun-dried brick, about the end of the eighth century, even large and important buildings were very perishable, and little now survives except mutilated foundations: it is rarely possible to restore the superstructures with confidence, or to assign them to any definite style. They are, in spite of this, of vital importance: but they cannot be interpreted except in the light of later remains. Their discussion is therefore postponed to a later point of this section. After 700 B.C. the evidence, though still scanty for a century, becomes rather fuller: and so much remains of the buildings of the early sixth century that restored elevations cease to be fanciful. It is true that few walls or columns of that period still stand, and that no building is even approximately perfect: but the styles resemble so closely those of the following centuries that a few fragments can give a great deal of information. Caution, however, is necessary, for small pieces of evidence sometimes show great abnormality where no one would readily have suspected it. But the two great classical styles, Doric and Ionic, were highly developed before the middle of the sixth century. Geographically they were clearly separated: with very few exceptions Doric was unknown to the east of the Aegean, and Ionic, though predominant in the islands, was

---

[1] 380, a.   [2] 374, d, e.   [3] 380, b.
[4] In this section † with numeral refers to plan on sheet facing p. 610.

unknown in Greece or the west (Treasuries at Delphi and Olympia belong architecturally to the cities of their builders). The products of these two styles differ so widely that it will be best to treat them separately. The main features of the earliest Doric will first be described: the external and internal evidence for its origins will then be considered, and this enquiry will be followed by a brief account of the chief developments of the Doric style down to 480 B.C. Ionic will then be treated on similar lines.

Little will be said except of temples and treasuries, and that only in the broadest outline: but the existence in this period of domestic, palatial and military architecture must not be forgotten, nor yet the execution of such grand engineering works as those which Herodotus admired at Samos, the aqueduct tunnel through Mount Ampelius, and the harbour mole (see p. 92 *sq.*).

The best preserved DORIC buildings of the first half of the sixth century are in Sicily and Italy. Two main types stand out at once: those that possess, and those that lack, a 'pteron,' or external colonnade. The pteron occurs before 700 B.C. on the Greek mainland, but until the middle of the sixth century it was not common in Doric east of the Adriatic. The old temple of Athena Polias †1 on the Athenian Acropolis, built in the first half of the sixth century, had originally no external colonnade, but was later adorned with one by Peisistratus or his sons (see p. 66)[1]. The main building, or 'cella,' itself takes many forms, but at all periods it was usually a rectangle, running east and west, and entered from the east end: early temples tend to be narrow. In Greece proper the temple seldom lacked an open porch, or 'pronaos,' produced by the extension of the long walls to the east, and generally containing two columns; but in Sicily a common alternative was a closed anteroom †3, entered by a central door. Such porchless buildings, which are not confined to Sicily and occur also in the Ionic area, cannot strictly be called Doric, for, except where they possess a pteron, they lack the chief distinctive features of the style. Other types of porch are less common. All temples, whether 'peripteral' (adorned with a pteron) or not, have a gabled roof, which covers the whole structure, closed in front, and, with rare exceptions, behind also, by a vertical wall, which forms the back of the triangular 'pediment.' The 'opisthodomos,' or false porch, at the west end (a replica of the pronaos, with no door in its back wall) is a very early feature, but was usually confined to peripteral buildings. In Sicily, especially, the cella often opens into an inner room †3, or 'adyton.' Circular Doric buildings are found as early as the first half of the sixth century, but they are rare. The forms

[1] 386, *b.*

of column[1], architrave, and frieze in the earliest Doric differ from classical types chiefly in their proportions. Generalization is difficult, for local variety is characteristic of the age, but the entablature is usually heavier and the echinus (the circular cushion, which forms the lower half of the capital) is more spreading and more curved. There is usually a deep groove[2] at the base of the echinus, and both the echinus and the abacus (the square block which carries the architrave) are sometimes carved. The frieze consists, as in later work, of grooved blocks, called triglyphs, one to each column, one to each intercolumnar interval, alternating with smooth slabs, called metopes: but the metopes (square in later work) are sometimes narrower than a square, and occasionally wider. The difficulties connected with the position of the angle triglyph, so acute in the fifth and fourth centuries, were scarcely felt in the surviving temples of the early sixth, chiefly because of the greater width of early triglyphs; but exceptionally close or wide spacing of columns raised awkward problems. Close spacing occasionally led to the omission of every other triglyph, wide spacing to the total omission of the frieze. Marble was rare in Doric work till after the Persian wars: but the stone was usually stuccoed, and the frieze and cornice painted, chiefly in broad masses of red and blue. Below the frieze painting was confined to details. Metopes often had sculpture in relief; early pediments often had reliefs, later ones free sculpture. The pediment of the early Temple C at Selinus was adorned with a large Gorgon's head in painted terracotta. Mouldings were painted but rarely carved. The temple of Assus in Mysia, perhaps of the later sixth century, the only archaic Doric temple in Asia, has sculpture on the architraves: but this is a unique imitation of Ionic.

The origin of this type of building is at present largely conjectural, but there is some evidence that in the preceding age temples were normally constructed of sun-dried brick, half-timbered, on low stone walls, with wooden columns. The inference that archaic Doric temples reproduce in stone the chief features of their predecessors was made in antiquity: and, despite the protests of many modern authorities, it is probably right. The best evidence for half-timber temples comes from three sites: Sparta, Olympia, and Thermum in Aetolia. At Sparta the buried remains of the sixth-century temple of Orthia proved on excavation to cover the flimsy relics of a building[3] which may be as old as the late ninth or early eighth century, and is perhaps the oldest surviving Greek temple. The lowest parts of the walls were of stone, but the main portion had clearly been of sun-dried brick,

---

[1] 384, *b*; 386; 388, *a*.   [2] 384, *b*; 386, *a*.   [3] 384, *a*.

with vertical timbers at intervals, of the full height of the walls.
To these timbers corresponded, inside the temple, isolated wooden
columns on stone slabs, probably a single central row (a common
archaic scheme). Not earlier than the seventh century, as the
examination of its subsoil has proved, is the surviving form of the
Heraeum of Olympia †2, long thought to be many centuries older.
Recent excavations, however, appear to have established the
existence of more than one stratum of earlier remains, the latest
of which is thought to have been peripteral. The stone portions
of the surviving building are wonderfully preserved. It is peripteral (six columns by sixteen), with pronaos and opisthodomos,
each containing two columns. The bulk of the walls was demon-
strably of sun-dried brick half-timbered, and all the columns were
originally of wood. In Pausanias' time (the second century A.D.)
one of the two columns in the opisthodomos was of oak. The rest
were then doubtless of stone, and many Doric stone columns were
found by the modern excavators: but these columns show the
widest variety in style and date, and must have been gradually
substituted for wooden ones. There was a flat ceiling under a
pitched roof, but there is no reason to think the pitched roof a
later addition. For Thermum (the religious centre of Aetolia, a
region traditionally connected with Olympia) the evidence is less
conclusive. The sanctuary was twice sacked at the end of the
third century B.C.: but abundant terracotta details survived the
disaster, and the ground-plans of three temples of the late seventh
or early sixth century can still be traced. The largest †4, dedicated
to the Thermian Apollo, in its final form had stone columns, but
these seem, as in the Olympian Heraeum, to have been gradually
substituted for wooden ones. The temple had wooden triglyphs
and also painted terracotta metopes, which it still retained in the
third century B.C. It was peripteral (five columns by fifteen) with
a single central row of interior columns: and the ground-plan has
many unusual features.

   There is no direct evidence for the forms of such wooden
columns, though they seem to be shown in early vase-paintings,
and these paintings closely resemble the slender stone columns[1],
with widely spreading capitals, which have been ascribed to the
seventh-century Temple of Athena Pronaia at Delphi: nor (except
at Thermum and a few other sites) can we prove the nature of
any frieze not made of stone: but the indirect evidence is overwhelming. Despite much local variety, the early Doric column
and the triglyph frieze are essentially the same wherever they are
found, and they appear almost simultaneously all over Greece

[1] 388, a.

and the Greek west. It is unlikely that they were sudden inventions, for the Greek instinct was for the gradual refinement of traditional forms: it is still more unlikely that such inventions should have spread so quickly and so far. The fashion of stone columns was probably due to acquaintance with Egyptian architecture, but the Doric column and frieze, despite the 'Proto-Doric' columns of Beni Hasan, were not borrowed from Egypt. There remains only one imaginable model, the half-timber temple of the preceding age. The history of the Olympian Heraeum strongly confirms this conclusion. Some of the forms of the triglyph frieze are suggestive of wooden technique: and it is not necessary to devise prototypes of wood, or wood and brick, in which every detail has a structural necessity, since arbitrary forms may develop in wood and brick, no less than in stone. The triglyphs are usually supposed to represent beam-ends, but it has recently been suggested that they are derived from brick crenellations faced with wood. There seems to be contraction of the angle intercolumniations in the Olympian Heraeum, a feature perhaps suggestive of the presence of triglyphs. Terracotta triglyphs occur at Thermum but were exceptional: though the casing of stone cornices in terracotta (common in early western Doric) is probably derived from timber traditions.

But if the archaic Doric temple gives us some notion of the plan and appearance of a half-timber temple of the eighth century, the question of origins remains. What is the pedigree of the half-timber temple? We think at once of the great hall or 'megaron' of the palaces of Tiryns and Mycenae, and the resemblance in ground-plan is very striking, though the temple is longer and narrower in its proportions. Like the temple, the megaron is a large rectangular half-timbered building with an open porch, often containing two columns: and the evidence of Cretan frescoes, and of the half-columns of the Treasury of Atreus, suggests that its columns may have been not unlike those of archaic Doric. In elevation, however, the resemblance of temple to megaron was probably not very great.

It is unlikely, though not inconceivable, that any Mycenaean palace was still standing in the eighth century. There is, indeed, at Tiryns a later building, erected on the ruins of the megaron, which some students have supposed to be a Doric temple of the early seventh century. This structure re-used one of the main walls of the megaron, and perhaps also its old pavement and some of its column-bases. Probably, however, it is not a temple at all, but a reconstruction of the megaron in late Mycenaean times.

But, even if porch and column can claim Mycenaean ancestry, this is certainly not the whole story. Megaron and porch have forerunners in the prehistoric architecture of Central Europe, Troy and Northern Greece: and there is evidence which suggests that the archaic temple was originally an independent offshoot from the same stock. At Thermum, in particular, we find a remarkable series of superimposed remains †4. First come hair-pin shaped buildings of a well-known prehistoric type—long narrow ellipses, sharply curved at one end, but entered through a straight cross-wall at the other, and divided internally by two or three cross-walls. Above one of these lies a unique structure, which has been named 'Megaron B.' It has been assigned to the early tenth century. It agrees in many features (the inward tilt of its walls, for instance) with its predecessors, and its chief walls, like theirs, are curved in plan. Yet these curves are so subtle that they escaped the notice of the first excavators, and the building produces the impression of an archaic temple of the western type, with closed antechamber, main cella, and adyton. It is still partially surrounded by an elliptical ring of stone slabs, which probably carried a verandah of wood—the earliest known forerunner of the pteron. The accumulation of ashes, perhaps sacrificial, proves that 'Megaron B' stood long: on its ruins the chief of the archaic temples (already mentioned) was built at the end of the seventh century. Remembering the connection of Aetolia with Olympia, we may reasonably suspect that 'Megaron B' is one of the ancestors of the Heraeum. There are classical buildings of primitive ground-plan at Olympia: and the apse was used in the sixth century on the Athenian Acropolis, possibly even in one of the largest temples. It is unlikely that Megaron B was a temple from the first: perhaps it was always a palace. Temples are gods' houses, modelled on kings' palaces, and they were perhaps little used till large images came into fashion. It has, however, been suggested that certain temples, and especially those of the porchless Sicilian type, are derived not from palaces but from sacred caves.

After the middle of the sixth century Doric style crystallized and local peculiarities disappeared. Capitals became more upright, and entablatures lighter. Ground-plans in particular became more regular, and greater care was taken to coordinate pteron and cella. To some extent this increased formality was a reaction. The Olympian Heraeum was remarkably regular, and this early regularity was perhaps connected with the technique of half-timber.

Of IONIC architecture before 480 B.C. scarcely a wall or a column
still stands, and very few buildings have been discovered, largely
for lack of excavation. Of those yet known two only were of the
first rank, the temple of Artemis at Ephesus and the temple of
Hera in Samos. Early Ionic temples have been found in Delos,
Chios, Naxos, Paros, and some other sites, and Naucratis in Egypt
has also left scanty traces: further, remains of four small Ionic
treasuries have been found at Delphi. All these buildings belong
to the sixth century. Again, Athens, Delos, and Delphi have
yielded many Ionic capitals of the same period, but the columns
to which they belonged were not architectural.

The early sixth-century Artemisium of Ephesus †5 lies upon the
ruins of successive earlier structures, the oldest perhaps of the
eighth century, but nothing definite is known of their architecture.
It was itself buried in the substructures of the great fourth-century
temple, but the main features of its plan, and many details of its
style, have been ascertained. Unlike any Doric temple, it had a
double pteron (eight columns by twenty in the outer row). There
was a deep pronaos, which probably contained eight columns, in
pairs: of the cella, and of a third room behind (adyton or opisthodomos) little is known. There are no certain remains of architrave
or frieze, but the roof had a large parapet, decorated with scenes
in relief. The columns agree in essentials with those of classical
Ionic, though the flutes are twice as numerous. The lowest drums
were in some cases sculptured. The shafts were mostly crowned
with a bead-and-reel moulding, on which rested a bold egg-and-
tongue. The volutes are very wide-spread, and have convex
channels. Some capitals substituted rosettes[1] for the volute spirals,
and these probably had leaf-patterns on their mouldings, in place
of bead-and-reel and egg-and-tongue. No angle capital survives
from this or any other archaic temple. The Heraeum of Samos
was a very similar building. The original temple was burnt in the
second half of the sixth century, and rebuilt about 500 B.C. on a
larger scale, but in the same style. Much of the earlier detail has
been found embedded in the later foundations. Another sixth-
century temple that has left remains of Ionic columns is the Temple
of Apollo at Naucratis, probably a simple non-peripteral structure.
The columns are interesting chiefly because they have necking-
bands, like those of the Erechtheum, carved with a lotus pattern.
Necking-bands also occur at Samos. At Delphi none of the Ionic
treasuries has columns with Ionic capitals, though all have open
porches with two free-standing supports. Two, the Cnidian and
Siphnian, built, it would seem, respectively in the middle and

[1] 388, b.

second half of the sixth century, substitute caryatids for columns: the other two (perhaps those of Massilia[1] and Clazomenae) had palm-capitals suggestive of Egypt: but about the character, identity, and history of these two buildings there is still much uncertainty. All four seem to have had the Ionic frieze, but no dentils, and sculpture was freely used. In all these buildings marble was used more lavishly than in contemporary Doric.

The origin of Ionic architecture is obscure. In the main features of the ground-plan, and in the use of the pteron, it is probably closely connected with Doric, and of mainland source. As for the Ionic capital of the classical type, structurally its form is suggestive of a rectangular block interposed between shaft and architrave. This is a familiar method of timber construction, and the Ionic capital is probably copied from wooden models. Other features of the style, especially the dentils under the cornice, are also suggestive of timber, and some of the rock-cut tombs of Lycia and Paphlagonia seem to be copied from analogous wooden structures. The dentils were probably not combined with the smooth frieze till the fourth century B.C., and possibly both members represent the same wooden feature—beam-ends exposed, or faced with planking. It is likely that Ionic is derived from a type of building more exclusively wooden than that which lies behind Doric. How far such timber structures had been influenced by Asiatic tradition is an unsolved problem.

We find on various sites, especially in Lesbos, and at Neandria, near Troy, an early type of capital, from which the decoration of classical Ionic may have been derived, as an adaptation to the structural form already described. This type has been called both 'Proto-Ionic' and 'Aeolic,' but the name 'Aeolic' is preferable, although the palm-capitals of Delphi have also been called 'Aeolic.' In this type the volutes spring vertically from the shaft: the effect is like that of a pliant stick, split at the top, with both halves curved spirally downwards and outwards: but the space between them is solid, and is treated as a large palmette. As a decorative motive this scheme, which was known to Minoan artists, is common in Greece and appears in sixth-century Doric in roof decoration. It occurs very early in Asiatic ornament, especially in Babylonia: and its original home was perhaps Egypt. Whether the 'Aeolic' scheme was employed to decorate capitals in Babylonia or Egypt is, however, uncertain, though a slightly different scheme, equally suggestive of Egypt, was almost certainly so used in Cyprus. The seventh-century temple at Neandria †6 was a simple porchless rectangle, entered from one end, and

[1] 390, a.

probably not peripteral. A single row of seven stone columns[1],
baseless and unfluted, ran down the centre. Below the volutes
the shafts seem to have carried two other elements: a large convex
moulding carved with a leaf-pattern, and below that an undercut
ring of carved leaves. Similar and even more elaborate capitals[2]
have been found at Larisa in Aeolis. The so-called Ionic 'echinus'
—a large moulding, adorned with egg-and-tongue, between shaft
and volutes—may be derived from this undercut leaf-moulding.
In developed Ionic it has the profile of the Doric echinus, but in
early work it is sometimes undercut. The numerous capitals[3] of
sixth-century votive columns found at Athens and Delos present
mixed 'Aeolic' and Ionic types. Possibly, however, the Ionic
volutes are independent of the 'Aeolic,' and represent the conventional side-view of a system of leaves hanging from each end
of the main block of the capital.

Some curious early buildings in Crete seem to anticipate certain
features of sixth-century Ionic. A temple at Prinia in particular
(between Cnossus and Phaestus) belonging to the seventh century,
had a heavy stone parapet, carved with a procession of horsemen,
which recalls the great parapet of the Ephesian Artemisium.

It may here be added that roof-tiles were nowhere used till
about the beginning of the seventh century B.C. Some of the
earliest types are found in the Olympian Heraeum and in the
temple of Neandria. They were at first always of terracotta:
marble tiles, when they appear in the sixth century, copy terracotta forms, and are sometimes confined to the lowest row, next
the eaves, where the various methods of rain-water disposal had
quickly led to a rich development of decorative treatment. Some
of the earliest tiles were bedded in clay, and this technique has
suggested the theory that they were invented for the paving of
flat terrace roofs, though in practice they are not known to have
been used except with sloping ones. It is in any case probable
that steeply sloping roofs existed before the invention of tiles. The
best evidence for this is perhaps provided by certain recently
published fragments of at least two clay models of houses or
temples, assigned to the eighth century B.C., which were found
many years ago at the Argive Heraeum: they resemble later
models of temples found in Etruria and Latium, and may well
represent the famous Heraeum itself. The type of building
imitated is rectangular in plan, with a 'prostyle' porch of two
columns standing in the line of the side walls, which barely
project, as shallow 'antae,' from the cross-wall containing the
door. There seems to be both a flat roof, which projects beyond

[1] 390, b.　　　[2] 392, b.　　　[3] 392, a.

the walls, and also, above that, a steep gabled one, set a little back. The whole roofing, as in classical types, probably reached to the porch columns, and there was a pediment at each end: the front one was pierced with a large door or window. The side walls of the building have triangular ventilation holes. No actual columns survive in the models, but horizontal struts seem to have connected them, near the top, with the 'antae' behind. The models are painted, but not realistically: it seems likely, however, that the building or buildings copied were of sun-dried brick half-timbered, with the sloping roof thatched or shingled, and with wooden columns. The curiously clumsy combination of flat and gabled roofing suggests a fusion of two rival traditions.

Had the Greeks of Asia retained their prestige, Ionic might well have explored new lines of development in the fifth century, which might have reacted on the more rigid Doric traditions. In the second half of the sixth century Ionic influence, helped by the Delphian treasuries, was spreading in Greece and the west. The huge temple of Olympian Zeus below the Acropolis at Athens was begun by the Peisistratidae as an Ionic temple with double pteron, after the fashion of Ephesus: but after the fall of the tyrants the work was abandoned till Hellenistic times (p. 67). In the same period the Spartans commissioned Bathycles of Magnesia to build the great 'Throne of Apollo' at Amyclae, an extraordinary structure which was almost more Ionic than Doric. Bathycles actually made Doric capitals which grew into Ionic consoles[1]: and other buildings of the period show similar influences. But political circumstances checked the growth of Ionic at home, and in Greece no real fusion of the two styles was effected. Ionic continued to attract mainland architects, but Doric remained predominant. Apart from a few isolated experiments—such as the 'Temple of the Giants' at Acragas—Doric architects in the fifth century showed little inclination to break with tradition. Instead, they turned aside to the elaboration of subtleties. Their road was a blind alley, but it led to the Parthenon.

[1] 394.

LIST OF ABBREVIATIONS

Abh.	Abhandlungen.
Abh. Arch.-epig.	Abhandlungen d. archäol.-epigraph. Seminars d. Univ. Wien.
Abh. K.M.	Abhandlungen für die Kunde des Morgenlandes.
A.J.A.	American Journal of Archaeology.
A.J.Ph.	American Journal of Philology.
Arch. Anz.	Archäologische Anzeiger.
Arch. Pap.	Archiv für Papyrusforschung.
Arch. Phil.	Archiv für Geschichte d. Philosophie.
A.S.A.E.	Annales du Service des antiquités de l'Egypte.
Ath. Mitt.	Mitteilungen des deutschen arch. Inst. Athenische Abteilung.
Bay. Abh.	Abhandlungen d. bayerischen Akad. d. Wissenschaften.
Bay. S.B.	Sitzungsberichte d. bayerischen Akad. d. Wissenschaften.
B.C.H.	Bulletin de Correspondance hellénique.
Beloch	K. J. Beloch's Griechische Geschichte. 2nd Ed.
Berl. Abh.	Abhandlungen d. preuss. Akad. d. Wissenschaften zu Berlin.
Berl. S.B.	Sitzungsberichte d. preuss. Akad. d. Wissenschaften zu Berlin.
B.I.C.	Bulletin de l'Institut français d'archéologie orientale au Caire.
B.P.W.	Berliner Philologische Wochenschrift.
B.S.A.	Annual of the British School at Athens.
B.S.R.	Papers of the British School at Rome.
Bull. d. I.	Bullettino dell' Istituto.
Bursian	Bursian's Jahresberichte.
Bury	J. B. Bury's History of Greece. 2nd Ed. 1922.
Busolt	G. Busolt's Griechische Geschichte.
C.A.H.	Cambridge Ancient History.
Cavaignac	E. Cavaignac's Histoire de l'antiquité.
C. Comp. G.	Cambridge Companion to Greek Studies. 3rd Ed. 1916.
C. Comp. L.	Cambridge Companion to Latin Studies. 3rd Ed. 1921.
C.I.A.	Corpus Inscriptionum Atticarum.
C.I.E.	Corpus Inscriptionum Etruscarum.
C.I.L.	Corpus Inscriptionum Latinarum.
C.J.	Classical Journal.
C.P.	Classical Philology.
C.Q.	Classical Quarterly.
C.R.	Classical Review.
C.R. Ac. Inscr.	Comptes rendus de l'Académie des Inscriptions et Belles-Lettres.
Diss.	Dissertation.
D.S.	Daremberg et Saglio, Dictionnaire des antiquités grecques et romaines.
E.Bi.	Encyclopaedia Biblica.
E.Brit.	Encyclopaedia Britannica. 11th Ed.
E.H.R.	English Historical Review.
E. Meyer	E. Meyer's Geschichte des Altertums.
F.H.G.	C. Müller's Fragmenta Historicorum Graecorum.
Geogr. Z.	Geographische Zeitschrift.
G.G.A.	Göttingische Gelehrte Anzeigen.
Gött. Nach.	Nachrichten von der Königlichen Gesellschaft der Wissenschaften zu Göttingen. Phil.-hist. Klasse.
Handbuch	Iwan Müller's Handbuch der klass. Altertumswissenschaft.
Harv. St.	Harvard Studies in Classical Philology.
Head H.N².	Head's Historia Numorum. 2nd Ed. 1912.
H.Z.	Historische Zeitschrift.

I.G.	Inscriptiones Graecae.
I.G².	Inscriptiones Graecae. Editio minor.
I. v. O.	Inschriften von Olympia.
Jahreshefte	Jahreshefte d. österr. archäol. Institutes in Wien.
J.D.A.I.	Jahrbuch des deutschen archäologischen Instituts.
J.E.A.	Journal of Egyptian Archaeology.
J.H.S.	Journal of Hellenic Studies.
J.I.d'A.N.	Journal internat. d'archéol. numismatique.
J.P.	Journal of Philology.
J.R.A.S.	Journal of the Royal Asiatic Society.
Klio	Klio (Beiträge zur alten Geschichte).
Lehrbuch	K. F. Hermann's Lehrbuch der griechischen Antiquitäten.
Liv. A.A.	Liverpool Annals of Archaeology.
M.B.B.A.	Monatsberichte der Berliner Akademie.
Mél. Arch.	Mélanges d'archéologie et d'histoire.
Mém. Ac. Inscr.	Mémoires de l'Académie des Inscriptions et Belles-Lettres.
Mon. d. I.	Monumenti Antichi dell' Istituto.
Mus. B.	Musée belge.
N.J. Kl. Alt.	Neue Jahrbücher für das klassische Altertum.
N.J.P.	Neue Jahrbücher für Philologie.
N.S.A.	Notizie degli Scavi di Antichità (Atti d. r. Accad. dei Lincei).
Num. Chr.	Numismatic Chronicle.
Num. Z.	Numismatische Zeitschrift.
O.L.Z.	Orientalistische Litteratur-Zeitung.
Phil.	Philologus.
Πρ.	Πρακτικά.
Proc. Brit. Acad.	Proceedings of the British Academy.
Proc. Cl. Ass.	Proceedings of the Classical Association.
P.W.	Pauly-Wissowa's Real-Encyclopädie der classischen Altertumswissenschaft.
Rec. Trav.	Recueil de Travaux relatifs à la philologie et à l'archéologie égyptienne et assyrienne.
Rend. Linc.	Rendiconti dell' Accademia dei Lincei.
Rev. Arch.	Revue Archéologique.
Rev. Bib.	Revue biblique internationale.
Rev. Eg.	Revue égyptologique.
Rev. E.G.	Revue des études grecques.
Rev. H.	Revue historique.
Rev. N.	Revue numismatique.
Rev. Phil.	Revue de philologie, de littérature et d'histoire anciennes.
Rh. Mus.	Rheinisches Museum für Philologie.
Riv. Fil.	Rivista di Filologia.
Riv. Stor. ant.	Rivista di Storia antica.
Röm. Mitt.	Mitteilungen des deutschen arch. Inst. Römische Abteilung.
Roscher	Roscher's Ausführliches Lexikon der griechischen und römischen Mythologie.
S.B.	Sitzungsberichte.
S.E.G.	Supplementum epigraphicum Graecum.
St. Fil.	Studi italiani di filologia classica.
Wien S.B.	Sitzungsberichte d. Akad. d. Wissenschaften in Wien.
Wien St.	Wiener Studien.
Z. Aeg.	Zeitschrift für ägyptische Sprache und Altertumskunde.
Z.D.M.G.	Zeitschrift der deutschen morgenländischen Gesellschaft.
Z.N.	Zeitschrift für Numismatik.

BIBLIOGRAPHIES

These bibliographies do not aim at completeness. They include modern and standard works and, in particular, books utilized in the writing of the chapters. Many technical monographs, especially in journals, are omitted, but the works that are registered below will put the reader on their track.

The works given in the General Bibliography for Greek History are, as a rule, not repeated in the bibliographies to the separate chapters.

N.B. Books in English and French are, unless otherwise specified, published at London and Paris respectively.

GENERAL BIBLIOGRAPHY FOR GREEK HISTORY

I. GENERAL HISTORIES

Beloch, K. J. *Griechische Geschichte*. Vols. I–II. Ed. 2. Strassburg, 1912–16.
Bury, J. B. *History of Greece*. Ed. 2. 1922.
Busolt, G. *Griechische Geschichte*. Vols. I–II. Ed. 2. Gotha, 1893–5.
Cavaignac, E. *Histoire de l'Antiquité*. Vols. I–II. 1913–19.
Cicotti, E. *Griechische Geschichte*. (Hartmann's Weltgeschichte.) Gotha, 1920.
De Sanctis, G. *Atthis. Storia della Repubblica Ateniese*. Ed. 2. Turin, 1912.
Freeman, E. A. *History of Sicily*. Vols. I–II. Oxford, 1891.
Glotz, G. *L'Histoire Générale*. I, Histoire Ancienne. 1925–.
Grote, G. *A History of Greece*. Vols. I–III. New ed. 1888.
——— ——— *From Solon to* 403 B.C. Condensed and edited with Notes and Appendices by J. M. Mitchell and M. O. B. Caspari, 1907.
Holm, A. *Geschichte Griechenlands*. Vols. I–II. Berlin, 1886–. Engl. trans. 1894–.
—— *Geschichte Siciliens im Altertum*. Vol. I. Leipzig, 1870.
Lehmann-Haupt, C. F. *Griechische Geschichte* in Gercke and Norden (below), vol. III.
Meyer, Eduard. *Geschichte des Altertums*. Vols. II–III. Stuttgart, 1893–1915.
—— *Forschungen zur alten Geschichte*. Halle, 1892–9.
v. Pöhlmann, R. *Griechische Geschichte und Quellenkunde*. Ed. 5. Munich, 1914. (In Iwan Müller's *Handbuch*, III, 4.)

II. WORKS ON CONSTITUTIONAL HISTORY, ETC.

Busolt, G. *Griechische Staatskunde*. I. (In Iwan Müller's *Handbuch*, IV, I. I.) Munich, 1920. (Very fully documentated.)
Gilbert, G. *Handbuch der Griechischen Staatsaltertümer*. Leipzig, 1881–5. Eng. trans. of vol. I, 1895.
Greenidge, A. H. J. *A Handbook of Greek Constitutional History*. 1902.
Halliday, W. R. *The Growth of the City State*. Liverpool, 1923.
Keil, B. *Griechische Staatsaltertümer* in Gercke and Norden (below), vol. III.
Swoboda, H. *Griechische Staatsaltertümer* (Hermann's *Lehrbuch*, I, iii). Tübingen, 1913.
v. Wilamowitz-Möllendorff, U. *Aristoteles und Athen*. 2 vols. Berlin, 1893.
—— *Staat und Gesellschaft der Griechen* (Kultur der Gegenwart, II, iv, I). Ed. 2. Leipzig and Berlin, 1923.
Zimmern, A. E. *The Greek Commonwealth*. Ed. 4. Oxford, 1924.

III. Works of Reference, Dictionaries, etc.

Clinton, H. Fynes. *Fasti Hellenici.* 3 vols. Oxford, 1834. (F.H.)

Daremberg et Saglio. *Dictionnaire des antiquités grecques et romaines.* 1877–1919. (D.S.)

Encyclopaedia Britannica. Ed. xi. Articles on Greek History. (E.Brit.)

Gercke, A. and Norden, E. *Einleitung in die Altertumswissenschaft.* Ed. 2. Leipzig and Berlin, 1914. Ed. 3, part appeared.

Hermann, K. F. *Lehrbuch der griechischen Antiquitäten.* New ed. Tübingen, various dates. (Lehrbuch.)

Iwan Müller. *Handbuch der klassischen Altertumswissenschaft.* Munich, various dates. (Handbuch.)

Lübkers Reallexikon des klassischen Altertums. Ed. 8. Edited by J. Geffcken and E. Ziebarth. Berlin, 1914.

Pauly-Wissowa-Kroll. *Real-Encyclopädie der classischen Altertumswissenschaft.* Stuttgart, 1893– (in progress). (P.W.)

Roscher, W. *Ausführliches Lexikon der griechischen und römischen Mythologie.* Leipzig, 1884– (in progress). (Roscher.)

Whibley, L. *A Companion to Greek Studies.* Ed. 3. Cambridge, 1916.

CHAPTERS I AND VII

THE FOUNDATION AND EXTENSION OF THE PERSIAN EMPIRE AND THE REIGN OF DARIUS

A. PERSIA (chapters I and VII, sections I–VI)

I. *Literary Sources*

Ctesias, *Persica*, ed. J. Gillmore, 1888.
Diodorus Siculus, IX–X.
Herodotus, books I–VI.
Strabo, *Geography*, XI–XVII.
Xenophon, *Cyropaedeia*.

II. *Inscriptions*

King, L. W. and Thompson, R. C. *Sculptures and inscriptions of Darius the Great.* 1907.
Rawlinson, H. *The Persian cuneiform inscription at Behistun*... J.R.A.S. XII, 70. (Of historical interest, see vol. I, p. 125.)
Smith, Sidney. *Babylonian historical Texts relating to the capture and downfall of Babylon.* 1924.
Stolze, F. *Persepolis: die Achaemenid. u. Sassanid. Denkmäler u. Inschriften* (with notes on the inscriptions by Nöldeke). 2 vols. Berlin, 1882.
Weissbach, F. H. *Abhandlungen.* Leipzig, 1913.
—— *Keilinschriften d. Achaemeniden.* Leipzig, 1911.
—— *Zur Kritik d. Achämenideninschriften.* Z.D.M.G. LXVII, 271.
Weissbach and Bang, W. *Die altpers. Keilinschriften.* Leipzig, 1908.

III. *General Works: Historical*

Champollion-Figeac. *Histoire de la Perse.* 1859.
Curzon, G. N. *Persia*, 1892.
v. Gutschmid, A. *Geschichte Irans u. seine Nachbarländer.* Tübingen, 1888.
Huart, C. *La Perse Antique et la civilisation Iranienne.* 1925.
Meyer, E. *Geschichte des Altertums.* III. Stuttgart, 1884.
—— Art. *Persia* in E.Brit.
Nöldeke, T. *Aufsätze zur persischen Geschichte.* Leipzig, 1887.
Otto, W. *Kulturgeschichte des Altertums.* Munich, 1925.
Prašek, J. V. *Forschungen zur Geschichte des Altertums.* Leipzig, 1897–1900.
—— *Geschichte der Meder und Perser.* Gotha, 1906, 1909.
Rawlinson, G. *Five great Monarchies.* Vol. III. 4th ed. 1879.
Sykes, Sir P. M. *History of Persia.* 2nd ed. 1921.
See also the histories of Hall, Helmholt, Maspero (above, vol. I, p. 635).

IV. *History*
(a) *Pre-Achaemenid.*

Dhorme, P. *Les Aryens avant Cyrus.* (Conférences de S. Étienne, 1910–11.)
Gune, P. D. *The Indo-Iranian migrations in the light of the Mitani records.* Journ. of the Iran. Assoc. X, 1921, p. 81.
Jackson, A. V. Williams. *Camb. Hist. of India*, chapter XIV. Cambridge, 1922. (With bibliography.)
Meyer, E. *Gesch. Alt.* I, i (*s.vv.* Iran, Persia, Zoroaster).

(*b*) *Achaemenid Period.*

Clay, A. T. *Gobryas, governor of Babylonia.* Journ. Amer. Orient. Soc. XLI, 1922.
Dhorme, P. *Cyrus le Grand.* Rev. Bibl., Jan. 1912.
Lehmann-Haupt, K. F. *Xerxes u. d. Babylonier.* Wochenschrift f. kl. Phil. 1900, p. 959.
Meyer, E. Arts. *Cyrus, Darius, Artaxerxes* in E.Brit.
Prašek, J. V. *Kyros der Grosse.* (Der alte Orient series.) Leipzig, 1912.
—— *Kambyses.* Leipzig, 1913.
—— *Dareios.* Leipzig, 1914.
Radet, G. *La première incorporation de l'Égypte à l'empire perse* (Rev. d. Ét. anciennes, July–Sept. 1909, p. 201).
Schulze, W. *Der Tod des Kambyses.* Berl. S.B., XXXVII, 1912, p. 702.
Swoboda. Art. *Dareios* in P.W.
Weissbach, F. H. Art. *Kyros* in P.W.
—— *Zur Chronologie d. Bīsutūn-Inschrift.* O.L.Z. XI, 485.

See also commentaries on Daniel, Ezra, Nehemiah and Esther. On Gobryas in particular, see W. Schwenzer, *Klio*, XVIII, 1923, p. 126, the references in *C.A.H.* III, 224 n., and S. Smith (11 above, pp. 104 *sq.*, 121 *sq.*) who publishes a text according to which the Gobryas who captured Babylon died shortly after the event, and therefore cannot be the later governor of that name. For the chronology, see especially, F. H. Weissbach, *Über einige neuere Arbeiten zur babylonisch-persischen Chronologie,* Z.D.M.G. LV, and for details Kugler, *Sternkunde und Sterndienst* (C.A.H. III, 712) and Weissbach, *Zeitschrift für Assyriologie* (N.F.) II, p. 55 and *Studia Orientalia* (Tallqvist Festschrift, I).

V. *Religion*

Zoroaster's date is keenly disputed; see, for an early discussion, A. V. Williams Jackson, Journ. of the Amer. Orient. Soc. XVII (1896). A date in the first half of the sixth century B.C., or even rather earlier, would be in general agreement with tradition; it would (on the analogy of Mohammed and Islam) fit in with the rise and rapid development of Persia; it could also be associated with the widespread religious activity in the East in and about the sixth century. On the other hand, evidence for the antiquity of the *name* of the god Mazda (eighth century B.C.), the close linguistic connection between Vedic and the early Avestan texts (Gāthās), and the admitted antiquity of early 'Iranian' culture (see vol. II, p. 331) have among other considerations led prominent authorities to place Zoroaster at about 1000 B.C., if not earlier. See *e.g.* E. Meyer (*E.Brit.* XXI, 205 *b*), C. Clemen, Lehmann, etc. A later date is maintained by Hertel (viz. *c.* 559–22), against whom see, especially, J. Charpentier, Bulletin of the School of Oriental Studies, London Institute, 1925 (III, 747 *sqq.*). On the whole, the usual history of religions makes it entirely probable that there was more than one great reforming period, and more than one outstanding reformer, in the early career of what we call Zoroastrianism; and clearer evidence is necessary before one can determine the religion of Medes and Persians prior to the Achaemenid age, and whether the Zoroaster of history had a forerunner or a successor.

Bartholomae, C. *Zarathuštras Leben u. Lehre.* Heidelberg Univ.-Reden. 1919.
Carnoy, A. J. Journ. Amer. Or. Soc. XXXVI, 300; Amer. Journ. Theol. XVII, 197; and Christus (ed. J. Huby, Paris, 1921).
—— *Iranian Mythology.* 1917.
Casartelli, L.-C. *La religion des rois achéménides d'après leurs inscriptions.* (IIIᵉ Congrès Scientif. Internat. d. Catholiques, 1894.) Brussels, 1895.
Clemen, C. *Fontes historiae religionis persicae* (Greek and Latin texts). Bonn, 1920.

Clemen, C. *Die griechischen u. lateinischen Nachrichten über d. persische Religion.* Giessen, 1920.

Dhorme, P. *La Religion des Achéménides.* Rev. Bib., Jan. 1913.

Geldner, K. Arts. *Zoroastrianism* in E.Bi. and E.Brit.

Gray, L. H. Art. *Achaemenians* in Hastings' Encyclopaedia of Religion and Ethics.

Harlez, C. de. *La rel. pers. sous les Achéménides.* Rev. de l'instruction publique en Belgique, xxxvii.

Hertel, J. *Die Zeit Zoroasters* (Indo-iran. Quellen u. Forschungen I.). Leipzig, 1924. (See Stein's review, O.L.Z. 1924, col. 727; also Charpentier, cited above.)

Jackson, A. V. Williams. *The religion of the Achaemenian kings,* I; with appendix by L. H. Gray on the non-Iranian inscriptions, Journ. Am. Orient. Soc. xxi; xxiv; also art. *Achaemenians* in Hastings, *op. cit.* See Geiger and Kuhn, Grundriss d. iran. Philologie, ii, 687.

—— *Zoroaster, the prophet of ancient Iran.* New York, 1899.

Lagrange, M.-J. *Religion des Perses.* 1904.

Lehmann, E., in Chantepie de la Saussaye, *Lehrbuch d. Rel.gesch.* (ed. by Bertholet and Lehmann, 1925).

Meyer, E. *Ursprung und Anfänge des Christentums,* ii, iii. Berlin, 1921.

Moore, G. F. *History of Religions.* 1913. Chapter xv *sq.*

—— *Zoroastrianism.* Harvard Theolog. Rev. v, 180.

Moulton, J. H. *Early Zoroastrianism.* 1913.

Oldenberg, H. *Die iranische Religion* (Die Oriental. Religionen, 1906).

Sayce, A. H. *The Medic origin of Zoroastrianism.* Academy, 1880, nos. 17, 18.

Scheftelowitz, I. *Altpersische Religion und das Judentum.* Giessen, 1920.

VI. *Astronomy*

Kugler, F. X. *Die babylonische Mondrechnung.* Freiburg, 1889.

—— *Sternkunde u. Sterndienst in Babel.* Münster, 1907–24.

—— *Von Moses bis Paulus.*

Schnabel, P. *Berossos u. die bab.-hell. Literatur.* Leipzig, 1923.

(Full references in these works.)

VII. *Alphabet* (see p. 201)

A full discussion of the origin of the Persian Alphabet may be found in Weissbach, *Keilinschriften der Achämeniden,* pp. liv–lx. There are four possibilities: (1) that the signs were borrowed from Babylonian cuneiform, much altered and adapted to alphabetic use; (2) that the signs were similarly borrowed from Elamite, (3) or some other, northern, script; (4) that it was an entirely new invention dependent only on the wedge-elements used in all cuneiform writing. As to the date when the writing was first used, the literature is quoted by Weissbach, *ibid.* pp. lx–lxix. Weissbach holds that Darius, in the Behistun inscription § 70, probably speaks of his own introduction of 'inscriptions in Aryan,' and that there is no proof of Old Persian inscriptions older than Darius. But the short inscription of Cyrus at Murghab is held by A. V. W. Jackson (*Persia Past and Present*), Herzfeld (*Klio,* viii) and many others, to belong to Cyrus the Great, and there are considerable difficulties in believing that it refers to the younger Cyrus.

VIII. *Art*

Dalton, O. *The Treasures of the Oxus, with other objects from ancient Persia and India.* (Franks Bequest, British Museum.) 1905.

Dieulafoy, M. *L'Art antique de la Perse.* 1884.

Herzfeld, E. *Islam,* xi, 127–137. (On the connection of Persian art with that of Urarṭu and Asia Minor.)

Mémoires de la Délégation en Perse, VIII. Recherches Archéol. 3ᵉ série (Ceramics). 1905.

Perrot, G. and Chipiez, C. *History of Art in Persia.* 1892.

Pottier, de Morgan, and Mecquenem. *Céramique peinte de Suse.* Mém. d. l. Délégation en Perse, XIII.

Sarre, F. *Die Kunst des Alten Persiens.* Berlin, 1922.

IX. *Miscellaneous*

Babelon, E. *Catalogue des monnaies grecques de la Bibliothèque nationale: les Perses Achéménides.* 1893.

Cowley, A. E. *Aramaic papyri of the Fifth Century B.C.* Oxford, 1923.

Gardner, P. *The gold coinage of Asia before Alexander the Great.* 1908.

Head, B. V. *The Coinage of Lydia and Persia from the earliest times to the fall of the Achaemenids.* 1877.

Herzfeld, E. *Pasargadae: Untersuchungen zur pers. Archaeologie.* Klio, VIII (1908), pp. 1–68.

—— *Am Tor von Asien, Felsdenkmale aus Irans Heldenzeit.* Berlin, 1920.

Hill, G. F. *British Museum Catalogue of the Greek Coins of Arabia, Mesopotamia and Persia.* 1922.

Hommel, F. *Grundriss d. Geographie u. Geschichte d. alten Orients.* 2nd ed. Munich, 1904.

Lehmann-Haupt, C. F. Art. *Satrap* in P.W.

Levy, R. *Persian Literature.* 1923.

Meyer, E. *Der Papyrusfund von Elephantine.* Leipzig, 1912.

Morgan, J. de. *Mission scientifique en Perse.* Vol. IV. 1896.

Moulton, J. H. *Early Religious Poetry of Persia.* Cambridge, 1911.

Pumpelly, R. *Explorations in Turkestan in 1903 and 1904.* (Washington, Carnegie Institution.) 2 vols. 1905, 1908.

Rostovtseff, M. *Iranians and Greeks.* Oxford, 1922.

Wilson, R. D. *Darius the Mede.* Princeton Theolog. Rev. 1922, p. 177.

B. THE SCYTHIAN EXPEDITION (chapter VII, section VII)

I. *Ancient Sources*

Herodotus, IV, 83–98, 118–144; V, 1–27.

II. *Modern Works*

Bonnell, E. *Beiträge zur Altertumskunde Russlands.* Petersburg, 1882. Vol. I, pp. 286–311.

Bury, J. B. Classical Review, 1897, pp. 277–82.

Grundy, G. B. *Great Persian War.* pp. 29–78.

How, W. W. and Wells, J. *Commentary on Herodotus.* Vol. I, pp. 429–34.

Macan, R. W. *Herodotus, Books IV–VI.* Vol. II, pp. 33–61.

Prašek, J. *Geschichte der Meder und Perser.* Gotha, 1906–10. Vol. II, pp. 75–108.

C. THE IONIAN REVOLT (chapter VII, section VIII)

I. *Ancient Sources*

Herodotus, V; VI, 1–43.

Plutarch, *De Herodoti Malignitate,* 24.

II. *Modern Books* (see also the General Bibliography)

(*a*) *General.*

Grundy, G. B. *The Great Persian War.* 1901. Chapter III.
Hauvette, A. *Hérodote historien des guerres médiques.* 1894. pp. 205–22.
Macan, R. W. *Herodotus, Books IV–VI.* 1895. Vol. II, pp. 62–70.

(*b*) *Special.*

Bury, J. B. *The Epicene Oracle concerning Argos and Miletus.* Klio, 1902, pp. 14–25.
Gardner, P. *The Coinage of the Ionian Revolt.* J.H.S. 1911, pp. 151–60; 1913, p. 105.
Heinlein, St. *Histiaios von Milet.* Klio, IX, 1909, pp. 341–51.
Lenschau, T. *Zur Geschichte Ioniens.* Klio, XIII, 1913, pp. 175–83.

CHAPTER II

THE REFORM OF THE ATHENIAN STATE

I. Ancient Sources

Solon: poems, editions Bergk, Hiller-Crusius, Diehl; and see Gilliard, Linforth, below.

Inscriptions: Sigeum stele, *C.I.G.* 8; Dittenberger³, 2; Hicks and Hill, 8; *I.G.* 1, 61 (*I.G.*² 1, 115); *I.G.*² 393.

Herodotus, I, 29–32, 34, 86; II, 177; V, 71, 94–6.

Thucydides, I, 126.

Lysias, X, 15–19.

Isocrates, *Panathenaicus*, 143 *sqq.*; *Areopagiticus*, 16, 20 *sqq.*

Cleidemus (*F.H.G.* I, 359–65).

Androtion (*F.H.G.* I, 371–7, esp. frags. 1, 4, 40).

Aristotle, *Constitution of Athens*, I–XIII, XXVIII, XXXV, XLI, XLVII; *Politics*, II, 7, p. 1266 b; II, 12, p. 1273 b *sq.*; III, 11, p. 1281 b; VI (IV), 11, 1296 a.

Papyrus ap. *Dikaiomata*, herausg. von der Graeca Halensis, pp. *64 sqq.* Berlin, 1913.

Philochorus (*F.H.G.* I, 384–417, esp. frags. 57, 58, 60, 94, 154).

Dionysius of Halicarnassus, *Antiq. Rom.* II, 26.

Diodorus, I, 77, 79, 96, 98; IX, 1–3, 17–18; XII, 18; XIX, 1; XXVI, 1.

Strabo, II, 102; XIII, 599–600.

Cicero, *ad Atticum*, X, 1, 2; *de legibus*, II, §§ 59–66.

Plutarch, *Solon*; *Solon-Publicola*; *Theseus*, esp. c. 25; *Moralia, passim*, esp. 295 C-D, 550 C, 823 F.

Gellius, *N.A.* II, 12.

Polyaenus, I, 20, 25.

Pausanias, I, vii, 25, 3.

Pollux, VII, 151; VIII, 22, 86, 108, 129 *sq.*

Diogenes Laertius, *Lives of Solon, Pittacus, Epimenides.*

Aelian, *Varia Historia*, III, 17; VIII, 10.

Gaius, *Digest*, X, 1, 13; XLVII, 22–4.

Heraclides, *Epitoma*, 1–5 (*F.H.G.* II, 208).

Hesychius, *s.v.* ἐκτήμοροι, ἐπίμορτος, σεισάχθεια.

Photius, *s.v.* ναυκραρία, πέλαται, σεισάχθεια.

Suidas, *s.v.* διάθεσις.

Other scattered references or repetitions of earlier authorities in rhetoricians, grammarians, chronological writers and lexicographers are to be found in the footnotes to Busolt, *Gr. Gesch.* II², 197–295. For citations and references to Solon's laws in the Attic Orators see Drerup, Schelling and Schucht below (III c).

II. Modern Writers on the Sources and Relations of the Ancient Authorities

For Aristotle's *Constitution of Athens*, see Sandys' second edition (1912) with bibliography up to that date, and add:

Busolt, G. *Griechische Staatskunde.* Munich, 1920. Vol. I, pp. 52 *sqq.*, 91 *sqq.*

Ledl, A. *Studien zur älteren athenischen Verfassungsgeschichte.* Heidelberg, 1914. pp. 1–76.

Mathieu, G. *Aristote: Constitution d'Athènes.* 1915.

Walker, E. M. *The 'Athenian Constitution'* in New Chapters in Greek Literature Oxford, 1921. pp. 133–46.

For Plutarch's *Solon*:

Adcock, F. E. *The Source of Plutarch, Solon, XX–XXIV.* C.R. xxviii, 1914, pp. 38–40.
Begemann, H. *Quaestiones Soloneae.* I. Diss. Holtzminden, 1875.
Keller, O. *Die Quellen in Plutarchs Lebensbeschreibung des Solons.* Saalfeld, 1867.
Prinz, R. *De Solonis Plutarchei Fontibus.* Diss. Bonn, 1867.

For Diogenes Laertius, *Solon*, see E. Schwartz, *s.v.* Diogenes (40) in P.W.

III. Modern Writers

See also General Bibliography

Bibliographies will be found in Gilliard (see below) up to 1907 and in Linforth (see below) up to 1919. Literature before 1895 is referred to by Busolt, see above.

A. *General*

Diels, H. *Epimenides.* Berl. S.B. 1891, pp. 387 *sqq.*
Gilliard, C. *Quelques Réformes de Solon.* Lausanne, 1907. (With app. on the poems.)
Jonas, J. *De Solone Atheniensi.* Diss. Münster i. W., 1884.
Ledl, A. *Die Zeit des Kylonischen Frevels* in Studien zur älteren athenischen Verfassungsgeschichte, pp. 77–104. Heidelberg, 1914.
Lehmann-Haupt, C. F. *Solon of Athens.* Liverpool, 1912.
v. Leutsch, E. L. *Die Griechischen Elegiker.* II. *Solon.* Phil. xxxi, 1872 *sqq.*, pp. 129–71.
Linforth, I. M. *Solon the Athenian.* Univ. of California Publ. 1919, vi, 1–318. (With text of poems and commentary.)
Mitchell, J. M. Art. *Solon* in E.Brit.
Niese, B. *Zur Geschichte Solons und seiner Zeit.* Historische Untersuchungen für A. Schäfer, Bonn, 1882, pp. 1 *sqq.*
Seeck, O. *Quellenstudien zu des Aristoteles Verfassungsgeschichte Athens.* Klio, iv, 1904, pp. 164–81, 270–326.
Toeppfer, J. *Quaestiones Pisistrateae.* Diss. Dorpat, 1886. (Also in Beiträge zur griech. Altertumswissenschaft, Berlin, 1897.)
—— *Attische Genealogie.* Berlin, 1889.
Wright, J. H. *The Date of Cylon.* Harvard Studies, iii, 1892, pp. 1–74.

B. *Constitutional*

Busolt, G. *Griechische Staatskunde.* Vol. i. Munich, 1920.
Cavaignac, E. *Sur les variations du cens dans les classes soloniennes.* Rev. Phil. 1908, pp. 36–47.
Cichorius, C. *Zu den Namen der attischen Steuerklassen.* Griechische Studien H. Lipsius dargebracht. Leipzig, 1894. pp. 135 *sqq.*
Droysen, J. G. *Die attische Kommunalverfassung.* Kl. Schriften, I, Berlin, 1893.
Glotz, G. Art. *Sortitio* in D.S.
Headlam, J. W. *Election by lot at Athens.* Cambridge, 1891.
Heisterbergk, B. *Die Bestellung der Beamten durch das Los.* Berl. Stud. f. kl. Phil. xvi, 1896.
Helbig, W. *Les vases du Dipylon et les Naucraries.* Mém. Ac. Inscr. xxxvi, 1898.
Ingle, C. *The original Function of the boule at Athens.* C.R. xxv, 1912, pp. 236–8.
Keil, B. *Die solonische Verfassung in Aristoteles' Verfassungsgeschichte Athens.* Berlin, 1892.
Ledl, A. *Studien zur älteren athenischen Verfassungsgeschichte.* Heidelberg, 1914

Lehmann-Haupt, C. F. *Schatzmeister- und Archontenwahl in Athen.* Klio, VI, 1906, pp. 304 *sqq.*

Miller, J. Art. *Drakon* in P.W.

Niese, B. *Über Aristoteles Geschichte der Athenischen Verfassung.* H.Z. LXIX, 1892, pp. 38 *sqq.*

Schjøtt, P. O. *Von Drakon bis Kleisthenes.* Videnskab Selskabs Skrifter, Christiania, 1909.

v. Schoeffer. Art. *Archontes* in P.W.

Wilbrandt, M. *Die politische und soziale Bedeutung der attischen Geschlechter vor Solon.* Phil. Suppl. Bd. VII, 1898, pp. 133–227.

Wilcken, U. *Zur Drakontischen Verfassung.* Apophoreton, Berlin, 1903, pp. 85–98.

See also articles in E.Brit. on *Archon, Athens, Constitution, Boule, Ecclesia,* etc.; in P.W. on βουλή, ἐκκλησία, etc.

C. *Economics, Law, etc.*

For coinage see the bibliography to chapter V and *H.N.*[2] pp. 365 *sqq.* with bibliography up to 1911.

Adler, G. *Solon und die Bauernbefreiung von Attika.* Vierteljahrsschrift für Staats- und Volkswirtschaft, IV, 1896, 107–32.

Andreades, A. M. Ἱστορία τῆς Ἑλληνικῆς δημοσίας οἰκονομίας. Athens, 1918.

Beauchet, L. *Histoire du droit privé de la république athénienne.* 1897.

—— Art. *Seisachtheia* in D.S.

Calhoun, G. M. *The early history of crime and criminal law in Greece.* Proc. Cl. Ass. 1922, pp. 86 *sqq.*

Christ, W. *Die solonische Münz- und Gewichtsreform.* Bay. S.B. 1900, pp. 118–32.

Cook, A. B. *Zeus.* Cambridge, 1914–25. Vol. II, p. 1093 *sq.* (on *Kyrbeis* and *axones*).

Dareste, R., Haussoullier, B. and Reinach, Th. *Inscriptions juridiques grecques.* 1891–1904.

Drerup, E. *Über die bei den attischen Rednern eingelegten Urkunden.* Jahrb. für Kl. Phil. Suppl. Bd. XXIV, 1898, pp. 221–336.

Gilbert, G. *Beiträge zur Entwicklungsgeschichte des griechischen Gerichtsverfahrens u.s.w.* Jahrb. für Kl. Phil. Suppl. Bd. XXIII, 1896, pp. 445–535.

Gleue, H. *De homicidarum in Areopago Atheniensi judicio.* Göttingen, 1894.

Glotz, G. *La solidarité de la famille dans le droit criminel en Grèce.* (With bibliography.) 1904.

—— *Études sociales et juridiques sur l'antiquité grecque.* 1906.

Hill, G. F. *Solon's Reform of the Attic Standard.* Num. Chr. XVII, 1897, pp. 284–92.

Kohler, J. and Ziebarth, E. *Das Stadtrecht von Gortyn und seine Beziehungen zum gemeingriechischen Rechte.* Göttingen, 1912. pp. 132 *sqq.*

Ledl, A. *Zum drakontischen Blutgesetz.* Wien. Stud. XXXIII, 1–36.

Lehmann-Haupt, C. F. Art. *Gewichte* in P.W. Suppl. Bd. III.

Lipsius, J. H. *Das attische Recht und Rechtsverfahren.* Leipzig, 1905–15. Esp. vol. I, pp. 1–133.

Niccolini, G. *Gli ectemori ateniese nell' Ath. Pol. di Aristotele.* Riv. Stor. ant. VII, 1903, pp. 673–81.

Partsch, J. *Griechische Bürgschaftsrecht.* Leipzig, 1909.

Pottier, E. *Études sur les lécythes blancs attiques à représentations funéraires.* Bibl. des écoles franç. d'Athènes et de Rome, 1883.

—— *Le commerce des vases peints attiques en VI*e *siècle.* Rev. Arch. 4e Série, III, 1904.

Ridgeway, Sir W. In *Notes on Text of the Athenaion Politeia.* C.R. V, 109.

Schelling, H. *De Solonis legibus apud oratores Atticos.* Berl. Diss. 1842.

Schreiner, J. *De corpore iuris Atheniensium.* 1913.

Schucht, H. *Über die Echtheit attischer Rednerurkunden.* B.P.W. 1919, cols. 1120–8, 1143–51.

Seltman, C. T. *Athens, its History and Coinage before the Persian Invasion.* Cambridge, 1924.

Sondhaus, K. *De legibus Solonis.* Jena Diss. 1909.

Swoboda, H. *Beiträge zur griechischen Rechtsgeschichte.* Zeitschrift der Savigny-Stiftung, xxvi (Romanistische Abt.), 1905, pp. 149 *sqq.*

Szanto, E. *Hypothek und Scheinkauf im griechischen Rechte.* Wien. Stud. ix, 1887, pp. 279–96. (=Ausgew. Abh. pp. 74–92.)

—— *Über die griechische Hypothek.* Arch. Epig. Mitt. xx, 101–14. (=Ausgew. Abh. pp. 121 *sqq.*)

—— *Zur drakontischen Gesetzgebung.* Arch. Epig. Mitt. xv, 180–2. (=Ausgew. Abh. pp. 328 *sqq.*)

Thalheim, T. *Griechische Rechtsaltertümer* in Hermann's *Lehrbuch.*

Usteri, P. *Aechtung und Verbannung im griechischen Rechte.* Berlin, 1903.

Vinogradoff, Sir P. *Historical Jurisprudence.* Vol. ii. The Jurisprudence of the Greek city. Oxford, 1922.

Vollgraff, W. *De origine hypothecae in iure Attico.* Mnemosyne, l, 1922, pp. 213–23.

v. Wilamowitz-Möllendorff, U. *Zum ältesten Strafrecht der Kulturvölker.* Leipzig, 1905.

Wilbrandt, M. *De rerum privatarum ante Solonis tempus in Attica statu.* Rostock Diss. 1895.

CHAPTER III

ATHENS UNDER THE TYRANTS

I. Ancient Sources

Solon: poems, esp. nos. 2, 8–10 (Diehl). See bibliography to chapter II, I.

Inscriptions: in *Hermes*, LVII, 478; *S.E.G.* I, 8; *B.C.H.* 140, 1920, p. 229; *C.I.A.* IV, i, p. 41, no. 373 E (=*I.G.*² I, 761, Hicks and Hill, 10).

Herodotus, I, 59–64; V, 55–65, 76, 90, 91, 94; VI, 34–9, 103, 121, 137–40; VII, 6.

Thucydides, I, 20; VI, 53–60.

Cleidemus (*F.H.G.* I, pp. 359–65).

[Plato], *Hipparchus*, p. 228 B–229 D.

Aristotle, *Constitution of Athens*, XIII–XIX; *Politics*, VIII (v), 12, p. 1315 b; *Rhetoric*, II, 24, p. 1401 b.

[Aristotle], *Oecon.* II, 4.

[?] Heraclides Ponticus, Ox. Pap. IV, no. 664.

Rylands Papyri, I (1911), no. 18 = Bilabel, Die kleineren Historikerfragmente, no. I.

Philochorus (*F.H.G.* I, 384–417, esp. frags. 69, 70).

Cornelius Nepos, *Miltiades*.

Diodorus, IX, 4, 20, 37; X, 16–17, 37; XIII, 95.

Plutarch, *Solon*; *Cato Major*, 24; *Moralia*, 794 F, 805 D, 807 D–E.

Polyaenus, I, 21.

Diogenes Laertius, *Life of Solon*.

Aelian, *Varia Historia*, VII, 19; VIII, 16; XI, 8.

Heraclidis *Epitoma*, 6 (*F.H.G.* II, 208).

Anth. Pal. XI, 4.

Justin, II, 7 *sq.*

For scattered references or repetitions of earlier authorities in grammarians, lexicographers and chronological writers, see footnotes to Busolt, *Gr. Gesch.* II², pp. 296–399: on criticism of the above sources see above, bibliography to chapter II, section II.

II. Modern Writers

See also General Bibliography

A. *General*

See Busolt, *Gr. Gesch.* II², pp. 295–6 for literature up to 1895.

Allen, T. W. *Homer, The Origins and Transmission*. Oxford, 1924. pp. 225–48.

Beloch, K. J. *Hipparchos und Themistokles*. Hermes, LV, 1920, pp. 311–18.

Berard, V. *Pisistrate, rédacteur des poèmes Homériques*. Rev. Phil. XLV, 1921, pp. 194–233.

Buschor, E. *Burglöwen*. Ath. Mitt. XLVII, 1922, pp. 92–105.

Busolt, G. *Die Lakedaimonier und ihre Bundesgenossen*. Leipzig, 1878.

Dickins, G. *The Growth of Spartan Policy*. J.H.S. XXXII, 1912, 1–42; XXXIII, 1913, pp. 111–12.

Dörpfeld, W. *Das Hekatompedon in Athen*. J.D.A.I. XXXIV, 1919, pp. 1–40.

Grundy, G. B. *The Policy of Sparta*. J.H.S. XXXII, 1912, pp. 261–9.

Heberdey, R. *Altattische Porosskulptur*. Wien, 1919.

Hill, B. H. *The Older Parthenon*. A.J.A. (N.S.), XVI, 1912, pp. 535–56.

Hirsch, M. *Die athenischen Tyrannenmörder in Geschichtsschreibung und Volkslegende*. Klio, XX, 1925, pp. 129–67.

Holland, L. B. *Erechtheum Papers*. I–IV. A.J.A. xxviii, 1924, esp. pp. 402 *sqq.*
Hude, K. *Zur Ermordung des Hipparchos*. Jahr. f. Phil. cxlv, 1892, pp. 170–6.
Jacoby, F. *Das Marmor Parium*. Berlin, 1904.
Kahrstedt, U. *Griechisches Staatsrecht*. I. Sparta und seine Symmachie. Göttingen, 1922.
Lenschau, T. Art. *Kleomenes* (3) in P.W.
Miller, J. Art. *Hipparchos* (1) and *Hippias* (1) in P.W.
Niccolini, G. *Per la storia di Sparta. La Confederazione del Peloponnese*. Rendiconti del r. istituto lombardo, xxxviii, 1905, pp. 538–57.
Oddo, A. *Pisistrato*. Palermo, 1903.
Petersen, E. *Die Burgtempel der Athenaia*. 1907.
Seltman, C. T. *Athens, its history and coinage before the Persian Invasion*. Cambridge, 1924.
v. Stern, E. *Hippias oder Hipparchos*. Hermes, lii, 1917, pp. 354–70.
—— *Solon und Peisistratos*. Hermes, xlviii, 1913, pp. 426–41.
Toeppfer, J. *Quaestiones Pisistrateae*. (See on chapter ii above.)
Ure, P. N. *The Origin of Tyranny*. Cambridge, 1922.
Welter, G. *Das Olympieion in Athen*. Ath. Mitt. xlvii, 1922, pp. 61–71.

B. *Chronology*

Adcock, F. E. *The Exiles of Peisistratus*. C.Q. xviii, 1924, pp. 174–81.
Bauer, A. *Die Chronologie des Peisistratos und seine Söhne*. Analecta Graeca, Festschrift zum 42 Philologentag. Graz, 1893.
Blass, F. *Album gratulatorium in honorem H. van Herwerden*. Traj. Rheni, 1902, pp. 28–31.
Cichorius, C. *Die Chronologie des Pisistratos. Kleinere Beiträge zur Geschichte*. Festschrift z. deutsch. Historikertag, 1894. Leipzig, 1894. pp. 11 *sqq.*
Herchensohn, M. In *Philologiciskoe Obozrenie*, x, 1896, pp. 119–23.
Köhler, U. *Die Zeiten der Herrschaft des Peisistratos in der* πολιτεία 'Αθηναίων. Berl. S.B. 1892. pp. 339 *sqq.*
Oddo, A. *Op. cit.* p. 23.
Pomtow, H. *Delphische Beilagen*. Rh. Mus. li, 1896, pp. 560 *sqq.*
Wells, J. *Studies in Herodotus*. Oxford, 1923. pp. 81–7. (On the date of the Plataean-Athenian Alliance.)

See also Beloch, i², 2, pp. 288 *sqq.*; Busolt, ii², p. 317, n. 4; E. Meyer, ii, p. 773; De Sanctis, pp. 276 *sqq.*; Wilamowitz, *Aristoteles und Athen*, i, pp. 21 *sqq.*

CHAPTER IV

THE OUTER GREEK WORLD IN THE SIXTH CENTURY

I. Introduction and Sources

Herodotus: commentaries by Macan, R. W., 1895–1908; How, W. W. and Wells, J., Oxford, 1912; Book II, Wiedemann, A., Leipzig, 1890.

On poets and philosophers see bibliography to chapters XIV and XV below.
See also Myres, J. L., *On the 'List of Thalassocracies' in Eusebius*, J.H.S. XXVI, 1906, pp. 84 *sqq.*; XXVII, 1907, pp. 123 *sqq.*; Fotheringham, J. K., *On the 'List of Thalassocracies' in Eusebius*, J.H.S. XXVII, 1907, pp. 75 *sqq.*

II. The Eastern Powers

See bibliography to chapters I and VII and vol. III, chapters XII–XV and XXI.

III. Miletus, Ephesus and Samos

A. *Ancient Literary Sources*

(*a*) *Miletus.*
Herodotus, I, 17–22; II, 178; IV, 137 *sqq.*; V, 23–5, 28–9, 92 ζ; VI, 21. Athenaeus, XII, 519 B.

(*b*) *Samos.*
Herodotus, II, 182; III, 39–60, 120–5; IV, 152. Thucydides, III, 104. Aristotle, *Pol.* VIII (V), p. 1313 b. Strabo, VII, 331, frag. 56; XIV, 637–8. Plutarch, *Qu. Gr.* 57 (*Moral.* p. 303). Athenaeus, XII, 540 D-F. Zenobius, III, 90. Eustathius *ad Dion. Perieget.* 534. Suidas and Photius, *s.v.* Σαμίων ὁ δῆμος. Malalas *ap.* Migne, *Bibl. Patr. Gr.* XCVII, 260. Cedrenus, *ib.* CXXI, 277.

(*c*) *Ephesus.*
Herodotus, I, 26, 92. Nicolaus Damasc. frag. 65 (*F.H.G.* III, 397). Polyaenus, VI, 50. Aelian, *Varia Hist.* III, 26. Athenaeus, VII, 289 c. Suidas, *s.v.* Πυθαγόρας Ἐφέσιος, Ἀρίσταρχος and Ἱππῶναξ.

B. *Archaeological Evidence*

British Museum Excavations at Ephesus, 1908.
Curtius, L. *Samiaca.* Ath. Mitt. XXXI, 1906, pp. 151 *sqq.*
Fabricius, E. *Altertümer auf der Insel Samos. Ib.* IX, 1884, pp. 165 *sqq.*
Wiegand, T. *Siebenter vorläufiger Bericht über Ausgrabungen in Milet und Didyma.* Berl. Abh. 1911.
—— *Erster vorläufiger Bericht über Ausgrabungen in Samos. Ib.* 1911.

C. *Historical Works*

Böhlau, J. *Aus ionischen und italischen Nekropolen.* Leipzig, 1898.
Dunham, A. G. *History of Miletus.* 1915.
Radet, G. *La Lydie et le monde grec au temps des Mermnades.* 1893.
Ure, P. N. *The Origin of Tyranny.* Chapters III and IX. Cambridge, 1922

IV. The Northern Ionian Cities

A. *Ancient Literary Sources*

(*a*) *Chios.*
Herodotus, I, 18, 160; IV, 138; VI, 8–16; VIII, 132.

(*b*) *Smyrna, Teos, etc.*
Herodotus, I, 15–16, 142, 164–70. Polyaenus, VII, 2, 2.

B. *Archaeological Evidence*

Dickins, G. *Catalogue of the Acropolis Museum.* Cambridge, 1912. I, 19 *sqq.*
Kourouniotis, K. Ἀνασκαφαὶ ἐν Χίῳ. Ἀρχ. Δελτ. I, 64 *sqq.*; II, 190 *sqq.*
Mavrogordato, J. *A Chronological Arrangement of the Coins of Chios.* Num. Chr. 1915, pp. 1 *sqq.*
Picard, Ch. and Plassart, A. *Sarcophages de Clazomènes.* B.C.H. 1913, pp. 378 *sqq.*, Pls. x–xvi.
Roberts, E. S. *Introduction to Greek Epigraphy.* Cambridge, 1887. p. 63 *sq.*
v. Wilamowitz-Möllendorff, U. *Nordionische Steine.* Berl. Abh. 1909, pp. 64 *sqq.*

C. *Historical Works*

Puchstein, O. *Die ionische Säule.* Leipzig, 1907.

V. Aeolians, Dorians and the Cyclades
A. *Ancient Literary Sources*

(*a*) *Cyme.*
Strabo, XIII, 622.

(*b*) *Mitylene.*
Herodotus, I, 27; II, 135; v, 94. Aristotle, *Pol.* III, 1285 a. Chron. Parium, 51 (*F.H.G.* I, 548). Cicero, *de legibus*, II, ch. 26, § 66. Plutarch, *Sept. Sap. Conv.* 13 (*Moral.* p. 156 A), *de malign. Herod.* 15 (*Moral.* p. 858). Athenaeus, XIII, 596 B. Diogenes Laertius, I, 74–81. Suidas, *s.v.* Πίττακος, Ῥοδώπιδος ἀνάθημα.

(*c*) *Dorian Settlements.*
Herodotus, I, 144, 174; II, 178; III, 4, 11. Thucydides, III, 88; VI, 4. Diodorus Siculus, v, 9. Pausanias, x, 11, 3.

(*d*) *Naxos.*
Herodotus, I, 61, 64; v, 30 *sqq.* Aristotle, *Pol.* VII (v), 1305 a. *Constit. of Athens*, xv; [Aristotle], *Oeconomica*, II, 1346 B. Polyaenus, I, 23. Plutarch, *de malign. Herod.* 21 (*Moral.* 859 D). Athenaeus, VIII, 348.

(*e*) *Paros.*
Herodotus, v, 28–9.

(*f*) *Siphnos.*
Herodotus, III, 57–8.

(*g*) *Delos.*
Thucydides, I, 13; III, 104.

B. *Archaeological Evidence*

Homolle, Th. *Statues trouvées à Délos.* B.C.H. 1879, pp. 99 *sqq.*, Pls. II, III, xiv, xv, xvii; 1880, pp. 29 *sqq.*
Joubin, A. *Relief archaïque de Thasos.* B.C.H. 1894, pp. 64 *sqq.* and Pl. xvi.
Kinch, K. F. *Fouilles de Vroulia.* Berlin, 1914.
Mendel, G. *Catalogue des Sculptures grecques...des Musées Impériaux Ottomans.* 3 vols. Constantinople, 1912–14.
Penoyre, J. *Thasos.* J.H.S. xxix, 1909, pp. 202 *sqq.*
Salzmann, A. *Nécropole de Camiros.* 1875.

C. *Historical Works*

See Puchstein, *op. cit.* above.

VI. The Black Sea and its Approaches

A. *Ancient Literary Sources*

(*a*) *Hellespont and Chersonese.*

Herodotus, IV, 137–8; VI, 34–41. Thucydides, VI, 59.

(*b*) *Cyzicus.*

Herodotus, IV, 76, 138. Athenaeus, I, 30 A.

(*c*) *Byzantium.*

Herodotus, IV, 87–8, 138, 144.

(*d*) *South Russia.*

Herodotus, IV, 17–18 and *passim.* Dio Chrysostom, *Or.* XXXVI. Eustathius, *ad Dion. Perieget.* 549.

B. *Archaeological Evidence*

See further bibliography to vol. III, chapter IX

Bulletin and *Compte-Rendu de la Commission Impériale Archéologique de St Pétersbourg, passim.*

Chamonard, J., Dhorme, E. and Courby, F. *La Nécropole d'Éléonte de Thrace.* B.C.H. XXXIX, 1915, pp. 135 *sqq.*; XLVI, 1922, pp. 539–41.

Pharmakowsky, B. *Archäologische Funde (Russland).* Arch. Anz. 1907–12.

C. *Historical Works*

Hasluck, F. W. *Cyzicus.* Cambridge, 1910.

Leaf, W. *The Commerce of Sinope.* J.H.S. XXXVI, 1916, pp. 1 *sqq.*

Lenschau, T. *Zur Geschichte Ioniens.* Klio, XIII, 1913, pp. 174 *sqq.*

Minns, E. H. *Scythians and Greeks.* Cambridge, 1913.

—— *C.A.H.* vol. III, chapter IX.

Rostovtzeff, M. *Iranians and Greeks in South Russia.* Oxford, 1922.

v. Stern, E. *Die politische und soziale Struktur der Griechenkolonien am Nordufer des Schwarzmeergebietes.* Hermes, L, 1915, pp. 161 *sqq.*

—— *Die griechische Kolonisation am Nordgestade des Schwarzen Meeres im Lichte archäologischer Forschung.* Klio, IX, 1909, pp. 139 *sqq.*

VII. The Greeks in Egypt and Cyrene

A. *Ancient Literary Sources*

(*a*) *Egypt.*

Herodotus, I, 30; II, 135, 153 *sqq.* Isocrates, *Busiris,* 28. Strabo, XVII, 801, 808. Plutarch, *Solon,* 25–6. Maspero, G., *Popular Stories of Ancient Egypt.* Tr. Johns, Mrs C. H. W. pp. 280–4, 1915.

(*b*) *Cyrenaica.*

Epicorum Graecorum Fragmenta. Ed. Kinkel, pp. 57–8. Leipzig, 1877. Pindar, *Pyth.* IV, 16, 56; IX, 105 *sqq.* Herodotus, II, 161, 181–2; III, 13, 91; IV, 150 *sqq.*; V, 42 *sqq.* Scylax, 108. Callimachus, *Hymns,* II, 86 *sqq.* Heracl. Pont. (*F.H.G.* II, 212). Sallust, *Jug.* 79. Diodorus Siculus, VIII, 30. Nicolaus Damasc. frag. 52 (*F.H.G.* III, 387). Pliny, *N.H.* XIX, 15; XXII, 49. Pausanias, III, 18; VI, 19. Polyaenus, VIII, 41. Eusebius, *Chron. ad Ol.* 53. Suidas, *s.v.* Βάττου σίλφιον.

B. *Archaeological Evidence*

(*a*) *Egypt.* (See also bibliography to vol. III, chapters XII–XIV, 3.)

Hogarth, D. G. and Edgar, C. C. *Excavations at Naukratis.* B.S.A. V, 26 *sqq.*

Hogarth, D. G., Lorimer, H. L. and Edgar, C. C. *Naukratis*. J.H.S. xxv, 1905, pp. 105 *sqq.*
Kourouniotis, K. Ἀνασκαφαὶ ἐν Χίῳ. Ἀρχ. Δελτ. ii, 192 *sqq.*
Petrie, W. M. F. *Tanis II, Nebesheh, and Defenneh.* 1888.
Petrie, W. M. F. and Gardner, E. *Naukratis I and II.* 1888.

(*b*) *Cyrenaica.*
Blinkenberg, C. *Die lindische Tempelchronik.* Bonn, 1915.
Deane, S. N. *Archaeological News: Cyrenaica.* A.J.A. 1922, pp. 113–14 and fig. 1.
Ferri, S. *Tre anni di lavoro archeologico a Cirene* (1919–22). Aegyptus, iv, 1923, pp. 167 *sqq.*
Ghislanzoni, E. *Notizie archeologiche sulla Cirenaica.* Notiziario Archeologico, i, 1915, pp. 67–239 and figs. 59 *a,b,* 60 *a,b.*
Hoppin, J. C. *The Excavations at Cyrene,* 1910–11. Bull. of the Arch. Inst. of America, ii, 1910–11, pp. 141 *sqq.*
Smith, R. M. and Porcher, E. A. *Discoveries at Cyrene.* 1864.
Weld-Blundell, H. *A Visit to Cyrene in* 1895. B.S.A. ii, 113 *sqq.*

C. *Historical Works*

See also bibliography to vol. iii, chapters xii–xiv

(*a*) *Egypt.*
Hall, H. R. *C.A.H.* vol. iii, chapters xii–xv.
Mallet, D. *Les premiers Établissements des Grecs en Égypte.* 1894.
Price, E. R. *Pottery of Naukratis.* J.H.S. xliv, 1924, pp. 180 *sqq.*
Prinz, H. *Funde aus Naukratis.* Klio, Beiheft vii, 1908.

(*b*) *Cyrene.*
Dickins, G. *Growth of Spartan Policy.* J.H.S. xxxii, 1912, pp. 28–9.
Keramopoullos, A. D. Καυλὸς σιλφίου. J. I. d'A. N. 1907, pp. 295 *sqq.*
Malten, L. *Kyrene.* Berlin, 1911.
Myres, J. L. *C.A.H.* vol. iii, chapter xxv, vi.
Niese, B. *Herodotstudien, besonders zur spartanischen Geschichte.* Hermes, xlii, 1907, pp. 419 *sqq.*
Studniczka, F. *Kyrene.* Leipzig, 1890.
Thrige, J. P. *Res Cyrenensium.* Copenhagen, 1828.

VIII and IX. Magna Graecia and the West, Trade, Industry, etc.

A. *Ancient Literary Sources*

(*a*) *Sybaris, Croton, Caulonia and Locri.*
Herodotus, iii, 125, 129–37; v, 44–7; vi, 21, 127. Diodorus, viii, 18–20; xii, 9. Justin, xx, 2–4. Strabo, vi, 253, 261–4. Pausanias, vi, 14. Athenaeus, xii, 519 b, 521 c, d, 522 c, d, 523 c. Pseudo-Scymnus, 341.

(*b*) *Tarentum.*
Strabo, vi, 282. Justin, iii, 4.

(*c*) *Zaleucus.*
Plato, *Laws,* iv, 722 d. Aristotle, *Pol.* ii, 1274 a; fr. 505 ed. Berolin. v, 1561. Diodorus, xii, 20, 21. Cicero, *de legibus,* ii, ch. 6, § 14, 15; *ad Atticum,* vi, 1, 18. Strabo, vi, 259. Athenaeus, xiv, 619 b. Pseudo-Scymnus, 315. Zenobius, *Centur.* iv, 10 (*ap.* Leutsch und Schneidewin, *Paroemiogr. Gr.* i, 87). Hieronymus, *Chron. ann. Abr.* 1354. Eusebius, *Chron. Vers. Arm. ann. Abr.* 1354.

(d) Cities on the West Coast.
Herodotus, I, 167; VI, 21. Livy, II, 21, 34. Dionysius of Halicarnassus, VI, 21; VII, 3 *sq.* Strabo, V, 220, 246; VI, 253 (cp. Pliny, *N.H.* III, 10). Plutarch, *Mul. Virt.* 26 (*Moral.* 261–2). Pseudo-Scymnus, 243, 306.

(e) Massilia.
Herodotus, I, 165 *sq.* Thucydides, I, 13. Diodorus, XIV, 93. Strabo, IV, 179; VI, 252. Justin, XLIII, 3–5. Athenaeus, XIII, 576.

(f) Agathe, Rhoda, Emporiae, Hemeroscopium, Maenaca.
Strabo, III, 156, 159, 160; IV, 182. Pseudo-Scymnus, 146, 204.

(g) Tartessus.
Herodotus, I, 163.

(h) Trade, etc.
Dionysius of Halicarnassus, I, 18, 28. Strabo, V, 214, 220. Plutarch, *Publicola*, 13.

B. *Archaeological Evidence*

British Museum Catalogue of Silver Plate (Greek, Etruscan and Roman), Pl. I.
Van Buren, E. *Figurative Terra-cotta Revetments in Etruria and Latium.* 1921.
—— *Archaic Fictile Revetments in Sicily and Magna Graecia.* 1923.
v. Duhn, F. *Funde und Forschungen, Italien*, 1914–20 (*Medma*). Arch. Anz. 1921, pp. 154 *sqq.*
Frickenhaus, A. *Griechische Vasen aus Emporion.* Anuari d'Estudis Catalans, 1908, pp. 195 *sqq.*
Gàbrici, E. *Cuma.* Mon. Lincei, XXII.
Noack, F. *Die thronende Göttin.* Arch. Anz. 1917, pp. 119 *sqq.*, Abb. 1–9.
Pellegrini, G. *Vasi greci dipinti delle Necropoli Felsinee.* Bologna, 1912.
Petersen, E. *Bronzen von Perugia.* Röm. Mitt. IX, 1894, pp. 253 *sqq.*
Pick, B. *Die thronende Göttin.* J.D.A.I. XXXII, 1917, pp. 204 *sqq.*
Quagliati, Q. *Rilievi votivi arcaici in Terracotta di Lokroi Epizephyrioi.* Ausonia, III, 1908, pp. 136 *sqq.*
De Sanctis, G. and Orsi, P. *Caulonia.* Mon. Lincei, XXIII, 685 *sqq.*, 699 *sqq.*
Vasseur, M. G. *Fouilles exécutées à Marseilles.* C.R. Acad. des Inscr. 1910, pp. 426 *sqq.*

C. *Historical Works*

Gandia, E. *La Estratificacion de la Ceramica en Ampurias.* Anuari d'Estudis Catalans, 1913–14, pp. 657 *sqq.*
Hübner, E. *Die Büste von Ilici.* J.D.A.I. XIII, 1898, pp. 114 *sqq.*, figs. 1, 2, 3.
Jullian, C. *Histoire de la Gaule.* Vol. I, chapter V. 1914.
—— *Arles grecque et romaine.* Journ. des Savants, 1922, pp. 103 *sqq.*
Koldewey, R. and Puchstein, O. *Die griechischen Tempel in Unteritalien und Sicilien.* Berlin, 1899.
Pais, E. *Origin of Siris.* Ancient Italy, 1908, pp. 67 *sqq.*
Paris, P. *Emporion.* Rev. Arch. ser. V, vol. IV, pp. 329 *sqq.*; vol. V, pp. 108 *sqq.*
Pinza, G. *Monumenti primitivi di Roma e del Lazio antico.* Mon. Lincei, XV.
Ponnelle, L. *Le Commerce de la première Sybaris.* Mél. Arch. XXVII, 1907, pp. 243 *sqq.*
Schulten, A. *Ampurias.* N.J. Kl. Alt. XIX, 1907, pp. 334 *sqq.*
—— *Avieni Ora maritima.* Berlin, 1922.
—— *Tartessos.* Hamburg, 1922.
Ure, P. N., *op. cit.* chapter VIII.
Waltz, P. *Les Artisans et leur Vie en Grèce, VII et VI siècles.* Rev. Hist. CXLI, pp. 161 *sqq.*; CXLII, pp. 14 *sqq.*; CXLVI, pp. 161 *sqq.*

CHAPTER V

COINAGE FROM ITS ORIGINS TO THE PERSIAN WARS

General reference should be made to the Bibliography in Head's *Historia Numorum*, 2nd ed. Oxford, 1911.

I. Materials

(*a*) The most important public collections containing Greek coins are the following (modern catalogues mentioned in brackets).

Athens, National Numismatic Museum. (Catalogues by A. Postolacca, 1868 and 1872.)

Berlin, Kaiser Friedrich-Museum. (Catalogues of Macedon, Thrace, part of S. Italy, by Friedländer, von Sallet, Dressel, 1888–94.)

Boston, U.S.A. (Catalogue of Warren Collection, by K. Regling, 1906.)

Brussels, Bibliothèque Royale.

Cambridge. (Catalogue by Leake of Leake Collection, 1854–9; of Maclean Collection by S. W. Grose in progress; vol. I, Spain to Sicily, 1923.)

Constantinople, Museum of Antiquities.

Copenhagen, Royal Collection and Thorwaldsen Collection. (Catalogue by L. Müller, 1851.)

Florence, Archaeological Museum.

Glasgow, Hunterian Museum. (Catalogue by G. Macdonald, 1899–1905.)

Gotha, Landes-Münzkabinett.

The Hague, Royal Collection. (Selection by F. Imhoof-Blumer, *Zeit. f. Num.* 1876.)

London, British Museum. (Catalogue by Poole, Head, Gardner, Wroth, Hill, 1873– (complete except Spain, Gaul, Later Kings of Macedon, and N. Africa, now in preparation). Also *Guide to the Coins of the Ancients,* by B. V. Head, 4th ed. 1895.)

Milan, Brera, etc. (in Castello Sforzesco).

Munich, (Königliche) Sammlung.

Naples, Museo Nazionale. (Catalogue by Fiorelli, 1866–72.)

New York, Metropolitan Museum. (Catalogue of Ward Collection, by G. F. Hill, 1901.)

Oxford, Ashmolean Museum (formerly Bodleian Library).

Paris, Bibliothèque Nationale. (Catalogue by Babelon of Persia, Satraps, Cyprus and Phoenicia, 1893; Waddington Collection, 1897; Luynes Collection, vols. I, II, 1924–6, in progress. All important coins of this collection are being included in Babelon's *Traité.*)

Turin, Royal Collection.

Vienna, Bundessammlung (formerly Hof-Museum). (Catalogue of Thessaly-Epirus by von Schlosser, 1893.)

(*b*) Of private collections, many important and finely illustrated catalogues have been issued for the auction-sales of Sotheby (London), Hirsch (Munich), Egger (Vienna), Naville (Geneva and Lucerne), Hôtel Drouot (Paris). To these may be added the Catalogue by R. Jameson (Paris) of his own collection (1913), and the Catalogue of the Sir Hermann Weber Collection by L. Forrer, in preparation (vols. I, II, Gaul to Cyclades, 1922, 1924).

(*c*) The chief periodicals to be consulted are *Journal International d'Archéologie Numismatique* (Athens), *Nomisma* (Berlin), *Numismatic Chronicle* (London), *Numismatische Zeitschrift* (Vienna), *Revue numismatique française* (Paris), *Zeitschrift für Numismatik* (Berlin).

(*d*) General works, other than catalogues of special collections, describing coins:

Babelon, E. *Traité des monnaies grecques et romaines.* Paris, 1901– (in progress).
Eckhel, J. *Doctrina numorum veterum.* Vienna, 1792–8. Addenda, 1826.
Head, B. V. *Historia Numorum.* 2nd ed. Oxford, 1911.
Imhoof-Blumer, F. *Monnaies grecques.* Paris, 1883.
—— *Griechische Münzen.* Abh. k. bayer. Akad. Munich, 1890.
—— *Kleinasiatische Münzen.* Sonderschr. oesterr. arch. Inst. Vienna, 1901–2.
Mionnet, T. E. *Description de médailles antiques grecques et romaines.* 1807–37.
Waddington, H., Reinach, Th., and Babelon, E. *Recueil général des monnaies d'Asie Mineure.* 1904– (in progress).

For monographs on more limited districts see the bibliographies in Head's *Historia Numorum.* Add:

Athens.
Seltman, C. T. *Athens, its History and Coinage before the Persian Invasion.* Cambridge, 1924.

Macedon.
Svoronos, J. N. *L'hellénisme primitif de la Macédoine prouvé par la numismatique.* Paris, Athens, 1916. Propagandist.

Elis.
Seltman, C. T. *The Temple Coins of Olympia.* Cambridge, 1921.

Cyzicus.
Fritze, H. von. *Elektronprägung von Kyzikos.* Nomisma. Berlin, 1912.

Chios.
Mavrogordato, J. *Chronological Arrangement of the Coins of Chios.* Num. Chron. 1918.

II. THEORY AND HISTORY

In addition to the works of Babelon, Eckhel and Head in 1 (*d*).

Babelon, E. *Origines de la Monnaie.* 1897.
Gardner, P. *Types of Greek Coins.* Cambridge, 1882.
—— *History of Ancient Coinage,* 700–300 B.C. Oxford, 1918.
Hill, G. F. *Handbook of Greek and Roman Coins.* 1899.
—— *Historical Greek Coins.* 1906.
Hultsch, F. *Griechische und römische Metrologie.* 2nd ed. Berlin, 1882.
—— *Metrologicorum Scriptorum Reliquiae.* Leipzig, 1864–6.
Lenormant, F. *La monnaie dans l'antiquité.* 1878–9.
Macdonald, G. *Coin Types.* Glasgow, 1905.
—— *Evolution of Coinage.* Cambridge, 1916.
Regling, K. *Die antike Münze als Kunstwerk,* 1924.
Ridgeway, Sir W. *Origin of Metallic Currency and Weight Standards.* Cambridge, 1892.
Viedebantt, O. *Forschungen zur Metrologie des Altertums.* Abh. sächs. Ges. d. Wiss. Leipzig, 1916.
—— *Antike Gewichtsnormen und Münzfüsse.* Berlin, 1923.

CHAPTER VI

ATHENS: THE REFORM OF CLEISTHENES

I. Ancient Authorities

Inscriptions: *C.I.A.* iv (1), p. 78, 334 a (= *I.G.*² 1, 394), Hicks and Hill, 12;
C.I.A. iv (2), 1 b (p. 1) (= *I.G.*² 11, 1), Hicks and Hill, 81, § 5; *I.G.* 11, 582, 589, 868.

Herodotus, 1, 60–3; 111, 80, 148; v, 39–54, 62–97; vi, 19, 34–41, 48–51, 61–93, 103, 104, 108–10, 131–6; vii, 148, 205, 239; ix, 73.

[Xenophon], *Athenian Constitution*, 1, 3.

Thucydides, 1, 18, 126; 11, 19, 55, 65; 111, 68 *ad fin.*

Aristophanes, *Lysistrata*, 274–82 *cum schol.*; schol. *ad Equites*, 855.

Xenophon, *Hellenica*, 11, iv, 30; *Memorabilia*, 111, 4.

Isocrates, *Areopagiticus*, 23.

Anaximenes, *Rhet. Gr.* 1, 2, p. 21. Ed. Hammer.

Ephorus, fr. 107.

Hellenica Oxyrhynchia, xi.

Aristotle, *Constitution of Athens*, xiii, 5; xvi; xx-xxii; xxv, 4; xxvi *ad fin.*; xxviii; xli; xliii–xlvii, 1; xlix; lxii, 3; *Politics*, 111, 2, 3, p. 1275 b *ad fin.*; 13, 18–24, pp. 1284 a and b; vii (vi), 2, 5, p. 1317 b; 4, 18–19, p. 1319 b; viii (v), 3, 7, pp. 1302 b and 1303 a.

Plato, *Hipparchus*, pp. 228–9; *Republic*, viii, p. 557.

Demosthenes, l, 8.

Dionysius of Halicarnassus, *Ant. Rom.* v, 77; vi, 6, 34.

Diodorus Siculus, xi, 86, 87.

Polyaenus, viii, 33.

Pausanias, 11, 20, 8–10; 111, 4, 1.

Strabo, ix, 396.

Plutarch, *Solon*, 19, 24; *Aristides*, 5, 7; *Themistocles*, 1–6; *de mul. virt.* 4, p. 245.

Aelian, *Var. Hist.* xiii, 24.

II. Modern Writers

A. *General*

Busolt, G. *Die Lakedaimonier und ihre Bundesgenossen.* Leipzig, 1878.

Dickins, G. *The Growth of Spartan Policy.* J.H.S. xxxii, 1912, pp. 1–42; xxxiii, 1913, pp. 111–12.

Grundy, G. B. *The Policy of Sparta.* J.H.S. xxxii, 1912, pp. 261–9.

How, W. W. and Wells, J. *Commentary on Herodotus.* Appendix xvii. Oxford, 1912.

Lenschau, T. Art. *Kleomenes* (3) in P.W.

Macan, R. W. *Herodotus IV–VI.* Appendix vii.

Niese, B. *Herodotstudien besonders zur spartanischen Geschichte.* Hermes, xlii, 1907, pp. 417–68.

Poralla, P. *Prosopographie der Lakedaimonier.* Breslau, 1913.

Wells, J. *Studies in Herodotus.* Oxford, 1923. Chapter iv.

B. *Constitutional*: see also bibliography to chapter 11, 111 b

Carcopino, J. *Histoire de l'ostracisme athénien.* Bibl. de la fac. des lettres, xxv, 1909, pp. 82–272. (Contains a review of previous literature.)

Ehrenberg, V. *Kleisthenes und das Archontät*. Klio, xix, 1923, pp. 106–10.
—— *Neugründer des Staates*. Munich, 1925.
Francotte, H. *La Polis grecque*. Paderborn, 1907.
Haussoullier, B. Art. *Demos* in D.S.
Kahrstedt, U. Art. *Kleisthenes* (2) in P.W.
Ledl, A. *Studien zur älteren athenischen Verfassungsgeschichte*. Heidelberg, 1914.
Loeper, R. *Die Trittyen und Demen Attikas*. Ath. Mitt. xvii, 1892, pp. 319–433.
Macan, R. W. *Herodotus IV–VI*. 1895. Appendix ix.
Martin, A. Art. *Ostrakismos* in D.S.
Milchhoefer, A. *Die attische Lokalverfassung*. Ath. Mitt. xviii, 1893, pp. 277–304.
—— *Untersuchungen über die Demenordnung des Kleisthenes*. Berl. Abh. 1892.
Sandys, J. E. *The Tribes of Cleisthenes and the Map of Attica*. Proc. Camb. Phil. Soc. 1911.
v. Schoeffer, V. Art. *Demoi* in P.W.
Szanto, E. *Die Kleisthenischen Trittyen*. Hermes, xxvii, 1892, pp. 312–15 (= *Ausgew. Abh.* pp. 183–6).
Toepffer, J. *Attische Genealogie*. Berlin, 1889.

CHAPTER VIII

MARATHON

A. Sections I–V

I. *Ancient Authorities*

(*a*) *Epigraphical.*
Athenian dedication at Delphi after the battle of Marathon: Hicks and Hill, 13;
  Dittenberger (3rd ed.), 23; Michel, 1117.

(*b*) *Literary.*
Herodotus, esp. vi, 31–50 and 94–124.
Cornelius Nepos, *Miltiades.*
Pindar, *Pyth.* vii, 16–17; viii, 79.
Thucydides, i, 18 (cf. 118); ii, 34; vi, 59.
Plato, *Menex.* 240; *Leg.* 698 c–e.
Demosthenes, *De fals. leg.* 303.
Aristotle, *Rhet.* iii, 1411 a, 5–10; *Constitution of Athens*, xxii.
Strabo, x, 448.
Justin, ii, 9.
Plutarch, *Arist.* 5; *Camill.* 19; *De Herod. malign.* 26–7; *Quaest. Conviv.* x, 3;
  De glor. Ath. 7, 8.
Pausanias, i, 15, 32; v, 11.
Suidas, *s.v.* χωρὶς ἱππεῖς.

  Further references in Macan's *Herodotus IV–VI*, vol. ii, Appendix x, §§ 12–30.

II. *Modern Works*

Boeckh, A. *Zur Geschichte der Mondcyclen der Hellenen.* Jahrb. f. class. Philologie,
  Suppl. i, 1, 1855, section 15.
Boucher, A. *Marathon d'après Hérodote.* 1920.
Bury, J. B. *The battle of Marathon.* C.R. x, 1896, pp. 95 *sqq.*
Busolt, G. *Die Lakedaimonier.* Leipzig, 1878. pp. 355–69.
Curtius, E. *Griechische Geschichte.* 4th ed. Berlin, 1874. Vol. ii, pp. 19–27.
Delbrück, H. *Die Perserkriege und die Burgunderkriege.* Berlin, 1887.
—— *Geschichte der Kriegskunst.* Berlin, 1900. Kap. v.
Duncker, M. *Strategie und Taktik des Miltiades.* Berl. Abh. 1886.
Finlay, G. *On the battle of Marathon.* Trans. R. Soc. of Literature, iii, ii, 1839,
  pp. 363–95.
Frazer, Sir J. G. *Pausanias's Description of Greece.* 1898. Vol. ii, pp. 431–43.
Grundy, G. B. *The great Persian war.* 1901. Chapter iv.
Hauvette, A. *Hérodote historien des guerres médiques.* 1894. Liv. i, chap. iv.
How, W. W. *On the meaning of* ΒΑΔΗΝ *and* ΔΡΟΜΩΙ. C.Q. xiii, 1919,
  pp. 40 *sqq.*
—— *Cornelius Nepos on Marathon and Paros.* J.H.S. xxxix, 1919, pp. 48 *sqq.*
—— *Arms, tactics and strategy in the Persian war.* J.H.S. xliii, 1923, pp. 117 *sqq.*
Kromayer, J. *Drei Schlachten aus dem griech.-röm. Altertum.* Abh. d. phil.-hist.
  Klasse d. Sächs. Akad. xxxiv, 1921.
Leake, W. M. *On the Demi of Attica.* Trans. R. Soc. of Literature, i, ii, 1829,
  pp. 158–94.
Lehmann-Haupt, C. F. *Herodots Arbeitsweise und die Schlacht bei Marathon.* Klio,
  xviii, 1923, pp. 65–78, 309–35.
Lolling, H. G. *Zur Topographie von Marathon.* Ath. Mitt. i, 1876, pp. 67 *sqq.*

Macan, R. W. *Herodotus, Books IV, V, VI.* 2 vols. 1895.
Milchhoefer, A. *Text zu Karten von Attika.* Heft III–VI. Berlin, 1889. Sect. v.
Mommsen, A. *Heortologie.* Leipzig, 1864. pp. 211–15.
Munro, J. A. R. *Some observations on the Persian wars.* J.H.S. XIX, 1899, pp. 185 *sqq.*
Schilling, W. *Die Schlacht bei Marathon.* Phil. LIV (N.F. VIII), pp. 253–73.
Staes, B. Ὁ ἐν Μαραθῶνι τύμβος. Ath. Mitt. XVIII, 1893, pp. 46 *sqq.*
Stein, H. *Herodotos, V, VI.* 4th ed. Berlin, 1882.

B. Sections VI–X

I. *Ancient Authorities*

Herodotus, II, 178; III, 59; V, 74–91, 93–7, 99–103; VI, 18–21, 33–41, 48–94, 103–4, 110–11, 125–36.
Thucydides, I, 14, 105, 108, 138.
Xenophon, *Hellenica,* III, 1, 6.
Aristotle, *Constitution of Athens,* XIII; XXII; XXVIII.
Marmor Parium, 49.
Nepos, *Miltiades; Themistocles,* 1; *Aristides; Cimon.*
Diodorus Siculus, X, 30–2.
Dionysius of Halicarnassus, *Ant. Rom.* V, 77; VI, 6, 34.
Justin, II, 9.
Plutarch, *Solon,* 24; *Themistocles,* 1–6; *Aristides,* 1–8.
Pausanias, III, 4.
Athenaeus, VI, 272.
Eusebius, *Chron. Can.* p. 337.

II. *Modern Writers*

See also bibliography to chapter VI, II A.

How, W. W. and Wells, J. *Commentary on Herodotus.* Oxford, 1912. Appendix XVII.
Jacoby, F. Art. *Herodotus* in P.W. Suppl. II, esp. col. 442–5.
Lenschau, T. Art. *Kleomenes* in P.W.
Macan, R. W. *Herodotus IV–VI.* 1895. Appendices VIII and XI.
Muelder, D. *Die Demaratosschrift des Dikaios.* Klio, XIII, 1913, pp. 39–69.
v. Wilamowitz-Möllendorff, U. *Aristoteles und Athen.* Berlin, 1893. Vol. II, pp. 280 *sqq.*

CHAPTERS IX AND X

XERXES' INVASION OF GREECE AND THE DELIVERANCE OF GREECE

I. Ancient Authorities

(*a*) *Epigraphical.*
(1) Inscription on the serpent column at Constantinople:
  Hicks and Hill, 19; Dittenberger (3rd ed.), 31; Michel, 1118.
(2) Epitaph on the Corinthians at Salamis: Ath. Mitt. xxii, 1897; Hicks and Hill, 18.
(3) Epitaph on the Megarians: *I.G.* vii, 53; Hicks and Hill, 17.

(*b*) *Literary.*
Herodotus, esp. vii, viii, ix.
Aeschylus, *Persae.*
Pindar, *Pyth.* i, 75–8; *Isth.* v (iv), 48–50; *Frag.* 77.
Thucydides, i, 14, 18, 20, 23, 73–4, 89, 132, 137; ii, 71–4; iii, 24, 54, 57–8, 62, 68, 92; iv, 109.
Xenophon, *Hell.* v, 4.
Ctesias, ed. Gilmore, 52–9.
Plato, *Lach.* 191 b, c.
Hellen. Oxyrh. xi, 3, 4.
Demosthenes, *De Cor.* 204.
Lycurgus, *c. Leocr.* 122.
Aristotle, *Constitution of Athens*, xxii–xxiii.
Sosylus, ed. Wilcken (Hermes, xli, 1906).
Laterculi Alexandrini. Ed. Diels. Berlin, 1904. Col. viii, ll. 8–11.
Diodorus Siculus, xi, 1–19, 27–37.
Livy, xxxvi, 15–19, 22–4.
Strabo, ix, 395, 398, 403, 408, 428–9; x, 445.
Plutarch, *Them.* 6–17, 21; *Arist.* 8–21; *Cim.* 5; *Lys.* 15; *Camill.* 19; *Cato Maj.* 13; *De Herod. malign.* 28–43; *De glor. Ath.* 7.
Pausanias, i, 40; v, 23; ix, 1, 2, 4; x, 1, 13, 19, 20–2.
Athenaeus, vii, 311.

II. Modern Works

Beloch, K. J. *Griechische Geschichte.* Vol. ii. 2nd ed. Strassburg, 1914, 1916. i, ii; ii, sect. 19–22, 27–32, 35–46.
Boeckh, A. *Zur Geschichte der Mondcyclen der Hellenen.* Jahrb. für class. Philologie, Suppl. i, i, 1855, section 16.
Boucher, A. *La bataille de Platées d'après Hérodote.* Rev. Arch. 1915. (With a topographical survey by Capt. Tribert, 1834.)
Bury, J. B. *The campaign of Artemisium and Thermopylae.* B.S.A. ii, 1896, pp. 83 *sqq.*
—— *Aristides at Salamis.* C.R. x, 1896, pp. 414 *sqq.*
Casson, S. ΑΠΟΔΕΙΞΙΣ, '*Inventory,*' *in Herodotus and Thucydides.* C.R. xxxv, 1921, p. 144 *sq.*
Custance, Sir R. *War at sea.* Part i. Edinburgh, 1919.
Delbrück, H. *Die Perserkriege und die Burgunderkriege.* Berlin, 1887.
—— *Geschichte der Kriegskunst.* Berlin, 1900.
Farrell, J. *Note on the position of Rhoduntia.* C.R. xxiv, 1910, p. 116 *sq.*
Frazer, Sir J. G. *Pausanias's Description of Greece.* 1898. Vol. v, pp. 2–18, 299–307.

Goodwin, W. W. *The battle of Salamis.* Papers of Amer. Sch. at Athens, I, 1885.
Grundy, G. B. *The topography of the battle of Plataea.* 1894.
—— *The great Persian war.* 1901. Chapters v–xiii.
Hauvette, A. *Hérodote historien des guerres médiques.* 1894. Liv. ii.
How, W. W. *Arms, tactics and strategy in the Persian war.* J.H.S. xliii, 1923, pp. 117 *sqq.*
Hunt, W. I. *Notes on the battlefield of Plataia.* A.J.A. vi, 1890, pp. 463 *sqq.*
Kromayer, J. *Antike Schlachtfelder.* Berlin, 1907. Bd. ii. i, i, with Karte v. Bd. iv, 1–4 (the Persian wars) with maps, Berlin, 1924, was published after these chapters had gone to press.
Leake, W. M. *On the Demi of Attica.* Trans. R. Soc. of Literature, i, ii, 1829, pp. 231–69.
—— *Travels in Northern Greece.* 1835. Chapters x, xvi, xvii.
Lolling, H. G. *Die Meerenge von Salamis.* Aufsätze E. Curtius gewidm. Berlin, 1884.
Macan, R. W. *Herodotus, Books VII, VIII, IX.* 3 vols. 1908.
Milchhoefer, A. *Text zu Karten von Attika.* Berlin, 1895. Heft vii, viii. Sect. iii. Berlin, 1900. Heft ix. Sects. iii, iv.
Mommsen, A. *Heortologie.* Leipzig, 1864. pp. 222–9, 253–6, 403–12.
Munro, J. A. R. *Some observations on the Persian wars.* J.H.S. xxii, 1902, pp. 292 *sqq.*; xxiv, 1904, pp. 114 *sqq.*
Obst, E. *Der Feldzug des Xerxes.* Klio, Beiheft xii, 1913.
Ramsay, Sir W. M. *Military operations on the N. front of Mt Taurus.* J.H.S. xl, 1920, pp. 89 *sqq.*
Rühl, F. *Herakleides von Mylasa.* Rhein. Mus. lxi, 1906, pp. 352–9.
Tarn, W. W. *The fleet of Xerxes.* J.H.S. xxviii, 1908, pp. 202 *sqq.*
Verrall, A. W. *The death of Cyrsilus, alias Lycides.* C.R. xxiii, 1909, pp. 36 *sqq.*
Wace, A.J. B. *The topography of Pelion and Magnesia.* J.H.S. xxvi, 1906, pp. 143 *sqq.*
Washington, H. S. *Description of the site and walls of Plataia.* A.J.A. vi, 1890, pp. 452 *sqq.*
—— *Discovery of a temple of archaic plan.* A.J.A. vii, 1891, pp. 390 *sqq.*
Wiegand, T. *Priene.* Berlin, 1904. Kap. i.
Wilcken, U. *Ein Sosylus-Fragment.* Hermes, xli, 1906, pp. 103 *sqq.*
—— *Zu Sosylus.* Hermes, xlii, 1907, pp. 510 *sqq.*
Woodhouse, W. J. *The Greeks at Plataiai.* J.H.S. xviii, 1898, pp. 33 *sqq.*
Wright, H. B. *The campaign of Plataea.* New Haven, 1904.

CHAPTER XI

CARTHAGE AND SICILY

I. Ancient Authorities

Inscriptiones Graecae Antiquissimae, ed. Roehl, 95, 512 A.
Sylloge Inscriptionum Graecarum. Dittenberger. 3rd ed. 33–5.
Pindar: *Olympians*, ii, iii; *Pythians*, i, ii, vi. Scholia vetera in *Pindari carmina*, ed. A. B. Drachmann (Teubner).
Simonides, *Epigram* 141 (Bergk).
Herodotus, i, 163–7; v, 43–7; vi, 22–4; vii, 153–67.
Thucydides, vi, 1–5.
Antiochus, Frags. 1 and 2; Ephorus, Frag. 111; Philistus, Frags. 8 and 17; Timaeus, Frags. 77–94; in *F.H.G.* (Müller), vol. i.
Diodorus Siculus, xi, 20–6.
Pseudo-Scymnus, 146–66, in C. Müller, *Geographi Graeci Minores*, vol. i, pp. 196 *sqq.*
Strabo, iii, 4, p. 156; vi, 2, pp. 265–75.
Polyaenus, *Strategemata*, i, 27–9; v, 6; vi, 51.
Justin, iv, 2; xix, 1.

II. General Histories

See General Bibliography

Gsell, S. *Histoire ancienne de l'Afrique du Nord.* Vols. i–ii. 1913.
Meltzer, O. *Geschichte der Karthager.* Vol. i. Berlin, 1879.
Pais, E. *Storia della Sicilia e della Magna Grecia.* (*Storia d' Italia*, Parte i.) Turin, 1894.

III. Chronology and Special History

See articles on separate states in P.W., *e.g. Acragas, Karthago, Selinus*

Blinkenberg, C. *Die lindische Tempelchronik.* Bonn, 1915.
Bury, J. B. *Bacchylides.* Cambridge, 1905. pp. 465 *sqq.*
Ciaceri, E. *Intorno alle più antiche relazione tra la Sicilia e la Persia.* Studi Storici Ant. Class. v, p. 1 *sq.*
—— *Cadmo di Coo.* Arch. Stor. per la Sicilia orient. viii, 68 *sqq.*
Dodd, C. H. *The Samians at Zancle-Messana.* J.H.S. xxviii, 1908, pp. 56 *sqq.*
Ender, H. *Die erste sizil. Expedition der Karthager.* Progr. Dillingen, 1913.
Mancuso, U. *Il sincronismo tra le battaglie di Himera e delle Termopyle sec. Timeo.* Riv. Fil. xxxvii, 1909, pp. 548 *sqq.*
Niese, B. *Herodotstudien besonders zur spartanischen Geschichte.* Hermes, xlii, 1907, pp. 417–68.
Pareti, L. *Studi siciliani ed italioti.* Florence, 1920.
de Sanctis, G. *Storia dei Romani.* Turin, 1907. i, 328 *sqq.*; ii, 251 *sqq.*
Schulten, A. *Tartessos.* Hamburg, 1922.
Sitzler, J. *Der Koer Kadmos.* Phil. lxviii, 1909, pp. 321 *sqq.*
Swoboda, H. *Zur Beurteilung der griechischen Tyrannis.* Klio, xii, 1912, pp. 341 *sqq.*
Täubler, E. *Imperium Romanum*, pp. 268 *sqq.* (on first Treaty between Rome and Carthage). Leipzig, 1913.
Tenney, Frank. *An Economic History of Rome*, pp. 29 *sqq.* Baltimore, 1920.

CHAPTER XII

ITALY IN THE ETRUSCAN AGE. A. THE ETRUSCANS

I. Geographical Distribution

A. *Inscriptions*

Corpus Inscriptionum Etruscarum: edd. Pauli, C., Danielsson, O. A., and Herbig, G. Leipzig, 1913– (in progress).

Until this is completed the only serviceable collection of Etruscan inscriptions (though it is less accurate than students are now wont to expect) is contained in the *Corpus Inscriptionum Italicarum* of A. Fabretti with supplements by G. F. Gamurrini. 1867–80.

Inscriptions of Novilara: published by E. Brizio, *Mon. d. I.* v, 178 *sqq.*, by E. Lattes, Hermes, xxxi, 1896, pp. 463 *sqq.* and xliii, 1908, pp. 325 *sqq.*

Inscriptions of Sondrio: Pauli, C., *Altitalische Forschungen*, I, 56, 63. Hanover, 1885.

Raetic Inscriptions: Whatmough, J., J.R.S. xi, 1921, p. 245; C.Q. xviii, 1923, p. 61.

Celto-Ligurian Inscriptions: Herbig, G., Anzeiger f. schweizerische Altertumskunde, vi, 1905–6, p. 187. (Cf. below, bibliography to chapter xiii, section i.)

B. *Literary Sources*

Pliny, *N.H.* iii, 50 *sqq.*

Strabo, v, 209–28.

Livy, v, 33, 4–11; Vergil, *Aen.* x, 198–203, with Servius *ad loc.*; Pliny, *N.H.* iii, 115, 130, 133 (Etruscans in Felsina and Mantua).

C. *Etruscan Names*

Herbig, G. *Kleinasiatisch-etruskische Namengleichungen.* Bay. S.B. 1914, p. 34. (Cf. Servius on Verg. *Aen.* xi, 598.)

Schulze, W. *Geschichte der lateinischen Eigennamen.* Berlin, 1904. pp. 62–421, esp. p. 388.

II. Traditional Data of Etruscan History

A. *Ancient Sources*

Herodotus, I, 94 *sqq.* Strabo, v, 219, 220 and 220, 221. Vergil, *Aen.* ii, 781; viii, 478; ix, 11; other authorities and discussion in B. Modestov, *Introduction à l'histoire romaine*, 1907, p. 347 *sq.* (Etruscan tradition of the Lydian origin of Etruscans.)

Dionysius Hal. i, 27; ii, 49. Pliny, *N.H.* iii, 50 and 112. (Umbri outside Umbria.)

Servius *ad* Verg. *Ecl.* ix, 47. (On Volcatius.)

Varro *ap.* Censorinum, xvii, 6. See Modestov, *op. cit.* p. 449, and Herbig, *op. cit.* p. 34. (The Etruscan saecula.)

Justin, xx, 5, and Inscriptions of Novilara and Sondrio above and of Marzabotto below. (The strata of population in North Italy.)

Livy, i, 34–60; iv, 37; viii, 14. Diodorus Sic. xii, 31. (The spread of Etruscan power.)

Thucydides, vi, 88, 103; vii, 57. (Tyrrheni with Athenians at Syracuse 414 B.C.)

Livy, i, 58–ii, 15. (The Fall of the Tarquins.)

Livy, iv, 37; xxvi, 14. Diodorus Sic. xii, 31. Servius *ad* Vergil, *Aen.* x, 145. (The Fall of Capua.)

Livy, iv and v; vii and ix. *C.I.L.* xi, part i *passim*. (The Roman conquest of Etruria.)

B. *Modern Writers*

Beloch, K. J. *Campanien.* 2nd ed. 1890, p. 245. Mommsen, *C.I.L.* x, p. 465. (Spread of Etruscan power.)
Conway, R. S. *Italic Dialects*, pp. 53, 94 *sqq.*, 99, 310 *sqq.* (The Fall of Capua.)
Montelius, O. *Civilisation primitive en Italie.* 1895; and Journ. R. Anthr. Inst. xxvi, 1896–7, p. 254. (Points of Etruscan Chronology.)

III. The Evidence of Etruscan Remains

Barnabei, F., Cozza, A., Pasqui, A., Gamurrini, G. F. *Scavi...nel Territorio Falisco.* Mon .d. I. iv, 1894, pp. 1–587. (This series of excavations at Narce yielded remarkably clear strata.)
Brizio, E. *Scavi eseguiti a Marzabotto.* Mon. d. I. i, 1891, punt. 2.
—— *La Necropole di Novilara.* Mon. d. I. v, 1895, pp. 85–464.
Déchelette, J. *Manuel d'archéologie.* ii, 1913, part ii, pp. 532 *sqq.*
Dennis, G. *Cities and Cemeteries of Etruria.* 3rd ed. 1883.
Falchi, I. *Scavi a Vetulonia.* Notizie d. Scavi, 1893, pp. 143 and 496; 1895, p. 272.
Gherardini, G. *Scavi a Corneto-Tarquinia.* Notizie d. Scavi, 1881, p. 342; 1882, p. 136; Mon. d. I., viii, 1898, p. 117. (On Volterra.)
Grenier, A. *Bologne villanovienne et étrusque.* 1912.
Gsell, S. *Fouilles dans les Nécropoles de Vulci.* 1891.
Koerte, G. Art. *Etrusker* in P.W.
Milani, L. A. *Scavi a Vetulonia.* Notizie d. Scavi, 1895, p. 22. See also *C.I.E.* 5213 (the warrior inscr.) and the whole section.
Perrot, G. et Chipiez, C. *History of Art in Phrygia, Lydia*, etc. p. 288 (the Tralles plaque), p. 326 (the Idrias tomb), pp. 128, 153, 367–71 and 385 (on chamber tombs in Asia Minor). For Etruscan parallels see Modestov, *op. cit.* p. 353 *sq.*

IV. Early Alphabets of Italy

On the history of Greek writing and alphabets derived from it, Kirchhoff, A., *Studien zur Geschichte des griechischen Alphabets*, ed. 4, Gütersloh, 1887, is still the chief authority.

i. *Alphabets of Formello and Caere.*

Mommsen, T. Bull. Inst. Arch. 1882, p. 91. (Facsimile of Formello alphabet.)
Roberts, E. S. *Greek Epigraphy.* Cambridge, 1887. Vol. i, p. 17.

ii. *Alphabets in Italy generally, Etruscan in Campania, Tarentine-Ionic.*

Conway, R. S. *op. cit.* ii, 458.

iii. *Origins and varieties of Etruscan script.*

Hammarström, M. *Beiträge zur Geschichte des etruskischen, lateinischen und griechischen Alphabets.* Helsingfors, 1890. Esp. pp. 41 *sqq.*, with Danielsson's comment *C.I.E.* 5213. (Vol. ii, p. 119.) See further *C.I.E.* 4943, 4952, 5005 (for *vh*).
Roehl, H., *Inscr. Gr. Antiquiss.* 131, 505, and Thumb, A., Indog. Forschungen, ix, 1898, p. 319, on ⅎh in Greek alphabets.

iv. *Lydian alphabet.*

Littmann, E. *Sardis*, vi, 11, 21. (For the symbol 8.)

v. *Phrygian alphabet.*

Kirchhoff, *op. cit.* p. 55.

vi. *Phocian alphabet.*

Kirchhoff, *op. cit.* p. 144.

vii. *Venetic alphabet.*

Conway, R. S. Art. *Veneti* in E.Brit.

Sommer, F. *Zur venetischen Schrift und Sprache.* Indog. Forschungen, XLII, 1924, p. 90.

viii. *Varieties of North Etruscan and East Italic scripts.*

Pauli, C. *Altitalische Studien.* Leipzig, 1885. I, 54 *sqq.* 1891. III, 216.

ix. *Script of Lemnos.*

Kirchhoff, *op. cit.* p. 54.

Pauli, *op. cit.* II, Abt. 2, p. 21. 1894. (On the date of the inscription, *ib.* p. 27.)

x. *The sign* ↑ .

Conway, R. S., in a review of *Kretschmer's Einleitung in d. Geschichte d. griech. Sprache.* C.R. XII, 1898, p. 462.

xi. *Lycian alphabet.*

Kalinka, E. *Tituli Asiae Minoris.* I. Vienna, 1901. (Caesareae Ac. Litt. Vindob.)

On Iberian ↑, see Hübner, *Mon. Ling. Ibericae*, Berlin, 1893, p. xxxvii *sq.* On the identity of Lat. Ϲ with the seventh letter of the Chalcid-Etruscan alphabet see G. Hempl, Trans. Amer. Philol. Assoc. xxx (1899), p. 24. On the Venetic puncts, see (pending the appearance of *The Prae-Italic Dialects*) R. S. Conway, Camb. Phil. Soc. Proc. 1915, p. 4, with Whitney, *Sanskrit Grammar*, section 87. The theory was accepted by G. Pellegrini and applied to inscriptions first published by him in Atti e Mem. d. R. Accad. Sci. Lett. Ant. Padova, XXXII, 1916, p. 206.

On the likeness in the method of denoting accent between the early Greek Papyri and the Pada text of the Rig-Veda see J. P. Postgate, *On Ancient Greek Accentuation*, Br. Acad. Proc. XI, 1925, p. 49.

V. The Etruscan Language

Conway, R. S. Art. *Etruscan Language* in E.Brit.

Corpus Inscriptionum Etruscarum. (See above, I, A)

Fraser, J. *The Lydian Language.* Anatolian Studies presented to Sir W. Ramsay, p. 139. Manchester, 1923.

Herbig, G. *Kleinasiatisch-etruskische Namengleichungen.* (See above, I, C.)

Kretschmer, P. *Einleitung in die Geschichte der griechischen Sprache.* Göttingen, 1896. p. 334.

Schulze, W. *Geschichte der lateinischen Eigennamen.* An indispensable mass of material, with an excellent index. (See above, I, C.)

Skutsch, F. Art. *Etruskische Sprache* in P.W.

Thomsen, V. *Remarques sur la parenté de la langue étrusque.* Bull. de l'Acad. R. des Sc. et Lett. Copenhagen, 1899.

In the articles of Conway and Skutsch earlier contributors to Etruscology are quoted with some fullness especially the works of E. Lattes, C. Pauli, and A. Torp. Pauli, C. *Altitalische Forschungen.* Vol. II. Leipzig, 1894. (On Lemnos epitaphs first published by Cousin and Durrbach in B.C.H. x, 1886, pp. 1 *sqq.*)

VI. Etruscan Custom and Religion

A. *Ancient Sources*

Livy, the early books *passim*, esp. I, 4; IV, 23, 61; V, 1, 17, 33. Strabo, V, 219–20. Vergil, *Aen.* VII, 695; VIII, 478–92; X, 689–908; *Georg.* II, 193.

C.I.L. v, 4057. See Conway, R. S., *Where was Vergil's Farm?* J. Rylands Library Bulletin, VII, 1923, p. 195 n. (On the pontifices of Mantua.)

Aristotle, *Politics*, III, 9, 6, 1280 a. Herodotus, I, 165 *sqq.* (On Etruscan early trade-alliances.)

Athenaeus, I, 28 B; xv, 700 C. (On bronze exports.)

Herodotus, I, 93. Timaeus *ap.* Athen. XII, 517 D. Plautus, *Cistellaria*, 562. Strabo, XI, p. 533 and p. 512. (On Etruscan manners.)

Varro, *Ling. Lat.* v, 36. (On Vertumnus.)

Vergil, *Aen.* x, 200. (On Manto.)

Pliny, *N.H.* xxx, 12 (cf. xxvIII, 12). Vergil, *Aen.* x, 518, and Servius *ad loc.* Herodotus, I, 167. Livy, vII, 15, 10; xxII, 56, 6; xxvI, 13, 15 (with v, 15, 11). Josephus, *Bell. Iud.* vII, 5, 6. (On human sacrifice.)

Servius *ad* Vergil, *Aen.* III, 168; IV, 56, quoting v, 483. (On the *hostiae animales*.)

Cicero. *De Harusp. Responso, passim*; *De Divinatione*, I, 11; II, 11–12, 28–51. Censorinus, *De Die Nat.* 17. (On the Etruscan *disciplina*.)

B. *Modern Writers*

i. *Political organization.*

Bormann, A. *Etruskisches aus römischer Zeit.* Arch. Epig. Mitt. xi, 1887, p. 94.

Müller-Deecke. *Die Etrusker.* Stuttgart, 1877. pp. 328 *sqq.*, with authorities there cited esp. *C.I.L.* xi, 3609, and Spartianus, *Vit. Hadriani,* 19.

Rosenberg, A. *Der Staat der alten Italiker.* Berlin, 1913. p. 51.

ii. *Manners and religion.*

Dieterich, A. *Kleine Schriften.* Leipzig, 1911. pp. 202 *sqq.*

Herbig, G. Art. in Hastings' Encyclopaedia of Religion and Ethics, 1912.

Koerte, G., *op. cit.* Also, *Die Bronzeleber von Piacenza.* Röm. Mitt. xx, 1905, p. 348.

Martha, J. *L'Art étrusque.* 1889. pp. 339 *sqq.*

Savignoni, L. *Nuovo Sarcofago di Caere.* Mon.d.I. vIII, 13, 14.

Additions:

Fell, R. A. L. *Etruria and Rome.* Cambridge, 1924.

Randall-MacIver, D. *Villanovans and Early Etruscans.* Oxford, 1924.

[These works appeared too late to be used in the writing of these sections. R. S. C.]

VII. ETRUSCAN ART

A. *General*

Dennis, G. *The cities and cemeteries of Etruria.* 2 vols. 1848. (There is a recent edition of this book in the Everyman Series.)

Fell, R. A. L. *Etruria and Rome.* Cambridge, 1924.

Frothingham, A. L. *Roman Cities in Italy and Dalmatia.* 1910.

Hausenstein, W. *Die Bildnerei der Etrusker.* Munich, 1922.

Martha, J. *L'Art étrusque.* 1889.

Randall-MacIver, D. *Villanovans and Early Etruscans.* Oxford, 1924.

Seta, A. Della. *Museo di Villa Giulia.* Rome, 1918.

—— *Antica Arte Etrusca.* Dedalo, I, p. 559.

B. *Painting*

Poulsen, F. *Etruscan tomb paintings.* Oxford, 1922.

Weege, F. *Etruskische Malerei.* Halle, 1921.

C. *Metalwork, gem-cutting and numismatics*

British Museum Catalogue of coins: Italy. 1873. pp. 1–24.

British Museum Catalogue of jewellery (Greek, Etruscan and Roman) by F. W. Marshall. 1911.

British Museum Catalogue of silver plate (Greek, Etruscan and Roman) by H. B. Walters. 1921.
British Museum Catalogue of terracottas by H. B. Walters. 1903.
Carcopino, J. *La Louve du Capitole*. 1925.
Furtwängler, A. *Die antiken Gemmen*. Leipzig and Berlin, 1900. Vol. I, pls. XVI–XXVI.
Hadaczek, K. *Die Ohrschmuck der Griechen und Etrusker*. Vienna, 1903.
Neugebauer, K. A. *Antike Bronzestatuetten*. Berlin, 1921.
Sambon, A. *Les monnaies antiques de l'Italie*. 1903. Vol. I, pp. 1–83.

D. *Terracottas*

Robinson, D. M. *Etruscan-Campanian antefixes and other terracottas from Italy at the Johns Hopkins University*. A.J.A. XXVII, pp. 1 *sqq.*
Strong, Mrs S. A. *The architectural decoration in terracotta from early Latin temples in the Museo di Villa Giulia*. J.R.S. IV, pp. 157 *sqq.*
Van Buren, E. D. *Figurative terracotta revetments in Etruria and Latium in the sixth and fifth century B.C.* 1922.
—— *Archaic fictile revetments in Sicily and Magna Graecia*. 1923.
—— *Archaic terracotta agalmata in Italy and Sicily*. J.H.S. XLI, pp. 203 *sqq.*

E. *Special subjects*

Ducati, P. *Le pietre funerarie felsinee*. Monumenti Antichi della Accademia dei Lincei, XX, 1910, pp. 357 *sqq.*
Minto, A. *Populonia, la necropoli arcaica*. Florence, 1922.
Pernier, L. *Il tempio Etrusco-Italico di Orvieto*. Dedalo, VI, p. 137.

CHAPTER XIII

ITALY IN THE ETRUSCAN AGE
B. THE INDO-EUROPEAN COMMUNITIES

I. THE LIGURES AND SICULI

Ancient Sources

Herodotus, v, 9; VII, 72. Thucydides, VI, 2. Lycophron, *Alex.* 1351. Polybius, II,
2 and 6. Strabo, IV, 202–4; VI, 257, 270. Seneca, *Consol. ad Helv.* VII, 9.
Pliny, *N.H.* III, 7. Servius *ad* Vergil, *Aen.* XI, 317.
Dionysius Hal. I, 10 *sqq.* (On the Aborigines.)
Tabula Genuatium, *C.I.L.* v, 7749.
Arch of Segusio, *ib.* 7231.

The names of Liguria, of which a large number are given in these inscriptions
and in Pliny, *loc. cit.*, will be recorded in Mrs S. E. Johnson's part of *The Prae-Italic
Dialects* (Conway, Johnson and Whatmough) which is in preparation. For a preliminary study of the names see Müllenhoff, *Deutsche Altertumskunde*, Brunswick,
1880–9, III, p. 173.

-asco names

Herbig, G. Art. *Ligurer* in Hoops Reallexikon d. germanischen Altertumskunde,
Strassburg, 1915. (For the objection to the Indo-European character of these
names.)

Ligurian origins

Whatmough, J. *The Ligurians.* Brit. Ass. Proc. Southampton, 1925.

Lepontic and Ornavasso Inscriptions

Conway, R. S. Speech following Sir W. Ridgeway's paper: '*Who were the Romans?*'
Proc. Brit. Acad. III, 1907.
Danielsson, O. A. *Zu den venetischen und lepontischen Inschriften.* Upsala and
Leipzig, 1909. p. 14.
Herbig, G. *Keltoligurische Inschriften aus Giubiasco.* Anzeiger f. schweizerische
Altertumskunde, VI, 1905–6, p. 187.
Kretschmer, P. *Die Inschriften von Ornavasso und die Ligurische Sprache.* Kuhns
Zeitschrift, XXXVIII, 1902, p. 97.

Siculi

For ancient authorities see Modestov, *Introduction à l'histoire romaine*, 1907,
pp. 127 *sqq.* The chief are: Thucydides, VI, 2; Philistus *ap.* Dionys. Hal. I, 22;
Dionysius Hal. I, 9, 16, 20, 21; Varro, *Ling. Lat.* v, 101; Pliny, *N.H.* III, 56, 111–12;
Silius Italicus, XIV, 37; Festus, *s.v.* Sacrani.

Sicel Inscription of Centuripa

Thurneysen, R. *Siculisch.* Kuhns Zeitschrift, XXXV, 1899, p. 212.
Since then there has been general agreement as to its Indo-European character.
See, *e.g.* Stolz, Fr., *Lat. Gramm.* ed. 4, Leipzig, 1910, p. 24.

Guttus type of vase

Walters, H. B. *History of Ancient Pottery.* 1905. I, 200, 211.

Sicel antiquities of Museum at Syracuse

Orsi, P. Studies in Notizie d. Scavi and in Bullettino di Paletnologia (from vol. XVI
onwards).
Peet, T. E. *The Stone and Bronze Ages in Italy.* Oxford, 1909. Chapter XVII.
Mr J. Whatmough has allowed the present writer the use in MS. of his edition
of the Sicel remains, to be published in *The Prae-Italic Dialects*.

Ligurian Rock-carvings

Bicknell, C. *The Prehistoric Rock-engravings in the Italian Maritime Alps.* Bordighera, 1902.

—— *Further explorations in the region of the Prehistoric Rock-engravings.* Bordighera, 1903.

See also Peet, *op. cit.*

The Romans in Liguria

Livy, Epit. 20, and Bks xxxviii–xlii.

II. THE GAULS OF N. ITALY

Livy, v, 33–4; xxxix, 55–8. Pliny, *N.H.* iii, 123–5.

Brizio, E. *Tombe e necropole galliche della Provincia di Bologna.* Atti e Mem. d. Reg. Deputaz. di Storia Patria per le prov. di Romagna, Serie iii, vol. v, Bologna, 1887.

Déchelette, J. *Manuel d'Archéologie.* Vol. ii, part iii. 1914.

Montelius, O. *La Civilisation primitive en Italie.* V. Stockholm and Berlin, 1895.

The Iapydes

Vergil, *Georg.* iii, 475. Livy, xliii, 5, 3. Strabo, vii, 314.

The Gallic Language

Dottin, G. *La Langue gauloise.* 1920. pp. 121 *sqq.*

Pedersen, H. *Vergleichende Grammatik der keltischen Sprachen.* Göttingen, 1909–13, vol. ii, p. 403.

III. THE VENETI

A. *Venetic Inscriptions*

Danielsson, O. A. *Zu den venetischen und lepontischen Inschriften.* Upsala and Leipzig, 1909.

Lattes, E. *Inscrizioni inedite Venete ed Etrusche.* Rend. Ist. Lombardo, xxxiv, 1901, p. 1133.

Pellegrini, G. *Alcune nuove Inscrizioni in lingua Veneta.* Atti e Mem. d. R. Accad. Lett. Ant. Padova, xxxii, 1916, p. 206.

Sommer, F. *Zum venetischen Schrift und Sprache.* Indog. Forschungen, xlii, 1924, p. 90.

Further linguistic evidence will be contained in the forthcoming work *The Prae-Italic Dialects*, of which the Venetic section has been used for the purposes of this chapter. The inscriptions quoted on p. 442 *sq.* are from the present writer's reading of them in 1908. Some 28 inscriptions are published in Camb. Phil. Soc. Proc. 1915, p. 6, where the value of the medial puncts is discussed.

B. *Ancient Sources*

Alcman, *Partheneion*, 50. Herodotus, i, 196; v, 9. Polybius, ii, 17. Livy, i, 1, 2; v, 33, 10; x, 2. Pliny, *N.H.* iii, 130; xxxv, 20. Strabo, iv, 195; v, 212; xii, 543–4; xiii, 608.

C. *Modern Works*

Braunholtz, G. E. K. *The Nationality of Vergil.* C.R. xxix, 1915, p. 106.

Conway, R. S. *Some Offerings to the Venetic Goddess Rehtia.* Journ. R. Anthr. Inst. xlvi, 1916, p. 227.

—— *New Studies of a Great Inheritance.* 1921. p. 193. (On Venetic art.)

Meyer, A. B. *Die Gurina in Obergailthal.* Dresden, 1885.

Pauli, C. *Die Veneter.* Leipzig, 1891.

Ridgeway, Sir W. *Origin and Influence of the Thoroughbred Horse.* pp. 104 *sqq.* (cf. p. 401). (On Venetic horsemanship.)

Whatmough, J. *Rehtia the Venetic Goddess of Healing.* Journ. R. Anthr. Inst. lii, 1922, p. 212.

IV. 'East-Italic' Group

A. *Ancient Sources*

C.I.L. III, 3364, 3401, 4857. (For the name *Meitime*.)
Pliny, *N.H.* III, 110; cf. 113. (Dolates cognomine Sallentini.)

B. *Modern Works*

Conway, R. S. *Italic Dialects*. Cambridge, 1897. p. 528.
Pauli, C., *op. cit.* p. 220, p. 428.

V. Messapii

A. *Ancient Sources*

Herodotus, I, 170. Aristotle, *Politics*, IV (VII), 10, 4, p. 1329 b. Strabo, VI, 261.
    Paul. Fest. 69 M.

B. *Modern Writers*

Conway, R. S. Art. *Messapian* in E.Brit. (where fuller particulars of the dialect and
    further references will be found).
Droop, J. P. *Messapian Inscriptions*. B.S.A. XII, 1905, p. 137.
Mommsen, T. *Die Unteritalischen Dialekte*. Leipzig, 1850. pp. 43 *sqq.*
Torp, A. *Zu den Messapischen Inschriften*. Indog. Forsch. V, 1895, p. 195.
Whatmough, J. *The Alphabet of Vaste*. C.Q. XIX, 1925, pp. 68–70.

The Messapic Inscriptions will be fully given in *The Prae-Italic Dialects.*

VI. Bruttii

A. *Ancient Sources*

Diodorus Siculus, XVI, 15. Strabo, VI, 254–5.

B. *Modern Writers*

Conway, R. S. *Italic Dialects*, pp. 3–10, 15. (On place-names and (Oscan)
    inscriptions of this district.)
Head, B. V. *H.N.*[2] p. 90.

VII. The Italic Peoples

Boni, A., Gamurrini, G. F. and others. Notizie d. Scavi. May, 1899. (On Forum
    Inscription.)
Brugmann, K. *Grundriss der vergleichenden Grammatik*. 2nd ed. Strassburg, 1902.
—— *Kurze vergleichende Grammatik*. Strassburg, 1904.
Conway, R. S. *The Italic Dialects*. Cambridge, 1897.
v. Planta, R. *Oskisch-umbrische Grammatik*. Strassburg, 1892–7.

VIII. The Co- and No- Peoples

Conway, R. S., *op. cit.* p. ix (where the two strata were first distinguished).
—— *I due strati nella popolazione indo-europea dell' Italia antica*. Atti d. Congresso
    internazionale di scienze storiche, Rome, 1903, vol. II, 1, p. 69.
—— Articles on all the tribes here discussed: E.Brit. esp. *s.v. Roma, Sabini, Volsci.*
        (The evidence from North Italy and its interpretation appear here for the
    first time.)
Ridgeway, Sir W. *Who were the Romans?* Proc. Brit. Acad. 1907–8, pp. 17 *sqq.*
    (On Sabines and Patricians.)

CHAPTER XIV

GREEK LITERATURE FROM THE EIGHTH CENTURY
TO THE PERSIAN WARS

I. Texts

Bacchylides. Ed. Jebb. Cambridge, 1905.
Berliner Klassikertexte, v, 2. Berlin, 1907.
Diels, H. *Fragmente der Vorsokratiker*. Band 1. Ed. 4. Berlin, 1922. (For Xenophanes, Parmenides, Empedocles.)
Fragments of Logographers and early writers on history, mythology, and geography in
(1) *Fragmenta Historicorum Graecorum*, ed. Müller, vol. 1, Paris, 1841;
(2) *Die Fragmente der griechischen Historiker*, ed. Jacoby, vol. 1, Berlin, 1923.
Hecataeus. See above, Fragments of Logographers.
Hesiod. Ed. A. Rzach. Leipzig, 1902.
Hymni Homerici. Edd. E. E. Sikes and T. W. Allen. 1904.
Lyric, Elegiac and Iambic Poets, Collections of their remains:
Poetae Lyrici Graeci. Ed. Bergk. Vol. 1 (= Pindar). Ed. 5 (by O. Schröder). 1900. Vols. 11 and 111. Ed. 4. Leipzig, 1882.
Supplementum Lyricum (papyrus fragments). Ed. E. Diehl. Bonn, 1917.
Lyra Graeca. Ed. J. M. Edmonds. Vols. 1–. 1922– (in progress).
ΣΑΠΦΟΥΣ ΜΕΛΗ. Ed. E. Lobel. Oxford, 1925.
Oxyrhynchus Papyri. Vols. 1, 1v, v, x, x11, x111, xv. Oxford, 1898–1922.
Pindar. Ed. Schröder. See above, Lyric Poets.
Stesichorus: Vürtheim, J. *Stesichoros' Fragmente und Biographie*. Leiden, 1919.
Theognis. Ed. T. Hudson Williams. 1910. See also E. Harrison, below.

II. Modern Works

Allen, T. W. *Homer, the origins and the transmission*. Oxford, 1924. (Contains studies on Hesiod and the Cyclic poets.)
Conybeare, F. C., Harris, J. R. and Lewis, A. S. *The Story of Aḥiḳar*. Ed. 2. Cambridge, 1913.
Cowley, A. E. *Aramaic Papyri of the Fifth Century B.C.* Oxford, 1923.
Croiset, A. and M. *Histoire de la littérature grecque*. Vols. 1 and 11.
Croiset, A. *La poésie de Pindare et les lois du lyrisme grec*. 1886.
Crusius, O. Art. *Alkman* in P.W.
Diels, H. *Alkmans Partheneion*. Hermes, xxxi, 1896, pp. 339 *sqq.*
Frere, J. H. *Theognis Restitutus*. In Works, 1872, 11, 313 *sqq.*
Halliday, W. R. *Notes upon European Folktales and the Problem of their Diffusion*. Folklore, xxxiv, No. 2, 1923, pp. 117 *sqq.*
Harrison, E. *Studies in Theognis*. Cambridge, 1902. (With text.)
Hausrath. Art. *Fabel* in P.W.
Hauvette, A. *Archiloque*. 1905.
Jebb, R. C. *Pindar*. J.H.S. 111, 1882, pp. 144 *sqq.*
Kalinka, E. *Der Ursprung der Buchstabenschrift*. Klio, xv11, 1920, pp. 302 *sqq.*
Kirchhoff, A. *Studien zur Geschichte des griechischen Alphabets*. Ed. 4. Gütersloh, 1887.
Mackail, J. W. *Lectures on Greek Poetry*. 1910.
Mure, W. *A Critical History of the Language and Literature of Ancient Greece*. Ed. 2. Vol. 111. 1854.

Murray, G. *History of Greek Literature*. 1897.

Rzach, A. Art. *Hesiodos* in P.W.

Schmidt, J. Art. *Alphabet* in P.W.

Sheppard, J. T. *The Partheneion of Alkman*. In Essays and Studies presented to William Ridgeway. Cambridge, 1913. pp. 124 *sqq*.

Symonds, J. A. *Studies of the Greek Poets*. First Series and Second Series. Ed. 2. 1877.

v. Wilamowitz-Möllendorff, U. *Textgeschichte der griechischen Lyriker*. Berlin, 1900.

—— *Die griechische Litteratur des Altertums* (= *Die Kultur der Gegenwart*, Teil I, Abt. VIII). Leipzig, Berlin, 1912.

—— *Sappho und Simonides*. Berlin, 1913.

—— *Pindaros*. Berlin, 1922.

—— *Der Chor von Hagesichora*. Hermes, XXXII, 1897, pp. 251 *sqq*.

On the Alphabet see further *C.A.H.* III, Bibliography to Chapters XVII to XX. p. 739 *sq*.

CHAPTER XV

MYSTICAL RELIGIONS AND PRE-SOCRATIC PHILOSOPHY

I. Eleusinian Mysteries

The available evidence is stated and discussed in the following works:

Farnell, L. R. *Cults of the Greek States*. Vol. III. Oxford, 1907. (Appendix of original authorities.)
Frazer, J. G. *The Golden Bough*. 3rd ed. Part V. Spirits of the Corn and of the Wild. 1912.
Foucart, P. *Les mystères d'Eleusis*. 1914.
Lenormant, F. Art. *Eleusinia* in D.S.
Lobeck, C. A. *Aglaophamus*. Regimontii Prussorum, MDCCCXXIX.

II. Orphism

A. *Fragments*

Abel, E. *Orphica*. Lipsiae, 1885.
Diels, H. *Die Fragmente der Vorsokratiker*. Ed. 3. Berlin, 1912. Vol. II, pp. 163 *sqq.*
Kern, O. *Orphicorum Fragmenta*. Berolini, 1922.

B. *Special Works*

Adam, J. *The Religious Teachers of Greece*. Edinburgh, 1908. (Lecture V.)
Cook, A. B. *Zeus*. Vol. I. Cambridge, 1914.
Dieterich, A. *Nekyia*. Leipzig, 1893.
Eisler, R. *Weltenmantel und Himmelszelt*. Munich, 1910.
Farnell, L. R. *Greek Hero-cults and Ideas of Immortality*. Oxford, 1921,
Gomperz, T. *Griechische Denker*. Vol. I. Leipzig, 1893.
Gruppe, O. *Orpheus*. Roscher, vol. III, Leipzig, 1897–1902.
Harrison, J. E. *Prolegomena to the Study of Greek Religion*. Cambridge, 1908. Chapters X–XII. (Critical Appendix on the Orphic Tablets by G. Murray.)
Kern, O. *Empedokles und die Orphiker*. Archiv f. Geschichte d. Philosophie, I (1888), p. 498.
—— *De Orphei Epimenidis Pherecydis Theogoniis quaestiones criticae*. Berolini, 1888.
—— *Orpheus*. Berlin, 1920.
Legge, F. *Forerunners and Rivals of Christianity*. Cambridge, 1915.
Lobeck, C. A. *Aglaophamus*. Regimontii Prussorum, MDCCCXXIX.
Maass, E. *Orpheus*. Munich, 1895.
Macchioro, E. *Nuovi Studi sull' Orphismo*. Bari, 1921.
Monceaux, P. Art. *Orpheus, Orphici* in D.S.
Nilsson, M. P. *A History of Greek Religion*. Oxford, 1925.
Reinach, S. *Cultes, Mythes et Religions*. 1906. II, 58 *sqq.*
Rohde, E. *Psyche*. Ed. 3. Tübingen und Leipzig, 1903.
Tierney, M. *A New Ritual of the Orphic Mysteries*. C.Q. XVI (1922), pp. 77 *sqq.*
—— *The Origins of Orphism*. Irish Theological Quarterly, XVII (1922), pp. 112 *sqq.*

III. Pre-Socratic Philosophy

A. *Fragments*

Diels, H. *Die Fragmente der Vorsokratiker*. Ed. 3. Berlin, 1912.
—— *Doxographi Graeci*. Berolini, 1879.
Ritter. H. et Preller, L. *Historia Philosphiae Graecae*. Ed. 9. Gotha, 1913.

B. *General Histories of Philosophy*

Burnet, J. *Early Greek Philosophy*. Ed. 3. 1920.
—— *Greek Philosophy*. Vol. 1. Thales to Plato. London, 1914.
Deussen, P. *Allgemeine Geschichte der Philosophie*. Vol. 11. Part I. Leipzig, 1911.
Döring, A. *Geschichte der griechischen Philosophie*. Vol. 1. Leipzig, 1903.
Gomperz, T. *Griechische Denker*. Vol. 1. Leipzig, 1893.
Joel, K. *Geschichte der antiken Philosophie*. Vol. 1. Tübingen, 1921.
Mieli, A. *La Scienza Greca*. I Prearistotelici. Vol. 1. Le Scuole Ionica, Pythagorica, ed Eleata. Florence, 1916. (Contains a full bibliography for these Schools.)
Windelband, W. *Geschichte der antiken Philosophie*. Ed. 3 (A. Bonhöffer). Munich, 1913.
Zeller, E. *Die Philosophie der Griechen in ihrer geschichtlichen Entwicklung*. Vol. 1. Ed. 5. Leipzig, 1892.

C. *Special Works*

Baeumker, C. *Das Problem der Materie in der griechischen Philosophie*. Münster, 1890.
Beare, J. I. *Greek Theories of Elementary Cognition*. Oxford, 1906.
Chiapelli, A. *L' Oriente e le Origini della Filosofia Greca*. Arch. Phil. N.F. xxi (1915), pp. 199 *sqq.* (Reviews recent works on oriental influences.)
Cornford, F. M. *From Religion to Philosophy*. 1912.
Cumont, F. *Astrology and Religion among the Greeks and Romans*. New York, 1912.
Eisler, R. *Weltenmantel und Himmelszelt*. 11. Munich, 1910.
Gilbert, O. *Die meteorologischen Theorien des griechischen Altertums*. Leipzig, 1907.
—— *Aristoteles und die Vorsokratiker*. Phil. lxviii (1909), pp. 368 *sqq.* (Collects Aristotle's judgments on the early schools.)
—— *Spekulation und Volksglaube in d. ionischen Philosophie*. Archiv f. Religionswissenschaft, xiii (1910), pp. 306 *sqq.*
—— *Griechische Religionsphilosophie*. Leipzig, 1911.
Heath, Sir Thomas. *Aristarchus of Samos*. Oxford, 1913.
—— *History of Greek Mathematics*. Oxford, 1921.
Heidel, W. A. *Qualitative Change in Pre-Socratic Philosophy*. Arch. Phil. xix (1906), pp. 333 *sqq.*
—— Περὶ φύσεως. Proc. American Academy of Arts and Sciences, vol. xlv, No. 4, 1910.
Milhaud, G. *Leçons sur les origines de la science grecque*. 1893.
—— *Les philosophes géomètres de la Grèce*. 1900.
Rohde, E. *Psyche*. Ed. 3. Tübingen und Leipzig, 1903. Eng. Trans. by W. B. Hillis, 1925.
Tannery, P. *Pour l'histoire de la science hellène*. 1887.
Teichmüller, G. *Studien zur Geschichte der Begriffe*. Berlin, 1874.

D. *Individual Schools*

(a) The Milesian School

Diels, H. *Ueber Anaximanders Kosmos*. Arch. Phil. x (1897), pp. 228 *sqq.*
—— *Ueber die ältesten Philosophieschulen d. Griechen*. Phil. Aufs. Zeller gewidmet, pp. 241 *sqq.*, Leipzig, 1887.
Heidel, W. A. *On Anaximander*. C.P. vii (1912), pp. 212 *sqq.*
Neuhäuser, J. *Anaximander Milesius*. Bonn, 1883.
Wellmann, E. Art. *Anaximandros* in P.W.
—— Art. *Anaximenes* in P.W.

(*b*) The Pythagoreans

Boeckh, A. *Philolaos*. Berlin, 1819.
Bywater, I. *On the fragments attributed to Philolaus the Pythagorean*. J.P. 1, 21 *sqq.*
Cornford, F. M. *Mysticism and Science in the Pythagorean tradition*. C.Q. XVI (1922), pp. 137 *sqq.*; XVII (1923), pp. 1 *sqq.* (These articles explain in detail the view of the development of Pythagoreanism taken in the text.)
Delatte, A. *Études sur la littérature pythagoricienne*. 1915.
Diels, H. *Ein gefälschtes Pythagorasbuch*. Arch. Phil. III, 1890, pp. 451 *sqq.*
Gilbert, O. *Aristoteles' Urteile über die pythagoreische Lehre*. Arch. Phil. XXII, 1908–9, pp. 28 *sqq.*, 145 *sqq.*
Heidel, W. A. Πέρας *and* ἄπειρον *in the Pythagorean Philosophy*. Arch. Phil. XIV, 1901, pp. 384 *sqq.*
Keith, A. B. *Pythagoras and the Doctrine of transmigration*. Journ. Roy. Anth. Inst. 1909, pp. 569 *sqq.*
Newbold, W. R. *Philolaus*. Arch. Phil. XIX, 1906, pp. 176 *sqq.*
Robin, L. *La théorie platonicienne des idées et des nombres d'après Aristote*. 1908.
Rostagni, A. *Il Verbo di Pitagora*. Turin, 1924.

(*c*) Heracleitus

Adam, J. *The Vitality of Platonism*. Essay III. Cambridge, 1911.
Bernays, J. *Gesammelte Abhandlungen*. 1. 1885.
Bywater, I. *Heracliti Ephesii reliquiae*. Oxonii, 1877.
Diels, H. *Herakleitos von Ephesos*. Ed. 2. Berlin, 1909.
Gilbert, O. *Heraklits Schrift* περὶ φύσιος. N.J.Kl.Alt. XXIII, 1909, pp. 161 *sqq.*
Heinze, M. *Die Lehre vom Logos*. Oldenburg, 1872.
Macchioro, V. *Eraclito*. Bari, 1922.
Patin, A. *Heraklits Einheitslehre*. Leipzig, 1886.
Pfleiderer, E. *Die Philosophie des Heraklit von Ephesos im Lichte der Mysterienidee*. Berlin, 1886.
Slonimsky, H. *Heraklit und Parmenides*. Giessen, 1912.
Wellmann, E. Art. *Herakleitos* in P.W.

(*d*) The Eleatics

Diels, H. *Parmenides Lehrgedicht*. Berlin, 1897.
Gilbert, O. *Die* δαίμων *des Parmenides*. Arch. Phil. XX, 1907, pp. 25 *sqq.*
Russell, Hon. B. *The Principles of Mathematics*. Cambridge, 1903. Vol. 1, pp. 347 *sqq.* (On Zeno's arguments.)
Slonimsky, H. *Heraklit und Parmenides*. Giessen, 1912.
Tannery, P. *La physique de Parmenide*. Rev. philosophique, XVIII, 1884, pp. 264 *sqq.*

(*e*) Empedocles

Bidez, J. *La biographie d'Empedocle*. Ghent, 1894.
Bignone, E. *Empedocle, studio critico, traduzione e commento delle testimonianze e dei frammenti*. Turin, 1916.
Diels, H. *Gorgias und Empedokles*. Berl.S.B. 1884, pp. 343 *sqq.*
—— *Studia Empedoclea*. Herm. XV, 1880, pp. 161 *sqq.*
Kern, O. *Empedokles und die Orphiker*. Arch. Phil. I, 1888, p. 498.
Millerd, C. E. *On the interpretation of Empedocles*. Chicago, 1908.
Stein, H. *Empedoclis Agrigentini fragmenta*. Bonn, 1852.
Wellmann, E. Art. *Empedokles* in P.W.
Ziegler, K. *Menschen- und Weltenwerden*. N.J.Kl.Alt. XXXI, 1913, pp. 529 *sqq.*

(*f*) Anaxagoras

The account of Anaxagoras' physics given in the text is based on that of Tannery (*Pour l'histoire de la Science hellène*) with some modifications.

Bury, R. G. *Philebus of Plato.* Cambridge, 1897. App. C.
Capelle, W. *Anaxagoras.* N.J.Kl.Alt. xxii, 1919, pp. 81 *sqq.*, 169 *sqq.*
Giussani, C. *T. Lucreti Cari De Rerum Natura.* Turin, 1898.
Krohn, F. *Der Νοῦς des Anaxagoras.* Münster, 1907.
Taylor, A. E. *On the date of the trial of Anaxagoras.* C.Q. xi, 1917, pp. 81 *sqq.*

(*g*) The Atomists

Brieger, A. *Die Urbewegung der Atome und die Weltentstehung bei Leukipp und Demokrit.* Halle, 1884.
Diels, H. *Leukippos und Diogenes von Apollonia.* Rh. Mus. xlii, 1887, pp. 1 *sqq.*
Liepmann, H. C. *Die Mechanik der leucipp-demokritischen Atome.* Berlin, 1885.
Zeller, E. *Zu Leucippus.* Arch. Phil. xv, 1902, pp. 137 *sqq.*

CHAPTER XVI

EARLY GREEK ART

A. Sections I–IV: Art

1. *General works on Greek art*

Curtius, L. *Die antike Kunst.* Berlin, 1913– (proceeding).
Lange, J. *Darstellung des Menschen in der älteren griechischen Kunst.* Strassburg, 1899.
Loewy, E. *The Rendering of Nature in early Greek Art.* 1907.
Carpenter, Rhys. *The Esthetic Basis of Greek Art.* Bryn Mawr, 1921.
Schweitzer, B. *Der bildende Künstler und der Begriff des Künstlerischen in der Antike.* Heidelberg, 1925.
Springer, Michaelis, Wolters. *Die Kunst des Altertums.* Leipzig, 1923. (Contains also a short bibliography.)
Winter, F. *Kunstgeschichte in Bildern*: neue Bearbeitung. I, *Das Altertum.* Leipzig, 1912– (proceeding).
Brunn, H. *Griechische Kunstgeschichte*, I–II. Munich, 1893–7.
—— *Denkmäler griechischer und römischer Skulptur.* 1890– (proceeding, continued by Arndt, P.).

2. *Sculpture*

Gardner, E. *A Handbook of Greek Sculpture.* 1920.
Bulle, H. *Der schöne Mensch im Altertum.* Munich, 1922.
Löwy, E. *Die griechische Plastik.* Vienna, 1920.

3. *Painting and Vases*

Pfuhl, E. *Malerei und Zeichnung der Griechen.* Munich, 1923. (A comprehensive work, with full bibliographies.)
Furtwängler, A. and Reichhold, K.: continued by F. Hauser and E. Buschor. *Griechische Vasenmalerei.* Munich, 1900– (proceeding). (From the sixth century onwards.)
Buschor, E. *Griechische Vasenmalerei.* Munich, 1914. Eng. trans. by G. C. Richards, 1921. (A good short work.)
Pfuhl, E. *Meisterwerke griechischer Zeichnung und Malerei.* Munich, 1924.
Walters, H. B. *History of Ancient Pottery.* 1905.
[Rumpf, A. *Chalkidische Vasen.* Munich, 1927.]

4. *Coins*

See also bibliography to chapter v

Head, B. V. *Historia Numorum.* 2nd ed. Oxford, 1911.
Gardner, P. *A History of Ancient Coinage, 700–300 B.C.* Oxford, 1918.
—— *The Types of Greek Coins.* Cambridge, 1883. (A short account.)

5. *Gems*

Furtwängler, A. *Die antiken Gemmen.* Leipzig, 1900.

6. *Geometric art*

Poulsen, F. *Die Dipylongräber und die Dipylonvasen.* Leipzig, 1905.
Schweitzer, B. *Untersuchungen zur Chronologie und Geschichte der geometrischen Stile in Griechenland*, II. Ath. Mitt. XLIII, 1918, pp. 1 *sqq.*

7. *Oriental influences and the earliest archaic art*

Poulsen, F. *Der Orient und die frühgriechische Kunst.* Leipzig, 1912.
Rumpf, A. *Die Wandmalereien in Veii.* Leipzig, 1915.
Johansen, K. Friis. *Les vases sicyoniens.* 1923.
Karo, G. *Orient und Hellas in archaischer Zeit.* Ath. Mitt. XLV, 1920, pp. 106 *sqq.*
Levi, D. *Arcadia, an early Greek Town*: new Italian excavations in Crete: in Liverpool Annals of Archaeology, XII, 1925.

8. *Seventh and sixth century sculpture*

[Langlotz, E. *Fruehgriechische Bildhauerschulen*, Nuremberg, 1927.]
Lechat, H. *La Sculpture attique avant Pheidias.* 1904.
Curtius, L. *Samiaca.* Ath. Mitt. XXXI, 1906, pp. 151 *sqq.*
Schrader, H. *Archaische Marmor-Skulpturen im Akropolis-Museum zu Athen.* Vienna, 1909.
Dickins, G. *Catalogue of the Acropolis Museum.* Vol. I. Cambridge, 1912.
Schrader, H. *Auswahl archaischer Marmor-Skulpturen im Akropolis-Museum.* Vienna, 1913.
Heberdey, R. *Altattische Porosskulptur.* Vienna, 1919.
Pace, B. *Arti ed Artisti della Sicilia antica.* (Memorie della R. Acc. dei Lincei, Rome, 1917.)
Gábrici, E. *Daedalica Selinuntia.* Naples, 1924.
Müller, V. K. *Gewandschemata der archaischen Kunst.* Ath. Mitt. XLVI, 1921, pp. 36 *sqq.*
Buschor, E. *Burglöwen*; and *Der Ölbaumgiebel.* In Ath. Mitt. XLVII, 1922, pp. 81 *sqq.*
Pfuhl, E. *Bemerkungen zur archaischen Kunst.* Ath. Mitt. XLVIII, 1923, pp. 119 *sqq.*

9. *Relations between archaic sculpture and archaic painting*

v. Lücken, G. *Archaische griechische Vasenmalerei und Plastik.* Ath. Mitt. XLIV, 1919, pp. 47 *sqq.*
Langlotz, E. *Zur Zeitbestimmung der strengrotfigurigen Vasenmalerei und der gleichzeitigen Plastik.* Leipzig, 1920.

10. *Sites*

The most important, for the early period, are the following:
Olympia.
Curtius, E., and others. *Olympia.* Berlin, 1890–6. (Especially vol. IV, *Die Bronzen*, by Furtwängler.) (A short account is given by E. Norman Gardiner, *Olympia, its History and Remains*, Oxford, 1925.)
Delphi.
Homolle, Th., and Perdrizet, P. *Fouilles de Delphes.* Vols. IV and V. 1902– (unfinished).
Pomtow, H. Art. *Delphoi* in P.W.
Poulsen, F. *Delphi.* 1920. And *Delphische Studien.* Copenhagen, 1924.
Sparta.
In *B.S.A.* vols. XII–XVI.

Ephesus.
Hogarth, D. G. *Excavations at Ephesus.* 1908.

Sicily.
Orsi, P. *Gela* (Mon. Lincei, XVII), and *Gli Scavi intorno all' Athenaion di Siracusa* (*ib.* XXV).

11. *Literary and epigraphical sources*

Overbeck, J. *Die antiken Schriftquellen zur Geschichte der Künste bei den Griechen.* Leipzig, 1868.
Loewy, E. *Inschriften griechischer Bildhauer.* Leipzig, 1885.
Brunn, H. *Geschichte der griechischen Künstler.* Stuttgart, 1889.
Jones, H. Stuart. *Select Passages from ancient writers illustrative of the History of Greek Sculpture.* 1895.
Sellers, E. *The elder Pliny's Chapters on the History of Art.* 1896.

B. Section V: Architecture

1. *General*

Anderson, W. J. and Spiers, R. P. *The Architecture of Greece and Rome.* 2nd ed. 1907. (A new edition in two volumes is announced, the Greek portion re-written by Dinsmoor, W. B.)
Bell, E. *Hellenic Architecture.* 1920.
Durm, J. *Die Baukunst der Griechen.* 3rd ed. 1910. (Invaluable. The 2nd ed. (1892) contains an excellent bibliographical index by von Duhn, F.)
v. Gerkan, A. *Griechische Städteanlagen.* 1924. Very important. Deals chiefly with matters not discussed in this section.
Leroux, G. *Les Origines de l'Édifice Hypostyle.* Bibl. des écoles franç. d'Athènes et de Rome, Fasc. 108. 1913.
Marquand, A. *Greek Architecture.* 1909.
Rodenwaldt, G. *Zur Entstehung der monumentalen Architektur in Griechenland.* Ath. Mitt. XLIV, 1919, pp. 175 *sqq.*

For many sites in Phocis, Boeotia, Attica, and the Peloponnese, full summaries and bibliographies are given in Sir J. G. Frazer, *Pausanias's Description of Greece,* six volumes, 1898. Among periodicals which regularly summarize the progress of excavation and research may be mentioned: Πρ., *Arch. Anz.* (printed with *J.D.A.I.*), *B.C.H., A.J.A., J.H.S., Year's Work in Classical Studies.*

2. *Archaic Doric and its antecedents*

(*a*) General

Many of the most important discussions will be found in the publications of individual sites: but see also:

Holland, L. B. *Primitive Aegean Roofs.* A.J.A. 2nd ser. XXIV, 1920, pp. 323 *sqq.*
Müller, K. *Gebäudemodelle spätgeometrischer Zeit.* Ath. Mitt. XLVIII, 1923 (1925), pp. 52 *sqq.* Illustrates and describes the clay models from the Argive Heraeum. Important for early roofing.
Van Buren, E. D. *Archaic Fictile Revetments in Sicily and Magna Graecia.* 1923.
Wilberg, W. *Die Entwicklung des dorischen Kapitells.* Jahreshefte XIX/XX, 1919, pp. 167 *sqq.*

(*b*) Important sites in alphabetical order. Those in Sicily and South Italy are grouped together

Aegina.
Furtwängler, A. and others. *Aegina.* 2 vols. Munich, 1906.

Recent work summarized in *B.C.H.* xlviii, 1924, pp. 460 *sqq.*, and in *A.J.A.* 2nd ser. xxix, 1925, pp. 107 *sqq.*

Amyclae.

Fiechter, E. *Amyklae.* J.D.A.I. xxxiii, 1918, pp. 107 *sqq.*

Klein, W. *Zum Thron des Apollo von Amyklae.* Arch. Anz. 1922, col. 6 *sqq.*

Assos.

Sartiaux, F. *Les Sculptures et la Restauration du Temple d'Assos.* Rev. A. 4ᵉ sér. 1913, ii, pp. 1 *sqq.*, 359 *sqq.*; 1914, i, pp. 191 *sqq.*, 381 *sqq.* (Contains full bibliography.)

Athens.

Buschor, E., in *Ath. Mitt.* xlvii, 1922, pp. 53 *sqq.*, 81 *sqq.*, 92 *sqq.*, 106 *sqq.*

Dickins, G. *Catalogue of the Acropolis Museum.* Vol. i. Cambridge, 1912.

D'Ooge, M. L. *The Acropolis of Athens.* 1908.

Dörpfeld, W. *Das Hekatompedon in Athen.* J.D.A.I. xxxiv, 1919, pp. 1–40.

Heberdey, R. *Altattische Porosskulptur.* Vienna, 1919.

Hill, B. H. *The Older Parthenon.* A.J.A. (N.S.) xvi, 1912, pp. 535 *sqq.*

Jahn, O. and Michaelis, A. *Arx Athenarum a Pausania descripta.* 2 vols. 3rd ed. Bonn, 1901.

Judeich, W. *Topographie von Athen.* Munich, 1905.

Petersen, E. *Die Burgtempel der Athenaia.* Berlin, 1907.

Wiegand, T. and others. *Die archaische Poros-Architektur der Akropolis zu Athen.* 2 vols. Cassel and Leipzig, 1904. (Very important.)

Corcyra.

Dörpfeld, W. *Die Ausgrabungen auf Korfu im Frühjahre,* 1914. Ath. Mitt. xxxix, 1914, pp. 161 *sqq.*

Dörpfeld, W. and Loeschke, G., in Arch. Anz. 1914, col. 46 *sqq.*

Rhomaios, K. A., in Ἀρχ. Δελτ. vi, 1920/1921, pp. 165 *sqq.*

Versakis, F., in Πρ. 1911, pp. 164 *sqq.*

Corinth.

Courby, F., in *Les Fouilles de Delphes,* ii, 1, 1915, p. 112. (See under Delphi.)

Powell, B. *The Temple of Apollo at Corinth.* A.J.A. 2nd ser. ix, 1905, pp. 44 *sqq.*

Delphi.

(*a*) General (including Ionic buildings).

Pomtow, H. *s.v. Delphoi,* in P.W. Suppl. iv, 1924, col. 1189 *sqq.*

Poulsen, F. *Delphi.* Translated by Richards, G. C. 1920.

(*b*) Temple of Apollo.

Homolle, T. and others. *Les Fouilles de Delphes.* 1902– (unfinished). Vol. ii: Courby, F. *La Terrasse du Temple.* Fasc. i, 1915; fasc. ii, 1921; plates, 1920.

Replat, J. *Questions d'Architecture delphique.* II. B.C.H. xlvi, 1922, pp. 435 *sqq.*

(*c*) Other early Doric buildings.

Dinsmoor, W. B. *Studies of the Delphian Treasuries.* I. B.C.H. xxxvi, 1912, pp. 439 *sqq.*

Les Fouilles de Delphes (see above). Vol. ii, iii, i, 1923, Le Sanctuaire d'Athéna Pronaia. Demangel, R., *Les Temples de Tuf.* Daux, G., *Les deux Trésors;* plates, 1925.

Eretria.

Furtwängler, A., in *Aegina,* 1906, i, pp. 321 *sqq.*

Karo, G., in *Arch. Anz.* 1911, col. 122 *sqq.*

Kuruniotis, K., in Πρ. 1900, pp. 53 *sqq.* and *Giebelskulpturen aus Eretria,* Ant. Denkm. iii, 3, 1914/1915.

Studniczka, F., in *Arch. Anz.* 1921, col. 323.

Olympia.

(*a*) General.

Curtius, E. and others. *Olympia.* Berlin, 1890–7. Textband II, Tafelband I, 1892, *Die Baudenkmäler,* by Dörpfeld, W. and others.

(*b*) Recent investigations of Heraeum.

Dörpfeld, W., in *Ath. Mitt.* XLVII, 1922, pp. 30–42.

Weege, F. *Einzelfunde von Olympia,* 1907–9. Ath. Mitt. XXXVI, 1911, pp. 163 *sqq.*

Sicily and South Italy.

Koldewey, R. and Puchstein, O. *Die griechischen Tempel in Unteritalien und Sicilien.* 2 vols. Berlin, 1899. (Invaluable.)

For later study of individual sites, see especially on

Locri.

Orsi, P., in *N.S.A.* 1912 (anno 1911—Supplemento), pp. 27 *sqq.*

Selinus.

Hulot, J. and Fougères, G. *Sélinonte.* 1910.

Syracuse.

Orsi, P., in *N.S.A.* 1915, pp. 175 *sqq.,* and in *Mon. Linc.* xxv, 1918, col. 353 *sqq.*

Sparta.

Dawkins, R. M. *Excavations at Sparta.* B.S.A. XIV, 1907/8, pp. 1 *sqq.*

Thermum.

Dörpfeld, W., in *Ath. Mitt.* XLVII, 1922, pp. 43 *sqq.*

Kawerau, G. and Sotiriades, E. *Der Apollotempel zu Thermos.* Antike Denkmäler, II, 5, 1902–8.

Rhomaios, K. A., in Ἀρχ. Δελτ. I, 1915, pp. 225 *sqq.*: also in Ἀρχ. Δελτ. VI, 1920/1, pp. 158 *sqq.*

Tiryns.

Blegen, C. W. *Korakou.* Boston and New York, 1921, pp. 130 *sqq.*

Frickenhaus, A. *Tiryns: Die Ergebnisse der Ausgrabungen.* I. Athens, 1912.

3. *Archaic Ionic and its antecedents*

(*a*) General

Braun-Vogelstein, J. *Die Ionische Säule.* J.D.A.I. xxxv, 1920, pp. 1–48.

Lehmann-Haupt, C. F. *Zur Herkunft der Ionischen Säule.* Klio, XIII, 1913, pp. 648 *sqq.*

von Luschan, F. *Entstehung und Herkunft der Ionischen Säule.* (Der Alte Orient, XIII.) 1912.

Puchstein, O. *Die Ionische Säule.* Leipzig, 1907.

Weickert, C. *Das lesbische Kymation.* Leipzig, 1913.

Wurz, E. and Wurz, R. *Die Entstehung der Säulenbasen des Altertums unter Berücksichtigung verwandter Kapitelle.* (Zeitschrift für Geschichte der Architektur, Beiheft 15.) Heidelberg, 1925.

(*b*) Important sites in alphabetical order

Athens. (Peisistratid Temple of Olympian Zeus.)

Welter, G. *Das Olympieion in Athen.* Ath. Mitt. XLVII, 1922, pp. 61 *sqq.*

Chios.

Kuruniotis, K., in Ἀρχ. Δελτ. I. 1915, pp. 64 *sqq.*

Delos.

The official publication is: Homolle, T. and others, *Exploration archéologique de Délos*, 1902– (unfinished). It has not yet dealt with anything of importance for archaic Ionic: but see its Appendix 1, Carte Archéologique, 1902.

The best summary is: Courby, F., *Le Sanctuaire de l'Apollon Délien*. B.C.H. xlv, 1921, pp. 174 *sqq.*

Delphi.

See under 2. *supra* (Doric). In *Fouilles de Delphes*, see vol. ii, iii, i (*Le Sanctuaire d'Athéna Pronaia*) mentioned above, and also vol. iv, 1904–9 (Sculpture).

Courby, F. *Sur le frise du Trésor de 'Cnide' à Delphes*. Rev. Arch. 4e sér. xvii, 1911, pp. 197 *sqq.*

Dinsmoor, W. B. See under 2. *supra* (Doric), and also *Studies of the Delphian Treasuries*, II, B.C.H. xxxvii, 1913, pp. 1–83. *The Aeolic Capitals of Delphi*, A.J.A. 2nd ser. xxvii, 1923, pp. 164 *sqq.*

Ephesus.

Benndorf, O. and others. *Forschungen in Ephesos*. Vol. i. Vienna, 1906.

Hogarth, D. G. and others. *Excavations at Ephesus*. The Archaic Artemisia. 1908.

Lethaby, W. R. *The Earlier Temple of Artemis at Ephesus*. J.H.S. xxxvii, 1917, pp. 1 *sqq.*

Larisa in Aeolis.

Kjellberg, L. *Gräfningarne i Larisa*. Uppsala Universitets Årsskrift, 1903, pp. 30 *sqq.* Also, lecture reported in *Arch. Anz.* xxi, 1906, col. 265.

Koch, H. *Studien zu den Campanischen Dachterrakotten*. Röm. Mitt. xxx, 1915, pp. 1–115. (Very important for the whole subject of terracotta decoration.)

Lesbos.

Koldewey, R. *Die Antiken Baureste der Insel Lesbos*. Berlin, 1890.

Wace, A. J. B. *Archaeology in Greece*. J.H.S. xli, 1921, p. 275.

Locri.

Koldewey, R. and Puchstein, O. *Die griech. Tempel in Unteritalien u. Sicilien*. 2 vols. Berlin, 1899.

Lycia.

Benndorf, O. and Niemann, G. *Reisen in Lykien und Karien*. Vienna, 1884.

Petersen, E. and F. v. Luschan. *Reisen in Lykien, Milyas und Kibyratis*. Vienna, 1889.

Naucratis.

Flinders Petrie, W. M., Gardner, E. A. and others. *Naukratis*. Part I. 1886. Part II. 1888.

Prinz, H. *Funde aus Naukratis*. VIIe Beiheft zu Klio. Leipzig, 1908.

Naxos and Paros.

Welter, G. *Ath. Mitt.* xlix, 1924, p. 17.

Neandria.

Koldewey, R. *LI. Programm zum Winckelmannsfeste*, 1891.

Paphlagonia.

Leonhard, R. *Paphlagonia*. Berlin, 1915.

Paros.

See under *Naxos*.

Samos.

Wiegand, T. and others. *Erster vorläufiger Bericht über die von dem Königl. Mus. unternommenen Ausgrabungen in Samos*. Berl. Abh. v, 1911.

4. *Archaic temples not definitely Doric or Ionic*

(*a*) Crete

Gortyn.

Savignoni, L. *Nuovi Studii e Scoperte in Gortyna.* Mon. Lincei, xviii, 1907, col. 181 *sqq.*

Palaikastro.

Bosanquet, R. C. *The Temple of Diktaean Zeus.* B.S.A. xi, 1904/5, pp. 298 *sqq.*

Prinia.

Pernier, L. *Templi arcaici sulla Patèla di Priniàs in Creta.* Ann. d. Reg. Scuola Arch. di Atene, i, 1914, pp. 18 *sqq.*

(*b*) Phrygia

Gordium.

Körte, G. and Körte, A. *Goraion.* J.D.A.I. Ergänzungsheft v, Berlin, 1904.

CHRONOLOGICAL NOTES

1. THE DATE OF CYLON'S *COUP D'ÉTAT*

Herodotus (v, 71) sets Cylon's attempt πρὸ τῆς Πεισιστράτου ἡλικίας; the source of Aristotle, *Ath. Pol.* 1 and Plutarch, *Solon*, 12, puts it before the legislation of Dracon. Cylon, according to Eusebius (1, 198), was a victor at Olympia in Ol. 35. 1 = 640 B.C. He was the son-in-law of Theagenes, tyrant of Megara (Thucydides, 1, 126; Pausanias, 1, 28, 1, etc.). Herodotus (1, 61) further assumes the story of the bloodguilt of the Alcmaeonidae as existing at the time of Peisistratus' marriage with Megacles' daughter, an event which he puts before *c.* 556 B.C.; see *C.Q.* 1924, p. 176. The expulsion of the Alcmaeonidae is put by Plutarch and Aristotle (*loc. cit.*) before the archonship of Solon, the purification of Athens by Epimenides is put by Diogenes Laertius, 1, 110, in Ol. 46 = 596 B.C. Thucydides (*loc. cit.*) says that the Alcmaeonidae were exiled as bloodguilty first by the Athenians after Cylon's attempt, and later by Cleomenes acting with an Athenian faction. Plutarch says that, in the disorders connected with the trial of the Alcmaeonidae, the Athenians lost Nisaea and Salamis again, but the confusion of ancient authorities about the Athenians' winning and losing of Salamis at least is too great to permit of any confident deduction from this statement. Finally, the amnesty law quoted as from the eighth law of the thirteenth axon, by Plutarch, *Solon*, 19, exempts from the amnesty people condemned to exile ἐπὶ φόνῳ ἢ σφαγαῖσιν ἢ ἐπὶ τυραννίδι. σφαγαί means either 'killing' or 'massacre'—the meaning of wounding as distinguished from killing is insufficiently supported. Killing is covered by ἐπὶ φόνῳ; there remains σφαγαί in the sense of massacre (cf. Xenophon, *Hell.* II, 2, 6, IV, 4, 2; Isocrates, v, 107, VIII, 96; Demosthenes, XIX, 260); ἐπὶ τυραννίδι implies an attempt at tyranny. The natural deduction is that the amnesty law, which is admittedly Solonian, refers to the *coup d'état* and the massacre of the Cylonians. In that case Cylon's attempt is earlier than 594 B.C.

The consensus of ancient tradition thus seems to place the attempt of Cylon towards the close of the seventh century.

Beloch, *Griechische Geschichte*, 1², 2, pp. 302 *sqq.*, and De Sanctis, *Atthis*², pp. 280 *sqq.*, advance arguments for a date about the middle of the sixth century.

Apart from his relations with Cylon there is no certain evidence for the date of Theagenes, and these scholars would place him about the middle of the sixth century and De Sanctis would attribute his fall to Spartan influence For a criticism of their arguments on this score see Ledl, A., *Studien zur älteren attischen Verfassungsgeschichte*, pp. 92 *sqq.* A Megacles was archon at the time of the Cylonian attempt, but there is no reason to make him the Megacles who opposed Peisistratus. It seems to the present writer impossible to make the first expulsion of the Alcmaeonidae 'by the Athenians' in Thucydides, 1, 126, refer to their flight or exile on the final return of Peisistratus. Beloch, *loc. cit.*, points out that Myron the accuser of the Alcmaeonidae appears as Φλυεύς in Plutarch, *Solon*, 12, that is, that he has a demotikon, and that there was a court of 300 to judge the Alcmaeonidae. He argues, therefore[1], that the story is a doublet of the events of 508 B.C., for then Cleomenes set up a council of 300 enemies of the Alcmaeonidae and the use of demotika comes in about that time. The demotikon presents a real difficulty; it is possible that Aristotle's source has blundered and that details referring to 508 B.C. are applied to the earlier expulsion But it is difficult, in the face of the ancient evidence, especially of the amnesty law, to deny that the earlier expulsion occurred; and occurred before the archonship of Solon. It may be legitimate to doubt the value of the early Olympian victor lists (but see vol. III, pp. 762 *sqq.*), but, at the least, they reflect some kind of genealogical calculation which put Cylon in the seventh century, and such a calculation is not likely to be at least two generations wrong. Cylon's attempt belonged to the history of the Alcmaeonid house who might well preserve a reasonably accurate tradition.

F. E. A.

2. REIGN OF BARDIYA (SMERDIS)

It is known that Bardiya became king in the spring of a certain year (independently of the evidence which determines the date of the death of Cambyses, see above, pp. 174 *sq.*). This year—in spite of a theory which would make it 523 B.C., the year previous to the death of Cambyses—must be the same year in which Cambyses died (522 B.C.). Tablets exist dated in the second and third months of the year of accession of Bardiya; others dated in the first (nineteenth day), third, fourth, fifth, sixth and seventh months of the first year of Bardiya. The fewest difficulties seem to be presented if it is assumed that in this case, exceptionally, the *accession year* and the *first year* are identical. Then the reign lasted, as Herodotus expressly says, seven months, and not at least eighteen as would be the case if they are not identical. Tablets exist for each of these seven months and there is no gap of ten consecutive months without a tablet, such as the theory of the longer reign would have to admit. In any case Bardiya was recognized as king as early as the second month (April–May) of the year of his accession. Darius (Behistun inscr.) dates two events in the revolt: Gaumata's proclamation that he was Bardiya, and his accession. For the first he gives the unambiguous date, 14th Viyakhria, the Persian name for the twelfth month (March) of the Babylonian year; for the second, the 9th Gharmapada. The identification of this month is disputed, some equating it with Tammuz, the fourth month (June–July) of the Babylonian year; others with the first month, and this alternative seems to be established by the fact that Bardiya was already king at least as early as the second month of the year of his accession.

G. B. G.

3. CHRONOLOGY OF THE CAMPAIGNS OF DARIUS IMMEDIATELY AFTER HIS ACCESSION

In the Behistun inscription Darius dates the main events accurately by the day of the month, but in no case names a year. But four times over he asserts that all the events recorded in the first four columns of the inscription

[1] So also O. Seeck, *Klio*, IV, pp. 318 *sqq.* who is answered by Ledl, *op. cit.* pp. 84 *sqq.*

(the fifth column was inscribed later and refers to later events) occurred *hamahyāyā tharda*, a phrase which, though formerly otherwise translated, should mean *in the same year*: 'in the same year after I became king I engaged in nineteen battles.' As a matter of fact month-dates given for the nineteen battles cannot all be brought strictly within a single year, and Darius indulges in a certain degree of exaggeration. But it is possible so to interpret the inscription that the period covered does not exceed seventeen months—from the autumn of 522 to the spring of 520, with the exception of the final battle against Vahyazdata dated the 5th day of Gharmapada and the final battle against the Parthians dated the 1st day of Gharmapada, which certainly did not occur in the first year of Darius, but presumably in the second. Thus all the events fall in the five months of the accession year, and the first year of the reign, as noted in the text (p. 176).

G. B. G.

45

INDEX TO MAPS

Each map has its own index and reference is made here only to its number. The aphabetical arrangement ignores the usual prefixes (lake, etc.).

Abae, 7
Abar-Nahara, 4
Abydos, 5
Achaea, 2
Acharnae, 1, 7
Aciris, R., 11
Acrae, 3
Acraephia, 7
Acragas, 3
Addua, R., 11
Adramyttium, 5
Adria, 11
Adria, R., 11
Aegaleos M., 1, 9
Aegina, 2
Aegina (town), 1
Aegosthena, 7
Aegyptus, 4
Aegytis, 2
Aenos, 5
Aeolian Islands, 3
Aeolis, 4
Aequi, 11
Aethiopes, 4
Aethiopia, 4
Aetna, 3
Aetna, Mt, 3
Ἄγκων, 11
Agrieliki, Mt, 6
Agyrium, 3
Ἀκράγας, 11
Alarodii ?, 4
Alba, 11
Albintimelium, 11
Alpeni, 7, 8
Alpes M., 11
Alpheus, R., 2
Amathus, 5
Amisus, 5
Amorgos, 5
Amphissa, 7
Amyclae, 2
Anaea, 5

Anapus, R., 11
Anauni, 11
Anio, R., 11
Antandrus, 5
Anthela, 7, 8
Aparytae?, 4
Aphidnae, 7
Aphorismos, Mt, 6
Apollonia, 3
Apotripi, F., 10
Appenninus M., 11
Apuli, 11
Arabia, 4
Arachosia, 4
Araxes, F., 4
Arcadia, 2
Arginusae I., 5
Argolid, 2
Argos, 2
Aria, 4
Arii, 4
Armenia, 4
Arnus, R., 11
Arx, 10
Asopus Fl., 7, 8, 10
Asopus, Gorge of the, 8
Asopus Ridge, 10
Aspendus, 5
Assyria, 4
Astacus, 5
Atalanta, 7
Aternus, R., 11
Ateste, 11
Athenians (Salamis), 9
Athens, 1, 7
Athesis, R., 11
Atria, 11
Attica, 2, 7
Aufidus, R., 11
Aulis, 7
Aurunci, 11
Avlona, 6

Babylon, 4
Bactra, 4
Bactria, 4
Bansa, 11
Barbara, C., 9
Baths (Thermopylae), 8
Benacus, L., 11
Boeotia, 2, 7
Bœum, 7
Boii, 11
Borysthenes, F., 4
Bovianum, 11
Brauron, 1
Bridge, 8
Brundisium, 11
Bruttii, 11
Budorum, 7
Byzantium, 5

Caicus, R., 5
Cale-Acte, 3
Callidromus, 8
Callidromus M., 7
Callipolis, 3
Camarina, 3
Camicus, 3
Camirus, 5
Cappadocia, 4
Capua, 11
Cardia, 5
Carduchi, 4
Caria, 5
Carpathos, 5
Carthage, 3
Casmenae, 3
Casos, 5
Caspii, 4
Caspium, Mare, 4
Casuentus, R., 11
Catana, 3
Caucasus M., 4
Caulonia, 3
Caunus, 5

INDEX OF PASSAGES REFERRED TO

NOTE: See further the General Index on separate writers and authorities